★ ★

Women in Politics: Outsiders or Insiders?

A Collection of Readings

Fourth Edition

Lois Duke Whitaker, Editor

Georgia Southern University

PEARSON
Prentice
Hall

Upper Saddle River, New Jersey 07458

Library of Congress Cataloging-in-Publication Data
Women in politics : outsiders or insiders? / [edited by] Lois Duke
Whitaker.—4th ed.
 p. cm.
 ISBN 0-13-134504-4
 1. Women in politics—United States. 2. Feminism—United States. I.
Whitaker, Lois Duke.
 HQ1236.5.U6W663 2006
 320'.082—dc22

                                    2005014342

VP, Editorial Director: Charlyce Jones Owen
Editorial Assistant: Suzanne Remore
Marketing Assistant: Jennifer Lang
AVP, Director of Production and Manufacturing: Barbara Kittle
Senior Managing Editor: Lisa Iarkowski
Project Liaison: Harriet Tellem
Production Editor: John Shannon
Manufacturing Manager: Nick Sklitsis
Manufacturing Buyer: Sherry Lewis
Composition: Pine Tree Composition
Printer/Binder: Courier Companies
Cover Design: Bruce Kenselaar

Credits and acknowledgments borrowed from other sources and reproduced, with permission, in this
textbook appear on the appropriate pages.

Pearson Education Singapore, Pte. Ltd
Pearson Education, Canada, Ltd
Pearson Education—Japan
Pearson Education Australia PTY, Limited
Pearson Education North Asia Ltd

Pearson Educación de Mexico, S.A. de C.V.
Pearson Education Malaysia, Pte. Ltd
Pearson Education, Upper Saddle River,
  New Jersey

10 9 8 7 6 5 4 3 2 1
ISBN 0-13-134504-4

Contents

★ ★

Preface

What began as a much smaller project about fifteen years ago has now developed into a fourth edition. Although the numbers of articles have increased somewhat, this fourth edition has attempted to maintain the major themes of the original edition. Unfortunately, four of the contributors to the first edition have departed this world. This fourth edition is especially dedicated to these four great women and colleagues: Joanne V. Hawks, Marcia Lynn Whicker, Wilma Rule, and Diane D. Blair. New contributors have also come on board for this fourth edition and are welcomed. These authors include Cynthia Burack, Sarah Brewer, Jennifer L. Lawless, Sean M. Theriault, Sarah Poggione, Robert P. Watson, D'Ann M. Campbell, Karen L. Padgett, and Brittany Penberthy. The editor especially thanks those contributors from the third edition who have continued to support the fourth edition. These include: Jennifer Ring, Nancie E. Caraway, Gertrude A. Steuernagel, Maureen Rand Oakley, Thomas E. Yatsco, Irene J. Barnett, Cal Clark, Janet M. Clark, Denise L. Baer, Susan A. MacManus, Charles S. Bullock, III, Carolyn Ellis Staton, Hedy Leonie Isaacs, Sara J. Weir, Karen O'Connor, Elaine Martin, Joan Hulse Thompson, Ruth Bamberger, Roberta Ann Johnson, Kathleen P. Iannello, and Elizabeth A. Kelly.

The basic thrust of the book is essentially unchanged. That is, this book is designed to provide a supplemental reader on the topic of women and politics to accompany texts for American government courses to aid in integrating the study of women in the political system, as well as for use in women and politics courses, and even as a supplement for graduate-level courses. This reader provides relevant research on women and politics across a spectrum of topics and perspectives;

therefore, the book can provide merely a "snapshot." Each author has added a "Further Reading" section at the conclusion of his or her article to help in explaining more fully where the essays fit into the overall picture of other research.

We begin with a feminist theoretical framework, examine some gender differences in political attitudes and voting, look at gender cultural reflections in the mass media and group politics, and examine how women have fared in competing for public office. Next we look at the various branches of government and see how women are (and in some cases still are not) participating in the functions of government. Then we explore women and national public policy, ending with women empowerment, changing roles, and cultural expression.

ORGANIZATIONAL FRAMEWORK

The book is organized into nine chapters, which are arranged into four parts. Part I includes an analysis of "Women, Equality, and Feminist Theory." Part II explores the topic of "Women and Politics," including how women and men have changed in their opinions about women's roles in politics; gender differences in voting and attitudes; the concept of occupational stratification and how this affects political attitudes; women, the media, and movement politics; and women and elections. Part III, "Gender and Government," examines women and their role as policy makers in political institutions. This topic includes females in the U.S. Congress and in state legislatures and projections for their future role, women as chief executives and first ladies' influence on presidents, females within the judicial system, and women's rights struggles and the U.S. Supreme Court's responses. Part IV looks at "Women and National Policy," in such public policy areas as family and medical leave, sex at risk in insurance classifications, and affirmative action. We conclude with a chapter on "Women, Empowerment, and Cultural Expression." This includes a new article on the role of women in the military and an article on coffee drinking and the importance of free speech. Brief summaries of the chapters included in the book follow.

Chapter 1   The Study of Women: A Theoretical Framework

Feminist Theory as Seeing
Jennifer Ring

Feminist theory is a way of seeing the world through the lens of gender, which is always present, but rarely recognized. In political science, as in most academic fields, gender is invisible, with the male gendered stance assumed to be neutral or objective. Here Jennifer Ring offers a feminist rereading of American slavery to demonstrate how the perspective of the most marginalized group in the social system, African-American women, actually permits access to the deepest, most revealing insight. Viewing social and political systems from the margins permits greater insights into the "center" or the whole. A more general discussion of the nature of feminist theory along with a survey of well-known theorists follows the description and analysis of slavery. "Feminist-compatible," approaches to theory, are identified as (1) liberalism and radicalism, (2) materialism, (3) a critique of objectivity, and (4) poststructuralist feminism, all of which presuppose a multicultural approach.

The Riddle of Consciousness: Racism and Identity in Feminist Theory
Nancie E. Caraway

Utilizing the political and epistemological contributions of contemporary black feminist theory, Nancie E. Caraway points up the intersections of gender, race, and class as determinants of oppression. She argues that the texts of black feminists teach us that feminist theory and politics should address this "multiple jeopardy." She cautions that feminists need to be wary of the damaging consequences of conceptions like identity and self, which have set up white norms. In her discussion of identity politics, Caraway questions many of the assumptions of mainstream white feminism. She proposes instead multicultural goals in which the themes of racism and identity come together in a configuration that can address the theoretical issues about the female subject. She argues that a critical identity politics cautions us not to become too comfortable too long in one spot with one identity lest we forget and stifle the ways in which we change, contradict, and grow in history.

Chapter 2   Gender Differences in Political Attitudes and Voting

Rethinking Pink and Blue: Gender, Occupational Stratification, and Political Attitudes
Gertrude A. Steuernagel, Maureen Rand Oakley, Thomas E. Yatsco and Irene J. Barnett

This article addresses questions concerning the effects of occupational stratification on women's political attitudes. It pays special attention to the intersection of occupational stratification and gender as it affects the political attitudes of women and men. Utilizing data from the University of Michigan/Survey Research Center's National Election Study and the U.S. Department of Labor, the authors look at political attitudes of groups of women and men in male-dominated, integrated, and female-dominated occupations.

The Gender Gap in the Early 21st Century: Volatility from Security Concerns
Cal Clark and Janet M. Clark

This article explores and describes the gender gap in the first two national elections in the 21st century. These elections produced dramatically different results in terms of the gender gap. In 2000, the normal gender gap emerged in both presidential and congressional elections, confirming that the significant difference in voting between women and men of the previous twenty years had seemingly been consolidated. Yet, for the 2002 elections, the gender gap virtually disappeared. One obvious factor that intervened between these two elections was the tragedy of September 11, 2001, which suggested (to journalists at least) that "soccer moms," heralded as the key to former President Bill Clinton's re-election in 1996, had been transformed into "security moms." This piece, hence, describes the gender gap in these two elections and explores the implications of the 2002 data for gender-based orientations toward American politics.

The New Right in American Politics: What Do Women Have to Do with It?
Cynthia Burack

In this essay, the author surveys some of the significant manifestations for women of contemporary New Right politics. She begins by briefly noting both some terminological issues that situate the New Right ideologically and some figures and groups that are connected to the right in one of a number of ways. Next, the author highlights some prominent themes of the New Right, moving from the social, or "culture war" strand to some brief reflections on links between cultural politics and what is variously referred to as the market, economic, or libertarian/laissez-faire strand. Throughout the essay, the author highlights women's roles as citizens, political actors, and scholar–critics. She concludes that, with regard to the American New Right, women are both insiders and outsiders.

Chapter 3   Women, Media, and Group Politics

Women and Sex Stereotypes: Cultural Reflections in the Mass Media
Lois Duke Whitaker

The editor explores some of the research that has been done concerning the manner in which the mass media have portrayed American political women in the news. Comparisons are drawn between the news about women and men in the American political environment. The editor considers influences on the newsmaking process, considers how specific agendas are passed through the media, looks at some of the myths and stereotypes about women that have been portrayed in the media, and describes the white male domination of the news organization. She concludes that clearly the role of women in all facets of American political life is changing; these changes have been and are being reported by the mass media. However, the question then becomes, What is the content of the media coverage? What has been the role of the media in assessing the "reality" of some of these changes? Do women in politics not deserve a great deal more coverage than the media give them? She concludes that additional studies appear warranted as the number of female candidates increases in American politics. Studies especially are needed using multiple methodological approaches that compare the coverage about women who run for elective office with that of male candidates.

What Kind of Women's Movement? Community, Representation and Resurgence
Denise L. Baer

Each successive wave of the women's movement from the 1830s to the present has created new organizations and a new sense of community that advances women's interests. This article reviews the history and groups of the women's movement in the United States, with particular emphasis on the current partisan divide on gender issues. Key factors related to group-based leadership on women's issues are analyzed. For example, if the movement portion of the women's movement is episodic, what are the key indicators of success? Are the activities of leading women's organizations different during periods of resurgence compared to periods of declining mass activists? How do the parties differ in the types of women represented? How influential are women in the 2004 conventions? It is argued that to effectively answer these questions requires debating whether there is a universal outcome to women's progress (e.g., involvement in the public sphere), or whether it is simply providing a range of quite diverse options for women to choose from (e.g., stay-at-home mom vs. working woman). Finally, two factors related to the prospects of the mass resurgence of the women's movement are discussed: (1) the growing gap in activism, partisanship, and consciousness between group leaders, intellectual leaders, and actual and potential "followers"; and (2) the continued nonpartisanship of leading women's organizations alongside the heightened polarization on issues associated with the women's movement. Paradoxically, both factors make it possible for party leaders to reach women voters directly without the mediation of women leaders—a devastating hurdle for expansion of women's gains.

Chapter 4   Women and Elections: The Uphill Struggle

Women Winning at the Local Level: Are County and School Board Positions Becoming More Desirable and Plugging the Pipeline to Higher Office?
Susan A. MacManus, Charles S. Bullock, III, Karen L. Padgett, and Brittany Penberthy

The Year of the Woman, 1992, produced sizable increases in the number of women serving in Congress and in state legislatures. During the early 1990s, more women also captured elective county offices. Expectations were that these women local officeholders would eventually run for higher state and national offices—the progressive ambition theory. At that time, higher offices were regarded as more desirable and prestigious. A decade later, the question is the degree to which local offices have become more appealing to women candidates. This article explores growth in the numbers of women holding elective county offices in two high-growth states (Florida and Georgia) since 1992. The results show that the proportion of women holding certain local elective offices surpasses the proportion of females in state legislatures across the country and in the U.S. Congress. Increased female representation has been incremental in the post-1992 period. Although increases in the proportion of local women officeholders have been greater in rural and suburban counties, women still hold a higher proportion of offices in urban counties (although the gap is narrowing somewhat).

On the Eve of Transition: Women in Southern Legislatures, 1946–1968
Joanne V. Hawks (Deceased) and Carolyn Ellis Staton

Many scholars considered the post–World War II era a quiescent time for white middle-class American women. After a period of wartime involvement, many women supposedly retreated into a more traditional lifestyle. Yet, between 1946 and 1968, almost 100 women entered legislatures in the South, a particularly traditional region. Data indicate that they were predominantly women who were already involved in the public sphere in one or more ways. Even though many were serious legislators, the press emphasized their domesticity and femininity instead of their legislative achievements.

Women Campaign Consultants: A New Actor in the Campaign Process
Sarah E. Brewer

This study highlights the unique working environment women face in the campaign consulting industry, the contributions they make to the profession by the ways in which their work differs from their male counterparts, and the reasons why there are so few women in the industry. The author finds gender-specific rules women face are upheld by continued assumptions about appropriate behaviors for men and women based on sex-role stereotypes. She concludes that women are not seen as strategic and competitive, have to work twice as hard as their male colleagues to achieve their goals, and are punished for being too aggressive in an environment that demands this trait in its professionals. The research also suggests that women may differ from the men in the consulting business in ways that, if they were to increase their numbers, could alter the way in which the campaign industry not only conducts its work internally, but also could change the nature of the campaigns.

Chapter 5   Legislatures, Women, and Policy Making

Women in the U.S. Congress: From Entry to Exit
Jennifer L. Lawless and Sean M. Theriault

This essay explores women's representation in Congress. The authors begin by outlining the traditional explanations for women's numeric underrepresentation on Capitol Hill.

The second section of their analysis explores the power women wield once they are elected to Congress and the manner in which women and men legislate differently, both in terms of issues and leadership style. The third section discusses the gender dynamics of congressional retirement. Together, the various components of their analysis culminate to suggest that trends toward gender parity in our political institutions are overstated. Contrary to the conventional wisdom, gender differences in political ambition and congressional retention suggest that, in the long run, at best case scenario, women will continue to comprise far less than 50 percent of the members of Congress. The authors' findings carry broad implications for women's substantive and symbolic representation.

Women State Legislators: Descriptive and Substantive Representation
Sarah Poggione

This article explores differences in men and women state legislators policy opinions and legislative behavior as well as the effect of women state legislators on a welfare policy. Although the author finds that women's participation in state legislatures does influence policy, the relationship between descriptive and substantive representation is not a simple one. She finds that women legislators' opportunities for influence are mediated by the institutions in which they serve. Specifically, the rules governing standing committees condition women's impact on policy. As other research demonstrates, increases in women's representation at the state level will continue to influence the agendas and policies adopted by state legislatures; however, even a small number of women legislators can significantly influence policy through service on independent standing committees. That is, even a small number of women legislators can influence policy if their policy preferences and legislative activities differ from those of their male colleagues and legislative rules and procedures advantage minorities in the policymaking process.

Chapter 6   The Executive Branch: Women and Leadership

Gendering the Political Executive's Space: The Changing Landscape?
Marcia Lynn Whicker (Deceased) and Hedy Leonie Isaacs

Women are slowly gaining access to the male-dominated political executive's space. Arguably, impulses that include leadership and policy consequences, access to education, the familial factor, and the media may enhance opportunities for women to rise to power. A counterargument is offered: In a political context in which a dialectic of exclusion and accommodation exists, these impulses are two-edged swords.

First Ladies and Their Influence on Politics, Policy, and the Presidency
Robert P. Watson

This article examines the growth of the first ladyship, the types of roles and duties performed by first ladies, and how first ladies have influenced politics, policy, and the presidency. The author concludes that first ladies can be understood more accurately as presidential partners than simply as spouses or hostesses. In each instance, the roles and duties fulfilled by first ladies have existed outside a formal office or official mandate. Instead, it has been through spousehood and the creative and inspired use of traditional roles women have been forced to assume that the first ladyship was forged. Yet, in politics, where importance is measured through access to power, the first lady has enjoyed physical proximity to power unequaled in government, irrespective of whether she held office or not. The author finds the first lady has therefore transcended her outsider status to become an insider capable of influencing politics, policy, and the presidency.

Four of the past five U.S. presidents have used the governorship as a pathway to the presidency. As more women are elected to the governorship, there is reason to expect that women candidates for high national office will come from the pool of U.S. governors. Drawing on the growing body of literature in the fields of women and electoral politics and state politics, this article describes and analyzes the campaigns and administrations of women seeking state elective executive offices and details a five-stage model that includes a new style of women governor labeled the "charismatic outsider."

Chapter 7   The Courts: Women and Decisions

Although Abigail Adams cautioned her husband, John, to make sure that women were remembered as the first national laws were drafted, women have yet to reach full equality under the U.S. Constitution. Over time, however, the U.S. Supreme Court has interpreted various provisions of the Constitution (as well as statutory law) to expand women's rights. This essay chronicles those efforts and highlights the ephemeral nature of rights based largely on interpretations of an unelected judiciary.

It has been more difficult for women to attain judicial office than to attain other public office, but the number of women judges continues to rise. There are indications that these new women judges may be making a difference in outcomes in gender-related cases. This raises the question as to whether women judges may be introducing bias into a presumably neutral system, or whether they may be providing a counterbalance to a system dominated by a male perspective. This article first presents data on the increase from 1976 to 2004 in the number of women judges, or numerical representation, and considers the eligible pool theory as an explanation for that increase. It then examines the potential impact of the increase in women judges on the diversification of gender perspectives on the judicial bench, or interest representation. Results from studies done in the 1970s and early 1980s suggested that men's and women's similar legal training and socialization as lawyers minimized any potential gender differences in judicial behavior. However, more recent studies indicate that, as women's numbers move beyond the token stage and as younger females educated after the women's movement become judges, differences based on gender emerge more clearly. Research on the current generation of women judges suggests that gender-based differences in experience may contribute to a widening gap between the behavior of men and women judges with respect to decisions in cases raising issues of gender discrimination and divorce/family law. This gap is attributed to a "gendered voice" expressed by both men and women judges. The conclusion of this article is that women judges may be providing a counterbalance to a previously all-male bias in family law.

Chapter 8   Public Policy: The Feminist Perspective

Working Women and Their Families: The Family and Medical Leave Act versus The Family Time Flexibility Act
Joan Hulse Thompson

The author examines congressional action on two proposals for helping working families, the Family and Medical Leave Act (FMLA) and the Family Time Flexibility Act (FTFA), both sponsored by congresswomen in leadership roles with the Congressional Caucus for Women's Issues. President Clinton signed the FMLA in 1993 and the Supreme Court affirmed its authority in 2003; in contrast the Republican House leadership acknowledged certain defeat and pulled the FTFA from the House floor in spring 2003. The conflicts over these bills illustrate both the impact of women in the House and the ongoing battle between interest groups representing business and labor organizations. When the Democrats controlled the House of Representatives, the Congressional Caucus for Women's Interests (CCWI) was a bipartisan organization able to advance an activist legislative agenda. Since the Republicans took control of the House in 1994, the CCWI has lost its office in the Rayburn House Office Building and become a less ideological organization.

Sex at Risk in Insurance Classifications? The Supreme Court as Shaper of Public Policy
Ruth Bamberger

Although numerous laws have been passed prohibiting sex discrimination in various areas of public policy, the insurance industry still retains sex as a classification in determining the price of insurance products. Is this practice unfairly discriminatory? The Supreme Court has answered this question within limitations, namely, some justices, as well as judges in the lower courts, maintain that their decisions in no way intend to revolutionize the insurance industry. Over the past 30 years, civil rights and women's groups have chipped away, through legislation, regulations, and litigation, the industry's use of the sex classification. The latest target of attack is in prescription benefits, where numerous insurance policies do not cover prescription benefits for birth control, while at the same time including drugs like Viagra. At best, the Supreme Court has changed public policy in insurance sex discrimination with restraint, though at some point it might have to act as final arbiter in deciding whether pricing by sex classification is unfair.

Affirmative Action and Women
Roberta Ann Johnson

Challenged from all sides, affirmative action, nevertheless, continues to live on as a highly charged issue. This article (1) defines affirmative action, (2) details the development of federal affirmative action guidelines, (3) describes Supreme Court decisions and congressional responses to affirmative action, (4) describes how the states and the lower courts have become battlegrounds on the issue of affirmative action, (5) considers the ways in which affirmative action is a woman's issue, and (6) considers the future of affirmative action.

Chapter 9   Women Empowerment, and Cultural Expression

The Political Is Personal: Third-Wave Feminist Perspectives on Power
Kathleen P. Iannello

Over the past two centuries women in America have been working toward the goal of obtaining greater power in the personal as well as public spheres. The first wave of feminism held as its prize the right of American women to participate in the political process, equal with men, in the act of voting. The second wave of feminism began with "consciousness-raising" groups in the 1960s and also was successful in obtaining power. Collaboration was a cornerstone of second-wave feminism in the practice of consensual organization. The goal of collaboration in consensual structure was to empower women as part of a group, and to share knowledge and information that served to advance the cause of the group. The notion of leadership *was* the group, and women gained power through this participation and group identity. Third-wave feminism, taking form in the 1990s, has just begun to make its contribution to women's progress with regard to power. This article argues that the story of the transition from second- to third-wave organization can be told through specific examples. The author uses an analysis of a feminist women's health clinic that has existed in three distinct forms over the past three decades. Based on the health clinic case, it seems that third-wave feminists seek the individual opportunity to explore, experiment, and focus on their own career development. The feminist struggle in the third wave becomes a personal one.

Inside or Outside? Women's Role in American Military History
D'Ann M. Campbell

American women have played many roles in wars from the Revolution to today. The changes are explained century by century, with special attention to the major wars, when change happened fast. Today, some women even serve in combat roles and combat units. What has not changed is that women continue to be in the minority in organized American military units. Thus, the majority of women in today's American military service remain outsiders looking "in."

Grounds for Criticism: Coffee, Passion, and the Politics of Feminist Discourse
Elizabeth A. Kelly

This essay explores the relationship between coffee and political discourse, paying particular attention to the role of coffeehouses as alternative public spheres. It also examines the often-complex relationships between coffee, coffeehouse cultures, and gender, along with how these relationships have shifted historically. The author concludes with a look at the countercultural institutions that have emerged in the last two decades that draw on the traditions of free speech and cultural and political criticism that were integral to the coffeehouse cultures of centuries past. She describes the GI coffeehouse movement during the Vietnam Conflict and the feminist community organizing and cultural work since the late 1960s, which has often centered around coffeehouses, sometimes in tandem with feminist bookstores and other forms of cultural expression. Finally, the author describes two feminist coffeehouses and the political struggles attached to building alternative social and cultural institutions that prioritize the concerns or needs of women.

Acknowledgments

★ ★

This book is specifically dedicated to the women and men who have contributed to, supported, and been loyal to this project from its inception more than fourteen years ago. I would also like to thank the members of the Women's Caucus for Political Science for their encouragement and advice—even though you are too numerous to name here, you know who you are, and I value and appreciate you. A special word of thanks to the three reviewers commissioned by Prentice Hall to study the essays in an earlier edition.

I would also like to thank Charlyce Jones Owen, Glenn Johnston, Suzanne Remore, editorial assistant, Political Science, and the staff at Prentice Hall.

Thanks to the following reviewers for their comments and suggestions: Kendra Stewart, Eastern Kentucky University; Sally Jo Vasicko, Ball State University; and Laurel Elder, Hartwick College.

And, finally a word of thanks to Andy, my most supportive husband.

Lois Duke Whitaker

The Study of Women: The Theoretical Framework

Until the 1960s, most of the research about movements for women's rights centered on women's suffrage in the nineteenth and early twentieth centuries (first wave of feminism). Since the 1960s, however, an enormous number of studies on women and politics has been added to the scholarly literature. Even a superficial review of the wealth of books, journal articles, and other publications analyzing the relationship between gender and politics reveals that the field of research in this area has grown substantially—and continues to grow.

Over the past forty years, the early scholars who wished to research the influence of women's political behavior in the American political process experienced numerous "growing pains." These included limited financial support for research on the topic, initial efforts to study a field that had established norms identified and defined from a male perspective and male-shaped understanding of the political world, and a tendency to view gender-related research as a "special-interest" focus, "outside" the normal theoretical framework. For all these reasons, many studies on women and politics turned out to be simply descriptive narratives drawn from traditional concepts, as opposed to empirically driven research studies.

The early pioneers of scholarly research on gender and politics, however, may currently reflect on a significant legacy of contributions. These include the present solid body of literature analyzing gender socialization, women's political behavior (at both the individual and the group level), and women's role (to include officeholding) in the political sector. However, it appears that the early scholars analyzing the issue of women in American politics have passed along to the next generation of researchers on this topic a clear challenge to ascertain why it is that, despite the gains women have made, women are still represented in such small numbers in both elective and appointive political offices. Clearly there is a continuing need to use the previously researched information to provide a new agenda in which findings on the role and performance of females in the public sector can be more conclusive. Why are more women not serving as elected and appointed officials in politics? Why are more issues of concern to women and families not being addressed in our public policies? Why are women still being discriminated against and still suffering sexual harassment and domestic violence? What are the political implications for women in the next decade as one looks at the congressional legislative agenda? Will the advances made during the women's rights movement of the 1960s (second wave of feminism) be sustained some forty years later during this third wave of feminism, taking form in the 1990s?

The next research agenda to explore further this issue of women and politics should address these questions. It would seem that only when women are able to mobilize continued support for further advancement in the equal rights arena will the women's movement remain viable. We begin this book by considering the issue of equality for women from the perspective of feminist theory. We will then move on to an examination of gender differences in political attitudes and voting and examine gender cultural reflections in the mass media. We will explore how women have competed for public office. We will look at women in U.S. government. We will then continue with an analysis of women and national policy. We will conclude with a look at a third-wave feminist perspective on power, the role of women in the American military organization, and the implications for political discourse among women centered around coffeehouses. Along the way we hope to provide some insight into the questions raised herein. First, however, let us consider several issues of concern to women from a theoretical feminist framework. For our purposes here, we define *feminist framework* as an overall analysis of the nature and causes of female inequality and an accompanying alternative or proposal for ending women's discrimination.

The first two articles analyze interlocking oppressions based on sex, gender, and race. In our first reading, Jennifer Ring critically argues that feminist theory is a way of seeing the world through the lens of gender, which is always present, but rarely recognized. In political science, as in most academic fields, gender is invisible, with the male gendered stance assumed to be neutral or objective. Ring offers a feminist rereading of American slavery to demonstrate how the perspective of the most marginalized group in the social system, African-American women, actually permits access to the deepest, most revealing insights. Viewing social and political systems from the margins permits greater insights into the "center" or the whole. A more general discussion of the nature of feminist theory along with a survey of well-known theorists, follows the description and analysis of slavery. "Feminist-compatible" approaches to theory are identified as (1) liberalism and radicalism, (2) materialism, (3) a critique of objectivity, and (4) poststructuralist feminism, all of which presuppose a multicultural approach.

Nancie E. Caraway uses the political and epistemological contributions of contemporary Black feminist theory to point up the intersections of gender, race, and class as determinants of oppression. She argues that the texts of Black feminists teach us that feminist theory and politics should address this "multiple jeopardy." She cautions that feminists need to be wary of the damaging consequences of conceptions such as *identity* and *self* that have set up white norms. In her discussion of identity politics, Caraway questions many of the assumptions of mainstream white feminism. She proposes instead multicultural goals in which the themes of racism and identity come together in a configuration that can address the theoretical issues about the female subject. She argues that a critical identity politics cautions us not to become too comfortable too long in one spot with one identity, lest we forget and stifle the ways in which we change, contradict, and grow in history. We begin with these two essays.

Feminist Theory As Seeing

Jennifer Ring

THE INVISIBILITY OF GENDER: CASE STUDIES

The most difficult problem feminist scholars of political science will encounter is the invisibility of gender. This may sound counterintuitive: Surely gender is highly visible. When political scientists wonder why women, despite having possessed the vote for eighty-five years, are not more highly represented in the arena of national political power, there is no ambiguity about who they mean. Women may be proportionally absent, or underrepresented, but few doubt that they know what gender is and can recognize it as an operative factor. So what can it mean to say that gender is invisible to political scientists? What I mean is that gender is omnipresent and pervasive, and yet its impact is all but denied by most political scientists. Feminist theory has as its task *seeing* gender at work when it is most often overlooked.

An eminent political scientist, a man of highly progressive political ideas, well acquainted with and respectful of a feminist perspective, recently lamented to me that so few women scholars seem attracted to the field of American political theory. He mused that perhaps the centrality of the "founding fathers" deterred women from pursuing the field. My response to him was that many women academics, although perhaps historians more than political scientists, were indeed teaching American political theory. Rather than focusing their courses or scholarly research on the writings of Franklin, Paine, Adams, Jefferson, and Lincoln, they

Reprinted by permission.

were teaching the same historical epoch from the standpoint of race and gender. They taught the Grimkes' writings on slavery and revolution, Stanton's, Anthony's and Sojourner Truth's responses to Lincoln on slavery, the debate over the Fourteenth and Fifteenth amendments from the standpoint of the conflict between race and gender, and the political writings of Elizabeth Cady Stanton, Frances Harper, Ida Wells Barnett, Frances Dana Gage, Alice Paul, and others on issues that range from the nature of liberal individualism, to treatises on direct political action, lynching, rape, racism, enfranciscement, and the rights of working people. My colleague had not been taught the works of these American political thinkers and activists, and so he, like many other academics, simply assumed that they were not central to the understanding of American political thought. They might belong in a course on "Women and American Politics," offered separately from "American Party Systems," "The Legislature," "State and Local Government," and so forth. But they were certainly not an essential component of "American Political Thought." He simply did not *see* that he was approaching the subject from his own gendered perspective. This is one example of the "invisibility of gender."

That the canon of American political science has survived as long as it has with so little impact from women's history and politics perpetuates the misconception that the traditional perspective is adequate, indeed complete, and that a course that omits the perspectives of the women who were also a part of history is not male-gendered but neutral. Women simply are not regarded as essential. In terms of the title of this volume, men are the insiders and women the outsiders.

But what do these terms mean? Feminist theory, as a way of *seeing,* must raise questions about the meaning of terms that are often used unthinkingly or uncritically. What does it mean to be an insider or an outsider in American politics? Is the presence of outsiders inevitable? Or, taking a cue again from the title of the book, can women achieve "insider" status in American politics without being interested in changing anything about the basic inequality of American society? In that case, is it necessary to demand that "women" as women be included as insiders? What difference does it make? Implicit in all these questions is the need to examine the nature of equality in the American polity. Why bother to distinguish between women and men elected to office if a feminist agenda plays no role in the politics of those elected? But these questions are all rather abstract. Let's take a look at what a feminist perspective might do to the standard reading of American political history.

In spite of caveats to the contrary, traditional views of political history adhere to an "add women and stir" perspective when it comes to women and politics. The "insiders" never doubt that they have the story right, or for the most part right. If they have left anybody out—blacks, women, and so forth—they can simply add their stories without fundamentally altering the traditional reading of American politics. But what happens to the traditional view when it is truly seen through the lens of gender, and race? For example, the phrase "blacks and women," which I used self-consciously above, has been standard throughout American history and became publicly problematic for the first time during the debate over the Fifteenth

Amendment to the constitution in 1869, which enfranchised black men. The move was regarded as progressive, and the dire political necessity for blacks in the south after the Civil War. Angela Davis observes in *Women, Race and Class,* "As far as Black people in the postwar South were concerned, a state of emergency prevailed. Frederick Douglass' argument for Black suffrage was based on his insistence that the ballot was an emergency measure. . . . For Douglass, the ballot . . . was basically a survival measure—a means of guaranteeing the survival of the masses of his people."[1] Douglass, the eminent abolitionist, former slave, and early "women's rights man" insisted,

> When women, because they are women, are dragged from their homes and hung upon lamp-posts; when their children are torn from their arms and their brains dashed upon the pavement; when they are objects of insult and outrage at every turn; when they are in danger of having their homes burnt down over their heads; when their children are not allowed to enter schools; then they will have [the same] urgency to obtain the ballot.[2]

When nineteenth-century feminists attempted to include the term "sex" along with the term "race" in the wording of the Fifteenth Amendment, they were rebuked, reminded that it was "the Negroes' Hour," and told to withdraw their demands for women's suffrage, lest the enfranchisement of black men go down to defeat under the unreasonable burden of demanding votes for women.

But conceptualizing the debate over passage of the Fifteenth Amendment in these terms is only "reality" from one distorted perspective. Certainly the demand that American feminists in 1869 (both white and black) "get real" was not without some validity: There is little doubt that had the Fifteenth Amendment proposed extending the franchise to women as well as to black men, it would not have passed. The "political realists" who insisted that women suffragists take a back seat on this issue were indeed realistic. Even Angela Davis, who approvingly notes that Frederick Douglass' statement had an unmistakable lucidity about it, nonetheless fails to notice that his position did not acknowledge that black women and white were indeed the victims of specifically anti-female violence; that they were, and continue to be "the objects of insult and outrage at every turn" in the form of public belittlement, ridicule, silencing, pornography, and in the general devaluation of the feminine; that when their homes were not owned by their husbands and fathers in the colonial United States, there had been a history of burning both their homes and themselves, most dramatically during the witchcraft trials; and that neither women nor their female children were admitted to academic schools, colleges, or universities in America until well into the nineteenth century, and even then only very selectively. But even more outrageous and usually not even noticed when rights in America are treated as a finite sum to be divided between "blacks and women," is that the phrase itself renders black women invisible to history. "Blacks and women" signifies that all blacks are men and all women are white, which is fairly devastating if you happen to be an African American woman, or any woman of color for that matter. Uncritical use of the phrase is another example of the invisibility of gender.

Still, our mainstream but progressive political scientist might respond, "African American women constitute a tiny minority of the American population. Empirically speaking, it is not tremendously significant to exclude their perspective on an issue of national importance and vital significance to the African American people as a whole." But that response only confirms that truth is defined by insiders, and that women are marginal figures in American political history. The term "Blacks" is assumed to be sufficient to include black women, because women's distinct experiences are insignificant to those telling the story.

But if we compare the traditional and the black feminist perspectives, for example, on slavery, we get a sense of the price paid for excluding the perspective of the outsider. The traditional liberal reading of slavery treats it as a violation of the rights of individuals: Slaves were forced to labor, had no control over their own destiny or the destiny of their children, and were the victims of terrible violence and physical brutality. All of this is conceived in the American imagination primarily as overwork, whippings, and perhaps other less commonly remarked upon forms of physical torture: branding, mutilation, and so forth. An important component of slavery thus conceived was the "emasculation" of the male slaves, particularly evident in their inability to protect "their" women from white sexual predators. Sexual abuse seen from the women's perspective is seldom associated with racial slavery per se. Rape of the slave women is regarded as incidental: "Oh yeah, and the white masters and their sons sometimes raped the slave women. That was a part of slavery, too." In the traditional liberal reading, the origins of slavery are usually regarded as greed, propelled perhaps by capitalism, and a general lack of morality among southern whites, who used the Christian Bible to justify the inferiority of the black race. Northern slavery is rarely even considered in standard accounts of American slavery.

The Marxist account does add class analysis, but neglects to add sexual analysis as well. To Marxists, slavery was the result of historical contradictions between an outmoded feudal system (southern agriculture) and burgeoning northern capitalism. The two systems were bound to clash. From this perspective, slavery was less a violation of individual rights than a systematic violation of the rights of working people. Racism, or the institutional encouragement of a hierarchy of whites over people of color, simply keeps the working class battling among itself, rather than perceiving their exploitation in class terms, and directing their anger at the appropriate objects: owners of the means of production, either industrial or agricultural. To Marxist analysts racism, and certainly sexism, are by-products of class oppression.

What, then, does a feminist analysis do? How can the perspective of the feminist outsider yield more fundamental insight than the prevailing perspectives? Consider bell hooks' chapter, "Sexism and the Black Female Slave Experience," from her book *Ain't I a Woman: Black Women and Feminism*.[3] hooks argues that racism and sexism may be separable, but slavery cannot be understood without understanding the centrality of sexism. She demonstrates that the abuse and exploitation of slave women, and the insistence upon dichotomizing female sexuality into entirely separate, hierarchically organized black and white experiences, kept not only slavery, but antebellum Southern society functioning. It was an exaggerated form of what has come to characterize much of American sexual dynamics. Slavery is understood as a template for understanding race and gender throughout American history. This should not be confused with a simplistic "all women are slaves" sort of reductionism.

According to hooks, sexual oppression of African women began on board the slave ships. The passage to America was regarded as a time for "socializing" the slaves in preparation for what awaited them. Since women were more likely to work in the household, in close proximity to the master's family, it was crucial that their spirits be broken. The women were kept naked, "allowed" to roam on shipboard (while the men were kept chained below), and raped at will by the ship's crew. Their babies were also the targets of extraordinary brutality at the hands of the crew.

hooks debunks the more conventional reading of slavery, which suggests that the model of brutality was the mistreatment of male slaves, who were "emasculated."

> Sexist historians and sociologists have provided the American public with a perspective on slavery in which the most cruel and de-humanizing impact of slavery on the lives of black people was that black men were stripped of their masculinity, which they then argue resulted in the dissolution and overall disruption of any black familial structure. . . . Implicit in this assertion is the assumption that the worst that can happen to a man is that he be made to assume the social status of a woman. (hooks 20)

While not minimizing the sufferings of male slaves, hooks points to an overlooked dimension of slavery: the explicitly sexual abuse of female slaves. She suggests that black women were the objects of misogynistic treatment that *can* be understood as distinct from racial oppression, and that was also used as a means of keeping white women in line. While black men were *not* emasculated, "not forced to assume a role colonial American society regarded as 'feminine'" (hooks 22), black *women were* masculinized, made to do the same physical labor as men, and sometimes made to wear men's clothing, which was regarded as degrading. No such role changes were forced upon the male slaves. In addition, slave women were viewed as sexual animals, available and unobjecting to any man who chose to impose himself sexually, and the polar opposite of white women, who were "ladies," "belles," models of femininity, but defined by their *lack* of sexual desire. "The brutal treatment of enslaved black women by white men exposed the depths of male hatred of women and woman's body." (hooks 29) And the hatred was harbored against white as well as black women.

> Forcing white women to deny their physical beings was as much an expression of male hatred of woman as was regarding them as sex objects. Idealization of white

women did not change the basic contempt white men felt towards them. . . . As American white men idealized white womanhood, they sexually assaulted and brutalized black women. The deep hatred of woman that had been embedded in the white colonizer's psyche by patriarchal ideology and anti-woman religious teachings both motivated and sanctioned white male brutality against black women. (hooks 32)

bell hooks' reading is corroborated by other women scholars, including Jacqueline Jones, Patricia Hill Collins, and Shirley Abbott.[4] What is eye-opening about hooks' feminist reading is the presentation of sexual oppression as both distinguishable from racial oppression and as a central dynamic in the social organization of slave society. Slavery would not have been the same without the abuse of black women and the sequestering of white women. The antebellum Southern economy thrived on forced "production" of new "labor"—babies—that were the result of the systematic, institutionally condoned rape of black women, as well as the managerial role imposed upon white women.[5] Sexual abuse of female slaves and the control of the sexual lives of white women to ensure the "purity" of the white race is central to any understanding of the functioning of slave society. Indeed, it may be regarded as the essential template. Before this sort of feminist analysis, the rape of slave women could be written off as idiosyncratic misbehavior on the part of individual slave holders, or worse, an example of "boys will be boys." But feminist analysis permits us to see that sexual abuse was systematic, endemic, and *necessary* to the perpetuation of the slave order.

There are no innocent victims in this view: *All* elements of southern slave society are implicated. bell hooks places responsibility not only on the shoulders of white men, who exhibited extraordinary violence against slaves of both sexes and did not even consider the impact of their rape of the slave women on the women, and also black men, black families in general, and the white women and girls who were the witnesses to the "infidelity" and brutality of their fathers, husbands, brothers, and sons. White women were also collusive. True, they were made to feel ashamed of their sexual feelings, and then accused of being cold and untouchable, enabling their menfolk to feel "compelled," and justified in turning to the "available" black women. But instead of confronting their men, white women, who had power over the blacks, but little over white men, blamed the slave women for seducing their husbands, and further punished them physically and emotionally, labeling them "prostitutes," and holding the black women responsible for the white men's infidelity. It was easier to cry "Whore!" than "Rape!"

Meanwhile, the black men, helpless to protect "their" women from the predatory slavers and feeling compromised by their ineffectiveness, were also likely to take out their frustration on the black women. It was easier, at least from time to time, instead of continually facing the reality of such complete oppression, to wonder if their own women hadn't in fact done something to bring on the sexual attentions of the master. hooks regards this as identifying with a model of white patriarchy that encouraged maintenance of male sexual privilege rather than recognizing slavery as both racially and sexually oppressive. It divided black men from women and undermined any chance of political resistance.

But hooks is also critical of black women's participation in this travesty. She acknowledges that

> Most white women regarded black women who were the objects of their husbands' sexual assaults with hostility and rage. Having been taught by religious teachings that women were inherently sexual temptresses, mistresses often believed that the enslaved black woman was the culprit and their husbands the innocent victims. (hooks 36)

But she also observes, "This same sexual morality was adopted by slaves. Fellow slaves often pitied the lot of sexually exploited females but did not see them as blameless victims." (hooks 36)

> They did not advocate social equality between the sexes. Instead they bitterly resented that they were not considered "women" by the dominant culture and therefore were not the recipients of the considerations and privileges given white women. Modesty, sexual purity, innocence, and a submissive manner were the qualities associated with womanhood and femininity that enslaved black women endeavored to attain. . . . (hooks 49)

ANALYSIS

What we see from this example is that a feminist reading acts as a *lens* that permits us to see historical and political dynamics from a previously ignored perspective. We can see the interconnectedness of various systems of oppression, and to the extent that sexual hierarchies are a necessary part of racial oppression, we can understand the position expressed by black feminists, that the oppression of any one group in society inevitably involves the oppression of others. There either *is* equality or there is not: There can be no liberation of black people as long as women are regarded as inferior. Nor can women be "free and equal" so long as racial hierarchies exist.

The "standpoint," or the perspective, of the group conventionally regarded as "most oppressed" is the one that gives us access to what Patricia Hill Collins refers to as "the simultaneity of race, class and gender oppression" in a way that members of more privileged groups are less likely to see, because it would require acknowledging their own unequal access to privilege.[6] But, paradoxically, the perspective of the "most oppressed" also undermines the validity of quantitative degrees of oppression. To ask whether during slavery white or black women were "more" oppressed is to ask a question that is politically useless.

To be more specific: Jacqueline Jones tells of a teenage slave performing one of her assigned duties, cleaning the master's bedchamber. While performing her tasks, she was raped by the master, who appeared unexpectedly in the room. During the rape, the mistress entered the room, discovered her husband and the slave, and severely beat the girl for "seducing" her husband. A more complete and concrete picture of oppression is difficult to imagine. But what is the basis for comparing it to the exploitation of the mistress? The social structure of the antebellum South insisted upon the white woman's silence about her husband's infidelity, drinking, and violence, in order to maintain the privilege of her class and race. In addition, the price she paid for her privilege included the denial of her own sexuality and her efficacy in the world, in the full knowledge that class and racial privilege were hers only so long as she behaved herself. She was forced to act in collusion with a society that publicly and systematically violated the bodies and spirits of women of color.[7] As bell hooks observes, "It takes little imagination to comprehend the significance of one oppressed black woman being brutally tortured while the more privileged white women look passively at her plight. . . . Surely, it must have occurred to white women that were enslaved black women not available to bear the brunt of such intense anti-women male aggression, they themselves might have been the victims." (hooks 38)

To protest, "But the black women *were* more oppressed! Physical oppression simply *is* worse than emotional oppression—if for no other reason than it is life-threatening!" is not entirely unproblematic. It offers only a distracting hierarchy, a rank ordering of suffering, that forecloses discussion by substituting blame rather than struggling to understand how similar problems plague us today. The enumeration of degrees of suffering is presumed to have objective validity, ignoring the subjective experience of oppression. It also patronizingly assumes that black women envy white women.

Rather than acknowledging the still existing sexual hierarchies lying at the core of racial—and economic—hierarchies, the conventional view avoids dealing with sexual oppression by defining sexual behavior in individual terms. In fact, while some masters were more brutal than others, the maintenance of sexual hierarchies lay at the heart of slavery. In order to understand the political and economic dynamics of slavery, we *must* understand the sexual dynamics. Feminist theory offers a perspective on how sexuality is usually rendered invisible by traditional political science approaches.

WHAT IS FEMINIST THEORY?

But what *is* feminist theory? Perhaps we have been able to see it "in action" as it were, from our feminist reinterpretation of American racial slavery. But can a theory be defined in the absence of an example of its practice? From one perspective, no theory possesses substantive content, nor can it influence content in a predictable way. If "feminist theory" always resulted in predictable political findings, it could not really be considered a theory: It would be more of an ideology, belonging in the realm of political action rather than scholarship. So how can there be a "feminist" theory, worthy of the title?

The word "theory" literally comes from the Greek, *theoreia,* "seeing." A theory is a way of seeing. But a theorist cannot approach the world believing that she knows what she is going to see. There are no inherent aspects to feminist theory that make it essentially feminist. However, there have emerged in the history of recent feminism several major identifiable tendencies that have been associated with

a feminist approach. Perhaps it is most accurate to say that there is a way of theorizing that is *compatible* with feminist political concerns, but not limited to feminism, nor capable, like a heat-seeking missile, of arriving at inherently feminist
perceptions. Let us consider the nature of these major "feminist-compatible" trends
in theory. Although most lists are too formal and schematized to accurately reflect
the fluidity of theory, consider the following four themes in feminist theory as handles to use to begin to get a grip on the subject: (1) liberalism and radicalism, (2)
materialism, (3) critique of objectivity, and (4) post-structuralism. These descriptive
titles are themselves both somewhat overlapping and somewhat contradictory.

Liberalism and Radicalism

The range of feminist theory parallels the range of more conventional "male" political theory in the sense that there are theories that view the world in a way that
makes political reform the more "rational" outcome of analysis of the possibilities
of change for women, and theories that lead us to the conclusion that change is
possible only with more radical, pervasive change. Liberal or reform feminism ac-
cepts the framework of existing liberal capitalism and believes the system can be
influenced to accept women into centers of political and economic power. This
moderate feminism takes its cues from Anglo-American liberal individualist theory
and views women as individuals fundamentally. "Idealist" notions such as the liberal profession of belief in freedom and equality are subject to persuasion from rational individuals who are capable of using the existing political structure to bring
about a more inclusive society, which includes women and minorities in increasing
numbers.

In contrast, various forms of radical feminism regard reform as illusory.
Grounded in Marxist class analysis, radical feminism argues that the liberal capitalist state is moved only by what is profitable, and that hierarchies are necessary for
capitalism's continued functioning. Women can "progress" in liberal capitalist society only by displacing others who in turn take their place as low-paid workers, or
unpaid domestic workers and child-care providers. "Equality" for women is a
chimera in liberal reform feminism, since it rests upon the inevitability of inequality
for others, as well as lack of acknowledgement that women come from different
class, racial, and ethnic backgrounds and do not necessarily share the same goals.
From the perspective of radical feminism, change is possible only when the economic system has changed to ensure that no class or group of people is economically exploited for the benefit of others. For purposes of radical analysis, women
are not viewed primarily as individuals, but as members of an economic class.
When the class structure is abolished, when institutionally protected hierarchies no
longer exist, then equality will be possible for women and others. As bell hooks remarks in *Killing Rage,* "There will be no feminist revolution without an end to
racism and white supremacy. When all women and men engaged in feminist struggle understand the interlocking nature of systems of domination, of white supremacist capitalist patriarchy, the feminist movement will regain its revolutionary
progressive momentum."[8]

The Marxist basis of radical feminist theory also lies at the heart of the black feminist contention that no freedom is possible so long as any one group is exploited or oppressed: what Collins refers to as the "simultaneity of oppression." Hierarchies are by definition incompatible with freedom and equality.

Materialism

Another aspect of radical feminist theory derived from Marxist is *materialism:* the belief that ideas are all grounded in concrete, economic reality. Nancy Hartsock coined the phrase "standpoint theory" derived from the Marxist contention that people who work with their hands and bodies have an essentially more complete view of the world than people who do not work with their hands and bodies, who do not mix their subjective human energy with the objective, material world.[9] Hartsock contends that since women do a disproportionate share of the manual and physical work of the world, including the physical experience of childbearing, their perspective, or "standpoint" is inherently more "essential" or complete than the view of others who give orders but have no direct experience of the hurly burly of daily life. The classic example is the wealthy corporate executive who may know how to maneuver in the world of high finance and politics, but who can't make his own dinner, buy socks or underwear, pick up his kids at school, or take them to the dentist or a music lesson without consulting his wife (or her maid). Patricia Hill Collins places this aspect at the center of her description of Black Feminism.

> Very different kinds of "thought" and "theories" emerge when abstract thought is joined with concrete action. Denied positions as scholars and writers which allow us to emphasize purely theoretical concerns, the work of most Black women intellectuals is influenced by the merger of action and theory. . . . Contemporary Black women intellectuals continue to draw on this tradition of using everyday actions and experiences in our theoretical work.[10]

Critique of Objectivity

But the centrality of materialism takes a different form in the legal theory of Catharine MacKinnon. Although her argument is more abstract, its applicability is perhaps most visible in terms of the impact of feminist theory on scholarship itself, specifically in political science. While the materialism of feminist theory is evident in the suggestion that a particularly acute perspective on reality is available to those who are most involved in the daily workings of life, MacKinnon challenges the privileging of objectivity itself. As she puts it,

> *Power to create the world from one's point of view is power in its male form.* The male epistemological stance, which corresponds to the world it creates, is objectivity: the ostensibly noninvolved stance, the view from a distance and from no particular perspective, apparently transparent to its reality. It does not comprehend its own perspectivity, does not recognize what it sees as subject like itself, or that the way it apprehends its world is a form of its subjugation and presupposes it.[11]

The implications of this position are more far-reaching than the "standpoint theory" that grants a privileged perspective to those who directly mix their labor with the mundane details of daily life, a theory that has the potential for creating an inverted hierarchy. Indeed, MacKinnon's challenge to the primacy of empirical reality goes to the heart of most social scientific methodology. It simply cuts off at the roots the traditional argument that the more tangible the suffering, the more oppressed is the "victim," which has been used to silence feminists whenever "more important" issues are at stake. The impulse to hierarchically organize oppression creates a sort of oppression sweepstakes, where the group who meets a certain externally defined conception of oppression wins the attention of whoever defines oppression. Thus, middle class white women rarely appear to have legitimate cause for making demands so long as poor and homeless people are more visibly distressed, or violent young male criminals frighten "respectable" middle-class citizens. Economic deprivation and violent criminal activity appear more urgent, because they are more empirically tangible and visible than the emotional deprivation and silencing suffered by many women. Even domestic violence is rendered invisible when it is regarded as a private, rather than a political problem.

Consider the difficulty of "proving" rape in a situation where no other visible violence occurred (such as beating or knifing), or the difficulty of "proving" sexual harassment. Consider the fact that domestic battery has not, until very recently, been regarded as an issue appropriate to public policy, or that the prevalence of government-condoned mass rapes in parts of the world, sexual slavery, forced genital mutilation of females, or female infanticide are *not* considered violations of *human* rights. Human rights advocates often use the rubric of "cultural relativism" to prevent their intervention in cases of specifically sexual crimes against women. That the offending cultures are entirely male-defined is not noticed, hence once again gender is rendered invisible. Returning to our example of American racial slavery, the impact of rape and forced breeding upon slave women is less comprehensible to the empirically inclined who dominate the social sciences, because it *looks* just like consensual heterosexuality, pregnancy, and childbirth. Being beaten, wearing rags, and working long hours in backbreaking field labor *looks* more oppressive, from this point of view, and so it becomes the very model for slavery.

Post-Structuralist Feminism

With the ability to challenge the primacy of conventional stories about reality, we are close to the stance of "post-modern" or "deconstructionist" feminist theory. And this brings us right back to the question of outsiders or insiders. Deconstructionist theory replaces the authority of traditionally held views with radical perspectives from the margins, much as we have done in this chapter. Instead of proceeding as a numerically minded empiricist might, by assuming that the perspective of the most populous group, or the people with the most power, money or education provides the most reliable account, deconstructionist, or post-modern feminism begins with the most marginal and overlooked viewpoint—in the case of American slavery, from the viewpoint of African American women—assumes its validity, if not its universality, then employs it to gain access to truths not available to those whose reality is more "central." Obviously, implicit in the deconstructionist stance is the assumption that there can be no *one* central, legitimate perspective. Only through a dialogue, or actually a dialectic of multiple and often conflicting perspectives can a (still transitory) purchase on reality be achieved. This can be a rather never-wracking approach to truth, but it has the radical potential to undermine the legitimacy of conventionally accepted authorities. It is a learning tool, a lens, as is all theory.

We have explored several dominant approaches in feminist theory to see how they alter our way of looking at history and politics, at least according to the single example of American slavery. What are the questions feminist theory is likely to raise when exploring the issues in the remainder of this book, about women in contemporary politics, seeking access to conventional centers of power?

NOTES

1. Angela Davis, *Women, Race and Class* (New York: Vintage, 1983), p. 80.

2. From Elizabeth Cady Stanton, *History of Woman Suffrage,* Vol. 2, p. 382. Quoted in Davis, *op. cit.,* p. 82.

3. bell hooks, *Ain't I a Woman: Black Women and Feminism.* (Boston: South End Press, 1981). Page references follow in parentheses in text.

4. See Jacqueline Jones, *Labor of Love, Labor of Sorrow: Black Women, Work and the Family, From Slavery to the Present.* (New York: Vintage, 1985); Patricia Hill Collins: *Black Feminist Thought: Knowledge, Consciousness, and the Politics of Empowerment.* (New York: Routledge, 1990); Shirley Abbott, *Womenfolks: Growing Up Down South,* (New York: Ticknor and Fields, 1983).

5. "Willing or not, thousands of Southern women in the first half of the nineteenth century were confronted with this scenario. Ladies were no longer a luxury of upper-class life in the Tidewater. They were a managerial necessity, and a psychological and moral one as well. For if slavery was to be the foundation of economic life, and if one important crop on any large farm includes healthy black babies, a plantation becomes a complex domestic mechanism that can hardly be expected to function without a white woman around to figure out the endless details. Not only that, without her supposedly softening and mitigating influence around the place—or her mere cosmetic value—the whole operation quickly turns too rotten for a Christian to contemplate." (Shirley Abbott, *Womenfolks: Growing Up Down South.* [New York: Ticknor and Fields, 1983] pp. 88–89).

6. "Viewing the world through a both/and conceptual lens of the simultaneity of race, class, and gender oppression and of the need for a humanist vision of community creates new possibilities for empowering Afrocentric feminist knowledge. Many Black feminist intellectuals have long thought about the world in this way because this is the way we experience the world." Patricia Hill Collins, *Black Feminist Thought.* (New York: Routledge, 1990) pp. 221–222.

7. Jones offers this account of one white women's misery: "Divorce petitions provide one of the few sources that reveal white wives' outrage in response to their husbands' provocative behavior. For example, a witness in a Virginia divorce case in 1848 offered the following testimony: A master one morning told his favorite slave to sit down at the breakfast table, 'to which Mrs. N [his wife] objected, saying . . . that she (Mrs. N) would have her severely punished.' The husband then replied 'that in that event he would visit her (Mrs. N) with a like punishment. Mrs. N then burst into tears and asked if it was not too much for her to stand.' Like at least some other masters, Mr. N freely admitted that his initial attraction to his future wife stemmed from her 'large Estate of land and negroes." (Thus a favorable marriage became one more consideration for the ambitious slaveholder.) However, this particular husband went out of his way to demonstrate his 'strong dislike and aversion to the company' of his bride by sleeping with the slave woman 'on a pallet in his wife's room' and frequently embracing her in the presence of his wife. Mrs. N's first response was to lay 'her hands in an angry manner on the said servant.' Her husband, besides threatening his wife with bodily harm, 'told her if she did not like his course, to leave his house and take herself to some place she liked better.'" p. 26

8. bell hooks, *Killing Rage, Ending Racism.* (New York: Henry Holt and Company, 1995) See especially the chapters "Revolutionary Feminism" and "Teaching Resistance", e.g., "It should have come as no surprise to any of us that those white women who were mainly concerned with gaining equal access to domains of

white male privilege quickly ceased to espouse a radical political agenda which included the dismantling of patriarchy as well as an anti-racist, anti-classist agenda. . . . Nor should it have surprised us that those individual white women who remained true to the radical and/or revolutionary vision of feminist politics . . . were soon marginalized as feminist politics entered the mainstream." (99) Also her discussion of the role of the mass media in "perpetuating and maintaining the values of white supremacy. Constantly and passively consuming white supremacist values both in educational systems and via prolonged engagement with mass media, contemporary black folks, and everyone else in this society, are vulnerable to a process of overt colonization that goes easily undetected. . . ." (111)

9. Nancy Hartsock, *Money, Sex and Power.* (New York: Longman, 1983) and "The Feminist Standpoint," in *Discovering Reality,* ed. Sandra Harding and Merrill B. Hintikka (Dordrecht, Holland: D. Reidel, 1983).

10. Collins, *op. cit.,* p. 29.

11. Catharine MacKinnon, "Feminism, Marxism, Method and the State" in *Feminist Theory: A Critique of Ideology,* ed. Nannerl O. Keohane, Michelle Z. Rosaldo, and Barbara C. Gelpi, (Chicago: University of Chicago Press, 1982). p. 23.

FURTHER READING

Collins, Patricia Hill, *Black Feminist Thought: Knowledge, Consciousness, and the Politics of Empowerment,* 1990. New York: Routledge.

Davis, Angela, *Women, Race and Class,* 1983. New York: Vintage.

Flax, Jane, *Thinking Fragments: Psychoanalysis, Feminism and Post-modernism in the Contemporary West,* 1990. Berkeley: University of California Press.

Hartsock, Nancy, *Money, Sex and Power,* 1983. New York: Longman.

hooks, bell, *Ain't I a woman: Black Women and Feminism,* 1981. Boston: South End Press.

hooks, bell, *Killing Rage, Ending Racism,* 1995. New York: Henry Holt and Company.

Keohane, Nannerl O., Michelle Z. Rosaldo, and Barbara Gelpi, *Feminist Theory: A Critique of Ideology.* 1982. Chicago: The University of Chicago Press.

MacKinnon, A. Catharine, *Towards a Feminist Theory of the State,* 1989. Cambridge: Harvard University Press.

Ring, Jennifer, *Modern Political Theory and Contemporary Feminism: A Dialectical Analysis,* 1991. Albany: State University of New York Press.

The Riddle of Consciousness: Racism and Identity in Feminist Theory

Nancie E. Caraway

INTRODUCTION

Feminist scholarship offers both an intellectual and a political stimulus to under-graduate students in political science. It may fruitfully be called syncretic because it "brings together" so many threads about knowledge, political action, and power—and the implications of scholarship in general. Formally, it is akin to African American studies, gay studies, and other moments in ethnic studies (Chicano, Latino, Asian, Arab, Native American) because it crosses disciplines and introduces students to historical, theoretical, empirical, and interpretive modes of inquiry. And, importantly, these academic initiatives recognize their ties to grass-roots constituencies and movements for social justice. Being explicitly tied to social movements belies the claims of "neutrality" and "objectivity" professed by much social science conventional wisdom.

The increasing encounter of feminist scholarship with traditional concerns of political science (such as the Constitution, the judiciary, and electoral politics) has been challenging and revitalizing. It has displaced naturalized taboos (as in, "It's not natural for women/Blacks to participate in the nation's civil life") and exposed as riddles what were considered universal truths (as in, "We all know that politics is about state and national security, not sexual double standards, parenting, or housework"). It has resulted in the inclusion of courses in feminist theory in most

Reprinted by permission.

political science departments at U.S. universities. This inclusion, however, carries with it the important caveat that one can't "just add women and stir."

The feminist imperative expands knowledge because it requires that we rethink old categories and accepted truths that have excluded women and women's experiences. What this means is that the concept of gender (the socially constructed "masculine" and "feminine" meanings attached to our biological plumbing) is now considered along with political authority, freedom, democracy, justice, race, and class as one of the important markers of political experience. The challenge requires as well new explanatory theories of "how things came to be this way" and new agendas for stimulating critical consciousness and accountability for oppression—whether oppression is practiced by the state, men, corporations, whites, *or* women.

The history of feminism itself is crucially a history of theory. Feminist scholarship has worked to demystify theory's abstractions by insisting, not only that the personal is political, but that the very meanings of the political and what counts as political experience are open to radical reinterpretation. This rethinking of traditional categories such as democracy, citizenship, and consciousness has enabled feminist theorists to ask subversive questions of the "canons" of political science: Which actions and experiences are considered political? How has the liberal public–private split rendered invisible women's contributions to culture? Who benefits from a social and political structure that subjugates women? What processes of identity and consciousness "produce" female and male political actors? And, importantly, how have traditional concepts of citizenship excluded women of all races?

So, although traditional concerns of political science remain legitimate, the perspectives from which they are examined are radicalized by feminist theory. Feminist political theorists have also turned to their own practices. They are attempting to examine the interlocking oppressions based on sex, gender, race, class, sexual preference, national origin, and ethnicity—and to devise strategies for overcoming those oppressions. Feminist theory describes (never unproblematically) the world from the perspectives of women by asking what kinds of political power and actions contribute to a more egalitarian society. This probing critique of traditional theories of citizenship and democracy has highlighted women's alternative political practices and the masculinist thought that has relegated women to inferior positions in the public world.

An analysis of grassroots activism of diverse women in the United States and other parts of the world historically has redefined the way "politics" is often thought of in our culture—as the actions of male elected officials. By making the activities of previously invisible women central, feminist scholars are helping to write both them and a new conception of democracy into the history of social change.

One of the most compelling turns in contemporary feminist theory is the emphasis on racism within feminists and the ways in which "women's oppression" has reflected the concerns of middle-class white women. This affords many new voices and feminisms the opportunity to negotiate community. Feminist women of color have insisted on articulating their own identities and experiences. In response, white feminists are working to contribute to this expanded understanding of "women" by interrogating their own racism, privilege, and the need for historical accountability for American apartheid and white supremacy. This is a painful but potentially liberating process that views racism and sexism not solely as "problems" but as textured ways of defining reality and living our lives. White feminists have learned that they too are "racialized."

The emphasis in feminist theory on identity politics, ethical commitments to creating coalitions of diverse women, and reflections on critical consciousness itself sets a new agenda for students of politics. These new configurations inhabit a challenging world of social theory to which I hope to introduce female and male political science students. A gentle warning to readers: Theoretical language provokes and often frustrates newcomers. But try to work with it. Think of theory's often technical terminology as an occasion for high-spirited translation (of the type required when we strain to "understand" the riffs of a Dylan concert)—and intellectual growth.

Multicultural feminist theory (the name for the dynamics I've been discussing) has its own mode of communicating—like rap, blues, jazz, or African American gospel testifying. The language of theory, however, does pose problems: It's dense, and it may ask that we read against the grain, follow the flow a bit while it teases us into a new coded way of thought. Much of these sentiments derive from something called *post-modernism* or *post-structuralism*—an intellectual attitude that offers skeptical insights, some of which are helpful to thoughtful feminists, some obfuscatory. This essay tries to sort out the criteria. Think of your frustration with theory-talk not as a declaration of verbal warfare, but as a meeting place of thought and spirit, a process of riddle solving.

As you travel the sometimes demanding terrain of this essay, remember the goal of creating a more robust "woman-friendly polity."[1] Toward this end, I employ two symbolic images of identity and consciousness in this essay as an entrée to these issues in current feminist theory: Toni Morrison's narrative in her novel of slavery, *Beloved,* and the autobiographical essay "Identity: Skin Blood Heart" by the white feminist Minnie Bruce Pratt.

KNOWING AND BEING: RACISM AND QUESTIONS OF FEMINIST THEORY

> Here, she said, in this place we flesh; flesh that weeps, laughs; flesh that dances on bare feet in grass. Love it. Love it hard. Yonder they do not love your flesh. They despise it. They don't love your eyes; they'd just as soon pick em out. No more do they love the skin on your back. Yonder they flay it. And O my people they do not love your hands. Those they only use, tie, bind, chop off and leave empty. Love your hands! Love them. Raise them up and kiss them. Touch others with them, pat them together, stroke them on your face 'cause they don't love that either. *You* got to love it, *you!*[2]

With this extraordinary declaration from her novel of enslavement,[3] Toni Morrison's "unchurched preacher" Baby Suggs articulates the passion of collective self-affirmation to her congregation of ex-slaves. Morrison's narrative speaks to the symbolic project that has defined the African American quest for agency and free space in the world the "whitethings" created.

This white world condemned by Morrison's text is a world in which African Americans have had their stories, identities, and very being defined by hegemonic white culture. I, as a white feminist, inhabit a similarly hegemonic terrain, that of the community of feminist scholars and activists whose legacy, too often, has been one of "whitethings" defining feminist life and aspirations for women of color. Fortunately, for our ethical health and our political direction, new stories, theories, and strategies voiced by feminist women of color are retooling feminist thought in penetrating and passionate modes to transform a deracinated "whitething" feminism. In this article, I want to chart some contours of this new multicultural direction, situate them within certain themes of identity politics, and provide a pedagogy about accountability for overcoming racism and developing critical consciousness, themes that come to us from Minnie Bruce Pratt.

As a political theorist, not a literary critic, I began to engage the coda of subjectivity and identity not through a technical philosophical discourse, but from the sheer emotional pull of Morrison's exhortation about the flesh of Black slaves—that is, the *identity* project of African Americans. The graphic physicality of Baby Suggs's statement concretizes for us that theory is truly never removed from the power-laden context of specific historical lives. When intellectuals consider utterances such as "deconstruction of the subject"—a provocative but often tediously hollow postmodernist challenge to certainties that we can truly "know" our "selves"—we need only return our thoughts to Morrison's prayerful *subjects* in the sun-dappled forest clearing to remember what social analysis is "about." This focus alerts us to the contributions of Black feminist theory to "our" (all women's) sense of the female subject. What can we learn about a revitalized polity and a newly committed series of feminisms if we look for the theoretical issues entangled within the arc narrated by Morrison?

Morrison's statement "*You* got to love it. *You!*" rejects the stigmas of otherness and difference inculcated by white supremacist culture, and validates, albeit tenuously, subjectivity and identity. This statement thus intersects in important ways with current epistemological debates—debates over "how we know what we know"—in feminist theory.[4] In particular, it demonstrates the creative challenges of Black feminism to feminist theory and politics.[5]

I have used Morrison's words to call attention to white racism within feminism and to validate feminist efforts at ending racist oppression as the central goal of feminist politics today. Let me note that the militant voices and courage of African American women were first to insist on the important task of decentering "whiteness" as the norm in feminist politics. In many historical moments, they have served as the conscience of feminist practice, the spirit that drives the movement back to the essential commitment feminist scholars ought to have toward enhancing the lives of marginalized women.

Contemporary Black feminist theory arises from the same spirit of affirmation and specificity reflected in Morrison's exhortation to the nineteenth-century Black community. The analysis that I will develop here characterizes such a project as "identity politics." But how do we reconcile this concern with agency and identity, given the red flags postmodernism sends up? The cultural power of our symbolic systems to seduce, delude, and encourage conceits about "self" and "authenticity" bear the footprints of metaphysics and take us away from the social and historical moorings in which such needs are produced. I want to think of identity politics as a contextual, not essentialist, process evolving out of political commitments and struggles for justice in multicultural feminist coalitions.[6] Identity is in the etched details of mediated lives and struggle. The reflective and reflexive political biography of the white feminist Minnie Bruce Pratt, to which I will return, is a luminous example of such a justice-seeking identity. Pratt's story is a chronicle of the fits and starts of seeking to know "how" one "is," a crucible of how a white feminist in a racist movement can be politicized through identity politics into a deeply personal interrogation of her own historical and racial roots.

What I hope to suggest in this essay is that questions about the self, about knowing and being, are not mutually exclusive. I am arguing that we must be able to articulate *some experiential foundation,* some notion of self, before we may act in the world. Rather than polarize antagonisms between feminists who "think" and feminists who "act," we need to see reflection and resistance as equally valid requirements of political and civic experience. Questions about and strategies for experiencing "identity" are crucial in this process. The perspectives derived from identity politics seek to emphasize the deep context, the "situated knowledges" (to use Donna Haraway's term), of our connected lives. Such a foundation is powerfully rendered in Morrison's preacher Baby Suggs's commentary: "In this place we flesh . . . *You* got to love it, *you!*" As Black feminist Cheryl Townsend Gilkes has pointed out, questions of identity have both historical and spiritual resonance for Black women *and* men. Black women's life experiences are grounded in a context that derives personal identity collectively, from a larger racially oppressed community "bound together by common interest, kinship, and tradition."[7] In charting the heroic and courageous activism of Black women in their struggle for dignity and equality ("uplift of the entire race") throughout American history, contemporary Black feminist historians *assume* the necessity of political agency, subjectivity, and identity as the very condition for social change.[8]

As a corollary to this understanding of the self as an entity that *is,* but is always in process, under seige, evolving as persons and events touch and change, African American women insist that for feminist discourse and politics to be relevant to their daily concerns, they must acknowledge the intersections of gender, race, and class as determinants of oppression, and not view gender as the *primary* form of oppression. This revolutionary paradigm shift is transforming feminism; we all are emerging from a new feminist "text" freshly educated about redefining the boundaries and connections of otherness. One need only observe the spectrum of contemporary feminist communities and activities to see the impact of such thinking. The writings of Black feminists are teaching us, in this regard, that feminist theory and politics should address the "multiple jeopardy" and "multiple consciousness" of Black women, in Deborah King's formulation.[9]

IDENTITY POLITICS: POSITIONAL RESISTANCE TO WHITE RACISM

As articulated by the Black feminist Combahee River Collective in a 1977 manifesto, "Our politics evolve from a healthy love for ourselves, our sisters, and our community. . . ." Their first commitment was to the cultural center they shared as women within the Black community.

> Even our Black women's style of talking, testifying in Black language about what we have experienced, has a resonance that is both cultural and political. We have spent a great deal of energy delving into the cultural and experiential nature of our oppression out of necessity because none of these matters have ever been looked at before. No one before has ever examined the multilayered texture of Black women's lives.[10]

The collective determined to align with progressive Black men in solidarity to resist racist oppression—struggling with them against sexism—and to frame their own oppression within the overlapping networks of family and community ties. More recently, Deborah King has spelled out these webbed commitments of Black feminists to the "special circumstances of our lives in the United States: the commonalities that we share with all women, as well as the bonds that connect us to the men of our race." King acknowledges the "distinctive context for Black womanhood," which she insists be defined and interpreted by Black women themselves: "While drawing on a rich tradition of struggle as blacks and as women, we continually establish and reestablish our own priorities."[11]

These statements argue for a politics of identity that is embodied in experiences and cultural spaces whose meanings are determined by those who live their daily lives in the tissue of interwoven contradictions. Alliances, priorities, and interpretations of self are relational and not responses to any set of given objective needs. Identity politics here finds affinity with a conceptualization of Donna Haraway in her explication of a feminist "objectivity" grounded in "partial local knowledges": "Feminism is about the sciences of the multiple subject with (at least) double vision. Feminism is about a critical vision consequent upon a critical positioning in unhomogeneous gendered social space."[12]

The operative phrase here is "critical positioning." For homophobes and chauvinists along with racists may well lay claim to a particular locus of cultural groundings and alliances that teach intolerance and racial and sexual revanchism. One might envision a mythologizing of David Duke as a southern populist, white male grass-roots expression of Arcadian-inspired public will, or even "white male, ex-Klansman and neo-Nazi"—that is to say, Duke's "identity." But it is not enough to issue a cultural–demographic schemata of one's identity-defining characteristics. In order to meet the politicized and justice-seeking criteria of identity politics, a fully articulated resistance and a critical positioning to oppression must be present. The multiple "subject" or shifting self that often comes to life in "nonfeminist" settings—as the women of the Combahee River Collective recognized—provides a more democratized terrain for feminist civic potential.

One colloquial way of stating this principle is to say that, as feminists, we need to "start where people are at," not insisting that feminist identity be based on shedding familial, regional, or religious local skins. How is it then that Black feminism's embodiment of identity politics demonstrates a *critical* and thus valorized stance?

One would be on dangerous ground in projecting a romanticized image of "the oppressed" as beyond criticism. We diminish our critical edge if we dismiss postmodernist admonitions about the human potential for culpability in projecting illusions, of adopting institutionalized discourses of truth, reason, and certainty as foundations for political life. At the same time, however, we can look to the political *knowledge* that comes from the oppositional worldview Black feminist bell hooks locates in living "on the edge" of white society.[13]

Such a critical and protean version of identity politics advances a space for political action and collective transformation. All feminists need to see value in the experience of those "on the edge" because such a vantage point embodies a negative moment, inherently attuned to flesh-and-blood deprivation and pain as central to political attention. As one feminist theorist has conceptualized such a stance, the knowledge gained by living "on the other side of the tracks" is justified by the critical positioning of those persons on the margins of societies.[14] The struggle against hierarchies of power is the substance that merits our allegiance to the practices and knowledge of the marginalized.

Toni Morrison in *Beloved* makes clear that "stories" and "identities" in America's apartheid have been far from reciprocal, far from the bridges of empathy and human understanding that ethical consciousness demands of human commerce. The "other" may indeed be alien and murderous. And one "identity" has not been as good as another. Morrison gives us a story about "subjects" struggling to wrest definition of what human beings are supposed to be from white masters. It is their *critical position* vis-à-vis the dominant racist society that must be endorsed, their determination to re-vision an "other" that does not annihilate, rather than their essence as "pure" petitioners.

BE THE RIGHT THING: POSITIONING WHITE FEMINIST IDENTITY AND RACIAL IMPERATIVES

This emerging portrait of identity politics tantalizes the theoretical imaginations of feminist scholars in its bonding of epistemological considerations with imperatives for historical political action. Feminist thinkers/activists may embrace knowledge about the "fluid" and unfixed construction of identity—albeit described in specific, historic local narratives. Such portraits need not be racially (or otherwise) specific; they surely fulfill the intertextual criteria of the most provocative multicultural feminist scholarship by speaking to "us all." Collectivities of multicultural, multiracial, sexually diverse feminists may find empowerment in the resources of identity politics about the shared and differentiated faces of female oppression.

Identity politics is the terrain of social outlaws.[15] It militantly asserts who "we" are and what "we" mean (this holds, especially so, for white feminists given the history of white assumptions in much feminist theory) and engages the potential for those explorations in coalition or affinity venues. It demands accountability for correcting the racism of everyday life which the expanded vision of multicultural feminism reveals to us. I want to briefly explore one of the most penetrating and transformative instances of identity politics work by a non-Black, non-person-of-color (to reverse the white solipsistic linguistic norm "non-white")—Minnie Bruce Pratt's 1984 essay "Identity: Skin Blood Heart."[16]

Pratt's text, an intensely probing mediation on her own shifting selves, is a powerful model for other white feminists to follow in order to question our own complicity in and accountability for correcting the myriad racist practices existing in the world around us—a precondition for successful coalition building. Pratt, a white, Southern-born, Christian-raised, lesbian woman, takes her reader inside an exploration of a divided consciousness, demonstrating the postmodernist feminist thesis that the "wholeness" of the self involves an inescapably protean encounter with others. The manner in which Pratt frames her experiential/political project of struggling to derive an "identity" from which the various layers of her life "fit," empowering her to act, foregrounds questions of otherness and accountability. Pratt uses her feminism, a politics of everyday life, as a springboard from which to investigate self-consciously those many "edges" on which she stands: ". . . I will try to be at the edge between my fear and outside, on the edge at my skin, listening, asking what new thing will I hear, will I see, will I let myself feel, beyond the fear."[17] Pratt is able to let her multiple experiences of otherness float in an uneasy alliance, allowing them to open her eyes to other scenarios of domination and oppression. Her own outsider status as a lesbian alerts her to the marginalization of others with whom she attempts to ally, without collapsing them all into one "grand polemics of oppression."[18]

Central to Pratt's articulation of her search for self and identity are two important metaprocesses that are important tools for white feminists' antiracist efforts. She has the ability to problematize, to evaluate reflectively, every encounter with another and to take nothing for granted in interracial relationships. These displacements provide a valuable corrective to status quo attitudes. Pratt encourages white women to scrutinize the historical and ideological layers attendant to encounters with "others"—paying particular attention to the concealments and exclusions, the buried "holes in the text,"[19] that submerge and mystify the violations of race, class, and gender.

Pratt is frustrated and doubtful of overcoming the chasm of racism. But Pratt keeps on keeping on. These painful incidents become challenges to overcome, not paralyzing dead ends in Pratt's story; they stand as markers of the quotidian signs of racism. As Pratt assays the cost to those whom her own protection and privilege as a southern white woman have disadvantaged, she is able to "free" herself from the poisonous racism by acknowledging her own family's participation in its system. She is empowered to locate the harm, to identify the victims that the vision of the society of her white childhood excluded. By seeking the absences, she may now "gain truth" when she expands her constricted eye, "an eye that has only let in what I have been taught to see."[20]

Revelation and psychological unpeeling continue when Pratt's professor husband takes her and their children to a new town, a Southern "market town." Geography and history again stimulate her questioning of the town whose center, tellingly, is not a courthouse, but a market house. With complacent, middle-class white friends at dinner in a private club overlooking the town's central circle, she queries them about the marketplace. They chat about the fruits and vegetables, the auctioned tobacco that were sold at the market. "But not slaves," they said. It is left to the Black waiter—a silent figure who boldly breaks through "the anonymity of his red jacket"—to assume the role of educator, disrupting white historical amnesia to tell them of the men, women, and children who were sold at the market near where they now dine.

> What he told me was plain enough: This town was a place where some people had been used as livestock, chattel, slaves, cattle, capital, by other people; and this use had been justified by the physical fact of a different skin color and by the cultural fact of different ways of living. The white men and their families who had considered Black people to be animals with no right to their own children or to a home of their own still did not admit that they had done any wrong, nor that there had been any wrong, in *their* town. What he told me was plain enough: Be warned: they have not changed.[21]

The narrative of Pratt's identity journey is a useful feminist teaching precisely because her project does not become a study in narcissism, a withdrawing from political reality. Her newfound knowledge of racist history through a probing of her own personal history serves as a spur toward further inquiry and action. Her ability to approach the world and structures of domination as interlocked, as "overlapping circles," elicits knowledge of other traditions of struggle whose experiences she might draw upon. And importantly in the framework of coalition politics, Pratt perceives scenarios of persons in whose service she might present herself as an ally in their struggles.

> I knew nothing of these or other histories of struggle for equality and justice and one's own identity in the town I was living in: not a particularly big town, not liberal at all, not famous for anything: an almost rural eastern North Carolina town, in a region that you, perhaps, are used to thinking of as backward. Yet it was a place with so many

resistances, so much creative challenge to the powers of the world: which is true of every county, town, or city in this country, each with its own buried history of struggle, of how people try to maintain their dignity within the restrictions placed around them, and how they struggle to break those restrictions.[22]

The potency of Pratt's story at this point in her account of the accumulated identities that she wrestles to incorporate has to do with her own connection to Southern racism. When she sought to find out what had been or was being done "in her name," the knowledge was shattering. "I had set out to make a new home with other women, only to find that the very ground I was building on was the grave of the people my kin had killed, and that my foundation, my birth culture, was mortared with blood."[23] The cracking and heaving and buckling Pratt experienced in what she describes as "the process of freeing myself" afforded no relief, no sanctimony. "This breaking through," she admits, "did not feel like liberation but like destruction." Her expanded sense of political accountability; her endeavors to locate a new "home," a chosen political community of women committed to justice; and her confession of loss are the flashpoints of Pratt's journey toward political conscience. This voice does not mute the pain and alienation such a process entails. Feel the drama in her telling:

> I think this is what happens, to a more or less extreme degree, every time we expand our limited being: it is upheaval, not catastrophe: more like a snake shedding its skin than like death: the old constriction is sloughed off with difficulty, but there is an expansion: not a change in basic shape or color, but an expansion, some growth, and some reward for struggle and curiosity. . . .
> As I try to strip away the layers of deceit that I have been taught, it is hard not to be afraid that these are like wrappings of a shroud and that what I will ultimately come to in myself is a disintegrating, rotting *nothing:* that the values that I have at my core, from my culture, will only be those of negativity, exclusion, fear, death. And my feeling is based in the reality that the group identity of my culture has been defined, often, not by positive qualities, but by negative characteristics: by the absence of: "no dogs, Negroes, or Jews"; we have gotten our jobs, bought our houses, borne and educated our children by the negative: no niggers, no kikes, no wops, no dagos, no spics, no A-rabs, no gooks, no queers [emphasis in original.][24]

Pratt's essay resonates in so many ways with wisdom and warnings vital to struggling antiracist feminists. The integrity with which she describes her story encourages our own probings. Her identity project can stand as a document of feminist politicization precisely because Pratt resists those self-destructive urges that are anathema to enacting social change: the reactionary extreme of abandoning her own complexly vexing Southern culture, the paralyzing guilt and fear that come with the knowledge of the enormity and barbarity of white privilege. Throughout this powerful essay, Pratt reveals herself determined to understand the volatile psychic hold of home, childhood, and patriarchal "protection" of white women in her class. There is no denouement in Pratt's search for "identity," only continued working-through. Hers, and ours, entails a long-term commitment, a meditation on consciousness that is grounded in daily actions that allow us to connect with or bypass the "others" with whom we seek community. This seeking is the riddle of consciousness to be grappled with through political struggle.

Pratt also shows her readers the psychic dangers of denial and its opposite, absorption into the other: the desire to cover her "naked, negative [self] with something from the positive traditions of identity which have served in part to help folks survive our people."[25] Finally Pratt can come to an awareness and acceptance of her own *whiteness*—while resisting the culture of white supremacy, on the one hand, and, on the other, avoiding the condescending trap of "cultural impersonation," of attempting to "become Black." We come to see such gestures for what they are—sentimental balms of political quietism.

In the language of postmodern thought, Pratt's essay provides a "genealogy," a deep sifting through the ideological and historical practices that render the tangle of "self." She asks how the contradictions that regulate her life came to be—in discourse, in history, in region, in family. Pratt offers a response to the issues of racism within feminism that takes us to the other side of paralyzing white guilt. In the "knowing and being" philosophical frame of feminist thought, Pratt's example ties reflection with the crucial next step of political engagement and activism for justice. She offers us the gift of openness to begin again each day that struggle to turn our received "identities" upside down.

CONCLUSION

The concept of identity politics I have attempted to sketch questions many of the troubling assumptions of mainstream white feminism. It brings to life the need for white feminists not only to endorse a call for *inclusion* and *diversity* within feminist organizations, but to go "beyond the inclusion of persons and texts," as Sandra Harding has recently argued, and ask "what should *we* be doing in order to be desirable allies from *their* perspectives?"[26] Identity politics with a postmodern tilt, then, facilitates such a commitment by rejecting the possibility of a common "woman's experience" that can be objectively derived. This reading follows Minnie Bruce Pratt's example in cautioning against the tendency to substitute a critical consciousness, or therapy, or other premises that assume we have an unchanging "essence." We are encouraged to focus instead on strategic discourse, by asking under which conditions we may work together democratically, and on political action toward common goals.

Feminists interested in multicultural goals may employ these ideas with the model of political action in strategic coalitions of diverse women. The themes of racism and identity come together in a configuration that can address the theoretical issues about the female subject so vital to current feminist thought. I hope my epigrammatic beginning, with Toni Morrison's searing accomplishment in *Beloved,* of textually imparting the criminal genealogy of Black flesh in America, reminds us all just what is at stake in questions of identity and racial memory.

We ought not forget how the construction of a "self" that sees its own reflection to those "semiotic technologies"[27] created by the culture that creates us can still feel injustice and endure pain. At the same time, a critical identity politics cautions us not to become too comfortable too long in *that spot* with *that identity,* lest we forget and stifle the ways in which we change, contradict, and grow in history. The achievement of identity itself must be viewed as one moment of political struggle, a struggle that precludes our standing, innocent, on the other side of our cultural mediations.

Identity politics calls for practices of deep contextualization, with accounts of persons that are always explicitly described, colored, gendered, situated—that, to borrow from Louis Althusser, resist simplification in the last instance. And, more importantly, it gives us grounds for politics and coalitions in the renegade terrain of that "real" world of shared struggle in feminist community.

NOTES

1. Kathleen B. Jones, "Citizens in a Woman-Friendly Polity,"*Signs* 15 (4) (Summer 1990), pp. 781–812.

2. Toni Morrison, *Beloved* (New York: Knopf, 1987), pp. 88–89.

3. Although most critics have characterized Morrison's novel as a novel "of slavery," I wish to adopt the term *enslavement.* Black feminist and longtime civil rights activist Ruby Sales has made a strong case for rejecting the word *slavery* in favor of *enslavement.* In her analysis, the former term suggests a passivity and renders the process of enslavement benign. Using the word *slavery* diminishes the moral and political responsibility demanded of the one who enslaves. If there's enslavement, there's an enslaver and an enslaved person. The term *enslaved,* according to Sales, doesn't mean a person is passive; it implies coercive force was used against that person. Further, importantly, the term implies that the enslaved person is resisting. See Ruby Sales, "In Our Own Words: An Interview with Ruby Sales," *Woman's Review of Books,* 7 (5) (February 1990), p. 24.

4. The problematic has been identified in these debates as one of "subject-centered discourse" and is occasioned by currents in what is intellectually framed as "postmodernist skepticism" of the founding categories of Western Enlightenment thought—truth, objectivity, the coherent self, agency, identity—all constructs from which feminism itself derived. For lucid discussions of these issues and feminism's encounter with postmodernism, consult Kathy Ferguson, "Interpretation and Genealogy in Feminism," paper presented at the Western Political Science Association, San Francisco, March

1988; Kathy Ferguson, "Subject-Centeredness in Feminist Discourse," in Kathleen B. Jones and Anna G. Jonasdottir (Eds.), *The Political Interests of Gender* (London: Sage Publications, 1985), pp. 66–78. Linda J. Nicholson (Ed.), *Feminism/Postmodernism* (New York and London: Routledge, 1990); Jane Flax, "Postmodernism and Gender Relations in Feminist Theory," *Signs,* 12 (4) (Summer 1987), pp. 621–643; Linda Alcoff, "Cultural Feminism versus Post-Structuralism: The Identity Crisis in Feminist Theory," *Signs,* 13 (3) (Spring 1988), pp 406–436; Leslie Wahl Rabine, "A Feminist Politics of Non-Identity," *Feminist Studies,* 14 (2) (Spring 1988), pp. 11–31; the entire volume on "Feminism and Epistemology: Approaches to Research in Women and Politics," in *Women & Politics,* 7 (3) (Fall 1987); Donna Haraway, "A Manifesto for Cyborgs: Science, Technology, and Socialist Feminism in the 1980s," in Nicholson, *Feminism/Postmodernism,* pp. 190–233; Donna Haraway, "Situated Knowledges: The Science Question in Feminism and the Privilege of Partial Perspective," *Feminist Studies,* 14 (3) (Fall 1988), pp. 575–599.

5. See bell hooks, *Feminist Theory: From Margin to Center* (Boston: South End Press, 1984); bell hooks, *Ain't I a woman* (Boston: South End Press, 1989); bell hooks, *Yearning: Race, Gender, and Cultural Politics* (Boston: South End Press, 1990); Audre Lorde, *Sister Outsider* (Trumansburg, NY: Crossing Press, 1984).

6. I am persuaded by Judith Butler's reading of the identity problematic in postmodern thinking that the deconstruction of identity need not lead to the deconstruction of politics. Through the dynamic of political

confrontation and coalition politics, we understand who we are and what we mean in our explication of feminist common differences. Butler argues the case "that there need not be a 'doer behind the deed,' but that the 'doer' is variably constructed in and through the deed." Butler does not, but I will, tip my voluntarist hat to Marx for the originary seeds of the insight about the self-defining character of political struggle. Judith Butler, *Gender Trouble: Feminism and the Subversion of Identity* (New York: Routledge, 1990), pp. 148, 142.

7. Cheryl Townsend Gilkes, "Dual Heroisms and Double Burdens: Interpreting Afro-American Women's Experience and History," *Feminist Studies,* 14 (3) (Fall 1989), pp. 573–590, esp. p. 573.

8. In reviewing Paula Giddings's excellent history of Black feminist activism, *When and Where I Enter: The Impact of Black Women on Race and Sex in America* (New York: William Morrow, 1984), Cheryl Townsend Gilkes states clearly that self-definition has historically been a major theme in Black feminist thought. Gilkes, "Dual Heroisms," p. 589, n. 4.

9. Deborah H. King, "Multiple Jeopardy, Multiple Consciousness: The Context of a Black Feminist Ideology," *Signs* 14, (3) (Autumn 1988), pp. 42–72.

10. "A Black Feminist Statement: The Combahee River Collective," in Gloria T. Hull, Patricia Bell Scott, and Barbara Smith (Eds.), *But Some of Us Are Brave* (Old Westbury, NY: Feminist Press, 1982), p. 17.

11. King, "Multiple Jeopardy," pp. 42, 72.

12. Haraway, "Situated Knowledges," p. 579.

13. hooks, *Feminist Theory,* preface.

14. Linda Alcoff has developed a related conceptual framework of positionality as a basis for feminist activism that does not depend on an identity that is "essentialized"—that is, on an identity that is idealized as "transcendent" and "pure," without fault. Positionality, as she defines it, is a contextual strategy of achieving one's subjectivity. Positionality views woman's identity "relative to a constantly shifting context, to a situation that includes a network of elements involving others, the objective economic conditions, cultural and political institutions and ideologies, and so on. . . . The position of woman is relative and not innate, and yet neither is it 'undecidable.'" *Alcoff,* "Cultural Feminism," pp. 433–434.

15. See Shane Phelan's highly original study of the political and theoretical dimensions of lesbian identity politics, *Identity Politics: Lesbian Feminism and the Limits of Community* (Philadelphia: Temple University Press, 1989).

16. Minnie Bruce Pratt, "Identity: Skin Blood Heart," in Elly Bulkin, Minnie Bruce Pratt, and Barbara Smith, (Eds.), *Yours in Struggle: Three Feminist Perspectives on Anti-Semitism and Racism* (Ithaca, NY: Firebrand Books, 1984).

17. *Ibid.,* p. 18.

18. I don't wish to replicate here the emphasis on the subjectivity question in Pratt's project taken up by Chandra Talpade Mohanty and Biddy Martin in their essay, "Feminist Politics: What's Home Got to Do with It?," in Teresa de Lauretis (Ed.), *Feminist Studies/Critical Studies* (Bloomington: Indiana University Press, 1986), p. 206. My approach in considering Pratt is to understand the powerful symbol of political transformation she represents vis-à-vis white racism and multicultural feminist politics. But I do want to acknowledge Mohanty and Martin's skepticism about the potential of identity politics to be incorporated into feminist work for social change. The translation of discourses of self-revelation into strategic grassroots work is not axiomatic; we need to insist that the achievement of critical consciousness is a political, not solely a psychological, achievement. In this sense, a heightened consciousness leads to and requires moving from the local to the global, moving from psychic transformation to concrete acts in the material world to subvert systematic forms of oppression.

19. This is the phrase Friedrich Nietzsche employs in his critique of representation. Friedrich Nietzsche, *The Dawn of Day,* section 523, in Oscar Levy (Ed.), *The Complete Works of Friedrich Nietzsche,* Vol. 9 (New York: Gordon, 1974).

20. Pratt, "Identity: Skin Blood Heart," p. 17.

21. *Ibid.,* p. 21.

22. *Ibid.,* p. 29.

23. *Ibid.,* p. 35.

24. *Ibid.,* p. 39.

25. *Ibid.,* p. 40.

26. Sandra Harding, "The Permanent Revolution," *Women's Review of Books,* 7 (5) (February 1990), p. 17.

27. Eloise Buker offers an incisive path through the dense thicket of semiotic discourse. She argues that feminists need not be "put off" by its technical jargon nor should they fall into a depoliticized passivity in the face of its abstractions. "In fact," Buker argues, "we may well find [postmodernism's skepticism of Enlightenment notions of truth] liberating because we do not have to pretend that we have found THE universal laws, or even patterns that characterize all persons for all times. We can figure out what we think best in our own limited worlds. We will not defer our decisions until we know for sure what to do since we will understand that we always act in the midst of both our knowledge and our ignorance. Putting-off politics is not possible." Eloise Buker, "Rhetoric in Postmodern Feminism: Put-offs, Put-ons and Political Plays," paper presented at the annual meeting of the American Political Science Association, San Francisco, August 30–September 2, 1990, p. 7.

FURTHER READING

Caraway, Nancie. *Segregated Sisterhood: Racism and the Politics of American Feminism.* Knoxville: University of Tennessee Press, 1991.

Bulkin, Elly, Minnie Bruce Pratt, and Barbara Smith. *Yours in Struggle: Three Feminist Perspectives on Anti-Semitism and Racism.* New York: Long Haul Press, 1984.

DuBois, E. C., and Vicki L. Ruiz (Eds.), *Unequal Sisters.* New York: Routledge, 1990.

Nicholson, Linda (Ed.), *Feminism/Postmodernism.* New York: Routledge, 1990.

Flax, Jane. "Postmodernism and Gender Relations in Feminist Theory." *Signs* 12 (4) (1987), pp. 621–643.

Giddings, Paula. *When and Where I Enter: The Impact of Black Women on Race and Sex in America.* New York: William Morrow, 1984.

Gender Differences in Political Attitudes and Voting

There have been revolutionary changes in the lives of twenty-first-century American women. Foremost among these changes are those related to women's employment outside the home. In 1880, for example, by far the largest segment of working women were single. Today, a majority of married women are numbered in the ranks of working women, and women with children are a significant part of the labor force. An emphasis on these changes, however, obscures an important reality concerning American women's working lives, one that is not likely to change in the near future. The fact is that most American women work in so-called pink-collar ghettos, a condition known as occupational stratification.

The next essay, by Gertrude A. Steuernagel, Maureen Rand Oakley, Thomas E. Yatsco, and Irene J. Barnett, examines the effects of occupation stratification on political attitudes and behavior. Utilizing data from the University of Michigan/Survey Research Center's National Election Study and the U.S. Department of Labor, the authors look at political attitudes of groups of women and men in male-dominated, integrated, and female-dominated occupations. They conclude that, as a result of sex-role socialization, life cycle demands, and discrimination, women tend to cluster in what they refer to as female-segregated jobs. The figures the authors looked at indicate that the experiences they have in these jobs affect their political attitudes.

Are women more alike than they are different in certain other aspects of political behavior? For example, some studies have shown that women tend to be more liberal on issues relating to social programs and economic security; that is, women have shown more humanitarian, social welfare–oriented attitudes. Women have also tended to be less supportive of militarist or aggressive action in foreign affairs. What does the record show about gender differences in voting behavior? Why and when do women and men support different political candidates? Why might we expect (or not expect) differences in voting patterns based on gender? Can security issues brought on by a national tragedy/terrorists attacks influence the voting preferences of women as compared with men?

Cal Clark and Janet M. Clark explore and describe the gender gap in the first two national elections in the twenty-first century. These elections produced dramatically different results in terms of the gender gap. In 2000, the normal gender gap emerged in both presidential and congressional elections, confirming that the significant difference in voting between women and men of the previous twenty years had seemingly been consolidated. Yet, for the 2002 elections, the gender gap virtually disappeared. One obvious factor that intervened between these two elections was the tragedy of September 11, 2001, which suggested (to journalists at least) that "soccer moms," heralded as the key to former President Bill Clinton's re-election in 1996, had been transformed into "security moms." This piece, hence, describes the gender gap in these two elections and explores the implications of the 2002 data for gender-based orientations toward American politics.

Voting behavior studies reflect shifts in choices for candidates and political parties. Traditionally, in our two political party system, this has reflected changes in political party and candidate support and emergence of ideological shifts within the two political parties. Cynthia Burack argues that when feminists turned to the American New Right at the turn of the twenty-first century, they confronted a web of ideologies, policies, practices, and institutions that were either explicitly or implicitly antifeminist. She maintains that the cultural and economic agendas of neoconservatives, business interests, and the Christian Right make up the three most prominent constituencies in the New Right constellation. First articulated as a shift from obsolete or discredit dimensions of the Old Right, compassionate conservatism is now one rhetorical device used to market a combination of laissez-faire market fundamentalism, unilateralism in foreign affairs, the erosion of civil rights and civil liberties, support for traditional gender roles and relationships, and the undermining of church–state separation.

In the author's essay, she surveys some of the significant manifestations for women of contemporary New Rights politics. She begins by briefly noting both some terminological issues that situate the New Right ideologically and some figures and groups that are connected to the right in one of a number of ways. Next, the author highlights some prominent themes of the New Right, moving from the social, or "culture war" strand to some brief reflections on links between cultural politics and what is variously referred to as the market, economic, or libertarian/laissez-faire strand. Through the essay, the author highlights women's roles as citizens, political actors, and scholar–critics. She concludes that, with regard to the American New Right, women are both insiders and outsiders.

Rethinking Pink and Blue:
Gender, Occupational Stratification,
and Political Attitudes

Gertrude A. Steuernagel
Maureen Rand Oakley
Thomas E. Yatsco
Irene J. Barnett

Revolutionary changes have dominated the lives of twentieth century American women. Foremost among these changes are those related to women's employment outside the home. This is not to imply, of course, that prior to the 1900s, women were not involved in paid employment. African-American women in particular have a history of combining family and work responsibilities. What is unprecedented about the current employment situation of American women are the numbers of married women and women with pre-school-age children who are employed as wage earners in a part-time or full-time capacity. A few statistics are useful in understanding the depth and scope of this major social restructuring. In 1880, women constituted 14 percent of this nation's workforce. One hundred years later, this figure had increased to 42.6 percent.[1] In 2001, women made up 54 percent of the workforce, and are expected to make up almost 60 percent of the nation's workforce by 2010.[2] During the same period, 1880 through 1980, the percent of all women who were employed outside the home increased from 16 percent to 51.2 percent.[3] By 2001, 59.7 percent of all women held paying jobs outside of the home.[4] Equally dramatic changes occurred in the demographic profile of working women. In 1880, most working women were single. Today, a majority of married women are numbered among the ranks of working women; and women with children are a significant part of the labor force. In 2001, 62.5 percent of married women with at least one child under the age of six participated in the labor force.[5]

Reprinted by permission.

WOMEN AND OCCUPATIONAL SEGREGATION

An emphasis on these changes, however, obscures an important reality concerning American women's working lives. There is a significant characteristic of women's employment that has not radically changed in recent times and is not likely to be altered in the near future. Most American women work in "pink collar ghettos." An employed American woman today is more likely than not to find herself in an occupationally segregated profession. She will work with other women in jobs traditionally held by women—jobs that reflect what society sees as appropriate to women's roles as wives, mothers, and care givers and that reflect women's supposed strengths as nurturers and helpmates. As of 2001, for example, women accounted for 97.8 percent of all dental assistants, 97 percent of all child care workers in private households, 81.9 percent of all data entry keyers, 82.5 percent of all elementary school teachers, 85.7 percent of all librarians, and 93.1 percent of all registered nurses. In contrast, women account for 19.9 percent of all dentists, 1.7 percent of all carpenters, 26.6 percent of all computer programmers, 43.3 percent of all college and university professors, 29.3 percent of all lawyers and judges, and 29.3 percent of all physicians.[6]

Women, despite their race or ethnic group, are concentrated in low-paying and low-status jobs. Certain factors, such as changing attitudes concerning appropriate sex roles and legislation outlawing sex discrimination, have led to a small decline in the degree of occupational segregation. However, familial responsibilities like child-rearing and elder care that traditionally falls on women's shoulders may continue to affect the types of occupations women choose. As such, there is substantial reason to believe that occupational segregation will continue to affect the lives of working women well into the next century.[7]

Some of the consequences of occupational segregation for women have been better documented than others. There is clear evidence that occupational segregation is involved in the wage gap. That is to say, it is one of the factors, possibly the most important, in explaining why women on the whole earn less than men.[8] In 2001, for example, median annual income for full-time male workers was $37,544, while women employed full-time earned just $28,184.[9] A recent government analysis found that women earned an average of 80 percent of what men earned in 2000 even after accounting for differences in men and women's work patterns like work experience and hours worked per year.[10]

In contrast, more information is needed on the impact of occupational segregation on women's conditions in the workplace. The area of workplace health hazards is a case in point. The risks to women in traditionally female occupations, for example, are less obvious than the risks to men in fields such as construction and welding.[11]

Another area which still needs to be explored deals with the effects of occupational segregation on women's political attitudes. Although there has been research into the effect of workforce involvement on women's political behavior,[12] little has been done on the specific effects of occupational segregation. If we want to understand the political behavior of American women, we need to understand the circumstances of their lives. Since there is considerable evidence that women's employment and their political behavior are related, we need to examine the relationship between the specific circumstances of that employment and their politics. Some research, for example, indicates that housewives and women employed in low status, low paying occupations (such as hairdresser and waitress) tend to show less support for feminism than women in higher status, higher paying jobs such as teacher and accountant.[13] This study, therefore, will address questions concerning the effects of occupational segregation on women's political attitudes and will pay special attention to the intersection of occupational segregation and gender as they affect the political attitudes of women and men.

FINDINGS

Fortunately, there are available data which permit us to examine the effects of occupational segregation on political attitudes. We utilize data from the 2000 University of Michigan/Survey Research Center's National Election Study as well as statistics on occupational segregation from the U.S. Department of Labor.[14] To give just one example of the selection process, consider the case of identifying women in female-dominated occupations at the managerial/professional level. Data from the Department of Labor for the year 2000 reveal that the two professional occupations with the heaviest concentrations of women are dental hygienists (98.5 percent) and secretaries (98.9 percent). In the National Election Study (NES) those occupations are clustered together into categories 14 and 24, respectively, on Variable #V000968; Respondent's Main Occupation; they contain totals of 12 and 35 women, respectively (and also 4 and 0 men, respectively). Thus, those 47 women comprise our sub sample of women in female-segregated, professional occupations (and the 4 men our sub sample of males in female-segregated, professional occupations). A similar pattern of identification was used for selecting the other sub samples, which then were aggregated across the different professional classifications to produce groups of men and women in male-dominated, integrated, and female-dominated occupations.[15] In the following analysis we utilize the .05 level of significance in determining statistical significance for each hypothesis we test.

Based on our review of the data, we examine in Tables 1 and 2 the differences between men and women generally in terms of their interest in and discussion of

TABLE 1   Attention to Campaign (V0001201)

	Men	Women
Very much interested	46.1%	37.7%
Somewhat interested	42.0	45.9
Not very interested	11.9	16.5

Chi square: $p = .001$; n = 1555

TABLE 2   Frequency of Political Discussion in the Last Week (V0001204)

	Men	Women
Everyday	54.7%	49.1%
5–6 days	10.4	10.8
3–4 days	17.7	20.5
1–2 days	15.6	17.9
No days in the last week	1.6	1.7

Chi square: $p = .367$; n = 1256

politics during the 2000 election season. The data indicate that men tend to express more interest in following the events and issues of the 2000 campaign—slightly more differences exist than we found in a previous study of the 1996 election season. However, we find that no statistically significant differences exist between men and women with regard to their frequency of political discussion during the campaign season.

That they follow politics less frequently than their male counterparts does not mean that women fail to perceive meaningful differences in social organization or levels of influence among the genders. Table 3 reveals that the majority of women believe that men exercise too much influence in American social and political life, while the majority of men believe they either exercise about the right amount or too little influence. Not surprisingly, a similar majority of women believe they exercise too little influence in society. An interesting finding is that men are about evenly split as to whether women exercise just the right amount or too little influence in American society and politics (see Table 4).

Similar differences between men and women can be observed when we focus our attention on substantive policy issues. Rather than examine a long series of individual issues in search of policy-relevant differences between the sexes, we have simplified our investigation by combining seven separate issue areas into a single index that measures liberalism and conservatism. Responses to questions are measured in terms of the SRC's traditional seven-point scale, which ranges from most liberal to most conservative. The following issues comprise the liberalism/conservatism index: governmental spending and services (Variable #000550 in the 2000 NES), defense spending (V000587), government-provided health insurance

TABLE 3   Men's Influence in American Life and Politics (V0001444)

	Men	Women
Too much influence	41.9%	64.5%
Just the right amount	49.0	33.1
Too little influence	9.1	2.4

Chi square: $p = .000$; n = 1519

TABLE 4   Women's Influence in American Life and Politics (V0001445)

	Men	Women
Too much influence	9.8%	4.6%
Just the right amount	43.1	31.3
Too little influence	47.1	64.1

Chi square: $p = .000$; n = 1527

(V000614), a government-guaranteed standard of living and job (V000620), governmental assistance for blacks (V000645), regulation of the environment (V000776), and women's role in society (V000760). Respondents were classified into three groups based upon the sums of their responses to the seven questions. As Table 5 illustrates, statistically significant differences between men and women exist on the overall liberalism–conservatism scale. As expected, women hold slightly more liberal views than do men and, conversely, men hold slightly more conservative views than do women. As was the case in our prior analysis of 1996 election data, the vast majority of respondents, however, fall into the moderate category.

A similar pattern emerges when we shift our attention from ideological-based issues to an assessment of differences among men and women in terms of their views on government spending. An index measuring preferences for governmental spending was constructed in much the same manner as the liberalism/conservatism index. For the spending index, the seven policy areas covered are Social Security (V000681), crime (V000684), child care (V000685), the environment (V000682), the poor (V000680), schools (V000683), and welfare (V000676). Based on their preferences, respondents were placed into one of three categories, as demonstrated in Table 6. Once again, statistically significant differences can be detected between men and women. Men are less likely to favor increased additional government spending, whereas women are more likely to exhibit the opposite tendencies.

A key argument of this analysis, however, is that concentrating on simple differences between men and women may draw attention away from the more critical dynamics that drive attitude formation. Instead, we argue that social roles—in this case, the effects of sex-based segregation in the workplace—may influence the formation of political opinions. With that in mind, we reformulate the tables above by controlling for occupational segregation.[16]

TABLE 5   Seven Issue Liberalism/Conservatism Index

	Men	Women
Liberal	6.3%	7.7%
Moderate	79.0	83.5
Conservative	14.7	8.8

Chi square: $p = .014$; n = 976

TABLE 6   Seven Issue Government Spending Index

	Men	Women
Increase spending	41.7%	53.9%
Maintain status quo	53.8	44.3
Decrease spending	4.5	1.8

Chi square: p = .000; n = 1659

We turn first to a re-examination of the political-interest and -discussion variables described in Tables 1 and 2. Table 7 reveals that females in male-dominated jobs (i.e., jobs where men make up 80 percent or more of the work force) are more interested in following politics than are females in either integrated or female-dominated occupations (for chi-square, p = .019). Interestingly, we do not see a similar pattern for men. Based upon a review of the data we can conclude that the level of interest in politics among men does not differ by occupational segregation [p (chi square) = .180].

With respect to discussing politics, we do not find statistically significant differences among the genders (with p (chi square) for men = .994, and for women = .150] (see Table 8). This is a change from the 1996 election season, when we did find differences between the genders regarding the frequency of political discussion.

Next, we re-examine the findings depicted in Tables 3 and 4, which pertain to the perceived power of women in our society. Whereas the simple breakdown by sex revealed statistically significant differences in both cases, controlling for occupational segregation here demonstrates significant occupational differences only among men regarding the perceived level of male influence in American society and politics. As Table 9 shows, a majority of the males in female-dominated occupations believe that men exercise too much influence, while the majority of men in male-dominated occupations believe their influence is just about right [p (chi square) = .010]. We find no significant occupational differences among women

TABLE 7   Attention to Campaign

	Male-Dominated Occupations		Integrated Occupations		Female-Dominated Occupations	
	Men	*Women*	*Men*	*Women*	*Men*	*Women*
Very much interested	47.4%	42.9%	44.3%	39.0%	60.0%	32.4%
Somewhat interested	42.9	19.0	43.4	46.2	20.0	50.5
Not very interested	9.7	38.1	12.2	14.8	20.0	17.1
	n = 154	n = 21	n = 221	n = 210	n = 25	n = 210

Chi square: Males p = .180, Females p = .019

TABLE 8 Frequency of Political Discussion

	Male-Dominated Occupations		Integrated Occupations		Female-Dominated Occupations	
	Men	*Women*	*Men*	*Women*	*Men*	*Women*
Everyday	53.7%	76.5%	55.6%	48.9%	59.1%	45.3%
5–6 days	11.8	——	9.2	10.6	9.1	15.7
3–4 days	19.9	11.8	19.9	22.9	22.7	20.9
1–2 days	14.0	11.8	14.3	17.6	9.1	16.3
No days this week	.70	——	1.0	——	——	1.7
	n = 136	n = 17	n = 196	n = 188	n = 22	n = 172

Chi Square: Males $p = .994$, Females $p = .150$

[p (chi square) = .398]. Conversely, we find significance only among females regarding the perceived levels of women's influences in American life and politics. As illustrated in Table 10, the vast majority of females in all three types of occupations believe they exercise too little political and societal influence [p (chi square) = .012]. No significant differences are detected among men, according to our review of the data [p (chi square) = .101].

We also re-evaluate the issue-based ideology and spending indexes, in Tables 11 and 12. Looking first at Table 11, we do not detect any significant ideological differences with regard to occupational segregation. Although we find that women tend to be more liberal than men, no significant differences can be detected among men or women based upon their location within an occupational category. In other words, occupational segregation does not impact upon the ideology of men and women [p (chi square for men) = .072, for women = .485].

For the spending index shown in Table 12, the data similarly reveal that no significant differences are found based on occupational segregation [p (chi square) for men = .623, for women = .073]. However, women do generally tend to favor more government spending than men.

TABLE 9 Men's Influence in American Life and Politics

	Male-Dominated Occupations		Integrated Occupations		Female-Dominated Occupations	
	Men	*Women*	*Men*	*Women*	*Men*	*Women*
Too much influence	35.5%	61.9%	46.6%	68.8%	64.0%	73.9%
Just the right amount	52.7	38.1	48.4	30.3	32.0	24.1
Too little influence	12.0	——	5.0	2.9	4.0	2.0
	n = 150	n = 21	n = 219	n = 208	n = 25	n = 203

Chi square: Males $p = .010$, Females $p = .398$

TABLE 10   Women's Influence in American Life and Politics

	Male-Dominated Occupations		Integrated Occupations		Female-Dominated Occupations	
	Men	*Women*	*Men*	*Women*	*Men*	*Women*
Too much influence	9.9%	14.3%	6.8%	2.4%	4.0%	2.5%
Just the right amount	46.7	14.3	44.3	31.1	24.0	24.6
Too little influence	43.4	71.4	48.9	66.5	72.0	72.9
	n = 152	n = 21	n = 219	n = 209	n = 25	n = 203

Chi square: Males *p* = .101, Females *p* = .012

Finally, we look at the degree of feminist consciousness found among men and women. Our main question is: do men and women differ in their degree of identification with an active role for women in society? To begin, we measure feminist consciousness by constructing a feminist consciousness score.[17] We take the feeling thermometers of eight groups—big business (V001313), labor unions (V001312), liberals (V001311), conservatives (V001310), whites (V001309), blacks (V001308), the military (V001306), and the poor (V001314)—and create a mean group rating for all groups. We then develop a measure of feminist consciousness based on the relationship of the individual's rating of the women's movement on the feeling thermometer (V001318), to their mean rating of all other groups. A second component of the feminist consciousness measure is based on the women's rights scale (V000760). This scale measures the degree to which individuals feel women should have an equal role in society (liberal), or should remain in the home (conservative). We have classified those who rate the women's movement 10 percent or more higher than the other groups combined, and who rate liberal on the women's rights scale, as feminists. Those who do not rate the women's movement 10 percent higher than other groups, but rate liberal on the women's rights scale are classified as potential feminists. Those who do not rate the women's

TABLE 11   Seven Issue Liberalism/Conservatism Index

	Male-Dominated Occupations		Integrated Occupations		Female-Dominated Occupations	
	Men	*Women*	*Men*	*Women*	*Men*	*Women*
Liberal	3.4%	8.3%	5.7%	7.5%	14.8%	9.5%
Moderate	79.8	75.0	75.4	87.2	81.5	81.0
Conservative	16.8	16.7	18.9	5.3	3.7	9.5
	n = 119	n = 12	n = 175	n = 133	n = 27	n = 116

Chi square: Males *p* = .072, Females *p* = .485

TABLE 12   Seven Issue Government Spending Index

	Male-Dominated Occupations		Integrated Occupations		Female-Dominated Occupations	
	Men	*Women*	*Men*	*Women*	*Men*	*Women*
Increase Spending	36.2%	27.3%	33.6%	55.3%	46.7%	52.3%
Maintain Status quo	57.1	72.7	61.0	43.9	46.7	45.5
Decrease Spending	6.7	—	5.4	.8	6.7	2.3
	n = 163	n = 22	n = 223	n = 237	n = 30	n = 222

Chi square: Males p = .623, Females p = .073

movement 10 percent higher than other groups and rate neutral or conservative on the women's rights scale are considered non-feminists. The idea behind the potential feminist category is that those individuals support an equal role for women, but may not have developed an identification with the women's movement.

Table 13 reveals significant differences between men and women in terms of levels of feminist consciousness [p (chi square) = .002]. Our trends reveal that most men and women can be classified as potential feminists, although more women than men have a feminist consciousness.

In Table 14 we discover that no significant differences exist among men and women with regard to occupational segregation. Consistent with our earlier findings, the vast majority of both men and women across all three occupational categories can be classified as either feminists or potential feminists. Therefore, men and women, who do not necessarily identify themselves with the women's movement, nonetheless support an active role for women in society.

As was the case in our prior analysis of data from the 1996 election, definitive answers to questions regarding gender attitudes are not possible with the given data. At this point, all we can do is reiterate the theme that emerges from our analysis here: gender segregation in the workplace does, in some cases, appear to play a role in the organization of various political attitudes. Although the simpler, broader distinction between men and women may be the more important influence on opinion formation, nevertheless anyone seeking to understand the differences

TABLE 13   Degree of Feminist Consciousness Among Men and Women

	Men	Women
Feminist Consciousness	27.1%	35.5%
Potential Feminist	54.4	49.9
Lack of Feminist Consciousness	18.5	14.6

Chi Square: p = .002; n = 1393

TABLE 14   Degree of Feminist Consciousness by Occupational Segregation

	Male-Dominated Occupations		Integrated Occupations		Female-Dominated Occupations	
	Men	Women	Men	Women	Men	Women
Feminist Consciousness	24.3%	40.0%	27.9%	39.7%	50.0%	38.7%
Potential Feminist	55.0	55.0	57.4	49.0	41.7	50.8
Lack of Feminist	20.7	5.0	14.7	11.3	8.3	10.5
Consciousness	n=140	n=20	n=204	n=194	n=24	n=191

Chi square: Males $p = .070$, Females $p = .927$

between the sexes must perform a more advanced analysis and attempt to identify the constellation of factors which could interact with gender to influence political attitudes. In the end, it appears that biology is not solely determinative; to a large extent, culture probably does matter.

SUMMARY

The findings of this study are consistent with much of the current research in the field of gender and politics. Research has indicated, for example, that women and men differ on certain "humanitarian" issues.[18] The women in our study, through their liberal positions on issues and their positions on spending, did display a more consistent pattern of support for humanitarian positions than did their male counterparts.

More importantly, however, our study suggests the need to look beyond the sex of the respondents if we want to understand the significance of gender and its relationship to political behavior. Biological males and females become gendered males and females in the context of particular cultures and particular historical periods. It is useful to think of gender in terms of what it represents for individuals. Gender viewed this way becomes for an individual a set of opportunity structures which a particular culture values. In the United States today, for example, gender is involved in the kinds of work experiences people choose or find themselves directed towards. As a result of sex-role socialization, life-cycle demands, and discrimination, women tend to cluster in what we have referred to as female-segregated jobs. The figures we have looked at indicate that the experiences they have in these jobs affect their political attitudes. We can also speculate that since adult socialization appears to affect political attitudes, the longer women remain in those positions the more their work experiences will affect their political attitudes. This is a subject for additional research. As the workplace changes so will American political life. The hows and whys of these changes present a challenge to citizens and political scientists alike.

NOTES

1. Lynn Weiner, *From Working Girl to Working Mother: The Female Labor Force in the United States, 1820–1980* (Chapel Hill, N.C.: The University of North Carolina Press, 1985), p. 4.

2. U.S. Bureau of the Census, *Statistical Abstract of the United States:2002* (122nd edition) Washington, DC, 2002, Table 561, p. 367.

3. Weiner, *From Working Girl,* p. 4.
Statistical Abstract of the United States: 2002, Table 561, p. 367.

4. *Statistical Abstract of the United States: 2002,* Table 561, p. 367.

5. *Statistical Abstract of the United States: 2002,* Table 570, p. 373.

6. *Statistical Abstract of the United States: 2002,* Table 588, pp. 381–383.

7. Andrea H. Beller, "Occupational Segregation and the Earnings Gap," in *Comparable Worth: Issue for the 80's, Vol. 1* (Washington, D.C.: U.S. Commission on Civil Rights, 1984), p. 23.

8. Beller, "Occupational Segregation," p. 32.

9. Statistical Abstract of the United States: 2001, Table 613, p. 403.

10. United States General Accounting Office, *Women's Earnings: Work Pattern Partially Explain Difference Between Men's and Women's Earnings.* GAO-04-35. Washington DC: October 2003, p. 2.

11. *Women's Health: Report of the Public Health Service Task Force on Women's Health Issues, Vol. II* (Washington, D.C.: U.S. Department of Health and Human Services), p. 16.

12. See, for example, Kristi Anderson and Elizabeth Cook, "Women, Work, and Political Attitudes." *American Journal of Political Science, 29*(3) (August 1985), pp. 439–455; Kristi Anderson, "Working Women and Political Participation, 1952–1972." *American Journal of Political Science, 19*(3) (August 1975), pp. 439–453.

13. Ethel Klein, *Gender Politics* (Cambridge, MA: Harvard University Press, 1984), p. 108.

14. The most recent NES data for 2002 could not be used as the occupational data essential to this analysis was not available in the 2002 dataset. This fact was verified by Angela Pok at NES.

15. The SRC's method for classifying occupations does not allow for a precise identification of individual occupations. Rather than list the respondent's occupation by means of the Census Bureau's 2000 Standard Occupational Classification (SOC) code, the SRC collapses several SOC categories into a single category of similar occupations. In utilizing the more generic categorizations in the NES for selecting our sub samples, we have been careful not to do harm to the segregated nature of the occupational categories identified from the Labor Department's tables. In other words, if too many non-segregated occupations were included in an SRC-encoded category, we chose to exclude all those respondents from our analysis, rather than contaminate the results.

16. In the discussion to follow, male-segregated occupations encompass jobs which are held by men at an 80% rate or higher; female-segregated jobs are those held by women at an 80% rate or higher; and integrated occupations generally fall into the 40%–60% range.

17. This is based on M. Margaret Conway, Gertrude A. Steuernagel, and David W. Ahern. *Women and Political Participation: Cultural Change in the Political Arena* (CQ Press, 1997).

18. See, for example, Sandra Baxter and Marjorie Lansing. *Women and Politics: The Invisible Majority* (University of Michigan Press, 1983); Cal Clark and Janet Clark, "The Gender Gap 1988: Compassion, Pacifism, and Indirect Feminism," in Lois Lovelace Duke, ed., *Women in Politics: Outsiders or Insiders* (Prentice Hall, 1993), 32–45; Nancy E. McGlen and Karen O'Connor. *Women, Politics, and American Society* (Prentice Hall, 1995), 71–72.

FURTHER READING

Bertrand, Marianne and Kevin F. Hallock. *The Gender Gap in Top Corporate Jobs.* Cambridge, MA: National Bureau of Economic Research, 2000.

Bhavnani, Kum-Kum, ed. *Feminism and "Race."* Oxford; New York: Oxford University Press, 2001.

Bridges, William, "Rethinking Gender Segregation and Gender Inequality: Measures and Meanings," *Demography,* 40, no. 1 (August 2003), 543–568.

Card, David E. and Rebecca M. Blank, eds. *Finding Jobs: Work and Welfare Reform.* New York: Russell Sage Foundation, 2000.

Cok, Jacklyn, and Alison Bernstein. *Melting Pots and Rainbow Nations: Conversations About Difference in the United States and South Africa.* Urbana, Ill.: University of Illinois Press, 2002.

Cohen, Philip N., and Matt L. Huffman, "Occupational Segregation and the Devaluation of Women's Work

Across Labor Markets," *Social Forces*, 81, no. 3 (March 2003), 881–908.

Creese, Gillian. *Contracting Masculinity: Gender, Class, and Race in a White-Collar Union, 1944–1994*. Toronto: Oxford University Press, 1999.

Diamant, Louis, and Jo Ann Lee, eds. *The Psychology of Sex, Gender, and Jobs: Issues and Solutions*. Westport, CT: Praeger, 2002.

Gardiner, Judith Kegan, ed. *Masculinity Studies and Feminist Theory: New Directions*. New York: Columbia University Press, 2002.

Hacker, Andrew, "How the B.A. Gap Widens the Chasm Between Men and Women," *Chronicle of Higher Education*, 49, no. 41 (June 20, 2003), B10, 2p, 1c.

Howell, Susan E., and Christine L. Day, "Complexities of the Gender Gap," *The Journal of Politics*, 62, no. 3 (August 2000), 858–874.

USEFUL WEB SITES

http://www.jobwatch.org. Produced by the Economic Policy Institute, this Web site tracks jobs and wages.

http://www.aflcio.org/issuepolitics/women/. This is the section of the Web site of the labor union, the AFL-CIO, devoted to issues affecting women. There are links to information on women in the global economy, equal pay, and concerns and priorities of women in the workforce.

http://www.idea.int/gender. The Web site of IDEA, the Institute for Democracy and Electoral Assistance, devotes this section to gender issues of women and political participation from an international perspective.

http://www.bls.gov/cps/. The Web site of the U.S. Department of Labor Bureau of Labor Statistics presents labor statistics from the Current Population Survey. The Current Population Survey is conducted monthly and provides data on issues such as weekly earnings, union affiliation, and employee absences.

http://aarp.org. This is the Web site of the American Association of Retired Persons. It provides information on the impact of occupational segregation on the retirement income of women and minorities.

http://www.iwpr.org. This is the Web site of the Institute for Women's Policy Research, a public policy research group that focuses on issues such as employment and earnings and work and family issues.

Web Sites for Further Information

United States General Accounting Office (GAO), http://www.gao.gov

United States Department of Labor, http://www.dol.gov

Women's Bureau, United States Department of Labor, http://www.dol.gov/wb

Women in Development, United States Agency for International Development http://www.usaid.gov/our_work/cross-cutting_programs/wid

Office of Women's Business Ownership, United States Small Business Administration, http://www.sba.gov/financing/special/women.html

Feminist Majority, Feminist Gateway—Internet resources, http://www.feminist.org/gateway

9 to 5, National Association of Working Women, http://www.9to5.org

Urban Institute, http://www.urbaninstitute.org

Women Employed, http://www.womenemployed.org

National Organization for Women, http://www.now.org

AFL-CIO, http://www.aflcio.org

National Election Study, http://www.umich.edu/~nes

2002 Statistical Abstract of the United States, http://www.census.gov/prod/www/statistical-abstract-02.html

The Gender Gap in the Early 21st Century: Volatility from Security Concerns

Cal Clark
Janet Clark

The 1980 presidential election marked an important new development in American voting behavior. Before then there had been little difference in how women and men voted in national elections; and, in the few elections when there was a significant difference, women were more supportive of Republicans than men. In 1980, in contrast, Democratic President Jimmy Carter received 45% of women's votes compared to just 36% of men's, creating a "gender gap" of nine percentage points. This turned out to be far from the idiosyncratic result of candidate personalities or events in the 1980 campaign. Rather, for the rest of the twentieth century similar gender gaps existed in presidential elections and emerged a little more slowly in the aggregate vote in congressional campaigns (see Table 1).

The attention that has been paid to this gender gap has varied considerably over time. Initially, feminist politicians and scholars trumpeted women's disproportionate support of Democratic candidates, presumably as a strategy for making that party more responsive to their primary issue concerns.[1] Then, the mainstream press seized on the gender gap in support for Bill Clinton in 1996 to herald "soccer moms" as the key to Clinton's re-election. More sophisticated analysis of public opinion data, incidentally, indicated that the underpinnings of the gender gap were quite complex and went far beyond any single group, such as feminists or soccer moms or women in the "pink collar proletariat." Rather than gainsaying the gender gap, though, such findings actually implied that it was more important and permanent because it represented the parallel attitudes and actions of disparate groups of women.[2]

The first two national elections in the twenty-first century produced dramatically different results in terms of the gender gap. In 2000, the normal gender gap emerged in both presidential and congressional elections, confirming that the significant difference in voting between women and men of the previous twenty years had seemingly been consolidated. Yet, for the 2002 elections, the gender gap virtually disappeared. One obvious factor that intervened between these two elections was the tragedy of September 11th 2001, which suggested (to journalists at least) that soccer moms had been transformed into "security moms." This article, hence, describes the gender gap in these two elections and explores the implications of the 2002 data for gender-based orientations toward American politics.

THE 2000 ELECTIONS: THE GENDER GAP AS USUAL

The 2000 elections were certainly dramatic in terms of their razor-thin outcomes for both the presidency and Congress. Yet, they represented "politics as usual" in terms of the gender gap in partisanship between men and women in four distinct ways. First, the gender gap itself of women's being supportive of Democratic candidates by approximately 8-to-10 percentage points more than men continued. Second, while this degree of difference in the partisanship of women and men may not appear extreme, it was actually in the same range as many other assumedly important cleavages in U.S. politics, such as those based on income, education, and region. Thus, the gender gap was far from trivial. Third, this pattern existed for an extremely diverse and encompassing set of demographic groups, indicating that gender itself was the primary causal agent. Finally, the gender gap in voting was undergirded by similar attitudinal differences between women and men on a wide array of political issues. Especially when taken together, therefore, these four factors implied that the gender gap had become a permanent fixture on the American political scene.

A Stable and Long-term Gender Gap

Table 1 presents estimates of the gender gap in vote for president and the House of Representatives between 1980 and 2000 based on two different sources: 1) extensive exit polls conducted by the media (which experienced highly embarrassing problems in 2000) and 2) the biennial National Election Surveys conducted by the Survey Research Center of the University of Michigan. The 2000 problems with exit polls certainly indicate that they are not infallible. Still, the parallel results from these two separate and independent sources are indicative of the strength and stability of the gender gap. The gender gap in voting for President grew slightly from about eight percentage points during the 1980s to just above ten percentage points

TABLE 1 Gender Gap in Voting for Democrats

	Measured by Exit Polls			Measured by NES Survey		
	Men	*Women*	*Gap*	*Men*	*Women*	*Gap*
		A. President				
1980	36%	45%	9%	36%	42%	6%
1984	37%	44%	7%	37%	45%	8%
1988	41%	49%	8%	43%	50%	7%
1992	41%	45%	4%	42%	52%	10%
1996	43%	54%	11%	47%	60%	13%
2000	—	—	—	45%	56%	11%
		B. House of Representatives				
	Men	*Women*	*Gap*	*Men*	*Women*	*Gap*
1980	49%	55%	6%	56%	53%	−3%
1982	55%	58%	3%	54%	60%	6%
1984	48%	54%	6%	53%	57%	4%
1986	51%	54%	3%	59%	62%	3%
1988	52%	57%	5%	59%	59%	0%
1990	52%	55%	3%	59%	69%	10%
1992	52%	55%	3%	57%	62%	5%
1994	42%	53%	11%	45%	49%	4%
1996	45%	54%	9%	44%	52%	8%
1998	29%	40%	11%	44%	48%	4%
2000	—	—	—	44%	53%	9%

Sources: Richard A. Seltzer, Jody Newman, and Melissa Voorhees Leighton. *Sex as a Variable: Women Candidates and Voters in U.S. Elections.* Boulder, CO: Lynne Rienner, 1997. pp. 34–35 & 38 for 1980–94.

New York Times. "Portrait of the Electorate: Gender." nytimes.com. for 1996 & 1998 exit polls.

Computations from the data sets of the National Election Studies of the Survey Research Center of the University of Michigan for 1996–2000 NES results, available at www.icpsr.umich.edu.

in the 1990s. The difference in the voting patterns of women and men for U.S. House candidates was more muted until the 1990s, but by the end of that decade it had grown to approximate equality with the gender gap in presidential voting.

The National Election Study found similar gender gaps in the 2000 elections. In the presidential race, Democrat Al Gore was supported by 56% of the women in the NES survey compared to only 45% of the men, creating a gender gap of 11 percentage points. For the entire U.S., Democratic House candidates received the votes of 53% of women compared to 44% of men for a difference of nine percentage points. Men and women, therefore, split almost exactly the same in 2000 as they had in 1996 and 1998. Consequently, it seemed that American politics was marked by a stable gender gap of about ten percentage points that remained fairly constant regardless of whether Democrats or Republicans came out on top in their fairly even biennial battles.

Comparing Gender to Other Political Cleavages

The next question, of course, is whether a gender gap of this size is important politically. For example, a difference of ten percentage points is certainly a long way from most women opposing most men. As Richard Seltzer and his associates argued, "the [gender] gap has not become a chasm, nor does it represent a war between the sexes."[3] One means for assessing the political importance of the gender gap is to compare it to other potential cleavages in American politics, such as class or presumed traditional orientations. Table 2, hence, compares the gender gap to other differences or gaps that are often considered politically relevant, such as family income, born-again Christian, community size, and race. Each of these is divided into two categories, which in some cases understates the difference (i.e., between the very poor and very rich). However, a much greater gender gap would also emerge if we only compared, say, feminist women to male devotees of Rush Limbaugh.

This comparative analysis indicates that, just as in 1996,[4] the gender gap appears equivalent in degree to the cleavages among Americans on class, traditional

TABLE 2   Gore's "Gaps" Among Selected Voting Groups in 2000 Election

	Gore Vote Among Less Supportive	Gore Vote Among More Supportive	Gap
Gender (male/female)	45%	56%	11%
Class			
Family Income (over/under $35,000)	48%	59%	11%
Education (Post-sec/high sch or less)	49%	55%	6%
Union Member in Family (no/yes)	49%	60%	11%
Traditional Orientation			
Born-again Christian (yes/no)	41%	53%	12%
Married (yes/no)	44%	59%	15%
Children (yes/no)	50%	54%	4%
Age (under/over 35)	49%	52%	3%
Community			
Population (under/over 100,000)	48%	69%	21%
Region (South & West/other)	43%	55%	12%
Race (white/black)	45%	91%	46%
Ideology (conservative/liberal)	30%	79%	49%

Source (for this and all following tables):

Computed from data from the National Election Studies of the Survey Research Center, distributed by the International Consortium for Political and Social Research. Available at www.icpsr.umich.edu. Reprinted with permission.

roles, and community characteristics, which might be more than a little surprising given the centrality of some of these to popular images of partisan competition and conflict in the United States. In particular, Gore's gender gap of 11 percentage points in the 2000 presidential election is almost exactly the same as the differences for income, union membership, being a born-again Christian, and region, all of which are generally considered politically important. Interestingly perhaps, there are even slightly bigger gaps between married and unmarried people (15 percentage points), and residents of large cities and small towns (21 percentage points), suggesting that life-style and value differences may be coming to the fore in American politics. However, among the fairly wide range of demographic factors included in Table 2 only race dwarfs the effects of gender. That the gender gap now approximates the ones associated with the "politics of rich and poor" and traditional roles, therefore, is quite striking and implies that it has become an important factor on our political scene.

The Pervasiveness of the Gender Gap in Many Social Groups

If women actually do form a distinct political group, one would expect that a gender gap would exist across many social categories rather than just a few. That is, significant differences would be expected between men and women regardless of income or education, religion or region, and so forth. If, in contrast, the gender gap only exists in a few social groupings (e.g., those who live in a particular region or have a particular level of education), it would become quite questionable whether women, by themselves, form a distinct political group. Table 3, therefore, breaks down the gender gap for categories in the major indicators of socioeconomic status. For example, under the first variable of family income, the votes of women and men are compared in four different income categories that range from approximately poverty level (under $15,000) to upper middle class and above (over $75,000).

These data generally demonstrate that the gender gap in 2000 presidential voting was extremely broad-based since a significant gender gap with women being more likely to vote for Al Gore exists for almost all the categories of the 10 SES indicators included in the table. In fact, of the 34 categories, the only one for which a gender gap of at least four percentage points did not emerge is people with family incomes under $15,000, among whom 67% of both women and men voted for Gore. More positively, the gender gap is at least seven percentage points for 30 of these 34 categories. In sum, the gender gap persists even when indicators of class, traditional roles, community, and race are controlled. Consequently, it would be hard to argue that women did not manifest the characteristics of a distinct political group in their 2000 presidential votes.

More particularly, the data in Table 3 can be used to disprove several attempts to downplay the significance of the gender gap because it is supposedly limited to a small number of socioeconomic groups. First, because African-Americans vote overwhelmingly Democratic, the gender gap has been attributed primarily to the much higher voting rate of African-American women than

TABLE 3   2000 Gender Gap on Gore Broken Down by SES Factors

	Men	Women	Gender Gap
Full Sample	*45%*	*56%*	*11%*
Class			
FAMILY INCOME			
Under $15,000	67%	67%	0%
$15,000–34,999	48%	61%	13%
$35,000–74,999	46%	68%	12%
Over $75,000	40%	44%	4%
EDUCATION			
Less than High School	53%	67%	14%
High School Degree	49%	56%	7%
Some Postsecondary	42%	54%	12%
College Degree	45%	54%	9%
Advanced Degree	41%	58%	17%
UNION MEMBER IN HOME			
No	42%	54%	12%
Yes	57%	63%	6%
Traditional Roles			
Born-again CHRISTIAN			
No	47%	58%	11%
Yes	36%	45%	9%
MARITAL STATUS			
Married	41%	48%	7%
Divorced	42%	62%	20%
Never married	50%	68%	18%
CHILDREN			
No	46%	61%	15%
Yes	44%	54%	10%
AGE			
18–34	40%	58%	18%
35–50	45%	54%	9%
51–65	45%	57%	12%
Over 65	49%	56%	7%

TABLE 3   2000 Gender Gap on Gore Broken Down by SES Factors (*continued*)

	Men	Women	Gender Gap
Full Sample	*45%*	*56%*	*11%*
Community			
COMMUNITY SIZE			
Under 25,000	38%	54%	16%
25,000–99,999	48%	52%	4%
100,000–500,000	59%	76%	17%
Over 500,000	57%	81%	24%
REGION			
Northeast	48%	62%	14%
South	36%	51%	15%
Midwest	45%	57%	12%
Plains/Mountains	38%	45%	7%
Pacific coast	57%	66%	9%
Race			
Non-Latino Whites	40%	50%	10%
Black	83%	97%	14%
Latinos	46%	59%	13%

African-American men. Yet, Table 3 displays a gender gap of 10 percentage points for non-Latino whites, which is almost exactly equal to the overall gender gap of 11 percentage points. Second, because the gender gap in the original movement of voters' party identification from Democratic to Republican during the late 1970s and 1980s was concentrated in the South, the gender gap has been seen by some as a fairly marginal regional phenomenon.[5] Yet, gender gaps of seven percentage points or more on Gore vote existed in all regions in 2000; and the Northeast with a gender gap of 14 percentage points is almost indistinguishable from the South's 15%.

Finally, the data in Table 3 do suggest that the gender gap may be especially pronounced among "nontraditional" groups. For example, the largest gender gaps in the table of 18% to 24% exist for people who live in cities with populations over 500,000 (24 percentage points), who are divorced (20 percentage points) or have never married (18 percentage points), and who are under 35 years of age (18 percentage points). Yet, significant gender gaps exist for all categories of community size, marital status, and age. Furthermore, several indicators of traditional roles clearly *do not* act to reduce the gender gap. For example, the gender gap is 17 percentage points in small towns and rural areas; and there is almost no difference in the tendency of women to have voted more strongly than men for Al Gore between those who do and do not consider themselves to be born-again Christians. In sum, no matter how we look at it, the gender gap in voting appears to have been extraordinarily pervasive in the 2000 presidential election.

The Issue Base for the Gender Gap in Voting

The gender gap in voting is presumed to reflect similar differences or gaps on a fairly broad array of issues; and, indeed, such differences were widely documented during the 1980s and 1990s.[6] Table 4, hence, provides data on the gender gap in four major areas: women's issues, an activist government regarding social policy, anti-violence positions, and overall political identification and allegiances. In this table, the issues are defined in such a manner so that a positive gender gap reflects the normally assumed difference in the position of women and men. For example, women are assumed to be more positive toward feminists and spending for public schools but more opposed to increasing defense spending than men. Table 4 certainly shows that the issue differences between the sexes that existed in the 1990s were little changed in 2000. Only one of the 20 gender gaps in the table is nega-

TABLE 4   2000 Gender Gap on Specific Issues

	Men	Women	Gender Gap
Women's Issues			
Warm to Feminists*	37%	47%	10%
Warm to Women's Movement*	57%	63%	6%
Pro-Choice on Abortion	41%	43%	2%
Support Nondiscrim for Gays	60%	73%	13%
Support Gay Adoptions	39%	50%	11%
Pro-Government & Redistribution			
Want More Government Services	34%	44%	10%
Govt Guarantee Job & Standard of Living	16%	22%	6%
Spend More on Poor	46%	56%	10%
Spend More on Public Schools	70%	81%	11%
Spend More on Child Care	57%	67%	10%
Spend More on Social Security	56%	69%	13%
Spend More on Welfare	15%	19%	4%
Oppose Using Surplus for Tax Cuts	40%	34%	−6%
Anti-Violence			
Support Tighter Gun Laws	46%	69%	23%
Oppose Spending More on Defense	57%	64%	7%
Pro-Environmental Regulation	43%	54%	11%
Oppose Death Penalty	17%	25%	8%
Spend More on Crime	59%	71%	12%
Political Loyalties			
Democratic Party Identity	46%	54%	8%
Liberal Ideology	33%	39%	6%

*A score of 51 or higher on a thermometer of 0 to 100.

tive; and 16 of the 19 positive ones meet the normal criterion for statistical significance of a difference of approximately six percentage points.

Obviously, the emergence of the gender gap within a few years of the blossoming of the Feminist Movement suggests that feminist *consciousness* played a major role in its development.[7] The first group of issue positions in Table 4 shows that the predicted gender gap on women's issues (including support for gays and lesbians) generally did hold in 2000. Women were more likely than men to have positive views of feminists (47% to 37%) and the Women's Movement (63% to 57%) by margins that were just under the gender gap in voting; and the gender gap in support for gays and lesbians on several issues was in the low double digits. The one issue here for which a significant gender gap did not emerge was abortion where almost an equal proportion of women and men (43% and 41%, respectively) took the unambiguously pro-choice position that abortion should always be legal. This might be somewhat surprising since abortion is probably the central issue of the Feminist Movement. However, for the last thirty years women have differed little from men on this issue,[8] so these 2000 results again indicate attitudinal continuity.

In addition to feminist issues, women have also been found to be more liberal than men on a wide array of social issues in the sense that they support governmental activism in combating social problems and in providing redistributive aid to the disadvantaged in society. This has been attributed both to the growing "feminization of poverty"[9] which gives them a direct interest in government redistribution and to women's fairly distinct values compared to men which leads them to place more emphasis upon "connectiveness" in personal and community relations rather than abstract rights and power considerations.[10] The data in Table 4 clearly confirm women's greater liberalism on almost all of these issues. Women wanted an expansion of government services by ten percentage points more than men (44% to 34%); and there were gender gaps of almost exactly the same size for spending on the poor, public schools, child care, and social security, although the differences between women and men on support for the government's guaranteeing people a job and standard of living and increasing welfare spending were more muted. In contrast, women were less likely to take the liberal position against using the federal government's budgetary surplus for tax cuts than men, probably primarily due to women's more stressed financial situation.[11]

Women have long been viewed as more strongly opposed to violence than men, as reflected in a variety of issues on domestic and foreign affairs.[12] Table 4 finds similar gender gaps to 1996 on these issues as well.[13] As in 1996, the largest gender gap on any issue (including many not reported here) occurred for gun control, where 69% of the women compared to 46% of the men favored making existing gun laws stricter, creating a gender gap of 23 percentage points. In terms of foreign affairs, women were seven percentage points more likely to oppose increased defense spending than men (64% to 57%) in line with data from the 1980s that attitudes on defense spending are an important component of the gender gap.[14] Women's greater opposition to violence is also apparent for domestic issues concerning the environment and public safety. In 2000, women were considerably more supportive of environmental regulation than men (54% to 43%) and were more likely to oppose the death penalty by a margin of 25% to 17%. The one departure in women's greater concern with safety and anti-violence from the normal liberal–conservative divide comes in attitudes about increasing spending to fight crime. Here, women were more supportive of this conservative position by a 12-percentage-point margin of 71% to 59%.

Given the existence of so many issue differences between women and men with women almost invariably taking the liberal position, it would be strange indeed if the gender gap did not extend to overall political orientations, such as ideology and party identification. In the United States over the last several decades, there has been something of a "disconnect" between ideology and partisanship in the sense that conservatives outnumber liberals by a comfortable three-to-two margin; yet, Democrats retain a slight edge in popular allegiance. Despite this small anomaly, though, women were more likely than men to be Democrats and liberals by almost exactly the same margins: 54% to 46% for party loyalty and 39% to 33% for ideology.

THE DISAPPEARING GENDER GAP IN 2002: THE NEW IMPACT OF SECURITY CONCERNS

The analysis of the gender gap in 2000 in the preceding section would certainly lead us to expect that a fairly similar pattern would have occurred in 2002. Yet, this was most certainly not the case! As Table 5 indicates, there was almost no difference whatsoever between the voting of women and men in these midterm congressional elections. Democratic candidates for the House received 45% of the votes of women in the NES sample compared to 46% of the men's votes. In Senate races, there was a positive Democratic gender gap, but it was only a minuscule three percentage points (48% to 45%). Furthermore, the two sexes agreed quite closely on how good a job President George W. Bush was doing at that time, as 71% of the men and 69% of the women approved his handling of the presidency. Clearly, something drastic had impacted in the normal difference between how women and men view American politics and society.

A search for suspects or factors that might have caused this change in the gender gap certainly does not have to be very far reaching. The tragedy of September 11th transformed the political landscape in the United States. In terms of the gender gap, a tempting hypothesis would be that heightened fears about personal and national security pushed enough women in the Republican direction to eradicate the gender gap. For this to have occurred, four conditions need to be found. First, positions on security issues must be correlated with partisanship, or else they would have little relevance for aspects of partisanship, such as the gender gap. Second, they would have to be salient or important in public opinion at the time of the 2002 elections. Third, some change must have occurred in how gender is related to views about national security between 2000 and 2002. Finally, explicitly

TABLE 5   Gender Gap in 2002 Congressional Elections and Bush Approval

A. House of Representatives

House Vote	Gender		
	Men	*Women*	*Gender Gap*
Democrat	46%	45%	−1%
Republican	50%	48%	−2%
Other	4%	7%	3%

B. Senate

Senate Vote	Gender		
	Men	*Women*	*Gender Gap*
Democrat	45%	48%	3%
Republican	49%	48%	−1%
Other	6%	3%	−3%

C. Approval of George W. Bush as President

Bush Approval	Gender		
	Men	*Women*	*Gender Gap*
Disapprove Strongly	19%	19%	0%
Disapprove	10%	12%	2%
Approve	22%	22%	0%
Approve Strongly	49%	47%	−2%

controlling for position on national security should at least partially explain the vanishing gender gap of 2002.

September 11th and the Security Issue in U.S. Politics

The image that the greatly enhanced security threat after September 11th made the public much more supportive of President Bush and his Republican party is so universally held that it would be shocking if the first two conditions specified above did not hold. Table 6, which is representative of almost all national elections during the last several decades, certainly confirms that people concerned about national security tended to vote Republican. This table uses a person's position on defense spending to explain her or his vote for the House of Representatives in 2002. Among those who wanted to increase defense spending, 62% voted for Republican candidates, while less than a sixth of that number (16%) voted Republican among advocates of cutting the defense budget. The data in the first column in Table 7 then show that concerns about security were quite high in 2002. Two-thirds

TABLE 6   Crosstabulation of House Vote by Position on Defense Spending, 2002

House Vote	Defense Spending			
	Cut	*Keep Same*	*Increase*	*Total*
Democrat	91%	57%	38%	48%
Republican	9%	43%	62%	52%

of Americans believed that another terrorist attack was somewhat or very likely; not so coincidentally, approximately equal percentages supported more spending for the war on terror, homeland security, protecting our borders, and national defense; and the military was almost universally perceived in a positive light.

A Shift in Women's Views on Security Issues

The third condition that some change should have occurred between 2000 and 2002 in the relationship between gender and views about national security might seem a little less certain. However, such a change is indicated by the data on the differences between women and men regarding national security issues in the last three columns of Table 7. Traditionally (and in 2000), women have been more liberal and pacifist on these issues. In fact, women's greater opposition to defense spending was a major cause of the gender gap during the 1980s.[15] The situation was much different in 2002, though. Women were more likely than men to believe that a terrorist attack was quite possible by a margin of 72% to 61%. Perhaps because of this, the normal pattern of women being less supportive of the military and security expenditures was eclipsed and, if anything, reversed in 2002. For example, women, compared to men, were more supportive of increasing expenditures for homeland security and defense by five percentage points (70% to 65%) and four percentage points (61% to 57%) respectively.

Table 8, which compares the difference between women's and men's positions on defense spending (the one question about national security policy included in both NES surveys) in 2000 and 2002, directly confirms the supposition that the association between gender and views about national security issues shifted significantly

TABLE 7   Gender Gap on National Security Concerns, 2002

Indicators of Security Concerns	Total	Men	Women	Gender Gap
Another terrorist attack somewhat or very likely	67%	61%	72%	11%
Positive view of military	85%	87%	84%	−3%
Want more spending for war on terror	64%	63%	66%	3%
Want more spending for homeland security	68%	65%	70%	5%
Want more spending for border security	71%	72%	70%	−2%
Want more spending for defense	59%	57%	61%	4%

TABLE 8   Reversed Gender Gap on Defense Spending

A. 2000

Defense Spending	Gender			
	Total	*Men*	*Women*	*Gender Gap*
Cut	13%	11%	14%	3%
Keep Same	48%	46%	51%	5%
Increase	39%	43%	36%	−7%

B. 2002

Defense Spending	Gender			
	Total	*Men*	*Women*	*Gender Gap*
Cut	7%	8%	7%	−1%
Keep Same	34%	36%	33%	−3%
Increase	59%	57%	61%	4%

between these two elections. In 2000, following the normal or conventional pattern, women were less supportive of increasing defense spending than men by seven percentage points (36% to 43%). Yet, two years later they were actually more supportive than men of increasing military spending by four percentage points (61% to 57%). The data in Table 8, incidentally, also reflect the vastly increased concern of Americans with security issues after September 11th as support for more defense expenditures was half again as high in 2002 (59%) as it had been two years earlier (39%).

The Impact of Security Issues on the Gender Gap in 2002

The existence of these first three conditions, though, only provides circumstantial evidence that the especial national security concerns of women explain the vanishing gender gap in 2002. In order to confirm that this really is the case, we need to control for position on these issues to see how it explicitly affects the gender gap. Tables 9 and 10, therefore, examine the nature of the gender gap in the 2002 vote for the House of Representatives (which, unlike the Senate, included all voters) controlling for whether or not a person wanted to increase spending for homeland security and for defense. The results in the first case are almost spectacular. Among those who did not want increased spending for homeland security, there was a *positive* gender gap of 14 percentage points in the vote for Democratic House candidates, as 61% of the women but only 47% of the men voted for Democrats. In stark contrast, among people who wanted more resources devoted to homeland security, women were actually *less* likely to vote Democratic than men by the almost similar margin of 11 percentage points (39% to 50%). Clearly, the increased salience of security issues had driven men and women in different directions in terms of their partisan loyalties.

TABLE 9   Gender Gap in 2002 House Vote Controlling for Position on Homeland Security Spending

A. Cut Homeland Security Spending or Keep It the Same

House Vote	Gender		
	Men	*Women*	*Gender Gap*
Democrat	47%	61%	14%
Republican	49%	35%	−14%
Other	5%	4%	−1%

B. Increase Homeland Security Spending

House Vote	Gender		
	Men	*Women*	*Gender Gap*
Democrat	50%	39%	−11%
Republican	48%	58%	10%
Other	2%	4%	2%

The data on the gender gap in the 2002 House elections controlling for attitudes about defense spending are far less dramatic. Yet, they repeat the same pattern. Among those who wanted the same or less defense spending, women were more likely to support Democratic candidates than men by the slightly less than "normal" gender gap of six percentage points (63% to 57%), while there was a small negative gender gap of four percentage points (34% to 38%) for Democrats

TABLE 10   Gender Gap in 2002 House Vote Controlling for Position on Defense Spending

A. Cut Defense Spending or Keep It the Same

House Vote	Gender		
	Men	*Women*	*Gender Gap*
Democrat	57%	63%	6%
Republican	40%	29%	−11%
Other	3%	8%	5%

B. Increase Defense Spending

House Vote	Gender		
	Men	*Women*	*Gender Gap*
Democrat	38%	34%	−4%
Republican	59%	60%	1%
Other	3%	6%	3%

TABLE 11   Gender Gap in 2000 Presidential Vote Controlling for Position on Defense Spending

A. Cut Defense Spending or Keep It the Same

Presidential Vote	Gender		
	Men	*Women*	*Gender Gap*
Al Gore	54%	63%	9%
George W. Bush	39%	33%	−6%
Other	7%	4%	−3%

B. Increase Defense Spending

Presidential Vote	Gender		
	Men	*Women*	*Gender Gap*
Al Gore	32%	37%	5%
George W. Bush	66%	62%	−4%
Other	2%	1%	−1%

among those who felt that more spending on defense was needed. This "reversal of gender gaps," moreover, represented a major change in the normal pattern. For example, Table 11 reports the gender gap in the 2000 presidential vote controlling for defense spending. Here, Al Gore received positive gender gaps both for opponents (nine percentage points) and supporters (five percentage points) of increased defense spending.

While the relatively even partisan division in the 2002 congressional elections represented "politics as usual," the elections were also marked by the absence of a gender gap between the voting behavior of women and men for the first time in twenty years. The data presented in this section imply very strongly that the tragedy of September 11th was the prime cause for this fairly fundamental change in the pattern of partisanship in American politics. This obviously raises the question of how permanent the vanishing gender gap is likely to be. Have increased threats of terrorism and national security transformed the manner in which a considerable number of women view government and political choice in the United States? Or, were the results in 2002 a temporary "blip" that will be replaced by a return to gendered voting in the near future?

WHITHER THE GENDER GAP?

At the dawn of the twenty-first century, the gender gap appeared to have assumed a significant role in American politics. While it was admittedly a "gap" rather than a "chasm,"[16] it had reached a size equivalent to such assumedly important political cleavages in the United States as income and region. Women, therefore, evidently had come to constitute a significant political group or constituency. This did not necessarily mean that women agreed on all issues. Rather, different but overlapping groups of women differed from comparable men on a variety of issues, leading women in the aggregate to be more supportive of Democratic candidates at the polls. As feminist theorist Iris Marion Young argued:

> Feminism itself is not a grouping of women; rather, there are many feminisms, many groupings of women whose purpose is to politicize gender and change the power relations between women and men in some respect.[17]

A collapse of the gender gap, therefore, could have profound implications for the role of women in American politics.

Continuing Issue Differences between Women and Men

One approach to assessing whether the transformation of how security issues affect the relationship between gender and partisanship is to see whether it ended or eroded the distinctiveness of women's positions on other issues. Table 12, therefore, examines the gender gap in 2002 on political loyalties, women's issues, and governmental redistributive policies, although unfortunately not all the issues covered in the 2000 NES study were included in the 2002 survey. In 2002, the gender gaps on party identification and ideology had decreased, but only slightly, from 2000 when there was a normal gender gap in voting, as they were five percentage points each compared to eight percentage points for Democratic party identifica-

TABLE 12   2002 Gender Gap on Specific Issues

	Men	Women	Gender Gap
Political Loyalties			
Democratic Party Identity	45%	50%	5%
Liberal Ideology	36%	41%	5%
Women's Issues			
Warm to Feminists[*]	33%	43%	10%
Support Equal Pay for Women Strongly	43%	54%	11%
Pro-Government & Redistribution			
Govt Guarantee Job & Standard of Living	25%	32%	7%
Spend More on Poor	49%	54%	5%
Spend More on Public Schools	68%	76%	8%
Spend More on Child Care	53%	56%	3%
Spend More on Social Security	58%	64%	6%
Spend More on Welfare	21%	20%	−1%
Disapprove Tax Cuts	31%	32%	1%

[*]A score of 51 or higher on a thermometer of 0 to 100.

tion and six percentage points for liberal ideology two years earlier. The slippage in the gender gap on the role of government and redistributive policies was even greater, as the gender gap on most of these issues fell from about ten percentage points in 2000 (see Table 4) to five percentage points, although the "negative" gender gap on taxes in 2000 disappeared as well. In contrast, there was little change in women's greater support for women's issues. Taken together, therefore, these data imply that, while the difference between women and men on these issues may have decreased slightly, these attitudinal bases for the gender gap in voting remained in place, even if they were ineffective in generating a gender gap at the polls.

More strikingly perhaps, there is even evidence of the continuation of women's greater pacifism in some areas, despite its eclipse regarding the war on terrorism. Table 13 demonstrates that gender gaps consistent with the previous pattern of women being more opposed to war and international violence existed on several items in 2002. First, women were more likely to oppose military action in Iraq than men by a margin of six percentage points (37% to 31%) in an unambiguously more pacifist position. A higher proportion of women than men also expressed substantial concern over the possibility of conventional war (39% to 27%) and especially nuclear war (34% to 15%). Such attitudes in the past led women to oppose aggressiveness in foreign policy.[18] Yet, as we have seen, concern about terrorism made women more supportive of a strong defense and of Republican candidates after September 11th. Thus, by themselves, these latter two gender gaps on being concerned about the outbreak of war are somewhat ambiguous in their implications.

This ambiguity can be resolved, though, by seeing how these attitudes actually affected the attitudes of women. Table 14, hence, examines how attitudes about national security influenced the voting preferences of *just women*. As would certainly be expected, women who expressed a concern with security matters by supporting military action in Iraq or more spending on defense and homeland security were substantially less likely to vote for Democratic House candidates than women who held opposing views: 29% to 69% for invading Iraq, 34% to 63% for defense spending, and 39% to 61% for spending on homeland security. Exactly the opposite pattern emerged, though, for women who expressed their concern in the security sphere by worrying a lot about conventional or nuclear war since they were very significantly *more* likely to support Democrats in the House elections

TABLE 13   Potentially Dovish Gender Gaps on Security Issues in 2002

	Men	Women	Gender Gap
Oppose Military Action in Iraq	31%	37%	6%
Worried a Lot about Conventional War	27%	39%	8%
Worried a Lot about Nuclear War	15%	34%	19%

TABLE 14   Impact of Security Concerns on Democratic Vote of Just Women in 2002 House Elections

	Percent Dem Vote
Security Concern Makes Less Democratic	
Increase Defense Spending	
No	63%
Yes	34%
Increase Homeland Security Spending	
No	61%
Yes	39%
Support Military action in Iraq	
No	69%
Yes	29%
Security Concern Makes More Democratic	
Worry about Conventional War a Lot	
No	37%
Yes	59%
Worry about Nuclear War a Lot	
No	40%
Yes	57%

than were women who were less fearful about the outbreak of war: 59% to 37% for conventional war and 57% to 40% for nuclear war. In sum, clearly women's greater pacifism continued in certain areas in 2002 even though it did not make its usual contribution to the gender gap in voting.

Portents of a Re-emerging Gender Gap in Voting?

Even in 2002, therefore, there was a significant attitudinal base for the resurrection of the gender gap in voting. Whether or not it will be activated is more problematic. Still, there are several "straws in the wind" suggesting that the gender gap may well re-emerge in the not too distant future. First, despite the absence of any difference in voting between themselves and men, women in 2002 were much more likely to believe that the Democratic Party was "better for women" than the Republican Party. As shown in Table 15, 70% of women believed that there was little difference between the two major parties in terms of how their policies affected women. Among the 30% who saw a significant difference between the parties, however, women picked the Democrats by an overwhelming margin of over four-to-one (24.5% to 5.6%). Second, in the summer of 2003, less than a year after the

TABLE 15   Women's Perception of Which Party is "Better for Women"

Republicans	5.6%
No Difference	69.9%
Democrats	24.5%
TOTAL	100%

2002 elections, a Zogby poll found a gender gap of 12 percentage points in support for President Bush's re-election as 56% of men but only 44% of women said that Bush deserved re-election, although this margin narrowed over the next few months.[19] It would probably be rash to predict or assert the resurrection of the gender gap. However, it would appear rasher still to proclaim its epitaph.

NOTES

1. Bella Abzug with Mim Kelber, *Gender Gap: Bella Abzug's Guide to Political Power for American Women* (Boston: Houghton Mifflin, 1984); Eleanor Smeal, *Why and How Women Will Elect the Next President of the United States* (New York: Harper & Row, 1984).

2. Cal Clark and Janet Clark, "The Gender Gap in 1996: More Than a 'Revenge of the Soccer Moms,'" pp. 68–84 in Lois Duke Whitaker, Ed., *Women in Politics: Outsiders or Insiders?* 3rd Ed. (Upper Saddle River, NJ: Prentice Hall, 1999).

3. Richard A. Seltzer, Jody Newman, and Melissa Voorhees Leighton, *Sex as a Variable: Women Candidates and Voters in U.S. Elections* (Boulder, CO: Lynne Rienner, 1997) p. 2.

4. Clark and Clark, "The Gender Gap in 1996," pp. 72–73.

5. Warren E. Miller, "Party Identification, Realignment, and Party Voting: Back to the Basics," *American Political Science Review* 85:2 (June 1991) pp. 557–568.

6. Carol M. Mueller, Ed., *The Politics of the Gender Gap: The Social Construction of Political Influence* (Beverly Hills, CA: Sage, 1988); Keith T. Poole and L. Harmon Zeigler, *Women, Public Opinion, and Politics: The Changing Political Attitudes of American Women* (New York: Longman, 1985); Seltzer, *et al., Sex as a Variable,* Chapter 2; Robert Y. Shapiro and Harpreet Mahajan, "Gender Differences in Policy Preferences: A Summary of Trends from the 1960s to the 1980s," *Public Opinion Quarterly* 50:1 (Spring 1986) pp. 42–61.

7. Susan L. Carroll, "Gender Politics and the Socializing Impact of the Women's Movement," pp. 306–339 in Roberta S. Sigel, Ed., *Political Learning in Adulthood: A Sourcebook of Theory and Research* (Chicago: University of Chicago Press, 1989); Pamela Johnston Conover,

"Feminists and the Gender Gap." *Journal of Politics* 50:4 (November 1988) pp. 985–1010; M. Margaret Conway, Gertrude A. Steuernagel, and David W. Ahern, *Women and Political Participation: Cultural Change in the Political Arena* (Washington, D.C.: Congressional Quarterly Press, 1997); Ethel Klein, *Gender Politics: From Consciousness to Mass Politics* (Cambridge: Harvard University Press, 1984); Patricia S. Misciagno, *Rethinking Feminist Identification: The Case for De Facto Feminism* (Westport, CT: Praeger, 1997); Sue Tolleson-Rinehart, *Gender Consciousness and Politics* (New York: Routledge, 1992).

8. Clark and Clark, "The Gender Gap in 1996;" Shapiro and Mahajan, "Gender Differences in Policy Preferences."

9. Steven P. Erie and Martin Rein, "Women and the Welfare State," pp. 273–291 in Carol M. Mueller, Ed., *The Politics of the Gender Gap: The Social Construction of Political Influence* (Beverly Hills, CA: Sage, 1988); Misciagno, *De Facto Feminism;* Gertrude Schiffner Goldberg and Eleanor Kremen, Eds., *The Feminization of Poverty: Only in America?* (New York: Greenwood, 1990).

10. Carol Gilligan, *In a Different Voice: Psychological Theory and Women's Development* (Cambridge: Harvard University Press, 1982).

11. More complex tables not reported here show, for example, that the greater support for tax cuts by women was most pronounced among the least affluent and educated and among the elderly.

12. Carole Chaney, R. Michael Alvarez, and Jonathan Nagler, "Explaining the Gender Gap in U.S. Presidential Elections, 1980–1992," *Political Research Quarterly* 51:2 (June 1998) pp. 311–339; Pamela Conover and Virginia

Sapiro, "Gender, Feminist Consciousness, and War." *American Journal of Political Science* 37:4 (November 1993) 1079–1099; Shapiro and Mahajan, "Gender Differences in Policy Preferences;" Emily Stoper, "The Gender Gap Concealed and Revealed: 1936–1984," *Journal of Political Science* 17:1–2 (Spring 1989) pp. 50–62.

13. Compare to Clark and Clark, "The Gender Gap in 1996," p. 75.

14. Martin Gilens, "Gender and Support for Reagan: A Comprehensive Model of Presidential Approval," *American Journal of Political Science* 32:1 (February 1988) pp. 19–49.

15. Conover and Sapiro, "Gender, Feminist Consciousness, and War;" Gilens, "Gender and Support for Rea-

gan;" Shapiro and Mahajan, "Gender Differences in Policy Preferences;" Stoper, "The Gender Gap Concealed and Revealed."

16. Seltzer, *et al.*, *Sex as a Variable*, p. 2.

17. Iris Marion Young, "Gender as Seriality: Thinking about Women as a Social Collective," *Signs* 19:3 (Spring 1994) p. 737.

18. Conover and Sapiro, "Gender, Feminist Consciousness, and War;" Shapiro and Mahajan, "Gender Differences in Policy Preferences;" Stoper, "The Gender Gap Concealed and Revealed."

19. Myriam Marquez, "President Needs Hughes' Assessment on Women Issues," *Birmingham News*, November 12, 2003, p. 9A.

FURTHER READING

Burrell, Barbara. *A Woman's Place is in the House: Campaigning for Congress in the Feminist Era.* Ann Arbor: University of Michigan Press, 1994.

Carroll, Susan L. "Gender Politics and the Socializing Impact of the Women's Movement," pp. 306–339 in Roberta S. Sigel, Ed., *Political Learning in Adulthood: A Sourcebook of Theory and Research.* Chicago: University of Chicago Press, 1989.

Chaney, Carole, R. Michael Alvarez, and Jonathan Nagler. "Explaining the Gender Gap in U.S. Presidential Elections, 1980–1992." *Political Research Quarterly* 51:2 (June 1998) pp. 311–339.

Clark, Janet and Cal Clark. "The Gender Gap: A Manifestation of Women's Dissatisfaction with the American Polity?" pp. 167–182 in Stephen C. Craig, Ed. *Broken Contract? Changing Relationships between Citizens and their Government in the United States.* Boulder, CO: Westview, 1996.

Conway, M. Margaret, Gertrude A. Steuernagel, and David W. Ahern. *Women and Political Participation: Cultural Change in the Political Arena.* Washington, D.C.: Congressional Quarterly Press, 1997.

Darcy, R., Susan Welch, and Janet Clark. *Women, Elections, and Representation,* 2nd Ed. Lincoln: University of Nebraska Press, 1994.

Dolan, Kathleen. "Voting for Women in the 'Year of the Woman.'" *American Journal of Political Science* 42 (January 1998) pp. 272–293.

Gilligan, Carol. *In a Different Voice: Psychological Theory and Women's Development.* Cambridge: Harvard University Press, 1982.

Klein, Ethel. *Gender Politics: From Consciousness to Mass Politics.* Cambridge: Harvard University Press, 1984.

Misciagno, Patricia S. *Rethinking Feminist Identification: The Case for De Facto Feminism.* Westport, CT: Praeger, 1997.

Mueller, Carol M., Ed. *The Politics of the Gender Gap: The Social Construction of Political Influence.* Beverly Hills, CA: Sage, 1988.

Norris, Pippa. "The Gender Gap: Old Challenges, New Approaches," pp. 146–170 in Susan J. Carroll, Ed. *Women and American Politics.* New York: Oxford University Press, 2003.

Poole, Keith T. and L. Harmon Zeigler. *Women, Public Opinion, and Politics: The Changing Political Attitudes of American Women.* New York: Longman, 1985.

Sapiro, Virginia. *The Political Integration of Women: Roles, Socialization, and Politics.* Urbana: University of Illinois Press, 1983.

Seltzer, Richard A., Jody Newman, and Melissa Voorhees Leighton. *Sex as a Political Variable: Women as Candidates and Voters in U.S. Elections.* Boulder, CO: Lynne Rienner, 1997.

Shapiro, Robert Y. and Harpreet Mahajan. "Gender Differences in Policy Preferences: A Summary of Trends from the 1960s to the 1980s." *Public Opinion Quarterly* 50:1 (Spring 1986) pp. 42–61.

Stoper, Emily. "The Gender Gap Concealed and Revealed: 1936–1984." *Journal of Political Science* 17:1–2 (Spring 1989) pp. 50–62.

Tolleson-Rinehart, Sue. *Gender Consciousness and Politics.* New York: Routledge, 1992.

Young, Iris Marion. "Gender as Seriality: Thinking about Women as a Social Collective." *Signs* 19:3 (Spring 1994) pp. 713–738.

The New Right in American Politics: What Do Women Have to Do with It?

Cynthia Burack

COMPASSIONATE CONSERVATISM?

Surveying the "clash of ideas" and policies between feminism and New Right conservatism from the late 1970s to the 1990s, Sylvia Bashevkin notes that "right wing leaders shaped organized feminism and vice versa" (Bashevkin, 1998:234). Bashevkin confirms that social and political movements do not exist in an intellectual or political vacuum. Feminist thought and practices develop in response to particular socio-political configurations, threats, and challenges as much as they do to the personal or collective aspirations of women who espouse them.

When feminists turn to the American New Right at the turn of the twenty-first century they confront a web of ideologies, policies, practices, and institutions that are either explicitly or implicitly antifeminist. During the 2000 presidential election campaign, Governor George W. Bush represented himself as a new kind of conservative against his more strident and exclusionary colleagues on the American right. Using the slogan "compassionate conservatism," Bush positioned himself as a centrist politician (Campbell, 2003). However, once in office, Bush consistently supported the cultural and economic agendas of neo-conservatives, business interests, and the Christian Right—the three most prominent constituencies in the New Right constellation. Indeed, some of the first initiatives of the Bush administration lay in the areas of tax policy, reproductive rights, "faith-based" initiatives, and American

Reprinted by permission.

independence from international treaties and cooperation—all subjects of particular concern to the New Right. First articulated as a shift from obsolete or discredited dimensions of the Old Right, compassionate conservatism is now one rhetorical device used to market a combination of laissez-faire market fundamentalism, unilateralism in foreign affairs, the erosion of civil rights and civil liberties, support for traditional gender roles and relationships, and the undermining of church–state separation. Although women are less visible than men in the ranks of New Right politics, women figure as participants, as commentators, and as citizens on whom the consequences of New Right political decisions fall. Feminist and other critics offer cogent critiques of the New Right's history, premises, claims, and policies. Certainly, feminists are not alone in responding politically and intellectually to the New Right. But feminist critical practices and attention to intersections of gender and other forms of identity distinguish feminist scholarship from that of many other critics.

In this essay, I would like to survey some of the significant manifestations for women of contemporary New Right politics. I begin by briefly noting both some terminological issues that situate the New Right ideologically and some figures and groups that are connected to the right in one of a number of ways. Next, I highlight some prominent themes of the New Right, moving from the social, or "culture war," strand to some brief reflections on links between cultural politics and what is variously referred to as the market, economic, or libertarian/laissez-faire strand. Throughout, I highlight women's roles as citizens, political actors and scholar–critics. With regard to the American New Right, women are both insiders and outsiders.

WHO'S RIGHT?

Overlapping terms and categories inevitably characterize discussion of the right in American politics. Many commentators have adopted the New Right as a general term, although the labels "neoconservative," "neoliberal," "social conservative," and "Christian conservative" continue to be used to distinguish different nuances of contemporary conservatism. Broadly, "neoconservatism" has been employed to denote the formerly Democratic anticommunism and cultural conservatism that emerged from the 1960s. Neoconservatives such as those in the Bush administration today are often identified by an aggressive and unilateral foreign policy and by socially conservative domestic policies. As many critics point out, there is less ideological difference between neoconservatives and social/Christian conservatives today than there was between these two conservative constituencies before the fall of the Soviet Union (Dorrien, 2001:74–75). "Neoliberalism" has been used to denote laissez-faire capitalist formations, especially as they affect relations between nation–states in a global context. Yet, as is true of many terms in popular political discourse, these terms refer to a diverse and shifting mapping of political positions, affiliations, and investments.

Of the constituencies of the New Right, the Christian Right has most ably responded to late twentieth and early twenty-first century appeals to moral regeneration and the protection of traditional practices and relations. Indeed, it is difficult to imagine the growth and efficacy of the New Right today without the reconstitution of conservative Christianity that began in earnest in the 1970s. Susan Friend Harding tells the story of this transformation through an examination of the "fundamentalist language and politics" associated with Jerry Falwell, the founder of the Moral Majority and an influential Christian Right opinion leader. According to Harding, Falwell took "conservative Protestant moral indignation" and refashioned it into a cultural and political movement that works to disrupt secular modernity and to save America from God's judgment (Harding, 2000:18; Burack, 2003).

Nor is this conservative Christian refashioning only theological and rhetorical; the political force of the Christian Right relies upon the institutionalization of born again Christian conservatism "in the broad spectrum of middle-class institutions that shape and produce American culture, society, and politics" (Harding, 2000:147). These include Christian public-interest law firms that avoid church–state separation issues in court cases by basing their arguments on the Free Speech Clause of the First Amendment (S. Brown, 2003). They also include colleges and universities such as Pat Robertson's Regent University and the more recently founded Patrick Henry College. These conservative Christian institutions of higher education work to "mold a vanguard of Christian leaders who will change the nation through their work in politics and culture" (Helderman, 2003).

Many popular narratives on the rise of the New Right identify its appearance with the election of Ronald Reagan—especially with the defection of "Reagan Democrats" from the Democratic Party—and with the founding of the fundamentalist and intensely political Moral Majority. However, historians locate the roots of New Right ideology and action in the political struggles of the 1950s and 1960s, particularly in conservative struggles against racial integration and federal government intrusions into the social and political prerogatives of segregated states (Diamond, 1995; Bendroth, 1999; Hardisty, 1999; McGirr, 2002). A new consensus emerged on the political right by the late 1970s and early 1980s (Hartmann, 1989). This consensus supported "traditional" practices at home and anti-communism abroad but now attracted a newly-politicized core of conservative Protestant Christians (Diamond, 1998). Since the mobilizing period of the Civil Rights Movement, the "key events" that mark the inception of the New Right revolve around issues—such as *Roe v. Wade* and the ERA—widely understood as "questions of morality, gender and family relations" (Diamond, 1998:63).

Feminist and mainstream accounts of the New Right alike emphasize its rise to prominence as a direct and vociferous response to both cultural and economic changes in American society. Culturally, the "disorder" associated with the African American, women's, and gay and lesbian civil rights movements sparked fears of loss of social order and masculine authority (Josephson and Burack, 1998). Economically, the 1970s saw declines in real wages and job security for working-class white men that made particular kinds of conservative cultural appeals attractive (Lienesch, 1993). To understand this dynamic, it is useful to turn to W.E.B. Dubois's claim that in a racist socio-economic system, white people receive a "psychological wage" that obscures from them the economic interests they share with similarly class-situated people of color (Dubois, 1992). Despite many differences between the political climates of the first and last quarters of the twentieth century, Dubois's analysis is still trenchant, if not sufficient. Hierarchies of gender, nationalism, sexual orientation, and race/ethnicity can trump and mystify the workings of class and economic interests at the same time that they promise order, security, and conformity with moral and social traditions.

Women have exercised political agency both in opposition to the New Right and as representatives of the New Right. A brief introduction to a few prominent women suggests the range of interests and activities of New Right women in the last four decades. Although she was identified with the anti-communist Old Right as early as the 1960s, Phyllis Schlafly is the founder of Eagle Forum and a prominent activist against the Equal Rights Amendment, "secular humanism" in education, and sexual minority rights (Klatch, 1987; Bashevkin, 1998; Rymph, 2000). Beverly La-Haye, founder of Concerned Women for America, is an author, lobbyist, and conservative Christian spokesperson (Kintz, 1997). With careers in government and academia, Condoleeza Rice serves as President George W. Bush's National Security Advisor and a powerful voice for neoconservative politics in his administration. Elizabeth Dole, U.S. Senator from North Carolina, is known as a consistent social and economic conservative, but she actually began her political career as a Democrat in the administration of President Lyndon Johnson (Zengerle, 1999). Like many successful New Right politicians of recent years, she became and then remained successful in the Republican Party by moving right with the Party.[1] A new breed of New Right women includes anti-feminist polemicists such as Ann Coulter and Laura Ingraham as well as ex-feminist academic provocateurs, such as Daphne Patai.

Other conservative women may be politically unknown but nonetheless exercise agency and leadership in New Right groups and in the maintenance of New Right ideology. Some of these women act within the constraints of doctrines that champion strict gender roles and hierarchies (Brasher, 1998).[2] Some support social, economic, and political interests that are antithetical to the well-being of poor women and children or members of other marginal or vulnerable groups. Some, including women of color, join male critics of affirmative action to champion "color-blindness" for a nation that historically has distributed its social, economic, and political benefits unequally by race. Many of these women, especially those with a particular concern about the decay of families, morality, and gender roles, engage in multiple forms of political action under the rallying cry of "family values."

FROM THE "CULTURE WAR" TO "FAMILY VALUES"

"Family values" is a relatively recent rallying slogan of the political right. Throughout the 1980s, the Republican Party moved away from a "moderate center" and pushed out Republican policy-makers who were not "true believers in a new conservative doctrine" (Bashevkin, 1998:31). By the early 1990s, the GOP was firmly situated as the party of the social and economic New Right. A watershed moment in the consolidation of the cultural New Right was Dan Quayle's June, 1992 broadside against "Murphy Brown" and the putative glamorization of single motherhood. Later that summer, Pat Buchanan delivered his infamous "culture wars" address at the 1992 Republican National Committee meeting in Houston, Texas. In the speech, he derided the Clintons and Democrats in general for imposing "radical feminism" on America and fighting on the wrong side of the "war for the soul of America" (Buchanon, 1992).

After the GOP lost the presidential elections of 1992 and 1996, Republican Party strategists began to worry about the ways in which Party activists projected intolerance for minority groups and social nonconformity. Even though the Republican Party's cultural politics had not changed, party strategists pleaded for "culture war" to be muffled under the "big tent" of GOP aspirations. Fearing that obvious appeals to cultural boundaries and exclusions would hurt the Republican Party with swing voters, and particularly with women, strategists prevailed upon party opinion leaders to exercise caution in characterizing even marginal groups such as lesbians and gay men. John A. Moran, a co-chair of the Republican Leadership Council, noted that the Republican Party needed to "soften the image of the party" and "avoid ideological purity" (Conn, 1999).

In many respects, an emphasis on family values promises to close, or at least obscure, some of the political fault lines visible among citizens drafted into the culture wars. The affirmative associations of family values are love and care for others, including vulnerable members of families and communities, especially children. Unfortunately, "family values" also mystifies a range of social, legal and policy positions such as "pro-life" anti-abortion activism, state and federal Defense of Marriage Acts (DOMAs), "father's rights" initiatives, and "abstinence only" sex-education programs for public school students. Yet two broad categories of identity and politics always threaten to reveal the exclusions that constitute "family values": race and sexual orientation and their associated political interests.

Race is a particularly vexing subject for critics of the New Right. Open and virulent racism remains a prominent feature of the white-supremacist far right. Although vehement conservative support for segregation and second-class citizenship for African Americans is often forgotten today, this support is an important part of the genealogy of the New Right. Like many contemporary political actors, the Reverend Jerry Falwell was a vocal supporter of racial segregation before he moved on to oppose abortion rights (Harding, 2000:22–27). And opposition to the civil rights movement continues to be a quiet motif for many conservatives, as evidenced by such events as Senator Trent Lott's commendation of Senator Strom Thurmond's political career on the occasion of Thurmond's 100th birthday party in 2002 (Mercurio, 2002). However, such racism is disowned within the contemporary mainstream New Right. Indeed, some New Right constituency groups have apologized to African Americans for their historical support of slavery and opposition to the Civil Rights Movement.[3] Nonetheless, mainstream political ideologies can disavow extreme manifestations of racism and still authorize the ordinary forms of white supremacy and privilege that characterize many aspects of social and political life (Ferber, 1998; Berlet, 2001).

The New Right treats the frequent racism and racialisms of factions of the Old Right in two ways: some strains of discourse continue to employ coded language that invokes and sustains racial attributions and inequities (Collins, 1998; R. Williams, 1999), while others explicitly disclaim racism and create an aura of racial tolerance (Smith, 1994; hooks, 1995). Conservatives frequently craft messages and launch initiatives to attract people of color with an ideology of spirituality and family values (Kintz, 1997:84–91).[4] These messages are aimed at communities of color, but they do not address racial issues directly. Instead, they bypass potentially divisive debates—over, for example, discrimination and poverty—and attempt to recruit African Americans and Latinas/os to New Right political goals (Diamond, 1996; hooks, 1995:202–203). The New Right goal of recruiting people of color relies upon the cooperation of those Angela Dillard calls "multicultural conservatives," many of whom try to differentiate themselves as individuals from what they perceive as a suffocating identity group of origin. However, the effort to achieve "freedom from group consciousness" is paradoxical. Those who flee the stifling orthodoxies of identity groups often end up pledging themselves to ideological groups that value them precisely for their minority-group affiliations (Dillard, 2001:14). Black male conservatives such as Clarence Thomas may support their own identifications with power by stigmatizing women of color and denying the intersections of racism and sexism that affect women's lives (E. B. Brown, 1995).

If the New Right reaches out to people of color who do not generally identify with its politics, it does not similarly recruit sexual minorities. Lesbians and gay men remain objects against which the right defines normality and sexual normativity. There is an appearance of outreach towards lesbians and gay men, particularly in what is known to adherents as the ex-gay movement. This movement is explicitly interested in reforming people with same-sex sexual orientation to heterosexuality, but its political purpose is to underscore the equation of minority sexual orientation with "choice." It is this tacit goal that makes the ex-gay movement the "right's kinder and gentler anti-gay campaign" (Hardisty, 1999:116). Lesbian feminists note that in spite of the virtual absence of "big tent" interest in queer constituencies by the New Right, many middle-class white gay men ignore the right's stereotyping of poor women, lesbians, and women of color and embrace cultural and economic conservatism (Phelan, 2001).

Through such political tactics as the passage of Amendment 2 in Colorado and the movement to amend the U.S. Constitution to obviate the possibility of same-sex marriage, the New Right attempts to circumvent pluralism and threaten sexual minorities. Urvashi Vaid notes that "the right undermines the gay and lesbian civil rights quest in two conflicting ways: by denying discrimination against gay people and by defending it" (Vaid, 1995:330). One of the most effective strategies of the right in the 1990s was the rhetoric of "special rights." Deploying "special rights" rhetoric, the right held that lesbians and gay men use the democratic political process to achieve legal protections unavailable to other American citizens

(Vaid, 1995; Stein, 2001). In *Roemer v. Evans* the Supreme Court rejected the majority's efforts to bar lesbians and gay men from equal political participation in the state of Colorado over the strenuous objections of Justice Antonin Scalia and social conservative interest groups.

Same-sex sexuality is not the only kind of sexuality that the political right monitors and attempts to regulate. The New Right poses a threat to women's intimate lives and reproductive choices. After all, the rise of the New Right was inspired in part by political battles for women's reproductive freedoms (Diamond, 1998; Nossiff, 2001). The political struggle over reproductive rights and access to abortion did not just heat up in the last quarter of the twentieth century. Women led controversial campaigns for reproductive rights throughout the century. In 1965, the Supreme Court decided a case that set the stage for the most politically polarizing decision decriminalizing abortion for American women. In *Griswold v. Connecticut,* the Court determined that a right of privacy implicit in a number of enumerated Constitutional rights invalidated laws against the dissemination of birth control information and devices, at least to married couples. Later, in 1972, this right was extended to single individuals by *Eisenstadt v. Baird,* and Americans finally enjoyed a protected constitutional right to birth control.

As controversial as this newly articulated right to contraception was, it was the 1973 Supreme Court decision in *Roe v. Wade* that changed the face of reproductive rights politics. In *Roe,* the Court employed the privacy argument it articulated in *Griswold* and invalidated remaining state laws that outlawed abortion. The right of a woman to have an abortion was limited by *Roe*—the Court installed the medical idea of trimesters as a framework for exercise of the right—but the women's movement largely understood the decision as a victory for women's autonomy and citizenship.[5]

Roe v. Wade was a key event in the formation of what has come to be known as the New Right in American politics. But political struggles over reproductive rights continue in a variety of forums, policy domains, and branches of government that make it difficult for partisans of abortion rights politics to determine that they have either won or lost (O'Connor, 1996). Today, along with resistance to sexual minority rights, resistance to abortion rights continues to be one of the most dependable pillars of domestic New Right cultural politics. Indeed, research into the belief systems of anti-abortion activists suggests that "pro-life" attitudes are deeply interconnected with attitudes about other social "evils" related to "sexuality and gender roles" (Williams and Blackburn, 1996: 174). Sympathetic to the anti-abortion rights position of the right, President George W. Bush acted against abortion rights on the first working day of his administration. Bush reinstalled the "global gag order" put into effect by Ronald Reagan and revoked by Bill Clinton; still in effect, the "gag order" keeps international family planning groups and facilities that receive federal U.S. funding for any programming from giving women information about abortion. In *Time* magazine, Tony Karon concludes that the policy sends the global message: "getting help from the U.S. requires conforming to the morality of the Christian Right" (Karon, 2001).

Far from being the threats to culture and children that social conservatives claim, feminists argue that diverse families and diverse forms of gender and sexuality are a valuable feature of desirable pluralist societies. One difficulty in these debates is factual and historical: New Right arguments often proceed by describing the history of family life, sexuality, or gender roles in ways that are not based on empirical reality. Hence, one problem with New Right politics is that they are premised on inaccurate and ideological accounts of history and social relations (Coontz, 1992; Stacey & Biblarz, 2003). However, it is also undeniable that what often separates feminists and antifeminists, progressives and conservatives, left and right, are differences of moral, social, and political goals and values. These goals and values cannot be established by recurring to some stable foundation of universal truths or incontrovertible logic, although those who take sides in political debates often pose their arguments in these terms. Rather, social, economic, and political ideals, practices, and institutions are contested matters over which democratic citizens disagree, often harshly. Not only is it difficult to adjudicate such disagreements, it is often difficult to even determine the nature of political attitudes and aims and where they fit into broader political belief systems.

SHIFTING THE CENTER OF AMERICAN POLITICS

The idea of a continuum of politics from left to right empirically fails to capture all the complexities of political identifications and ideologies. This is not to say that the left–right continuum fails to be useful at all. As Norberto Bobbio argues, the continuum expresses a range of positions from a commitment to equality on the left to a commitment to hierarchy on the right (Bobbio, 1996). Feminists emphasize the ways in which the political right resists gender equality, sexual pluralism, and the existence of a social safety net for vulnerable citizens. However, another problem with the fruitful fiction of a political continuum is the way it might suggest a stable set of positions that correlate with the contents of political beliefs and policies. To the contrary, the substance of beliefs at points on political continua shift over time; the "center" of American politics may move to the left or to the right over time.

Anna Marie Smith points out that the majority of Americans wish to understand themselves as occupying a tolerant political center rather than a position on an extreme of the political continuum. For her, right wing movements and ideologies succeed when they are constructed in such a way that they permit citizens to understand themselves as reasonable centrists in spite of the substance of their political beliefs. The genius of the New Right has been in repackaging inegalitarian racial, gender, and sexual politics as egalitarian and even compassionate. The result is that those with intolerant beliefs "misrecognize themselves as tolerant" (Smith, 1994:19). One example of this rescripting of intolerance into tolerance is the way in which the discourse of the Civil Rights Movement, rejected at one time by the American political right, becomes the basis for a new antiegalitarian "rights" discourse (Smith, 2001:151–52).

Just as many inegalitarian and intolerant "cultural" beliefs are understood by those on the New Right as moral, natural, or traditional, many previously marginal economic beliefs are now understood as centrist and mainsteam. These include the constellation of policies associated with revoking the New Deal, such as regressive tax policies, "privatized" social security, and welfare "reform." As Ann Withorn notes about recent New Right interventions into welfare, "opposition to welfare has successfully become not only a unifier for the Right but a wedge issue for infusing right-wing ideology into mainstream social policy and social thought" (Withorn, 1998:127). In fact, like the beliefs of social and Christian conservatives, the market assumptions and policies associated with the neoliberal New Right are not new in the last twenty years of American history. Economic conservatism has always been central to American thought and practice, as Kevin Phillips suggests when he argues that the Republican and Democratic parties are the first and second most enthusiastic laissez-faire political parties in the world (Phillips, 1991:32). But market fundamentalism received great ideological support from the collapse of the Soviet Union and the perception that there is no viable alternative to a global regime of unfettered capitalism. Political observers on the left chart the progress of New Right economic thought and practice from the economic policies of the Reagan and H. W. Bush administrations to the ineffectually disputed dominance of global capitalism (Lind, 1996; Bashevkin, 1998).

Most critiques of New Right economics do not explicitly analyze the effects of these policies and practices on women. Nevertheless, gendered, raced, and other social locations influence the impact on individuals of economic policies. Policies that purport to satisfy market imperatives frequently have differential race and gender effects. For example, a policy such as workfare allows New Right conservatives to uphold personal responsibility by advocating that poor women work outside the home even as they advocate against such work for middle and upper-class women. Throughout much of the history of America's welfare state, African American women were systematically excluded from receiving benefits that poor and widowed white women could receive. Given this history, the intersection of race and gender is significant for welfare policy even though it is little discussed in mainstream analysis. Both the stereotyping of black "welfare queens" and the passage of welfare "reform" that puts an end to a social safety net have come on the heels of women of color finally gaining access to public benefits (Roberts, 1997).

Besides affecting differently-situated individuals in different ways, New Right economic policies frequently are constructed to reconcile laissez-faire economic principles with social conservative ideals such as complementary gender roles and social reliance on women's care work. Traditional families with complementary gender roles—male provision and female care-giving—create economic disadvantages for women (Ferber and Nelson, 1993). Although it is not financially compensated, women's care work is often assumed in economic models. Feminists propose different kinds of reposts to these assumptions. Martha Fineman argues that caregivers should be provided economic and legal advantages such as tax breaks to compensate for their care-giving work and to recognize the social and economic benefits that caregivers provide (Fineman, 1995). Other feminists prefer strategies that give women greater access to living wage work and more support services for working parents (Bergmann, 1997; Young, 1997). When New Right economic thinkers oppose such egalitarian ideas they do not do so by recourse to ostensibly natural gender roles. This open social conservatism would make it more difficult for New Right ideologists to "center" their political ideas for mainstream citizens. However, New Right conceptions of fixed and natural gender roles tacitly under-gird and validate these economic ideas.

NEW RIGHT CONSERVATISMS

At the core of both economic and social strands of the New Right is an ideology of individual responsibility and commitment to the "basic values of work, faith, and family" (Withorn, 1998:140). But there is more to the relationship between different arenas and constituencies of the New Right than ideological principles. A series of compromises, common interests, spheres of influence, and emotional appeals forge bridges between economic and social conservatism. Feminist and other critics of the right identify four kinds of linkages: the construction of common enemies, patterns of financial support, the manipulation of symbolic and emotional appeals that bring together constituencies of the right, and a division of influence between New Right constituencies that enables cooperation among them.

The first form of convergence between the conservatisms relates to the belief in threats and enemies to American society, especially the refocusing of targets of resentment from outsiders to insiders in the wake of communism and the Cold War. It is no accident that antigay and lesbian activism, antiabortion rights activism, welfare "reform," and the broader elimination of a safety net of social provisioning accelerated and became central New Right political goals during the decline and after the fall of the U.S.S.R. As Chip Berlet points out, the Christian Right antici-pated this transformation by emphasizing the internal domestic threat of secular humanism. The conservative Christian analysis of the threat to American culture and values was taken up by the rest of the right throughout the 1990s (Berlet, 2001:27). A more strategic reading of this shift is that the "culture war" "divert[s] the wrath of wage-earning populist voters from Wall Street and corporate America to other targets: the universities, the media, racial minorities, homosexuals, immi-grants" (Lind, 1996:154). Like their New Right male counterparts, economically and socially conservative women, in spite of their many differences, "converge in nam-ing the forces responsible for America's decline" (Klatch, 1987:195).

A second kind of convergence follows from the injunction to "follow the money." Critics of the right point to material support extended by corporations, foundations and other loci of economic conservatism for the intellectual and ac-tivist enterprises of social conservatism. Actors and organizations of the New Right do not just act spontaneously on small budgets but, instead, rely on corporate donors like billionaire Richard Mellon Scaife, who contributes to the operation of organizations such as the American Enterprise Institute, the Heritage Foundation, and Stanford University's Hoover Institution.[6] In sites such as the Heritage Foundation and Empower America, large financial donations and interests support purveyors of both economic and social conservative doctrines with sophisticated lobbying and communication networks (Diamond, 1996).

Third, some analyses of the New Right focus on the manipulation of symbols and emotional appeals that link economically and socially conservative factions. Linda Kintz ties the intimate and familial meanings embedded in major social issues to newly-reconfigured subtexts of raced, gendered, and (hetero)sexualized meanings in free market ideology. Kintz posits the construction of a "transparent American subject" that fuses working class cultural resentments against the American government with the economic resentments of the wealthy (Kintz, 1997:25). Such a discursive and symbolic fusion mystifies the gender, race, and sexual exclusions and oppressions that serve the interests of political power and transnational capitalism. Women are not merely bit players in the creation of this ideological synthesis. Conservative women have "helped establish a symbolic framework that returns manliness to the center of culture and brings the traditional morality of fundamentalist religion together with the fundamentalism of the market" (Kintz, 1997:2).

Finally, it is frequently true that when we look past the symbolic performances that represent the public face of politics, cultural and economic conservatives exercise different kinds and degrees of influence in different arenas of decision-making. For example, neoconservative foreign policy and neoliberal business considerations drive administration foreign policies.[7] Meanwhile, the Bush administration actively courts the Christian Right in areas of domestic policy related to reproductive rights, lesbian, gay, bisexual, and transgender (LGBT) issues, and faith-based provision of public services. This is not to say that the Christian Right does not also extend its influence into the international arena; as Doris Buss and Didi Herman point out, Christian Right initiatives are well-institutionalized in the broad area of family policy (Buss and Herman, 2003). It is merely to suggest that there is a tacit division of authority over particular spheres and kinds of decision-making that enables New Right constituencies to cooperate rather than conflict.

From local school boards to state legislatures, from courts to congressional elections, the political agenda forged by social and economic conservatives remains central to the politics of the nation. When we examine the American New Right today across its multiple actors, issue areas, and strategies of action, it is useful to bear in mind that even when women are out of sight, women have a great deal to do with the right. Women are both actors—agents and shapers of right wing beliefs and policies—and acted upon. Not only that, women and women's issues are frequently invoked by the right as symbols and objects of right-wing apprehensiveness. Anxiety surrounding women's roles, rights, and demands catalyze and shape the interests and political action of the right as much as right-wing politics catalyze and shape feminism and progressive women's politics.

NOTES

1. For example, Dole modified her early support for the Equal Rights Amendment and affirmative action to conform to more conservative Republican positions. As a CNN profile put it, "her ideological transformations were perfectly in synch with each of her moves up the Washington hierarchy" (Stengel, 1996).

2. Rank and file women on both the antifeminist New Right and on the fascist or white supremacist far Right may share a common sense of empowerment in the context of groups and ideologies characterized by masculine dominance and strict gender roles. As Kathleen Blee points out, pro-White women often experience "a sense of control over the circumstances of life, a feeling of self-empowerment, and an expectation that they have authority over others" (Blee, 2002:163).

3. In 1995, the Southern Baptist Convention passed a non-binding resolution expressing regret for Southern Baptist support for slavery and racial discrimination and calling for the elimination of racism.

4. One such initiative is the Christian Coalition's Samaritan Project, launched in 1997.

5. It is important to note that some feminists find the legal foundation of reproductive liberty based on privacy and choice problematic. (See, e.g., Petchesky 1984 and Solinger 2001).

6. Scaife foundations contributed nearly $3.5 million to the Heritage Foundation between 1994 and 1996 (Jackson, 1998).

7. Even military campaigns can effect legal, political, and economic transformations abroad that accord with New Right goals. A recent example is "Operation Iraqi Freedom," which brought to that country both Christian Right missionary activity and a tax structure that is championed by market conservatives in the United States.

REFERENCES

Bashevkin, Sylvia. 1998. *Women on the Defensive: Living Through Conservative Times*. Chicago and London: Chicago University Press.

Bendroth, Margaret Lamberts. 1999. "Fundamentalism and the Family: Gender, Culture, and the American Pro-Family Movement." *Journal of Women's History*. 10(4). 35–54.

Bergmann, Barbara R. 1997. *Saving Our Children from Poverty: What the United States Can Learn from France*. New York: Russell Sage Foundation.

Berlet, Chip. 2001. "Following the Threads." In Amy E. Ansell, editor, *Unraveling the Right: The New Conservatism in American Thought and Politics*. Boulder, Colo.: Westview Press. 17–40.

Blee, Kathleen M. 2002. *Inside Organized Racism: Women in the Hate Movement*. Berkeley: University of California Press.

Bobbio, Norberto. 1996. *Left and Right: The Significance of a Political Distinction*. Chicago: University of Chicago Press.

Brasher, Brenda E. 1998. *Godly Women: Fundamentalism and Female Power*. New Brunswick, N.J.: Rutgers University Press.

Brown, Elsa Barkley. 1995. "Imaging Lynching: African American Women, Communities of Struggle, and Collective Memory." In Geneva Smitherman, editor, *African American Women Speak Out on Anita Hill–Clarence Thomas*. Detroit: Wayne State University Press. 100–124.

Brown, Steven P. 2003. *Trumping Religion: The New Christian Right, the Free Speech Clause and the Courts*. Tuscaloosa, Ala: University of Alabama Press.

Buchanan, Patrick J. 1992. "Address By Patrick J. Buchanan," in *Official Report of the Proceedings of the Thirty-Fifth Republican National Convention Held in Houston, Texas*. Washington, D.C.: Republican National Committee. 371–376.

Burack, Cynthia. 2003. "Getting What 'We' Deserve: Terrorism, Tolerance, Sexuality, and the Christian Right." *New Political Science*. 25(3). 329–349.

Buss, Doris and Didi Herman. 2003. *Globalizing Human Values: The Christian Right in International Politics*. Minneapolis, Minn.: University of Minnesota Press.

Campbell, Nancy D. 2003. "Reading the Rhetoric of Compassionate Conservatism." In Cynthia Burack and Jyl J. Josephson, editors, *Fundamental Differences: Feminists Talk Back to Social Conservatives*. Lanham, MD: Rowman and Littlefield. 113–126.

Collins, Patricia Hill. 1998. *Fighting Words: Black Women and the Search for Justice*. Minneapolis and London: University of Minnesota Press.

Conn, James L. April 1999. "Rift on the Right: Right-Wing Strategist Paul Weyrich Says The Culture War Is Lost, But Dobson, Robertson and Other Religious Right Leaders Insist They've Just Begun To Fight," *Church and State*. http://www.au.org/churchstate/cs4991.htm (November 16, 2001).

Coontz, Stephanie. 1992. *The Way We Never Were: American Families and the Nostalgia Trap.* New York: Basic Books.

Diamond, Sara. 1998. *Not by Politics Alone: The Enduring Influence of the Christian Right.* New York: Guilford Press.

Diamond, Sara. 1996. *Facing the Wrath: Confronting the Right in Dangerous Times.* Monroe, ME: Common Courage Press.

Diamond, Sara. 1995. *Roads to Dominion: Right Wing Movements and Political Power in the United States.* New York: Guilford Press.

Dillard, Angela D. 2001. *Guess Who's Coming to Dinner Now? Multicultural Conservatism in America.* New York: New York University Press.

Dorrien, Gary. 2001. "Inventing an American Conservatism: The Neoconservative Episode." In Amy E. Ansell, editor, *Unraveling the Right: The New Conservatism in American Thought and Politics.* Boulder, Colo.: Westview Press. 56–79.

Dubois, W.E.B. 1992. *Black Reconstruction in America, 1860–1880.* New York: MacMillan.

Ferber, Abby L. 1998. *White Man Falling: Race, Gender, and White Supremacy.* Lanham, MD: Rowman and Littlefield.

Ferber, Marianne A. and Julie A. Nelson, editors. 1993. *Beyond Economic Man: Feminist Theory and Economics.* Chicago: University of Chicago Press.

Fineman, Martha. 1995. *The Neutered Mother, the Sexual Family, and Other Twentieth-Century Tragedies.* New York: Routledge.

Fitzgerald, Jenrose 2003. "A Liberal Dose of Conservatism: The 'New Consensus' on Welfare and Other Strange Synergies." In Cynthia Burack and Jyl J. Josephson, editors, *Fundamental Differences: Feminists Talk Back to Social Conservatives.* Lanham, MD: Rowman and Littlefield. 95–110.

Hardisty, Jean. 1999. *Mobilizing Resentment: Conservative Resurgence from the John Birch Society to the Promise Keepers.* New York: Beacon Press.

Harding, Susan Friend. 2000. *The Book of Jerry Falwell: Fundamentalist Language and Politics.* Princeton, N.J.: Princeton University Press.

Hartmann, Susan M. 1989. *From Margin to Mainstream: American Women and Politics Since 1960.* New York: Alfred A. Knopf.

Helderman, Rosalind S. 2003. "Outfitted with Placards and Prayer: Students from Va's New Patrick Henry College Planting Political Seeds." *Washington Post.* October 20. P. B1.

hooks, bell. 1995. *Killing Rage: Ending Racism.* New York: Henry Holt and Company.

Jackson, Brooks. 1998. "Who is Richard Mellon Scaife?" *CNN.Com.* http://www.cnn.com/ALLPOLITICS/1998/04/27/scaife.profile/ (February 4, 2004).

Josephson, Jyl J. and Cynthia Burack. 1998. "The Political Ideology of the Neo-Traditional Family." *Political Ideologies.* 3(2). 213–231.

Karon, Tony. 2000. "For Bush, Humility and the Global Gag Order Don't Mix." *Time Online Edition.* http://www.time.com/time/world/article/0,8599,96407,00.html (February 4, 2004).

Kintz, Linda. 1997. *Between Jesus and the Market: The Emotions that Matter in Right-Wing America.* Durham and London: Duke University Press.

Klatch, Rebecca E. 1987. *Women of the New Right.* Philadelphia: Temple University Press.

Lienesch, Michael. 1993. *Redeeming America: Piety and Politics in the New Christian Right.* Chapel Hill, N.C.: University of North Carolina Press.

Lind, Michael. 1996. *Up From Conservatism: Why the Right is Wrong for America.* New York: Free Press.

McGirr, Lisa. 2002. *Suburban Warriors: The Origins of the New American Right.* Princeton: Princeton University Press.

Mercurio, John. 2002. "Lott Apologizes for Thurman Comment." http://www.cnn.com/2002/ALLPOLITICS/12/09/lott.comment/. CNN.Com/Inside Politics (February 4, 2004).

Nossiff, Rosemary. 2001. *Before* Roe: *Abortion Policy in the States.* Philadelphia: Temple University Press.

O'Connor, Karen. 1996. *No Neutral Ground? Abortion Politics in an Age of Absolutes.* Boulder, Colo.: Westview Press.

Petchesky, Rosalind Pollack. 1984. *Abortion and Woman's Choice: The State, Sexuality, and Reproductive Freedom.* Boston: Northeastern University Press.

Phelan, Shane. 2001. *Sexual Strangers: Gays, Lesbians, and Dilemmas of Citizenship.* Philadelphia: Temple University Press.

Phillips, Kevin. 1991. *The Politics of Rich and Poor: Wealth and the American Electorate in The Reagan Aftermath.* New York: HarperPerennial.

Roberts, Dorothy. 1997. *Killing the Black Body: Race, Reproduction, and the Meaning of Liberty.* New York: Pantheon.

Rymph, Catherine E. 2000. "Neither Neutral nor Neutralized: Phyllis Schlafly's Battle Against Sexism." In Linda K. Kerber and Jane Sherron De Hart, *Women's America,* fifth edition. New York: Oxford University Press. 501–507.

Smith, Anna Marie. 2001. "Why Did Armey Apologize? Hegemony, Homophobia, and the Religious Right." In Amy E. Ansell, *Unraveling the Right: The New Conservatism in American Thought and Politics.* Boulder, Colo.: Westview Press. 148–172.

Smith, Anna Marie. 1994. *New Right Discourse on Race and Sexuality: Britain, 1968–1990.* Cambridge University Press.

Solinger, Rickie. 2001. *Beggars and Choosers: How the Politics of Choice Shapes Adoption, Abortion, and Welfare in the United States*. New York: Hill and Wang.

Stacey, Judith and Timothy Biblarz. 2003. "(How) Does the Sexual Orientation of Parents Matter?" In Cynthia Burack and Jyl J. Josephson, editors, *Fundamental Differences: Feminists Talk Back to Social Conservatives*. Lanham, MD: Rowman and Littlefield.

Stein, Arlene. 2001. *The Stranger Next Door: The Story of a Small Community's Battle over Sex, Faith, and Civil Rights*. Boston: Beacon Press.

Stengel, Richard. 1996. "Liddy Makes Perfect." *CNN ALLPolitics*. http://www.cnn.com/ALLPOLITICS/1996/analysis/time/9607/01/stengel.shtml (February 5, 2004).

Vaid, Urvashi. 1995. *Virtual Equality: The Mainstreaming of Gay and Lesbian Liberation*. New York: Doubleday.

Williams, Rhonda M. 1999. "Unfinished Business: African-American Political Economy During the Age of 'Color-blind' Politics." In Audrey Rowe, editor, *The State of Black America 1999: The Impact of Color-Consciousness in the United States*. New York: National Urban League.

Williams, Rhys H. and Jeffrey Blackburn. 1996. "Many Are Called but Few Obey: Ideological Commitment and Activism in Operation Rescue." In Christian Smith, editor, *Disruptive Religion: The Force of Faith in Social-Movement Activism*. New York: Routledge.

Withorn, Ann. 1998. "Fulfilling Fears and Fantasies: The Role of Welfare in Right-Wing Social Thought and Strategy." In Amy E. Ansell, *Unraveling the Right: The New Conservatism in American Thought and Politics*. Boulder, Colo.: Westview Press. 126–147.

Young, Iris Marion. 1997. *Intersecting Voices: Dilemmas of Gender, Political Philosophy, and Policy*. Princeton, N.J.: Princeton University Press.

Zengerle, Jason. February 1, 1999. "Liddy Lite." *The New Republic*. 222 (5). 9–10.

Women, Media, and Group Politics

★ ★ ★ ★ ★ ★ ★ ★ ★ ★ ★ ★ **3** ★ ★ ★ ★ ★ ★ ★ ★ ★ ★ ★ ★ ★

The media serve as sex-role socialization agents for young women and men. However, women are basically underrepresented in the top management positions within the mass media organizations; consequently, women have had less control in determining media content and in how women are depicted in the news. Does this influence how accurately and realistically the changing role of women in American political society is portrayed in the mass media? Do the media set an agenda that helps the general public better understand the political participation of American women within our society? The first essay in this chapter examines some of the research that has been done concerning the manner in which the mass media have reported news about American political women. Comparisons are drawn between the news about women and men in the U.S. political environment. The author concludes that clearly the role of women in all facets of American political life is changing; these changes have been and are being reported by the mass media. However, she cautions that additional studies employing multimethodological approaches appear warranted as the number of female candidates increases in American politics to further determine the content of this media coverage, the "reality" of political gender roles, and how the media cover these and to compare the coverage about women who run for elective office with the coverage given male candidates.

We next move from news about women and men in the American political environment to a review of the history and groups of the women's movement in the United States, with particular emphasis on the current partisan divide on gender issues.

Scholars agree that there is no intrinsic or organic political interest that unites all women. Each successive wave of the women's movement from the 1830s to the present has created new organizations and a new sense of community that advance women's interests. Denise Baer's essay analyzes key factors related to group-based leadership on women's issues. For example, if the movement portion of the women's movement is episodic, what are the key indicators of success? Are the activities of leading women's organizations different during periods of resurgence compared to periods of declining mass activists? How do the parties differ in the types of women represented? How influential are women in the 2004 conventions? It is argued that to effectively answer these questions requires debating whether there is a universal outcome to women's progress (e.g., involvement in the public sphere), or whether it is simply providing a range of quite diverse options for women to choose from (e.g., stay-at-home mom vs. working woman).

Finally, two factors related to the prospects of the mass resurgence of the women's movement are discussed: (1) the growing gap in activism, partisanship, and consciousness between group leaders, intellectual leaders, and actual and potential "followers"; and (2) the continued nonpartisanship of leading women's organizations alongside the heightened polarization on issues associated with the women's movement. Paradoxically, both factors make it possible for party leaders to reach women voters directly without the mediation of women leaders—a devastating hurdle for the expansion of women's gains.

Women and Sex Stereotypes: Cultural Reflections in the Mass Media

Lois Duke Whitaker

Walter Lippmann believed that people act on the basis of pictures they carry around in their heads, pictures of the way they think things are. These pictures constitute what is "real" for us, and, according to Lippmann, much of what we know about the world and our relationship to it reaches us indirectly. Lippman, who was analyzing public opinion more than eighty years ago, believed that what each person does is based not on direct observation or certain knowledge but on pictures made by the individual or given to her or him.[1] This is especially important when one considers how the mass media shape our perceptions by transmitting information.

Many images of what we interpret as real are conceived based on second-hand accounts provided by the mass media, or what Nimmo and Combs describe as "mediated" realities.[2] These mediated realities are perceptions, which are focused, filtered, and fantasized by the mass media. Because these perceived realities are shared with others, a group fantasy takes on an aura of truth that the private fantasies of individuals do not.[3] As Ben H. Bagdikian points out, the mass media become the authority at any given moment for what is true and what is false, what is reality and what is fantasy, what is important and what is trivial.[4]

A previous version of this article was presented at the 1994 Western Political Science Association Meeting, Albuquerque, New Mexico, March 10–12. I would like to thank David L. Paletz and Doris A. Graber for reading and critiquing an earlier version of this article.

All too often, the news about women is reported based on these "mediated" realities or on other myths driven by cultural norms and standards of what are deemed "appropriate" roles for women in American society; in some instances, it is determined by institutionalized discrimination and common socialization within the news organization itself.

This article will explore some of the research that has been done concerning the manner in which the mass media have portrayed American political women in the news. Comparisons will be drawn between the news about women and men in the American political environment. For the purposes of this article, mass media will include newspapers, network television news, fiction and entertainment television programs, political advertisements, and magazines. Numerous other studies about women and the mass media have been done—far too many to cite here. For example, these studies include research into the various media cited earlier as well as analyses of movies, talk shows, music videos as shown on MTV and other stations, and commercial advertisements that explore many issues of concern to women (e.g., rape, sexual violence, aging, pornography, female health matters, sexual harassment, and the beauty myth).

INFLUENCES ON NEWS MAKING

Scholars, including among others W. Lance Bennett, Doris A. Graber, Todd Gitlin, Robert Entman, and Gaye Tuchman argue that journalists construct reality in deciding what's news rather than merely providing a "picture of reality." This portrayal of what is real is influenced by the journalists' interpretation of reality or shaping the news story by framing—reporting the news from a particular perspective so that some aspects of the situation come into close focus and others fade into the background.[5] Tuchman further cites certain "strategic rituals" journalists follow in striving for "objectivity."[6] Included in these "rituals" is the process of presenting conflicting possibilities, as seen when "both sides" of a story are presented. Tuchman and other scholars also explain how "topical chains of command" and the gatekeeping process in the hierarchy of news organizations affect the news product and the events of day-to-day happenings that culminate as news.[7]

Other internal influences on news determination cited in previous research include recruitment, socialization, and control of the reporting staff. Lee Sigelman and Warren Breed, among others, argue that news is affected by organizational structure and relationships between reporters and editors.[8] Roshco, Bennett, and Graber maintain that news making is also affected by journalists' beats, sources, and organizational constraints of time and space.[9] Prior studies have also concluded that internal influences on the news from within the newspaper organization stem from the more liberal political ideology of reporters as compared with their generally more conservative editors or publishers.[10]

These internal factors have determined the construction of the news, but women, other minorities and those less influential in our society also have not had equitable access to the news organization. Thus, in many instances, issues of concern to these groups have not been addressed in the mass media. For example, Edie N. Goldenberg researched the access of resource-poor groups to the metropolitan press in Boston.[11] Goldenberg discovered that sources rich in resources within the political system enjoy certain advantages that place them in a much stronger position to manage the news than do resource-poor interest groups. That is, the groups who maintain continuing interaction with the mass media will have much greater access than most resource-poor groups, who are unable to establish and maintain an ongoing exchange with news personnel.[12]

SPECIFIC AGENDAS PASSED THROUGH THE MEDIA

The mass media not only favor certain classes and races of news story subject matter; they also are selective in what they write about, how they play up or play down a story, the "saturation" coverage they can give, sources of their stories and how balanced these sources are, endorsement and legitimacy given to the status quo by the media, and other means of conveying information.[13]

McCombs and Shaw maintain that editors, newsroom staff, and broadcasters, in choosing and displaying news, play an important part in shaping political reality.[14] That is, readers learn not only about a given issue but also how much importance to attach to that issue from the amount of information in a news story and its position. Therefore, in reflecting what candidates are saying during a campaign, the mass media may well determine the important issues—that is, the media may set the "agenda" of the campaign.[15]

Even though women and other minorities have made recent strides into the public and governmental arena, for the most part the mass media still reflect a "cultural" lag in depicting these advances through realistic news portrayal. Lang argues the "news media are both potential agents of change and captives of their own assumptions."[16]

As but one example of the coverage given African Americans in the news, previous research into how newspapers reported on issues of race and southern politics over a thirty-year time frame revealed that four Carolina newspapers reflected more bias in the news content about issues of intense social conflict during the civil rights movement (*Brown v. Board of Education* decision and school desegregation) than in the news coverage about those issues less socially threatening to the white community (the 1964 Civil Rights Act, the 1965 Voting Rights Act, and Senate reapportionment of the South Carolina General Assembly).[17] The bias of the dominant white influence was significantly more negative in direction when the news coverage was about a more socially and politically threatening issue. Bias appeared to be directly related to the degree of the social and political threat to the White community.

Thus, as politicians used the issue of race and fear of integration in their campaign rhetoric as they sought state and national office, this negativity toward blacks

became an entrenched part of the culture. Newspapers picked up on this nega-
tivism, as reflected by their bias on the news pages and in their editorials against
progressive change. The newspapers, in most instances, were basically a mouth-
piece for the dominant social, cultural, and political views of the White southern
community.[18]

MYTHS AND STEREOTYPES ABOUT WOMEN PORTRAYED IN THE MEDIA

Women also have been subjected to sex-role stereotypes, cultural standards, and
myths established by societal norms and passed along through the news media.
Maria Braden describes a journalist who referred to former Vermont governor
Madelein Kunin's arguments as "hysterical" may not have realized that the word he
used reflected a view that women are emotional and irrational. Braden cites Boston
University journalism professor Caryl Rivers who has written, "We have come far
from the days when a respectable woman's name appeared in the press only on
the day she was married and the day she died, but old myths about female unrelia-
bility and weakness still drift through the modern media like smoke. Many journalists—women among them—are so accustomed to these myths as to be only barely
aware of their existence."[19]

For example, some research into how the press covered the contemporary
women's movement revealed evidence of sex stereotypes. David Broder explains
that when the National Organization for Women (NOW) was formed in 1966, it
was not considered news in the eyes of the *Washington Post*. Even though the
New York Times reported the event, the news was reported on the "Food, Fashion,
Family and Furnishings" page. According to Broder, this news was placed "down at
the bottom of the page, under the recipes for the 'traditional Thanksgiving menu'
and the picture of 'the culinary star of the day, the turkey, roasted, stuffed and surrounded by other festive Thanksgiving specialties.'"[20] Alger also points out that in
assessing themes depicting women in the media, women's activities have most
often been portrayed as concerned with the home or with men.[21]

Broder goes on to explain that the women's movement did not make the
front pages of the *Post* or the *Times* until August 1970. This happened after Betty
Friedan, a key figure in the women's movement and founder of NOW, organized a
strike of women workers (housewives as well as office and factory workers) and
protest marches in Washington, New York and other cities throughout the United
States. The tactic worked, the movement became news, and issues of concern (discrimination in pay and employment opportunities, passage of the Equal Rights
Amendment, provision of child care and abortion facilities) were finally debated.[22]
Kahn and Goldenberg also examined news coverage of the women's movement;
they found that the early media coverage of the women's movement did not help
the movement to grow. In fact, they argue that the press coverage of the women's
movement—when there was any at all—was unflattering. Their findings indicate
that the movement grew despite the media.[23] Ashley and Olson examined the print

media's framing of the women's movement over a span of twenty years (1966–1986). Their content analysis included a total of 499 articles from the *New York Times, Time,* and *Newsweek.* Coverage of both women who organized to promote and deter the movement was studied. Results showed that both groups were not considered important. The strongest evidence for framing techniques was the delegitimation of feminists; this included reporting aspects of the women's appearance, using quotation marks around such words as "liberation," and emphasizing dissension within the movement. Conversely, the anti-feminists were described as well-organized and attractive. The movement's goals were rarely mentioned, while surface details were commonly presented.[24]

Decades later, this media trend of stereotyping females by portraying women as primarily concerned with home and family is still in existence in other studies. According to Clara Bingham, forty female members of Congress met with Hillary Rodham Clinton in 1993 to discuss politics and policy. When the *Washington Post* published a story about the first meeting of the women's caucus with the First Lady, the story ran on the front page of "Style," the newspaper's section devoted to lifestyle features and cultural happenings. To contrast coverage along these same lines, the First Lady met several weeks before with a group of members of Congress (the black caucus and the Hispanic caucus) and the story appeared in the "A" section of the newspaper.[25]

Still other scholars have identified certain patterns in the manner in which women are portrayed in the mass media. For example, Vande Berg and Streckfuss studied 116 prime-time television program episodes that covered two weeks of programming in the mid 1980s for each of the three major U.S. commercial networks (CBS, NBC, and ABC).[26] Male characters were found to outnumber female characters by a factor of about two to one. Females were seen far more frequently than males in household occupations and as students. The researchers also found that, proportionately, female characters were far more likely than male characters to be portrayed as enacting a humane, interpersonally focused, cooperative, concerned, information-sharing side of working and managing. Male characters, on the other hand, were far more likely to be seen fulfilling decisional, political, and operational functions in organizations. These studies concluded that relatively little has changed over forty years of prime-time television in terms of the portrayal of working women—that the overall image of women continues to be one in which they are defined primarily through stereotypical domestic roles.[27]

Lana F. Rakow and Kimberlie Kranich observe that feminists have long noted the relationship of news to the political and economic interests of men. Journalists' "hard news–soft news" distinction has institutionalized a gendered division between "serious, important" news that is overwhelmingly masculine and "human interest, lifestyle" news that is more likely to be the purview of women reporters and readers. That is, news is largely "men talking to men."[28] M. Junior Bridge of Unabridged Communications had similar findings in a research project she conducted for *Women, Men, and Media,* the media monitoring group. The study was conducted during July and August 1992. Seven major, general-interest newspapers and three news magainzes were examined. The publications included *Newsweek, Time, U.S. News & World Report, Chicago Tribune, Houston Chronicle, Los Angeles Times,* the *New York Times,* the *Philadelphia Inquirer, USA Today,* and the *Washington Post.* Among the observations:

- White, male political candidates and professionals are simply referred to by name and title, whereas the opposite gender's gender usually precedes her title, as in "lady lawyer" or "female candidates"—with one exception: homemaker.
- "Women's issues" is a favorite media catchphrase. Bridge questions just what exactly is meant by "women's issues"? Usually, the implication is day care, health care, reproduction, education. These issues, as Bridge points out, are no more the exclusive property or responsibility of women than war is of men. These issues affect all manner of people, no matter the gender, race, creed or ethnic background.
- There were many articles on mothers' impact on children, and by implication, mother's total responsibility for children.[29]

Penny M. Miller, University of Kentucky, conducted a series of hands on exercises at the University of Kentucky in courses on American government, introduction to political science, political behavior, campaigns and the media, women and politics, and state and local politics. Students in these courses content-analyzed front pages of Kentucky's major newspapers, the *New York Times,* and the college daily. The conclusion in every class was clear: when it comes to front-page reporting, Kentucky's major newspapers, the *New York Times,* and the college daily significantly underrepresented coverage of women and were often unflattering in the coverage they did provide.[30]

Recognizing that the role of women has changed in American society, one wonders how and why myths and stereotypes about contemporary American women continue to appear in the mass media. One explanation for this is the male control of the internal news organization. That is, the male viewpoint is still dominant in the hierarchy of the news organization and in the recruitment and socialization of media personnel.

WHITE MALE DOMINATION OF THE MEDIA

Bridge points out that the majority of editors, columnists and reporters are white males who tend most often to seek out other white males for commentary and showcasing.[31] Kay Mills points out there remain countless newsrooms where women still are underrepresented or where they feel reluctant to speak their minds, and those newspapers and news programs still feel less effect of women's experiences.[32] Mills further describes how newsrooms where some progress was being made on hiring more women and people of color now face tensions from white males who feel they are not getting the good jobs, the good assignments, although in many cases they still are. She concludes that the top people at the major news outlets still are men.[33]

Other studies point out that male and female editors and publishers seem to disagree about sexism in the newsroom, according to a survey released in September 2002. Many women editors believe there is a lack of opportunity for promotion, with only one in three of top female editors saying they expect to move up the ladder at their present newspaper. Of the women who say they find discrimination in their ability to advance, 64 percent believe employers favor male candidates. In excess of half expect to end employment with their present company, or expect to leave newspapers behind entirely. On the other hand, men who have been in the news business for decades believe there isn't really any sexism at high levels.[34]

Does the gender of the reporter/editor determine the slant or frame of the news story? Mills describes an interview with Joanne Byrd in the mid-1980s, who at the time was editor of the *Everett Herald* in Everett, Washington. Byrd said that she did not think there was any difference between men and women on the question of news judgment. Byrd later said, "I take it all back. Now I use that as practically the opening line of half the talks I give. In my first couple of years as an editor of a newspaper, I was practicing news judgment that I had learned from my predecessors, and of course they were all men. I knew what journalism was and I knew what news was. Several years later I said, well, hey, who says that's what news is? Why aren't those things that interest me news?" Day care, nanny problems, she said, would never have been considered news twenty-five years ago.[35]

James Devitt found the differences in coverage in female and male gubernatorial candidates in 1998 were due to stories written by male reporters who covered the gubernatorial campaigns; that is, newspaper readers were more likely to read about a female candidate's personal traits, such as her appearance or personality, than those of a male candidate. By contrast, they were more likely to read about a male candidate's stand or record on public policy issues than about a female candidate's. Devitt found that female reporters employed about the same percentage of issue and personal frames for both men and women within the same campaign. By contrast, male reporters used different proportions of frames to cover female and male candidates within each of the races studied.[36]

Stephanie Craft and Wayne Wanta studied issue agendas and story focus at newspapers with relatively high percentages of women in editorial positions with those at newspapers with lower percentages of female editors. Content analysis of stories from thirty newspapers' Web sites showed few differences in issues covered, but differences in what male and female reporters covered related to the predominant editor gender. Newspapers with a high percentage of female editors appeared not to differentiate between male and female reporters when assigning beats, as is apparently the case at male-dominated newsrooms. That is, male-dominated newsrooms tended to have male reporters cover political beats. Female reporters at these newspapers, conversely, were more likely to cover business and education beats. Male-dominated newsrooms thus rewarded male reporters with what has traditionally been considered a prestigious beat. They also found that papers with predominately male editors contained news with a more negative

focus.[37] Cory L. Armstrong studied the influence of reporter gender on source selection in newspaper stories. He analyzed the frequency and placement given to
male and female sources and story subjects in 889 newspaper stories. He found
that male sources and subjects received more mentions and were placed more
prominently in the stories.[38]

What does this mean for the element of bias one might expect in news coverage of the contemporary American woman and her changing role? As Maria Braden
points out, "The presence of women in journalism doesn't guarantee that news will
be free of sexist reporting, editing, or headline writing. It takes a conscious effort
by a journalist, male or female, to become more sensitive to gender-based stereotypes, to seek gender balance in stories, and to generate and promote stories of
concern to women."[39] However, generally speaking, women and other minorities,
the poor, those outside the power order and those with differing ideological perspectives that clash with the system will, in all probability, continue to be subject
to disparities in media coverage. There is a cultural, social, political, and economic
redefinition of what is news and how it should be reported. Let us next look at
some of the studies that have been completed about news coverage of women in
political elections and campaigns.

WOMEN, POLITICS, AND THE MEDIA

As women advance in all political arenas, including elective and appointive offices,
how do the mass media respond? Kahn analyzed newspaper coverage in forty-
seven statewide campaigns between 1982 and 1988. Findings show that the media
differentiated between male and female candidates in their campaign coverage. The
differences were found to be more dramatic in U.S. Senate races, but the distinctions were evident in gubernatorial contests as well. In senatorial races, women received less campaign coverage than their male counterparts; the coverage they received was more negative—emphasizing their unlikely chances of winning. In both
senatorial and gubernatorial races, women received consistently less issue attention
than their male counterparts. Finally, the news media seemed more responsive to
the messages sent by male candidates. The media's agenda more closely resembled
the agenda issued by male candidates in their televised political advertisements.[40]

Geralyn Miller examined newspaper coverage in Illinois state legislative races
in 1996. A content analysis of newspaper articles appearing in a sample of 21 legislative races indicate there are differences in coverage along lines of gender, but
these differences are subtle. While overall quantity and quality of coverage are similar for male and female candidates, a closer look reveals that differences, including
those along lines of candidate status and issue choice, may cause concern for female candidates in these races. The findings suggest that newspapers may affect
our democratic electoral processes negatively by introducing subtle forms of bias
into contests at the local and state levels, making it more difficult for women to run
successfully at the state level.[41]

A study by Bystrom, Robertson & Banwart of newspaper coverage of women and men running for their party's nomination for U.S. Senate and governor in the 2000 primary races found that these women received more coverage than did men in terms of quantity and that the quality of their coverage—slant of the story and discussion of their viability, appearance, and personality—was mostly equitable. Still, these female candidates were much more likely to be discussed in terms of their role as mothers and their marital status, which can affect their viability with voters. That is, the media can have a great impact on the public's perceptions of women candidates and their campaigns by portraying them as less viable and by describing them in terms of their image characteristics, rather than their issue stances. In their coverage of women candidates, the media often reflect the biases and stereotypes of the public.[42] Aday and Devitt compared newspaper coverage of Elizabeth Dole's presidential campaign with that of former Texas Governor George W. Bush, Arizona Senator John McCain, and publisher Steve Forbes. The authors examined three months of coverage in the *Des Moines Register,* the *New York Times,* the *Los Angeles Times, USA Today,* and the *Washington Post.* The authors found qualitative differences in coverage that they attributed to Dole's gender. Compared to her male opponents, Dole received less coverage on her positions on the issues but more coverage on her personal traits. That is, news stories about Dole did not tell voters much about what she stood for.[43]

Still, a study of statewide campaigns in 1994 indicates that portrayals of female candidates seem to have been more positive. Kevin B. Smith found much smaller coverage differences than in studies relying on pre-1990 data. Although systematic gender-based patterns are still detectable, they are not so glaring as reported in previous studies, and not always to the disadvantage of female candidates.[44] Banwart, Bystro, and Robertson also found some evidence of more equal treatment of female candidates. Their study analyzed the media's portrayal of candidates in mixed-gender gubernatorial and U.S. Senate races through a comparison of primary coverage to general election coverage in 2000. The study relied on content analyses of more than 1,200 articles from major newspapers to understand how female and male candidates might be framed differently when running for their party's nomination as opposed to during the general election. Their study confirmed that in the 2000 election, female candidates received more newspaper coverage than did male candidates in U.S. Senate and gubernatorial races. It also suggests that the slant of male candidates' news coverage became more negative, whereas female candidate coverage remained more neutral from the primary to general election. Yet, they found female candidates continue to face some stereotypical biases in the news coverage of their campaigns.[45] Thus, one could conclude that there is some evidence to indicate a shift may be underway and that one could expect even more equal treatment of female candidates in the press in the future.

But, let's move from studies reflecting how the mass media report on female candidates for public office to briefly assess how the mass media cover women who are elected or appointed to office.

Patty Murray (D-WA), the woman who ran for the U.S. Senate in 1992 as the "mom in tennis shoes," not only was successful in her bid for election; she also landed an assignment to the powerful Senate Appropriations Committee on her first day on the job. How did the *Seattle Times* report this committee assignment? The news was reported in the local pages instead of on the front page.[46] One has to question the placement decision by newspaper personnel, which unquestionably downplayed this news item. Would the same "news" have been subjugated to inside pages if the Washington senator had been male?

Analysis of the newspaper coverage given the nominations for attorney general of Zoe Baird and Kimba Wood revealed newspapers set an agenda that depicted typical female stereotypes. That is, the newspaper accounts tended to highlight and focus not just on the issue of lawbreaking but on the problems of female professionals and the issue of child care.[47] Of course, child care has traditionally been perceived to be a female responsibility. Our society and our government leaders have delegated the nurturing role to women, which, to many, means women are the prime caretakers of children.

To contrast perceptions of male and female roles in child care, more than twenty years ago it was learned that then-Deputy Attorney General William Ruckelshaus had an alien woman with an improper visa working in his home. Stories in the media attributed this arrangement to his wife, and the story quickly died.[48] Thus, even though the nominee in question had employed an alien woman, the basic issue of child care was linked to the wife's responsibility—and not that of a male nominee—and the issue was put to rest.

The nominations of Baird and Wood were withdrawn by the Clinton administration, and Janet Reno, a single woman without child care responsibility, was nominated and confirmed as the first female U.S. attorney general. Shortly thereafter, Commerce Secretary Ronald H. Brown reported that he had failed to pay Social Security taxes for a household worker. Newspaper accounts explained this double-standard in the following manner:

> What is the distinction between Mr. Brown and Judge Wood? In the screening process for Presidential nominees, Mr. Brown was not asked about his compliance with immigration and tax laws. By contrast, Judge Wood was asked several times and "she was not completely forthcoming," Mr. Stephanopoulos (Clinton spokesperson) said.
>
> Judge Wood said that she was asked if she had a 'Zoe Baird problem' and that she interpreted that to mean had she ever hired an illegal alien, when it was against the law and not paid Social Security and other taxes for that worker, as Ms. Baird had. She said she had replied truthfully that she had not.[49]

Thus, we have a situation in which a woman was not confirmed although she had broken no law and a man who had not complied with the law avoided the same critical scrutiny by the press during the confirmation process. The mass media play into this double standard in other ways. The press provides not only information but the particular "spin" the public and our government officials associate with this news report or this issue.

As another example, Susan J. Carroll and Ronnee Schreiber studied 291 distinct articles on women in the 103rd Congress published in twenty-seven major newspapers throughout the United States in the months between January 1993 and October 1994. Even though the women who were elected to Congress for the first time during 1992 clearly received more media attention than their first-term male colleagues, there were examples of stories with the theme of juggling family and career. One story was a lengthy article that made the front page of the *New York Times* with the headline, "Even Women at Top Still Have Floors to Do" (*New York Times,* 31 May 1993). Carroll and Schreiber point out that, among other fascinating facts about women in Congress, one learns from the article that Senator Dianne Feinstein picks up bath towels her husband refuses to hang up and that people are surprised to find that Congresswoman Lucille Roybal-Allard would be interested in a recipe.[50]

Thus, the mass media interpret what is perceived as a "female" burden or problem and pass this along to the general populace. Public opinion coalesces around this issue, elected and other officials within government interpret this stereotypical role for women, and female professionals often are the losers.

CONCLUSION

The very nature of the news-making process dictates that reporters, journalists, editors, and/or publishers, by necessity, must make news decisions. Judgments as to what is news and what is not; decisions of how to "play" a story as far as importance; judgments regarding placement of news; the amount of coverage to be given a particular issue, event or personality; and other internal decisions within the media organization will always be determined by institutional norms of what is and ought to be "news." These internal constraints of media organizations and personnel, by necessity, dictate the ultimate news product. As Paletz and Entman have observed, "Seeking neither to praise nor deplore, we have shown that much of the news is determined less by external 'reality' than by the internal logic of media organizations and personnel.[51]

In addition, mass media professionals bring their own culture, their own social norms, and their own political views and preferences to the news-making procedure. Despite the professionalism of the individual reporter and her or his news organization, the final news product will be influenced by any number of internal and external factors.

Thus, whether the issue is women seeking elective or appointive public office, ethnicity in the Northeast, the environment in the West, or religion or race in the Deep South, specific issues and events will be selected for coverage, while others will be ignored or downplayed. Still other issues will be addressed by giving the story a different "spin" in the newspapers' pages or in the nightly television news. And the sociological and cultural influences of the individuals making these decisions will always be a human determination.

If falls, then, to the American public to recognize media coverage for what it is and to work beyond the stereotypes that do end up in the news. The role of women in all facets of American life has changed significantly over the past four decades, and is continuing to change. Clearly, these changes have been and are being reported by the mass media. But, a number of questions remain: What is the content of this media coverage? What has been the role of the media in assessing the 'reality' of some of these changes? How have these changes subsequently been reported by the mass media? Do women not deserve a great deal more coverage, even under the present constraints as outlined above, than the media give them?

And, should not the coverage focus on issues, opinions, assessments by female candidates and policymakers as much as is now given to men? Women have made strides in American politics. But much remains to be rectified such that we do not have newspaper columns as this one reported by Paula LaRocque: "At 36, she's still a knockout, her clear English skin and sparkling blue eyes set off by auburn curls . . . (column about a woman who had won political office)."[52]

Obviously, this is a preliminary article written to synthesize some of the research that has been done in the area of press coverage of women in American politics. As the number of female candidates increases and the number of women in other important positions within our government grows, further studies are indicated that will examine and analyze the media coverage given women by the press. Studies that would further explore how the news is reported about women who run for elective office and how this coverage compares with that of male candidates especially appear to be warranted. This area of research for political scientists is still basically untapped. As Kahn has outlined, while research in the last twenty years has shown us ways in which the media can influence women's role in the political system, many important questions have yet to be explored. Kahn outlines five areas for future research: (1) news media treatment of women officeholders (2) effectiveness of men's and women's campaign strategies (3) gender differences in political-press relationships (4) how the gender of journalists influences the news and (5) how the media affect the political socialization of children.[53] As more women seek and are elected to public office, one hopes that additional research can be done in these areas.

NOTES

1. Walter Lippman, "The World Outside and the Pictures in Our Heads," in *Public Opinion* (New York: Macmillan, 1922), chap. 1; see also "Newspapers Walter Lippman," in Doris A. Graber (Ed.), *Media Power in Politics,* 4th ed. (Washington, D.C.: Congressional Quarterly Press, 2000), pp. 36–43.

2. Dan Nimmo and James E. Combs, *Mediated Political Realities,* 2nd ed. (New York: Longman, 1990), p. 2.

3. *Ibid.,* pp. 1–20.

4. Ben H. Bagdikian, The Media Monopoly (Boston: Beacon Press, 2000), p. 1iii.

5. W. Lance Bennett, *News: The Politics of Illusion,* Fifth Edition (New York: Longman, 2003), pp. 130, 134–139; Doris A. Graber, *Mass Media & American Politics* (Washington, D.C.: Congressional Quarterly Press, 2002), pp. 173–175; Todd Gitlin, *The Whole World Is Watching.* (Berkeley: University of California Press, 1980), pp. 1–18 and pp. 249–282; Gitlin, *Inside Prime*

Time (London: Routledge Publishers, 1994), pp. 203–220 and pp. 325–335; Robert Entman, "Framing: Toward Clarification of a Fractured Paradigm," *Journal of Communication* 43 (Autumn 1993), pp. 51–58; and Gaye Tuchman, *Making News: A Study in the Construction of Reality* (New York: Free Press, 1978), p. 23.

6. Tuchman, *Making News,* p. 667.

7. *Ibid.,* p. 12; Bennett, *News: The Politics of Illusion,* pp. 2–4 and pp. 15–17. Graber, *Mass Media & American Politics,* 99–131; Stephen D. Reese, Jane Ballinger, "The Roots of a Sociology of News: Remembering Mr. Gates and Social Control in the Newsroom," *Journalism and Mass Communication Quarterly* 78, (4) (Winter, 2001), pp. 641–659.

8. Lee Sigelman, "Reporting the News: An Organizational Analysis," *American Journal of Sociology,* 79 (July–November 1973), pp. 132–151; Warren Breed, "Social Control in the Newsroom: A Functional Analysis," *Social Forces,* 33 (May 1955), pp. 326–335.

9. Bernard Roshco, *Newsmaking* (Chicago: University of Chicago Press, 1975), pp. 4–5; Bennett, *News: The Politics of Illusion,* pp. 160–189; Graber, *Mass Media & American Politics,* p. 104.

10. Bob Schulman, "The Liberal Tilt of Our Newsroom," *Bulletin of the American Society of Newspaper Editors,* 654 (October 1982), pp. 3–7; Graber, *Mass Media & American Politics,* pp. 92–95.

11. Edie N. Goldenberg, *Making the Papers* (Lexington, MA: Lexington Books, 1975), pp. 1–6.

12. *Ibid.,* pp. 145–146, 148.

13. Among others, see Michael Parenti, *Inventing Reality: The Politics of News Media,* 2nd ed. (New York: St. Martin's Press, 1993), pp. 191–210. Also, see Daniel C. Hatlin, "Sound Bite News," in Gary Orren (Ed.) *Blurring the Lines* (New York: Free Press, 1990); Martin A. Lee and Norman Solomon, *Unreliable Sources* (New York: Carol Publishing Group, 1991).

14. Maxwell E. McCombs and Donald L. Shaw, "The Agenda-Setting Function of Mass Media," *Public Opinion Quarterly,* 36 (Summer 1972), pp. 176–187. Also see Everett M. Rogers and James W. Dearing, "Agenda-Setting Research: Where Has It Been and Where Is It Going?" in James A. Anderson (Ed.), *Communication Yearbook,* vol. 2 (Beverly Hills, CA: Sage, 1988) and reprinted in Graber, *Media Power in Politics,* pp. 68–85.

15. Maxwell E. McCombs and Donald L. Shaw, "The Agenda-Setting Function of Mass Media," *Public Opinion Quarterly* 36 (Summer 1972), p. 177; W. Lance Bennett, *News: the Politics of Illusion,* 5th ed. pp. 6–8; Graber, *Mass Media & American Politics,* 6th ed.; pp. 175–184.

16. Gladys Engel Lang, "The Most Admired Women: Image-Making in the News," in Gaye Tuchman, Arlene Kaplan Daniels, and James Benet (Eds.) *Hearth and Home* (New York: Oxford University Press, 1978), p. 147.

17. Lois Lovelace Duke, "Cultural Redefinition of News: Racial Issues in South Carolina, 1954–1984," Ph.D. diss., University of South Carolina, 1986; see also J. Fred MacDonald, *Blacks and White TV,* 2nd Edition (Chicago: Nelson-Hall Publishers, 1992), pp. 278–301; Douglas M. McLeod, "Communicating Deviance: The Effects of Television News Coverage of Social Protest," *Journal of Broadcasting & Electronic Media* 39 (Winter, 1995), pp. 4–19; and Herman Gray, *Watching Race* (Minneapolis: University of Minnesota Press, 1995), pp. 1–13 and 162–176.

18. Among others who discuss basic distortions in the media, see Michael Parenti, *Inventing Reality: The Politics of News Media,* 2nd ed. (New York: St. Martin's Press, 1993), pp. 191–210; Kathleen Hall Jamieson and Karlyn Kohrs Campbell, *The Interplay of Influence* (Belmont, CA: Wadsworth, 1992), especially pp. 98–124; and Kathleen Hall Jamieson, *Beyond the Double Bind: Women and Leadership* (New York: Oxford University Press, 1995), pp. 167–170, 172, 177–180.

19. Maria Braden, *Women Politicians and the Media,* (Lexington, Ky.: The University Press of Kentucky, 1996), p. 10. See also Caryl Rivers, "Women, Myth, and the Media," in Bernard Rubin (Ed.), *When Information Counts: Grading the Media* (Lexington, MA: D.C. Heath, 1985), p. 4.

20. David S. Broder, *Behind the Front Page* (New York: Simon and Schuster, 1987), p. 126.

21. Dean E. Alger, *The Media and Politics* (Englewood Cliffs, NJ.: Prentice Hall, 1989), p. 26. See also Mike Budd, Steve Craig & Clay Steinman, *Consuming Environments: Television and Commercial Culture* (New Brunswick, N.J.: Rutgers University Press, 1999), p. 56.

22. Broder, *Behind the Front Page,* pp. 125–127.

23. Kim Fridkin Kahn and Edie N. Goldenberg, "The Media: Obstacle or Ally of Feminists?" *Annals of the American Academy of Political and Social Science,* 515 (1991), pp. 104–113.

24. Laura Ashley and Beth Olson, "Constructing Reality: Print Media's Framing of the Women's Movement, 1966 to 1986," *Journalism & Mass Communication Quarterly,* Vol. 75, No. 2 (Summer, 1998), pp. 263–277.

25. Clara Bingham, *Women on the Hill* (New York: Times Books, 1997), p. 82.

26. Leah R. Vande Berg and Diane Streckfuss, "Prime-Time Television's Portrayal of Women and the World of Work: A Demographic Profile," *Journal of Broadcasting and Electronic Media,* 36 (Spring 1992), pp. 195–208.

27. *Ibid.*

28. H. L. Molotch, "The News of Women and the Work of Men," in Gaye Tuchman, A. K. Daniels, and J. Benet (Eds.) *Hearth and Home: Images of Women in the Mass Media* (New York: Oxford University Press, 1978), pp. 176–185 as cited in Lana F. Rakow and Kimberlie Kranich, "Women as Sign in Television News," *Journal of Communication* 41 (1) (Winter, 1991), p. 11.

29. M. Junior Bridge, "Report Traces Media's Polarizing Influence in Society, Politics," *Women, Men and Media Study* (Washington, D.C.: Unabridged Communications, 1992), p. 3.

30. Penny M. Miller, "Teaching Women in the News: Exposing the 'Invisible Majority,'" *PS: Political Science & Politics,* September 1996, pp. 513–517.

31. Bridge, "Report Traces Media's Polarizing Influence in Society, Politics," p. 4.

32. Kay Mills, "What Difference Do Women Journalists Make?" in Pippa Norris (Ed.), *Women, Media, and Politics* (New York: Oxford University Press, 1997), p. 54.

33. *Ibid.*

34. "Some Male Editors Don't See Newsroom Sexism," *Quill Magazine,* December 2002, p. 6.

35. Mills, "What Difference Do Women Journalists Make?" p. 55.

36. James Devitt, "Framing Gender on the Campaign Trail: Female Gubernatorial Candidates and the Press," *Journalism & Mass Communication Quarterly,* Vol. 79, No. 2 (Summer 2002), pp. 445–463.

37. Stephanie Craft and Wayne Wanta, "Women in the Newsroom: Influences of Female Editors and Reporters on the News Agenda," *Journalism and Mass Communication Quarterly,* Vol. 81, Iss. 1 (Spring 2004), pp. 124–139.

38. Cory L. Armstrong, "The Influence of Reporter Gender on Source Selection in Newspaper Stories," *Journalism and Mass Communication Quarterly,* Vol. 81, Iss. 1 (Spring 2004), pp. 139–155.

39. Braden, *Women Politicians and the Media,* p. 182.

40. Kim Fridkin Kahn, "The Distorted Mirror: Press Coverage of Women Candidates for Statewide Office," *Journal of Politics,* 56 (1) (February 1994), pp. 154–174; see also Kahn and Edie N. Goldenberg, "Women Candidates in the News: An Examination of Gender Differences in U.S. Senate Campaigns," *Public Opinion Quarterly* 55 (1) (Summer, 1991), pp. 180–199; Kahn, "Does Being Male Help? An Investigation of the Effects of Candidate Gender and Campaign Coverage on Evaluations of U.S. Senate Candidates," *Journal of Politics* 54, 1992, pp. 497–517; Kahn, "Gender Differences in Campaign Messages: The Political Advertisements of Men and Women Candidates for U.S. Senate," *Political Research Quarterly* 46 (3), 1993, pp. 481–503; Kahn, "Does Gender Make a Difference? An Experimental Examination of Sex Stereotypes and Press Patterns in Statewide Campaigns," *American Journal of Political Science* 38 (1), 1994, pp. 162–195; and Kahn, *The Political Consequences of Being a Woman* (New York: Columbia University Press, 1996), pp. 131–134.

41. Geralyn Miller, "Newspaper Coverage and Gender: An Analysis of the 1996 Illinois State Legislative House District Races," *Women & Politics,* Vol. 22(3) (2001).

42. Dianne G. Bystrom, Terry A. Robertson, and Mary Christine Banwart, "Framing the Fight: An Analysis of Media Coverage of Female and Male Candidates in Primary Races for Governor and U.S. Senate in 2000," *American Behavioral Scientist,* Vol. 44 No. 12 (August 2001), pp. 1999–2013.

43. Sean Aday and James Devitt, "Style over Substance: Newspaper Coverage of Elizabeth Dole's Presidential Bid," *Harvard International Journal of Press/Politics* Vol. 6, Issue 2 (Spring 2001), pp. 52–72.

44. Kevin B. Smith, "When All's Fair, Signs of Parity in Media Coverage of Female Candidates," *Political Communication* 14 (1997), pp. 71–82.

45. Mary Christine Banwart, Dianne G. Bystrom, and Terry Robertson, "From the Primary to the General Election," *American Behavioral Scientist,* Vol. 46, No. 5 (January 2003), pp. 658–676.

46. Junior Bridge, "The Media Mirror: Reading between the (News) Lines," *Quill,* January/February 1994, pp. 18–19.

47. See numerous accounts in major newspapers during the period January–February 1993. In particular, see Anna Quindlen, "The Sins of Zoe Baird," *New York Times,* January 20, 1993, p. A23. See also Jamieson, *Beyond the Double Bind,* pp. 62–63.

48. "It's Gender, Stupid," *New York Times,* February 8, 1993, p. A17.

49. "Nominees Are Screened for Illegal Hiring," *New York Times,* February 9, 1993, p. A1.

50. Susan J. Carroll and Ronnee Schreiber, "Media Coverage of Women in the 103rd Congress," in Pippa Norris (Ed.), *Women, Media, and Politics* (New York: Oxford University Press, 1997), pp. 131–148.

51. David L. Paletz and Robert M. Entman, *Media Power Politics* (New York: Free Press, 1981), p. 24.

52. Paula LaRocque, "Political Correctness has its Roots in Cultural Condition," *Quill* 84 (4) (May, 1996), p. 34.

53. Kim Fridkin Kahn, "Assessing the Media's Impact on the Political Fortunes of Women," in Susan J. Carroll (Ed.) *Women and American Politics* (New York: Oxford University Press, 2003) pp. 173–189.

FURTHER READING

Bagdikian, Ben H. *The Media Monopoly,* 6th ed. Boston: Beacon Press, 2000.

Braden, Maria, *Women Politicians and the Media.* Lexington, Kentucky: University Press of Kentucky, 1996.

Bennett, W. Lance. *News: The Politics of Illusion,* 5th ed. New York: Addison Wesley Longman, 2003.

Carroll, Susan J. (Ed.), *Women and American Politics.* New York: Oxford University Press, 2003.

Cook, Timothy E. *Making Laws and Making News*. Washington, D.C.: The Brookings Institution, 1989.

Foerstel, Karen and Herbert N. Foerstel. *Cllimbing the Hill Gender Conflict in Congress*. Westport, Connecticut: Praeger, 1996.

Fox, Richard Logan. *Gender Dynamics in Congressional Elections*. Thousand Oaks, California: Sage Publications, 1997.

Gitlin, Todd. *Inside Prime Time*. Berkeley: University of California Press, 2000.

Graber, Doris A. *Mass Media and American Politics*, 6th ed. Washington, D.C.: Congressional Quarterly Press, 2002.

Garber, Doris A. *Media Power in Politics*, 4th ed. Washington, D.C.: Congressional Quarterly Press, 2000.

Iyengar, Shanto. *Is Anyone Responsible? How Television Frames Political Issues*. Chicago: University of Chicago Press, 1991.

Jamieson, Kathleen Hall. *Beyond the Double Bind*. New York: Oxford University Press, 1995.

Kahn, Kim Fridkin. *The Political Consequences of Being a Woman*. New York: Columbia University Press, 1996.

Rivers, Caryl. *Slick Spins and Fractured Facts: How Cultural Myths Distort the News*. New York: Columbia University Press, 1996.

Tuchman, Gaye. *Making News: A Study in the Construction of Reality*,. New York: Free Press, 1978.

Tuchman, Gayr, Arlene Kaplan Daniels, and James Benet (Eds.) *Hearth and Home Images of Women in the Mass Media*. New York: Oxford University Press, 1997.

What Kind of Women's Movement? Community, Representation, and Resurgence

Denise L. Baer

What kind of women's movement is the contemporary women's movement? This is not a simple question to answer. In part, it is because the role of women has not only changed historically and therefore the terms of reference have themselves changed—from Victorian womanhood in the nineteenth century to the Year of the Woman in 1992. The answer grows more complex when we consider that the women's movement is both the result and the architect of these changes, so that cutting edge becomes a matter of relativism also. Votes for women, for example, once viewed as radical, now is taught to American school children and advocated abroad as a matter of policy by the U.S. government as an essential ingredient for democracy. Finally, the partisan divide over women's issues means that the terms of evaluation are themselves contested. The Republican Party and the Democratic Party offer very different visions of women's rights on issues ranging from abortion, to domestic violence, to childcare and education, poverty assistance and the workplace. It is well-known that the Democratic Party has become more closely allied with the major women's organizations. Yet, if, as was proclaimed at the 2004 Republican Convention, that "W stands for Women," does this mean that both parties have equally valid claims to representing women?

As will be discussed below, the answer may be, as former Republican National Committee Chair Mary Louise Smith exclaimed, "But what kind of woman!" That is, not all women may agree, but we may still identify some "universal" or at least "cross-cutting" interests that intersect in women's lives. It is argued that these complexities must be at least confronted, if not resolved at an analytical level to ensure the continued empowerment of women. To address these questions, this article will examine the factors related to group-based leadership on women's issues, and the current strength of the women's movement—organizationally, within the two major parties, and within the academy.

THE WOMEN'S MOVEMENT IN SOCIETY AND7 THE ACADEMY

Social movements and theories about them have a moral essence to them. It derives from the moral agency of subordinated groups to change embedded power relations. Specifically social movements are a new form of action and mobilization through which *nonelites* can influence elites. In other words, social movements are a distinctive formation of the have-nots. Unlike traditional methods of participation and action (e.g., voting, campaigning, volunteering for an existing group), *social movements are not constrained by alternatives already determined by existing leaders*. Social movements create new leadership, and they expand the public policy agenda as well as broader social relations in new and unique ways. Social movements are normative in that they expand democracy by including new groups and leaders internal to that group. Establishing these points in the academy was a hard-fought battle, and many of the early scholars were also themselves activists. Early social movement theory (described here as "classic social movement theory") engaged and challenged mainstream social science, which treated social protest and mobilization as pathological and irrational, and women's issues as not worthy of serious study.

Winning these two battles has produced an extensive array of new paradigms such as the *resource mobilization*[1] (stressing resources external to the movement), the *political process*[2] (emphasizing strategies for public goods) and the *cultural perspectives*[3] (emphasizing aspects of identity and consciousness) models. Each of these perspectives, drawing primarily from sociology, has brought considerable theoretical insights to our understanding of social movements. For example, the resource mobilization and political process models have stressed the role of political opportunities and governmental and private sector resources external to movements as creating opportunities. The cultural perspectives model has pointed out that social movements can also change culture as well as the public sphere.

However, it is also true that the professionalization of social movement studies in the academy has directed attention away from core elements of social movements from a political science or power perspective.[4] As Richard Flacks has pointed out, there is a lack of relevance and moral compass as "the work of younger scholars is driven by the efforts to refine theory rather than to contribute to public knowledge about movements."[5]

Specifically, in terms of the women's movement, other facets at risk of receiving short shrift in the current emphasis on existing political opportunities and resources or non-political goals include:

- Viewing movements as primarily a war of ideas rather than primarily embedded in the world of action, which can, if overemphasized, become elitist, and lack engagement with the all too concrete political fray of the growing partisan divide over women's issues;

- Failing to incorporate the importance of "critical mass" support critical for successful collective action can minimize the factors essential for political clout using organized activity;

- Treating social movements as indistinguishable from political movements[6] or causes and campaigns[7] can blind us to the transformation process through which causes can become genuine movements;

- Viewing the incorporating of women and politics and women's studies in the academy as a leading part of the movements, regardless of whether scholars are active in the public sphere or not, can equate intellectual movements with genuine social and political action;

- Losing the ability to look at the cumulative life cycles of movements as they achieve successes, recede from the public sphere, and are regenerated can make invisible the risk to current gains if they are not maintained.

If it is true of the women's movement that "The peak period has now passed . . . consciousness has diminished, and organizations . . . are now preoccupied with just maintaining themselves,"[8] these theoretical gaps are not merely abstract. It is about community, representation and resurgence of the women's movement.

THE MOVEMENT BASIS OF WOMEN'S ADVANCES

Central to the classic social movement approach is defining the women's movement in concrete organizations and specific successes within the broader public agenda, rather than using the idea of "waves."[9] Certainly, women's associations have indeed formed in "waves." And it is true that policy advocacy and reform have always been a central part of women's organizations, whether within or outside of the active phase of women's movements. As Mildred Wells stated in her history of the GFWC, "the early history of every women's club shows it to be the group in each community which sponsored the progressive movements which were later taken over by the municipal government or by specialized welfare organizations."[10] The history of women's clubs finds them moving issues from the private sphere to the public sphere. According to Anne Scott, women's volunteerism serves as an "early warning system" in "identifying emergent social needs and trying to deal with them, first on their own and then by persuading some government body to undertake responsibility."[11] Pendleton Herring found women's lobby groups only second in number to trade associations in the 1920s, and that the women's suffrage associations introduced new techniques of lobbying in their systematic campaign to gain suffrage.[12] However, it still remains useful to consider the specific goals, organization, and successes and failures of specific historical phases of women's mobilization.

According to classic social movement theory, there have been three distinct, organized movements for women: the **Equal Rights Movement** arising from the 1848 Seneca Falls Declaration of Sentiments; the **Suffrage Movement** developing in 1890 out of the merger of the two rival woman suffrage groups; and the contemporary **Women's Rights Movement** originating in 1961 when the Presidential Commission on the Status of Women was appointed by President Kennedy. Each movement is divided into an active and a latent phase, and prior movements may lay a foundation for a later movement. The distinctive features of each of these movements, ranging from leadership to organization, activities, policy successes and postmovement activities are compared in Table 1.

According to this classic social movement model focused on collective action, which is described in greater detail elsewhere,[13] social movements can be analyzed using four basic elements:

1. Leadership, including social networks, communication and social ties;
2. Organizational base and structure, including resources provided internal to the group;
3. A sense of collective oppression and a need for a common solution based in the ordinary lives of group members; and
4. The critical mobilizing event, which can occur differently for leaders and for mass followers.

A few key points bear emphasis. First, leadership networks may work for as long as 8–10 years (or more) prior to their efforts igniting and mobilizing women at the mass level. Second, movements are episodic, spontaneous, and autonomous, with multiple groups, and multiple leaders working on a variety of issues in both the public and the private spheres. Third, social movement recruitment is intensely personal, primarily occurring through personal friendships at the grass-roots levels. Other forms of new media (Internet, broadcast media) may be used by social movements, but these supplement, rather than replace concrete, face-to-face organizing. Fourth, the active phases of movements are short-lived, lasting twenty years or so. Unless success is imminent, social group members have little incentive to actively participate. Following an active phase, social movement organizations may disappear or else evolve into traditional interest groups offering selective incentives available only to those who join the organization. Fifth, each movement is organized around different problems, and has distinct concrete successes. And sixth, social movements, which represent the have-nots, act to socialize political conflict and, as such, are successful as movements only when they focus on national issues framed in the social as well as the public spheres using groups based in and organized around the social identity of women.

Movements "end" their active phase with an event—either a success or a significant failure (which may not be recognized as such at the time) that time shows

TABLE 1 Distinctive Features of the Three American Women's Movements Compared Using the Collective Action Approach of Classic Social Movement Theory[a]

Factor	Equal Rights (1848–1869)	Suffrage (1890–1920)	Women's Rights (1961–1994)
Critical Mobilizing Event	*Mass:* 1848 Seneca Falls Declaration *Leadership:* Refusal to seat women as part of delegates to 1840 World Anti-Slavery Convention in London	*Mass:* 1913 Washington March *Leadership:* 1890 Merger of AWSA and NWSA; 1879 endorsement of suffrage by Women's Christian Temperance Union (WCTU)	*Mass:* 1970 event and media-driven "Mushroom Event" *Leadership:* 1961 Presidential Commission on Status of Women; 1963 publication of *Feminine Mystique*, 1966 refusal of EEOC to enforce on behalf of women; 1966 formation of NOW; 1968 Sandy Springs meeting of New Left women's leaders
Initial Leadership Networks	Abolition movements and conventions Female Anti-Slavery Societies	Settlement house movement Temperance/anti-domestic violence movement Child and women's labor movement Women's club movement	Washington community of women Civil rights movement Anti-war movement
Group Organizational Resources	Churches Abolitionist newspapers	Women's colleges Women's Christian Temperance Union Women's Trade Union League National Consumers League	Women's colleges Women's party organizations and clubs National Student Association Student Mobilization Committee to End the War in Vietnam Student Non-Violent Coordinating Committee
New Organizations	American Equal Rights Association (1866) National Women Suffrage Association (1869) American Women Suffrage Association (1869)	National American Woman Suffrage Association (NWSA) (1890) General Federation of Women's Clubs (GFWC) (1890) National Pan-Hellenic Association (1891) National Association of Colored Women (1896)	National Organization for Women (1966) National Women's Political Caucus (1971) Women's Equity Action League (1968) Women's Campaign Fund National Political Congress of Black Women (1984) Emily's List (1988)
Major Leaders	Elizabeth Cady Stanton Lucretia Mott Susan B. Anthony Lucy Stone Sojourner Truth	Anna Howard Shaw Carrie Chapman Catt Jane Addams Alice Paul Ida B. Wells	Betty Friedan Gloria Steinem Eleanor Smeal C. DeLores Tucker
Major Actions	Lecture circuit Petition drives Direct action (e.g., voting)	Meetings Petition drives/referenda Marches (1913) D.C. March greeting Pres. Wilson's inauguration Direct action/protests/arrests/hunger strikes launched from Sewell Belmont House	Organized protest through marches, sit-ins, strikes, pickets, boycotts Legal challenges, new legislation, policy Organized new groups including within major professional organizations Symbolic efforts (take back the night marches)

Major Achievements	Right of women to speak in public Married Women's Property Act(s) Founding of Women's Colleges Admission of women to major universities 1867 Kansas Referendum on suffrage 1868–1869 Federal Suffrage Amendment introduced in House and Senate 19 states grant limited suffrage by 1890 3 states grant suffrage for tax and bond measures	Suffrage Amendment Ratified (1920) Women accepted as delegates to major party conventions beginning in 1900 Equal Division Rule for Democratic and Republican National Committees (1920–1924) First women elected to state legislatures (1894)	Equal Pay Act (1963) Equal Employment Act (1964/1972/1991) Equal Education (Title IX, 1972) Equal Credit (1974) Pregnancy Nondiscrimination (1978) Affirmative Action Plans Party Reform (increase in women delegates, Equal Division for Democratic Party Delegates in 1980) Establishment of Women's Policy "think tanks" and PACs Growth of Women's Studies in Higher Education Family and Medical Leave Act (1993)
Partisan Alignments	Third Party activity Whigs cease to exist Republicans formed in 1860 Democrats continue in era of Republican dominance	Third party activity Progressive Party endorses suffrage (1912) Democrats and Republicans both include women via 50/50 Rule	Democratic Party reform from within Republican Party responds without making rules changes; development of Christian Right within GOP; drives out many feminist women
End of Active Phase	Split of AERA into two rival women suffrage organizations (NWSA and AWSA)	Ratification of 19th Amendment, August 26, 1920	Election of Republican House Majority in 1994
Post Movement Activities	State referenda in Michigan (1874); Colorado (1877); Nebraska (1882); Oregon (1884); Rhode Island (1887); Washington (1889) International movement develops Direct action between 1871 and 1872 150 women tried to vote in DC and in 10 states Continued growth of national women's organizations: AAUW (1881); YWCA (1881)	Increased adoption of 50/50 Rule at state party level Introduction of Equal Rights Amendment Removal of last legal restrictions on election of women to office (1928) Election of women to state legislatures in all 48 states (1936) Continued slow progress NAWSA becomes League of Women Voters (LWV) Formation of National Council of Negro Women (NCNW) (1929)	Partisan split women's movement Selection of Nancy Pelosi Majority Leader International activities expand 1996 Get-Out-the-Vote activities 2001 Election of Nancy Pelosi Democratic Majority Leader in the U.S. House 2004 March for Women's Lives in D.C. 2004 Revolutionary Women Formed; Hosts Events at Democratic National Convention

[a] This chart is not meant to be comprehensive. It is a selective, summary listing stressing major highlights of the three women's movements at the organizational level.

greatly reduces their capacity to expand their gains. The contemporary women's movement is dated from 1961 to 1994, with the year selection based on the Republican majority elected to the U.S. House of Representatives (which will be discussed below). Of course, these dates do not mean the cessation of activities or even some successes. First, a number of advances can still be made by existing women's groups and leaders, although these tend to build on the already committed and reflect demonstrations of existing support or defense of existing gains, rather than a growing movement making new demands. Both the extensive Get Out the Vote activities of women's organizations in 1996,[14] and the highly successful 2004 March for Women's Lives, which brought an estimated 400,000 marchers to Washington, D.C., are examples of this.

And second, the contemporary women's movement has produced some significant advances that may well constitute a continuing infrastructure that previous women's movements lacked. In addition to the creation of women's studies programs and centers in the academy, there are also foundations devoted just to women and girls (e.g., the Girls Best Friend Foundation and SisterFund, in addition to the MS Foundation), as well as policy institutes or think tanks focusing on women's issues (e.g., the Center for Women Policy Studies, the Institute for Women's Policy Research (IWPR), the Women's Research and Education Institute (WREI), the National Women's Law Center, and the Center for Policy Alternatives (CPA)). An additional institutional power base is the women's funding community, organized as free-standing political action committees (PACs). PACs usually only donate funds,[15] while the goal of the women's funding community is to elect more women—it is not to lobby for economic profit for a business. Yet another critical institutional power base is the rise of feminist associationalism within the workplace environment, which Mary Fainsod Katzenstein describes as "mushrooming" in the 1970s and beyond.[16] The key to retaining institutional capacity for a fourth women's movement will depend on the degree to which this existing infrastructure retains an associational base with ordinary women.

THE ORGANIZATIONAL BASE OF THE WOMEN'S MOVEMENT

The women's movement is based in concrete organizations, and women's organizations are distinctive. While most interest groups represent economic interests, this is not true of women's organizations.[17] A 1980 survey of women's organizations found that seven out of ten women's organizations were citizens groups, as opposed to nonprofit organizations or for profit business groups.[18] This is also true of the women's political action committees (PACs). Women's organizations are diverse. They vary from those whose mission serves women or girls *(Girl Scouts, AAUW)*, to those whose membership is primarily women but whose mission is not primarily women or girl-serving *(e.g., the National Education Association)*, to those which are the women or girl-serving affiliate of a larger non-women's organization *(e.g., National Baptist Women's Division)*, and those which are women-led, but whose mission is not primarily women or girl-serving *(e.g., Children's Defense Fund)*. The variety of women's organizations include women's rights groups *(e.g., NOW, NWPC, MANA: A National Latina Association)*, religious *(e.g., Hadassah)*, Greek letter *(Delta Sigma Theta)*, social and fraternal orders *(e.g., Soroptomist)*, community organizations *(e.g., Young Women's Christian Association (e.g., YWCA))*, children and youth *(e.g., Girls Speak Out)*, women's clubs *(e.g., GFWC, NCNW)*, labor *(Coalition of Labor Union Women (CLUE))*, international affairs *(Women's International League for Peace and Freedom)*, women elected officials and support groups *(e.g., National Foundation for Women Legislators (NFWL), Women Executives in State Government (WESG))*, business *(e.g., (BPW), National Assn. of Women Business Owners)*, health professionals *(e.g., American Medical Women's Association)*, partisan *(e.g., National Federation of Republican Women (NFRW), National Federation of Democratic Women (NFDW))*, media *(e.g., American Women in Media and TV)*, and senior citizens *(e.g., Older Women's League)*.

What are considered traditional women's organizations today began as movement organizations. The older generation of women's organizations themselves arose at a time when the creation of a women's sphere was a radical innovation; mobilizing women was previously confined to the home, in order to engage in the public sphere.[19] Prior to the 1830s, it was unheard of for women to speak in public at events men attended. In the 1880s and 1890s, women's clubs, as forums for social and political expression went beyond political speaking to become political instruments for women through separate institution building. While the newly federated organizations in the early twentieth century did become increasingly specialized,[20] they continued to cooperate to a degree unparalleled by other groups. Women's organizations have increasingly crossed class barriers.[21] This has been particularly true of black women's organizations which began forming in large numbers during the late 1800s, and later in white women's organizations.[22]

What we know about women's organizations is that they organize around elements of ordinary life. Prior to the Civil War, there were two distinct phases of local organization: religiously based benevolent societies during the early 1800s and reform organizations springing from religious values during the mid 1800s. As Harriet Martineau noted in 1827, during this era, religion was the only "occupation" open to women besides marriage. And historically, women's organizations and "clubs held a more significant place in women's lives than men's clubs and organizations did for men."[23]

Another facet of organization involves women of color, who have organized separately even as they also fought for women's rights. There is considerable variation by ethnic and racial group, although African American women are the only women of color to organize significantly—as a group—before 1920. Delta Sigma Theta (an African American social reform sorority) formed on the Howard University campus in 1913 just to march in the historic suffrage parade which greeted President Wilson at his inauguration.[24] Other early leaders include Maria Stewart

(who dared to speak in public in 1832), Sojourner Truth (a popular speaker traveling the abolitionist and women's rights lecture circuits from the 1840s and on),
Anna Julia Cooper (who wrote *A Voice From the South* (1892)) and Ida B. Wells
(known for her anti-lynching campaign) who formed the Alpha Suffrage Club in
Chicago in 1913 and marched in the suffrage parade with the Chicago contingent
rather than at the end as a black woman, have viewed the vote as essential, and
actively organized for the right to vote. Black women's rights activists found
strength in their spirituality (Burton 1996), and have traditionally valued children.[25]
Abortion, the major criterion for endorsement of women's organizations like
NWPC, EMILY's List, Women's Campaign Fund and others—has never been at the
forefront of African American women's rights organizations.

Latina women's organizations are small, but growing in number: MANA is
new name for National Mexican Women's Association, which aims to now provide
leadership for all Latina women; the National Conference of Puerto Rican Women
(organized in 1972); the National Hispana Leadership Institute, and the recent
Cuban American Women's Conference all focus on Latina issues. Chicanos were
the only Latino/Latina minority to reside in the U.S., who as a group prior to
woman suffrage also possessed citizenship. Because of the legacy of discrimination
in California and Texas, only in New Mexico did the Hispanos have a continuous
heritage of leadership since the nineteenth century.[26] Puerto Ricans, permitted to
vote in American elections only since 1917 (once they have attained a mainland
residency) and Cubans, who emigrated after the Cuban revolution of 1959, are
post-woman-suffrage additions.

Women among other ethnic minorities continue to mobilize. The Association
of Chinese American Women was founded in 1990. Among Asian Americans a
legacy of racist immigration laws (beginning with the Chinese Exclusion Act of
1882, not repealed until 1943) prevented most Asian Americans from becoming
naturalized citizens (and thus eligible to vote) until 1952, and large-scale Chinese
immigration did not occur until after the 1965 Immigration Act. Native Americans,
while increasingly present as delegates to Democratic conventions and in elective
office, evince little in the way of separate women's organizations.[27] The continued
mobilization of women of color, while exacerbating the divisions among women's
groups, nonetheless demonstrates that movement politics is part of all women's organizations—whether white or non-white.

In terms of associationalism, the most fundamental change has been the increasing empowerment of women. It seems to make a great deal of difference if
women are able to represent themselves. Schlozman, for example, found that in
terms of ideology, the policy agenda, and their willingness to work in coalition
with other women's organizations, organizations of women *represented by men*
were less feminist than those represented by women.[28] Alan Rosenthal, in his
analysis of lobbyists and lobbying in the states, believes that the increase in the
1980s among women lobbyists is tied directly to the increase in women state legislators, which has changed the legislative culture. The key question is the degree to
which women's organizations can survive the gendered partisan divide.

THE ORIGINS OF THE GENDERED PARTISAN DIVIDE

We now know that the parties are realigned on women's rights issues,[29] a process which began in 1976.[30] One of the triggers of this realignment has been the issue of abortion,[31] but it has also been related to the different cultures of the two parties,[32] the gender realignment in voting,[33] and the drive for parity in party power with the contemporary women's movement. By 2004, this has culminated in a gendered partisan divide, where the two parties now represent different types of women. Some may place the decline of the women's movement earlier than 1994—perhaps in 1983 when the Equal Rights Amendment failed to be ratified. But the continued organization of women, and the role of the gender gap in re-energizing women, as well as motivating Democratic and Republican leaders to battle for the women's vote extended the clout of women through the 1990s, even as the Republican Party gained majority control of the U.S. Congress. The events of 2000–2001, however, dramatically changed the political landscape, and have exposed some serious weaknesses in women's political power—and potential for political power.

This history of this change is important because prior women's movements did not result in a partisan alignment, and because key women's movement organizations still maintain a bipartisan stance toward the political parties. And it is becoming more critical because the parties are strengthened, and the partisan game is increasingly the only game for genuine political power.[34] Paradoxically, the rise of the gendered partisan divide makes it possible for party leaders whose incentives are only to win election, not to be inclusive, to reach women voters without the mediation of women leaders—a potentially devastating hurdle for expansion of women's gains.

The Early Non-Partisan Stature of Women's Movements

The Democratic Party, founded in 1796, and the Republican Party, formed in 1860, both predate the three identified women's movements, a fact which greatly limited opportunities for forming a political party for women. In fact, as Jo Freeman has noted, women entered political parties "one room at a time" as they also engaged in women's movement activities.[35] While there have been many third party efforts in American history, "suffrage activism normally institutionalized itself in interest group activism," rather forming a new party.[36] Each of the three women's movements sought different goals, which impacted their relationship to the political parties. The Equal Rights Movement sought to give women legal existence and rights; the Suffrage Movement political rights and identity; today's Women's Rights Movement focuses on parity in political representation in both formal and informal political institutions.

Suffrage leaders were aware of the need to include women in party leadership roles. The 50/50 campaign was the chosen vehicle used to achieve parity. Adopted in Colorado in 1910 by state statute, the 50/50 Rule gained momentum at the state level after adoption of the Nineteenth Amendment on August 20, 1920 guaranteeing women the right to vote. Nationally, the Democratic Party adopted the 50/50 Rule in 1920, the Republicans in 1924. In 1940, the Republican Convention passed Rule 29, providing for equal representation of women on all committees of the RNC. These were major advances. But the decline of movement politics meant that increasingly women found the inner circles of party power closed to them in the immediate post-suffrage era.[37] As a consequence, the representation of women rested more heavily upon party culture and traditions.

Gender Parity and the Campaign for the 50/50 Rule

In the absence of organized pressure, the Republican Party was relatively more open to including Republican women based on their contributions to the party, than was true of the Democratic Party, with its machine politics and ethnic and blue-collar supporters. When Alice Paul sought a partisan strategy to get suffrage adopted, it was the Democratic Party that she targeted as the opposition party. The Republican Party took the lead in adding the Equal Rights Amendment to its party platform in 1940, followed by the Democrats in 1944. By the 1960s, one study found as many as half of Democratic national committeewomen, but only one-third of Republican committeewomen were rated quite unimportant by their peers.[38] The 50/50 balance on the RNC (but not RNC committees) ended in 1952 with the addition of Republican state chairs to the RNC—an overwhelmingly male group. Today, the RNC has a minimum of one-third female representation. In 1960, Republican women gained a significant advance when the Convention adopted a rule providing for 50/50 representation of women delegates with men on all Convention committees.

The new political cleavages developing with the Women's Rights Movement reversed the Republican partisan advantage in 1972. The watershed event was the demand for parity at the conventions—the Democrats reformed and the Republicans refused. Prior to the 1970s, there had been no organized efforts to demand parity in convention delegate selection. *This meant that the nominating conventions*—where control of the party by a dominant faction and the selection of party leaders as well as recruitment and vetting of cabinet and subcabinet appointees were determined—*remained in the control of the informal but closed "old boy" network.*

Party Reform and the Drive for Gender Parity in Conventions

Political opportunities expanded for women in 1968 when the Democratic Convention authorized the appointment of a reform commission (later known as the McGovern–Fraser Commission) to study Democratic Party rules.[39] The newly organized NWPC took the lead and chose as its inaugural initiative the reform of the Democratic and Republican parties. This was an important political battle, which succeeded in doubling and tripling women's representation in the post-party reform era (see Figure 1).

The dominance of the Democratic Party by the southern wing (traditionally least supportive of women's rights) and by organized labor (then quite hostile to the

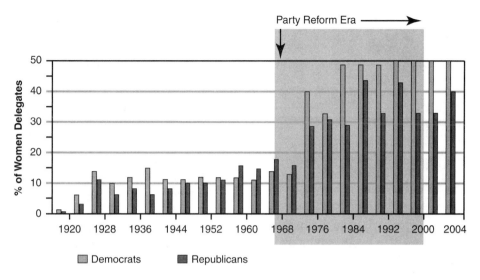

FIGURE 1   Proportion of Women in Major Party Conventions, 1916–2004 *Source:* Data for 1988–2004 calculated by the author from official lists of delegates provided by the national parties: data for earlier years from the Center for the American Woman and Politics, Rutgers University: Eagleton Institute.

women's movement) meant no change would come easily. It was McGovern–Fraser, under pressure from NWPC (and other groups) in 1971–1972, which *mandated* proportional representation for women, blacks, and youth (those under 30) for the 1972 Democratic convention. As a result, the proportion of women tripled from 13% in 1968 to 40% in 1972. Following McGovern's defeat, party reform came under attack by dominant party forces. In response, the Mikulski Commission rewrote delegate selection rules, banning "quotas" in favor of affirmative action efforts. Since states that field an affirmative action plan were granted immunity from credentials challenges, efforts to include women were dependent upon local party culture and traditions. The proportion of women dropped sharply in 1976 to 34%.

In 1974, Democratic women gained a significant advance by using the historical precedent of the 50/50 Rule. *First,* the 1974 Democratic Party Charter established the supremacy of national party law, a move which permanently reduced the power of sectional and local interests to oppose inclusion of women. *And second,* while the McGovern–Fraser quotas were "banned," the Charter expressly exempted equal division of men and women from the ban (Article Ten, Section 11). This was done at the behest of women delegates to the 1974 Mid-Term Convention following a contentious session in which both black and women delegates walked out protesting efforts to undermine party reform. In 1980, the Democratic National Committee, acting under the Charter exemption, adopted the 50/50 Rule for delegates.[40] In 1988, at the behest of presidential candidate Jesse Jackson, the 1988 Convention amended the Charter to extend the 50/50 Rule from the *final* statewide delegation to *each* candidate's delegation within each state.

The Republican Party has traditionally regarded the selection of delegates as a state matter. While there were two reform commissions appointed (DO—Delegates and Organization—and Rule 29 committees), party traditions prevailed. The Republican Party, adamantly refusing to mandate parity, remains unreformed. However, following the dramatic upsurge of Democratic women delegates in 1972, the proportion of Republican women delegates also rose in the years in 1972–1980 to about one-third of the delegates.

The Gender Gap Battleground Conventions

Even as women's organizations found the 1980s more difficult for organizing, discovery of the gender gap after the 1980 election focused increased attention on women's issues and representation of women. In particular, Republican leaders have grown more concerned about how the low proportion of women at Republican conventions makes the party look unresponsive. In the absence of official rules, however, efforts to include women rests with the traditional mechanism of personal intervention by influential leaders[41]—which is affected by whether an incumbent is running for re-election. In 1984, the proportion of Republican women increased to a record 44%, largely through the intervention of President Reagan's campaign manager, Ed Rollins, who personally called each state party. In 1988, however, when the race involved a contested primary and no incumbent, the proportion of women delegates returned to one-third. With an incumbent president, Republican women delegates increased to 41% in 1992, only to drop in 1996 and 2000 to 33% following a contested primary campaign. In 2004, with efforts from the Republican National Committee, the proportion of women delegates rose to 40%. Without extraordinary efforts, there seems to be an informal "glass ceiling" for Republican women of about one-third of the delegates (see Figure 2).

These party differences are structured by partisan culture. Despite the lack of parity, Republican women have achieved considerable influence at the leadership levels—an achievement without parallel in the Democratic Party. In 1985, the DNC under Chair Paul Kirk disestablished the DNC Women's Caucus. In contrast, in 1988, the NFRW was granted a voting seat on the 28 member Council which governs the RNC between its quadrennial meetings.

In 1996, EMILY's List developed a structural relationship with the DNC to conduct research on the gender gap, to coordinate GOTV, to recruit women volunteers for the coordinated state campaigns, and to raise money. As an external organization with no real members in local groups, one must wonder if this represents greater party power for Democratic women, or whether it merely means the attempted exploitation of the women's funding community by (male) Democratic party leaders for their own purposes. It may be that women's influence has actually dropped within the Democratic Party even as parity has increased the number of women delegates. As Cotter and Hennessy concluded of the pre-reform party system, "In most states, at most levels of the party organization, women have *equal representation* with men; there is no evidence that they have ever had *equal influ-*

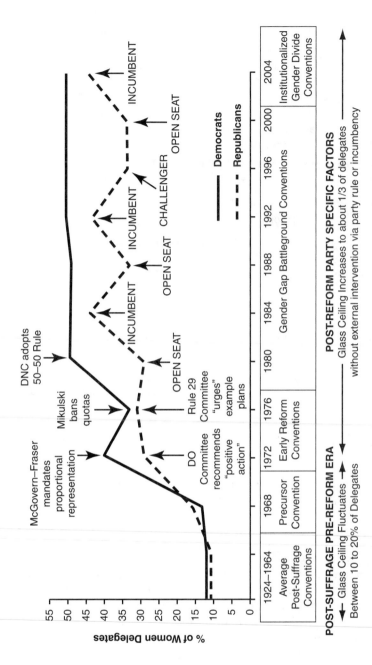

FIGURE 2 Party-Specific Factors Affecting Representation of Women Delegates in the Pre- and Post-Reform Major Party Conventions, 1924–2004 *Source:* Data for 1988–2004 calculated by the author from official lists of delegates provided by the national parties; data for earlier years from the Center for the American Woman and Politics. Rutgers University: Eagleton Institute.

ence."[42] In 1984 and 1988, the power of the convention women's caucus was such that key platform debates were brokered during its daily meetings. By 1992, the daily Women's Caucus meetings formerly sponsored by the Democratic Task Force of the National Women's Political Caucus were now hosted by the Democratic National Committee. In 1996, while the pro-choice plank has become an unquestioned party of the Democratic Party platform, President Clinton's signing of the welfare reform bill immediately before the convention provided no cause for complaint—despite the fact that most major women's organizations opposed the bill.

The 2004 Partisan Gender Divide Conventions

The 2004 Conventions were qualitatively different from prior conventions, as they were the first that occurred after:

- The contested 2000 presidential election which left so many Democrats angry when George Bush, who lost the popular vote, became President following a Supreme Court decision;
- The passage of the BiPartisan Campaign Finance Act, which banned soft money, and altered the funding strategies of the national party committees at the conventions and during the 2004 campaign; and
- The terrorist attacks of September 11th, which altered the policy landscape, impacted the nomination and primary processes, as well as heightened security at the conventions;
- The war in Iraq and the war against "terror," which have sparked a growing anti-war movement and protests on each day of the 2004 Republican convention.

Each of these factors conspired to reduce the political importance of the gender gap, even as gender issues sharply divided the two parties.

Revolutionary Women. The 2004 Democratic Convention occurred after a "frontloaded" process that resulted in early agreement on a nominee—Senator John Kerry, after the campaign of the early front runner, Governor Howard Dean, lost steam. Democratic National Committee Chair Terry McAuliffe sought to create a controlled convention that provided a platform to introduce Sen. Kerry with maximum public relations benefit. In contrast to earlier conventions, when the women's caucus met on all four days of the convention, a reduced schedule provided for only 2 hours of meetings on two of the four days of convention. This provided opportunities for women delegates to attend other formal DNC-sponsored caucus meetings, but also reduced the stature of the women's caucus meetings. Other groups, including the NWPC and NOW held meetings and receptions, but for the most part, these constituted fundraisers rather than efforts at political organizing. The largest meeting was held by a new organization called Revolutionary Women, which trained over 4,000 women during a one-day conference on July 27, 2004. Revolutionary Women is a nonpartisan organization headed by Barbara Lee, a philanthropist of the Barbara Lee Family Foundation.

"W Stands for ~~Women~~ Wife. "W Stands for Women" is a Republican organization, which boasts over 55,000 women who are actively campaigning for the re-election of George Bush. The steering committee for the organization is highly populated with the spouses of major Republican elected officials. This group hosted a large event at the 2004 Republican Convention. Signs on the convention floor stated that "W Stands for Women!" and press releases for the 2004 Republican Convention bragged that the convention provided historic representation of women—44%. Typically, the larger numbers of women included alternate delegates rather than regular delegates. This increases the proportion of women since the Republican Party traditionally includes more alternate slots than delegates slots. A careful perusal of the delegate allocations, and the delegate roll reveals a more complicated picture. By matching names and addresses, it is obvious that a large number of state delegations represented married couples and families. Among the smaller states, this amounted to a large proportion of the women delegates or alternates being the wife of another delegate. For example, Idaho, Montana and Utah included 12 couples each in their state delegations, and South Dakota included 11 couples. Other states with a larger number of couples included Arizona (5), Nevada (6), Oregon (8), West Virginia (6), and Wyoming (5). In a number of states, the substantial proportion of women (as many as 25 to 40%) who are delegates received their position as a "delegate wife."

The more traditional roles among Republican women delegates in 2004 is consistent with early studies of delegates. For example, in past conventions, less than half of Republican women (42%) were employed full-time, compared to two-thirds (66%) of Democratic women. By contrast, a similar proportion of Republican men (82%) and Democratic men (85%) were employed full-time.

Republican Party elites are much more likely to be married and living in "traditional" families. Over four-fifths of Republicans are married, and of these, 28% of the women identify themselves as housewives and 44% of the Republican men say their wife is a housewife. By contrast, only 7% of Democratic women are housewives, and only 28% of Democratic men so identify their wives. To the extent that more Republican women are housewives, this becomes an identity that structures their participation as well as affecting male/female status differentials.[43]

WHITHER THE WOMEN'S MOVEMENT_____? THE STAKES FOR WOMEN

This article raises two key questions. First, women's organizations have by and large employed a bipartisan strategy, and have organized outside of the parties. For groups with declining electoral or political power, seeking power within a political party is a viable strategy. But it is one that the women's movement has eschewed. Is this a dated strategy given the events outlined in this essay? In the pre-reform party system, women were recruited to political activism and office holding primarily outside of the party system via women's organizations. The significance of factional conflict is that the advent of true factions within the institutionalized party system in the 1970s enhances the impact of informal associations, apprenticeships and recruitment among party activists within the parties. Therefore the more active women are within the party, the more opportunity they have to be recruited via party-linked factions and groups—a fundamentally decentralized and "privatized" process beyond the reach of party rules. No longer is recruitment in the hands of a few party bosses. This means that women are increasingly dependent on the extent to which they have organized clout *as a movement within* the party—a more difficult hurdle. With the decline of the mass level of the contemporary women's movement reduces resources for women's leaders and women's organizations. This, combined with the loss of institutional power within the national parties and the majority status of the Republican Party (now hostile to policy issues of the women's movement) raises a serious question: what kind of woman and what kind of women's movement is being represented in parties and in government?

Second, how should leaders of the women's movement orient themselves toward the women's movement? Should women leaders and aspiring women leaders now look toward building the necessary infrastructure for a fourth women's movement rather than lobbying an increasingly hostile government? Perhaps the study of women's power should emphasize rebuilding the associational context with a focus on women's everyday lives. This, of course, has always been an aspiration of the women's movement. For many, the universal interest is the ability to have a "choice"—in work, in education, and in family. While it may be controversial to consider, it might also be critical to take another look at the degree to which the gendered partisan divide structures these choices, so that women's political power is undermined until and unless the partisan divide in which kind of woman is represented is addressed.

NOTES

1. John D. McCarthy and Mayer N. Zald, *The Trends of Social Movements in America: Professionalization and Resource Mobilization* (Morristown, NJ: General Learning Press, 1973).

2. Doug McAdam, Political Process and the Development of Black Insurgency, 1930–1970 (Chicago: University of Chicago Press, 1982), pp. 36–59; Anne N. Costain, *Inviting Women's Rebellion: A Political Process Interpretation of the Women's Movement* (Baltimore, MD: Johns Hopkins University Press, 1992), pp. xi–xx and pp. 1–25; Lee Ann Banaszak, Karen Beckwith, Dieter Rucht, *Women's Movements Facing the Reconfigured State* (Oxford: Cambridge University Press, 2003).

3. See, for example, Alberto Melucci, "The Symbolic Challenge of Contemporary Movements," *Social Research* 52, pp. 789–816.

4. See Denise L. Baer, "Women, Women's Organizations, and Political Parties," in Susan J. Carroll (Ed.), *Women and American Politics: New Questions, New*

Directions (London; Oxford University Press, 2003), pp. 114–117.

5. Richard Flacks, "Knowledge for What? Thoughts on the State of Social Movement Studies," in Jeff Goodwin and James M. Jasper (Eds.), *Rethinking Social Movements* (Lanham, MD: Rowman and Littlefield, 2004), p. 136.

6. Denise L. Baer and David A. Bositis, *Politics and Linkage in a Democratic Society* (Englewood Cliffs, NJ: Prentice Hall, 1993), pp. 165–68.

7. Flacks, "Knowledge for What?"

8. Costain, *Inviting Women's Rebellion,* p. 14. In addition, lobbying by women's rights organizations has declined. WEAL has ceased to exist, and both NOW and the NWPC no longer have full-time lobbyists on staff.

9. Examples of the "wave" metaphor include Costain, Ibid., and Christina Wollbrecht, *The Politics of Women's Rights: Parties, Positions, and Change* (Princeton, NJ: Princeton University Press, 2000). The drawback of using the wave analogy to reflect degrees of mass support for "the women's movement" is that it seems to

imply a linear advance in women's rights, as well as grouping together distinct "movements" which I have argued elsewhere are best understood as episodic, concrete, organic, phenomena that have organized differently at different points in American history.

10. Mildred White Wells, *Unity in Diversity: The History of the General Federation of Women's Clubs* (Washington, DC: General Federation of Women's Clubs, 1975), p. 461.

11. Anne Firor Scott, "Women's Voluntary Associations: From Charity to Reform," in Kathleen D. McCarthy (Ed.) *Lady Bountiful Revisited: Women's Philanthropy and Power* (New Brunswick, NJ: Rutgers University Press, 1990), p. 46.

12. Herring, E. Pendleton, *Group Representation Before Congress.* (Baltimore: The Johns Hopkins Press, 1941[1929]), pp. 34–46; 186.

13. This model is more fully described in Baer and Bositis, *Politics and Linkage,* pp. 152–197.

14. In 1996, there were four, major national women's Get-Out-the-Vote efforts. The 1996 Women's Vote Project, chaired by Irene Natividad, which involved a large coordinated effort by 110 women's organizations. This effort was more sophisticated than earlier efforts launched in 1988 and 1992 which relied on media efforts. The 1996 Project utilized grassroots efforts to identify and register previously inactive women, and targeted ten states where women's voting had been historically low. The African American Women's Voter Crusade, a coalition of over 100 African American women's groups including the NPCBW, the NCNW and the major sororities and women's clubs targeted states with a large black voting age population. In addition, there were large-scale parallel efforts initiated by individual partisan women's organizations—NFRW for the Republicans and EMILY's List for the Democrats. In all, some 38 states were selected for targeted GOTV efforts for women.

15. Even the more influential mainstream PACs limit their influence to other similar PACs (e.g., the so-called "lead PACs" like BIPAC and the AFL-CIO handicap upcoming races and make recommendations to other organizations).

16. Mary Fainsod Katzenstein, "The Reconfigured U.S. State and Women's Citizenship," in Lee Ann Banaszak, Karen Beckwith, and Dieter Rucht, *Women's Movements Facing the Reconfigured State* (Oxford: Cambridge University Press, 2004), p. 213. See also Mary Fainsod Katzenstein, *Faithful and Fearless: Moving Feminist Protest into the Church and the Military* (Princeton, NJ: Princeton University Press, 1998).

17. Even women lobbyists have more often been *less* associated with business interests. According to Kay Lehman Schlozman ("Representing Women in Washington: Sisterhood and Pressure Politics," a paper presented at the annual meeting of the American Political Science Association, Washington, D.C. 1986), in 1985,

61 percent of male representatives compared to only 49% of women representatives represented business organizations. In another study looking at economic policy domains, women lobbyists were much more common in government affairs offices (a staff position) than as higher status executives of Washington organizations, and only 7 percent of women were executives in business organizations and 17 percent were business government affairs representatives. While citizen and good government associations were a small portion of the economic policy domain study, women lobbyists were most prevalent as citizen group executives (29%) and government affairs representatives (19%) (John P. Heinz, Edward O. Laumann, Robert L. Nelson, and Robert H. Salisbury, *The Hollow Core: Private Interests in National Policy Making* (Cambridge, MA: Harvard University Press, 1995), pp. 222–224).

18. Jack L. Walker, Jr., *Mobilizing Interest Groups in America: Patrons, Professions and Social Movements* (Ann Arbor: University of Michigan Press, 1991), p. 188.

19. Estelle B. Freedman, "Separatism as Strategy: Female Institution Building and American Feminism, 1870–1930," *Feminist Studies* 5, pp. 512–529.

20. Sophonisba P. Breckinridge, *Women in the Twentieth Century* (New York: ARNO Press, 1972 [1933]).

21. Wendy Kaminer, *Women Volunteering: The Pleasure, Pain and Politics of Unpaid Work from 1830 to the Present* (Garden City, NY: Anchor, 1984).

22. Margit Misangyi Watts, *High Tea at Halekulani: Feminist Theory and American Clubwomen* (Brooklyn, NY: Carlson, 1993).

23. Karen J. Blair, *History of American Women's Voluntary Organization, 1810–1960* (Boston, G.K. Hall, 1989), p. x.

24. Paula Giddings, *In Search of Sisterhood: Delta Sigma Thete and the Challenge of the Black Sorority Movement* (New York: William Morrow, 1988).

25. Niara Sudaraska, "African American Female Headed Households: A Different Perspective." In Julianne Malveaux (Ed.), *Voices of Vision: African American Women on the Issues,* (Washington, D.C.: National Council of Negro Women), pp. 50–57.

26. The 75,000 Mexican nationals (Hispanos) residing in the U.S. after the end of the Mexican-American War which annexed Texas, California, and most of Arizona and New Mexico to the U.S., were granted citizenship after one year, but quickly lost political power (they were driven out of California by the 1880s, and subject to a full-scale war in Texas).

27. Initially treated as a foreign nation and segregated on reservations after the 1830 Relocation Act, national Native American organizations appeared first only recently: in 1944 with the National Congress of American Indians, and then in 1968 with the American Indian Movement which signaled a more activist stance following the Bureau of Indian Affairs relocation of Indi-

ans to urban areas beginning in 1952 (about one in four by 1968).

28. Scholzman, "Representing Women in Washington."

29. Tanya Melich, *The Republican War Against Women* (New York: Bantam Doubleday, 1998); Christina Wollbrecht, *The Politics of Women's Rights: Parties, Positions and Change* (Princeton, Princeton University Press, 2000); Kira Sanbonmatsu, *Democrats, Republicans and the Politics of Women's Place* (Ann Arbor: University of Michigan Press, 2002).

30. Jo Freeman, "Women at the 1992 Democratic and Republican Conventions," *PS: Politics and Political Science* 26, pp. 21–28.

31. Sanbonmatsu, *Democrats, Republicans and the Politics of Women's Place;* Wollbrecht, *The Politics of Women's Rights: Parties, Positions and Change.*

32. Jo Freeman, "The Political Culture of the Democratic and Republican Party," *Political Science Quarterly* 101, pp. 327–356.

33. Pippa Norris, "The Gender Gap: Old Challenges, New Approaches," in Susan J. Carroll (Ed.), *Women and American Politics* (Oxford: Cambridge University Press, 2004), pp. 146–172.

34. Denise L. Baer, "Who Has the Body? Party Institutionalization and Theories of Party Organization," *Political Research Quarterly* 46, pp. 547–576.

35. Jo Freeman, *A Room at a Time: How Women Entered Party Politics* (New York: Rowman and Littlefield, 2000).

36. J. David Gillespie, *Politics at the Periphery: Third Party Politics in Two-Party America* (Columbia: University of South Carolina Press, 1993), p. 143. Rare exceptions include the Equal Rights Party which ran Belva Lockwood for President in 1884 and 1888; Alice Paul's National Women's Party (organized in 1916) which did not formally nominate candidates, and the 21st Century Party, launched by NOW in August, 1992 and has yet to run candidates under its own label.

37. Cornelius P. Cotter and Bernard Hennessey, *Politics Without Power* (New York: Atherton Press, 1964).

38. *Ibid.*

39. Bella Abzug with Mim Kelber, *Gender Gap* (Boston, MA: Houghton Mifflin, 1984); Denise L. Baer and David A. Bositis, *Elite Cadres and Party Coalitions* (Westport, CT: Greewood Press, 1988).

40. The Charter was also amended in 1980 to provide equal division *for all party groups*—namely "the Democratic National Committee, the Executive Committee, Democratic state central committees, commissions, and like bodies" (Article Eleven, Section 16). Interestingly, the DNC has not tried to demand compliance with this rule since an early and incomplete effort in 1981–1982.

41. At the state level, some state parties have voluntarily chosen to employ equal division (e.g., the California Republican delegation in 1988).

42. Cotter and Hennessey, *Politics Without Power,* p. 58.

43. Denise L. Baer and Julie A. Dolan, "Intimate Connections: Political Interests and Group Activity in State and Local Political Parties," in Sarah P. Morehouse and Malcolm E. Jewell (Eds.) *Comparative State Parties,* Special Issue of *American Review of Politics* 35, pp. 257–289.

FURTHER READING

Baer, Denise L. 1993. "Political Parties: The Missing Variable in Women and Politics Research." *Political Research Quarterly,* 46 (1993), pp. 547–576.

Banaszak, Lee Ann, Karen Beckwith, and Dieter Rucht. *Women's Movements Facing the Reconfigured State.* Oxford: Cambridge University Press, 2003.

Freeman, Jo. *A Room at a Time: How Women Entered Party Politics.* New York: Rowman and Littlefield, 2000.

Goodwin, Jeff and James M. Jasper. *Rethinking Social Movements: Structure, Meaning and Emotion.* Lanham, MD: Rowman and Littlefield, 2004.

Sanbonmatsu, Kira. *Democrats, Republicans and the Politics of Women's Place.* Ann Arbor: University of Michigan Press, 2002.

★ ★ ★ ★ ★ ★ ★ ★ ★ ★ ★ ★ ★ ★ 4 ★ ★ ★ ★ ★ ★ ★ ★ ★ ★ ★ ★ ★ ★

Women and Elections: The Uphill Struggle

Even though the political role of women is changing when one examines the history of women in politics over the last two centuries, women still are stifled in their attempts to seek elective and appointive office in the United States. For example, while breaking into this new arena, women have had to deal with establishing fund-raising networks, proving to the voters that women have qualifications to seek office, handling campaign strategy to deal with potential bias of women by voters (that is, "Who will take care of your children if you should win?"), the effect of fewer women in "launching roles" in the recruitment of qualified women for public office, women's limited roles in party organizations, and the effect of family responsibilities on women seeking careers in politics.

The following three articles examine women and elections at two levels of government: women holding elective county offices and women in Southern legislatures in the post–World War II era. The third article examines the unique working environment women face in the campaign consulting industry. We begin with an article that explores whether 1992 (dubbed the Year of the Woman with sizable increases in the number of women serving in Congress) also marked a significant departure in the growth in the numbers of women holding elective county offices in Florida and Georgia. Susan A. MacManus, Charles S. Bullock, III, Karen L. Padgett, and Brittany Penberthy found that the proportion of women holding certain local elective offices surpasses the proportion of females in state legislatures across the country and in the U.S. Congress. Increased female representation has been incremental in the post-1992 period. Although increases in the proportion of local women officeholders have been greater in rural and suburban counties, women still hold a higher proportion of offices in urban counties (although the gap is narrowing somewhat).

Next, Joanne V. Hawks (Deceased) and Carolyn Ellis Staton provide a critique of women in Southern legislatures during the period 1946–1968. Many scholars considered the post–World War II era a quiescent time for white, middle-class American women. After a period of wartime involvement, women supposedly retreated into a more traditional lifestyle. Between 1946 and 1968, however, almost 100 women entered legislatures in the South, a particularly traditional region. Data indicate that they were predominantly women who were already involved in the public sphere in one or more ways. Even though many were serious legislators, the press emphasized their domesticity and femininity instead of their legislative achievements. The authors critique this period of transition—and reflect on the political environment for these Southern women.

Finally, Sarah E. Brewer focuses on the contributions women make to the campaign consulting profession by highlighting the ways in which their work differs from their male counterparts and the reasons why there are so few women in the industry. The author finds gender-specific rules women face are upheld by continued assumptions about appropriate behaviors for men and women based on sex-role stereotypes. She concludes that women are not seen as strategic and competitive, have to work twice as hard as their male colleagues to achieve their goals, and are punished for being too aggressive in an environment that demands this trait in its professionals. The research also suggests that women may differ from the men in the consulting business in ways that, if they were to increase their numbers, could alter the way in which the campaign industry not only conducts its work internally, but could also change the nature of campaigns.

Women Winning at the Local Level: Are County and School Board Positions Becoming More Desirable and Plugging the Pipeline to Higher Office?

Susan A. MacManus

Charles S. Bullock, III

Karen Padgett

Brittany Penberthy

The "Year of the Woman," 1992, focused attention on efforts to increase the numbers of females winning national and state offices.[1] The proportion of women holding local offices also rose in some states,[2] fueling expectations that these women would later run for higher, more prestigious offices (the progressive ambition theory). Local offices were viewed as the entry point into the pipeline to state and national elected posts. The question in the 2000s is whether local offices have become more prestigious, or desirable, over the past decade since there have been no sharp increases in the proportion of women state legislators or members of Congress after the immediate post-1992 jump. (See Table 1.)

We find that in the decade following the Year of the Woman, female representation levels have fluctuated across local offices. Our data show that women are winning some types of county and school district posts more than others and that women officials have become more numerous in the types of counties in which they had traditionally been most underrepresented (rural and suburban).

THE GROWING DESIRABILITY OF LOCAL OFFICES: HIGHER PAY, BETTER RATINGS

The 2002 Census of Governments identifies 3,034 counties and 13,522 school districts in the United States,[3] yet studies of local women officials have focused more

TABLE 1   Incremental Increases in Proportion of Females in State Legislatures and U.S. Congress Across the U.S. After 1992 Gains

				% Females				
Collegial Body	Year of Women 1992	1994	1998	2000	2002	2004	Increase 1994–2004
U.S. Congress	102nd	103rd	105th	106th	107th	108th	+3.5
	5.9	10.1	11.8	12.1	13.6	13.6	
State Legislatures	18.4	17.7	21.8	22.5	22.7	22.4	+4.7

Source: Center for the American Women in Politics.

on successes capturing municipal offices (mayor, city council)[4] than county[5] or school district[6] posts. Now in the early years of a new century, there are powerful reasons to believe that counties and school districts may be increasingly attractive venues for women interested in public office.

County, rather than city, elective positions are likely to be the local government of choice for many since in recent years county governments have acquired responsibilities far beyond the traditional tasks of paving roads and law enforcement.[7] Term limits which many states have imposed on state legislative service may make county offices more attractive than state legislative seats.[8] So, too, might the salaries of some county offices which are higher than legislative salaries in states where being a legislator is a part-time job. Local offices often have longer terms requiring less frequent campaigns than state legislative posts, particularly in the lower chamber. (See Florida as an example; Table 2.) Georgia county office terms run four years while members of both legislative chambers face the electorate every two years. As with Florida data in Table 2, administrators in Georgia counties earn more than the $16,000 paid legislators annually. In many Georgia counties, school board and commission members receive little compensation for what are seen as part-time positions.

Women have become more interested in running for school board or school superintendent posts (where elected) but for different reasons. For years, more women than men have taught in the elementary and secondary grades; more recently, female teachers have made in-roads into school administrator positions. The percentage of women principals jumped from 16 percent in 1982 to 34 percent in 1993.[9] By 2000, the percentage of female public school principals was 44 percent.[10] Experience in these posts has given some women more confidence in their ability to manage a school system and served as the impetus to run for office.

Not all women serving on boards of education come from the classroom. Today, more women are charged with almost singular responsibility for their children's education, often as single parents. The more interaction mothers have with

TABLE 2   Local Governments in Florida 2004: Pipeline or Plug In the Recruitment Path to the Statehouse?

Elected Posts	% of Women Currently in Post	Salary Range (Fiscal Year 2003–2004[*]) $	Term of Office	Term Limits
	Florida Legislature			
House (n = 120)	25	29,916	2	Yes
Senate (n = 40)	25	29,916	4	Yes
	County Level			
County Commissioners (n = 371)	25	20,861–84,213	4	No
School Board (n = 359)	48	20,945–37,428[**]	4	No
School Superintendent[a] (n = 67)	10	80,015–152,716[*]	4	No
Tax Collector (n = 67)	49	81,644–156,168	4	No
Property Appraiser (n = 67)	13	81,644–156,168	4	No
Clerk of the Circuit Court (n = 67)	34	81,644–156,168	4	No
Supervisor of Elections (n = 67)[b]	72	66,490–138,401	4	No
Sheriff (n = 67)	0	89,504–164,028	4	No
	Municipal Level			
Mayor (n = 404)	20	$1–$150,000[c]	2–4	Some (26%)
Council Members (n = 1805)	29	$1–29,661[c]	2–4	Some (25%)

Notes: [a]44 are elected (of the 44 elected, 4 are female; of 23 appointed, 3 are women;

[b]66 are elected, one is appointed (Miami Dade). The appointed Supervisor is a female.

[c]The wide range of salaries of municipal officials is due to tremendous population size differences among the cities. The population of Florida's smallest city is 6; of its largest city, more than 800,000.

[*]Last formula used to calculate elected school superintendent was for 2002–2003 fiscal year.

[**]"School Board Member Salaries," 2003–2004 Commission Recommendation by the Legislative Committee on Intergovernmental Relations, October 21, 2003.

Sources: "Finalized Salaries of County Constitutional Officers for Fiscal Year 2003–2004. Pursuant to the Salary Formula in Chapter 145, Florida Statutes." Legislative Committee on Intergovernmental Relations, October 2003. Materials provided by the Hillsborough County School Board, March 2004. Term limit information for municipal officials: 2001 International City/County Management Association (Florida data); salary for council officials—ICMA. School board and constitutional officer composition from websites. Mayor and council member gender composition data extracted from list supplied by the Florida League of Cities, effective March 30, 2004.

the school system, the more concerned some become. Although little empirical research has been done on the topic, cursory examinations of the backgrounds of school board members show that a high percentage first ran when they had school-age children.

Finally, the 1990s emphasis on grassroots governance, decentralization, and devolution has thrust local governments into the limelight. National polls consistently show that Americans give higher marks to their local officials than to state or national politicos. Citizens regard local officials as more approachable and better capable of resolving problems that matter to the average person in the street. The typical American cares more about property taxes, potholes, traffic congestion, and local schools than about U.S. efforts at nation building in Haiti, the space program, or fast track authority for the president. More voters now realize that *local* offices impact their lives more directly than do the higher profile decisions rendered in Congress or the state legislature. Local officials often get better marks from the public on their job performance than state or national officials. (See Figures 1 and 2 for Florida as an example.)

NATIONAL TRENDS: WOMEN IN COUNTY ELECTED OFFICES[11]

Counties are often called "the forgotten governments."[12] As if to bear out that assessment, data on female county office-holding have been sparse until recently. (See Table 3.) Even now, most studies focus on women on county commissions rather than on executive or judicial posts. But statistics do show a higher proportion of women serving on local collegial bodies (county commissions; school boards) than in Congress or in the state legislature.

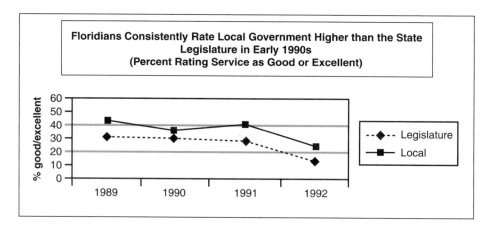

FIGURE 1   Floridians Consistently Rate Local Government Higher Than the State Legislature in Early 1990s (Percent Rating Service as Good or Excellent) *Source:* J. Arthur Heise, Hugh Gladwin, and Douglas McLaughen, *1992 FIU/Florida Poll.* Miami: Florida International University Institute for Public Opinion Research, pg. 111, 112. Note: Respondents were asked: "How would you rate the job that the Florida state legislature did this year—using the same system we all know from school, would you give the legislature an A, B, C, D, or F?" Excellent = A and Good = B.

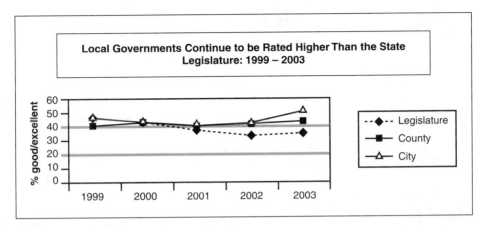

FIGURE 2   Local Governments Continue to be Rated Higher Than the State Legislature: 1999–2003
Source: FSU Florida Annual Policy Survey, 1999–2003. Tallahassee: Florida State University, Public Opinion Laboratory.
Note: Respondents were asked: "How would you rate the job _____ is doing? Would you say excellent, good, fair, or poor?"

County Commissions

Between 1975 and 1988, the number of women serving on county governing boards rose from 456 to 1,653, or from 3 percent of all county commission seats to 9 percent.[13] By the end of 1997, the percentage had risen to 24%, a remarkable increase in 11 years. But the percentage since 1997 has remained somewhat flat, increasing just 1 percent by 2001.

Women have made greatest progress in large, urban, cosmopolitan areas.[14] For example, a 1993 survey of the nation's largest counties (1990 populations over

TABLE 3   National Trends: Women in Elective County and School District Offices

Elective Position		Year/% Women Office-Holders Across the U.S.							
		1975		1988		1998			2001
County Commission		3%		9%		24%			25%
	1971	1975	1980	1985	1990	1992	1993		2000
School Superintendent[1]	0.6%	0.5%	1.0%	2.7%	6.0%	6.6	7.1%		14%
		1978		1986/87		1992	1997		2001
School Board[1]		25.7%		36.6%		39.9%	44.0%		38.9%

Notes: [1]These data include both elected and appointed positions.

Sources: International City/County Management Association (1975, 1988 county commission data); National Association of Counties (1998 county commission data); American Association of School Administrators (school superintendent data); National Association of School Boards (school board data).

423,000) found that the percentage of women on these boards was 27.5 percent—above the national average.[15] Within metropolitan areas, there are more women's groups (professional, social, political) that may provide critical support and more women professionals willing to run.[16]

Few studies have focused on the backgrounds of women commissioners. The first, and perhaps most, extensive study (in the 1970s) found that women commissioners were most likely to be 40–59 years old (68%), with some college (75%), and in professional or technical occupations (50%).[17] A high proportion belonged to a political organization (65%) while over half (53%) had held a political party position at one time or another.

Other Elective County Offices

A variety of other county officers are elected such as the sheriff, probate judge, clerk of the court, some type of revenue officer (tax collector, tax commissioner, property appraiser), and the supervisor of elections, to name the most common. Because of the wide variation in the number and type of county elective posts, there are no national aggregate statistics available for these positions.

Past research has shown that women are more likely to capture some of these positions than others. A 1989 study of women county office-holders in Georgia and South Carolina found that the positions most frequently held by women have a record-keeping or book-keeping component.[18] Positions that have the greatest discretion (sheriff and solicitor) have largely been beyond the reach of women.

The 1989 study found that approximately three of every five clerks of court in these states were female. Women also held approximately half of the revenue-related elected positions in the two states and about 40 percent of the probate judgeships. On the other hand, neither state had a female sheriff in 1989 and women coroners, solicitors, and surveyors were extremely rare. In summary, the administrative positions to which women are most frequently elected are ones which bear some similarity to traditional female occupations.

NATIONAL TRENDS: WOMEN IN SCHOOL DISTRICT POSITIONS

Women have been more successful at winning seats on school boards than at capturing school superintendent positions. Data reported by the National School Boards Association show that between 1978 and 1992, the percent of women school board members jumped from 25.7 percent to 39.9 percent and by 1997, it had risen to 44 percent, but then dipped to 38.9 percent in 2001. (Some speculate the drop may have been prompted by the recession which may have affected the personal finances of women more than men. There was a drop-off in school board candidacies nationwide during that time.)[19] But women still hold more school board seats than county commission, state legislative, or congressional seats.

A couple of theories suggest why women occupy a much higher proportion of school board seats than of any other legislative body. The first involves desirability theory. Some years ago, school boards were viewed as "lower in the prestige order" than other elective positions, thereby explaining why women were more likely to run for them.[20] But more recent research suggests just the opposite: "Increased attention to all facets of education by the media and the public at-large and the higher stakes attached to controlling educational policy and expenditures have suddenly weakened the 'lower prestige' or 'occupational segregation' explanation for increases in female school board representation."[21] If anything, school board seats have become more desirable.

Another theory is that women are more successful at winning school board seats because their service on school boards is not threatening to men since it is consistent with the traditional roles of motherhood and child-rearing.[22]

The *American School Board Journal* and the Virginia Polytechnic Institute gather descriptive data on school board members annually. A longitudinal look at these data showed that between 1982–1992, the most dramatic increase in the proportion of women serving on school boards occurred in the South (22.3% to 40.2%).[23] Studies focusing on *elected* school boards states have concluded that women do better in larger, urban, and more cosmopolitan district settings.[24]

Women are less successful at becoming school superintendents, although the percentage of women holding such posts doubled between 1992 (6.6%) and 2000 (14%). In the past, scholars have offered several explanations for the shortage of women in such posts:

> Women don't imagine themselves in leadership roles. . .and neither do school boards [which often hire superintendents]. Others say the traditional path to the superintendency—becoming a high school principal or central office business administrator—favors male candidates. Women are more likely to be elementary school principals or curriculum coordinators, jobs that are not considered stepping stones to the superintendency.[25]

To the extent that superintendents are recruited from the ranks of high school principals, women are disadvantaged since those principals often come from the ranks of coaches.

More recently, some scholars are predicting that the number of women school superintendents will escalate now that "the academic standards movement has pushed school boards to look for superintendents with curriculum backgrounds to become instructional leaders for their districts," thereby benefiting female superintendent candidates.[26] In jurisdictions where school superintendents are elected, voters may be searching for the same qualities.

TESTING THEORIES IN TWO LARGE STATES

In this reading, we look at changes in women's successes at the county and school district levels using data collected from Florida and Georgia, the nation's fourth and ninth largest states. A full descriptive analysis of women officeholders in all U.S. counties and school districts would be a massive undertaking and well beyond our resources. Even the National Association of Counties does not have longitudinal data on the number and percent of women commissioners, county executives, sheriffs, clerks, supervisors of election, etc.

The wide variance in which posts are elected at the county and school district levels makes national comparisons difficult. For example, the American Association of School Administrators does not distinguish between elected and appointed school superintendents. Even within the *same* state, counties and school districts may vary in what positions are elective and which are appointive under their separate charters.

Florida and Georgia: Rapidly Changing Population Profiles

At first blush, there may be the temptation to discount any patterns observed in these two southern states as being "aberrant." However, the changing demographics of Florida and Georgia due to tremendous growth in the 1980s and 1990s[27] have made them much less southern. (The 2000 Census showed that only 32.75% of Florida's residents were born in the state; the comparable figure for Georgia was 57.8%.) In-migrants from other regions of the country and, in the case of Florida, from other countries have also changed their political profiles considerably. At the outset of the twenty-first century, Florida and Georgia—currently the nation's fourth and ninth most populous states—mirror .the nation much more closely in terms of partisan identification, party competitiveness, and race/ethnicity.[28]

County and School District Offices Examined

We have collected information on a wide range of county-level offices. Each has a four-year term but not all counties choose local officers on the same cycle. Some counties elect their local officials in presidential years, others in off-years, while still others stagger the terms of county commissioners and school board members. (Staggered terms mean that some members of a collegial body are elected in presidential years while the remainder of the board is chosen in non-presidential election years.)

All Florida (67) and Georgia (159) counties have *county commissions* although the number of commissioners varies considerably. In Georgia, they range from ten members down to one as eleven counties retain the sole commissioner form of government.[29] Almost two-thirds of Georgia's counties elect five commissioners with between 11 and 15 counties each electing one, three, six or seven commissioners. In Florida, most county commissions (85%) have five members, 10 percent have seven members, one county has nine commissioners (Broward), and two counties have at least ten (Miami-Dade, 13; Jacksonville-Duval, 19).

Each Georgia county has an elected *sheriff, probate judge, clerk of the court,* and all but five a *tax commissioner*. Most Georgia counties also elect a coroner and/or a surveyor. In Florida, county-level elected "constitutional officers" are the *sheriff,*[30] *clerk of the court,*[31] *supervisor of elections,*[32] *tax collector,*[33] *and property appraiser.*[34] (One county has an appointed tax collector or revenue officer and one has an appointed supervisor of elections.)

In both states, all *school board* members are elected. Almost 65 percent of Georgia school boards have five members and another 20 percent elect seven members although the range is from four to nine. In Florida, 87 percent are five-member boards; the remainder range from 6 to 9. The larger boards are in more urban areas.

Since 1992 all Georgia *school superintendents* have been appointed.[35] In Florida, 44 of 67 (66%) counties *elect* their school superintendent while in the remaining counties the school board selects the superintendent. The method of selection (appointment v. election) has made little difference in women's successes in Florida.[36]

SHARP OR INCREMENTAL CHANGE SINCE 1992?

In 1992, unprecedented numbers of women ran for Congress and met with historically high levels of success. The number of women in the U.S. Senate, which had never before exceeded three, went to seven and California became the first state to have an all-female Senate delegation. The ranks of women in the House jumped from 29 to 48. By 2003 Congress had 14 female senators and 59 representatives—both unprecedented numbers. Maine and Washington had joined California with a pair of women U.S. senators.

Women also became more numerous in state legislatures, jumping from 18.3 percent in 1991 to 20.5 percent in 1993.[37] The 2.2 percentage point increase following the 1992 election was the second largest since 1969 and probably the second largest ever. As with Congress, the numbers of female legislators has risen since 1993 although the rate of growth has slowed. In 2004, women filled 22.4 percent of the state legislative seats with their most pronounced success being in Washington where 36.7 percent of the lawmakers are women.

But was "the Year of the Woman" phenomenon, so clearly observable at the national and state levels, fact or fiction at the *local* level? Is there any evidence of the same sharp increase in women holding county and school district offices after 1992? And have women subsequently made greater strides in winning local offices than in capturing state legislative or congressional seats? In other words, have women's gains at the local level been incremental in nature as have their gains in state legislatures and in the U.S. Congress?

Georgia

Table 4 presents biennial data on the percent of females in various Georgia offices at ten points in time—from 1981 to 1997 along with figures for 2003. A look at the data for all county offices indicates the presence of a "Year of the Woman" bump—a 4.7 percentage point rise in female officeholders. This increase was more than three times greater than the second largest, a rise of 1.5 points produced by the 1988 election. The elections since 1992 have witnessed a three-percentage growth in women county officials, a smaller increase than from 1983 to 1991 and only two-thirds as large as the change associated with the Year of the Woman.

TABLE 4   Percentage Female Make-up of Various County Offices in Georgia

County Office	% Female									
	1981	1983	1985	1987	1989	1991	1993	1995	1997	2003
Summary of 8 Local Offices	14.2	15.5	16.6	17.8	19.3	19.2	23.9	24.2	24.9	26.9
County Commn.	5.1	5.5	5.2	5.1	5.8	6.3	7.8	10.0	10.4	9.9
Clerk of Court	45.9	47.8	51.6	53.5	59.1	57.2	68.6	66.7	68.6	71.7
Probate Judge	42.1	37.3	39.6	39.0	39.6	39.6	49.1	50.3	48.4	53.5
Coroner	2.6	3.2	3.8	3.8	6.5	7.2	9.3	8.8	9.9	10.9
Sheriff	0.0	0.0	0.0	0.0	0.0	0.0	.6	.6	.6	.6
Tax Commr.	36.7	39.2	43.7	47.5	49.1	47.7	54.5	52.8	61.7	67.7
Surveyor	1.1	1.1	2.0	1.9	2.3	2.3	1.3	1.3	2.7	0.0
School Board	12.5	15.0	17.8	21.2	22.9	21.6	27.9	27.7	28.1	31.8

Source: Created by authors.

The 1992 upsurge was not constant across offices. As Table 4 shows, the most dramatic gain came among women serving as clerk of court—a rise from 57.2 percent in 1991 to 68.6 percent two years larger. The Year of the Woman also coincided with the largest increases up to that time in women serving as probate judge (+9.5 percentage points), tax collector (+6.8 points), and school board member (+6.3 points). The percentage of female coroners rose by 2.1 points after the 1992 election, an increase of more than 25 percent over the 1991 election although women increased by 2.7 points in 1989. The 1992 election also saw the first woman elected sheriff in many years.

As with congressional and state legislative offices, *the increases post-1992 have generally been smaller.* The last decade saw more women serving as clerk of court (+3.1 percentage points), probate judge (+4.4 points), coroner (+1.6 points), and school board member (+3.9 points). One office for which a one-election increase exceeds that for the Year of the Woman came in 1997 when the percentage of female tax commissioners rose from 52.8 to 61.7. Another office that registered a larger gain post-1992 was county commissioner where women's share rose from 7.8 to 10 percent following the 1994 election. The third office, surveyor, saw women briefly double their percentage to 2.7 in 1997. During the decade since the Year of the Woman, the share of offices filled by women has increased in all but two categories. Georgia continues to have only one female sheriff and the few female surveyors ceased to hold office by 2003.

A distinguishing feature between offices in which women made sizable gains and those that lagged is the extent to which women already served in an office before 1992. Women made unprecedented gains in each of the four offices in which they were already relatively numerous (held more than 20 percent of the positions) while not scoring major breakthroughs in offices that heretofore eluded them. The Year of the Woman phenomenon had less impact on posts that have been least accessible to women. Thus, the number of women serving as chief law enforcement officers in their county rose from zero to one but the number of female surveyors actually dropped slightly.

Despite gains registered in the share of school board and county commission posts filled by women, Georgia is still well below national percentages. Indeed, women held smaller shares of board of education seats in Georgia than in the South overall. The disparities between women in Georgia and nationally serving on these two local collegial bodies are greater than the disparity of women legislators where Georgia is less than a percentage point below the proportion of female legislators nationally.

A final test of whether the gains registered in 1992 were unique involves the use of times series analysis. This analytic technique is appropriate when a researcher has collected data from multiple points in time (a longitudinal data set). Using this technique, the year 1992 is coded as 1 and the other years as 0 so that the Year of the Woman is a "pulse" variable. In addition to the "pulse" variable the model includes a "counter" variable in which the first election (1980) is coded zero and each successive year is coded one greater so that 1982 is coded 1, 1984 is coded 2, and so forth. Both the pulse and counter variables are entered as independent variables into a model to predict the proportion of women in the position being analyzed. If the Year of the Woman had a unique impact, the pulse variable will be statistically significant in the model. A separate model is estimated for each office in Table 4.

The clearest evidence that the 1992 elections made a significant difference in the number of women officials between 1981 and 1997 shows up for three offices: one in which the dependent variable is the proportion of all eight county offices filled by women, another is the model for coroners, and the third is the model for clerks of court. For these three models, the pulse variable (1992) is a statistically significant predictor (at the .05 level) of female representation. The Year of the Woman had an impact on school board elections although the pulse variable just misses statistical significance at the .05 level. Overall, women became substantially more visible in Georgia courthouses at the same time they made historic gains in Congress and state legislatures.

Evidence of the uniqueness of 1992 is unimpressive for two of the three offices most often filled by women. While the sign for the pulse variable is positive, it is not a statistically significant predictor of female representation among tax commissioners or probate judges. The Year of the Woman was not significant for tax commissioners because of the increase in female incumbents after the 1996 election, an increase that exceeds 1992. Of offices to which women gravitate, only that of clerk of the superior court experienced a major jump in 1992.

While percentage gains may appear unimpressive, it is important to note that the share of county offices filled by women in Georgia (27%) still exceeds the percentage female in the Georgia General Assembly (22%) or in Georgia's U.S. House delegation (8%). Service on county commissions (10%), however, remains largely elusive for Georgia women who are only slightly more likely to serve in that capacity than in Congress.

Florida

Data for Florida's county officials are more limited and to the extent that longitudinal comparisons are possible, they suggest incremental, rather than sharp, increases during the 1990s for most county posts. (See Table 5.) However, Florida already had larger shares of women officeholders than a number of other states due to increases that occurred in the 1980s. In 1950, there were only two female county commissioners. The number rose to eighteen by 1976, still a small percentage of all commissioners.[38] By 1991, the number had increased to 72 (19.5%), more than three times the rate in Georgia. By 1997, 20.6% of all Florida county commissioners were female and by 2004, 25%—a steady improvement.

Women have also been much more likely to serve on Florida than Georgia school boards. Florida's earlier and more extensive urbanization may help account for these inter-state differences.

Another pattern similar to Georgia's is that the Florida administrative positions most frequently held by women bear some similarity to traditional female occupations. Nearly three-fourths (72%) of Florida's supervisors of elections are female, as are 49 percent of its tax collectors and 34 percent of its clerks of the courts. Women do not dominate the clerk of court and tax administration jobs in Florida to the degree that they do in Georgia but they have made gains in each of those posts even since 1997 (see Table 5). Another difference is that in Florida, women

TABLE 5   Percent Female Make-up of County and School District Offices in Florida: 1991–2004

Elective Position	% Females in Office			
	1991	1997	2004	Percent Change 1997–2004
COUNTY (n = 67)				
County Commission	19.5	20.6	25.0	+4.4
Sheriff	0	0	0	—
Clerk of the Court	NA	31.3	34	+2.7
Tax Collector	NA	37.3	49	+11.7
Property Appraiser	NA	10.4	13	+2.6
Supervisor of Elections	76% (1988)	68.7	72	+3.3
SCHOOL DISTRICT (n = 67)				
Superintendent	NA	11.6	10	−1.6
School Board	38.1	40.7	48	+7.3

Note: NA = not available.

Sources: 1991 data are from telephone surveys by Susan A. MacManus, 1991 data; 1997 figures were calculated from data reported in Tom Fiedler and Lance deHaven-Smith, *Almanac of Florida Politics 1998* (Dubuque, IA: Kendall/Hunt Publishing Company, 1998) and from telephone surveys by Susan A. MacManus. 2004 data were collected by Susan A. MacManus via Website analysis and phone calls.

hold a larger share of two administrative positions (supervisor of elections, tax collector) than of school boards, while in Georgia, it is three.

Florida has had no female sheriffs since the 1950s. All eleven women who served as sheriff between 1938 and 1959 "secured the position after their husband, the then incumbent sheriff, died in office."[39] Most served only a few months, usually just until the next election. The few who have run for sheriff in the 2000s have been from metropolitan area counties (urban; suburban).

BIGGEST GAINS AFTER 1992: URBAN, SUBURBAN, OR RURAL AREAS?

Prior to The Year of the Woman, women had more success capturing county and school district offices in large urban areas. (See Tables 6 and 7.) During the 1990s, there was some evidence that the percentages of women office-holders in suburban and rural areas also rose, although incrementally and unevenly depending upon the state and the region. Among students of women in politics, there is still the perception that rural and suburban areas are less female-friendly, characterized by more traditional patriarchal cultures thereby inhibiting female candidacies and victories. But is this perception still true?

Georgia

To test whether the degree of urbanization is associated with the incidence of women in county office, we divided counties into three groups: rural, suburban, and urban. Georgia's eight urban counties are ones that contain the central city of a metropolitan area. The 34 suburban counties are in metropolitan areas but do not contain the central city while the 117 rural counties lie outside a metropolitan area as defined in the early 1990s.

Table 6 compares the presence of women across three types of counties in 1991, just before the Year of the Woman, and again in 1997 and 2003. For the two collegial offices, the female percentage increases as we move from rural to suburban and then to urban counties in each year. The linkage between urbanization and the incidence of women is strong on county commissions. In 1991 women were more than twice as likely to be commissioners in suburban than rural counties and the female percentage in urban counties was twice that for suburban counties. In 1997, the percentage female increased by five percentage points between each category. By 2003, the difference in percent women between rural and suburban counties had slipped to only 2.5 points while the female percentage on urban commissions continued to be twice that for rural commissions. However only in rural counties did the percentage of women commissioners increase from 1991 to 2003, lending some support to the diffusion hypothesis.

The percent female on school boards increased by ten percentage points for each increasing level of urbanization in 1991, reaching 39 percent in urban counties. Women continued to hold substantially more suburban than rural school

TABLE 6 Incidence of Female Officeholding in Georgia by Level of Urbanization: 1991–2003

	% Females								
Office	Rural			Suburban			Urban		
	1991	*1997*	*2003*	*1991*	*1997*	*2003*	*1991*	*1997*	*2003*
Commission	4.5	8.4	8.5	11.0	13.1	11.0	23.0	18.2	18.5
School Board	19.2	25.3	28.2	29.0	34.0	38.5	39.1	37.3	41.2
All Offices	17.4	23.2	25.4	29.0	28.3	29.2	29.1	30.3	36.0
N of counties		117			34			8	

board slots but the difference between suburban and urban boards dropped to about three points for the two more recent years. Although the percent female increased by eight points after 1991 in rural counties, the increase in urban counties was almost as large (6.9 points).

A different pattern characterized the "All Offices" category. Here differences between suburban and urban counties were nearly non-existent in 1991 and 1997. By 2003, urban counties, where women held 36 percent of the offices, were distinguishable from suburban counties where women showed no gains across time and continued to fill 29 percent of the slots. In each of the three years, women held much smaller shares of the offices in rural counties than in the more urbanized ones indicating little support for the diffusion hypothesis.

Focusing on extremes, two counties in 1991 had most offices filled by women and in another six counties women held at least 40 percent of the offices. These eight counties included four of the six *least* populous in the state. By 2003, women held most of the offices in four counties. Included here were the state's least populous county where women constituted 69 percent of officialdom but also the most populous (57 percent female officeholders). The other two counties with predominantly female leadership were the two majority-black counties at the center of the Atlanta metro area. In another 12 counties, at least 40 percent of the officeholders were women. Over a dozen years, heavy concentrations of women officials went from being most common in tiny rural counties to a phenomenon that occurred frequently in major urban counties.

In 1991 DeKalb, the state's second most populous county, had a commission dominated by women while another four counties, three of which are in the Atlanta suburbs, had 40 percent female commissions. Twelve counties had at least 50 percent female school boards. Included here were four suburban counties and two urban ones. A dozen years later, the state's smallest county had a female-majority commission while counties, including the state's two most populous and two suburban counties had commissions at least 40 percent female. In 2003, 26 counties had school boards at least 50 percent female, including the three most populous counties and eight other suburban counties. This provides evidence of growing ranks of female officials that often put women in position to control collegial bodies, if they present a united front.

At the other extreme, in 1991, thirteen counties had an all-male corps of officials and in another sixteen women held between 1 and 9 percent of the offices. Over the next twelve years the number of counties in which women officials were rare declined. In only six counties did women fill less than ten percent of the offices in 2003 with a mountain county having only male officials.

Florida

Collegial bodies in Florida's urban counties, like those in Georgia, have higher levels of female representation than in rural counties (see Table 7). The fact that a much higher proportion of Floridians than Georgians live in metropolitan areas (93% v. 69%)[40] helps account for generally higher levels of female representation in Florida across all county and school district positions.

There was a much more uneven pattern to female representation gains in Florida's rural, suburban, and urban counties in the 1991–1997 period than between 1997–2004. There has been much more fluctuation in the female composition of school boards than of county commissions.

Between 1991 and 1997, female representation on Florida's rural school boards went up 5.4 points, more than in either urban (+1.8 points) or suburban (−8.8 points) counties. The sharp gains in rural areas has continued (+25.7 points), followed by gains on suburban boards (+7.2 points) but losses on urban boards (−11.5 points). By 2004, female composition on rural and suburban boards surpassed that on urban school boards. This rather dramatic rank order shift lends credence to the theory that women are more likely to be elected to school boards from areas with higher proportions of married persons and families. The state's heavily urbanized areas have higher incidences of single persons of voting age than rural or suburban districts.

Changes in the female composition of Florida's 67 county commissions over time have been much more incremental. Between 1991 and 1997, rural commissions experienced a slight decline (−2.4 points) in their proportions of female

TABLE 7   **Incidence of Female Officeholding in Florida by Level of Urbanization: 1991–2004**

	\multicolumn{9}{c}{% Female Makeup}								
	Rural			Suburban			Urban		
Office	1991	1997	2004	1991	1997	2004	1991	1997	2004
Commission	9.7	7.3	11.0	21.7	25.7	28.1	33.7	34.6	36.2
School Board	27.3	32.7	58.4	50.5	41.7	48.9	48.7	50.5	39.0
N of counties		29			17			21	

members while suburban and rural counties experienced slight gains (+4 and + 1). From 1997–2004, gains across the three types of counties were even narrower: +3.7 (rural), +2.4 (suburban), and +1.6 (urban). Urban counties still have the highest incidence of female officeholders in spite of the gains of rural and suburban counties. However, over the entire period, 1991 to 2004, women have made the greatest strides in capturing suburban county commission posts. (See Table 7.)

In 2004, the percentage of Florida counties with a majority female county commission is higher in urban areas (23.8%) than in suburban (11.8%) or rural (0%) locations. The percentage of counties with majority female school boards exceeds that of county commissions across all types of areas: (urban—76.2%; suburban—41.2%; and rural—37.9%). As in Georgia, the counties with majority female commissions and school boards shifted across time. Undoubtedly, changing partisan politics and term limits in the case of county commissioners prompted some of the fluctuations.

In summary, both the Florida and Georgia data show there is volatility in the levels of female representation even at the local level. There is no guarantee that once a county has a large number of women in a particular office, the number will remain stable. In other words, gains in female representation on individual collegial boards are not necessarily permanent. Shifts in levels of representation tend to be incremental, paralleling changes in demographic and socioeconomic composition. Suburban and rural areas have gained female representation at slightly higher rates in places where rural and suburban growth rates have outstripped those of core counties of Metropolitan Statistical Areas.

CONCLUSION

Both states examined experienced growth in the numbers of female county officials during the 1990s and early 2000s. Generally, gains were incremental rather than sharp. There were fluctuations across positions, even within the same state.

In offices for which longitudinal comparisons can be made, Florida has had more women on collegial bodies than Georgia, perhaps reflecting the sunshine state's more cosmopolitan, less traditional population make-up. On the other hand, women have done slightly better in winning administrative posts in Georgia than in Florida. In both states, women have been most successful at winning administration positions that have a record-keeping or book-keeping component (e.g., tax collector, clerk of the court, probate judge, supervisor of elections) than those related to law enforcement (sheriff) or property (surveyor, property appraiser).

While women officials continue to be more common in urban counties, the growth produced in the 1990s and early 2000s has not been in big city counties. In both states, the ranks of women have expanded in rural and suburban counties where, if there is a glass ceiling, greater opportunity for growth remains.

Perhaps our most significant finding is that local elective offices—collegial and administrative—are becoming increasingly more desirable posts for women seeking public office. At the same time, other research has shown that fewer women are seeking state and national posts. The unanswered question remains: "Has [or will] the growing popularity of local offices put a plug in the pipeline of women candidates seeking state and national offices?" If the answer is "Yes," we may need to revisit the progressive political ambition theory that so dominates the literature on political career paths.

We appreciate the help given in the preparation of this manuscript by Keith Gaddie.

NOTES

1. See Elizabeth Adell Cook, Sue Thomas, and Clyde Wilcox, eds. *The Year of the Woman: Myths & Realities.* Boulder, CO: Westview Press, 1994.

2. See Charles S. Bullock, III, Susan A. MacManus, Frances E. Akins, Laura Jane Hoffman, and Adam Newmark, " 'Winning in My Own Back Yard': County Government, School Board Positions Steadily More Attractive to Women Candidates," in Lois Duke Whitaker, ed. *Women in Politics: Outsiders or Insiders?* 3rd edition. Upper Saddle River, NJ: Prentice Hall, 1999: 121–137.

3. U.S. Census Bureau, "Government Units in 2002," 2002 Census of Governments, GC02-1(P), issued July 2002, p. 1.

4. See for example: Denise Antolini. "Women in Local Government: An Overview," in Janet Flammang, ed., *Political Women*. Beverly Hills, CA: Sage, 1984; Susan Abrams Beck. "Rethinking Municipal Governance: Gender Distinctions on Local Councils," in Debra L. Dodson, ed., *Gender and Policymaking: Studies of Women in Office*. New Brunswick, NJ: Center for the American Woman and Politics, Eagleton Institute of Politics, Rutgers University, 1991, pp. 103–113; Timothy Bledsoe. *Careers in City Politics: The Case for Urban Democracy*. Pittsburgh, PA: University of Pittsburgh Press, 1993; Janet K. Boles. "Advancing the Women's Agenda Within Local Legislatures: The Role of Female Elected Officials," in Debra L. Dodson, ed., *Gender and Policymaking: Studies of Women in Office*. New Brunswick, NJ: Center for the American Woman and Politics, Eagleton Institute of Politics, Rutgers University, 1991, pp. 39–48; Charles S. Bullock, III and Susan A. MacManus. "Municipal Electoral Structure and the Election of Councilwomen," *Journal of Politics* 53 (February) 1991: 75–89; Janet A. Flammang. "Filling the Party Vacuum: Women at the Grass-Roots Level in Local Politics," in Janet A. Flammang, ed., *Political Women: Current Roles in State and Local Government*. Beverly Hills, CA: Sage, 1984, pp. 87–114; Arnold Fleischman and Lana Stein. "Minority and Female Success in Municipal Runoff Elections, *Social Science Quarterly* 68 (June). 1987: 378–385; Joyce Gelb. "Seeking Equality: The Role of Activist Women in Cities," in Janet K. Boles, ed., *The Egalitarian City*. New York: Praeger, 1986, pp. 93–109; Jeanette Jennings. "Black Women Mayors: Reflections on Race and Gender," in Debra L. Dodson, ed., *Gender and Policymaking: Studies of Women in Office*. New Brunswick, NJ: Center for the American Woman and Politics, Eagleton Institute of Politics, Rutgers University, 1991, pp. 73–79; Albert Karnig and B. Oliver Walter. "Election of Women to City Councils," *Social Science Quarterly* 56 (March), 1976: 605–613; Albert K. Karnig and Susan Welch. "Sex and Ethnic Differences in Municipal Representation," *Social Science Quarterly* 60 (December) 1979: 465–481; Susan A. MacManus. "How to Get More Women in Office: The Perspectives of Local Elected Officials (Mayors and City Councilors)," *Urban Affairs Quarterly* 28 (September), 1992: 159–170; Susan A. MacManus and Charles S. Bullock, III. "Women on Southern City Councils: A Decade of Change," *Journal of Political Science* 17 (Spring), 1989: 32–49; Susan A. MacManus and Charles S. Bullock, III. "Electing Women to City Council: A Focus on Small Cities in Florida," in Wilma Rule and Joseph F. Zimmerman, eds., *United States Electoral Systems: Their Impact on Women and Minorities*. New York: Greenwood Press, 1992, pp. 167–181; Susan A. MacManus and Charles S. Bullock, III. "Women on Southern City Councils: Does Structure Matter?" in Lois Lovelace Duke ed., *Women and Politics: Have the Outsiders Become Insiders?* Englewood Cliffs, NJ: Prentice Hall, 1993, pp. 107–122; Susan A. MacManus and Charles S. Bullock, III. "Women and

Racial/Ethnic Minorities in Mayoral and Council Positions," in International City/County Management Association, *The Municipal Year Book 1993* (Washington, DC.: ICMA), 1993, pp. 70–84; Sharyne Merritt. "Winners and Losers: Sex Differences in Municipal Elections," *American Journal of Political Science,* 21 (November), 1977: 731–744; Susan Welch and Rebekah Herrick. "The Impact of At-Large Elections on the Representation of Minority Women," in Wilma Rule and Joseph F. Zimmerman, eds., *United States Electoral Systems: Their Impact on Women and Minorities.* New York: Greenwood Press, 1992, pp. 153–166; Susan Welch and Albert K. Karnig. "Correlates of Female Office-Holding in City Politics," *Journal of Politics* 41 (May), 1979: 478–491; Susan A. MacManus and Charles S. Bullock, III. "Second Best? Women Mayors and Council Members: A New Test of the Desirability Thesis," in Lois Lovelace Duke, ed., *Women and Politics: Have the Outsiders Become Insiders?,* 2nd ed. Englewood Cliffs, NJ: Prentice Hall, 1996, pps. 590–610; Susan A. MacManus and Charles S. Bullock, III. "The Form, Structure, and Composition of America's Municipalities in the New Millennium," in *The Municipal Year Book 2003* (Washington, DC: International City/County Management Association): 3–18.

5. Susan A. MacManus and Charles S. Bullock, III. "Electing Women to Local Office," in Judith A. Garber and Robyne S. Turner, eds. *Gender in Urban Research,* Thousand Oaks, CA: Sage, 1995, pps. 155–177; Charles S. Bullock, III. "Women Candidates and Success at the County Level." Paper presented at the Annual Meeting of the Southern Political Science Association, Atlanta, GA, November 8–10, 1990; Victor DeSantis and Tari Renner. "Minority and Gender Representation in American County Legislatures: The Effect of Election Systems," in Wilma Rule and Joseph F. Zimmerman, eds., *United States Electoral Systems: Their Impact on Women and Minorities.* New York: Greenwood Press, 1992, pp. 143–152; Susan A. MacManus. "Representation at the Local Level in Florida: County Commissions, School Boards, and City Councils," in Susan A. MacManus, ed., *Reapportionment and Representation in Florida: A Historical Collection.* Tampa, FL: Intrabay Innovation Institute, University of South Florida, 1991, pp. 489–538; Susan A. MacManus. "Politics, Partisanship, and Board Elections," in Donald C. Menzel, ed., *The American County,* 1993, pps. 53–79.

6. Trudy Haffrom Bers. "Local Political Elites: Men and Women on Boards of Education," *Western Political Quarterly* 31 (September), 1978: 381–391; Peter J. Cistone. "The Recruitment and Socialization of School Board Members," in Peter J. Cistone, ed., *Understanding School Boards: Problems and Prospects.* Lexington, MA: Lexington Books, 1975, pp. 47–61; Kenneth Greene. "School Board Members' Responsiveness to Constituents," *Urban Education* 24 (January), 1990: 363–375; Marilyn Johnson and Kathy Stanwick. "Local

Office Holding and the Community: The Case of Local School Boards," in Bernice Cummings and Victoria Schuck, eds., *Women Organizing.* Metuchen, NJ: Scarecrow Press, 1979, pp. 61–81; Rebecca Luckett, Kenneth E. Underwood, and Jimmy C. Fortune. "Men and Women Make Discernibly Different Contributions to Their Boards," *The American School Board Journal,* 174 (January), 1987: 21–41; Susan A. MacManus. "Representation at the Local Level in Florida: County Commissions, School Boards, and City Councils," in Susan A. MacManus, ed., *Reapportionment and Representation in Florida: A Historical Collection.* Tampa, FL: Intrabay Innovation Institute, University of South Florida, 1991, pp. 489–538; Susan A. MacManus and Rayme Suarez. "Female Representation on School Boards: Supportive Constituency Characteristics," *The Political Chronicle* 4 (Fall/Winter), 1992: 1–8; National School Boards Association. "School Boards: The Past Ten Years." Alexandria, VA: National School Boards Association, 1993; Ted Robinson and Robert E. England. "Black Representation on Central City School Boards Revisited," *Social Science Quarterly* 62 (September), 1981: 495–502; Joseph Stewart, Jr., Robert E. England, and Kenneth J. Meier. "Black Representatives in Urban School Districts: From School Board to Office to Classroom," *Western Political Quarterly* 42 (June), 1989: 287–305. Leon Weaver and Judith Baum. "Proportional Representation on New York City Community School Boards," in Wilma Rule and Joseph F. Zimmerman, eds., *United States Electoral Systems: Their Impact on Women and Minorities.* New York: Greenwood Press, 1992, pp. 197–205; Frederick M. Wirt. "Social Diversity and School Board Responsiveness in Urban Schools," in Peter J. Cistone, ed., *Understanding School Boards: Problems and Prospects.* Lexington, MA: Lexington Books, 1975, pp. 189–216. Harmon L. Zeigler, M. Kent Jennings, and Wayne G. Peak. *Governing American Schools: Political Interaction in Local School Districts.* North Scituate, MA: Duxbury, 1974; Frederick M. Hess, "School Boards at the Dawn of the 21st Century," A Report prepared for the National School Boards Association, 2002.

7. Donald C. Menzel, ed. *The American County: Frontiers of Knowledge.* Tuscaloosa, AL: University of Alabama Press, 1996; J. Edwina Benton, *Counties as Service Delivery Agents: Changing Expectations and Role.* Westport, CT: Praeger, 2002; Tanis J. Salant, "Trends in County Government Structure," *The Municipal Year Book 2004,* Washington, DC: International City/County Management Association, 2004, pps. 35–41.

8. See Robert A. Bernstein and Anita Chadha, "The Effects of Term Limits on Representation: Why So Few Women?" in Rick Farmer, John David Rausch, Jr. and John C. Green, eds. *The Test of Time: Coping With Legislative Term Limits.* Lanham, MD: Lexington Books, pps. 147–158; Susan J. Carroll and Krista Jenkins (2001). "Unrealized Opportunity? Term Limits and the

Representation of Women in State Legislatures," *Women and Politics* 23 (4): 1–30.

9. See Xenia Montenegro, *Women and Racial Minority Representation in School Administration.* Arlington, VA: American Association of School Administrators, 1993.

10. National Center for Educational Statistics. Digest of Education Statistics 2002, Chapter 2, Elementary and School Education, Table 85; http://nces.ed.gov\ programs\digest\do2\tables\dt085, accessed April 30, 2004.

11. Much of the following discussion of trends is from MacManus and Bullock, "Electing Women to Local Office."

12. Vincent Marando and Robert D. Thomas. *The Forgotten Governments: County Commissioners as Policy Makers.* Gainesville, FL: University Presses of Florida, 1977.

13. Center for the American Woman and Politics (CAWP) (1992). "Fact Sheet: Women in Elective Office 1992." New Brunswick, NJ: CAWP, Eagleton Institute of Politics, Rutgers University.

14. For a review of this literature, see MacManus and Bullock, "Electing Women to Local Office."

15. Susan A. MacManus. "Politics, Partisanship, and Board Elections," in Donald C. Menzel, ed., *The American County,* 1993, pps. 53–79.

16. Robert Darcy, Susan Welch, and Janet Clark (1987). *Women, Elections, and Representation.* New York: Longman.

17. Marilyn Johnson and Susan Carroll (1978). "Statistical Report: Profile of Women Holding Offices, 1977," in Center for the American Woman and Politics, *Women in Public Office,* 2nd ed. Metuchen, NJ: The Scarecrow Press, 1A–65A.

18. Charles S. Bullock, III. "Women Candidates and Success at the County Level." Paper presented at the Annual Meeting of the Southern Political Science Association, Atlanta, GA, November 8–10, 1990.

19. Carol Chmelynski. "In Some Communities, Fewer People Are Willing to Run for the School Board," National School Boards Association, August 12, 2003. www.nsba.org/site/doc_sbn.asp?TRACKID=&VID=58&CID=199&DID=31684, accessed April 24, 2004.

20. Roger D. Rada. "A Public Choice Theory of School Board Member Behavior," *Educational Evaluation and Policy Analysis,* 10 (Fall), 1988: 225–236.

21. Susan A. MacManus and Rayme Suarez. "Female Representation on School Boards: Supportive Constituency Characteristics," *The Political Chronicle* 4 (Fall/Winter), 1992: 1–8.

22. Trudy Haffrom Bers. "Local Political Elites: Men and Women on Boards of Education," *Western Political Quarterly* 31 (September), 1978: 381–391.

23. Unfortunately, the study does not distinguish between elective and appointive positions.

24. MacManus and Bullock, "Electing Women to Local Office;" Kathleen Vail. "The Changing Face of Education," *Education Vital Signs,* December 2001: www.asbj.com/evs/ol/people.html, accessed April 26, 2004.

25. Vail, "The Changing Face of Education."

26. Vail, "The Changing Face of Education."

27. The percent change in Georgia's population from 1980–1990 was 18.6%; ffrom 1990–1995, 11.2%. For Florida, the percent change from 1980–1990 was 32.7%; 9.5% from 1990–95. Source: *Statistical Abstract of the United States 1996,* p. 29.

28. Susan A. MacManus. "Demographic Shifts: The Old South Morphs into the New," paper presented at The Citadel Symposium on Southern Politics, Charleston, SC, March 4–5, 2004.

29. Georgia is the only state to have a sole commissioner local government and the number of counties using this format is declining although the U.S. Supreme Court upheld this system in the face of a challenge brought under Section 2 of the Voting Rights Act (*Holder v. Hall,* 512 U.S. 874 (1994)).

30. The sheriff is the chief law enforcement officer and executive officer of the courts. The sheriff is responsible for: the execution of all process, writs, warrants, and other papers issued by the state and county courts; maintaining law and order; apprehending violators of the law; and operating the county jail.

31. The clerk is responsible for all circuit and county court records. Other duties include: serving as ex officio Clerk of the Board of County Commissioners, auditor, recorder, custodian of all county funds, recording documents such as deed, mortgages, and satisfaction of liens; disbursing of court-ordered alimony and child support payments; and issuing of marriage licenses.

32. The Supervisor administers all elections, conducts voter registration, issues voter identification cards, updates voter registration lists, and handles absentee registration and voting. The supervisor is also responsible for qualifying candidates for local offices, receiving candidate campaign finance reports, maintaining election equipment, hiring and training poll workers, and keeping registration and election statistics.

33. The collector bills, collects, and disburses the annual property taxes levied by all governments in the county. The office also collects other types of taxes and issues various types of licenses.

34. The appraiser is responsible for identifying, locating, and fairly valuing real and tangible personal property within the county for ad valorem tax purposes.

35. Some counties used to elect their school superintendent. In 1992, legislation was passed making all school district superintendents appointive posts.

36. In 2004, four female superintendents were elected and three appointed.

37. Center for the American Woman and Politics, "Fact Sheet." 1997 New Brunswick, NJ: author.

38. Joan Carver. "Women in Florida," *Journal of Politics* 41 (August), 1979: 941–955.

39. Tom Berlinger, Director of Operational Services, Florida Sheriffs Association, faxed document sent January 27, 1998.

40. *Statistical Abstract of the United States 2003,* p. 28.

FURTHER READING

Carroll, Susan J. *Women as Candidates in American Politics,* 2nd ed. Bloomington, IN: Indiana University Press, 1994.

Carroll, Susan J., ed. *Women and American Politics: New Questions, New Directions.* Oxford: Oxford University Press, 2003.

Darcy, R., Susan Welch, and Janet Clark. *Women, Elections & Representation,* 2nd ed. Lincoln: University of Nebraska Press, 1994.

Faucheux, Ronald A. *Running for Office: The Strategies, Techniques and Messages Modern Political Candidates Need to Win Elections.* New York: M. Evans & Co., 2002.

Gruber, Susan. *How to Win Your First Election,* 2nd ed. Boca Raton, FL: St. Lucie Press, 1997.

Guzzetta, S. J. *The Campaign Manual: Definitive Study of the Modern Political Campaign Process,* 6th ed. Flat Rock, NC: AmeriCan GOTV Enterprises & Political Publications, 2002.

Seltzer, Richard A., Jody Newman, and Melissa Voorhees Leighton. *Sex as a Political Variable: Women as Candidates and Voters in U.S. Elections.* Boulder, CO: Lynne Rienner Publishers, 1997.

Strachan, J. Cherie. *High-Tech Grass Roots: The Professionalization of Local Elections.* Boulder, CO: Rowman & Littlefield Publishers, Inc., 2003.

Thomas, Sue and Clyde Wilcox. *Women and Elective Office: Past, Present, and Future.* Oxford: Oxford University Press, 1998.

Witt, Linda, Karen M. Paget, and Glenna Matthew, *Running as a Woman: Gender and Power in American Politics.* New York: Macmillan, 1994.

On the Eve of Transition: Women in Southern Legislatures, 1946–1968

Joanne V. Hawks, deceased
Carolyn Ellis Staton

This study focuses on women who served in southern legislatures in the period following World War II, beginning with the election of 1946 and culminating in 1968. During this period—especially in the earlier years—middle-class women received many signals that their proper sphere encompassed home, family, and related activities. The willingness of women to enter the legislature against society's traditional expectations of them may have been a mild form of rebellion, but it was nonetheless real. To some extent the women serving between 1946 and 1968 were transitional figures, standing between an earlier group of legislative women whose mere presence made them important and a later group of more activist women. They set the stage for the political women of the 1970s and 1980s, the activist women who benefited directly or indirectly from the women's movement.

The postwar legislators followed a group of trailblazers, women who had emerged from the suffrage movement with new rights and imperatives. These earlier women had begun moving into southern legislatures in a slow but steady stream in the decade of the 1920s.[1] Most were short-term legislators; few served more than one or two terms. For the most part, they could be characterized as southern progressives, people who wanted to use state government as a means of ameliorating conditions in their communities.[2] Many of them were especially concerned with the needs of women, children, and persons with mental, physical, and moral handicaps. Even though much of their proposed legislation did not pass, they brought certain needs

Part of the research for this paper was supported by a Basic Research Grant from the National Endowment for the Humanities.

into focus as matters of public concern. Just as importantly, they established the right and ability of women to serve competently as state legislators.

In the Great Depression and World War II years, a slightly larger group of women were elected. By 1936 all eleven of the former Confederate states had female as well as male legislators.

After a period of wartime involvement in paid employment or volunteer services, many women in the late 1940s and early 1950s supposedly retreated into a more traditional lifestyle.[3] According to many historical and sociological treatises, the post–World War II era was a quiescent time for U.S. women, especially middle-class white women. Andrew Sinclair has called the postwar attitude New Victorianism because of its emphasis on sharp distinctions between male and female roles and proper behavior by women.[4] The prescription for the times called upon women to immerse themselves in private concerns surrounding their families and homes and to surrender activity in the public realm to the returning veterans.

In light of these generally observed patterns, it is interesting to consider the movement of women into southern legislatures in the years following the war. In a region of the nation considered to be particularly traditional, where proper sex roles had been carefully defined and political participation had long been regarded as a white male preserve, women began entering southern legislatures in increasing numbers. Although the incidence varied from a low of one person in Alabama to a high of nineteen in the neighboring state of Mississippi, a total of ninety-three women were seated in the legislatures of the eleven former Confederate states between 1946 and 1968.

HOW WOMEN ENTERED THE LEGISLATURE

One means by which women entered legislatures was what has been termed "the widow's route," a method whereby a wife succeeded to a seat formerly held by her deceased husband. During this period, twenty-four women from the eleven states in this study entered via succession. Twenty-one were widows elected or appointed to complete their husbands' legislative terms. Two were wives who ran when their husbands resigned before their terms were completed. One, Maud Isaacks, was a daughter who succeeded her father. Most were elected to office, although a few were appointed. Of the entire group of successors, only Maud Isaacks of Texas served for an extended period of time.[5] Most finished the husband's unexpired term and then retired from office. A few ran for reelection, but most of those who were reelected served only one additional term before retiring or being defeated. Their positions seemed to be regarded by many voters as a gesture of courtesy. For instance, when Governor Earl Long of Louisiana appointed Mrs. E. D. Gleason to complete her husband's term, he expressed doubt about his authority to make the appointment, but he assured his audience that she was a nice lady and had promised not to run again.[6]

Thus, approximately 25.5 percent of the total group of women serving between 1946 and 1968 were "fill-ins" for seats that were deemed to "belong" to their predecessors. But what of the remaining 74.5 percent? Who were they, and what motivated them to seek office?

Data indicated that they were predominantly women who were already involved in the public sphere in one way or another, as professional or business women, local officeholders, political party workers, or active members of women's organizations. Fifty-four had a profession or business in which they were contemporaneously engaged or which they had previously practiced. By far the largest single group—twenty women—were teachers. Nine women were attorneys. Ten were owners or co-owners of businesses. Two were farmers, two journalists, two physicians, and two government workers. The remainder held various other positions in the business world.

At least six women had held local political office before running for the legislature, most of them as city or county council members. Even more had served on local and state executive committees of their party, worked with the women's division, or helped in the campaigns of others before seeking office themselves. Of the nine Republican women elected during this period, most had been heavily involved in Republican party politics and were committed to strengthening two-party politics in their states. Several of the women were from political families.

In addition to these two groups—professional and business women and those with political activity of one kind or another—most of the other women were involved significantly in one or more women's organizations. At least two women became interested in politics as a result of their participation in Parent–Teacher Associations (PTAs). Other women were involved in Federated Women's Clubs, Business and Professional Women, the League of Women Voters, the American Association of University Women, the Farm Bureau (or related Home Demonstration groups), garden clubs, and other groups. Through these organizations they became aware of issues and gained a sense of how to accomplish things through their club work. In many cases, their legislative interests mirrored the concerns of the organized groups in which they had worked or held leadership positions. Maxine Baker of Florida (1963–1973) said. "I wanted to serve in the Legislature to try to accomplish some of the things I had been working for during my years as member and President of the Florida League of Women Voters. . . ."[7] Others, like Carolyn Frederick of South Carolina (1964–1976), a member of the American Association of University Women, had lobbied legislators in behalf of interests supported by their organizations, only to find that legislators tended to be longer on promises than on favorable action. Kathryn Stone of Virginia (1954–1966), a national vice president of the League of Women voters, admonished women to join service and civic organizations to learn skills and to move on to the political arena from there.[8] She believed that women should not confine themselves to any one civic group but should become involved in party politics.[9]

Stone's comments were closely echoed by Grace Hamilton of Georgia:

If you are concerned about working in the legislative branch of government, you had better get some experience in working other than in the legislature on the matters that concern you. . . . If you look at people who have been effective legislators, they usually have been effective in something that was non-political, related to issues before them. I personally think that the League of Women Voters is a good training, very good training to have, but I think sometimes you need to graduate from the League.[10]

Some of the women worked primarily with one particular organization; many were active in several and held membership in many more. At least eighteen women appeared to be heavily involved in club work. A few of these could also be grouped with one or both of the categories previously discussed. In fact, women who had several connections with the public sphere seemed to be especially likely at some point to consider public office.

LEGISLATIVE ISSUES

A survey of the issues in which the female legislators expressed interest leads to rather predictable findings. Many issues came readily to their attention as mothers and community volunteers. Education was a key interest, with many in favor of strengthening the public schools, providing child care and kindergartens, and raising teachers' pay. Other concerns included health, mental health, aid to the handicapped, problems of children and youth, care of the aged, alcohol and drug abuse, consumer and environmental protection, and election reform. Rural legislators often focused on agricultural problems while those elected from urban districts concentrated their efforts on urban problems, including the need for adequate representation in the legislature and better services in their areas.

A few of the women expressed concern for the so-called women's issues of the day. Jury service for women appeared to be the most generally supported proposal. A federal equal rights amendment was a more problematic issue. The few who were outspoken supporters of equal rights for women were balanced by a similar number who opposed the concept. Many women preferred to equivocate or to avoid the issue altogether.

Middle-class, mature women, long trained to be conciliatory persons—peacemakers—often seemed reluctant to take on highly controversial issues. In a period when civil rights, women's rights, youth protest, and antiwar and antiestablishment issues were eroding society's postwar complacency, most of the southern legislative women avoided identification with any of these divisive movements. They concentrated instead on gradual elimination of community problems and provision of government services to segments of the society who had unmet needs.

Civil Rights Issues

Of all the contemporary issues, the civil rights issue struck nearest to home. Clearly, the easiest way to deal with the problems of the day was to ignore them, and it is amazing how many of the legislators during this period managed to do just that. But for others the issues had to be confronted, and women, like their male counterparts, lined up on both sides of the civil rights question.

In Virginia, in particular, women could not avoid the issue. In the aftermath of the United States Supreme Court's decision in *Brown v. Board of Education,* Virginia almost immediately sought to forestall school integration by a number of measures, some as extreme as closing whole school systems. One is struck by the courage of the moderates and liberals during this time in Virginia politics. Most of the women legislators favored compliance with the law and opposed massive resistance. The usually ultrachivalrous male-dominated assembly proved that it had its raw side: it could behave rudely toward them when they tried to keep the Virginia schools open.[11]

Although most of the Virginia women delegates supported compliance, such was not the case everywhere. In Mississippi, for instance, just the opposite situation prevailed. The segregation establishment reigned supreme. As Jack Bass and Walter DeVries have stated,

> These were not ordinary times. The executive director of the Citizens Council . . . had begun preparing [Governor] Barnett's speeches. Citizens Council members were named to the State Sovereignty Commission, the official state segregation committee and a propaganda arm of the Citizens Council. . . . The Citizens Council claimed 80,000 members in the state. . . .[12]

The female legislators seemed to oppose attempts to integrate the schools as stridently as most of the male delegates. At least two women were part of the segregation establishment, the White Citizens Council and the State Sovereignty Commission. Occasionally, a legislator who proclaimed that she was a segregationist would, however, champion the rights of others. A notable example occurred in Mississippi when Senator Orene Farese argued vehemently against passage of a bill that would have eliminated the property tax exemption for churches that used their facilities on an integrated basis.[13]

Because of these stands, Farese felt compelled in her next senatorial campaign to proclaim staunchly her segregationist views. In her campaign literature she maintained that her purpose in opposing the removal of tax exemptions for integrated churches was to keep segregation intact and preserve tax exemptions for churches.[14] Perhaps, like many other politicians of the day, Farese maintained a certain façade of segregation that did not always conform to other ideas that she held.

By 1967, the civil rights movement had begun to have a significant impact on portions of the South, legislative resistance notwithstanding. Because of the movement and *Baker v. Carr,* the United States Supreme Court decision that mandated "one man, one vote," legislative redistricting was required. One result of redistricting was to increase voting strength in urban areas—places where there might be a large population of Blacks. It is not surprising, then, that in 1967 three Black women in the South entered their state legislatures: Barbara Jordan of Texas, Dorothy Brown of Tennessee, and Grace Hamilton of Georgia. The civil rights movement, by changing both the social climate and the laws, gave them opportunities for political office that they had previously lacked.

PRESS IMAGES

The times were changing, but the public's image of women in politics was not changing at the same pace. This was best indicated by contemporary press coverage, which emphasized femininity. The renewed emphasis on femininity may have been a result of a convert campaign to force women out of the traditionally male jobs that many had held during the war years. It may also have been an effort to glamorize the homemaker so that she, as consumer, might aid in the improving economy. Moreover, as the country recovered from the difficult war period, some people longed to return to a less confused, less complicated world.

In the postwar period, press treatment of female legislators primarily covered personal rather than political aspects of their lives. Articles on these women tended to focus on specific female roles. A prevalent form of feature article was the portrait of the lady legislator as family member, either wife, mother, homemaker, or grandmother. Orene Farese, who served along with her husband in the Mississippi legislature during the 1950s, was consistently spotlighted in her domestic roles. The following excerpt from a feature story about her is characteristic of the coverage she received:

> Mrs. Farese, though public minded, is a very domestic and home loving person. . . .
>   She is a capable housekeeper and a wonderful homemaker. With the help of a full time maid she cares for their four bedroom, two bathroom home. . . .[15]

Farese discussed her cooking, sewing, and home decorating abilities.[16] The article proceeded to describe her to the readers:

> When you see this lovely senator-elect . . . she will most likely be wearing a stunning tailored dress or suit in one of her favorite colors, the blues, aqua or yellow in medium tone.[17]

The newspaper account contained virtually no mention of Farese's legislative and political interests. She was treated primarily as a housewife who went to the legislature.

A somewhat more muted example of the lady legislator as homemaker occurred with Grace Rodenbough of North Carolina. Although Rodenbough, who served in the legislature from 1953 to 1966, was a woman of considerable stature, the press on several different occasions focused on her fondness for her antebellum home.[18] Rodenbough might play a significant role in the legislature, but she was still seen as the southern aristocratic lady.

Rodenbough's fellow North Carolinian, Mary Faye Brumby, was subjected to similar treatment. When Brumby went to the legislature, she took her eleven-year-old son along. Her child care arrangements were highlighted in the press.[19] By taking her son with her to the capital rather than leaving him at home, she avoided being seen as the abandoning mother who pursued her own interests.

Although some accounts were brief in their mention of the legislators' children, comment was usually made. For instance, Iris Blitch of Georgia, who later went to Congress, was simply described as devoted to her children.[20]

The epitome of the legislator-as-wife stories involves Lillian Neblett Scott of Tennessee. Scott, always referred to as Mrs. Scott, was being routinely interviewed by a reporter from the Nashville *Banner* when her husband entered the room. The spotlight of the article immediately became *Mr.* Scott and his stories of marital harmony: "Somebody asked me how I made out with Lillian so active in politics, I just tole 'em that I still have my hot biscuits 365 days a year."[21] Scott continued his antics: "As the couple exchanged a look of deep affection and long understanding, 'I've never had to spank her.' "[22] Throughout the article, Lillian Scott is seen not as the incredibly active woman she was, but as a wife who knew her place. As is true of all of these features, there is an implicit statement that these women legislators were all right because, first and foremost, their principal roles were as wives and mothers.

Domesticity, Femininity, and Beauty

When they were viewed primarily as domestic creatures, female legislators lost their "strangeness." The same principle applied if the emphasis was on their femininity rather than their domesticity. Moreover, by their being pigeonholed as either a domestic or a feminine type, these women, working in a nontraditional forum, threatened no one. For example, articles such as the following 1954 feature in the *Jackson Daily News* made the idea of female legislators more palatable to the public:

> The universal feminine preoccupation with weddings, babies, and bringing up children reaches strongly into the Mississippi legislature. . . .
> Far from being a sentimental interest, confined to cooing over the newlywedded or recently born, theirs is an informed concern aimed at changes in the laws. . . .[23]

The article went on to provide an apologia for these women:

> . . . it is, perhaps, to the state's advantage to number among its lawmakers those whose beliefs are conditioned by the previous primary experience of wife, mother, and frequently teacher.[24]

Since the days of Scarlett O'Hara, femininity and gracious beauty have been part of the mystique of southern womanhood. The beauty queen has been a consistent southern type, one with which southern society felt comfortable. In many instances, by emphasizing pulchritude, southern society was able to accept women on its own terms, and by doing so, could avoid accepting them as serious legislators. Ruth Williams of South Carolina was linked with "the rustle of silk and the faint scent of perfume" and managed "somehow, to cling to her femininity and still compete with men. . . ."[25]

Mary Shadow of Tennessee, like Williams, was young and single when she entered the legislature. Shadow, however, married during her legislative stint. News of the marriage was widely featured. Shadow, a college teacher, was quoted as saying that in her forthcoming marriage she wanted to cook, keep house, and raise a large family. One article was captioned "Miss Shadow Plans to Keep House, Raise Family."[26] Upon Shadow's marriage it was assumed that she would become a traditional housewife.

Because of the emphasis on femininity, there was a never-ending discussion of physical appearance. To some extent this focus suggested to the public that, after all, these female legislators were more female than legislator. Blitch was often described as "an attractive brunette"[27] with "a perfect size 12 figure."[28] Shadow was described as a "pretty, charming legislator,"[29] and Betty Jane Long of Mississippi was depicted as "lovely."[30] Mississippi's Mary Lou Godbold and Orene Farese "add[ed] much to the lustre of [the legislature]. And the men [were] all in favor of the ladies."[31]

Kathryn Stone of Virginia, in particular, was the topic of much publicity about her physical appearance. The press found it noteworthy that one Virginia senator said to another upon seeing Stone presiding in the senate," 'Have you ever seen a lovelier creature presiding from the chair of the president of the Senate?' whereupon the other senator then responded. 'I yield to the lovely creature. . . .'"[32] On another occasion, the press claimed that "Mrs. Stone . . . is the prettiest thing to hit the General Assembly since Sarong Siren Dorothy Lamour dropped in at the Capitol one day a few years ago. Besides looks . . . she has brains."[33] Another feature described her clothing and home decor.[34] No matter how significant these women were as legislators and politicians, their colleagues and the press trivialized them in many instances by focusing on irrelevant considerations.

As if to stereotype them even further, the press played up the emotional nature of these women. Blitch is depicted as on the verge of tears when an adverse amendment was added to her original bill.[35] When Orene Farese opposed taxing churches that did not practice segregation, she was choked with tearful emotion.[36] Although the situation may have warranted tears, no comment is made in the coverage of the heated senate debate about the emotions of her male colleagues.

How Women Legislators Were Treated

During this period when there was an emphasis on the female attributes of the women politicians, several of them were singled out for what was then considered a chivalrous tribute. When only one woman served in a legislative body, she might be entitled sweetheart of the senate or house or some honorific variation. Blitch was named queen of the Georgia General Assembly.[37] Collins was elected sweetheart of the Alabama house,[38] and Berta Lee White of Mississippi was designated sweetheart of the senate.[39] In Collins's case, this meant that the house members might on occasion be addressed as "Mister Speaker, gentlemen of the House and sweetheart of the House."[40] In some instances the chivalry was rather overdone. For example, in making seat assignments at the beginning of the session, the speaker of the Georgia house announced that "the Lady of the House [Blitch] and the physically handicapped will get their first choice of seats."[41] Sometimes the chivalry became quite time-consuming. When the speaker of the Virginia house instructed Kathryn Stone, the sole female legislator, to make a communiqué to the senate, Stone was accompanied by the entire Virginia house delegation to the senate chambers. The newspaper described the event as a "chivalry safari."[42]

When the female legislators occasionally acted out of character from the role in which the public had cast them, it was definitely noted. Thus, when the women were perceived as politicians rather than as ladies, they were likened to males. For instance, the newspaper remarked that "Mrs. Blitch had to fight like a man."[43] Perhaps it was her ability to fight like a man that won Blitch the sobriquet "the wench from Clinch."[44] In Mississippi when three women were elected to the legislature in the same term, it was noted that they could fare well against strong male opposition.[45] The tenacity of Clara Collins was editorialized as "stubbornness, albeit justified."[46] It was with Martha Evans of North Carolina that the press had a field day. Practically every story about Evans mentioned that she was a redhead with a temper to match. For instance, in one article she was referred to as "a red-headed pepper-pot."[47] Evans, who was held in a certain amount of esteem for her work, was excused by the press from stepping out of the traditional role of southern womanhood:

> In Raleigh she'll stand on her own small feet. . . . That's because she's always felt she is the equal of the male politician. And she's "been around," as the saying goes among office seekers.[48]

The women were newsworthy. When they conformed to the stereotyped version of southern womanhood, they were viewed as nonthreatening. When they did not conform to the standard image, the media nevertheless tried to force them into that mold. When they were not susceptible to being molded, they were excused, as was Evans, on the basis of being an "outsider." They were less novel than the women who preceded them in the earlier decades, but the public was still not quite comfortable with them and still regarded them as curiosities.

SUMMARY

Female legislators of the post–World War II era tried to live up to societal expectations of them as women while they practiced their political skills. For some, the substance of lawmaking was secondary to their role as lady legislator. For most, the legislature was not a stepping stone to greater political heights but it was a forum for public service. By their service these women set the stage for the more activist, more ambitious, and more political women who succeeded them.

NOTES

1. Anne Firor Scott, *The Southern Lady: From Pedestal to Politics, 1830–1930* (Chicago: University of Chicago Press, 1970), pp. 186–211.

2. Dewey W. Grantham, *Southern Progressivism: The Reconciliation of Progress and Tradition* (Knoxville: University of Tennessee Press, 1983), pp. 410–422.

3. William H. Chafe, *The American Woman, Her Changing Social, Economic, and Political Roles, 1920–1970* (New York: Oxford University Press, 1972), pp. 176–178, 199–212. Chafe's bibliography includes many other treatises on the subject.

4. Andrew Sinclair. *The Emancipation of the American Woman* (New York: Harper & Row, 1965), pp. 354–367.

5. Mary Beth Rogers (Ed.), *Texas Women: A Celebration of History* (Austin: Texas Foundation for Women's Resources, 1981), p. 100.

6. Baton Rouge *State-Times,* August 5, 1959, Sec. A, p. 11.

7. Questionnaire completed by Maxine Baker, January 21, 1986, in possession of the authors.

8. Richmond *Times-Dispatch,* March 23, 1954.

9. *Ibid.*

10. Taped interview with Grace Hamilton, conducted by the authors, August 8, 1984, in possession of the authors.

11. See, e.g., Richmond *Times-Dispatch,* February 23, 1958.

12. Jack Bass and Walter DeVries, *The Transformation of Southern Politics: Social Change and Political Consequence since 1945* (New York: Basic Books, 1976), p. 196.

13. Unnamed, undated clipping in possession of the authors.

14. *The Southern Advocate,* July 23, 1959.

15. *Jackson Advertiser—TV News,* September 15, 1955, p. 6.

16. *Ibid.*

17. *Ibid.*

18. *The News and the Observer* (Raleigh), January 17, 1963, p. 8.

19. Unnamed clipping, February 14, 1965.

20. *Atlanta Constitution,* October 6, 1949, p. 26.

21. Nashville *Banner,* January 10, 1957, p. 8.

22. *Ibid.*

23. *Jackson Daily News,* January 24, 1954.

24. *Ibid.*

25. *The State* (Columbia), November 6, 1964, Sec. A, p. 1.

26. *The Nashville Tennessean,* November 19, 1950, Society Section, p. 1.

27. *Atlanta Constitution,* October 6, 1949, p. 27.

28. *Ibid.,* October 24, 1954.

29. *The Nashville Tennessean,* January 7, 1948, p. 8.

30. *Jackson Daily News,* August 29, 1955, p. 2.

31. Unnamed clipping, January 12, 1958.

32. Richmond *Times-Dispatch,* March 15, 1954, p. 4.

33. *Ibid.* January 13, 1954, p. 16.

34. *Ibid.,* November 11, 1953.

35. *Atlanta Constitution,* January 27, 1953, p. 1.

36. Jackson *Clarion-Ledger,* March 27, 1956, p. 1.

37. *Atlanta Constitution,* October 6, 1949, p. 26.

38. *Advertiser-Journal* (Montgomery), Alabama Sunday Magazine, August 16, 1965, p. 12.

39. Questionnaire completed by Berta Lee White, in possession of the authors.

40. *Advertiser-Journal* (Montgomery), Alabama Sunday Magazine, August 15, 1965, p. 12.

41. *Atlanta Constitution,* January 11, 1949, p. 1.

42. Richmond *News Leader,* March 9, 1954.

43. *Atlanta Constitution,* October 24, 1954.

44. *Ibid.,* December 28, 1970.

45. *Jackson Daily News,* August 29, 1955, p. 2.

46. *Montgomery Advertiser,* August 13, 1967.

47. *Durham Morning Herald,* November 18, 1962, Sec. C, p. 9.

48. *Ibid.*

FURTHER READING

Baxter, Sandra, and Marjorie Lansing. *Women and Politics.* Rev. ed. Ann Arbor: University of Michigan Press, 1983.

Carroll, Susan J. *Women as Candidates in American Politics.* Bloomington: Indiana University Press, 1985.

Chafe, William H. *Paradox of Change: American Women in the Twentieth Century.* New York: Oxford University Press, 1991.

Diamond, Irene. *Sex Roles in the State House.* New Haven, CT: Yale University Press, 1977.

Dodson, Debra L., and Susan J. Carroll. *Reshaping the Agenda: Women in State Legislatures.* New Brunswick, NJ: Eagleton Institute of Politics, Rutgers, State University of New Jersey, 1991.

Fowlkes, Diane. *White Political Women: Paths from Privilege to Empowerment.* Knoxville: University of Tennessee Press, 1992.

Githens, Marianne, and Jewel L. Prestage (Eds.). *A Portrait of Marginality: The Political Behavior of the American Woman.* New York: David McKay, 1977.

Jewel, Malcolm Edwin, and Marcia Lynn Whicker, "The Feminization of Leadership in State Legislatures." *Quarterly of American Political Science Association,* 26 (4) (December 1993), pp. 705–712.

Johnson, Louise B. *Women of the Louisiana Legislature.* Farmerville, LA: Greenbay Publishing, 1986.

Jones, Leslie Ellen. "The Relationship between Home Styles and Legislative Styles and Its Implication for Representation: A Comparison of Women and Men in a Southern State Legislature." Ph.D. diss., Georgia State University, 1990.

Kirkpatrick, Jeane J. *Political Woman.* New York: Basic Books, 1974.

Klein, Ethel. *Gender Politics.* Cambridge, MA: Harvard University Press, 1984.

Mandel, Ruth B. *In the Running: The New Woman Candidate.* Boston: Beacon Press, 1981.

Nelson, Albert J. *Emerging Influentials in State Legislatures: Women, Blacks, and Hispanics.* New York: Praeger, 1991.

Thomas, Sue. *How Women Legislate.* New York: Oxford University Press, 1994.

Women Campaign Consultants: A New Actor in the Campaign Process

Sarah E. Brewer

In his groundbreaking work, *The Rise of Political Consultants: New Ways of Winning Elections,* Larry Sabato defined a political consultant as "a campaign professional who is engaged primarily in the provision of advice and services (such as polling, media creation and production, and direct mail fund-raising) to candidates, their campaigns, and other political committees."[1] Early research provided descriptive accounts of this emerging actor in the campaign process.[2]

Recent research has examined consultants' attitudes on a variety of campaign factors including the role of the political parties, consultants, and the news media in elections, and the quality of candidates over time.[3] And another new line of research empirically analyzes the effects of campaign consultants on a candidate's fund-raising efforts and electoral success.[4] The higher the level of professionalization, measured by the number of consultants on a campaign, the greater the candidates total dollars raise and votes garnered on Election Day.[5]

This recent work compares the differences **between** consultants' attitudes and abilities on a variety of dimensions—party affiliation, area specialty, years of experience, effectiveness, and level of notoriety. What is not explored by these scholars is the differences between men and women consultants. The research to date has failed to address adequately the impact of the gender composition of the industry on its findings. Sabato's classic study of campaign consultants relied on forty-nine interviews; three of his subjects were women. More recently, only 18 percent of the consultants surveyed by Thurber and his colleagues were women.[6] As a result, claims made by these scholars and conclusions drawn about political consultants' attitudes and behaviors may be biased systematically toward the experiences and beliefs of the males in these studies. Feminist critiques of political science research have demonstrated that conclusions based on the experience of the male majority are not necessarily accurate for women in politics.[7]

Political scientists have examined the differences between men and women and the political consequences of women's unequal representation in other political vocations including: (1) legislators; (2) party leaders; (3) lobbyists; and (4) congressional staffers. First, research has found fewer numbers of women than men engaging in several forms of elite political participation. Fewer women are legislators,[8] political party leaders,[9] lobbyists working at the state and federal level,[10] and congressional staffers.[11]

And more importantly, this research has found that women political actors differ in significant ways from their male counterparts in these different political vocations.[12] For example, women legislators vote differently on issues with women voting generally more liberally than men and men and women legislators also have different priorities and issue agendas. Studies have found that with the increase of women in office, issues such as women's health, childcare, and family planning have received more legislative attention.[13]

Studies also have found that while women and men lobbyists generally engaged in similar lobbying techniques to further their organizations' interests, testified at hearings, drafted legislation, and built coalitions to advance their agendas, women were far less likely to do personal favors for public officials than their male counterparts. And similar to gender differences between men and women lobbyists, research has found that women congressional staffers are less likely to do favors for friends or local government or party officials than their male counterparts.[14] These differences between men and women working in different political vocations implicitly suggests that increasing the number of women working in these professions could significantly change the character and nature of those professions. More women legislators could produce different policy output and more women lobbyists and staffers could change the way those professions conduct government business.

The research above suggests that there could be similarities between women consultants and women legislators, lobbyists and staffers. This reading presents findings from a larger study on gender and the campaign industry and focuses on three questions asked in interviews with 40 men and women D.C.-based consultants. To understand more about gender and the campaign consulting profession, the respondents were asked to explain the unique environment of women working in the consulting profession, if and how their work differs from their male counterparts, and why there are so few women political consultants.

ARE THERE DIFFERENT RULES OF THE GAME
FOR MEN AND WOMEN CONSULTANTS?

A majority of women consultants, 72 percent, believed that women consultants operated under a different set of game rules than their male counterparts, as shown in Table 1. In contrast, only 60 percent of men believed that there were different rules of the game for women. Interestingly, also shown in Table 1, the party breakdown of the men and women consultants showed that a greater proportion of Democratic women, 84.6 percent compared to 58.3 percent of Republican women believed there are different rules of the game for women than men consultants. In contrast, a similar proportion of Democratic men consultants, 57.1 percent, compared to 62.5 percent of Republican men consultants believed that women have to play by different rules. Thus, Democratic women consultants were more likely than any other group of consultants to believe that there are different rules of the game for women in the consulting business. This finding suggests that Democratic women are more likely to see the political environment as different for men and women than their Republican women counterparts.

Following up with consultants who believed that there were different rules of the game for women, respondents were asked to describe these rules. Ten consultants, seven women and three men, said that women had to work twice as hard as men consultants. One woman consultant noted, "I feel for one, you always have to be thoroughly prepared, more so than men—there is no such thing as winging it." A young man consultant noted, "Like other jobs, I think women have to work harder." Two other consultants noted that women consultants couldn't make the same mistakes that men make. One woman noted, "Women have to be smarter—more careful about making mistakes. They cannot do dumb things or say dumb stuff." Similarly, another woman consultant noted, "Men can get away with things a little more and still bounce back. We get one shot." These perceptions suggest that women consultants face a professional environment in which their skills and abilities are questioned and that they have to work harder than their male counterparts to demonstrate that ability. Working harder can establish a credibility that women are not immediately granted like their male counterparts.

TABLE 1   Gender and Partisan Differences of Whether There Are Different "Rules of the Game" for Women Political Consultants

Percent	Women	Men	Dems	Reps	Dem Women	Rep Women	Dem Men	Rep Men
YES	72.0 (18)	60.0 (9)	75.0 (15)	60.0 (12)	84.6 (11)	58.3 (7)	57.1 (4)	62.5 (5)
NO	28.0 (7)	40.0 (6)	25.0 (5)	40.0 (8)	15.4 (2)	41.7 (5)	42.9 (3)	37.5 (3)
TOTAL	100 (25)	100 (15)	100 (20)	100 (20)	100 (13)	100 (12)	100 (7)	100 (8)

Note: Figures in parentheses are cell Ns.

Six consultants, four women and two men, believed that women consultants were not taken seriously or seen as credible as their male counterparts. One young woman consultant commented, "Women may not get taken as seriously off the bat—it's hard for them (clients or potential clients) to think of me in a hard core strategic session." A man consultant echoed her statement saying, "I think that women have the burden of proof on being strategic. . . . I don't think that candidates envision their consultants as women." Another young woman consultant noted, "I think we have to be better—to be taken seriously. And the younger you are the more you have to come out of the box with a punch in the nose!"

Women officeholders have often faced questions of their credibility, particularly with economic and foreign policy issues.[15] In addition, recent reports on the status of women in the legal and the financial services sectors have noted that women in these sectors also experience questions about their credibility in their professions.[16] In the 2001 American Bar Association's Commission on Women in the Profession, the report notes, "Women do not receive the same presumption of competence as their male counterparts. In large national surveys, between half and three-quarters of female attorneys believe that they are held to higher standards than their male counterparts or have to work harder for the same results."[17] As a result, this demonstrates that the political consulting profession is not immune to the societal assumptions about women's professional credibility that spread across many vocational sectors.

In addition to questions regarding women's credibility and their need to work harder, respondents provided two additional rules for women consultants. Seven consultants, four men and three women, specifically mentioned different rules for men and women consultants regarding sex or perceptions of sexual relationships with either clients or other consultants. One male consultant noted, "One rule of the game that is different is a male candidate with a female consultant can't be seen traveling all over day and night—rumors would start." In addition, two women consultants who had male partners in their firms mentioned that often people would wonder about their relationship with these men, implying that they were sleeping with them for their jobs. One woman noted, "I can walk into a meeting with him (her male partner) and people get the wrong impression—they think we are just sleeping together." The role of sex or perceived sexual availability contributes to the way in which women's credibility is questioned and undermined in the profession.

Finally, four women consultants believed that women could not be as aggressive as men consultants. Women, who engaged in highly aggressive behavior come across as "bitchy," as noted by one young woman consultant, "I think men can be assholes easier than women can be. You are strong and tough as a woman and you are bitchy and annoying. There are a lot of women consultants that men hate—and they had to be a certain way to be heard." Another woman consultant noted more mildly, "Men just get away with more yelling." This finding is significant because of the characteristics of the professional environment. In a business that is characterized by competition and conflict, women's need to sensor themselves and their behavior for fear of being labeled a "bitch" works against their ability to assert themselves as tough, hard-nosed operatives. For the political consultant man, getting angry, aggressively arguing his perspective, and going after the opposition is looked at as a positive quality for the profession. Women, however, have to walk a fine line—not too angry, not too aggressive or argumentative, not too competitive. These social expectations on the differences in appropriate behaviors for women could work to women consultants' disadvantage in this industry.

Deviation from socially ascribed gender characteristics have been barriers to women running for office and women officeholders and women in other professional sectors. In Keys to the Governor's Office, the Barbara Lee Family Foundation presents data that noted, "Female candidates walk a tightrope in attempting to present a persona that's neither too strong and aggressive—too 'male'—nor too soft."[18] Similarly, in the ABA report mentioned above, the Commission concluded, "Female lawyers often face a double standard and a double bind. They risk appearing too 'soft' or too 'strident,' too aggressive or not aggressive enough."[19] In addition, a study on women in the financial sector found that 61.0 percent of the women interviewed believed that stereotyping and preconceptions of women's roles and abilities were barriers to women's advancement in the industry.[20]

As a result, a majority of consultants believed that women consultants face different rules of the game than their male counterparts. These rules included that they are questioned about their credibility and they have to work twice as hard to establish that credibility. Their credibility is undermined by assumption that they got their job by sleeping with their clients or their boss and they must tone down aggressive behaviors so as not to come across "too bitchy." All of these rules could be barriers for women who find this vocation attractive and also could weed out many women early on. If women consultants' levels of credibility are underestimated and clients do not believe that they can engage in strategic thinking, women consultants will get less business than their male counterparts. If women consultants' participation on campaigns is undermined with perceptions of their sexual availability to campaign actors, their credibility is undermined. Finally, if women cannot be aggressive and tough in a business that demands aggressive and tough people, they are immediately disadvantaged in the field.

DO WOMEN CONSULTANTS APPROACH AND EXECUTE THEIR WORK IN WAYS QUALITATIVELY DIFFERENT FROM MEN?

A majority, 57.5 percent, of consultants believed that women consultants approached and performed their work in a qualitatively different way than their male counterparts. As shown in Table 2, a greater proportion of women believed that women consultants had a different approach to their work than their male counterparts, 68 percent compared to 40 percent. In addition, as shown in Table 2, a higher proportion of Democratic, than Republican consultants, 65 percent compared to 50 percent, believed that women consultants were qualitatively different

TABLE 2   Gender and Partisan Distribution of Whether Women Consultants Approach and Execute their Work in a Qualitatively Different Way Than Their Male Counterparts

Percent	Women	Men	Dems	Reps	Dem Women	Rep Women	Dem Men	Rep Men
YES	68.0 (17)	40.0 (6)	65.0 (13)	50.0 (10)	76.9 (10)	58.3 (7)	42.9 (3)	37.5 (3)
NO	32.0 (8)	60.0 (9)	35.0 (7)	50.0 (10)	23.1 (3)	41.7 (5)	57.1 (4)	62.5 (5)
TOTAL	100 (25)	100 (15)	100 (20)	100 (20)	100 (13)	100 (12)	100 (7)	100 (8)

Note: Figures in parentheses are cell *N*s.

than their male counterparts. As was the case above between Democratic and Republican women, more Democratic women believed that women consultants approached and executed their work in a qualitatively different way than their male counterparts, 76.9 percent compared to 58.3 percent, respectively. And again, there was not as great of a difference between the men on this measure—42.9 percent of Democratic men compared to 37.5 percent of Republican men.

Consultants provided three broad qualitative differences between men and women consultants. First, six women consultants and four men consultants noted that women consultants bring a different perspective to the table that specifically could be used to reach women voters. One woman Democratic consultant noted, "I think that part of what has changed is the issues that women consultants bring to the table—to help the party understand women voters." One Republican woman consultant noted, "People say Kim Alfano won a race in Pennsylvania because she brought a woman's perspective to the table."

Second, two women consultants believed that more women would change overall campaign messages and suggested that more women could radically alter the campaign environment. A Republican woman consultant noted, "Campaign messages would be different, not just to reach out to women voters, but in general." She argued that women consultants are better at addressing the needs and interests of women voters, and an increase in the number of women consultants and their control over the strategy and message of the campaign could move women voters' interests to dominate the whole campaign agenda. Much like research findings that women legislators bring different priorities to the legislature, such as women's health, more women campaign consultants would not only result in different messages but could also bring different message *priorities* to the campaign. Different issue priorities radically would change the electoral process in the U.S., not by style, but by substance.

There were several consultants, five men and five women, who noted that while they did not believe women consultants would change the messages of a campaign, they had a different working style. A Democratic man consultant noted there could be differences "maybe in style, but I don't know about output." Another Democratic male consultant noted, "If it was 50-50 the way we do campaigns would be different. Women are easier than men to work with. It would not be night and day, however, but subtle. We would still do negatives and still work with the formula that works to win campaigns. The differences would be in the shades of gray."

Several consultants identified the stylistic differences between men and women consultants. Four women and two men noted that women consultants were more collaborative than their male counterparts. In addition, one woman and one man believed that women consultants were more detail oriented than men consultants. Carol Gilligan, in her groundbreaking study of the gender differences in psychological development of men and women, found that young girls were more "other-oriented" and were different from their male counterparts in that they were more collaborative and tried to build consensus in their decision-making. This is in contrast to men's hierarchical and competitive decision-making styles.[21] Building on Gilligan's model, subsequent research has found evidence of these gender differences in the leadership styles and decision making processes of other political actors, namely between men and women legislators.[22]

As it pertains to political consultants, if women are more collaborative, more women consultants in the profession could result in more inclusive campaigns and major campaign decisions would be decentralized to include more perspectives. If women consultants do their work differently, the changes that would result in the business by an increase in their numbers would be experienced internally, or by the people who work in campaigns. This is in contrast to changes that would be experienced externally in the messages received by the public, discussed above. More specifically, if women differ in style, more women would change the way campaigns are run and as a result only the individuals who work in campaigns would notice a change in the industry.

WHY ARE THERE SO FEW WOMEN POLITICAL CONSULTANTS?

The 40 consultants interviewed were asked at the end of the interview why they believed that there were so few women campaign consultants. Consultants came up with four general reasons for women's under-representation in the consulting industry: (1) family demands; (2) business climate; (3) sexist clients; and (4) early career decisions, as shown in Table 3.

Family Demands

The most frequently cited reason that there are so few women campaign consultants was family. Twelve consultants discussed the difficulty women have raising children and being campaign consultants. Ten of the twelve consultants that mentioned family as a barrier to women's increased numbers in the profession were women. As a result, women disproportionately provided family demands as the reason for their low numbers in the profession. As shown in Table 3, family rea-

TABLE 3   Gender and Partisan Distribution of Why There Are So Few Women Political Consultants

Percent	Women	Men	Dems	Reps	Dem Women	Rep Women	Dem Men	Rep Men
Family Demands	40.0 (10)	13.3 (2)	30.0 (6)	30.0 (6)	46.2 (6)	33.3 (4)	0.0 (0)	25.0 (2)
Competitive Business Climate	12.0 (3)	40.0 (6)	20.0 (4)	25.0 (5)	7.7 (1)	16.7 (2)	42.9 (3)	37.5 (3)
Risk-Taking Business Climate	20.0 (5)	13.3 (2)	20.0 (4)	15.0 (5)	15.4 (2)	25.0 (3)	28.6 (2)	0.0 (0)
Sexist Clients	12.0 (3)	13.3 (2)	15.0 (3)	10.0 (2)	15.4 (2)	8.3 (1)	14.3 (1)	12.5 (1)
Early Career Decisions	16.0 (4)	20.0 (3)	15.0 (3)	20.0 (4)	15.4 (2)	16.7 (2)	14.3 (1)	25.0 (2)
TOTAL	100 (25)	100 (15)	100 (20)	100 (20)	100 (13)	100 (12)	100 (7)	100 (8)

Note: Figures in parentheses are cell Ns.

sons represented 40 percent of women consultants' answers to this question. One young woman consultant noted, "I desperately want a family, to settle down and get married. I would feel comfortable doing a presidential and then calling it quits." A more seasoned woman consultant explained, "Young smart women want to get married and have a family life—and this is not a business where that is easy to do. You can go off and be a million different things." Another seasoned woman said, "There are quality of life issues—women still have children. You get in this business and the next thing you know we wake up and are 40 with no kids and not married."

A woman consultant noted, "Regardless of gender, if you are married and have kids, this job will eat you alive." Another young woman consultant said, "It is not much different than other high powered jobs. No women with kids. Anyone who decides to get married and have kids, you cannot be a consultant—the travel and the time. I don't think there is something more sexist about the consulting profession than other professions in this aspect." While the business can be hard on men and women with children, this research suggests that children and families disproportionately affect women consultants compared to their male counterparts.

Other women and politics scholars generally attribute women's late entry into politics as a result of their responsibility as the primary caretaker of their children. Congresswoman Nancy Pelosi (D-CA), for example, did not seek elective office until she was 47 and had raised her five children. Perhaps not surprisingly then, research has found that female legislators and political appointees were more likely to be unmarried and childless than their male counterparts.[23] A survey by *National*

Journal found that in the current Bush White House, 39 percent of the women were single as opposed to 10 percent of the men in upper level advisory positions.[24] An example from the current Bush White House of the problems women face balancing a career in politics and their families is political counselor Karen Hughes' decision to leave Washington D.C. and return to Texas to raise her 15-year-old son.

A recent comprehensive study about the interaction between the personal and political lives of men and women state legislators found that family concerns were significantly more important, and more hindering, to women politicians' careers than to the careers of their male counterparts. Thomas and Braunstein asked men and women state legislators for details about their private lives regarding their marriages and children. They found "women officeholders are much more likely than men in office to be primarily responsible for cleaning, cooking, shopping, dishes, and laundry. They have primary care of children and are more often than not, the ones to stay at home when the children are ill."[25] In addition, in their study, 73 percent of men had spouses who "do not or have not worked during at least some of their time in office" compared to 27 percent of women legislators. As a result, they conclude, "family status affects who runs for office, when, how they may perceive their role in office, the time commitments to public life, and the implications for how ideas about family participation affect the structure of public sphere careers."[26]

Business Climate

Two aspects of the campaign consulting industry's business climate were used to explain why there were so few women in the business—competition and risk-taking. Nine consultants, three women and six men, believed that the low number of women consultants in the business was a reflection of the fact that women were not attracted to the competitive and often combative environment of campaigns. The competitive nature of the campaign environment was the number one reason that men cited for women's low levels of participation in the business. One man noted, "My whole professional life has revolved around conflict—managing conflict, creating conflict, minimizing conflict, avoiding conflict. Maybe men are more likely to want to engage in conflict." One man consultant said, "For field operations, there is a Texas Rangers approach, to go into a room ripping off the arms and legs of the local people—I don't think people think women want to do that." Two men consultants compared the profession to sports. One noted, "It's a game in some respect, and we, men, are more motivated by the game. It is so ego driven and women may not be attracted to that climate." Another man consultant said, "This is a very competitive sport. It's a contact sport. How many girls do you know who like to play tackle football?" One woman echoed the assessments of her male colleagues and stated, "Maybe women just don't find the process of politics exciting, the competition." Another woman said, "Women may not like the hand to hand combat of campaigns."

Two additional aspects of the work climate were identified by respondents as reasons that there are so few women consultants—travel and financial security—and both were used as examples to argue that women, in general, are less likely to be risk-takers than men. This aversion to risk is why there are fewer women in the business. Four consultants, three women and one man mentioned the problem of financial security. These consultants noted the cyclical nature of the campaign business and believed that women in particular are attracted to jobs with a more stable income. One woman consultant believed that the aspect of the profession where a consultant leaves the party or the Hill to start their own business is very "scary" and she believed that women are not as encouraged to make those professional moves the same way that men are. Similar to concerns about financial security, three consultants, two women and one man, noted that they believed that women were more risk averse to the travel required in the profession than men. One consultant noted that she believed that women in general were not as likely to want to travel around the country working on campaigns as men. She believed that the travel demanded from the job was very disruptive on one's life and very isolating and believed that women, particularly young women, were turned-off by this quality of the profession. One woman noted that the travel part of the profession, particularly early in one's career, is risky, and women are not as big of risk-takers. She argued, "Moving away from friends and family is a huge risk—and it is harder for women because they are not encouraged by parents or society to do it. I think there are perceptions that it is more dangerous for women than men to be on the road." As a result, the consultants suggested that women were less likely to be risk-takers than men, both financially and personally, and in a career that has high risk, this is a reason why there are so few women in the business.

Sexist Clients

Five consultants noted that the sexist expectations of potential candidate-clients, most of whom are men, could also be a reason why there are so few women consultants in the profession. Three women and two men noted the impact of candidate perceptions on women consultants' careers. One woman noted, "All the consultants are men because the men are more comfortable working with men." Another women argued, "There are a lot of men in this business—candidates and others—and they all think that the strategy side of politics is a man's business." A man consultant explained, "I think a lot of members and candidates see women as staff. More candidates are men, and men are more comfortable with men consultants. Campaigns are wars and I think they probably want their top general to be a man to lead them into battle."

Early Career Decisions

Seven consultants, four women and three men, believed there were few women consultants due to early career decisions. Specifically the way in which early career moves either set up an individual for a future as a consultant or lead them down another vocational path. A senior Republican woman consultant noted, "It still comes down to the Hill offices—entry level jobs. Men are LAs (Legislative Assistants) and women are receptionists." She went on to tell a story of how when she was a Hill staffer she was going to take a job as a scheduler. Some of her male colleagues told her not to—specifically because that position is looked at as a "woman's job" and as a result it would be professionally limiting. She concluded, "Often women's strengths, particularly their attention to detail, are turned into their weakness."

The importance of campaign experience, however, was an explanation as to why there are so few women consultants offered by a number of respondents. A senior man consultant noted women's lack of campaign experience as well and said, "There are so few women at senior levels in campaigns. Campaign managers with campaign backgrounds are mostly men. Campaigns are a lot of grunt work— hauling boxes and hanging signs, and I don't think women like to do that." One man consultant reflected on his years at the DCCC (Democratic Congressional Campaign Committee) and commented that in terms of career paths he saw two things going on with young women and their careers in politics. First, he said, "I think they don't stick with it. The women choose other options, the Hill, etc." However, he argues, "there are clearly barriers, turning points of opportunity. Women don't get to manage big campaigns because they are underestimated."

This early career track division of labor, driven by women's lack of campaign experience and sex-role stereotyping for men and women in entry-level positions, is a major obstacle for women trying to gain the experience necessary to become political consultants. When young women are funneled into gender specific jobs at the political parties and in the consulting profession, they fail to get the professional experiences necessary to move into consulting jobs where they can significantly influence the campaign process.

CONCLUSION

This study has highlighted the unique working environment women face in the campaign consulting industry, the contributions they make to the profession by the ways in which their work differs from their male counterparts, and the reasons why there are so few women in the industry. The gender specific rules women face are upheld by continued assumptions about appropriate behaviors for men and women based on sex role stereotypes. Women are not seen as strategic and competitive, have to work twice as hard as their male colleagues to achieve their goals, and are punished for being too aggressive in an environment that demands this trait in its professionals. The research also suggests that women may differ from the men in the consulting business in ways that if they were to increase their numbers could alter the way in which the campaign industry not only conducts its work internally, but could change the nature of the campaigns. Future research should pay attention to these dynamics in other political professions. With a thorough understanding of the way in which men and women candidates and legislators behave, it is time to critically analyze the supporting political vocations and how the lack of parity of women in the top positions of paid government jobs significantly affect our political life and public discourse.

NOTES

1. Sabato, Larry. *The Rise of Political Consultants: New Ways of Winning Elections.* (New York: Basic Books, 1981), p. 8.

2. Baus, Herbert M. and William B. Ross. *Politics Battle Plan.* (New York: MacMillan Company, 1968); Leuthold, David A. *Electioneering in a Democracy.* (New York: John Wiley & Sons. 1968); Perry, James M. *The New Politics: The Expanding Technologies of Political Manipulation.* (London: Weidenfeld and Nicolson, 1968); Agranoff, Robert. *The New Style in Election Campaigns.* (Boston: Holbrook Press, Inc, 1972); Rosenbloom, David Lee. *The Election Men: Professional Campaign Managers and American Democracy.* (New York: Quadrangle Books; 1973); Heibert, Ray, Robert F. Jones, Johns d'Arc Lopenz, & Ernest A. Lotito. *The Political Image Merchants: Strategy for the 70s.* (Washington DC: Acropolis Books, Ltd, 1976); Nimmo, Dan. *The Political Persuaders: The Techniques of Modern Election Campaigns.* (Englewood Cliffs, NJ: Prentice Hall, 1976); Blumenthal, Sidney. *The Permanent Campaign: Inside the World of the Elite Political Operations.* (Boston: Beacon Press, 1980); Luntz, Frank L. *Candidates, Consultants and Campaigns.* (New York: Basil Blackwell, 1988); Petracca, Mark C. "Political Consultants and Democratic Governance." *PS: Political Science & Politics.* 22 (1) (1989). pp. 11–13; Sabato, Larry. "Political Influence, the News Media, and Campaign Consultants." *PS: Political Science & Politics.* 22 (1): (1989), pp. 14–15.

3. Thurber, Nelson and Dulio, "'Campaign Consultants: A Portrait of the Industry"; Dulio, *For Better or Worse?*

4. Herrnson, "Hired Guns and House Races"; Medvic, "Effectiveness of the Political Consultant as a Campaign Recourse"; "Professionalization in Congressional Elections"; *Political Consultants in US Congressional Elections.*

5. Herrnson, "Hired Guns and House Races"; Medvic, *Political Consultants in US Congressional Elections;* Dulio, *For Better or Worse?*

6. Thurber, Nelson and Dulio, "'Campaign Consultants: A Portrait of the Industry"; Dulio, *For Better or Worse?*

7. Burns, Nancy. "Gender: Public Opinion and Political Action." (2000); Flammang. Janet A. *Women's Political Voice: How Women Are Transforming the Practice and Study of Politics.* (Philadelphia: Temple University Press, 1997); Carroll, Susan J. and Linda M. G. Zerilli.

"Feminist Challengers to Political Science." (Washington, DC: American Political Science Association, 1993).

8. Saint-Germain, Michelle. "Does their Difference make a Difference? The Impact of Women on Public Policy in the Arizona Legislature." *Social Science Quarterly.* 70 (4) (1989) pp. 956–968; Thomas, Sue. "Voting Patterns in the California Assembly: The Role of Gender." *Women & Politics.* 9 (1) (1990) pp. 43–56; Thomas, Sue. "The Impact of Women on State Legislative Politics." *Journal of Politics.* 53 (4) (1991) pp. 958–976; Thomas, Sue. *How Women Legislate.* (New York: Oxford University Press, 1994); Thomas, Sue. "Why Gender Matters: The Perceptions of Women Officeholders." *Women & Politics.* 17 (1) (1997) pp. 27–53; Thomas, Sue & Susan Welch. "The Impact of Gender on Activities and Priorities of State Legislatures." *Western Political Quarterly.* 44 (2) (1991) pp. 445–456; Mandel, Ruth B. and Debra Dodson. "Do Women Officeholders Make a Difference?" In *The American Woman: 1992–1993, A Status Report.* Eds. Paula Ries and Anne J. Stone. (New York: W.W. Norton, 1992); Rosenthal, Cindy Simon. "The Role of Gender in Descriptive Representation." *Political Research Quarterly.* 48 (3) (1994) pp. 599–611; Rosenthal, Cindy Simon. "A View of Their Own: Women's Committee Leadership Styles and State Legislatures." *Political Studies Journal.* 25 (4) (1997) pp. 585–600; Rosenthal, Cindy Simon. "Getting Things Done: Women Committee Chairpersons in State Legislatures." In *Women and Elective Office: Past, Present and Future.* Eds. Sue Thomas and Clyde Wilcox. (New York: Oxford University Press, 1998); Rosenthal, Cindy Simon. *When Women Lead: Integrative Leadership in State Legislatures.* (New York: Oxford University Press, 1998); Rosenthal, Cindy Simon. "Divided Lives: Revisiting Considerations of the Personal and Political." *Women & Politics.* 22 (1) (2001) pp. 37–62; Rule, Wilma. "Why are More Women State Legislators?" in *Women in Politics: Outsiders or Insiders? A Collection of Readings.* Ed. Lois Duke Lovelace. (Upper Saddle River, NJ: Prentice Hall, 1999); Reingold, Beth. *Representing Women, Sex and Gender in Legislative Behavior in Arizona and California.* (Chapel Hill, NC: University of North Carolina Press, 2001); Dolan, Kathleen and Lynne E. Ford. "Women in the State Legislature: Feminist Identity and Legislative Behavior." *American Political Quarterly.* 23 (1) (1995) pp. 96–108.

9. Burrell, Barbara C. "Party Decline, Party Transformation and Gender Politics: The USA." In *Gender and Party Politics*. Eds. Joni Lovenduski and Pippa Norris. (Thousand Oaks, CA: Sage Publications, 1993); Burrell, Barbara C. "Women's Political Leadership and the State of the Parties." *The State of the Parties*. David Shea and John C. Green. Eds. (Lanham, MD: Roman & Littlefield, Publishers, 1994); Burrell, Barbara C. *A Woman's Place Is in the House: Campaigning for Congress in the Feminist Era*. Ann Arbor: (University of Michigan Press, 1994); Jennings, M. Kent and Barbara G. Farah. "Social Roles and Political Resources: An Over-Time Study of Men and Women Party Elites." *American Journal of Political Science*. 25 (3) (1981) pp. 462–482; Paddock, Joel and Elizabeth Paddock. "Differences in Partisan Style and Ideology Between Female and Male State Party Committee Members." *Women & Politics*. 18 (4) (1997) pp. 41–56.

10. Salisbury, Robert H. "Washington Lobbyists: A Collective Portrait." in *Interest Group Politics*. 2nd ed. Allan J. Cigler and Burdett A. Loomis. Eds. (Washington, DC: Congressional Quarterly Press, 1986); Schlozman, Kay Lehman. "Representing Women in Washington: Sisterhood and Pressure Politics." In *Women, Politics, and Change*. Louise A. Tilly and Patricia Gurin. Eds. (New York: Russell Sage, 1990); Rosenthal, Alan. *The Third House: Lobbyists and Lobbying in the States*. (Washington DC: Congressional Quarterly Press, 1993); Thomas, Clive S. and Ronald J. Hrebenar. "Interest Groups in the States." *Politics in the American States: A Comparative Analysis*. 6th ed. Virginia Grey and Herbert Jacobs. Ed. (Washington DC: Congressional Quarterly Press, 1996); Nownes, Anthony J. and Patricia K. Freeman. "Female Lobbyists: Women in the World of 'Good Ol' Boys." *Journal of Politics 60* (4) (1998) pp. 1181–1201; Bath, Michael G., Anthony J. Nownes, and Jennifer Gayvert. "Women Lobbyists: The Gender Gap and Interest Representation." (Paper presented at the Midwest Political Science Association Annual Meeting, Chicago, IL, 2002).

11. Beverly, Sheree L. *2000 House Staff Employment Survey*. (Washington DC: Congressional Management Foundation, 2000; Rosenthal, Cindy Simon and Lauren Cohen Bell. "Invisible Power: Congressional Staff and Representation Behind the Scenes." (Paper presented at the Women Transforming Congress Conference, Norman, OK, 2000); Johannes, John R. "Women as Congressional Staffers: Does It Make a Difference?" *Women & Politics*. 4 (2) (1984) pp. 69–81; Fox, Harrison W. and Susan Hammond. *Congressional Staffs: The Invisible Force of American Lawmaking*. (New York: The Free Press, 1997).

12. Burrell, "Women's Political Leadership and the State of the Parties." Nownes and Freeman. "Female Lobbyists: Women in the World of 'Good Ol' Boys"; Carroll, "Representing Women: Congresswomen's Perceptions of Their Representational Roles." Reingold, *Representing Women, Sex and Gender in Legislative Behavior in Arizona and California;* Rosenthal, "Divided Lives: Revisiting Considerations of the Personal and Political." Rosenthal and Bell. "Invisible Power: Congressional Staff and Representation Behind the Scenes."; Shogan, Colleen J. "Speaking Out: An Analysis of Democratic and Republican Woman-Invoked Rhetoric of the 105th Congress." In *Women and Congress: Running, Winning, and Ruling*. Ed. Karen O'Connor. (New York: The Haworth Press, Inc, 2001); Swers, Michele. *The Difference Women Make: The Policy Impact of Women in Congress*. (Chicago: University of Chicago Press, 2001). Bath, Nownes, and Gayvert. "Women Lobbyists: The Gender Gap and Interest Representation."

13. Dolan and Ford. "Women in the State Legislature: Feminist Identity and Legislative Behavior"; Dodson, Debra "Representing Women's Interests in the US House of Representatives." In *Women in Elective Office: Past, Present, and Future*. Eds. Sue Thomas and Clyde Wilcox. (New York: Oxford University Press, 1998); Kathlene, Lyn. "In a Different Voice: Women and the Policy Process." In *Women in Elective Office: Past, Present and Future*. Eds. Sue Thomas and Clyde Wilcox. (New York: Oxford University Press, 1998); Little, Thomas H., Dana Dunn and Rebecca E. Deen. "A View from the Top: Gender Differences in Legislative Priorities Among State Legislative Leaders." *Women & Politics 22* (4): (2001) pp. 29–50; Reingold. *Representing Women, Sex and Gender in Legislative Behavior in Arizona and California*. Swers. *The Difference Women Make: The Policy Impact of Women in Congress*.

14. Nownes and Freeman, "Female Lobbyists: Women in the World of 'Good Ol' Boys." Johannes, "Women as Congressional Staffers: Does it Make a Difference?" Bath, Nownes, and Gayvert. "Women Lobbyists: The Gender Gap and Interest Representation."

15. Lee, Barbara. "Keys to the Governor's Office." (Boston: The Barbara Lee Family Foundation, 2001); The White House Project. Barriers & Opportunities to Women's Executive Leadership. www.thewhitehouse project.org/research/barriers_research.html.(2002).

16. American Bar Association (ABA): Commission on Women in the Profession. "The Unfinished Agenda: A Report on the Status of Women in the Legal Profession." (Chicago: American Bar Association, 2001); Catalyst. "Women in Financial Services: The Word on the Street." (New York: Catalyst, 2001).

17. American Bar Association, "The Unfinished Agenda" p. 15.

18. Lee, Barbara. "Keys to the Governor's Office." (Boston: The Barbara Lee Family Foundation, 2001).

19. American Bar Association, "The Unfinished Agenda" p. 15.

20. Catalyst. "Women in Financial Services: The Word on the Street."

21. Gilligan, Carol. *In a Different Voice: Psychological Theory and Women's Development*. (Cambridge: Harvard University Press. 1982).

22. Thomas, *How Women Legislate;* Rosenthal, "Getting Things Done: Women Committee Chairpersons in State Legislature."

23. Carroll, Sue *Women as Candidates in American Politics.* 2nd ed. (Bloomington IN: Indiana University Press, 1994); Gertzog, Irwin. *Congressional Women: Their Recruitment, Integration, and Behavior.* 2nd ed. (Westport CT: Praeger 1995); Thomas, Sue and Matt Braunstein. "Legislative Career: The Personal and the

Political." (Paper Presented at the Carl Albert Center's Women Transforming Congress Conference. OK, 2000).

24. Kamen, Al. 2001. *The Washington Post,* June 25. A 13.

25. Thomas and Braunstein. "Legislative Career: The Personal and the Political." pp. 16.

26. Thomas and Braunstein. "Legislative Career: The Personal and the Political." pp. 22.

FURTHER READINGS

Dulio, David. *For Better or Worse? How Political Consultants Are Changing Elections in the United States.* (New York: SUNY, 2004).

Gertzog, Irwin. *Congressional Women: Their Recruitment, Integration, and Behavior.* 2nd Ed. (Westport CT: Praeger, 1995).

Johnson, Dennis. *No Place for Amateurs: How Political Consultants are Reshaping American Democracy.* (New York: Routledge. 2001).

Kelley, Stanley, Jr. *Professional Public Relations and Political Power.* (Baltimore: Johns Hopkins University Press, 1956).

Medvic, Stephen. *Political Consultants in US Congressional Elections.* (Columbus OH: Ohio State University Press, 2001).

Nimmo, Dan. *The Political Persuaders: The Techniques of Modern Election Campaigns.* (Englewood Cliffs, NJ: Prentice Hall, 1976).

Rosenthal, Cindy Simon. *When Women Lead: Integrative Leadership in State Legislatures.* (New York: Oxford University Press., 1998).

Rosenthal, Cindy Simon (Ed). *Women Transforming Congress.* (Norman, OK: University of Oklahoma Press, 2002).

Sabato, Larry. *The Rise of Political Consultants: New Ways of Winning Elections.* (New York: Basic Books, 1981).

Sanbonmatsu, Kira. *Democrats, Republicans and the Politics of Women's Place.* (Ann Arbor, MI: University of Michigan Press, 2002).

Swers, Michele. *The Difference Women Make: The Policy Impact of Women in Congress.* (Chicago: University of Chicago Press, 2001).

Thurber, James A., Candice J. Nelson, and David Dulio. (Eds) *Campaign Warriors: The Role of Political Consultants in Elections.* (Washington DC: Brookings Institution Press, 2000).

5

Legislatures, Women, and Policy Making

Do female legislators make a difference in their impact on public policy? If we have greater numbers of women in our legislative bodies, can we expect a shift in issues that deal explicitly with women's concerns? For example, Michele L. Swers, in her article, "Transforming the Agenda Analyzing Gender Differences in Women's Issue Bill Sponsorship," published in *Women Transforming Congress,* edited by Cindy Simon Rosenthal (Norman: University of Oklahoma Press, 2002, pp. 260–283) examined bill sponsorship activity on women's issues during the 103rd (1993–94) and 104th (1995–96) Congresses. She found evidence that women are transforming the institution of Congress by bringing new issues to the national agenda, particularly feminist issues. That is, they are asking their male colleagues to consider how policy changes will affect women, and they are using their scarce political capital to shine a spotlight on such feminist issues as domestic violence, reproductive rights, and family leave. Thus, one could argue that female legislators can make a difference in the public policy decisions about such matters as child care, health benefits, sex discrimination, and other issues of concern to women and families.

How, then, have women fared in running for Congress and state legislative bodies? Jennifer L. Lawless and Sean M. Theriault explore women's representation in Congress. The authors begin by outlining the traditional explanations for women's numeric underrepresentation on Capitol Hill. The second section of their analysis explores the power women wield once they are elected to Congress and the manner in which women and men legislate differently, both in terms of issues and leadership style. The third section discusses the gender dynamics of congressional retirement. Together, the various components of their analysis culminate to suggest that trends toward gender parity in our political institutions are overstated. That is, contrary to the conventional wisdom, gender differences in political ambition and congressional retention suggest that, in the long run's best-case scenario, women will continue to comprise far less than 50 percent of the members of Congress.

On the other hand, currently women hold about 22 percent, or 1,655, of the 7,382 seats in the U.S. state legislatures; 30 years ago, women only held about 8 percent of the seats. What does this mean as far as legislative outcomes and women's policy concerns? Sarah Poggione's essay explores differences in men and women state legislators' policy opinions and legislative behavior as well as the effect of women state legislators on a welfare policy. Although the author finds that women's participation in state legislatures does influence policy, the relationship between descriptive and substantive representation is not a simple one. She finds that women legislators' opportunities for influence are mediated by the institutions in which they serve. Specifically, the rules governing standing committees condition women's impact on policy. As other research demonstrates, increases in women's representation at the state level will continue to influence the agendas and policies adopted by state legislatures; however, even a small number of women legislators can significantly influence policy through service on independent standing committees. That is, even a small number of women legislators can influence policy if their policy preferences and legislative activities differ from those of their male colleagues and legislative rules and procedures advantage minorities in the policy-making process.

Women in the U.S. Congress: From Entry to Exit

Jennifer L. Lawless
Sean M. Theriault

In 1991, the Senate readied for a vote on Clarence Thomas' appointment to the U.S. Supreme Court. Shortly before the confirmation hearings concluded, Anita Hill, an accomplished law professor at the University of Oklahoma, accused Mr. Thomas of making unwanted sexual advances toward her when she worked under his supervision at the Equal Employment Opportunities Commission. Many members of the all male Senate Judiciary Committee criticized Ms. Hill for coming forward so many years after the incidents occurred and questioned the validity of her claims. Ultimately, the 98 percent male Senate voted 52–48 to confirm Clarence Thomas.

Angered by the manner in which the Senate handled Clarence Thomas's confirmation to the Supreme Court, a previously unprecedented number of women candidates sought and won congressional seats in 1992.[1] As Barbara Boxer summarized:

> The American public realized that Anita Hill struck an honest chord; Clarence Thomas struck a disturbing chord; and the Senate Judiciary Committee, looking like a relic from another time and place, struck a chord of irrelevancy. And all of these chords played together had a very dissonant sound. America, and in particular, American women, were uncomfortable with the way the whole issue was handled, were uncomfortable with the way the Senate looked—and the Anita Hill incident became a catalyst for change.[2]

Thanks to Richard Fox for comments on earlier drafts.

More specifically, Carol Moseley Braun, who had been serving as the Recorder of Deeds for Cook County, challenged incumbent senator Alan Dixon in the Democratic primary in Illinois. Not only did Moseley Braun use Dixon's vote in favor of Thomas to win the primary, but she also rode the issue to victory in the general election. In another example, Dianne Feinstein, whose campaign slogan was "Two percent may be good for milk, but it's not good enough for the United States Senate," defeated John Seymour in a race to fill the California Senate seat vacated by Pete Wilson, who was elected governor. The "male" face of the U.S. Congress spurred many women to run for office at the national level. Widely heralded as the "Year of the Woman," the 1992 congressional elections were thought to have changed the gender dynamics of the political landscape.[3]

On November 5, 2003—more than a decade after the Clarence Thomas confirmation hearings—six white men beamed down on President Bush as he signed into law a bill that banned partial birth abortion. Numerous explanations were proffered for the exclusive presence of smiling men modifying policy pertaining to women's reproductive rights, although none is particularly compelling. It is not true that only men in the Congress supported the bill. GOP Conference Chairwoman Deborah Pryce, the fourth ranking Republican in the House, was an early and constant supporter of the ban on partial birth abortion. It is not true that only male representatives attended the signing event. Congresswomen Sue Myrick and Ileana Ros-Lehtinen were simply relegated to seats in the audience. It is not true that only the bill's chief advocates earned a place on the stage. Congresswoman Melissa Hart, who also attended the event, was a forceful advocate for the ban; in fact, she was a featured speaker of the GOP Conference during a discussion of the bill with the media. The only reasonable explanations are simple oversight and outright insensitivity. As Representative Pryce fumed, "Somebody dropped the ball over there."[4]

Put simply, men continue to represent the face of the United States' political institutions. Women occupy only 14 percent of the seats in the House of Representatives and Senate. No woman chairs a House committee and only one woman—House Minority Leader Nancy Pelosi—ranks among the top three party leaders in either chamber of Congress. It may be nearly 30 years since Armed Services Chairman Edward Hebert admonished Congresswoman Patricia Schroeder with the advice that she would get a lot further on his committee if she kept her mouth closed and her legs open. But Congress remains far from exhibiting any semblance of gender parity.

In this article, we explore women's representation in Congress. We begin by outlining the traditional explanations for women's numeric under-representation on Capitol Hill. The second section of our analysis explores the power women wield once they are elected to Congress and the manner in which women and men legislate differently, both in terms of issues and leadership style. The third section discusses the gender dynamics of congressional retirement. Together, the various components of our analysis culminate to suggest that trends toward gender parity in our political institutions are over-stated. Contrary to the conventional wisdom, gender differences in political ambition and congressional retention suggest that, in the long run's best case scenario, women will continue to comprise far less than 50 percent of the members of Congress. These findings carry broad implications for women's substantive and symbolic representation.

ENTER WOMEN: EXPLANATIONS FOR WOMEN'S NUMERIC UNDER-REPRESENTATION

When the 108th Congress convened, 86 percent of its members were male.[5] Although this percentage is low, it represents a marked improvement (Figure 1 documents this increase). Over the course of the last 20 years, alone, the number of women in Congress has more than tripled. Since the end of World War II, the number of women serving in the House of Representatives and the Senate has grown by more than 800 percent. In fact, California's Democratic congressional delegation, which is the largest state party delegation in Congress, is comprised of more women than men.

A closer examination of the Figure 1 indicates, however, that whereas the 1980s saw a gradual increase in the numbers of women holding these positions, and the 1990s experienced a rather dramatic surge in women's presence in Congress, the last several election cycles suggest a plateau in Democratic and Republican women's entry into the political sphere; fewer new women are entering the congressional ranks. In fact, the United States now places 60th worldwide in terms of the number of women serving in the national legislature, a ranking that falls

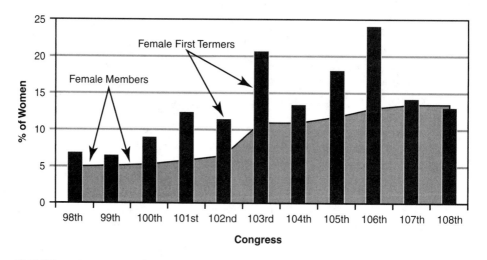

FIGURE 1   Percentage of Women in Congress, 1983–2004
Notes: Gray shaded area indicates the percentage of women in Congress. The black bars represent the percentage of female newcomers in each Congress.

TABLE 1 World Rankings of Women in National Legislatures

World Rank/Country	Percentage Women
1. Sweden	45.3
2. Denmark	38.0
3. Finland	37.5
4. Netherlands	36.7
5. Norway	36.4
6. Cuba	36.0
7. Costa Rica	35.1
8. Iceland	34.9
9. Austria	33.9
10. Germany	32.2
11. Argentina	30.7
12. Mozambique	30.0
13. South Africa	29.8
14. Seychelles	29.4
15. New Zealand	28.3
16. Spain	28.3
17. Vietnam	27.3
18. Grenada	26.7
19. Namibia	26.4
20. Bulgaria	26.2
21. East Timor	26.1
22. Turkmenistan	26.0
23. Rwanda	25.7
24. Australia	25.3
25. Uganda	24.7
60. United States	14.3
World Average	15.2

Note: Entries indicate the percentage of women serving in national legislatures; in bicameral systems, the percentage is for the lower house.

Source: Inter-Parliamentary Union, "Women in National Parliaments," March 28, 2003, http://www.ipu.org/wmn-e/classif.htm.

below the worldwide average (Table 1).[6] Whether we consider recent election cycles, or the United States' global ranking on women in politics, therefore, it is difficult not to conclude that our political institutions continue to be overwhelmingly male-dominated.

The glaring gender disparities in Congress have motivated political scientists to gain a better understanding of why so few women occupy positions of political power in the United States. We classify four general explanations for women's under-representation, each of which we discuss and evaluate in this section.

The Discrimination Explanation

The earliest research in the women and elections subfield expected overt discrimination to account for the gender disparities in office-holding. Women candidates, in other words, experienced bias in the electoral arena and at the voting booth. As a result, they did not win elections. Reflecting on the political arena for women in 1972, for example, Barbara Boxer recounts that being a woman was a "distinct, quantifiable disadvantage," at least when she ran for the Board of Supervisors in Marin County, California:

> [T]o be a woman in politics was almost a masochistic experience, a series of setbacks with not a lot of rewards. If I was strong in my expression of the issues, I was strident; if I expressed any emotion as I spoke about the environment or the problems of the mentally ill, I was soft; if I spoke about economics, I had to be perfect, and then I ran the risk of being "too much like a man."[7]

It is easy to compile a list of similar experiences women candidates endured.[8]

In the contemporary political environment, though, individual accounts of women who face overt gender discrimination once they enter the public arena are increasingly rare.[9] Barbara Boxer, herself, notes that, when she ran for the Senate two decades later, "It was different. Being a woman running for public office in 1992 was a distinct advantage. The polls showed it."[10]

The public's attitudes toward women in politics also seem to have evolved, thereby corroborating the experiences of women candidates. As we see in Figure 2, an overwhelming majority of Americans no longer believe that men are better suited emotionally for politics than are women. An even greater proportion of citizens express a willingness to support a qualified, female party nominee for the presidency.

Of course, this is not to say that gender does not play a role in the electoral process. In depth examinations of campaigns continue to show that gender stereotypes affect the manner in which voters, the media, party recruiters, and candidates assess men and women's electoral prospects.[11] We need only take a closer look at Figure 2 to realize that nearly one in every four Americans still agrees that "Most men are better suited emotionally for politics than are most women."[12] It is also important to note the sharp decrease in the most recent levels of support for a woman presidential nominee. In September 2002, only 65 percent of respondents were sure they would be willing to vote for a woman for president, even if she were qualified and their political party's nominee. Although levels of direct bias against women were about the same as they have been since the mid-1990s (7 percent), the 28 percent of sample respondents who were unsure whether they were willing to vote for a woman represents a substantial shift away from an unequivocal willingness to support a woman presidential party nominee. These results suggest that stereotyping about candidate competence to govern in a political context dominated by the "war on terrorism" may work to the detriment of women candidates, at least at the presidential level.[13] This is particularly damning considering the issues and obstacles the United States must address for the foreseeable future.

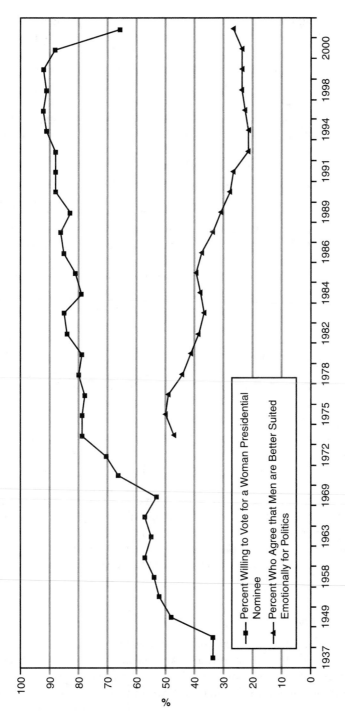

FIGURE 2 Attitudes Toward Women in Politics

Notes: Data depict citizens' responses to the following questions: "If your political party nominated a woman for president, would you be willing to vote for her if she were qualified for the job?" and "Tell me if you agree or disagree with this statement: Most men are better suited emotionally for politics than are most women." The data for the "willingness to vote for a women president" question are drawn from multiple sources: Gallup (1937–1971, and 1984); the National Opinion Research Council (1972–1998); CBS (1999); the *Wall Street Journal* (2000); and *Knowledge Networks* (2002). The "men better suited emotionally" data are from the National Opinion Research Council's General Social Survey and begin in 1972, the first year the question was asked. The GSS did not include the question in its 2002 battery, so the data for 2002 are from *Knowledge Networks*.

Yet these lingering biases do not appear to hurt women candidates at the end stage of the electoral process—at least in congressional elections. When we turn to fundraising receipts and vote totals, often considered the two most important indicators of electoral success, researchers find that women congressional candidates fare just as well as, if not better than, their male counterparts.[14] Thus, as Kathleen Dolan concludes, based on a series of public opinion polls and election results, "Levels of bias are low enough to no longer provide significant impediments to women's chances of election."[15] When women run, women win, at least at percentages similar to their male counterparts.

The Incumbency Explanation

In light of the seeming contradiction between a political system that elects few women and an electoral environment that is unbiased against women candidates, political scientists have also turned to more institutional explanations for women's numeric under-representation. Perhaps most notably, they point to the incumbency advantage. Not only do incumbents tend to seek reelection in more than 75 percent of congressional elections, but their reelection rates are also consistently above 90 percent.[16] In most of these races, the average incumbent receives well over 60 percent of the vote.[17] Under these circumstances, increasing the number of electoral opportunities for previously excluded groups can be glacial.[18]

Figure 1 offers more insight into the degree to which the incumbency advantage serves as a structural barrier for women. The gray shaded area of the figure represents the percentage of women in the House of Representatives. The black bars indicate the percentage of newcomers to each Congress—i.e., it is their first term in the chamber—who are women. For the 20 years following 1983, the percentage of newcomers who were women consistently exceeded the total percentage of female members. In 1992, for example, women comprised 20 percent of the new members in the House, compared to only 11 percent of the overall House membership. Likewise, in 1998, women accounted for 24 percent of the new members who entered the 87 percent male chamber. Over the course of the last couple of congresses, however, the trend is less promising. In 2000, the percentage of new women entering Congress was nearly the same as the percentage of women already in Congress; and in 2002, for the first time since before Ronald Reagan's presidency, the percentage of new women was actually smaller than the percentage of women already in the House.

The Eligibility Pool Explanation

A clear consensus indicates that the most prominent professions for aspiring politicians are law, business, and education. An analysis of the professional occupations of members in the 107th Congress, for example, reveals that law and business are the top two professions for men, followed by education and politics. For women, the numbers are reversed, with education and politics as the leading two professions, followed by business and law.[19] Similar patterns exist among state legislators: men are most likely to be attorneys, followed by business leaders and educators, whereas women are most likely to be teachers or school administrators, followed by business leaders and attorneys.[20] Despite the fact that both women and men candidates yield from these professions, far more men than women work in the professions that serve as pipelines to careers in politics. As Janet Clark explains, "Women are not found in the professions from which politicians inordinately are chosen—the law and other broker-type businesses. Therefore, they do not achieve the higher socioeconomic status that forms the eligibility pool for elective office."[21]

The "eligibility pool" explanation suggests that as more and more women come to occupy the careers that are most likely to lead to a political candidacy— and it appears that they are; women now enter law schools and MPA programs at equal levels as men—we can assume that more and more women will run for office, contest open seats, and face no discrimination at the polls. This explanation has become widely accepted in the political science literature. Morris Fiorina and Paul Peterson state in a leading American government textbook, for instance, that "The under-representation of women . . . will naturally lessen as women's career patterns become more like those of men."[22]

There is no question that, as women increase their proportions in the pipeline professions that precede a political career, there will be an increase in the number of women candidates. The data on career patterns, however, suggest that these increases may be more incremental than some optimists purport. The National Association for Law Placement finds that women account for only 15 percent of the partners in the nation's major law firms.[23] This number represents relative stagnation over the course of the last decade, when 13 percent of the partners in major law firms were women. In the business world, only two *Fortune* 500 companies have women CEOs, and 71 of these companies do not have any women corporate officers. If we move beyond *Fortune* 500 companies, women comprise only 16 percent of the corporate officers at the nation's largest companies.[24]

The Political Ambition Explanation

The three previous explanations for gender disparities in elective office suggest that we are on a steady course, albeit slow, toward equity in women's numeric representation in elective office. After all, voters and campaign contributors support women candidates. As an increasing number of open seats become available, women have an equal opportunity to seek and win them. And, at least in terms of objective qualifications, women are acquiring an increasing proportion of the degrees and professional experiences typical of candidates for public office. Embedded in each prognosis is the assumption that women and men, when well positioned, will be equally likely to decide to run for office.

These explanations for women's under-representation do not, however, take into account the selection process by which potential candidates become actual candidates. A recent national survey of women and men situated in the "candidate eligibility pool" finds that these conventional institutional explanations that account for women's numeric under-representation are incomplete and somewhat misleading. Richard Fox and Jennifer Lawless find that women who share the same personal characteristics and professional credentials as men express significantly lower levels of political ambition to hold elective office.[25] Accordingly, women are far less likely than men to emerge from the pool of eligible candidates and seek elected positions. Thus, even though women who run for office are just as likely as men to emerge victorious, the substantial winnowing process in candidate emergence yields a smaller ratio of women than men.

The gender gap in political ambition among the pool of eligible candidates can be attributed to two critical aspects of the candidate selection process. First, women are significantly less likely than men to receive encouragement to run for office. This difference is very important, since potential candidates are twice as likely to think about running for office when a party leader, elected official, or political activist attempts to recruit them as candidates. Second, women are significantly less likely than men to deem themselves qualified to run for office, yet more likely to rely on their self-perceived qualifications when considering whether to enter the electoral arena. In other words, women, even in the top tier of professional accomplishment, tend not to consider themselves qualified to run for political office. And recruitment patterns—or lack thereof—appear to solidify women's self-perceptions.

Together, these findings also suggest that the end stage of the electoral process may not be as "gender neutral" as it is commonly described. After all, if women are more likely than men to doubt their own qualifications, then it stands to reason that women who think they are "qualified" are actually more qualified than men who self-assess this way. And if party leaders and other recruiters are less likely to encourage women to run, then women whom party leaders suggest for candidacy may also be more "qualified" than men they encourage. If women must meet higher standards in their selection to feeder positions for high-level office, the apparent absence of voter bias against women candidates might reflect the higher average quality of women candidates, as compared to men.

The explanations for women's under-representation offer a mixed bag for the prospects of gender parity in Congress. While women can compete effectively in terms of campaign contributions and election margins, they continue to face several hurdles. First, even though women and men now enter the professions that precede politics at similar rates, women's rise to power in those professions is glacial. Second, women face higher standards—both self-imposed and by political kingpins—when deciding whether to throw their hats into the electoral ring. Consequently, the relatively rapid increases in women's presence in Congress in the 1990s have all but stagnated.

THE FEMININE GAVEL: POWER EXERCISED BY WOMEN IN CONGRESS

Whether we subscribe to the somewhat optimistic prospects for gender parity, or the less promising prognosis, it is important to address the implications of women's presence in Congress. After all, the push to increase women's numeric representation in the House and Senate is predicated on the notion that women will bring a "different voice" to the legislature. Perhaps no "voices" are as important as those of the congressional leadership.

When Richard Gephardt stepped down as Minority Leader in the House of Representatives, proponents of gender equity hailed the Democrats' move to promote Nancy Pelosi into that leadership role. A new day, so it was argued, dawned for women throughout the Capitol. A systematic review of women's roles in Congress, however, indicates that Pelosi's ascension is the lone bright spot in a sea of despair. With the exception of Pelosi, no woman has ever approached the top of the parties' leadership pyramids, either in the House or the Senate. The record from the 108th Congress, while poor, is the most gender inclusive Congress in congressional history. The highest ranking woman in the Republican leadership in the House is Conference Chairwoman Deborah Pryce. The highest ranking female Senate Democrat is Conference Secretary Barbara Mikulski. Conference Vice Chairwoman Kay Bailey Hutchison serves as the highest ranking female Senate Republican. No more than one woman occupies the top echelon of leadership in either political party.

The record is, perhaps, even more dismal when we move from party leadership to committee leadership. Exclusive committees are the real plums on the committee assignment tree. By virtue of their expansive jurisdictions and important policy areas, the House's Appropriations, Rules, and Ways and Means Committees, and the Senate's Appropriations, Armed Services, Finance, and Foreign Policy Committees have been deemed the most important in Congress. No woman has *ever* served as the chair of any of these committees. Further, the data presented in Table 2 indicate that in the 108th Congress (2003–4), of the 21 subcommittees of the exclusive committees in the House, only Deborah Pryce and Nancy Johnson wielded gavels. Kay Bailey Hutchison was the only female subcommittee chairwoman (out of the 30) within the exclusive committees in the Senate.

Women are not excluded only from the leadership ranks of the most important committees; no woman in the House chairs a nonexclusive committee either (this has been the case for the last four congresses). In fact, only 5 women—6.6 percent—even serve as subcommittee chairs. Women are completely absent from committee leadership positions in Armed Services (7 men), Energy (6 men), Judiciary (5 men), Education (5 men), Homeland Security (5 men), and Transportation (6 men). Although Susan Collins and Olympia Snowe chair, respectively, the Government Affairs and Small Business Committees in the Senate, neither is particularly powerful.

The record among informal caucuses and coalitions is no better. Caucuses act as brokers between members and parties, frequently serving as the venue in which

TABLE 2 Committee Leaders in the 108th Congress

House of Representatives

	Chairs	Subcommittee Chairs
Exclusive Committee		
Appropriations	Man	13 Men
Rules	Man	Man and Deborah Pryce
Ways and Means	Man	5 Men and Nancy Johnson
Female Exclusive Committee Chairs		0.0%
Female Exclusive Subc. Chairs		9.5%
Other Committees		
Agriculture	Man	5 Men
Armed Services	Man	6 Men
Budget	Man	
Education	Man	5 Men
Energy	Man	6 Men
Financial Services	Man	4 Men and Sue Kelly
Government Reform	Man	6 Men and Jo Ann Davis
House Administration	Man	
International Relations	Man	5 Men and Illeana Ros-Lehtinen
Judiciary	Man	5 Men
Resources	Man	4 Men and Barbara Cubin
Science	Man	3 Men and Judy Biggert
Select Home Security	Man	5 Men
Select Intelligence	Man	4 Men
Small Business	Man	4 Men
Standards of Conduct	Man	
Transportation	Man	6 Men
Veterans	Man	3 Men
Female Other Committee Chairs		0.0%
Female Other Subc. Chairs		6.6%

Senate

	Chairs	Subcommittee Chairs
Exclusive Committee		
Appropriations	Man	10 Men and Kay Bailey Hutchison
Armed Services	Man	6 Men
Finance	Man	5 Men
Foreign Relations	Man	7 Men
Female Exclusive Committee Chairs		0.0%
Female Exclusive Subc. Chairs		3.3%
Other Committees		
Agriculture	Man	3 Men and Elizabeth Dole
Banking	Man	5 Men
Budget	Man	
Commerce	Man	7 Men, Snowe, and Hutchison
Energy	Man	6 Men
Environment	Man	3 Men and Lisa Murkowski
Environment	Man	4 Men
Government Affairs	Susan Collins	3 Men
Health	Man	4 Men
Indian Affairs	Man	
Judiciary	Man	6 Men
Rules	Man	
Select Ethics	Man	
Select Intelligence	Man	
Small Business	Olympia Snowe	4 Men
Special Aging	Man	
Veterans Affairs	Man	
Female Other Committee Chairs		11.8%
Female Other Subc. Chairs		8.2%

to hammer out party positions and policy statements. The Blue Dog Coalition, the New Democrat Coalition, and the Republican Main Street Partnership are led, aggregately, by 10 men and no women. Only one member of the Republican Study Group's board is a woman (Sue Myrick), although the Progressive Caucus is co-chaired by a woman (Barbara Lee). We are happy to note that the Women's Caucus continues to be co-chaired by women (Carolyn Maloney and Sue Kelly).

The lack of women's voices emanating from committees and party leadership roles would be somewhat less disconcerting if the words coming from members' mouths did not appreciably differ across gender lines. But such is not the case. From a policy perspective, men and women legislators' priorities differ.[26] Women are more likely than their male counterparts to promote legislation geared to ameliorate women's economic and social status, especially concerning issues of health care, poverty, and education.[27] Debra Dodson reminds us, for example, that the Women's Health Initiative was enacted only because women in Congress appealed to the General Accounting Office to fund the research.[28] Prior to this enactment, even though women were twice as likely as men to suffer from heart disease, the majority of the research was conducted on male subjects.[29]

Similarly, Susan Moller Okin explains that the presence of women legislators allows issues such as marital rape, domestic violence, and child custody—all of which have traditionally been deemed private matters—to receive public attention and debate.[30] Barbara Burrell confirms this claim with her analysis of House members' support for women's rights. Even after controlling for party, region, and constituency characteristics, she finds that women are more supportive than men of issues related to gender equity and women's issues, including day care, flex time, abortion, minimum wage increases, and the extension of the food stamp program.[31]

In addition to content, the tone of voice differs between men and women. Studies suggest that female legislators are more likely than their male counterparts to conduct business in a manner that is egalitarian, cooperative, communicative, and contextual.[32] Lyn Kathlene's analysis of the gender differences in how state assembly members debate and discuss crime provides compelling evidence that women are more concerned with context and environmental factors when determining the reasons for crime and the best way to punish criminals.[33] She also uncovers significant gender differences in the manner in which male and female state legislature committee chairs conduct themselves at hearings; women are more likely to act as "facilitators," but men tend to use their power to control the direction of the hearings.[34] Sue Tolleson Rinehart, in a study of male and female mayors, also finds that women tend to adopt an approach to governing that emphasizes congeniality and cooperation, whereas men tend to emphasize hierarchy.[35]

We can extrapolate from these state and local-level studies to the U.S. Congress: women's presence in high-level elective office not only decreases the possibility that gender-salient issues will be overlooked, but it also brings a different voice to the legislative process. Thus, women's numeric under-representation is exacerbated by the fact that women are less likely than men to climb the career ladder within Congress and wield the kind of policy influence that could considerably affect women constituents.

EXIT WOMEN: GENDER DYNAMICS OF CONGRESSIONAL TENURE AND RETIREMENT

In December 2000, Strom Thurmond celebrated his 100th birthday, 29 days before his eighth and final term in the Senate would end. In 1999, he relinquished the Armed Services Committee gavel even though he would serve on the committee for another two years. In the 103rd Congress, another Southern icon—Jamie Whitten—became the longest serving member in the history of the U.S. House. After 14 years as the chairman of the Appropriations Committee, the Democrats turned his gavel over to the sprite, 82-year-old William Natcher. While the stories of these long-serving men are legendary, the most attuned political observer would be hard pressed to come up with a similar story for a woman in Congress. When Patricia Schroeder retired in 1996, after 24 years in the House, she was a subcommittee chair in the Armed Services Committee. Likewise, Small Business Committee Chairwoman Jan Meyers, Labor and Education Chairwoman Nancy Kassebaum, and Conference Vice Chairwoman Tillie Fowler all voluntarily departed from Congress when they still had the potential to rise in stature.

Powerful positions in the Congress are contingent on seniority.[36] If women are more likely than men to retire prematurely, then it is not, necessarily, institutional discrimination, but rather, their early retirements, that preclude them from attaining powerful committee positions and influencing the legislative agenda. A more systematic assessment of voluntary retirement from the U.S. House of Representatives suggests that a gender dynamic does, indeed, underlie patterns of congressional retirement. From the 98th Congress (1983–4) until the 107th Congress (2003–4), the average tenure for men who retire is approximately 30 percent longer than the average for women (slightly more than 17 years, compared to about 12 years; difference significant at $p < .01$). As a result, only 2 of the 20 oldest members of the House to retire during this time period were women (Virginia Smith at 79 and Carrie Meek at 75); only 3 of the 75 oldest members seeking reelection were women; and of the 35 members who died in office, only two were women (Sala Burton and Patsy Mink).[37]

In other work, we more closely examine the dynamics underlying voluntary retirement from the House.[38] We find few gender differences. Women, like men, are more likely to retire if they are older, if they are electorally weak, or if they have been victims of redistricting. The one important gender difference we do uncover pertains to "positional considerations." Based on an analysis of the 102nd Congress (1991–2), Sean Theriault finds that members who served in the House for a long time, but who had not yet accrued powerful positions, were more likely to retire than both long-serving powerful members and newly elected members.[39] In other words, they faced "career ceilings." Samuel Fisher and Rebekah Herrick corroborate Theriault's findings with a survey of retired members. They find that "the more satisfied that members [a]re with their House careers, the longer they stay in office."[40]

While it is true that those members who have hit a congressional career ceiling are more likely to retire, the effect is much greater for women. The coefficient for women is more than 33 percent greater than it is for men.[41] In real terms, this means that if a male member moves from being a chair of a policy committee (e.g., the Agriculture Committee) to simply being a member on that committee, his probability of retirement increases nearly 50 percent. The same position change yields almost a quadrupling of a female member's likelihood of leaving the House.[42] This finding comports well with Richard Fox's study of congressional candidates. He finds men more likely than women to be motivated to run for office by the raw desire to hold office; women often chose to run because of a specific policy issue.[43] More specifically, surveys suggest that women are more likely to become involved in politics when motivated by concerns pertaining to women and children.[44] This same type of issue motivation plays a role in voluntary departures from the House as well. Whereas men seem to be satisfied—at least in part—by mere service in the House, women appear to need policy influence to satisfy their career goals.

Further, we should note that although women are more likely than men to retire from Congress when faced with a seemingly stalled career, they are no more likely than men to seek higher office when they reach the same career ceiling. In other words, all members, regardless of sex, are more likely to leave the House when their position is stunted, but women are more likely than men to respond by leaving politics altogether.

CONCLUSION: REPRESENTATION, EQUALITY, AND DEMOCRATIC LEGITIMACY

The political system may be "gender neutral," at least in terms of vote shares and fundraising returns, but gender differences continue to persist in terms of entry into, power within, and departure from the United States Congress. Certainly, many of the barriers to women's advancement in formerly male fields are drastically changing, and women's presence in the fields of business and law has increased dramatically over the last thirty years.[45] But female potential candidates remain less likely than similarly situated men to receive encouragement to run for office and to deem themselves qualified to hold elected positions, both of which decrease their likelihood of throwing their hats into the electoral arena. Moreover, even when women make it to the House, they face more obstacles than do their male counterparts in terms of achieving leadership positions. This inability to affect the policy agenda as thoroughly as they might like leads women to serve significantly shorter terms than men. If female seats in Congress turn over more rapidly, a higher proportion of women will have to run and win just to keep pace with the status quo percentage of women in Congress.

As we conclude this article, it is important also to mention briefly an additional implication of women's under-representation: symbolic representation, or the role model effects that women's presence in positions of political power confers to women citizens.[46] Symbolic effects are difficult to quantify, but the logic underlying symbolic representation is compelling.[47] Barbara Burrell captures the argument well when she explains:

> Women in public office stand as symbols for other women, both enhancing their identification with the system and their ability to have influence within it. This subjective sense of being involved and heard for women, in general, alone makes the election of women to public office important because, for so many years, they were excluded from power.[48]

In other words, there is a potentially powerful and positive relationship between women's presence in elective office and their female constituents' political attitudes and behavior.

The inclusion of more women in positions of political power would change the nature of political representation in the United States. At the very least, the government would gain a greater sense of political legitimacy, simply by virtue of the fact that it would be more reflective of the gender breakdown of the national population. As Sue Thomas explains, "A government that is democratically organized cannot be truly legitimate if all its citizens from . . . both sexes do not have a potential interest in and opportunity for serving their community and nation.[49] It also seems clear that the election of more women would substantially reduce the possibility "that gender-salient issues [will be] overlooked."[50] Some political scientists, however, would offer even bolder conclusions. Many would predict that a fuller inclusion of women in our governing bodies would dramatically change the style by which policy is made. Some would also argue that a greater presence of women in elective office would send a signal to other women that the political system is fair, open, democratic, and worthy of engagement. Despite the policy and symbolic importance of increasing women's presence in our political institutions, the overview data we presented in this article suggest that achieving any semblance of gender parity in Congress is bleak.

NOTES

1. Center for American Women and Politics, Women in Elective Office 2003 Fact Sheet (New Brunswick: Center for American Women and Politics, 2003).

2. Barbara Boxer, *Politics and the New Revolution of Women in America* (Washington, DC: National Press Books, 1994), pp. 39–40.

3. See Marjorie Margolies-Mezvinsky, *Woman's Place: The Freshman Women Who Changed the Face of Congress* (New York: Crown, 1994) for an account of the importance various women candidates placed on the

Hill–Thomas hearings when deciding to pursue elective office.

4. Quoted in Ethan Wallison, Pryce Declares White House 'Dropped the Ball' (*Roll Call*, November 20, 2003), p. 3.

5. The dearth of women in elective office in the United States is also evident at the state and local levels: 86 percent of state governors, 85 percent of big city mayors, and 78 percent of state legislators are male (CAWP 2003).

6. Certainly, nuanced cultural and political components factor into the total number of women who hold seats in any nation's legislature. But Table 1 demonstrates that the nations that surpass the U.S. in terms of women's numeric representation do not share a particular political system, geography, region, or culture.

7. Boxer (1994), pp. 73–4.

8. Linda Witt, Karen Paget and Glenna Matthews, *Running as a Woman* (New York: Free Press, 1994).

9. Harriet Woods, *Stepping Up to Power: The Political Journey of American Women* (Boulder: Westview Press, 2000); Patricia Schroeder, *24 Years of House Work . . . and the Place is Still a Mess* (Kansas City: Andrews McMeel, 2000). Witt, Paget and Matthews (1994).

10. Boxer (1994), p. 74.

11. David Niven, "Party Elites and Women Candidates: The Shape of Bias," *Women and Politics* 19 (2) (1998): 59–84; Janet Flammang, *Women's Political Voice: How Women Are Transforming the Practice and Study of Politics* (Philadelphia: Temple University Press, 1997); Richard L. Fox, *Gender Dynamics in Congressional Elections* (Thousand Oaks: Sage, 1997); Kim Fridkin Kahn, *The Political Consequences of Being a Woman* (New York: Columbia University Press, 1996).

12. In the late 1990s, approximately 15 percent of General Social Survey respondents also agreed that "women should take care of running their homes and leave running the country up to men."

13. Jennifer L. Lawless, "Women, War, and Winning Elections: Gender Stereotyping in the Post September 11th Era," *Political Research Quarterly* 57 (2004): forthcoming.

14. Eric R.A.N. Smith and Richard L. Fox, "A Research Note: The Electoral Fortunes of Women Candidates for Congress," *Political Research Quarterly* 54 (2001): 205–21; Richard L. Fox, "Gender and Congressional Elections," (In S. Tolleson-Rinehart and J. Josephson (eds.), *Gender and American Politics,* Armonk: M. E. Sharpe, 2000); Barbara Burrell, *A Woman's Place Is in the House* (Ann Arbor: University of Michigan Press, 1996); Kathleen Dolan, "Voting for Women in the Year of the Woman," *American Journal of Political Science* 42 (1998):272–93.

15. Kathleen Dolan, *Voting for Women: How the Public Evaluates Women Candidates* (Boulder: Westview Press, 2004), p. 50.

16. Georgia Duerst-Lahti, "The Bottleneck, Women as Candidates," (In S. Thomas and C. Wilcox (eds.), *Women and Elective Office,* New York: Oxford University Press, 1998), p. 19.

17. Gary C. Jacobson, *The Politics of Congressional Elections,* 5th edition (Boston: Allyn and Bacon, 2000).

18. R. Darcy, Susan Welch and Janet Clark, *Women, Elections, and Representation* (Lincoln: University of Nebraska Press, 1994). Some researchers contend that, with the implementation of term limits, women can

overcome the incumbency advantage (but see Susan J. Carroll and Krista Jenkins, "Do Term Limits Help Women Get Elected?" *Social Science Quarterly* 82 (2001):197–201). From the five congressional elections in the 1990s, for instance, 90 percent of all incumbents sought reelection. If members of Congress were barred from serving more than three terms, only 39 percent of these incumbents could have stood for reelection. Even with a less stringent 12 year limit, 28 percent of incumbents who chose to seek reelection would have had to give up their seats.

19. Information pertaining to members' professional backgrounds was drawn from the *Almanac of American Politics.* See also Richard L. Fox and Jennifer L. Lawless, "Entering the Arena? Gender and the Decision to Run for Office," *American Journal of Political Science* 48 (2004): 264–80.

20. Center for American Women and Politics, Women State Legislators: Past, Present, and Future, (New Brunswick: Eagleton Institute of Politics, 2001).

21. Janet Clark, "Getting There: Women in Political Office," (In Marianne Githens, Pippa Norris, and Joni Lovenduski (eds.), *Different Roles, Different Voices,* New York: Harper-Collins, 1994), p. 106.

22. Morris P. Fiorina and Paul E. Peterson, *The New American Democracy, 2nd Edition* (Boston: Longman, 2002), pp. 340–1.

23. National Association for Law Placement Foundation, Presence of Women and Attorneys of Color Continues to Rise at Large Law Firms (NALP Foundation, 1999), accessible at http://www.nalp.org/press/divers98.htm.

24. These data were provided by Catalyst, a New York based non-profit organization.

25. The following discussion draws heavily from Fox and Lawless (2004).

26. Michele L. Swers, *The Difference Women Make* (Chicago: University of Chicago, 2002); Susan J. Carroll, Debra L. Dodson and Ruth B. Mandel, *The Impact of Women in Public Office: An Overview* (New Brunswick: Eagleton Institute of Politics' Center for American Women and Politics, 1991); Sue Thomas, "The Impact of Women on State Legislative Policies," *Journal of Politics* 53 (1991): 958–76.

27. Flammang (1997); Sue Thomas, *How Women Legislate* (New York: Oxford University Press, 1994); Michael B. Berkman and Robert E. O'Connor, "Do Women Legislators Matter?" *American Politics Quarterly* 21 (1993): 102–24; Sue Thomas and Susan Welch, "The Impact of Gender on Activities and Priorities of State Legislators," *Western Political Quarterly* 44 (1991): 445–56.

28. Debra L. Dodson, "Representing Women's Interests in the U.S. House of Representatives" (In S. Thomas and C. Wilcox (eds.), *Women and Elective Office,* New York: Oxford University Press, 1998).

29. Sarah Glazer, Women's Health Issues, (*CQ Researcher,* May 13, 1994), p. 414.

30. Susan Moller Okin, *Justice, Gender, and the Family* (New York: Basic Books, 1989).

31. Burrell, Barbara, "Campaign Finance: Women's Experience in the Modern Era," (In S. Thomas and C. Wilcox (eds.), *Women and Elective Office,* New York: Oxford University Press, 1998), p. 159.

32. Cindy Simon Rosenthal, *When Women Lead* (New York: Oxford University Press, 1998); Thomas (1994).

33. Lyn Kathlene, "Alternative Views of Crime: Legislative Policymaking in Gendered Terms," *Journal of Politics* 57 (1995): 696–723.

34. Lyn Kathlene, "Power and Influence in State Legislatures; the Interaction of Gender and Position in Committee Hearing Debates," *American Political Science Review* 88 (1994): 560–76, p. 527.

35. Sue Tolleson Rinehart, "Do Women Leaders Make a Difference? Substance, Style, and Perceptions" (In D. L. Dodson (ed.), *Gender and Policymaking: Studies of Women i–n Office,* New Brunswick: Rutgers University, 1991). Not all studies uncover such differences: Debra L. Dodson and Susan J. Carroll, *Reshaping the Agenda: Women in State Legislatures* (New Brunswick: Eagleton Institute of Politics' Center for American Women and Politics, 1991), and Diane D. Blair and Jeanie R. Stanley, "Personal Relationships and Legislative Power: Male and Female Perceptions," *Legislative Studies Quarterly* 16 (1991): 495–507 find that both men and women state legislators choose to employ "feminine" leadership styles. Georgia Duerst-Lahti and Cathy Marie Johnson, "Management Styles, Stereotypes, and Advantages" (In M. E. Guy (ed.) *Women and Men of the States: Public Administrators at the State Level,* Armonk: M. E. Sharpe, 1992) find few differences in the traits men and women public administrators value. More importantly, they conclude that the most valued traits (conscientiousness, reliability, and efficiency) are gender neutral. According to Beth Reingold, "Conflict and Cooperation: Legislative Strategies and Concepts of Power among Female and Male State Legislators," *Journal of Politics* 58 (1996):464–85, the one factor that distinguishes the studies that have found sex differences from those that have not is the presence of strong institutional norms of behavior (468). The successful rational actor is aware of the dangers of "ruffling feathers, stepping on toes, and burning bridges" (483).

36. Barry Weingast and William Marshall, "The Industrial Organization of Congress," *Journal of Political Economy* 96 (1988): 132–63; Douglas H. Price, "Careers and Committees in the American Congress: The Problem of Structural Change," (In W. O. Aydeloote (ed.) *The History of Parliamentary Behavior,* Princeton: Princeton University Press, 1977); Nelson Polsby, "The Institutionalization of the U.S. House of Representatives," *American Political Science Review* 62 (1968): 144–68.

37. These figures are not a result of women's relatively recent entry into the House. If we focus only on those members who entered the chamber after the 97th Congress and voluntarily retired, women's tenure is still 18 percent shorter than men's.

38. Jennifer L. Lawless and Sean M. Theriault, "Will She Stay or Will She Go? Women's Retirement from the U.S. Congress," paper presented at the annual meeting of the Midwest Political Science Association, Chicago, April 3–6, 2003.

39. Sean M. Theriault, "Moving Up or Moving Out: Career Ceilings and Congressional Retirement," *Legislative Studies Quarterly* 23 (1998): 419–33.

40. Samuel H. Fisher and Rebekah Herrick, "Whistle While You Work: Job Satisfaction and Retirement from the U.S. House," *Legislative Studies Quarterly* 27 (2002): 445–57, p. 453.

41. See Lawless and Theriault (2003) for the regression analysis on which this discussion is based.

42. Length of service exerts a strong effect as well. The exact same female representative is four and a half times more likely to retire if we double her years of service from 15 to 30. Although the slope for men is not as large as it is for women, it still, nonetheless, has quite an impact. Doubling the 25 year career of a male representative more than triples his retirement probability. Regardless of the manner in which we present the data, career ceilings significantly affect congressional retirement, especially for female representatives.

43. Fox (1997). See also Helen S. Astin and Carole Leland, *Women of Influence, Women of Vision: A Cross-generational Study of Leadership and Social Change* (San Francisco: Jossey-Bass, 1991); Timothy Bredsoe and Mary Herring, "Victims of Circumstances: Women in Pursuit of Political Office," *American Political Science Review* 84 (1990): 213–23; Edmond Constantini, "Political Women and Political Ambition: Closing the Gender Gap," *American Journal of Political Science* 34 (1990): 74–70.

44. Dodson (1998); Thomas (1994).

45. Beth Reingold, *Representing Women: Sex, Gender, and Legislative Behavior in Arizona and California* (Chapel Hill: University of North Carolina, 2000); Darcy, Welch, and Clark (1994).

46. Lonna Rae Atkeson, "Not All Cues are Created Equal: The Conditional Impact of Female Candidates on Political Engagement," *Journal of Politics* 65 (2003): 1040–61; Jane Mansbridge, "Should Blacks Represent Blacks and Women Represent Women? A Contingent "Yes," *Journal of Politics* 61 (1999): 628–57; Cindy Simon Rosenthal, "The Role of Gender in Descriptive Representation," *Political Research Quarterly* 48 (1995): 599–612; Sue Tolleson-Rinehart, "The California Senate Races: A Case Study in the Gendered Paradoxes of Politics," (In E. A. Cook, S. Thomas, and C. Wilcox (eds.),

The Year of the Woman, (Boulder: Westview, 1994); Hanna F. Pitkin, *The Concept of Representation* (Berkeley: University of California, 1967).

47. Jennifer L. Lawless, "Politics of Presence: Women in the House and Symbolic Representation," *Political Research Quarterly* 57 (2004): 81–99.

48. Burrell (1996), p. 151.

49. Thomas (1998), p. 1.

50. Phillip Paolino, "Group-Salient Issues and Group Representation: Support for Women Candidates in the 1992 Senate Elections," *American Journal of Political Science* 29 (1995): 294–313, pp. 309–10.

FURTHER READING

Blair, Diane D. and Jeanie R. Stanley. (1991) "Personal Relationships and Legislative Power: Male and Female Perceptions," *Legislative Studies Quarterly* 16:495–507.

Bledsoe, Timothy and Mary Herring. (1990) Victims of Circumstances: Women in Pursuit of Political Office, *American Political Science Review* 84:213–23.

Burrell, Barbara. (1996) Campaign Finance: Women's Experience in the Modern Era, In S. Thomas and C. Wilcox (eds.), *Women and Elective Office,* New York: Oxford University Press.

Carroll, Susan, Debra L. Dodson and Ruth B. Mandel. (1991) The Impact of Women in Public Office: An Overview, New Brunswick: Eagleton Institute of Politics' Center for American Women and Politics.

Center for American Women and Politics (CAWP). (2003) Women in Elective Office 2003 Fact Sheet, New Brunswick: Center for American Women and Politics.

———. (2001) Women State Legislators: Past, Present, and Future. New Brunswick: Eagleton Institute of Politics.

Clark, Janet. (1994) Getting There: Women in Political Office, In Marianne Githens, Pippa Norris, and Joni Lovenduski (eds.), *Different Roles, Different Voices,* New York: Harper-Collins.

Constantini, Edmond. (1990) Political Women and Political Ambition: Closing the Gender Gap, *American Journal of Political Science* 34:741–70.

Dodson, Debra L. (1998) Representing Women's Interests in the U.S. House of Representatives, In S. Thomas and C. Wilcox (eds.), *Women and Elective Office,* New York: Oxford University Press.

Duerst-Lahti, Georgia and Cathy Marie Johnson. (1992) Management Styles, Stereotypes, and Advantages, In M. E. Guy (ed.) *Women and Men of the States: Public Administrators at the State Level,* Armonk: M. E. Sharpe.

Fox, Richard L. and Jennifer L. Lawless. (2004) Entering the Arena? Gender and the Decision to Run for Office, *American Journal of Political Science* 48(2): 264–80.

Inter-Parliamentary Union. (2003) Women in National Parliaments, http://www.ipu.org/wmn-e/classif.htm.

Kahn, Kim Fridkin. (1996) *The Political Consequences of Being a Woman,* New York: Columbia University Press.

Lawless, Jennifer L. (2004) Politics of Presence: Women in the House and Symbolic Representation, *Political Research Quarterly* 57(1):81–99.

Lawless, Jennifer L. and Sean M. Theriault. (2003) Will She Stay or Will She Go? Women's Retirement from the U.S. Congress, paper presented at the annual meeting of the Midwest Political Science Association, Chicago, April 3–6.

National Association for Law Placement Foundation. (1999) Presence of Women and Attorneys of Color Continues to Rise at Large Law Firms, NALP Foundation. http://www.nalp.org/press/divers98.htm

Niven, David. (1998) Party Elites and Women Candidates: The Shape of Bias, *Women and Politics* 19(2):57–80.

Paolino, Phillip. (1995) Group-Salient Issues and Group Representation: Support for Women Candidates in the 1992 Senate Elections, *American Journal of Political Science* 29:294–313.

Pitkin, Hanna F. (1967) *The Concept of Representation,* Berkeley: University of California.

Reingold, Beth. (1996) Conflict and Cooperation: Legislative Strategies and Concepts of Power among Female and Male State Legislators, *Journal of Politics* 58(2):464–85.

———. (2000) *Representing Women: Sex, Gender, and Legislative Behavior in Arizona and California,* Chapel Hill: University of North Carolina.

Rosenthal, Cindy Simon. (1995) The Role of Gender in Descriptive Representation, *Political Research Quarterly* 48:599–612.

Theriault, Sean M. (1998) Moving Up or Moving Out: Career Ceilings and Congressional Retirement, *Legislative Studies Quarterly* 23(3):419–33.

Thomas, Sue. (1998) Introduction: Women and Elective Office: Past, Present, and Future, In S. Thomas and C. Wilcox (eds.), *Women and Elective Office,* New York: Oxford University Press.

Wallison, Ethan. (2003) Pryce Declares White House "Dropped the Ball," *Roll Call,* November 10:3.

Women State Legislators: Descriptive and Substantive Representation

Sarah Poggione

Currently women hold about twenty-two percent or 1,655 of the 7,382 seats in the U.S. state legislatures; thirty years ago, women only held about eight percent of the seats.[1] In response to the dramatic increase in women's presence in statehouses, scholars have documented differences between men and women state legislators. Early research found that women state legislators of 1970s were less educated, older, and less likely to have professional careers outside the legislature than men; in surveys, women state legislators reported that civic concerns and the desire to help people motivated them to seek public office and that they were unlikely to pursue politics as a career or seek higher office.[2] Women legislators reportedly spent more time on constituent service and less time in committee hearings or meeting with lobbyists than men legislators.[3]

As the career paths and socio-economic characteristics of men and women converged in the 1980s, more women were elected to office and many of the differences between men and women legislators diminished or disappeared entirely.[4] The growing number of women serving in state legislatures in the 1980s and 1990s, while still slightly older, were just as likely as men to have a college degree. In the 1980s, differences between men and women legislators' levels of political ambition and experience, known as the professionalization gap, shrank considerably. A recent study finds that contemporary women legislators are more likely than men to view politics as a career, seek reelection, and run for higher office.[5] Although women continue to see themselves as more attuned to constituency interests, they are no less likely to participate in committees, speak on the floor, or deal with lobbyists than men legislators.[6]

As differences in men and women legislators backgrounds, characteristics, and participation in legislative activities diminished, gender differences in their policy preferences and related legislative behaviors increased. Based on these differences, scholars have turned their attention to the effects of women's representation in state legislatures, particularly women legislators' impact on policy. In this article, I explore differences in men and women state legislators' policy opinions and legislative behavior as well as the effect of women state legislators on policy by discussing previous work and by investigating gender differences and women's influence on a welfare policy.

This work concentrates specifically on welfare policy because previous work suggests that women will hold more liberal policy preferences and exhibit greater commitment to policies, like welfare, that concern women, children, and families.[7] Welfare policy also provides a unique opportunity to study women's impact because federal welfare reform has prompted a great deal of state activity. The Personal Responsibility and Work Reconciliation Act of 1996 replaced the categorical grant-in-aid program, Aid to Families with Dependent Children (AFDC), with Temporary Assistance to Needy Families (TANF). TANF delegates considerably more control over welfare policy from the federal government to the states. This devolution has prompted many state legislatures, for the first time, to review prior administrative reforms and take an active role in shaping state welfare programs. The large volume of state activity created by this reorganization of program responsibilities provides ample variation in policy to be explained by the participation of women legislators.[8]

Consistent with previous work on women state legislators, I find significant gender differences in legislators' welfare policy preferences and welfare-related activities. Women state legislators hold more liberal policy preferences and are more active on the issue of welfare than their male colleagues. In addition, women's representation in state legislatures has significant effect on policy. Women's presence on welfare committees, particularly when these committees have greater autonomy in the policymaking process, produces more liberal state welfare policies.

WOMEN'S REPRESENTATION IN STATE LEGISLATORS

Although scholars cite numerous potential benefits of women's increasing representation in government, including greater competition for public office and improved legitimacy for the political system, researchers consider women's potential impact on public policy one of the most important. Debra Dodson and Sue Carroll explain,

> Proponents of increased representation for women can and do argue for the election or appointment of more women public officials as a matter of justice and equity. They assert that democratic principles require that all citizens regardless of gender should have an equal opportunity to participate in politics. Many question the quality of rep-

resentation in a nation where women are half of the citizens, but a small minority of officeholders. However, their arguments become more compelling if, in fact, women officeholders bring to office important perspectives and priorities that are currently underrepresented in the policymaking process.[9]

As a result, scholars have examined women's representation in a variety of contexts, including federal, state, and local government as well as the executive, legislative, and judicial branches. While studies at nearly every level and in every branch of government suggest that women public officials have an impact on public policy,[10] a great deal of research has focused on women in state legislatures.

State legislatures continue to be an important context for exploring the policy impact of women officials for several reasons. First, state legislatures are the highest level of government institutions with substantial numbers of women members. Figure 1 compares the percentage of women elected to the U.S. House, the Senate, and the upper and lower houses of state legislatures. Not only do a greater percentage and a greater number of women serve in both the lower and upper houses of state legislatures compared to the U.S. House and Senate, the increase in women's representation in the 1970s and 1980s has been more dramatic.

Second, state legislatures formulate policy in response to a growing number of important issues like violence against women, healthcare, education, and welfare, which are of particular interest to women. The continuing devolution of policy responsibilities from the federal government to the states has increased the importance of state legislatures and their members in the policymaking process. Increased women's representation in state legislatures affords women legislators a greater opportunity to influence the content and direction of state policy on a growing number of important issues.

However, increases in women's representation may not produce comparable changes in policy. In order for women's descriptive representative, the presence of women in governing institutions, to produce substantive representation, legislative agendas and policies reflecting women's interests, women legislators' policy preferences must differ from those of their male colleagues. If men and women legislators, after accounting for the effects of political party or constituency concerns, have similar attitudes on policy then increases in women's representation may have little effect on legislative decisions.

Gender differences in policy opinions are also not sufficient to establish a connection between women's descriptive and substantive representation; women must also act on their distinctive policy preferences. If the policy preferences of men and women legislators differ, but their legislative behavior does not, then the increased representation of women in state legislatures will not alter legislative agendas and policies. If gender differences exist in men and women legislators' policy preferences and legislative activities, then women's representation in state legislatures may influence state policies.

Given significant gender differences in policy preferences and legislative behavior, the relationship between descriptive and substantive representation is still

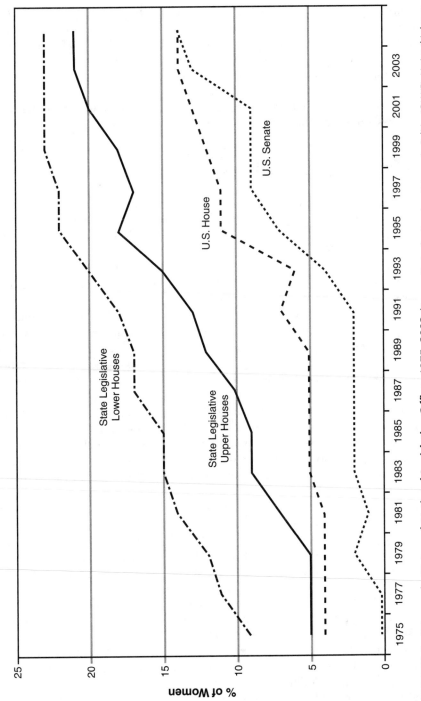

FIGURE 1   Women in State and National Legislative Office, 1975–2003 (*Source:* Center for American Women in Politics (CAWP), National Information Bank on Women in Public Office, Eagleton Institute of Politics, Rutgers University.)

185

not automatic. Women, currently a numerical minority in all 99 state legislative chambers, must successfully navigate legislative institutions in order to influence legislative agendas and state policies. As a legislative minority, women legislators may face institutional obstacles that hamper their ability to influence policy. However if women state legislators have distinct policy attitudes, pursue legislative activities that reflect their preferences, and succeed in influencing legislative decisions despite their minority status, then the increasing presence of women in state legislatures will shape the content and direction of state policy.

GENDER DIFFERENCES IN POLICY PREFERENCES

The notion that men and women state legislators have different preferences on policy has considerable theoretical and empirical support. Scholars expect the policy attitudes of men and women legislators differ due to men and women's distinct experiences and responsibilities in the private sphere.[11] As Karin Tamerius summarizes, "Simply put, women's experiences happen to women while men's experiences happen to men."[12] This explanation is largely based on the work of gender theorists who contend that men and women develop differently, both psychologically and socially.[13] Dodson and Carroll note that although these difference theorists explore diverse explanations for observed gender differences, their work collectively suggests that women in comparison with men are more relational, have a greater sense of connection with others, are more empathetic and caring and less likely to think in terms of rights and more likely to think in terms of responsibilities.[14]

Based on these theoretical foundations, a great deal of work on women and politics hypothesizes that women state legislators will express greater interest in representing women's issues and hold more liberal policy opinions than their male colleagues. Early empirical work finds that women state legislators do hold more liberal policy positions than their male colleagues, particularly on issues that affect children, women, and families. For example, a study of four New England states in the 1970s finds that women state legislators favored addressing poverty rather than using force as a solution to urban unrest and were more supportive of providing daycare services and repealing restrictive state abortion laws than men.[15]

While a few studies find mixed results concerning the effect of gender on men and women legislators' policy preferences,[16] a great deal of evidence demonstrates that women legislators continue to exhibit more liberal policy preferences than men. Dodson and Caroll find that women legislators policy attitudes concerning private sector solutions to economic problems, the death penalty, government provision of child care services, nuclear power, parental consent for abortion for minors, increasing state and local taxes for social services, the Equal Rights Amendment, and prohibiting abortion are more liberal and feminist than their male colleagues.[17] Significant differences in men and women's policy preferences remain even after accounting for political party.[18]

Using data collected from a mail survey of more than 2,500 legislators in twenty-four states as well as information from state legislative Web pages, I evaluate the independent effect of gender on state legislators' welfare policy preferences. The survey, conducted in 2000, was mailed to 2,526 state legislators, all members of the lower houses of 24 selected state legislatures.[19] To measure legislators' welfare policy preferences, I develop a summative index of welfare policy liberalism composed of 17 dichotomous items indicating legislators' support or opposition to principles of welfare reform and initiatives designed to help recipients or populations at risk.[20] The index of welfare policy liberalism ranges from a low of zero, indicating the most conservative position on welfare policy, to a high of 17, indicating the most liberal position. The mean score for all respondents is 9.13. The mean scores for men and women legislators are reported in Table 1.

On average, women legislators score an 11.4 on the welfare liberalism index and men score an 8.5, resulting in a three point gender difference in men and women's mean scores. The results of the difference in means test, reported in the final column of the Table 1, indicate that the difference in men and women's average scores is statistically significant. The probability that the observed difference in

TABLE 1   Gender and Welfare Policy Preferences

	Mean Welfare Liberalism Score		Diff. in Means	t^b
	Women[a]	*Men*[a]		
(All Legislators)	11.4 (114)	8.5 (388)	3.0	8.6*
(By Party)				
Democrats	12.4 (80)	11.0 (161)	1.5	3.8*
Republicans	9.1 (29)	6.7 (216)	2.5	4.4*
(By Ideology)				
Liberals	13.1 (48)	12.4 (73)	.79	1.8
Moderates	11.1 (34)	9.7 (93)	1.4	2.4*
Conservatives	8.9 (26)	6.6 (213)	2.3	3.9*
(By Constituency)				
Rural	10.8 (42)	8.0 (197)	2.8	4.8*
Suburban	10.6 (32)	7.9 (102)	2.7	4.8*
Urban	12.9 (38)	10.1 (80)	2.8	4.7*

[a]Cell entries relfect the mean welfare index score for particular groups of women and men legislators with number of legislators in the group in parentheses.

[b]The calculated *t* value for the test of equality of men and women's mean scores (equal variances not assumed).

*$p < .05$

means could occur due to chance variation in the sample if there was no real difference between men and women's average scores in the population is quite small, less than .05. This probability is small enough to conclude that the mean scores for men and women are not equal and that men and women hold different preferences on welfare policy.

These results provide evidence of women's greater liberalism; however, these apparent gender differences may be driven by party or ideological differences among men and women legislators or differences in the type of constituencies they represent. Studies of gender differences in state legislators attitudes that have included control variables like party and constituency characteristics find that these measures are related to legislators' attitudes and may reduce the observed effect of gender.[21] In order to control for the influence of factors like party, ideology, and constituency interests, I compare the mean scores of men and women of the same party, ideological position, and type of constituency.[22] Returning to Table 1, notice that even within the same party, ideology, or constituency, women legislators have a higher average score and exhibit more liberal welfare policy preferences then their male counterparts. For example, the average score for Democratic women is 12.4 and only 11.0 for Democratic men. With only one exception, the differences between women and men's mean scores within these various subgroups are statistically significant. While party, ideology, and constituency characteristics also influence members policy preferences, gender differences persist even after controlling for these factors.

These results also indicate that the effect of gender is not constant across legislators. Gender differences are larger among Republicans and conservatives compared to Democrats and more liberal legislators. For example, while the difference in means between Democratic men and women is 1.5 points, the difference in means among Republicans is 2.5 points. Regardless of party, women are more liberal in their opinions on welfare policy than men, but Republican women are substantially more liberal in their opinions than Republican men. This finding is consistent with prior work that finds that Republican women are more likely to defect from their party and cast liberal votes, introduce bills, and act in other ways that do not reflect their party's more conservative agenda.[23]

The results also demonstrate gender differences are less pronounced among liberal legislators and more pronounced among conservatives. For the most part women hold more liberal policy attitudes on welfare than men, and these gender differences are larger among conservatives. Conservative women are actually far less conservative with respect to welfare policy than their male colleagues. These results suggest that the increasing presence of women in state government has the potential to produce more liberal state policies. In fact, increases in women's representation may have a larger, relative impact on policy where we might least expect it—when conservative and Republican women replace their male counterparts. However, in order to conclude that women's representation in state legislatures will alter policy, women must also act differently in the legislature.

GENDER DIFFERENCES IN LEGISLATIVE ACTIVITIES

Based on men and women private sphere experiences, scholars also expect that men and women legislators will pursue different legislative activities. As Sue Thomas notes, although women as a group do not have a single set of priorities or a single lens through which they view politics, it is true that they have distinctive life experiences to bring to their deliberations and decisions.[24] Early research found that women elected officials not only express more liberal policy opinions but also behaved in ways that reflected their greater interest in social welfare, education, and issues dealing with family life.[25] Women state legislators were more likely to serve on committees with jurisdiction over traditional women's concerns like health and welfare issues rather than committees dealing with taxes or business.[26]

Contemporary research confirms that women's legislative activities continue to reflect their more liberal preferences, and that they remain more likely to work on women's issues than men. Women state legislators are more likely to sponsor legislation and work on issues related to traditional women's concerns and feminist issues than men.[27] Although women now serve on a more diverse set of committees, they are still more likely to sit on health or welfare committees and less likely to sit on business or economic committees than men.[28] Research finds that women are also more likely to chair health, education, and human services committees and less likely to chair banking and financial, energy, insurance, and rules committees.[29]

Susan Carroll and Ella Taylor report that this skew in committee assignments reflects women's preferences rather than discrimination.[30] In addition, the results of the 2000 survey of state legislators also support this conclusion. Over 88 percent of women legislators report that they were generally pleased with their committee assignments compared to eighty-seven percent of men. In addition, eighty-nine percent of members who serve on welfare committees report satisfaction compared to eighty-seven percent of members who do not serve on these committees. It appears that women choose committee assignments in line with their own personal and political agendas and are not relegated to these committees by chamber or party leaders.

Using data from the survey of state legislators, I find that women are more active on the issue of welfare than men. I examine gender differences in legislative activities related to welfare policy, including working on welfare legislation and serving on welfare committees. Both activities relate to important parts of the legislative process. When legislators actively work on a bill by influencing the committee to which a bill is referred, testifying or arranging for witnesses to testify on behalf of the bill, and negotiating with committee members, bills are more likely to pass.[31] Legislators who choose to take part and be actively involved in committee deliberation on a given bill have an opportunity to influence policy in a way that is not easily observed by the public and therefore less constrained by constituency demands.[32] As a result, legislators' decisions to work on welfare legislation or specialize on welfare committees are likely to influence the content of state welfare policies.

From the survey, I record the number of welfare related bills that state legislators reported actively working on in the previous session. This ranges from zero for members who did not report working on any welfare-related legislation to five for members who reported actively working on five pieces of welfare-related legislation. The mean number of welfare bills that men and women legislators actively worked on is presented in Table 2.

The average among all women legislators is about 1.06 welfare bills per session. The average for all men is only .60 bills per session. As indicated by the t-test in the final column of the table, this .45 difference between men and women is statistically significant. Women state legislators do actively work on more welfare legislation than men. Generally, these significant gender differences remain even after accounting for party, ideology, and constituency characteristics. Similar to gender differences in policy preferences, differences in the average number of bills men and women legislators work on are more pronounced among Republicans and conservative legislators compared to Democrats and more liberal legislators. However, even among Democrats and moderates, women are significantly more active on the issue of welfare than their male colleagues.

Using the survey, I also determine whether or not legislators serve on welfare committees. Table 3 indicates the percentage of men and women who serve on welfare committees in their legislatures.

TABLE 2   Gender and Working on Welfare Legislation

	Mean No. Welfare Bills		Diff. in Means	t^b
	Women[a]	Men[a]		
(All Legislators)	1.06 (108)	.60 (318)	.45	4.20*
(By Party)				
Democrats	1.13 (77)	.83 (133)	.30	2.03*
Republicans	0.89 (28)	.45 (175)	.45	2.68*
(By Ideology)				
Liberals	1.09 (46)	.89 (64)	.20	.95
Moderates	1.16 (32)	.72 (77)	.43	2.14*
Conservatives	1.04 (24)	.43 (169)	.60	3.29*
(By Constituency)				
Rural	1.03 (40)	.63 (167)	.39	2.29*
Suburban	1.19 (31)	.53 (76)	.67	3.50*
Urban	1.03 (35)	.61 (67)	.42	1.97*

[a]Cell entries relfect the mean number of welfare related bills that particular groups of women and men legislators reported working on in previous session with number of legislators in the group in parentheses.

[b]The calculated t value for the test of equality of men and women's mean number of bills (equal variances not assumed).

*$p < .05$

TABLE 3   Gender and Working on Welfare Committees

	% Serving on Welfare Committee		Diff. in Percentages	t^b
	Women[a]	Men[a]		
(All Legislators)	21 (121)	12 (407)	9	2.31*
(By Party)				
Democrats	26 (85)	11 (171)	15	2.88*
Republicans	9 (32)	14 (224)	−4	−.78
(By Ideology)				
Liberals	22 (50)	8 (76)	14	2.11*
Moderates	29 (35)	11 (102)	18	2.13*
Conservatives	18 (28)	14 (221)	3	.44
(By Constituency)				
Rural	15 (47)	13 (209)	2	.26
Suburban	21 (33)	8 (105)	14	2.21*
Urban	31 (39)	13 (83)	18	2.09*

[a]Cell entries relfect the percentage of particular groups of women and men legislators that serve on welfare committees with the number of legislators in parentheses.

[b]The calculated t value for the test of equality of men and women's proportions (equal variances not assumed).

*$p < .05$

About twenty-one percent of women legislators serve on welfare committees compared to only twelve percent of men. This nine percentage point difference is statistically significant. Comparing men and women's welfare committee service within the parties, gender differences are greater among Democrats than Republicans. While Democratic women are substantially more likely to serve on welfare related committees than Democratic men, Republican men are slightly more likely to serve on welfare committees (fourteen percent) than their female counterparts (nine percent), although the difference is not significant at traditional levels. Similarly, the effect of gender is also stronger among liberals and moderates than conservatives.

These gender differences in legislators activities suggest that Republican and conservative women as well as Democratic and liberal women have the potential to influence state policy. Although Republican women are not more likely than Republican men to serve on welfare committees, Republican and conservative women have markedly more liberal preferences and work on more welfare legislation than male counterparts. As a result, the replacement of Republican or conservative men with Republican or conservative women has the potential to liberalize policy. Although the policy preferences of liberal men and women and Democratic men and women are similar, replacing Democratic or liberal men with Democratic or liberal women also has the potential to liberalize policy through women's greater participation on welfare committees.

WOMEN STATE LEGISLATORS' IMPACT ON POLICY

Based on empirical evidence confirming women state legislators' distinctive preferences and legislative behaviors and theoretical expectations of gender difference, women and politics scholars generally conclude that the presence of women in governing institutions will fundamentally alter the policies considered and adopted by these institutions. Increased women's representation is expected to bring, not only new issues to the attention of government, but also new governmental solutions to what were previously considered individual.[33] Thomas and Welch contend, "It is likely that as women move further away from token status, they will feel ever more encouraged to bring forth distinctive solutions to problems closest to home."[34]

Women's presence in state legislatures has been linked to policy changes. For example in her longitudinal study of the Arizona state legislatures, Michelle Saint-Germain finds that as the number of women in the legislature increased over time the legislature paid more attention to women's issues and passed more legislation addressing women's concerns.[35] Cross-sectional research on a number of states also finds a positive relationship between women's representation in state legislatures and policy. In her study of twelve states legislatures, Thomas finds that more bills concerning women, children, and families were introduced and that somewhat more of these bills were passed in legislatures with moderate (ten to twenty percent) or high proportions (over twenty percent) of women members; she explains, "In short, in states within the high category with respect to percentage of women in the legislature, women introduced a greater amount of bills dealing with women, and children, and the family than did men. In states in the low category, no such pattern is displayed."[36] Focusing specifically on abortion policy, Michael Berkman and Robert O'Connor find that states with more women legislators are less likely to impose parental notification requirements than states with fewer women in the statehouse.[37]

While research on women in state legislatures finds considerable support for a positive relationship between descriptive representation and substantive representation, there is little evidence to suggest that it is a simple linear relationship.[38] Given that decisions in state legislatures are made by majority rule, women legislators' minority status makes it unlikely that they will be able to alter the policymaking process and other legislative procedures to their advantage. Consequently, women representatives may have to work through existing and often inconvenient legislative procedures in order to influence policy. Prior work acknowledges that although women legislators may desire to change legislative structure, they typically must work within the existing legislative structure to affect policy. As Sue Thomas observes, "Women's distinctive contribution has focused on policy, not procedure."[39] Although previous research on women in state legislatures has not focused explicitly on legislative institutions and procedures, some scholars have observed that particular characteristics of legislative institutions may prevent women from successfully pursuing their objectives and diminish their impact on policy, and other researchers suggest that some institutional arrangements may allow women to have a substantial influence on policy despite their small numbers.[40] These observations confirm the importance of legislative structure in explaining women legislators success in shaping public policy.

Formal models of legislative organization in Congress suggest that standing committees provide small groups of legislators the opportunity to substantially influence legislative outcomes.[41] Based on the survey of state legislators, the eighty-eight women who did not serve on welfare committees in their states worked on an average of .90 welfare bills in the previous session. The twenty women welfare committee members worked on about 1.75 bills per session. In addition, fifty-one percent of the women who did not serve on welfare committees succeeded in passing at least one of the welfare bills they worked on. Over sixty percent of women welfare committee members succeeded in passing some of the welfare legislation they worked on.[42] It appears that committees do provide women legislators with a greater opportunity to influence welfare policy.

The extent to which committees can dominate the policymaking process depends on the structure of the legislature. Rules and procedures that minimize or eliminate the participation of non-committee member in decisions about the composition and activities of committees foster committee independence.[43] A key element of committee independence is the self-selection of committee members. When individual legislators are able to determine their own committee assignments, the resulting composition of committees is ill-suited to representing the interests of the chamber leaders or party caucuses. The potential policy bias that results from the self-selection of committee members is reinforced by the rules and procedures that structure the legislative process.[44]

Rules governing committees vary across the states. In states where non-committee members have little control over the composition and activities of committees, committees have greater autonomy and control over policymaking. As a result, women legislators have a greater opportunity to effect policy through their committee service when committees have a high degree of independence in the policymaking process. To determine the degree of committee autonomy in policymaking, I consider the selection of committee leaders and members, the jurisdiction of committee issues, the process of bill referral, the rules associated with committee hearings, and the provision of committee staff in state legislatures from *The Book of the States.*

The resulting index of committee independence varies from a low of—6.07, indicating that committees have little autonomy, to a high of 7.64, indicating that committees have a great deal of autonomy and control over policymaking.[45] States with negative values on the index have committees with less than average levels of independence, and states with positive values have committees with more independence than average. I divide states into high levels of committee independence (positive values on the index) and those with low levels of committee independence (negative values on the index). Twenty states are characterized by a high degree of committee independence including Arkansas, Hawaii, Massachusetts, and Texas. Thirty states have low levels of autonomy including Colorado, Georgia, Michigan, and North Dakota.

In order to examine how committees and legislative structure provide or constrain opportunities for a minority of women legislators to influence policy, I compare the relationship between women's participation on welfare committees and significant aspects of state welfare policy in legislatures with high and low levels of committee autonomy. The correlation coefficients presented in Table 4 summarize the relationship between women's participation and important aspects of state welfare policy including eligibility for pregnant women, time limits on assistance, as well as welfare effort—the percent of state budgets spent of welfare services.[46] Person's correlation coefficient r measures the amount of linear association between two interval or dichotomous variables like the percentage of women on state welfare committees and whether or not states extend TANF eligibility to pregnant women. It ranges from negative one, a perfect negative relationship in which high values of one variable are always associated with low values of the other, to positive one, a perfect positive relationship in which high values of one variable are always associated with high values of the other. Smaller negative or positive coefficients indicate weaker relationships, and an r of zero indicates that the two variables are unrelated. Spearman's ρ provides a similar assessment of the relationship between two variables when one or both are ordinal or ranked data.

For the twenty states characterized by a high level of committee independence, the relationship between TANF eligibility for pregnant women and women's participation on welfare committees is a moderate positive one ($r = .37$). Higher proportions of women serving on welfare committee are associated with states extending eligibility to pregnant women. For the 30 states with less independent committees, the relationship is still positive but much weaker ($r = .13$). A similar pattern holds for

TABLE 4   Committee Independence and Women's Influence on Welfare Policy

	Committee Independence	
	High	*Low*
Eligibilty for Pregnant Women[a]	.37 (20)	.16 (30)
Time Limits[b]	.39 (20)	−.03 (30)
Welfare Effort[a]	.67 (20)	−.32 (20)

[a]Cell entries relfect Pearson correlation coefficients with the number of states in parentheses.
[b]Cells reflect Spearman rank order correlations with the number of states in parentheses.

time limits on assistance as well as welfare effort. When committees have a high degree of autonomy in the policymaking process, women's participation on welfare committees is associated with longer life-time limits ($\rho = .39$) and a greater proportion of state budgets being spent on welfare programs ($r = .67$). When committees have less autonomy, women's participation has essentially no effect on TANF time limits ($\rho = -.03$) and is actually negatively related to welfare effort ($r = -.32$). (See Table 4.)

While these results suggest that women's participation in state legislatures does influence policy, the relationship between descriptive and substantive representation is not a simple one. Women legislators' opportunities for influence are mediated by the institutions in which they serve. Specifically, the rules governing standing committees condition women's impact on policy. As other research demonstrates, increases in women a representation at the state level will continue to influence the agendas and policies adopted by state legislatures; however, even a small number of women legislators can significantly influence policy through service on independent standing committees. We might expect that women legislators in Colorado, where they make up thirty-seven percent of the lower house, are likely to influence state policy. This research also suggests that women legislators in Alabama may also influence policy even though they make up only about ten percent of the lower house. Even a small number of women legislators can influence policy if their policy preferences and legislative activities differ from those of their male colleagues and legislative rules and procedures advantage minorities in the policymaking process.

NOTES

This research would not have been possible without the generous support of the National Science Foundation (SES 9905432) and assistance from the College of Liberal Arts at the Pennsylvania State University. I would also like to thank Janna Deitz for her helpful comments.

1. CAWP Fact Sheet. (New Brunswick, NJ: Center for American Women in Politics, 2004).

2. Carol Nechemias. Changes in the Election of Women to U.S. State Legislative Seats. *Legislative Studies Quarterly* (1987), 12: 125–142; Carol Nechemias. "Geographic Mobility and Women's Access to State Legislatures." *Western Political Quarterly* (1985), 38: 119–131; Wilma Rule. "Why Women Don't Run: The Critical Contextual Factors in Women's Legislative Recruitment." *Western Political Quarterly* (1983), 34: 60–77.

3. Irene Diamond. *Sex Roles in the State House* (New Haven, CT: Yale University Press, 1977); Jeane Kirkpatrick. *Political Woman* (New York: Basic Books, 1974).

4. R. Darcy, Susan Welch, and Janet M. Clark. *Women, Elections and Representation,* 2nd ed. (Lincoln, NE: University of Nebraska Press, 1994); Irwin Gertzog. *Congressional Women: Their Recruitment, Treatment, and Behavior* (New York: Praeger, 1984).

5. John M. Carey, Richard G. Niemi, and Lynda W. Powell. "Are Women State Legislators Different?" ed. Sue Thomas and Clyde Wilcox, *Women and Elective Office: Past, Present, & Future* (New York: Oxford University Press, 1998).

6. Carey, Niemi, and Powell, "Are Women State Legislators Different?"; Sue Thomas. *How Women Legislate* (New York: Oxford University Press, 1994); Sue Thomas and Susan Welch. "The Impact of Gender on the Activities and Priorities of State Legislators: Legislative Styles and Policy Priorities." *Western Political Quarterly* (1991) 44: 445–456.

7. Thomas, *How Women Legislate.*

8. Jack Tweedie. "Welfare: What Now?" *State Legislatures* (1997) 23: 21–24.

9. Debra L. Dodson and Susan J. Carroll. *Reshaping the Agenda: Women in State Legislatures* (New Brunswick, NJ: Center for the American Woman in Politics, 1991), p. 2.

10. For research that examines the policy impact of women elected officials in a variety of government settings, see: Debra Dodson, ed. *Gender and Policymaking: Studies of Women in Office.* (New Brunswick, NJ: Center for the American Woman in Politics, 1991).

11. See for example: Ruth Mandel and Debra L. Dodson. "Do Women Officeholders Make a Difference?" eds. Paula Ries and Anne J. Stone. *The American Woman, 1992–1993* (New York: Norton, 1993); Susan Gluck Mezey. "Increasing the Number of Women in Office: Does it Matter?" eds. Elizabeth Adell Cook, Sue Thomas, and Clyde Wilcox, *The Year of the Woman: Myths and Realities* (Boulder, CO: Westview Press, 1994); Thomas, *How Women Legislate.*

12. Karin L. Tamerius. "Sex, Gender, and Leadership in the Representation of Women". eds. Georgia Duerst-Lahti and Rita Mae Kelly, *Gender, Power, Leadership, and Governance* (Ann Arbor, MI: University of Michigan Press, 1995).

13. See for example: Nancy Chodorow. *The Reproduction of Mothering, Psychoanalysis and the Sociology of Gender* (Berkeley: University of California Press, 1978); Carol Gilligan. *In a Different Voice, Psychological Theory and Women's Development.* (Cambridge, MA: Harvard University Press, 1982); Sara Ruddick. "Maternal Thinking." *Feminist Studies* (1980), 6: 342–367.

14. Dodson and Carroll, *Reshaping the Agenda: Women in State Legislatures,* p. 4.

15. Diamond, *Sex Roles in the State House;* see also Shelah Gilbert Leader. "The Policy Impact of Elected Women Officials." eds. Louis Maisel and Joseph Cooper, *The Impact of the Electoral Process* (Beverly Hills, CA; Sage, 1977).

16. See for example: Sue Thomas. "The Impact of Women on State Legislative Policies." *Journal of Politics* (1991), 53: 958–976; Thomas and Welch, "The Impact of Gender on the Activities and Priorities of State Legislators: Legislative Styles and Policy Priorities."

17. Dodson and Carroll, *Reshaping the Agenda: Women in State Legislatures;* see also Dodson, *Gender and Policymaking: Studies of Women in Office.*

18. See Carey, Niemi, and Powell, "Are Women State Legislators Different?" ; Thomas, *How Women Legislate;* Thomas and Welch, "The Impact of Gender on the Activities and Priorities of State Legislators: Legislative Styles and Policy Priorities."

19. The 24 selected legislatures include the unicameral legislature of Nebraska and the lower houses of Arkansas, California, Colorado, Connecticut, Delaware, Idaho, Illinois, Louisiana, Maine, Michigan, Missouri, Montana, Nebraska, New Jersey, North Dakota, Ohio, Pennsylvania, South Carolina, South Dakota, Tennessee, Texas, Vermont, West Virginia, and Wyoming. These 24 states were randomly selected to represent varying levels of legislative professionalism, party control, and the percent of women in the legislature. After three separate mailings, 530 legislators responded to the survey, including 407 men and 123 women, producing an overall response rate of about 21 percent and a response rate of 21 percent for both men and women.

20. For each of the 17 items, legislators scored a one when they indicated the more liberal position (allowing recipients to save money for education, starting a business or buying a home while remaining eligible for benefits; matching recipients savings; assisting recipients with moving expenses; providing tuition vouchers for recipients to attend community or technical college; increasing access to public transportation for working recipients; increasing child care for working recipients; increasing job training for recipients; rewarding recipients who complete educational or job training objectives with cash incentives; providing child-care services to prepare at-risk children for kindergarten; supporting teenage pregnancy prevention; providing job counseling and GED assistance to teen parents; providing shelters for homeless families; providing a state earned income tax credit for low income families; opposing time limits, family caps, and the elimination of government funded welfare; and opposing requirements that all able-bodied recipients work) and zero otherwise. All 17 items are positively correlated with one another as well with the index computed without the item; this, combined with the large and significant coefficient of reliability for the scale (Cronbach s α = .84), indicates that the items do reflect the underlying dimension, welfare policy liberalism.

21. See Carey, Niemi, and Powell, "Are Women State Legislators Different?; Thomas and Welch, The Impact of Gender on the Activities and Priorities of State Legislators: Legislative Styles and Policy Priorities."

22. Constituency type indicates whether or not legislators represent an urban, rural, or suburban constituency. See William Lilley III, Laurence J. DeFranco, and Mark F. Bernstein. *The Almanac of State Legislatures: Changing Patterns 1990–1997* (Washington D.C.: Congressional Quarterly, Inc., 1998).

23. See for example: See Carey, Niemi, and Powell, "Are Women State Legislators Different?"

24. Thomas, *How Women Legislate,* p. 105.

25. Emmy E. Werner. "Women in State Legislatures." *Western Political Quarterly* (1968), 21: 372–380.

26. Diamond, *Sex Roles in the State House;* Jeane Kirkpatrick, *Political Woman.*

27. Kathleen A. Bratton and Kerry L. Haynie. "Agenda Setting and Legislative Success in State Legislatures: The Effects of Gender and Race." *The Journal of Politics* (1999), 61: 658–679; Michelle A. Saint-Germain. "Does Their Difference Make a Difference? The Impact of Elected Women on Public Policy in Arizona." *Social Science Quarterly* (1989), 70(4): 956–968; Thomas, "The Impact of Women on State Legislative Policies;" Thomas and Welch, "The Impact of Gender on the Activities and Priorities of State Legislators: Legislative Styles and Policy Priorities."

28. Thomas and Welch, "The Impact of Gender on the Activities and Priorities of State Legislators: Legislative Styles and Policy Priorities."

29. R. Darcy. "Women in the State Legislative Power Structure: Committee Chairs." *Social Science Quarterly* (1996), 77: 888–898.

30. Susan J. Carroll and Ella Taylor. "Gender Differences in the Committee Assignments of State Legislators: Preferences or Discrimination?" Paper presented at the annual meeting of Midwest Political Science Association, Chicago, IL, 1989.

31. Wayne L. Francis. *The Legislative Committee Game: A Comparative Analysis of Fifty States* (Columbus, OH: Ohio State University Press, 1989).

32. Richard L. Hall. *Participation in Congress* (New Haven, CT: Yale University Press, 1996).

33. Mandel and Dodson, "Do Women Officeholders Make a Difference?;" Mezey, "Increasing the Number of Women in Office: Does it Matter?;" Virginia Sapiro. "Research Frontier Essay: When Are Interests Interesting? The Problem of Political Representation of Women." *American Political Science Review* (1981), 75: 701–716; Thomas, *How Women Legislate.*

34. Thomas and Welch, "The Impact of Gender on the Activities and Priorities of State Legislators: Legislative Styles and Policy Priorities," p. 455.

35. Saint-Germain, "Does Their Difference Make a Difference? The Impact of Elected Women on Public Policy in Arizona."

36. Thomas, *How Women Legislate,* p. 94.

37. Michael B. Berkman and Robert E. O Connor. "Do Women Legislators Matter? Female Legislators and State Abortion Policy." *American Politics Quarterly* (1993), 21: 102–124.

38. For example, theories of critical mass posit a nonlinear relationship between the number of women in the institution and policy outputs. See for example: Rosabeth Moss Kanter. "Some Effects of Proportion on Group Life: Skewed Sex Ratios and Response to Token Women." *American Journal of Sociology* (1977), 82: 965–990; Cynthia Fuchs Epstein. *Deceptive Distinctions: Sex, Gender, and the Social Order* (New Haven, CT: Yale University Press, 1988).

39. Thomas, *How Women Legislate,* p. 105.

40. Berkman and O. Connor, "Do Women Legislators Matter? Female Legislators and State Abortion Policy;" Dodson and Carroll, *Reshaping the Agenda: Women in State Legislatures;* Jeanie R. Stanley and Diane D. Blair. "Gender Differences in Legislative Effectiveness: The Impact of the Legislative Environment." ed. Debra Dodson, *Gender and Policymaking: Studies of Women in Office* (New Brunswick, NJ: Center for the American Woman in Politics, 1991).

41. See for example: Kenneth A. Shepsle and Barry R. Weingast. "The Institutional Foundations of Committee Power." *American Political Science Review* (1987), 81: 85–104.

42. In comparison, the 282 men who did not serve on welfare committees only worked on about .56 welfare bills in the previous session, and the 36 male welfare committee members worked on about .92 welfare bills. Thirty-two percent of men who did not serve on welfare committees and 47 percent of men who did serve on welfare committees succeeded in passing at least one welfare initiative that they worked on.

43. Forrest Maltzman. *Competing Principals: Committees, Parties, and the Organization of Congress* (Ann Arbor: University of Michigan Press, 1997).

44. See David P. Baron and John A. Ferejohn. "Bargaining in Legislatures." *American Political Science Review* (1989), 89: 1181–1206; Shepsle and Weingast, "The Institutional Foundations of Committee Power;" Steven Smith. *Call to Order: Floor Politics in the House and Senate.* (Washington DC; Brookings Institution, 1989).

45. Because the items are measured on different metrics, I standardize the items (express the items in units of standard deviation from their means). The six standardized items of the committee independence scale are positively correlated with each other and the scale computed without the item. The alpha coefficient of reliability for the scale of committee independence is .44. Because this is relatively low coefficient of reliability, I created a similar scale using different data provided by Keith E. Hamm and Ronald D. Hedlund as part of their data collection for National Science Foundation Grant SBR-9511518. The correlation of the index I created using information from the *Book of the States* and the index using Hamm and Hedlund's data is .66, confirming the validity of the index despite its somewhat low coefficient of reliability.

46. Data on state welfare policies were collected from the State Policy Documentation Project (SPDP), a project of the Center for Law and Social Policy and the Center on Budget and Policy Priorities. Eligibility for pregnant women is coded one if states permit pregnant women without children to be eligible for TANF benefits and zero otherwise. Time limit is coded three if states have no limit on the amount of time recipients can receive benefits over the course of their lives, two if recipients can receive benefits for a maximum of five years, one if recipients can receive benefits for a maximum of two to four years, and zero if recipients can only receive benefits for less than two years over the course of their lives. Welfare effort is the percentage of state budgets spent TANF programs.

FURTHER READING

Berkman, Michael B., and Robert E. O Connor. 1993. "Do Women Legislators Matter? Female Legislators and State Abortion Policy." *American Politics Quarterly* 21: 102–124.

Bratton, Kathleen A., and Kerry L. Haynie. 1999. "Agenda Setting and Legislative Success in State Legislatures: The Effects of Gender and Race." *The Journal of Politics* 61: 658–79.

Carey John M., Richard G. Niemi, and Lynda W. Powell. 1998. "Are Women State Legislators Different?" In *Women and Elective Office: Past, Present, & Future,* ed. Sue Thomas and Clyde Wilcox, 87–102. New York: Oxford University Press.

Darcy, Robert, Susan Welch, and Janet M. Clark. 1994. *Women, Elections and Representation.* 2cd rev. ed. Lincoln: University of Nebraska Press.

Thomas, Sue. 1994. *How Women Legislate.* New York: Oxford University Press.

The Executive Branch: Women and Leadership

A growing list of nations in this century have selected female heads. These have included Great Britain, the Philippines, Argentina, Israel, Iceland, and India. Female world leaders who hold/have held office since the 1990s up to the present include Canada, Panama, Peru, Nicaragua, Philippines, Bangladesh, Indonesia, Ireland, New Zealand, and Turkey. However, the United States has not yet succeeded in electing a woman as our chief executive. The U.S. presidency has remained a bastion of maleness.

Marcia Lynn Whicker (deceased) and Hedy Leonie Isaacs maintain that women are slowly gaining access to the male-dominated political executive's space. This article argues that impulses including leadership and policy consequences, access to education, the familial factor, and the media may enhance opportunities for women to rise to power. A counterargument is offered: In a political context in which a dialectic of exclusion and accommodation exists, these impulses are two-edged swords. That is, decision-making structures and institutions in many societies have not been transformed to facilitate the emergence of women in the political executive's space in a manner that negates bias. Thus, the factors that seem to serve as drivers for women's access to political leadership roles, namely, leadership style and policy consequences, access to education, familial links, and the media, may facilitate as well as limit access.

When, who, and how will Americans finally elect our first female president? Will the route to this office be as Diane Kincaid describes in her article, "Over His Dead Body: A Positive Perspective on Widows in the U.S. Congress," *Western*

Political Quarterly, March 1978, pp. 96–104? That is, will the route to the White House for women be similar to that of women who first gained entrance to the Congress—widows of congressmen who had served in that district? These widows had campaign advantages often associated with an incumbent candidate, such as name recognition and campaign experience because many had campaigned with their husbands. Will a first lady who gains the public eye by being the wife of the president end up being our first female president? The first lady is a prominent figure in American political life. Robert P. Watson in his article examines the growth of the first ladyship, the types of roles and duties performed by first ladies, and how first ladies and how first ladies have influenced politics, policy, and the presidency. The author concludes that first ladies can be understood more accurately as presidential partners than simply as spouses or hostesses. In each instance, the roles and duties fulfilled by first ladies have existed outside a formal office or official mandate. Instead, it has been through spousehood and the creative and inspired use of traditional roles women have been forced to assume that the first ladyship was forged. Yet, in politics, where importance is measured through access to power, the first lady has enjoyed physical proximity to power unequaled in government, irrespective of whether she held office or not. The author finds the first lady has therefore transcended her outsider status to become an insider capable of influencing politics, policy, and the presidency.

Sara J. Weir focuses on the growing importance of the governorship in U.S. politics. In recent years, the governorship has served as a proving ground for aspiring presidential candidates—of the five most recent U.S. presidents, four gained much of their political experience and national reputation by serving as governors. This article provides insights into the careers of the twenty-seven women who served or are serving as governor. It highlights patterns emerging in the 21st century, in light of the growing body of literature on women and electoral politics, arguing that as negative stereotypes regarding women in high executive elected positions diminish, women seeking the governorship face challenges similar to those of their male counterparts. Drawing on the experiences of the most recent women governors, the article suggests that a new pattern of gubernatorial leadership is emerging. Labeled "The Charismatic Outsider," the women governors who fall into this category possess qualities that make them attractive to a broader audience.

Gendering the Political Executive's Space: The Changing Landscape?

Marcia Lynn Whicker (Deceased)
Hedy Leonie Isaacs

INTRODUCTION

The notion that men will continue to dominate the political executive's space is arguably changing slowly. In certain jurisdictions this change is imperceptible, as political leaders, their deputies and other elected officials are predominantly male. This trend runs true to form in jurisdictions including the United States, where traditionally, factors including the presidential system itself, the paucity of women gaining experience in the presidential "launching roles" of the vice presidency, limited access to campaign funding, and the image of female candidates, have diminished the opportunity for women to compete for the presidency.[1]

"Facilitating" factors are arguably juxtaposed to these traditional limiting factors. In jurisdictions, in Europe, Asia, within the Caribbean region and elsewhere, although electoral politics is generally regarded as the "stronghold of males" there is evidence of women increasingly assuming leadership roles. Other factors apparently provide impulses that influence women's access to positions of political leadership. These factors include leadership style and policy consequences, access to education, the familial factor and the media. These "drivers" for success are often two edged swords: While a leadership style characterized by assertiveness and dominance seems to fit the bill as a criterion for entry to and maintenance of a woman's space in the political executive's arena, these very traits seem to attract ubiquitous male resistance and sometimes female lack of support. This leads one to question the world view about women, and the need for increased support in the forms of civic education and legislation to shore up the opportunities for women.

The purpose of this essay is to explore whether there are linkages between these "facilitating" factors and enhanced opportunities for women to rise to power in a political context in which the dialectic of exclusion and accommodation exists.

THE CONTEXT: DIALECTIC OF EXCLUSION AND ACCOMMODATION

There are recognizable difficulties in generalizing about the factors that "facilitate" access to the political leadership space in different regions of the world, bearing in mind that women's histories are context specific. At this level of abstraction, one also has to control for cultural, class, age and other differences. The argument that the dialectic of exclusion and accommodation exists that limits women's access is not likely, however, to provoke dispute.

The impulses for changing women's "subordinate position in society" that began with women's movements, that persist and underpin related discourse and action are seeking to challenge and change gender stereotypes and decision-making structures and institutions. The perception that the woman's place is in the home is changing, but slowly. Women are mothers, homemakers, entrepreneurs, engineers and scientists among other professions. While women contend with a manifestly exclusionary bias there is also evidence that they are taking their places in the political space.

During the decade of the 90s, despite the existence of the glass ceiling, women have increasingly joined the ranks of parliamentarians. The world average, of women in national parliaments (both houses combined) has increased from 11.7% (in 1997) to 15.3% (in 2004). In terms of the current regional averages, using 1997 as the base year, Nordic countries have the highest average (39.7%, moving up from 36.4%), followed by the Americas 18.2%, (moving up from 12.7%); Europe–OSCE member countries 17.3%, (moving up from 12.6%); sub-Saharan Africa 15.3%, (moving up from 10.4%); Asia, 14.8% in 2004 (there is no data for 1997 from this source); Pacific, 12.2% (up from 11.6%); Arab States, 6.2% (up from 3.3%).[2]

It is apparent that the numbers of female parliamentarians as well as world leaders in various regions have increased. Female world leaders, by country, who hold/have held office since the 1990s up to the present, are indicated in Table 1.

Women who have found a way around or over the exclusionary bias are generally considered to be strong leaders, have had access to education, may have been influenced by family members, who themselves, may have held positions of political leadership. It is also arguable that public opinion has contributed to the rise or fall of women in politics.

TABLE 1   Women Political Leaders by Country

Name/Position	Years of Rule	Country
Prime Minister Kim Campbell	1993 (4 months)	Canada
Governor–General Adrienne Clarkson	1999–present	Canada
President Mireya Moscoso	1999–present	Panama
Prime Minister Beatriz Merino	2003–present	Peru
President Violeta Barriosde Chamorro	1990–1997	Nicaragua
Prime Minister Gloria Macapagal-Arroyo	2001–present	Philippines
Prime Minister Khaleda Zia	1991–1996, 2001–present	Bangladesh
President Megawati Sukarnoputri	2001–present	Indonesia
Prime Minister Junichiro Koizumi	2001–present	Japan
Prime Minister Benazir Bhutto	1993–1996 (held position 1988–1990)	Pakistan
President Chandrika Kumaratunga	1994–present	Sri Lanka
Prime Minister Sirimavo Bandaranaike	1994–2000 (held this office periodically during the 1960s and 1970s)	Sri Lanka
Prime Minister Luisa Dias Diogo	February 2004–present	Mozambique
Prime Minister Maria Das Neves	2002–present	Sao Tome & Principe
Mame Madior Boye	2001–2002	Senegal
Prime Minister Agathe Uwilingiyimana	1993–1994	Rwanda
President Mary Robinson	1990–1997	Ireland
President Mary McAleese	1997–present	Ireland
President Vaira Vike-Freiberga	1999–present	Latvia
President Tarja Halonen	2000–present	Finland
Prime Minister Susanne Camelia-Romer	1993, 1998–1999	Netherlands Antilles
Prime Minister Mirna Louisa-Godett	2003–present	Netherlands Antilles
Governor–General Dame Silvia Cartwright	2001–present	New Zealand
Prime Minister Jenny Shipley	1997–1999	New Zealand
Prime Minister Helen Clark	1999–present	New Zealand
Prime Minister Gro Harlem Brundtlandt	1990–1996 (held position also 1981, 1986–1989)	Norway
Premier Hanna Suchocka	1992–1993	Poland
Prime Minister Tansu Ciller	1993–1996	Turkey
Governor–General Dame Ivy Dumont	2001–present	Bahamas
Premier Jennifer Smith	1998–present	Bermuda
Governor–General Dame Pearlette Louisy	1997–present	St. Lucia
President Janet Jagan	1997–1999	Guyana
Provisional President Ertha Pascal-Trouillot	1990, 1991	Haiti
Prime Minister Claudette Werleigh	1995–1996	Haiti

Sources: Compiled from "World Leaders Page" home.att.net/~r.c.culp/wleader.htm www.infoplease.com/ipa/A0801534 March 2004.

THE LEADERSHIP STYLE

It has been argued that the complex power structures that many societies have inherited have led to inequities that are evident in the leadership of the state, among others. To be a leader one has to display a certain style of leadership. Leadership characteristics that are usually linked to masculinity are still demanded for effective management.[3] Even though the style of leadership may turn on one or other of two pillars, namely, "a soft style of cooperation, influence and empowerment or a hard style of leadership that stresses hierarchy, dominance and order," the former is usually attributable to females while the latter is the "male style."[4] This is of course arguable as there are women, including Indonesia's current president who may not be described as displaying a male style. The argument that women leaders develop their own identities that suit the context may have greater value.

Documented cases however suggest that women who have had some measure of success at electoral politics and have held or hold positions of political leadership are generally deemed as strong personalities, who perceive themselves to be in control. According to political scientists, a possible explanation for this style that Indira Ghandi, Margaret Thatcher and Prime Minister Edith Cresson of France possessed, is that women leaders feel compelled to cultivate a style that conveys strength in traditional male terms.[5] This style of leadership however, often leads to ubiquitous male resistance and to criticisms being leveled at the female politicians, particularly by their male counterparts.

Benazir Bhutto perceived herself as a strong personality. She was however criticized as being too imperious, domineering and arrogant. Bhutto is charismatic, but charisma is rarely honored in a women, and some of her male colleagues had trouble working with her.[6] Male resistance led to defections or dismissals, weakening the political party that Bhutto led. Former Prime Minister Gro Harlem Brundtlandt was also considered to be a strong leader.

Thatcher was a bold ideological leader. Her leadership style has been described as personalized and imperious. She is also alluded to as populist radical who relied on a strong sense of self, a warrior image, self confidence, determination and "conviction." By the same token, Thatcher's leadership traits have been described as demonstrating a paradoxical quality, and could be seen a series of dichotomies: Her single mindedness was often dogmatic; conviction was often rigidity; strength was often an aggressive drive for control; her determination was often contentiousness; her forcefulness was combative; her moralism was often quarrelsome. For a British Prime Minister she was extraordinarily assertive. This assertive style was essential to Thatcher's success.[7]

The Caribbean perceptions of the leadership style for "successful" female politicians sometimes resonate those paradoxes existing elsewhere. Strong individuals are sometimes perceived as aggressive and arrogant: A forthright, strong, dominant political leader may be variously described as articulate, forthright, fearless, independent, and outspoken; but also as arrogant and aggressive. Women in one of these "male-dominated" political settings have been alluded to as "men in dresses."

One's personality may also play a role in one's acceptability as a female political leader. In the election of the first female president in Finland, Tara Halonen, the "personality" factor apparently played a decisive role. "Her personality decided this election. Halonen is a person who with her own individuality, her openness and her genuine character appealed across party lines."[8]

The emergence of women in political leadership roles has policy consequences. It is argued that there is greater transparency in the political process. "Political action has become more sensitive to the needs of the population, especially of women and the most disadvantaged sectors of society."[9] Paradoxically, the policy agenda of female political leaders often tends to be characterized as feminist even where there are efforts to address issues other than women's issues, including issues related to the economy, foreign relations.

It may well be that while an assertive and dominant style may be credible, that as women's unique styles become visible and accepted that these may provide the benchmarks for acceptability and enhance their credibility.

THE FAMILIAL FACTOR AND THE RISE TO POWER

It is argued that familial power/inherited power from either one's father, mother or husband may play an influential role in a woman's rise to power in the political arena. Women from Europe, Asia, the Americas and elsewhere have arguably benefited from strong bonds with familial figures. Women political leaders, including, Megawati Sukarnoputri, Chandrika Kamuratunga, Kaleda Zia, Benazir Bhutto, former Prime Minister of Pakistan and Margaret Thatcher former British Prime Minister have had strong bonds with family figures, some of whom were politicians. The same is true of a number of Caribbean female politicians.

"Megawati Sukarnoputri was born into the nation's [Indonesia's] political elite. Her father Sukarno led the country to independence from Dutch colonial rule after World War II and became its first president. He is still revered as a charismatic national hero and that status has been automatically transferred to Megawati."[10]

Benazir Bhutto's father was her inspiration and hero, and she cultivated and used his mystique."[11] This familial link helped to propel her into the political executive's space and to maintain her place.

Margaret Thatcher's father instilled in her a need to win, an ethic of work and a drive to succeed. When Thatcher became Britain's first woman Prime Minister, she attributed her success to her father. Her father was a community activist and lay preacher, school governor, borough councilor, alderman, and finally mayor. According to Michael Genovese, Margaret was thus reared on a life of public affairs and learned about politics at her father's knee (partially paraphrased). Mrs. Thatcher in turn expressed this view about her father: He brought me up to believe all the things I do believe and they are the values on which I fought the election. I owe almost everything to my father.

In 2000, the then first lady of the United States, Hillary Rodham Clinton, became the first president's wife to seek political office. Isabel Peron and Eleanor Roosevelt benefited from the positions of power held by their husbands as heads of state. Isabel assumed power when Juan Peron died. Prime Minister Khaleda Zia, is the widow of late General Ziaur Rahman, the country's ruler in the late 1970s and early eighties. In the mid 1990s, Sirimavo Bandaranaike, became the world's first woman premier on the death of her husband Solomon, the then premier of Sri Lanka. She is mother of Chandrika Bandaranaike Kumaratunga, Sri Lanka's first woman president. These familial linkages apparently contributed to the rise to power.

In certain new states, namely Barbados, and the Bahamas the current Deputy Prime Ministers are women. While these women are articulate, assertive and well educated individuals who hold their own in the political leadership space, some of these individuals also have "familial links." Incites concerning the rise of women to positions of power in the political arena in the Caribbean, with an emphasis on Barbados have been editorialized. The role of women in politics in the case of Barbados is particularly note worthy as six members of the current fifteen member cabinet in that jurisdiction are women:

"Gertrude Eastmond pushed open doors for women in Barbados politics when she contested and won a seat in the 1971 general elections, 20 years after Ermie Bourne became the first woman to enter Parliament as the senior representative for St. Andrew. Since then, Billie Miller, daughter of former Minister of Health, Freddie Miller, Mia Mottley, granddaughter of the last Mayor of Bridgetown, [Barbados] the late Earnest D. Mottley, a political firebrand of his time and Elizabeth Thompson, niece of Barbados' first woman MP Ermie Bourne, have successfully contested political elections in Barbados."

Miller was the Deputy Prime Minister in 2001. Mottley, who was the Attorney General then, has acted as Prime Minister. She is currently the Deputy Prime Minister and is considered the heir apparent to the country's political leadership.

"Elsewhere in the Caribbean other women political leaders have served to inspire. Dame Eugenia, sometimes called the Caribbean's 'Iron Lady,' ruled Dominica—one of the most difficult countries in the Caribbean to govern—for 15 years (1980 to 1995) as its Prime Minister and inspired fresh ambition in a whole generation of Caribbean women. Dame Hilda Bynoe, who served Grenada as Governor before she quit public office during pre-independence upheavals in 1974, also demonstrated there should be no limits to women's horizons."[12]

While we cannot be dismissive of good [family] connections, as a prerequisite for women entering politics, additional pre-requisites according to one writer include "a tough hide and extremely high self esteem."[13] It must also be reiterated that strong political pedigrees do not politicians make. Successful female politicians are also effective and resolute. They generally possess the intellectual capacity and the seriousness of purpose required to maintain their place in the political arena.

ACCESS TO EDUCATION

Access to education is reflected in the growing female population in educational institutions, in professions that were once male dominated and more importantly in state legislatures.

More women have joined the ranks of college students. A recently published "public lecture" revealed that at the collegiate level, women now constitute the majority of students on college campuses in the U.S. . . .so that in 8 years women will earn 58% of the bachelor's degrees in U.S. colleges. Doomsayers lament that women outnumber men in the social and behavioral sciences by about 3 to 1, and how they have invaded such traditionally male bastions as engineering (where they now make up 20%) and biology and business virtually par.[14] Women generally also outnumber men on university campuses in the Caribbean region.

In terms of the level of education of the increasing number of women who have entered politics, it is evident that many of these women have had access to high school as well as tertiary education.

A 1999 survey of 187 female parliamentarians from 65 countries (including respondents from the Americas, Asia, Europe, sub-Saharan Africa, Latin America and the Caribbean) conducted by the Inter-Parliamentary Union (IPU) speaks to this issue: [The survey population included] women who ranged in age from 70–31. The largest proportion—60 percent—were married. Seventy-three percent were mothers; with a combined total of 381 children.

All the women had access to education, ranging from seven percent with a high school diploma, to 15 percent with post graduate degrees. Seventy-three percent had an undergraduate degree. Most held positions as public or civil servants before entering parliament; while 17 percent had been teachers, another 10 percent were lawyers. Six respondents were journalists, six were doctors, four nurses and four were social workers.[15]

Again, the two edged sword is at work. The question may be asked of what value is leadership that has access to education when those who follow may have limited access? The "followership" is therefore not able to add value to the extent that it could. Advocacy for civic education may have merit in these circumstances. Civil society, in particular women, may benefit from ongoing political education so that they are better able to appreciate the challenges faced by women in politics, better understand the issues that these politicians address, as well as provide support, that female politicians in their "lonely"[16] jobs at the top face.

THE MEDIA

The media according to the IPU Survey mentioned can make the female politician. As a two edged sword it may also be a hindrance. This is the case especially if the media still holds to traditional stereotypes and focuses on her looks or her private life instead of political activities. It is also argued that "femininity is used as a weapon and one's personal life is subjected to outrageous and unkind speculation. Even women's normal physiological functions are ridiculed on political platforms and cited as reasons why they should not assume public office. This demoralizing tactic along with allusions about women's emotional nature, are strategies to keep women in a bind of powerlessness despite their educational, social and economic mobility."[17]

On the other hand it has also been reported (in the IPU Survey) that the fact of a female politician sometimes piques the curiosity of the press. As a result the politician in question receives many requests for interviews or articles.

Advocacy for mandating aspects of women's socialization has merit in these circumstances by making it illegal for women to be the target of unkind speculation about their personal life. Other appropriate legislation may also curb outrageous onslaughts against female politicians.

CONCLUSION

Decision-making structures and institutions in many societies have not been transformed to facilitate the emergence of women in the political executive's space in a manner that negates bias. In addition some of the factors that seem to serve as drivers for women's access to political leadership roles, namely, leadership style and policy consequences; access to education; familial links, and the media, are manifestly two edged swords. They may facilitate as well as limit access. The context is the dialectic of exclusion and accommodation.

Nations are reminded that if they "exclude women from decision-making, or rest content with low levels of participation by women, [that] they are surely depriving themselves of a rich reservoir of talent and wisdom."[18]

NOTES

1. Marcia Lynn Whicker and Hedy Leonie Isaacs, "The Maleness of the American Presidency" in Lois Duke Whittaker (ed) *Women in Politics: Outsiders or Insiders* (Prentice Hall, Upper Saddle River, N.J.).

2. The Inter Parliamentary Union file://A:\ Women%20in%20Parliaments%20World%20and%20Regional%20Averages%203.htm Date accessed March 2004.

3. Bernard M. Bass (ed) *Handbook of Leadership: Theory Research and Managerial Applications* (New York: Free Press, 1990).

4. Michael Genovese, "Women as National Leaders: What do we know?" in Michael Genovese (Ed) *Women as National Leaders* (Beverly Hills, CA, 1993).

5. Patricia Lee Sykes, "Women as National Leaders: Patterns and Prospects" in Michael A. Genovese (Ed.) *Women as National Leaders* (Beverly Hills, CA, 1993).

6. Nancy Fix Anderson, "Benazir Bhutto and Dynastic Politics" in Michael A. Genovese (Ed.) *Women as National Leaders* (Beverly Hills, CA, 1993).

7. Michael A. Genovese, "Margaret Thatcher and Conviction Leadership" in *Women as National Leaders* (Beverly Hills, CA, 1993).

8. Quote taken from, *Daily Gleaner,* February 7, 2000 "Finland: Finns Elect their first female President" (Kingston, Jamaica).

9. Quote taken from *The Daily Observer,* March 20, 2000 "What its really like for Women in Politics" (Kingston, Jamaica).

10. Quote taken from the BBC News, Monday 23 July, 2001. "Profile: Megawati Sukarnoputri." http://news.bbc.co.uk/I/hi/world/monitoring, media-reports/1453088.stm

11. Nancy Fix Anderson, "Benazir Bhutto and Dynastic Politics" in *Women as National Leaders* (Beverly Hills, CA, 1993).

12. Editorial, "Breaking the Barriers of Time" in the *Barbados Advocate,* Sunday, November 11, 2001.

13. Betty Holford, "Women and Politics" in the the *Advocate,* Wednesday, October 7, 1998, and submitted by the Caribbean Association of Feminist Research and Action CAFRA/Women's Forum of Barbados.

14. Quote taken from Professor Michael Kimmel's 2004 Lucille Mathurin Mair Public Lecture "Men, Masculinites and Development," March 11 2004. The University of the West Indies, Mona, Kingston Jamaica.

15. Editorial providing a synopsis of the IPU survey "What its really like for Women in Politics" in the *Daily Observer,* March 20, 2000 (Kingston: Jamaica).

16. According to politician Sheila Flinstone, Canadian politician, "when she became a minister, she found high office intrinsically isolating and sought to overcome this by going out of her way to keep in touch with party colleagues and fellow parliamentarians in Commonwealth Secretariat, Gender and Youth Affairs publication.

17. CAFRA/ Women's Forum of Barbados "Women and Politics" in the *Advocate,* Wednesday, October 7, 1998.

18. Quote taken from the "Commonwealth Plan of Action on Gender and Development." Commonwealth Secretariat, Gender and Youth Affairs Division.

FURTHER READING

Barriteau, Eudine (Ed.). *Confronting Power: Theorizing Gender.* Mona, Kingston: The University of the West Indies Press, 2003.

Commonwealth Secretariat. *Women in Politics: Voices from the Commonwealth.* London: United Kingdom, 1999.

Genovese, Michael A. (Ed.). *Women as National Leaders.* Newbury Park, CA: Sage, 1993.

Kellerman, Barbara. *Political Leadership: A Source Book.* (Pitt Series in Policy and Institutional Studies). University of Pittsburgh, 1986.

Massiah, Joycelin. *Still a Long Way to Go.* In Women as Leaders Series. Interpress Service, June 1, 2000.

Northhouse, Peter G. (Ed.). *Leadership: Theory and Practice.* Thousand Oaks, CA: Sage, 1997.

Phillips, Anne (Ed.). *Feminism and Politics.* Oxford: Oxford University Press, 1998.

The World's Women 2000: Trends and Statistics. New York: United Nations.

First Ladies and Their Influence on Politics, Policy, and the Presidency

Robert P. Watson

First ladies are unelected and unappointed. Yet, even a cursory review of American history reveals that first ladies have influenced presidential decision making and White House social affairs. Indeed, the first ladyship has a long history of social and political influence dating to the nation's founding, and one finds the first ladies' fingerprints on everything from presidential speeches, to executive and Cabinet staffing decisions, to White House renovations. While the sheer extent and scope of influence wielded by first ladies might seem surprising, it is consistent with the examples set by other female leaders throughout history; it has also been manifested through what, at first glance, may appear to be an usual basis for influence.

Denied the right to vote, hold public office, own property, or litigate, women have been political outsiders in every way, legally and otherwise, for most of the country's history. Nevertheless, even though women faced legal and social obstacles to educational, commercial, and political opportunities, women's voices were not silenced during the great American experiment in popular governance. Forced to find unofficial means to offset disenfranchisement, women often exerted political influence through actions, institutions, and roles deemed by society to be within "acceptable" gender mores. For instance, women produced "homespun" clothing during the American Revolution, Civil War, and the "Great War" (WWI), led relief missions for the urban poor, organized charities, were often the foot soldiers in the effort to end slavery—and later in the Civil Rights Movement—marched against the abuse of alcohol before and during Prohibition, and agitated on behalf of a wide array of worthy social and humanitarian causes. All these accomplishments were, however, done from the auspices of feminine gender roles. Not surprisingly, American first ladies were among the women who participated in many of these activities.[1] How? Through their marriage to the president they were able to both bring the requisite notoriety and credibility to these causes and emerge as leaders of them.

TRADITION AND SPOUSEHOOD

To understand the many contributions of first ladies to the nation, it is important to note that one of the few avenues to political influence available to women historically was spousehood. Marriage to men of public stature and financial success offered opportunities to influence the public and social agenda. On one extreme, history reveals that political wives often stood in for and served as replacements for their husbands. Known as the "widow's mandate," it was not uncommon for widows to be selected to complete their deceased husband's term in office.[2] But, party insiders and gender norms precluded these widows from continuing in elected office in the subsequent election. Interestingly, this phenomenon continues to some extent. In recent times, several prominent women in politics shared such a traditional starting point for their careers. This includes Margaret Chase Smith of Maine, who was elected to both the U.S. House of Representatives and U.S. Senate, and ran for the presidency in 1964, and Jean Carnahan of Missouri, who served in her late husband's Senate seat after his untimely and tragic death in a plane crash during the 2000 campaign.[3] Hillary Rodham Clinton used her first ladyship as a stepping stone to launch her own successful bid to be New York's junior senator and Elizabeth Dole joined Senator Clinton in that esteemed body after being the spouse of the Republican Party's presidential nominee in 1996. That women are gaining entry to politics should not be surprising, as direct familial ties have always benefitted men (the *sons* of the powerful). Countless governors and members of Congress have been the sons of previous office holders; and, it is doubtful that John Quincy Adams, Benjamin Harrison, or George W. Bush would ever have achieved the pinnacle of political power had their fathers or grandfathers before them not served as president.[4]

On the other hand, spousehood permitted first ladies intimate access to power, even if it has been hard to detect. Even though many first ladies have held a deep passion for politics, sexism in society forced them to camouflage their political desires and activities in public. Although they exerted "bully" influence behind-the-scenes, first ladies were forced to employ a "white glove pulpit" in public in accordance with societal expectations about the "proper" role for women in political life.[5] Herein is the story (and lesson) of the first ladies. They have been political *outsiders*—they faced sex-role constraints, disenfranchisement, and served in an office lacking legal standing—who managed to become political *insiders* through the unlikely and ironic path of spousehood.

As the person closest to the president, first ladies had political access. Few presidential aides, after all, could claim to have known the president well even prior to his political career. Table 1 lists the years first couples were married *prior* to the presidency and reveals that many couples spent over a quarter-century together before the inauguration.

Another lesson of the first ladies is that, even though their basis for influence derives from marriage, individually and as a group they have transcended both their identity as solely a spouse and their influence solely on the president. First ladies have become public figures in their own right, advancing important social causes, their own political agendas, and, most recently, their own political careers.[6] In doing so, they have been aided through another trait they shared with early women leaders: the presidential spouses were a highly capable and impressive lot. Many came from prominent families, were talented musicians, spoke other languages, had a well rounded education, held deep convictions about equality and justice, and were robust, charismatic, and politically savvy. For instance, even though Senators Hillary Rodham Clinton and Elizabeth Dole benefitted from their

TABLE 1   Years Married Prior to Presidency

Years	First Couple
45	William & Anna Harrison
45	George & Barbara Bush
41	James & Elizabeth Monroe
38	Zachary & Margaret Taylor
37	Andrew & Eliza Johnson
35	Dwight & Mamie Eisenhower
32	John & Abigail Adams
30	George & Martha Washington
30	Herbert & Lou Hoover
30	Jimmy & Rosalynn Carter
29	Warren & Florence Harding
29	Lyndon & Lady Bird Johnson
29	Ronald & Nancy Reagan
28	John & Letitia Tyler
28	Franklin & Eleanor Roosevelt
28	Richard & Pat Nixon
27	John Q. & Louisa Adams
27	Woodrow & Ellen Wilson
26	William & Ida McKinley
26	Harry & Bess Truman

Note: The years do not include months, which would add to the years.

husbands' political positions, both had distinguished themselves in the fields of law and politics long before their forays into elected politics and were widely regarded as accomplished, influential women of their right. Mrs. Clinton, with a Yale law degree, had worked with the legendary children's advocate Marian Wright Edelman and the Children's Defense Fund, practiced law with one of the top law firms[7] in Arkansas, was recognized as one of the 100 most influential attorneys in the United States,[8] and led several successful educational reform measures during her tenure as Arkansas's first lady. Mrs. Dole, with a Harvard law degree, held senior administrative positions in the federal government, and was a Cabinet secretary in the administrations of Ronald Reagan and George Bush.[9] While these examples might be unusual in terms of attaining elected office, they are less the exception than they are the rule in terms of being capable, intelligent, influential political spouses.

EMERGENCE OF AN UNOFFICIAL OFFICE

Much was made by the press and the political opponents of Bill Clinton of his remark during the 1992 presidential campaign that, if he were elected, the public would, as the old sayings go, "buy one, get one free" and get "two for the price of one." Critics took Clinton's comment as a nearly unprecedented and inappropriate endorsement of the influence Hillary Rodham Clinton would wield in a Clinton

TABLE 2   The Education of First Ladies

First Lady	College/University
Lucy Hayes	Ohio Wesleyan University
Lucretia Garfield	Hiram College; Western Reserve Eclectic; Geauga Seminary
Frances Cleveland	Wells College
Ellen Wilson	Rome Female College
Helen Taft	Miami University (OH)
Grace Coolidge	University of Vermont
Lou Hoover	San Jose Normal School; Stanford University
Jacqueline Kennedy	Vassar; Sorbonne; George Washington University
Lady Bird Johnson	University of Texas
Pat Nixon	University of Southern California
Betty Ford	Bennington College
Rosalynn Carter	Georgia Southwestern College
Nancy Reagan	Smith College
Barbara Bush	Smith College
Hillary Clinton	Wellesley College; Yale Law School
Laura Bush	Southern Methodist University; University of Texas

White House. Yet, the response was inaccurate. Although she was an activist first lady, Mrs. Clinton was less the trailblazer than she was simply the latest in a long line of influential and active presidential spouses. "Two for the price of one" was nothing new for the office. In effect, the country had "been there, and done that." For example, when Abraham Lincoln received word that he had won in 1860 he shouted, "Mary, Mary *we* are elected," and Florence Harding announced to her husband after his election in 1920, "Well, Warren, I've gotten you the White House, now what are you going to do with it?"[10]

So, how did an unelected, unappointed position become an office of influence? The Constitution is silent on even the existence of a presidential spouse, making the first ladyship an "extra-constitutional" development. This lack of statutory or constitutional guidelines has been a mixed blessing. The absence of defined parameters for the first lady means she is somewhat free to fashion her duties as she sees fit, but at the same time she is open to criticism for everything she does (and does not do). To be sure, one of the common experiences of most first ladies is that they have been subject to attacks from the press and their husband's opponents, often times unfairly so.[11]

First ladies to an extent have approached the office according to their own inclinations and abilities, with respect to the nature of the presidential marriage. Eleanor Roosevelt and Bess Truman served back-to-back first ladyships, as did Barbara Bush and Hillary Rodham Clinton. Yet, neither set of first ladies could have been more different: First Ladies Clinton and Roosevelt enjoyed politics and were active in a bewildering array of policy issues, and First Ladies Bush and Truman preferred to remain behind the scenes as private citizens. Likewise, factors such as age and health impacted the approach presidential wives have pursued. Some wives such as Julia Tyler, Frances Cleveland, and Jacqueline Kennedy were very young and in good health, allowing them to rigorously pursue renovations to and restorations of the Executive Mansion, an active hosting role, and a vigorous and highly public agenda.[12] On the other hand, Margaret Taylor and Anna Harrison were older, in poor health, and were disinterested in public life, all of which were reflected in their first ladyships.[13] Elizabeth Monroe, Abigail Fillmore, and Letitia Tyler were all capable women who enjoyed productive and close marriages, yet each one suffered from poor health which seriously limited their activism in office.[14]

Presidents John Adams and Jimmy Carter saw their wives as equals and valued their advice, while Presidents Dwight Eisenhower and Richard Nixon did not. The dynamic of these marriages framed the prominent and influential roles of the first set of wives, as it did the rather unremarkable, subdued first ladyships of the latter spouses. Taken together, all these factors have shaped the individual roles and duties first ladies have undertaken.

However, the office is not entirely an empty bucket into which first ladies pour their objectives and preferences. Over time historical precedents have been set that—just as is the case for the presidency—subsequent holders of the office have been expected to follow.[15] Two notable differences between the precedents and expectations surrounding the presidency and first ladyship are that presidents are elected, first ladies are not, and the parameters restricting first ladies have been rigidly set and restricted by societal notions of gender. American society has not been comfortable with women in positions of leadership, especially in such non-traditional areas as politics and especially when influence derives from the wedding band. First ladies have had to walk a careful line, being supportive wives who uphold the history of the office, yet mindful of not being too active or giving the appearance of having influence. The saying "damned if you do, and damned if you don't" comes to mind.

The "founding mothers" also faced the challenge of establishing a role or function for the president's wife with virtually no guidelines, and certainly no direction from the founding fathers and their discussions in Philadelphia. While Martha Washington and Abigail Adams looked to the customs of European courts in forging the official social protocol for the new nation and its commander-in-chief, they had to balance royal pomp and pageantry with the American preference for democratic simplicity. The nation was fortunate to have women of such extraordinary ability among the early presidential spouses, because they managed to provide both an aura of prestige, one worthy of the ambitions of the young nation and visiting dignitaries, yet one free of from old World exclusivity and extravagance.

Prior to George Washington's inauguration as the first president, Martha Washington had earned a reputation as a gracious hostess and as "Lady Washington," the beloved symbol of the American Revolution. She was uniformly praised for her ability to manage large, frequent crowds of guests at her bustling Mount Vernon home and admired for her tireless support of the colonial troops. As first lady,[16] Martha Washington forged an office responsible for the social affairs of state and positioned the presidential spouse as the foremost woman in the capital city and country, aspects of the office that hold true to the present day. The second presidential spouse, Abigail Adams, had long been a valued counselor to her husband, a role she continued while living in the president's house.[17] That John Adams, considered by his fellow framers as an important intellectual force in the Revolution, viewed his wife as his intellectual equal—the two avid readers were passionate in their discussions of literature, philosophy, and politics—speaks to her intelligence and influence.[18] As first lady, Abigail Adams added to the first ladyship the role of political confidante. It is difficult to overstate the popularity of the third presidential spouse. Dolley Madison presided over the social affairs of her husband's two terms, frequently hosted for Thomas Jefferson and James Monroe during their combined four terms in office, and would return to the nation's capital after her husband's death to again pick up the mantle of the nation's hostess. Charismatic, with an ability to read people and an innate understanding of politics, "Queen Dolley" hosted the most successful parties in the history of the presidency—events that combined the social and political in a way that influenced politics and policy—and emerged as the dominant figure in Washington affairs for nearly a half century.

These early presidential spouses crafted a first ladyship that was defined by the social realm, containing unofficial yet public roles and duties consistent with the status of women at the time, yet one poised to influence the presidency and the nation. Their precedents continue to define the actions of modern first ladies, many of whom shared the early founding mothers' ability to influence politics.

In the twentieth century, the notion of an "office" of first lady has been formalized, adding another important avenue to political influence.[19] Beginning with Edith Roosevelt, who employed the services of Belle Hagner, a former clerk in the War Department reassigned to assist the First Lady with her correspondence, more recent first ladies have had the benefit of staff, resources, and office space. Jacqueline Kennedy had upwards of forty individuals assisting her with her famous historic restoration of the White House. First ladies from Lady Bird Johnson through the present have employed a staff of between a dozen and two dozen aides with responsibility for such areas as special projects, scheduling and advance, and media relations. The emergence of an Office of the First Lady, with office space typically in the East Wing of the White House and Eisenhower Old Executive Office Building, and replete with a Chief of Staff, has allowed recent first ladies to expand the scope of their activities and influence.[20]

In addition to the advent of an office and resources, the first ladyship has emerged as an institution. Most presidencies were served with a first lady as part of them. Only one president remained a bachelor: James Buchanan, the fifteenth president. Grover Cleveland entered the office a bachelor but married during his presidency. Both John Tyler and Woodrow Wilson lost wives during their presidencies (Letitia and Ellen, respectively), but the two widowers soon remarried (to Julia Gardner and widow Edith Bolling Galt, respectively) so that first ladies served for much of their presidencies. In total, only five presidencies were without first ladies: Thomas Jefferson, Andrew Jackson, Martin Van Buren, and Chester A. Arthur were widowers and Buchanan was a bachelor.[21]

ROLES AND DUTIES OF FIRST LADIES

Even though women were disenfranchised for most of the country's history and even though first ladies have not enjoyed constitutional or legal recognition of their office, over a two century period the presidential spouses have through custom, public expectation, and personal fortitude established identifiable roles and duties for the first ladyship. These roles can be traced to the actions of the earliest presidential spouses and have evolved in a gradual manner, mirroring the enlargement of the presidency and reflecting in recent times progress made in the status of women. The list offered in Table 3 is neither mutually exclusive nor collectively exhaustive, nor have all first ladies invested equal emphasis in the various duties, but it is a compilation of the core functions performed by most first ladies in the modern era. Interestingly, all ten functions are performed in an unofficial capacity, as none of them are mandated by statute or any other formal authority.

TABLE 3   Basic Roles of First Ladies

1. Public figure
2. Nation's social hostess
3. Symbol of the American woman
4. White House manager and preservationist
5. Campaigner
6. Social advocate
7. Presidential spokesperson
8. Presidential–national booster
9. Diplomat
10. Policy advocate

Public Figure

First ladies have been among the nation's most admired women since the founding. Indeed, since the poll began in the 1940s, first ladies have topped Gallup's annual poll of the most admired women, and frequently more than one former first lady has appeared in the poll's top 10.[22] In recent times, first ladies grace the cover of popular magazines, are covered daily by the press, and perform a wide range of ceremonial duties and public appearances. Such public visibility has allowed presidential spouses to develop their own identity and has enabled them to focus public attention on social and political issues of their choosing.

Nation's Social Hostess

Absent a monarchy and large presidential staff, early presidents were forced to take on the responsibility (and costs) of entertaining on their own. Given the notions of gender prevalent at the time, it should not be surprising to learn that the planning and administration of everything from official state dinners, to informal teas, to receptions and levees fell to the first ladies, along with many of the ceremonial and social facets of the presidency. These duties are neither discussed in the Constitution nor required by statute, but the functions have become associated with the first ladyship to the extent that presidential spouses do not have the luxury of declining to hostess. It is expected, even for such a politically active first lady as Eleanor Roosevelt, who was not fond of the responsibility. Moreover, it has been expected even during times of war and economic crisis, and has been defined by societal notions of gender.

But, such a role has permitted first ladies to meet dignitaries and heads of state, put a personal face on the presidency for the public, and promote foods and performers of their liking. In short, in official Washington, as elsewhere, the *social* is the *political* and first ladies have figured prominently in the capital city's social affairs. Today, the White House is staffed with chefs, ushers, and protocol specialists responsible for the day-to-day discharge of presidential events. However, the first lady ultimately remains responsible for what is served and how it is served, where guests are seated, and the overall tone of White House social functions.

Symbol of the American Woman

From Julia Tyler, to Grace Coolidge, to Jacqueline Kennedy, first ladies have influenced everything from fashion, to names for children, to popular culture in general. Whether she has desired the "role" or not, wives of presidents have been held up by the media and patriarchal establishment as symbols of American womanhood, reflecting prevailing gender ideals. First ladies failing to conform to such standards have often been criticized.

White House Manager and Preservationist

The White House has been since its completion in November 1800 one of the most open, accessible residences of a head of government in the world. As "the people's house," it remains a living museum and monument to popular governance. Yet, few steps were taken legally to preserve the historic integrity of the building and early presidents were not provided with sufficient staff or budget to manage the mansion in a way befitting its purpose. The building that is today recognized worldwide and cherished by the American people owes its status to first ladies.[23]

When Abigail Adams moved into the residence, she found a cold, damp unfinished building strewn with tell-tale signs of construction, only six rooms complete, and no place to hang her laundry. First ladies since Abigail Adams have overseen the building's day-to-day operation, decorating, and renovations. The wear and tear of a daily stream of visitors and employees have necessitated frequent restorations, and with time and the growth of both presidential family size (the building has not only been the president's office and centerpiece of national government, but it has had to function as the first family's private residence) and the powers of the presidency, the building has proved to be too small. The Executive Mansion was also damaged by fire during the War of 1812 and again during the Coolidge presidency, and it had to be gutted and rebuilt during the Truman presidency.

First lady Caroline Harrison established the White House china collection, while Edith Roosevelt organized the first lady portrait gallery. Mrs. Harrison and Mrs. Roosevelt also had plans drawn for everything from a complete renovation of the building to the construction of another presidential residence. Jacqueline Kennedy's famous restoration of the White House, shown to the American public in an Emmy-award winning tour, was only one of many such attempts to preserve the historic quality of the home. Mrs. Kennedy inventoried the White House's objects and furnishings, uncovered historically important items in storage, established commissions to oversee future renovations and decorations, and employed leading art historians to assist her in returning the presidential residence to the glory of the Federalist period.

Campaigner

It is common in modern times for the presidential candidates' wives to not only campaign beside them but to speak on their behalf and campaign independently for their husband. Most recent first ladies have shown themselves to be popular, effective campaigners, and a few have even raised funds for their husband and their political party. All recent first ladies have delivered major addresses at the national party conventions that nominate their husband, and the trend of first ladies campaigning dates to the late 1800s and the "front porch" campaigns of Grover Cleveland, Benjamin Harrison, and Ida McKinley.[24] The name and likeness of these spouses were featured on campaign literature, and they opened their homes to glad-hand with the public. From the back of his whistle stop train campaign, Harry Truman would introduce Bess Truman to the audience as "The Boss," which produced a rousing applause, George Bush, the President's strategists, and the media all joked only half-heartedly that Barbara Bush was her husband's secret weapon on the campaign stomp, and, Betty Ford gave her husband's concession speech in 1976 because he was too hoarse to deliver it.[25]

Indeed, more than simply campaign, first ladies have often been considerable assets to presidential campaigns. Hillary Rodham Clinton's reassuring support at her husband's side during the 1992 campaign helped him to deflect concern about his marital infidelity, while Lyndon Johnson called on his wife to rally support for him in the South for the 1964 election. In an effort to limit the defection of Whites from the Democratic Party because of the President's support of the 1964 Civil Rights Act, Lady Bird Johnson was dispatched on a whistle stop train campaign through the region. Although she encountered threats and opposition from racists, she met with numerous key politicians and delivered dozens of public speeches, helping her husband to victory at the ballot box. Perhaps most amazing of all examples is that Eleanor Roosevelt actually accepted on behalf of her husband the unprecedented renomination for a third term at the Democratic National Convention in 1940, then delivered the keynote speech because of President Roosevelt's absence.

Social Advocate

First ladies have been prominent advocates of an array of worthy causes. Although this advocacy has at times been derisively deemed a first lady "pet project," the reality is that first ladies have brought valuable public attention to social issues and even enjoyed success in impacting the policy agenda through their advocacy. For example, Lady Bird Johnson championed "beautification," a politically salient term that masked a larger, more important conservation effort, Pat Nixon advocated volunteerism, and Barbara Bush spoke out for literacy, to name a few. Historically, first ladies led aid societies in the drive for food, clothing, and funds for the poor, helped establish children's hospitals, and were leaders in supporting veterans.

Arguably the most profound advocacy work of first ladies has been for human rights. A number of presidential wives and future presidential wives worked to oppose slavery, including Abigail Fillmore, Jane Pierce, Mary Todd

Lincoln, Lucy Hayes, and Lucretia Garfield. Later, Eleanor Roosevelt proved to be a tireless crusader for human rights: helping integrate public facilities; serving on the board of the NAACP; supporting the Tuskegee Airmen; promoting the hiring of women and Blacks in her husband's administration; improving the living conditions of the impoverished in Appalachia; and taking personal offense to the discrimination of the Black contralta Marian Anderson, speaking out against the refusal to allow her to perform in Constitution Hall and scheduling a performance for her at the Lincoln Memorial. This admirable trend has continued in recent times, with Rosalynn Carter traveling to Africa on aid missions and Hillary Rodham Clinton voicing support for women's rights in China, to name a few examples.

Presidential Spokesperson

In addition to campaigning with and for their husbands, first ladies frequently make appearances on behalf of and champion causes related to the presidential policy agenda. Jimmy Carter sent his wife on a seven-nation tour through Latin America in the capacity as his envoy, and aides, lobbyists, and members of Congress recognize that they are speaking to more than the first lady when they meet a president's spouse.

Presidential–National Booster

First ladies have been among the most staunch defenders and supporters of their husbands. This has involved coming to his defense in the face of criticism, to speaking on behalf of his character and qualifications for the office, to campaigning tirelessly for his candidacy and, later, his policies. This unqualified loyalty, however, along with repressive gender norms in society, have caused some first ladies to remain quiet about any personal disagreements they have with their husband over policy and politics. For instance, Barbara Bush admitted in her memoirs that she kept silent about her support for gun control because her husband opposed the issue.[26] Yet, Betty Ford was open about her beliefs, even when they ran contrary to her husband's policies.[27]

Relatedly, first ladies have become boosters for the political parties, campaigning on behalf of party nominees and appearing at party events. They might also be said to serve as boosters of the nation, American business, the armed forces, and other "politically patriotic" institutions and causes. In this capacity, first ladies such as Eleanor Roosevelt and Barbara Bush visited the troops during times of war, Laura Bush prayed for the victims of the September 11, 2001 terrorist attacks, Lucy Hayes initiated what would become the famous Easter egg roll on the White House lawn, and most presidential spouses have presided over holiday ceremonies.

Diplomat

All first ladies since Betty Ford have made high profile trips abroad, some with the president, some alone, but all in an "official" capacity. These diplomatic missions included cultural exchanges and performances—such as the visits to China by

Betty Ford and Nancy Reagan—meetings with heads of state and dignitaries such as the Pope, and speeches on various social and political causes, such as Hillary Rodham Clinton's address in Beijing on behalf of women and Laura Bush's comments on a Voice of America broadcast from Europe. One of the most memorable diplomatic missions was Jacqueline Kennedy's visit with Charles DeGaulle, whereby the French leader was so visibly smitten by Mrs. Kennedy and her knowledge of French literature and culture that President Kennedy joked on his return to the United States that he will forever be remembered as "the man who accompanied Jackie Kennedy to Paris." Another historic mission was when Edith Wilson joined her husband around the negotiating table during the Treaty of Versailles after World War I.

Policy Advocate

President Woodrow Wilson's first wife, Ellen, worked to improve the living conditions of the descendants of slaves living in the capital city. Herself descended from slave holders, her interest in the issue was in part to atone for previous wrongs, and she was successful in building interest among members of Congress and proposing improvements in the slums in the city. Her tragic death in 1914, only a year into her husband's presidency, helped muster the final support needed to pass the bill she advocated. Mrs. Wilson was one of the first presidential spouses to take an active role in policy and the legislative process—Dolley Madison, Sarah Polk, and other first ladies enjoyed attending sessions of Congress—but she was certainly not the only to do so.

Several presidential spouses—Eleanor Roosevelt, Rosalynn Carter, Hillary Rodham Clinton, Laura Bush—have testified before Congress as policy experts, as have such "second ladies" as Joan Mondale, Marilyn Quayle, Tipper Gore, and Lynne Cheney. Other presidential spouses, such as Rosalynn Carter and Hillary Rodham Clinton, have headed presidential policy task forces. Mrs. Carter's mental health reform commission succeeded in producing arguably the most comprehensive mental health care initiative in the country's history in 1980. Other first ladies have been involved in the policy process by lobbying for congressional or public support, such as was the case when Rosalynn Carter and Betty Ford publically supported the Equal Rights Amendment, and Nancy Reagan raised awareness of drug abuse among children.

FIRST LADIES AS PRESIDENTIAL PARTNERS

To varying degrees, first ladies have always functioned as presidential partners. The "two for the price of one" analogy has held true in most of the presidencies where the spouse was living. In the capacity of partners, first ladies have served perhaps their most vital role—one encompassing the entire list from the previous section—as the president's most trusted political confidante. Critics have alleged that, as an extra-constitutional development, the president's wife is without official portfolio.[28] But, she is thus without the constraints of official jurisdictional boundaries as, for instance, those that would restrict a Secretary of the Interior from influencing defense readiness or foreign policy. The legendary "turf battles" that occur in Washington, along with official requirements, would prevent the Interior Secretary from such grandiose designs. But, acting as a free-ranging advisor or ombudsperson, the first lady is unrestricted by formal parameters.

Often presidential decision making has taken on a pattern of joint, consultative, or collaborative decision making:[29] The notion of a "plural presidency," whereby it is not simply the president who is responsible for White House actions, but the large cast of aides and advisers that staff the Executive Office of the President. The reality of this model has often included at its epicenter a small group or "inner circle" of advisers known as the "Kitchen Cabinet."[30] These key aides function as presidential spokespersons in the administration and partners in the decision process. Many presidents, after all, such as Warren Harding and Ronald Reagan, were notorious for their reliance on staff and delegation of authority. Only a handful of first ladies, such as Hillary Rodham Clinton, were a part of the inner circle of advisers, but many others were a viable part of the plural presidency and participated in the decision process: Edith Wilson was with her husband at the Treaty of Versailles and at his side throughout his recovery from a stroke; Rosalynn Carter scheduled weekly working business lunches with her husband; Sarah Polk clipped newspaper articles for her husband to read and edited his speeches; and Nancy Reagan's role in her husband's travel and public scheduling is not to be minimized.

Table 4 lists first ladies who have functioned as presidential partners. Some can be considered as "full" partners, sharing in every facet of the presidency: they have assisted with the social facets of the presidency; served as his most trusted counselor; understood his strengths and weaknesses better than any aide; supported and defended him politically and personally; discussed politics and policy

TABLE 4   Presidential Partners

Full Partners	Partial Partners
Abigail Adams	Dolley Madison
Sarah Polk	Julia Tyler
Helen Taft	Mary Todd Lincoln
Florence Harding	Frances Cleveland
Eleanor Roosevelt	Caroline Harrison
Rosalynn Carter	Ellen Wilson
Hillary Rodham Clinton	Edith Wilson
	Lou Hoover
	Lady Bird Johnson
	Betty Ford
	Nancy Reagan

with him "after hours;" and have been a formidable presence in the highly public presidency. Other spouses can be considered as "partial" partners, sharing in many parts of the presidency but not functioning as full partners in political decisions and policy matters. Only a very few first ladies have failed to exert themselves as partners in the presidency. This includes: Letitia Tyler and Ida McKinley, who were severely debilitated by illness; Anna Harrison and Margaret Taylor, both of whom were advanced in years and disinterested in the presidency; and Jane Pierce, whose depression as a result of the tragic death of her only surviving son just prior to the inauguration consumed her first ladyship.

Presidents have often expressed frustration with the inability to fully trust those around them. Many an aide have leaked information to the press, written "kiss and tell" books about their White House service, or functioned as little more than "yes men." As a result, presidents have turned to the person closest to them for advice. At the least, even politically inactive, traditional first ladies, such as Bess Truman and Pat Nixon, have functioned as sounding boards for their husbands. The type of support and counsel offered by first ladies transcends the paycheck received by White House aides for their counsel.

First ladies have been presented in the this article and can be understood more accurately as presidential partners than simply as spouses or hostesses. Conceptually, their partnership in the presidency and path to political and policy influence have been portrayed in this article and can be understood as occurring through three distinct spheres: the political sphere; the public sphere; and the personal sphere. In each instance, the roles and duties fulfilled by first ladies have existed outside of a formal office or official mandate. It has been through spousehood and the creative and inspired use of traditional roles women have been forced to assume that the first ladyship was forged, something many first ladies shared with many other notable women leaders in history. Yet, in politics where importance is measured through access to power, the first lady has enjoyed physical proximity to power unequaled in government, irrespective of whether she held office or not. She has therefore transcended her outsider status to become an insider capable of influencing politics, policy, and the presidency.

NOTES

1. See, for example, Carl Sferrazza Anthony, *First Ladies: The Saga of the Presidents' Wives and their Power,* 2 vols (New York: William Morrow, 1990 & 1991), reprint 1993 by Perenial; Betty Boyd Caroli, *First Ladies* (New York: Oxford, 1987), reprint 1995 by Oxford; Robert P. Watson, *The Presidents' Wives: Reassessing the Office of First Lady* (Boulder, Colo.: Lynne Rienner Publishers, 2000).

2. When a seat became available because of death, it was not uncommon historically for the governor to appoint the widow to complete the deceased office holder's term or for the political party to nominate her to a single term. Rarely, however, did the widow receive support to run for election on her own.

3. Mel Carnahan, Democratic nominee for the Senate in Missouri, died in a plane crash just weeks prior to the November 2000 election. The deceased candidate's name remained on the ballot and he defeated Republican challenger John Ashcroft. Missouri's governor asked Jean Carnahan, the late candidate's widow, to serve in his place, which she did until her defeat in 2002 in a reelection bid.

4. John Adams (1797–1801) and John Q. Adams (1825–1829) were father and son. William Henry Harrison (1841) and Benjamin Harrison (1889–1893) were grandfather and grandson. George Bush (1989–1993) and George W. Bush (elected in 2000) are father and son.

5. Teddy Roosevelt made famous the "Bully Pulpit," emphasizing the president's ability to capture public attention and lead through speaking directly to the public. In so doing, the president can expand his influence beyond the narrow powers assigned to the office. First ladies have done the same, but from a social—or "white glove" pulpit.

6. Hillary Rodham Clinton's election to the U.S. Senate after her first ladyship (technically, just weeks before the end of it) marked the first time a first lady was elected to public office. However, several first ladies served on the boards of schools and philanthropies, Grace Coolidge served on the board of a school for the blind, Eleanor Roosevelt was asked by President Harry Truman to serve as a U.S. delegate to the United Nations, and so on.

7. The Rose Law Firm in Arkansas was founded in 1820 and was one of the oldest and most prestigious law firms in the region. Hillary Rodham Clinton began work there in 1977.

8. Hillary Rodham Clinton was named as one of the "100 Most Influential Lawyers in America" by the *National Law Journal*.

9. Elizabeth Dole served in the administrations of Ronald Reagan and George Bush, as Secretary of Labor and Secretary of Transportation.

10. See William O. Foss, *First Ladies Quotations Book* (New York: Barricade Books, 1999).

11. Most first ladies have been criticized, often times on a personal level and unfairly so. For a general critique of activism in the first ladyship, see Gil Troy, *Affairs of State: The Rise and Rejection of the Presidential Couple Since World War II* (New York: The Free Press, 1997), reprinted as *Mr. and Mrs. President: From the Trumans to the Clintons* (Lawrence: University Press of Kansas, 2000).

12. The three youngest first ladies are: Frances Cleveland (21), Julia Tyler (24), and Jacqueline Kennedy (31).

13. Margaret Taylor (60) and Anna Harrison (65) were among the oldest first ladies at the time of their husband's election. They were both in poor health and neither wanted to be the first lady. Anna Harrison even delayed her departure from her home to Washington until after the inauguration. Tragically, President William Henry Harrison became ill after the inaugural and died only one month later—before his wife's arrival in the capital city.

14. Elizabeth Monroe (1817–1825), Letitia Tyler (1841–1842), Abigail Fillmore (1850–1853) were all in poor health during their husband's presidency. Before her years as first lady, Mrs. Monroe had been a gracious hostess who traveled with her husband abroad and was active in his political career. Mrs. Tyler was an invalid when her husband ascended to the presidency from the vice presidency, and died one year later. Abigail Fillmore did participate in some facets of the first ladyship, but her health precluded her from taking an active role. Earlier in life she was active, even working outside of her marriage, and she did help to establish and stock a new library in the Executive Mansion.

15. Article II of the Constitution says little about the specific powers of the presidency. Much of the presidential powers are implied or are byproducts of the enlargement of the nation and office in the Twentieth Century. Consequently, many of the precedents set by George Washington—such as serving only two terms—influenced the actions of subsequent presidents and the general development of the office over time.

16. The title of "First Lady" was not used during Martha Washington's time. Scholars remain uncertain as to when the title was first used, but most place it around the time of the Civil War or shortly thereafter during the first ladyship of Lucy Hayes (1877–1881). See Watson, *The Presidents' Wives*, 7, 10–11.

17. The "White House" was not finished until November 1800, and the term *White House* was not officially used until the presidency of Theodore Roosevelt (1901–1909). Initially, the building was known simply as The President's House or The Executive Mansion. See, Robert P. Watson, ed., *Life in the White House: A Social History of the First Family and the President's House* (Albany: SUNY Press, 2004).

18. See David McCollough, *John Adams* (New York: Simon & Schuster, 2002). It is clear in McCollough's well received biography that the author found Abigail Adams a most worthy subject as well.

19. See Anthony J. Eksterowicz and Kristen Paynter, "The Evolution of the Role and Office of the First Lady: The Movement Toward Integration with the White House Office," *The Social Science Journal* 37 (2000): 547–562; Watson, *The President's Wives*, 108–116.

20. Still, however, aides to the first lady typically have a joint appointment and are both assigned through and paid by the Office of the President, and the first lady remains unpaid.

21. When presidential spouses were either deceased or in poor health, presidents utilized the services of younger female relatives (sisters, daughters, daughters-in-law, etc.) to preside over social hosting and other ceremonies. For more information on these "surrogate" or "proxy" hostesses, see Watson, *The Presidents' Wives*, 57–66.

22. Gallup has done an annual poll on "The Most Admired Women" since 1948. See www.gallup.org.

23. For information on the history, challenges, and approaches to preserving and renovating the White House, see Watson, *Life in the White House,* 2004.

24. So-called "front porch" campaigns date to the late 1800s and essentially mark the first time in the country's history that candidates actually campaigned for the presidency. The name derives from the practice of inviting potential voters to visit with the candidate on the front porch of the candidate's home. Spouses played a role in these campaigns, also marking the debut of campaigning by political spouses.

25. President Gerald Ford had lost his voice and was thus unable to deliver his concession speech on election night in 1976. So, too, was he visibly shaken on the stage. Betty Ford delivered the speech on his behalf and was very professional in her delivery.

26. See Barbara Bush, *Barbara Bush: A Memoir* (New York: Scribner's, 1994).

27. See Betty Ford, *The Times of My Life* (New York: Ballantine Books, 1987).

28. See Troy, *Affairs of State,* 1997.

29. For good discussions on presidential decision making, see George C. Edwards III and Stephen J. Wayne, *Presidential Leadership: Politics and Policy Making,* 6th ed. (New York: Wadsworth, 2003); Michael A. Genovese, *The Presidential Dilemma: Leadership in the American System,* 2nd ed. (New York: Longman Publishers, 2003).

30. "Kitchen Cabinet" is the name for close friends and advisers to the president. The first Kitchen Cabinet dates to Andrew Jackson, in response to a weak and divided Cabinet.

FURTHER READING

Carl Sferrazza Anthony. *First Ladies: The Saga of the Presidents' Wives and their Power,* 2 vols. New York: William Morrow, 1990 & 1991. [Reprinted in 1993 by Perennial.]

Betty Boyd Caroli. *First Ladies.* New York: Oxford University Press, 1987. [Reprinted in 1995 by Oxford.]

Anthony J. Eksterowicz and Kristen Paynter. "The Evolution of the Role and Office of the First Lady: The Movement Toward Integration with the White House Office." *The Social Science Journal* 37 (2000): 547–562.

Lewis L. Gould, ed. *American First Ladies: Their Lives and their Legacy.* New York: Greenwood Press, 1996.

Myra G. Gutin. *The President's Partner: The First Lady in the Twentieth Century.* New York: Greenwood Press, 1989.

Karen O'Connor, Bernadette Nye, and Laura Van Assendelft. "Wives in the White House: The Political Influence of First Ladies." *Presidential Studies Quarterly* 26 (1997), 835–853.

Robert P. Watson. "Ranking the First Ladies: Polling Elites to Assess Performance." *PRG Report* (Presidency Research Group) 26 (Fall 2003): 15–22.

Robert P. Watson. "Toward the Study of the First Lady: The State of Scholarship." *Presidential Studies Quarterly* 33 (June 2003): 423–441.

Robert P. Watson. *The Presidents' Wives: Reassessing the Office of First Lady.* Boulder, Colo.: Lynne Rienner Publishers, 2000.

Robert P. Watson. "The First Lady Reconsidered: Presidential Partner and Political Institution." *Presidential Studies Quarterly* 27 (1997), 805–818.

Molly Meijer Wertheimer, ed. *Inventing a Voice: The Rhetoric of American First Ladies of the Twentieth Century.* Boulder, Colo.: Roman & Littlefield, 2004.

Women Governors in the 21st Century: Re-Examining the Pathways to the Presidency

Sara J. Weir

INTRODUCTION

The governors of the 21st century have emerged to become initiators and administrators of large annual budgets and major public programs. Their work as national executives has allowed many to gain experience by dealing directly with international trading partners—states such as New Jersey, Texas, and Washington each depend on international trade for jobs (as well as for tax revenues). The governorship has evolved and today's governors are politically astute in ways that would have been unheard of in previous generations.

The ongoing study of state governorship is increasingly important to scholarly work in the fields of state government and women in politics. As witnessed by the growing impact of state governance within the United States' political system, the study of the governorship in the new millennium offers new research opportunities.

In recent years, the governorship has also served as a proving ground for aspiring presidential candidates—of the five most recent U.S. presidents, four gained much of their political experience and national reputation by serving as governors.

While much has been written about gubernatorial races and of governors as central figures in sub-national governance, a new area of scholarly inquiry explores women as governors. As more women seek (and win) gubernatorial elections; the theories, patterns and expectations emerging from the literature on women and politics becomes more applicable.

Reprinted by permission.

This article provides insights into the careers of the twenty-seven women who served or are serving as governor. It highlights patterns emerging in the 21st Century, in light of the growing body of literature on women and electoral politics, arguing that as negative stereotypes regarding women in high executive elected positions diminish, women seeking the governorship face challenges similar to those of their male counterparts.

Candidate sex, the level of gendered information and other factors related to gender belief stereotypes in a particular race or electoral season still matter. But in many cases, political party and the availability of an open seat outweigh other factors in explaining electoral outcomes.[1]

Drawing upon the experiences of the most recent women governors, the essay suggests that a new pattern of gubernatorial leadership is emerging. Labeled "The Charismatic Outsider," the women governors who fall into this category possess qualities that make them attractive to a broader audience. These women possess positively viewed gender-linked personality traits that overcome the typical maleness of the governorship, while at the same time holding policy positions that are not necessarily reflective of traditional women's issues.[2] The "outsider" status reflects the degree to which voters have looked to governors and others who are not Washington insiders as presidential material in the post WWII era. The combination of these personality traits and issue positions make these women governors politically appealing on a larger national stage.

THE STUDY OF WOMEN AS GOVERNORS

Very few studies of the governorship have focused on women as governors. However in the eighty years of history from the 1925 administration of the first woman governor Nellie Tayloe Ross (D-Wyoming) to the women seeking the governorship in the current electoral cycle, 27 women (17 Democrats, 9 Republicans, and 1 Popular Democratic Party), have served as governors in 21 states and the U.S. commonwealth of Puerto Rico.

While the number of women governors remains small when compared with the proportion of women elected to statewide offices or with men elected as governors, a growing number of women are running for and winning in gubernatorial contests and others are positioning themselves to run for governor by serving in other statewide elected offices.

Because so few women were elected to state executive offices (especially to the governorship), the early literature on women governors was more journalistic than scholarly. For example, books like former governor Madeleine Kunin (D-Vermont)'s autobiography, *Living a Political Life,* are rich sources of information about gender and the exercise of power and leadership. Other autobiographical and biographical works include former governor Ann Richards (D-Texas)'s *Straight From the Heart* and Christine Todd Whitman (R-New Jersey)'s *Growing Up Republican.*[3] Beyond these biographical works, the early literature also focuses on particular gubernatorial races involving women,[4] and comparative case studies of the campaigns of women running for governor.[5]

Like the presidency, the governorship has historically been viewed as a highly gendered office. For example, political pollster Celinda Lake noted that the qualities that make a good governor—toughness and executive ability—are most often associated by voters with men.[6]

The picture today is both more promising and more complicated. As suggested earlier, candidate sex and gender related issues still matter—but in today's political world being a female is not necessarily a disadvantage. For example, recent studies have shown candidate sex seems to matter more in some elections than in others and the degree to which being a woman candidate is a potential liability depends upon the region of the country and other factors (such as local political culture and the power of gendered information in individual elections).[7]

PATTERNS IN THE CANDIDACY OF WOMEN GOVERNORS

The history of women governors is best understood as a progression from surrogacy to independent candidacy and beyond.

Before seeking the governorship, most of the women elected governor have solidified their reputations and increased their visibility by holding positions in local and state government.[8] As illustrated by Table 1, this experience—whether in elected positions, involvement with party politics or community activism—moves women up the "pipeline" of viable candidates within political parties and gives them the experience, partisan connections and name recognition necessary to seek the governorship.[9]

STAGE ONE: THE SURROGATE GOVERNORS

Three women served as state governors in a "surrogate" capacity. Acting initially as replacements or surrogates for their husbands, all three were appointed or elected because their husbands were governors who could not, for one reason or another, hold office any longer.

Nellie Tayloe Ross was elected to the governorship in a special election following the death of her husband and she served the remaining years of his term. Ross was then the Democratic Party candidate for re-election in 1926, but was defeated by her Republican challenger in a close race (36,651 votes to 34,286 votes). She remained active in Democratic Party politics—at one point she served as Vice-Chair of the Democratic National Committee and in 1933 newly elected President Franklin D. Roosevelt appointed her to the position of Director of the Mint.

First appointed to the governorship when her husband resigned under threat of impeachment, Miriam Ferguson (D-Texas) went on to be active in Texas politics for two decades. During that time, she ran for governor five times and won once, serving again as governor from 1933–1935.

TABLE 1
Before (and After): The Experience of Selected Women Governors

Governor	Before Taking Office	After Leaving Office
Nellie Tayloe Ross (D—Wyoming) 1925–1927	Active in the Cheyenne Woman's Club, which concentrated on intellectual self-improvement.	Active in Democratic Party politics—at one point she served as Vice-Chair of the Democratic National Committee. FDR appointed her Director of the Mint; a position she held throughout the Roosevelt and Truman administrations. Ross died in 1977.
Miriam "Ma" Ferguson (D—Texas) 1925–1927; 1933–1935	Devoted her energies almost exclusively to her husband and two daughters. This fact, and the combination of her first and middle initials, led her supporters to call her "Ma" Ferguson.	Went on to be active in Texas politics for two decades. During that time, she ran for governor five times and won twice. Ferguson died in 1961.
Ella Grasso (D—Connecticut) 1975–1980	Assistant director of research for the War Manpower Commission in Connecticut during World War II. Elected to the state legislature in 1952 and again in 1954. Elected secretary of state in Connecticut in 1958 and served two terms as a U.S. representative. Worked with John Baily, national chairman of the Democratic Party under President John F. Kennedy.	Resigned due to ill health during second term, Grasso died in 1981.
Dixy Lee Ray (D—Washington) 1977–1981	Director of the Seattle's Pacific Science Center and a personality on public television, where she gave lesson on seashore. In 1972 Richard Nixon appointed her to the Atomic Energy Commission, which she later chaired. Gerald R. Ford later appointed Ray to become the first Assistant Secretary of State for the Bureau of Oceans, International Environment and Scientific Affairs.	Stayed out of politics, published two books about the environment. Ray died in 1992.
Martha Layne Collins (D—Kentucky) 1984–1987	Began her political career as coordinator of women's activities in a number of political campaigns. Served as Clerk of the Supreme Court of the Commonwealth of Kentucky from 1978 to 1979, and was elected Lieutenant Governor. She chaired the Democratic National Convention in 1984.	Served as president of St. Catharine College for six years. Since 1998, Collins has served as Executive Scholar in Residence at Georgetown College in Georgetown.
Madeleine Kunin (D—Vermont) 1985–1991	Elected to the Vermont House of Representatives as a Democratic representative from Burlington. She served two three-year terms and became a minority whip. Served two terms as Lieutenant Governor.	Became U.S. Deputy Secretary of Education. Appointed U.S. ambassador to Switzerland during Clinton administration.

(continued)

TABLE 1 (continued)
Before (and After): The Experience of Selected Women Governors

Governor	Before Taking Office	After Leaving Office
Kay Orr (R—Nebraska) 1987–1991	Chief of staff for Gov. Charles Thone from 1979 to 1981 when Thone appointed her Nebraska State Treasurer. She was elected to the position the following year, becoming the first woman elected to a statewide constitutional office in Nebraska.	Member of the Family First board of directors. She also is involved with the Lincoln People's City Mission, the national board of Prison Fellowship, local prison ministry, and some corporate boards.
Ann Richards (D—Texas) 1991–1995	Travis County commissioner, teacher and activist. Served two terms as state treasurer.	Senior adviser with Verner, Liipfert, Bernhard, McPherson and Hand, a Washington, D.C. based law firm, serves on the boards of J. C. Penney, T.I.G. Holdings and the Aspen Institute.
Barbara Roberts (D—Oregon) 1991–1995	Began her career in public service as an advocate for handicapped children. Elected to the Oregon House of Representatives in 1981. In 1984 she was elected secretary of state.	Director of the Harvard Program for Senior Executives in State and Local Government and later as a senior fellow to the Women and Public Policy Program.
Joan Finney (D—Kansas) 1991–1995	Elected State Treasurer in 1974, a position she held for 16 years.	Two years after leaving office, Finney ran for U.S. Senate, losing in the primaries. A long-time advocate for the sovereignty and self-determination of Native Americans, Finney died in 2001.
Christine Todd Whitman (R—New Jersey) 1994–2001	Somerset County Board of Chosen Freeholders. Appointed to the New Jersey Board of Public Utilities.	Appointed Director of Environmental Protection Agency by George W. Bush.
Jeanne Shaheen (D—New Hampshire) 1997–2003	Active in New Hampshire Democratic Party. Served three-terms as State Senator.	Candidate for the U.S. Senate seat in 2004 election.
Judy Martz (R—Montana) 2001–Present	Field representative for U.S. Senator Conrad Burns from 1989 to 1995. President of the Butte Chamber of Commerce in the early 1990's, and vice-chair of the St. James Hospital Board of Directors.	

Ruth Ann Minner (D—Delaware) 2001–Present

Served as a page for the Delaware House of Representatives and was later elected as a state representative for four terms and as a state senator for three terms. Elected Delaware's first woman lieutenant governor in 1992.

Jennifer M. Granholm (D—Michigan) 2003–Present

Served as a federal prosecutor in the U.S. Attorney's Office in Detroit, and was appointed Wayne County Corporation Counsel in 1994. In 1998 she was elected state attorney general.

Linda Lingle (R—Hawaii) 2003–Present

Member of the Maui County Council. Elected mayor of Maui County in 1990. Elected Hawaii Republican Party chair in 1999.

Janet Napolitano (D—Arizona) 2003–Present

Nominated by President Bill Clinton to serve as U.S. Attorney for the District of Arizona. Elected Arizona attorney general in 1998.

Kathleen Sebelius (D—Kansas) 2003–Present

Daughter of former Ohio Governor John Gilligan. Served as a state representative for eight years. Elected Insurance Commissioner of Kansas for eight years.

Kathleen Blanco (D—Louisiana) 2004–Present

First woman ever elected to represent the people of Lafayette in the state legislature. Five years later she became the first woman elected to the Louisiana Public Service Commission and serve as its chairperson. In 1996, she was elected to her first of two terms as lieutenant governor.

Sila Calderon (Popular Democratic Party— Puerto Rico) 2004–Present

Special assistant for the secretary of labor, and later special assistant on economic development and labor issues. First woman chief of staff for the commonwealth. Puerto Rico's secretary of state.

Sources: Center for American Women and Politics (CAWP), Eagleton Institute of Politics Rutgers, The State University of New Jersey 191 Ryders Lane, New Brunswick, NJ 08901-8557—www.cawp.rutgers.edu); National Governors Association (NGA), Hall of States, 444 N. Capitol St., Washington, D.C. 20001—www.nga.org).

Ross and Ferguson—who first held office because their husbands were governor—each went on to serve in appointed and elected positions based on their own ability. Their lifelong careers as public servants have many elements that are similar to the careers of later women governors.

Stage Two: Winners of Open Seat Contests

The 1974 election of Ella Grasso (D-Connecticut) marked the beginning of a new era for women as gubernatorial candidates. Grasso was the fourth woman governor, but the first to be elected independent of a husband—she defeated her Republican challenger, Robert Steele, in an open-set contest, receiving 59% of the vote.

Of the seventeen women elected to the governorship in the years since Ella Grasso's historic victory, fifteen began their administrations by winning election in open seat contests.[10] Grasso is followed by a series of other independently elected governors who defeated male candidates, including Dixie-Lee Ray (D-Washington) in 1976, Martha Layne Collins (D-Kentucky) in 1983, and Madeleine Kunin (D-Vermont) in 1984.

The 1986 election of Kay Orr (R-Nebraska) as governor marked two firsts in gubernatorial races involving women. Orr had served as state treasurer before running for governor and not only was she the first Republican woman to be elected governor of any state, but her 1986 race was the first gubernatorial contest between two women candidates of major political parties. Orr defeated her Democratic opponent Helen Boosalis by receiving 53 percent of the vote "in a state where Republicans outnumber Democrats by 75,000 registered voters."[11]

Barbara Roberts (D-Oregon) and Ann Richards were elected in open seat contests in 1990. In 1994, nine women ran for state governor in the 36 gubernatorial contests held—none were elected.

In 1996 Jeanne Shaheen was elected governor of New Hampshire in an open-seat contest. Shaheen's three terms in office signaled the beginning of a new era for women as governors. Her election builds upon the successful campaigns of Joan Finney (D-Kansas) and Christine Todd Whitman (see Stage Four: Defeating Incumbents).

In the elections held since 2000, eight women candidates have become governor in open seat contests: Judy Martz (R-Montana), Ruth Ann Minner (D-Delaware), Jennifer M. Granholm (D-Michigan), Linda Lingle (R-Hawaii), Janet Napolitano (D-Arizona), Kathleen Sebelius (D-Kansas), Kathleen Blanco (D-Louisiana) and Sila Calderon (Popular Democratic Party-Puerto Rico).

STAGE THREE: WINNING RE-ELECTION

Five women governors have won re-election (many more have been elected, but did not seek another term). Winning elections as an incumbent candidate or former governor shows an ability to put a program in place and maintain the electoral support needed to defend it against challengers.

TABLE 2   The Stages of Women Governors

Stage One:	Nellie Tayloe Ross (D-Wyoming) 1925–1927
	Miriam "Ma" Ferguson (D-Texas) 1925–1927; 1933–1935
	Lurleen Wallace (D-Alabama) 1967–1968
"The Surrogate"*	
Stage Two:	Ella Grasso (D-Connecticut) 1975–1980
	Dixy Lee Ray (D-Washington) 1977–1981
	Martha Layne Collins (D-Kentucky) 1984–1987
"Winners of Open Seat Contests"	Madeleine Kunin (D-Vermont) 1985–1991
	Kay Orr (R-Nebraska) 1987–1991
	Ann Richards (D-Texas) 1991–1995
	Barbara Roberts (D-Oregon) 1991–1995
	Jeanne Shaheen (D-New Hampshire) 1997–2003
	Judy Martz (R-Montana) 2001–Present
	Ruth Ann Minner (D-Delaware) 2001–Present
	Jennifer M. Granholm (D-Michigan) 2003–Present
	Linda Lingle (R-Hawaii) 2003–Present
	Janet Napolitano (D-Arizona) 2003–Present
	Kathleen Sebelius (D-Kansas) 2003–Present
	Kathleen Blanco (D-Louisiana) 2004–Present
	Sila Calderon (Popular Democratic Party-Puerto Rico)
Stage Three:	Ella Grasso
	Madeine Kunin
	Christine Todd Whitman
"Winning Re-election"	Jane Dee Hull*
	Jeanne Shaheen
Stage Four:	Joan Finney (D-Kansas) 1991–1995
	Christine Todd Whitman (R-New Jersey) 1994–2001
"Defeating the Incumbent"	
Stage Five:	Jeanne Shaheen
	Christine Todd Whitman
	Jennifer M. Granholm
"The Charismatic Outsider"	Kathleen Sebelius
	Sila Calderon

*This table does not include a sub-category of women governors who were independently appointed for shortened terms. These include (in chronological order): Vesta Roy (R-New Hampshire), Rose Mofford (D-Arizona), Jane D. Hull (R-Arizona), Nancy Hollister (R-Ohio), Jane Swift (R-Massachusetts), and Olene Walker (R-Utah). Of these women, only Hull went on to become a "Stage Three" governor by winning re-election independent of her appointment.

Source: Center for the American Women and Politics (CAWP), National Information Bank on Women in Public Office, Eagleton Institute of Politics, Rutgers University.

Four women in the modern era have won re-election: Ella Grasso was not only the first independently elected woman governor, she was also the first to be re-elected as an incumbent. During her second term, she was forced to resign due to illness and died shortly after her resignation. Madeleine Kunin went on to be re-elected to two additional two-year terms. Christine Todd Whitman won re-election in 1997, but left office to take a presidential appointment as Commissioner of the Environmental Protection Agency. She resigned as head of the EPA in 2003. Jeanne Shaheen won re-election for a second three-year term in 2000. While technically not re-elected (since she initially became governor by appointment), Jane Dee Hull (R-Arizona) went on to be elected to a full term as governor in 2000.

STAGE FOUR: DEFEATING THE INCUMBENT

Although women governors are most commonly elected in open seat contests, there have been two cases—Joan Finney (D-Kansas) and Christine Todd Whitman—where women candidates defeated male incumbents.

With her defeat of incumbent governor Mike Hayden in 1990, Finney became the first Stage Four governor. She did not seek re-election in 1994. After a failed attempt to gain the nomination of her party for the U.S. Senate race in 1996, Finney continued her political career by working to bring about state government reform. She died in 2001.

In 1993, Christine Todd Whitman (R-New Jersey) defeated incumbent governor James Florio. Whitman was re-elected to a second term as governor in 1997. Like her narrow victory over the incumbent governor in 1993, she defeated her Democratic Party challenger Jim McGreevey by only one percent (27,000 votes).[12]

STAGE FIVE: THE CHARISMATIC OUTSIDER

As detailed in the introduction, the "Charismatic Outsider" presents the newest stage in the progression of women governors.

Former governors Jeanne Shaheen and Christine Todd Whitman could be considered the first to exemplify the characteristics of this stage.

As a state senator and as governor of New Hampshire, Shaheen was known as a leader in the fight for health care reform. A long-time political activist, she was a highly visible presence in Democratic party circles, eventually becoming the only woman to appear on presidential candidate Al Gore's final vice-presidential short list for the 2000 Democratic nomination.

Christine Todd Whitman was a role model for many Republican women seeking office in the mid-to-late 1990s. She possessed the administrative experience that came with the goverance of a highly populated coastal state while embracing the conservatism of her political party. Whitman made history in 1995 by becoming the first Republican governor—male or female—to deliver the response to a State of the Union Address. Her speech following President Clinton's address helped to solidify her national visibility within the Republican party.

Both Whitman and Shaheen developed political reputations that bridged the gap between popularity within a state and recognition on a national level—characteristics necessary to become a Stage Five "Charismatic Outsider."

Three women who are currently serving as governors fall into this category as well. They include Michigan governor Jennifer Granholm, Puerto Rico's governor Sila Calderon and Kansas governor Kathleen Sebelius.

Although Sebelius is the only one of the three current governors who is eligible to serve as president,[13] all of these women have cultivated personal styles that combine both "the toughness and executive ability" once associated primarily with men, tempered by leadership qualities that are built upon problem solving orientations and other attributes more traditionally associated with women.

What makes the "Charismatic Outsider" unique is the positive way in which being female adds to the appeal of these women governors.

SUMMARY AND CONCLUSION

What predictions can be made about the future of women as governors and the governorship as an avenue of mobility to the presidency for women? The progress made in the election of women governors has been mixed, but there are several positive developments.

According to the Center for the American Woman and Politics, women have been elected and appointed to statewide executive offices in all but two of the fifty states. Twenty-seven women have served as state governors. At the time this article was written, nine women currently hold office as governors (in eight states and Puerto Rico), seventeen women serve as lieutenant governors and many more hold statewide elected offices such as secretary of state or state treasurer—positions that were stepping stones for most of the women serving today.[14]

In 2004, 11 states will have gubernatorial elections and in at least five of those states—Montana, North Dakota, Utah, Washington and West Virginia—the races will be open seat contests.

Several women have already indicated they will be running for governor. They include Christine Gregoire (D-WA); Claire McCaskill (D-MO); Fran Shubert (R-NC); Jennie Lee Sievers (R-MO) and Karen Skelton-Memhardt (R-MO).[15]

Several current women governors serve in states where there will be a 2004 gubernatorial race. Ruth Ann Minner (D-Vermont) is running for re-election. Judy Martz (R-MT) and Olene Walker (R-Utah) have each decided they will not run for an additional term in office. In addition, Sila Calderon (PDP-PR) has also indicated that she will leave office when her term expires.

In the thirty years since the election of Ella Grass, the numbers of women holding the governorship remains relatively small, but the visibility of women in state office and the disappearance of the most extreme negative stereotypes regarding women in public life has created a more even playing field for women candidates. The pattern of progress includes:

- More women are running for and holding statewide elected positions—putting themselves in the "experience pool."
- Women remain highly visible in their respective political parties following their gubernatorial successes.
- Women candidates have experienced success in open-seat elections.
- Women governors have proven they can be re-elected.
- Female candidates have proven they can beat incumbents.
- Women are gaining increased national visibility. Described here as "Charismatic Outsiders," they are successful in their states and attractive to a national audience.

At the time I first wrote about women governors, the numbers were small and the broader research on women in elected positions was limited. In the new century all of this is changing. The opportunities for women who wish to seek the governorship are, in most parts of the country, similar to those of their male counterparts. They may serve with little notoriety outside of the state in which they were elected, or come to be known nationally as public figures.

This article chronicles the progress of women as state elected executives and the progress of women in the governorship and begins to analyze them in light of the emerging research on women in electoral politics. It is a period of transformation in attitudes toward women as viable candidates for high office and an exciting time to examine the governorship as an important leadership position for women.

NOTES

1. Kathleen A. Dolan, *Voting for Women: How the Public Evaluates Women Candidates* (Boulder, CO: Westview Press, 2003).

2. Leonie Huddy and Nayda Terkildsen, "Gender Stereotypes and the Perception of Male and Female Candidates," *American Journal of Political Science 37* (1993a): 119–147.

3. Madeleine Kunin, *Living a Political Life* (New York: Vintage, 1995); Ann Richards, *Straight From the Heart* (New York: Simon and Schuster, 1989); and Patricia Beard, *Growing Up Republican, Christie Whitman: The Politics of Character* (New York: HarperCollins Publishers, 1996).

4. John Barrette (Ed.), *Prairie Politics: Kay Orr vs. Helen Boosalis, The Historic 1986 Gubernatorial Race* (Lincoln, Nebraska: Media Publishing and Marketing, 1987).

5. Celia Morris, *Storming the Statehouse: Running for Governor with Ann Richards and Dianne Feinstein* (New York: Simon and Schuster, 1992).

6. Celinda Lake, as cited in Eleanor Clift, "Not the Year of the Woman," *Newsweek,* October 25, 1993, p. 31.

7. Dolan, *Ibid.*

8. Center for American Women and Politics (CAWP), Eagleton Institute of Politics Rutgers, The State University of New Jersey 191 Ryders Lane, New Brunswick, NJ 08901-8557—www.cawp.rutgers.edu); National Governors Association (NGA), Hall of States, 444 N. Capitol St., Washington, D.C. 20001—www.nga.org).

9. Georgia Duerst-Lahti, "The Bottleneck: Women Becoming Candidates," in Sue Thomas and Clyde Wilcox, *Women and Elected Office: Past, Present and Future* (New York: Oxford University Press, 1998), p. 155.

10. A sub-category of the open seat contest is illustrated by the appointment of independent women governors. The state of Arizona has seen this happen twice following the resignation or impeachment of the elected governor—former Secretary of State Rose Mofford replaced Evan Mecham as governor in 1988 and Jane Dee Hull replaced Fife Symington as governor in September 1997.

11. Barrette, *Ibid*.

12. *Ibid*.

13. Granholm was born in Canada, Calderon in Puerto Rico—each is constitutionally ineligible to serve as President.

14. Center for American Women and Politics (CAWP), Eagleton Institute of Politics Rutgers. (The State University of New Jersey 191 Ryders Lane, New Brunswick, NJ 08901-8557—www.cawp.rugers.edu).

15. *Ibid*.

FURTHER READING

Beard, Patricia. "Growing Up Republican, Christie Whitman: The Politics of Character". New York: Harper Collins, 1996.

Burrell, Barbara C. *A Woman's Place Is in the House: Campaigning for Congress in the Feminist Era*. Ann Arbor: University of Michigan Press, 1994.

Dodson, Debra (Ed.). *Gender and Policymaking: Studies of Women in Office*. New Brunswick, New Jersey: Center for the American Woman in Politics, 1991.

Genovese, Michael A. (Ed). *Woman as National Leaders,* Thousand Oaks, California: Sage, 1993.

Githens, Marianne, et al. (Eds). *Different Roles, Different Voices: Woman and Politics in the United States and Europe*. New York: Harper Collins, 1994.

Kunin, Madeleine M. *Living a Political Life*. New York: Vintage, 1994.

Morris, Celia. *Storming the Statehouse: Running for Governor with Ann Richards and Dianne Feinstein*. New York: Scribners, 1992.

Richards, Ann, with Peter Knobler. *Straight from the Heart*. New York: Simon and Schuster, 1989.

Thomas, Sue. *How Women Legislate*. New York: Oxford University Press, 1994.

The Courts: Women and Decisions

Does gender make a difference when it comes to the judicial branch? Karen O'Connor points out that, although Abigail Adams cautioned her husband, John, to make sure that women were remembered as the first national laws were drafted, women have yet to reach full equality under the U.S. Constitution. The author traces the intertwined quest for expanded rights for women and the U.S. Supreme Court's responses to those actions. She begins with an overview of the colonial period, moves to the Civil War years, addresses the suffrage movement litigation, reviews the press for state laws and for the Supreme Court to address the issue of gender, and explores the legal status of women at the workplace as well as more contemporary attempts to expand women's rights. She finds that fewer and fewer constitutional cases involving sex discrimination are coming before the Supreme Court each year—perhaps because women's rights groups are using their time and money to fend off challenges to a series of decisions adverse to abortion rights. Also, the author maintains that most of the "easy" constitutional cases have been decided, and there is fairly uniform application of the intermediate standard of review in the lower courts. Thus, most cases involving sex discrimination that the Court chooses to hear now involve employment or educational discrimination litigated under Title VII of the Civil Rights Act or Title IX of the Educational Amendments of 1972. Over time, however, the U.S. Supreme Court has interpreted various provisions of the Constitution (as well as statutory law) to expand women's rights. This essay chronicles those efforts and highlights the ephemeral nature of rights based largely on interpretations of an unelected judiciary.

If we had more female judges, could we expect to see more judicial decisions favorable to women? Elaine Martin maintains that even though it has been more difficult for women to attain judicial office than to other public office, the number of women judges continues to rise. The author points out there are indications that these new women judges may be making a difference in outcomes in gender-related cases. This raises the question as to whether women judges may be introducing bias into a presumably neutral system, or whether they may be providing a counterbalance to a system dominated by a male perspective. This article first presents data on the increase from 1976 to 2004 in the number of women judges, or *numerical representation* and considers the eligible pool theory as an explanation for that increase. It then examines the potential impact of the increase in women judges on the diversification of gender perspectives on the judicial bench, or *interest representation*. Results from studies done in the 1970s and early 1980s suggested that men's and women's similar legal training and socialization as lawyers minimized any potential gender differences in judicial behavior. However, more recent studies indicate that, as women's numbers move beyond the token stage and as younger females educated after the women's movement become judges, differences based on gender emerge more clearly. Research on the current generation of women judges suggests that gender-based differences in experience may contribute to a widening gap between the behavior of men and women judges with respect to decisions in cases raising issues of gender discrimination and divorce/family law. This gap is attributed to a "gendered voice" expressed by both men and women judges. The conclusion of this article is that women judges may be providing a counterbalance to a previously all-male bias in family law.

Litigating for Social Change: The Role of Women's Groups in Advancing Women's Rights

Karen O'Connor

As early as March 31, 1776, Abigail Adams wrote to her husband John, who was attending the Second Continental Congress, urging him to "remember the Ladies, and be more generous and favorable to them than your ancestors" as he and others struggled to fashion the laws to govern the new union.[1] Adams's admonitions to her husband had little impact on either the Articles of Confederation or later to the U.S. Constitution. It was not until 1920 that the Nineteenth Amendment was added to the Constitution, offering women that most basic element of citizenship—suffrage. And, today despite long years of a concerted drive by women's rights groups to have an amendment guaranteeing equal rights ratified, the Constitution continues to afford women less protection from discrimination than it does to men.

In this essay, the role of the U.S. Supreme Court in the evolution of women's rights in the United States is traced. The Supreme Court often is looked upon as ahead of its time, or at least public opinion, in the expansion of rights to minorities. This has not been the case with the rights of women. Instead, as a general rule, the Court has lagged behind societal mores and realities when it has dealt with issues of concern to women. Thus, while today women still can technically be barred from combat positions in the U.S. military (in spite of the fact that several women in military uniform have been killed in Iraq), for example, the U.S. Supreme Court has upheld laws creating a male only draft should it be necessary. Even while there is evidence that some women served in a variety of positions in the Revolutionary and Civil Wars (although often disguised as men), Abigail Adams was one of the few women at the time to call for greater rights for women.[2]

FROM THE COLONIAL PERIOD TO THE CIVIL WAR AMENDMENTS

During the colonial period, the right to vote was determined largely by local custom and usage. While we know of instances where a few women, usually wealthy landowners, were allowed to vote, once individual states began to draft written constitutions, however, woman suffrage evaporated. Women also were excluded by the gradual shift from gender-neutral property-owning requirements to near universal male suffrage. This emphasis on male suffrage also fostered the passage of a host of laws that actually codified many of the informal customs that Abigail Adams had denounced as contributing to second-class citizenship for women. These regulations, for example, allowed husbands to beat their wives so long as the implement was no larger than their thumb ("the rule of thumb").[3]

Recognition of their legal inferior status, however, did not come to women overnight. In 1848, in what is widely hailed as the first major step toward female equality under the Constitution, a women's rights convention was held in Seneca Falls, New York. Eight years earlier, in 1840, two women active in the American abolitionist movement had traveled to London for the annual meeting of the World Anti-Slavery Society. After that long trip, Elizabeth Cady Stanton and Lucretia Mott were denied seating on the floor of the convention solely because they were women. As they sat in the balcony overlooking the proceedings, they could not help but begin to see parallels between their status and that of the slaves they sought to free. They resolved to call a meeting to discuss women's second class status, but the anti-slavery movement and issues in their own lives kept them from sending out a call to Seneca Falls until 1848.

At Seneca Falls, and at a later meeting in Rochester, New York, a series of resolutions and a Declaration of Sentiments were drafted calling for expanded rights for women in all walks of life. Both documents reflected dissatisfaction with contemporary moral codes, divorce and criminal laws, and the limited opportunities for women to obtain an education, participate in the church, and to enter careers in medicine, law, and politics. None of the participants at Seneca Falls or subsequent conventions for women's rights, however, saw the U.S. Constitution as a source of potential rights for women. Women's rights activists did, however, eventually see the need to amend the Constitution to achieve the right to vote.[4]

While women continued to press for changes in state laws to improve their inferior legal status, they also continued to be active in the abolitionist movement. During the Civil War, most women's rights activists concentrated on the war effort and abolition. Many who had been present at Seneca Falls or active in subsequent efforts for women's rights joined the American Equal Rights Association (AERA), an association dedicated to abolition and woman suffrage. AERA members saw the issues of slavery and women's rights as inextricably intertwined, believing that woman suffrage would occur when the franchise was extended to newly freed slaves.

Even the AERA, however, soon abandoned the cause of woman suffrage with its support of the proposed Fourteenth Amendment. When a majority of its members agreed "Now is the Negro's hour," key women's rights activists including Stanton and

Susan B. Anthony were outraged. They were particularly incensed by the text of the proposed amendment, which introduced the word *male* into the Constitution for the first time. Although Article II of the Constitution does refer to the president as "he," the use of the word *male* to limit suffrage was infuriating to many women. Not only did Stanton and Anthony argue that women should not be left out of any attempt to secure fuller rights for freed slaves, but they were concerned that the text of the proposed amendment would necessitate the passage of an additional amendment to enfranchise women. How right they were. Soon after passage of the Fourteenth Amendment, the Fifteenth Amendment was added to the Constitution to enfranchise African-American males previously ineligible to vote. Feverish efforts to have the word *sex* added to the amendment's list of race, color, or previous condition of servitude as improper limits on voting were unsuccessful. Women once again were told that the rights of African American men must come first.

Passage of the Fifteenth Amendment, and AERA's support of it, led Anthony and Stanton to found the National Woman Suffrage Association (NWSA) in 1869. Soon thereafter, more conservative women founded the American Woman Suffrage Association (AWSA). This schism in the women's movement was the first of many that was to plague and distract women from attaining additional rights under the Constitution. The women of AWSA were shocked by Stanton and Anthony's association with a known proponent of free love and their penchant for unconventional dress, which they ultimately abandoned.

LITIGATING FOR SUFFRAGE

In 1869, to lend credibility to its cause, as well as to short-circuit the possibility of a long battle for a woman suffrage amendment, NWSA launched a campaign to win the right to vote by bringing a series of test cases to the federal courts. A number of legal scholars and judges had publicly voiced the opinion that a case could be made that women were due the right to vote under the Privileges Immunities Clause of Article IV, section 2 of the Fourteenth Amendment. A Committee in the House of Representatives even appeared to encourage NWSA's strategy when it noted that if a right to vote was vested by the Constitution, that right could be established in the courts without further legislation. More importantly, the newly appointed chief justice, Salmon P. Chase, had suggested that women test the parameters of the Constitution to determine if they were already enfranchised by its provisions.[5]

Despite Chase's encouragement, prior references to women by the Supreme Court had generally defined a limited role for them. In 1857 in *Dred Scott v. Sanford,* for example, Chief Justice Taney noted, "Women and minors, who form a part of the political family, cannot vote. . . ."[6] It was not all that surprising, then, after the Supreme Court heard one of NWSA's test cases, *Minor v. Happersett* (1875), the Court failed to depart from this logic.[7] Unfortunately for NWSA, before *Minor* could be heard by the Supreme Court, the justices heard another case challenging gender discrimination under the Fourteenth Amendment. *Bradwell v. Illi-*

nois (1873) involved a challenge to the Illinois State Supreme Court's refusal to admit Myra Bradwell to the practice of law because she was a married woman.[8] Interestingly, Bradwell, as well as her lawyer, were active members of AWSA. He based her claim for bar admission on the Privileges and Immunities Clause of the Fourteenth Amendment. Because Bradwell's lawyer was well aware of the suffrage test cases, he specifically rejected the notion that women were enfranchised under the same provisions. He carefully differentiated the practice of a chosen profession from the right to vote, putting the Court on notice that not even all women were in agreement over the scope and reach of the Fourteenth Amendment. Despite the care he took to disassociate his client from NWSA's tactics, the Court ruled 8 to 1 against Bradwell's petition.

The majority opinion in *Bradwell*—the first pronouncement from the Supreme Court on the issue of gender—was based on two grounds. First, because Bradwell was a citizen of Illinois, the Privileges Immunities Clause of Article IV, section 2 of the Constitution was held inapplicable to her claim and to apply only to matters involving U.S. citizenship. Second, since admission to the bar of a state was not one of privileges and immunities of U.S. citizenship, the Fourteenth Amendment, said the Court, also did not secure that right.

Far more damaging to women's rights, however, was a concurrence written by Justice Joseph P. Bradley, which is often referred to as the promulgation of the "Divine Law of the Creator." Writing for himself and two other justices, Bradley observed "a wide difference in the respective spheres and destinies of man and woman" and went on to insist that the "natural and proper timidity and delicacy which belongs to the female sex evidently unfits it for many of the occupations of civil life. . . . The paramount destiny and mission of woman are to fulfill the noble and benign offices of wife and mother. This is the law of the Creator."[9]

Two years later, in *Minor v. Happersett* (1875), the Court again ruled against the claim of women's rights.[10] The Court rejected the argument that the judiciary was empowered to read into the Fourteenth Amendment the right of suffrage as a natural privilege and immunity of citizenship. Writing for a unanimous Court, the newly appointed chief justice, Morrison R. Waite, argued that the states were not inhibited by the Constitution from committing "that important trust to men alone."[11] Nevertheless, the Court stressed that women were "persons" and might even be "citizens" within the meaning of the Fourteenth Amendment.

All of the gender discrimination cases heard by the Supreme Court during this era involved construction of the Privileges and Immunities Clause, and not the Due Process or Equal Protection Clauses of the Fourteenth Amendment. In fact, in the same year as *Bradwell,* while limiting the constitutional significance of the Privileges and Immunities Clause, the Court had also concluded that the Equal Protection Clause was "so clearly a provision to that race [the Negro] that a strong case would be necessary for its application to any other."[12]

This kind of language as well as the Court's decisions in *Bradwell* and *Minor,* led women in both NWSA and AWSA to seek the vote through more traditional means at the same time that both groups began to suffer from losses in membership as the first efforts for woman suffrage faltered. By 1890 and the dawn of the

Progressive era, these two groups would combine to form the National American Woman Suffrage Association. Litigation was abandoned as NAWSA turned its attentions on obtaining the right to vote, first on a state-by-state basis, and later as a constitutional amendment. Other Progressive era groups, however, were quick to adopt litigation as a means of securing their goals, in this case, to secure maximum hour and minimum wage laws to protect women workers.[13]

LITIGATING TO PROTECT WOMEN

As early as 1873, the Supreme Court began to plant the seeds for judicial adoption of a very broad state police power to enact laws to protect the public health, welfare, safety, and morals of state citizens and by 1887, the Court announced that it was ready to examine the *substantive* reasonableness of state legislation. According to the Court, when state laws involving "the public morals, the public health, or the public safety" were at issue, the Court would "look to the substance of things" so as not to be "misled by mere pretenses."[14] Ten years later, the Court, for the first time, actually invalidated a state statue on substantive due process grounds.[15] In 1905, the Court similarly invalidated a law regulating the work hours of bakers.[16]

Until then, the Court rarely looked to the substance of legislation in addressing its validity. The Court's earlier reading of the Due Process Clause of the Fourteenth Amendment (or the Fifth Amendment when federal legislation was involved) only guaranteed that legislation be passed in a fair manner, even though it might have an arbitrary or discriminatory impact. Now according to the Court, state laws would fail *unless* the provisions at issue were deemed reasonable under "common knowledge."[17] Thus, the Court refused to accept New York's claim that a ten-hour maximum-hour law for bakers was reasonable to ensure the health of bakers. Instead, the Court found that it unreasonably interfered with the employers' and employees' freedom of contract protected by the Fourteenth Amendment, and found no "common knowledge" to justify such actions by New York.

The importance of common knowledge cannot be understated in chronicling the Court's treatment of gender. Often, "common knowledge" has been a substitute for the personal views of individual justices or societal mores. As Bradley's, "Divine Law of the Creator" opinion made quite clear, that view could easily lead to restrictions on the rights of women.

In the early 1900's, concern about the health, welfare, and morals of women led activists, particularly those closely allied with the growing woman suffrage movement, to press for state laws to upgrade the status of working women. Large numbers of women had begun to enter the labor force out of necessity. Most were confined to low paying jobs in substandard conditions, a circumstance highlighted by the 1911 Triangle Shirtwaist factory fire in New York City, in which many young female workers lost their lives. Even before that time, however, efforts had begun to improve the working conditions of women and children. And, whether out of civic concern, moral outrage, or a sense of noblesse oblige, beginning in the 1890's, resolutions were adopted annually at suffrage conventions calling for improved conditions for women workers.

The organization most responsible for change, and for the Court's again addressing issues of gender, was the National Consumers' League (NCL). Through the hard work of its national staff and numerous affiliates, the NCL secured maximum hour or other restrictions on night work for women in eighteen states. Its leaders, therefore, immediately recognized how much they had at stake when the Supreme Court decided to review *Muller v. Oregon* (1908), a case challenging the constitutionality of an Oregon law that prohibited the employment of women for more than ten hours a day.[18] (Muller, the owner of a small laundry, had been found guilty of violating the statute). When *Muller* was accepted for review and oral argument, the NCL went to work immediately. Its general secretary quickly asked Louis D. Brandeis, the brother-in-law of one of its most active members and already a famous progressive lawyer, to take the case. Brandeis did so under one condition— that he have sole control of the litigation, a condition to which Oregon gladly acceded, thus allowing the NCL to represent it in Court.

Numerous state court decisions involving protective legislation for women, as well as the Supreme Court's recent decision in *Lochner,* made it clear to Brandeis that a victory could be forthcoming only by presenting information or "common knowledge" that could persuade the Court that the dangers to women working more than ten hours a day made them more deserving of state protection than the bakers in *Lochner,* and by proving that there was something different about women that justified an exception to the freedom of contract doctrine enunciated in *Lochner.* Brandeis and the NCL would not challenge the Supreme Court's right, under substantive due process, to make that judgment.

At Brandeis's request, NCL researchers compiled information about the possible detrimental effects of long hours of work on women's health and morals, as well as on the health and welfare of their children, including unborn children. Brandeis stressed women's differences from men and the reasonableness of the state's legislation. In fact, his brief had but three pages of strictly legal argument and 110 pages of sociological data culled largely from European studies of the negative affects of long hours of work on women's health and reproductive capabilities. The information presented by Brandeis was not all that much different (except in quantity) than that presented on behalf of New York in *Lochner,* yet, the Court appears to have been keenly persuaded by the contents of what has been come to be called the "Brandeis brief," although Josephine Goldmark led his team of researchers and her name also actually was on the brief.

In holding that the Oregon law was permissible, the Court unanimously concluded "[t]hat woman's physical structure and the performance of maternal functions place her at a disadvantage in the struggle for subsistence."[19] Such a condition meant the state had an interest in protecting women's health through appropriate legislation. *Muller's* impact was immediate. State courts began to hold other forms of protective legislation for women constitutional, whether or not they involved the kind of ten-hour maximums at issue in *Muller*. Thus, eight hour maximum work laws in a variety of professions, outright bans on night work for women, and minimum wage laws for women routinely were upheld under the *Muller* rationale.

The NCL's efforts to protect women from unscrupulous employers won the approval of the Supreme Court in several additional cases, but then ran into trouble in the early 1920's. In *Stettler v. O'Hara* (1917), a lower court decision upholding Oregon's minimum-wage law for women was appealed to the Supreme Court.[20] Forces opposed to governmental inference in contractual rights feared that a decision supporting additional protective legislation would open floodgates to more governmental regulation. Stettler's lawyers argued that a labor agreement between an employer and an employee could not be disturbed by the government. Because the Fourteenth Amendment forbade the state from denying any individual liberty without due process of law, they argued that freedom of contract was protected by the Fourteenth Amendment. The Court had been amenable to this kind of argument, as attested to by its *Lochner* decision.

Building on the Court's far-ranging discussion of women and their physical, social and legal differences from men, Brandeis, again presenting the state's case, structured his arguments similarly to those offered in *Muller,* stressing the importance of a living wage to the health, welfare and morals of women. Before the Court could decide the case, however, a vacancy occurred on the Court and Brandeis was appointed to fill it. *Stettler* was reargued in 1917 with Brandeis not participating. The Court divided 4 to 4, thus sustaining the lower court's decision.

The next NCL-sponsored case, *Bunting v. Oregon* (1917), attracted a significant amount of attention. Felix Frankfurter, Brandeis's hand-picked successor as NCL counsel, used the same kind of arguments Brandeis had used in *Muller* and *Stettler*. In a 5 to 3 decision (with Brandeis again not participating) the Court extended *Muller* to uphold an Oregon statute that established maximum hours for all factory and mill workers.[21]

Although the NCL was victorious in these two cases, it had not anticipated the impact that the controversy within the suffrage movement over protective legislation would have on pending litigation. Many of its members were also active in NAWSA. During the early twentieth century, women had come together to lobby for passage and then ratification of the Nineteenth Amendment. Once it was ratified, attempts were made to secure other rights for women. Women in the more radical branch of the suffrage movement, represented by the National Woman's Party (NWP), proposed the addition of an equal rights amendment to the Constitution. Progressives, former NAWSA members, and those in the NCL were horrified because they believed that an equal rights amendment would immediately invalidate the protective legislature they had lobbied so hard to enact.

When *Adkins v. Children's Hospital* (1923) came to the Court, the NWP was ready. *Adkins* involved the constitutionality of a Washington D.C., minimum wage law for women. The NWP filed an amicus curiae brief urging the Court to rule that, in light of the Nineteenth Amendment, women should be viewed on a truly equal footing with men. The division among women concerning equal rights and protective legislation was now exposed to public view. It was a debate that was to be resurrected again and again in the Court and public through the 1990s.

In *Adkins,* the Court ruled 5 to 4 that minimum wage laws for women were unconstitutional thus resurrecting *Lochner.*[22] The Court, however, was unwilling to overrule *Muller* and thus simply distinguished it because it involved maximum hours and not wages. Nevertheless, the justices clearly believed that the Nineteenth Amendment conferred more rights upon women than just the right to vote. In noting women's newly emancipated status, the Court undoubtedly was responding at least in part to the pro-equality arguments offered by the National Woman's Party.

Adkins, unlike *Muller,* was decided by the narrowest of majorities. But it stood as a good law and as a ringing endorsement of the notion of freedom of contract regarding minimum-wage laws for women until 1937 (although the Court continued to uphold state maximum-hour provisions). In *West Coast Hotel v. Parrish* (1937), the Court finally abandoned its endorsement of substantive due process, explicitly overruled *Adkins,* and upheld Washington State's minimum-wage law for women.[23] Four years later, the Court completely abandoned substantive due process (and an equally insidious and excessively narrow view of the power of Congress under the commerce clause) when it upheld the validity of the federal Fair Labor Standards Act, which prescribed maximum hours and minimum wages for all workers.[24] In hammering in the last nail in the coffin of substantive due process, the Court also appeared to be escaping from the constitutional need to establish a difference between men and women.

While the Court was enunciating a view that men and women were equal as the permissible objects of regulation, clearly they were not. Most states continued to bar or limit highly lucrative night work for women, unless, of course, they were nurses. And while a separate minimum wage for women could no longer be valid, employer practices of clustering women into certain positions at far lower wages than those paid to men continued to exist. Male and female "Help Wanted" ads were the norm and further served to highlight the pervasive employment discrimination suffered by women. Even in fields where women dominated such as teaching, many states or local governments prohibited married women from working; later these policies were "liberalized" to allow married women to stay on the job so long as they were not pregnant. At the first news of a woman's pregnancy, or in more liberal school districts, by the fourth month of pregnancy, women were forced to leave their jobs.

Interestingly, during World War II, the U.S. government actually launched a campaign to recruit women workers telling them that it was their responsibility to help the war effort and "man" the positions left open in factories when men went off to war. It is not surprising, then, that no new cases came to the Court involving women's rights until 1948. The NCL had obtained what it wanted, and the coalition of women's groups that had pressed for suffrage had largely disintegrated. Women were urged to support the war effort and, after the war ended, to return to their homes to their traditional roles as wives and mothers. Thus, few groups were left to press for women's rights in the legislatures or through the courts. The National

Woman's Party continued to press for equal rights, and in fact, was able to see a proposed equal rights amendment (ERA) introduced into every session of Congress after 1923. But it chose to stay out of litigation until the 1970s.

NEW ATTEMPTS TO EXPAND RIGHTS

In *Goesaert v. Cleary* (1948)[25] and *Hoyt v. Florida* (1961),[26] the Court again made it clear that women were not guaranteed additional rights under the Fourteenth Amendment or elsewhere in the Constitution. Although the Fourteenth Amendment is a pledge of protection against state discrimination, over the years the Court generally had applied a two-tiered level of analysis to claims advanced under its provisions. Classifications based on race or national origin are considered suspect classifications and are entitled to be judged by a severe test of strict scrutiny. As such, they are presumed invalid unless the government can show that they are "necessary to a compelling state interest" and that there are no less-restrictive alternative ways to achieve those goals. In contrast, when the Court applies the less stringent level of ordinary scrutiny, which until 1976 included all other legislative classifications, a state need show only a conceivable or reasonable rationale for its action.

Until 1971, the Court routinely applied this minimal rationality test to claims involving discrimination against women. In *Goesaert,* for example, it sustained a statute that prohibited a woman from dispensing drinks from behind a bar unless she was the wife or daughter of the bar owner. Thus, forty years after *Muller,* the Court continued to justify differential treatment of women by deferring to a state's special interest in her social and "moral" problems. Under the reasonableness test, some rational basis for the law was all that needed to be shown. And, of course, cynics noted that state legislators wanted to make certain that women didn't take jobs from men just returning from protecting their country overseas.

In *Hoyt,* the Supreme Court accepted sex-role stereotypes as a sufficient reason to uphold a state statute that required men to serve on juries while women could merely volunteer for jury service. When Hoyt was convicted by an all-male jury of second-degree murder for killing her husband with a baseball bat, she argued that her conviction violated her rights to equal protection of the laws and her Sixth Amendment right to be judged by a jury of her peers. The Supreme Court disagreed, holding that the Florida statute was not an arbitrary and systematic exclusion of women. Justice John M. Harlan concluded that "Despite the enlightened emancipation of women from the restrictions and protections of bygone years, and their entry into many parts of community life formerly considered to be reserved to men, woman is still regarded as the center of home and family life."[27]

It was not until the dawn of the most recent women's movement that judicial perspectives on what was reasonable discrimination against women began to change. In 1966, the National Organization for Women (NOW) was founded. Soon after, a plethora of other women's rights groups were created. Most of these groups renewed the call for passage of an equal rights amendment (ERA) to the Constitution. While significant lobbying was carried out on that front, some groups, cognizant of the successes that the NAACP had in securing additional rights for African-Americans through the courts, began to explore the feasibility of a litigation strategy designed to seek a more expansive interpretation of the Fourteenth Amendment. Although prior forays into the courts had ended unfavorably, some women lawyers, in particular, believed that the times had changed enough for the justices (or some of the justices) to recognize that sex-based differential treatment of women was unconstitutional. Many believed that the status of women and the climate for change was sufficiently positive to convince even a conservative Court that some change was necessary. And, as more and more women were entering the legal profession, there were more women schooled to handle this litigation, many of whom had personally experienced sex discrimination.

The American Civil Liberties Union (ACLU), long a key player in the expansion of constitutional rights and liberties, led the planning for a comprehensive strategy to elevate sex to suspect classification status entitled to strict scrutiny. Under this standard, most state gender-based discrimination against women would be unconstitutional.

The ACLU's first case was *Reed v. Reed* (1971).[28] Ruth Bader Ginsburg, a member of the ACLU Board, argued the case before the Supreme Court. Her enthusiasm and interest in the expansion of women's rights via constitutional interpretation, in fact, was the impetus for the founding of the Women's Rights Project within the ACLU (WRP).

At issue in *Reed* was the constitutionality of an Idaho statute that required males be preferred to otherwise equally qualified females as administrators of estates for those who die intestate. NOW, the National Federation of Business and Professional Women, and the Women's Equity Action League (an organization that later disbanded) all filed amicus curiae briefs urging the Court to interpret the Fourteenth Amendment to prohibit discrimination against women on account of sex. Senator Birch Bayh (D-IN), a major sponsor of the ERA (and later Title IX), wrote one of the briefs in which he attempted to apprise the Court of the glaring legal inequities faced by women and to link those inequities, at least in part, to the Court's own persistent refusal to expand the reach of the Equal Protection Clause to gender discrimination. Judicial decisions such as *Goesaert* and *Hoyt*, which allowed states to discriminate against women on only minimally rational grounds, made it clear to women's rights activists that a constitutional amendment was necessary if women were ever to enjoy full citizenship rights under the Constitution. But, *Reed* was just a critical first step.

Chief Justice Warren Burger, writing for a unanimous Court in *Reed,* held that the Idaho statute, which provided "different treatment . . . to the applicants on the basis of their sex . . . establishes a classification subject to scrutiny under the Equal Protection Clause."[29] With these simple words, the Supreme Court, for the first time, concluded that sex-based differentials were entitled to some sort of scrutiny under the Fourteenth Amendment. But, what type of scrutiny? According to Burger, who quoted a 1920's case not involving sex discrimination, the test was whether the differential treatment was "reasonable, not arbitrary," and rested "upon some ground of difference having a fair and substantial relation to the object of the legislation, so that all persons similarly circumstanced will be treated alike." The Court then found that the state's objective of reducing the workload of probate judges was insufficient justification to warrant this kind of sex-based statute. In fact, according to the Court, this was "the very kind of arbitrary legislative choice forbidden by the Equal Protection Clause."[30]

This major breakthrough heartened women's rights activists. It also encouraged the WRP to launch a full-blown test case strategy akin to the one pursued by the NAACP Legal Defense and Education Fund that culminated successfully in *Brown v. Board of Education* (1954).[31] WRP attorneys jumped at the opportunity to assist the Southern Poverty Law Center of Alabama with the next major sex-discrimination case to come before the Supreme Court, *Frontiero v. Richardson* (1973).[32] At issue in *Frontiero* was the constitutionality of a federal statute which, for the purpose of computing allowances and fringe benefits, required female members of the armed forces to prove that they contributed to more than 50 percent of their dependent husbands' support. Men were not required to make a similar showing about their wives.

By an 8 to 1 vote, the Court struck down the statute, which gave male members of the armed forces potentially greater benefits than females. More importantly, though, a plurality of four justices voted to make sex a suspect classification entitled to the strict scrutiny standard of review. While four other Justices agreed that the statute violated the Equal Protection Clause, they did not agree that sex should be made a suspect classification. In fact, three justices, specifically noted the pending ratification of the ERA as a reason to wait to allow the political process to guide judicial interpretation.

Three years later, in *Craig v. Boren* (1976), Justice William J. Brennan, author of the plurality opinion in *Frontiero,* formulated a different test, known as "intermediate" or "heightened scrutiny" test to apply in sex discrimination cases.[33] *Craig* involved a challenge to an Oklahoma statute that prohibited the sale of 3.2 percent beer to males under the age of twenty-one and females under the age of eighteen. In determining whether this kind of gender-based differential violated the Equal Protection Clause, Brennan wrote that "classifications by gender must serve important governmental objectives and must be substantially related to achievement of those objectives."[34] He also specifically identified two governmental interests that would not justify sex discrimination: neither administrative convenience nor "fostering 'old' notions of role typing" would be considered constitutionally adequate rationalizations of sex classifications.[35] Shedding many of the stereotypes that had been at the core of *Muller, Hoyt,* and *Goesaert,* the Court specifically noted there was no further place for "increasingly outdated misconceptions concerning the role of females in the home rather than in the 'marketplace and world of ideas.'"[36] Continuing in this vein, in *Personnel Administrator of Massachusetts v. Feeney* (1979), the Court even went on to clarify this new standard, noting that any state statute that was "overtly or covertly designed to discriminate against women would require an exceedingly persuasive justification."[37] In *Feeney,* however, the Court concluded that a veteran's preference law was intended to discriminate against non-veterans—not women.

This new intermediate standard of review subsequently was used to invalidate a wide range of discriminatory practices including some Social Security, welfare and workmen's compensation programs, alimony laws, age of majority statutes and jury service exemptions. This is not to say that the Court no longer continued to be swayed by sex-role stereotypes. In *Rostker v. Goldberg* (1981), for example, the Court considered congressional combat restrictions sufficient to rationalize the exclusion of women from the new draft registration requirements of the Military Selective Service Act. A majority of the Court accepted the government's position that the statutory exclusion of women from combat positions combined with the need for combat-ready troops was a sufficiently important justification to meet the burden of the intermediate standard of review.[38] And, in *Michael M. v. Superior Court of Sonoma County* (1981), the Court held that a California rape law, which applied only to males, did not violate the Equal Protection Clause. Justice William H. Rehnquist, noted that the state's concern about teenage pregnancy was a sufficiently strong state interest to justify the statute. Rehnquist's opinion pointedly did not apply intermediate scrutiny.[39]

In late 1981, the Court was joined by its first female member, Sandra Day O'Connor. It was not long before she and the other justices were faced with another sex-based claim made under the Fourteenth Amendment. *Mississippi University for Women v. Hogan* (1982) involved a state policy that restricted enrollment in one state supported nursing school to females. Writing for the five-member majority, O'Connor noted that when the purpose of a statute was to "exclude or 'protect' members of one gender because they are presumed to suffer from an inherent handicap or to be innately inferior, the objective itself is illegitimate."[40] As one commentator noted, "she out-Brennaned Justice Brennan."[41] For example, not only did she go further than Justice Brennan had in recent opinions by suggesting in a footnote that sex might best be treated by the Court as a suspect classification, she also went on to resurrect the *Feeney* language saying that the state fell short of "establishing the exceedingly persuasive justification needed to sustain the classification."[42]

Justice O'Connor's strong opinion in *Hogan* again brought to four the number of justices on the Court who apparently favored some sort of strict standard of review for sex-based classifications that need "exceedingly persuasive justification" to withstand challenge. The elevation of William H. Rehnquist to chief justice and the appointments of Justices Antonin Scalia, Anthony Kennedy and David Souter by Republican presidents, however, were taken by supporters of expanded women's rights as a signal that the courts were no longer a viable strategy to see strict scrutiny applied to sex-based classifications. Thus, supporters of women's rights were heartened by the appointments of Ruth Bader Ginsburg and Stephen Breyer to the Court by Democratic president Bill Clinton.

In 1994, shortly after Justice Ginsburg's appointment to the Court, *J.E.B. v. Alabama* was decided. J.E.B. sought review of a lower court decision that had denied his claim that the use of peremptory challenges to exclude men from a jury deliberating a paternity claim against him, violated the Fourteenth Amendment.

Justice Harry Blackmun, writing for the Court, concluded that the state was unable to provide the exceedingly persuasive justification needed to justify these gender-based peremptory challenges. The use of gender-based stereotypes to select a jury pool, said the Court, must be condemned.[43]

By the late 1990s, it was to become clear that a narrow majority of the Court had reformulated the intermediate standard of review announced in *Craig,* replacing a state's need to show that a gender-based classification "serve important governmental objectives" with the need for a state to show an "exceedingly persuasive justification" for the practice or law. In *United States v. Virginia* (1996), a challenge to Virginia's maintenance of the male-only Virginia Military Institute (VMI), Justice Ginsburg, writing for a five-person majority, used the exceedingly persuasive justification test in a manner "all but indistinguishable from strict scrutiny" to find the state support of VMI unconstitutional.[44] Chief Justice Rehnquist's concurring opinion echoed this assessment of the standard used by the majority. At the very least, it appears that gender-based classification will now be examined more skeptically than under the *Craig* standard. This "skeptical scrutiny" test recognizes the long history of gender discrimination and seeks to give substance to a standard used by the Court.

Still, under this standard, the Court has upheld challenged practices as constitutional. In *Nguyen v. INS* (2001), for example, five members of the Court concluded that a federal law that imposed different requirements for a child's acquisition of citizenship depending upon whether the citizen parent was male or female, did not violate the Equal Protection Clause. Writing in sharp dissent, however, were Justices O'Connor, Souter, Ginsburg, and Breyer, who concluded that the INS had failed to show an exceedingly persuasive justification for the sex-based classification.[45]

Recognizing the fragile nature of even the heightened middle tier standard of review and the Court's uneven application of its standards, women's rights groups continue to seek the addition of an equal rights amendment to the Constitution. Most see an ERA as the only way to guarantee that women ever will be recognized as fully equal under the Constitution, but they are not particularly optimistic about its chances of success. In fact, as proposals for a constitutional amendment to define marriage or to limit it to persons of different genders abound, calls for an equal rights amendment are increasingly silent.

The Court has never been at the fore in the development of full equality for women. Yet, its decisions clearly add to a climate that frowns on blatant discrimination. Given the increasingly conservative nature of the Court, however, and the increasingly complex patterns of discrimination that are being presented to it, it is unlikely that the scope of constitutional protections for women will grow unless other societal changes take place. Women's active combat roles in Iraq, for example, could possibly foreshadow a Court that would uphold a challenge to the discriminatory provisions of the Military and Selective Service Act.

Moreover, it is important to note that fewer and fewer cases involving constitutional issues of sex discrimination come before the Court each year, perhaps because women's rights groups are using their time and money to fend off challenges to *Roe v. Wade* (1973) and to keep abortion safe and legal.[46] The April 2004 March for Women's Lives that drew nearly one million to the nation's Capitol underscores continued concern over this issue. Moreover, most of the "easy" constitutional cases involving women's rights have been decided, and there is fairly uniform application of at least the intermediate standard of review in lower courts. Thus, most cases involving sex discrimination that the Court chooses to hear now involve employment or educational discrimination litigated under Title VII of the Civil Rights Act or Title IX of the Educational Amendments of 1972. In *Johnson Controls, Inc. v. International Union, UAW* (1990), for example, which involved a company fetal protection policy that required women in certain hazardous positions to be sterilized as a condition of their continued employment, the Court ruled unanimously that the company's policies were not valid bona fide occupational qualifications permitted by Title VII.[47] Likewise, in *Davis v. Monroe County Board of Education* (1999), the Court found that a school board was responsible for sexual harassment and thus violating Title IX when the school board acted with deliberate indifference.[48] Still, repeated efforts from the Bush Administration to limit the reach of Title IX in athletics, or more recently to allow local school boards to reintroduce single sex schools, are likely to prompt a new wave of litigation should any of these proposals be implemented. And, at the forefront of those efforts is likely to be the National Women's Law Center, which was founded in 1972 and takes on more than 50 issues that cut to the core of the equality of women and girls, including issues of employment, economic security, and health.

Without groups such as the Women's Rights Project of the ACLU, and more recently, the National Women's Law Center, gains through litigation would have been unlikely. It has taken devoted attorneys willing to take cases—often on behalf of women without the resources to hire a private attorney—to bring these cases to Court. Litigation, although often an effective mechanism for gaining expanded rights for women, is very expensive and often risky for private attorneys. Thus, the importance of women's rights groups, as early as the late 1860's in securing rights through the courts cannot be ignored or minimized.

NOTES

1. L. H. Butterfield, Marc Friedlaender, and Mary Jo-Kline eds, *The Book of Abigail and John: Selected Letters of the Adams Family, 1762–1784*. Boston, MA: Northeastern University Press 2003, p. 21.

2. This is not to say that there were not many women active in the struggle. See, for example, Cokie Roberts, *Founding Mothers: The Women Who Raised Our Nation*. New York: William Morrow, 2004.

3. Maria Bevacqua and Carrie Baker, "Pay No Attention to the Man Behind the Curtain: Power, Privacy, and the Legal Regulation of Violence Against Women." *Women & Politics* 26(3): Forthcoming.

4. See Nancy E. McGlen, et al, *Women, Politics, and American Society,* 4th ed. New York: Longman, 2004.

5. Karen O'Connor, *Women's Organizations' Use of the Courts.* Lexington, MA: Lexington Books, 1980.

6. *Dred Scott v. Sandford,* 60 U.S. 393 (1857) at 422.

7. *Minor v. Happersett,* 88 U.S. 162 (1875).

8. *Bradwell v. Illinois,* 83 U.S. 130 (1873).

9. Id. at 141.

10. *Minor v. Happersett,* 88 U.S. 162 (1875).

11. Id. at 178.

12. *The Slaughterhouse Cases,* 83 U.S. 36 (1873).

13. O'Connor, *Women's Organizations* and Clement E. Vose, "The National Consumers' League and the Brandeis Brief," *Midwest Journal of Political Science* 1 (November 1957): 178–190.

14. *Mugler v. Kansas,* 123 U.S. 623 (1887) at 661.

15. *Allgeyer v. Louisiana,* 165 U.S. 578 (1897).

16. *Lochner v. New York,* 198 U.S. 45 (1905).

17. Id.

18. 208 U.S. 412 (1908).

19. Id. at 241.

20. 243 U.S. 629 (1917).

21. 243 U.S. 426 (1917).

22. 261 U.S. 525 (1923).

23. 300 U.S. 379 (1937).

24. *United States v. Darby Lumber Co.,* 312 U.S. 100 (1941).

25. 335 U.S. 464 (1948).

26. 368 U.S. 57 (1961).

27. Id. at 61–62.

28. 404 U.S. 71 (1971).

29. Id. at 75.

30. *Royster Guano v. Virginia,* 253 U.S. 412 (1920) at 76.

31. 347 U.S. 483 (1954).

32. 411 U.S. 677 (1973).

33. 429 U.S. 190 (1976).

34. Id. at 197.

35. Id. at 198.

36. Id. at 198–99.

37. 442 U.S. 256 (1979) at 273.

38. *Rostker v. Goldberg,* 453 U.S. 57 (1981).

39. 450 U.S. 464 (1981).

40. 458 U.S. 718 (1982) at 725.

41. Wendy Williams, "Sex Discrimination: Closing the Law's Gender Gap." In Herman Schwartz, ed. *The Burger Years.* New York: Smithmark, 1987, 112.

42. 458 U.S. 718 (1982) at 724.

43. 511 U.S. 127 (1994).

44. 518 U.S. 515 (1996); Deborah Brake, "Reflections on the VMI Decision," 6 *American University Journal of Gender and the Law* 35 (1997): 35.

45. 533 U.S. 53 (2001).

46. 410 U.S. 113 (1973).

47. 499 U.S. 187 (1991).

48. 526 U.S. 629 (1996).

FURTHER READING

Baer, Judith. 1978. *The Chains of Protection: Judicial Response to Women's Labor Legislation.* Westport, CT: Greenwood.

———. 2003. *Women in American Law: The Struggle Towards Equality from the New Deal to the Present,* 3rd ed. New York: Holmes & Meier.

Cochran III, Augustus B. 2003. *Sexual Harassment and the Law.* Lawrence: University Press of Kansas.

DuBois, Ellen Carol. 1978. *Feminism and Suffrage: The Emergence of an Independent Women's Movement in America 1848–1869.* Ithaca, NY: Cornell University Press.

Evans, Sara M. 1989. *Born for Liberty: A History of Women in America.* New York: Free Press.

Hartmann, Susan M. 1989. *From Margin to Mainstream: American Women and Politics Since 1960.* New York: McGraw-Hill.

Kay, Herma Hill, and Martha S. West. 1996. *Sex Based Discrimination: Text, Cases, and Materials,* 4th ed. St. Paul: The West Group.

Levit, Nancy. 2000. *The Gender Line: Men, Women, and the Law.* New York: New York University Press.

Lynn, Naomi B., ed. 1990. *Women, Politics, and the Constitution.* New York: Haworth.

McGlen, Nancy E. et al. 2004. *Women, Politics and American Society,* 4th ed. New York: Longman.

O'Connor, Karen. 1980. *Women's Organizations' Use of the Courts.* Lexington, MA: Lexington Books.

Vose, Clement E. 1972. *Constitutional Change.* Lexington, MA: Lexington Books.

Bias or Counterbalance?:
Women Judges Making a Difference

Elaine Martin

It has always been, and remains, difficult for women to succeed in attaining and re-taining high political office in the United States. It has been even more difficult for women to attain judicial office than other public office for several reasons, two of which are particularly important. First, women judges must meet high standards of education and experience to be eligible for judicial office. Aspirants must have graduate law degrees, often successful candidates must also have at least five to ten years or more of trial experience. Second, judges are selected in complicated ways that make women judicial candidates dependent on their ability to build strong professional and personal reputations in the mostly male, and often conser-vative, legal circles that influence judicial selections. For example, the American Bar Association Committee on Federal Judiciary plays an important role in federal judicial selection by ranking nominees into three categories: Well Qualified, Quali-fied, and Not Qualified. There is ample evidence to suggest that such evaluators prefer the career patterns more closely associated with male lawyers.[1]

There are two major interrelated issues relevant to any discussion of women as judges: why has the increase in the number of women judges been so slow, and do women judges behave any differently than men judges? Both are important. If the slow rate of increase in the number of women judges is due to gender discrim-ination, it may cast doubt on the legitimacy of our justice system. If women judges decide cases or administer their courts differently from men, their increasing num-bers may create profound changes in our justice system.

These issues are often discussed in terms of whether women judges merely "stand for" other women in the numerical sense or whether they "act for" women.[2] In these terms, all women judges would necessarily "stand for" other women merely because they are also women. Women judges would not, however, necessarily "act for" other women. That is, although they would symbolically represent women, they might or might not act in a manner to further the interests and perspectives of other women. There seems to be strong support for the notion that it is only fair that women should be better represented numerically on the bench than they are at present. Justice Linda Trout of Idaho's supreme court has said: "Without women, the bench does not fully represent the fabric of society." However, it is not so clear that a numerical increase will result in an increase in the representation of women's interests.

This article will first present data on the increase from 1976 to 2004 in the number of women judges, or numerical representation, and consider the eligible pool theory as an explanation for that increase. It will then examine the potential impact of the increase in women judges on the diversification of gender perspectives on the judicial bench, or interest representation. It will be demonstrated that the rate of increase in the number of women judges has accelerated in recent years and that this new generation of women judges is contributing to a growing diversification of perspectives on the American bench, especially with respect to issues of gender fairness and family law. In conclusion, the present study will discuss whether this added female perspective introduces new bias into the law or provides a counterbalance to a pre-existing bias.

THE INCREASE IN WOMEN JUDGES

"Times are changing. The president made that clear by appointing me, and just last week, naming five other women to Article III courts." Ruth Bader Ginsberg made these remarks on August 20, 1993, following her inauguration as an associate justice and as the second woman member of the U.S. Supreme Court. Times, indeed, are changing. Just 17 years before Ginsberg's inauguration, when President Carter took office in 1976, no women sat on the U.S. Supreme Court, one woman sat on the U.S. Appeals Court, and five women sat on the district courts. Carter broke all records to appoint 40 women or about 15 percent of his total judicial appointments. President Clinton, who appointed Justice Ginsberg, broke Carter's long-standing record to give nearly one-third of his federal judicial nominations to women. He appointed 60 women to federal district and appeals courts in his first term of office and appointed another 24 during his second term, despite 'slowdowns' in judicial confirmations by the Republican majority on the Senate Judiciary Committee. From January 2000 to February 2003, President George W. Bush appointed 32 women accounting for almost one-fifth of his 165 appointments. By February of 2004, women occupied two of the nine seats on the U.S. Supreme

Court, women occupied 202 of the 680 judgeships on the federal district courts and there were 54 women out of 140 judgeships on the U.S. Appeals Courts.

From 1976 to 2003, the number of women who held seats on their state's supreme court increased by more than tenfold, from 9 women justices to 98. In 2003, four states, New York, Vermont, Washington and Wisconsin, had female majorities. Two other states, Minnesota and Michigan, for a time, had a female majority on their state supreme courts. Over-all, almost 30 percent of the nation's state supreme court justices were women in 2004, although half of them had been in office seven years or less.

Despite recent increases at these upper levels of federal and state courts, the proportion of women state trial and intermediate appellate court judges lags far behind the proportion of women lawyers. Estimates are that 30 percent of lawyers are women, and only about 15 percent of judges nation-wide. Judicial office in the United States has long been dominated by white, middle-class male lawyers with strong local connections. Because of the high visibility of United States Supreme Court Justices Sandra Day O'Connor and Ruth Bader Ginsberg, many people don't realize that there are proportionately far fewer women judges than other kinds of women politicians. Although there are many thousands of judges in the United States, only in the last twenty years have there been more than a few women judges in office at any given time, regardless of the level of government. An increase in the eligible pool of women lawyers from which judges are drawn, and changing attitudes on the part of those who are influential in selecting judges has fueled the recent acceleration of the numbers of women judges.

THE ELIGIBLE POOL THEORY

The eligible pool theory holds that because relatively few women possess the requisite educational, political, and career credentials to be judges, they are unable to compete successfully for office. This theory essentially provides a gender-neutral explanation for the dearth of women judges. However, the lack of a sizable pool of qualified women lawyers does not fully account for the low representation of women on the bench or the wide range from state to state in the gender composition of their courts. For example, in 2003, there were twenty-one women intermediate appellate court judges in the state of Ohio, but only seven women in the neighboring state of Michigan. Cook[3] concludes that one major barrier to increased numbers of women judges is the resistance of those who control access to career opportunities that traditionally pave the way to the bench. Githens[4] asserts that a major deciding factor that leads to the selection of women as state court judges in many states is simply the lack of interest in the relatively poorly paid positions by more 'successful' male attorneys. Martin[5] thinks that the real key to explaining the variation among states in the number of women judges is the ability of women to capture a significant percentage of newly created judgeships. These two notions, that women lawyers are less likely to have the career opportunities that men do, and that women's best chances for judgeships are newly created seats help us see that the eligible pool theory does not operate in a gender-neutral manner.

Judges are drawn exclusively from the legal profession, and historically that profession has been overwhelmingly white and male. By the 1980s there were important changes in the gender composition of the legal profession, and therefore in the pool of lawyers from which judges are drawn. In 1980 only 8 percent of lawyers were women, by 1992 that figure had risen to 19 percent and by 2004, 30 percent of lawyers were women. In 24 years the size of the eligible pool of women lawyers almost quadrupled. Yet, this increase in the proportion of women lawyers has not been matched by a similar increase in the proportion of women judges. See Table 1 for a comparison of eligible pool changes and increases in the percentages of women judges.

Several researchers have concluded that a major barrier to better judicial representation for women is the resistance of official gatekeepers, such as Governors, Presidents, bar associations and political parties, as well as resistance by those who control access to legal career opportunities that traditionally pave the way to the bench. In the past, many women lawyers were not considered for jobs that would give them the experience useful for prospective judges; for example as law clerks to federal judges, or as partners in major law firms. Although this is changing to some extent, women lawyers still do not have the same career patterns as men lawyers. Women lawyers are clustered in the lower prestige ranks of their profession, such as public sector employment; making less money, having less opportunity for advancement, and often subjected to varying degrees of gender bias.[6] This may be because women lawyers do not have the same range of opportunities as men lawyers, and are excluded from higher ranked positions. It could also be that women lawyers choose public service employment over more lucrative private practice, to have more job security, more regular hours, and less stress, so that they may combine career and family responsibilities.

In any case, so long as the male career pattern remains the standard for judgeships, the eligible pool of women lawyers will continue to appear smaller

TABLE 1   Percentage of Female Judges, Percentage of Women Receiving Law Degrees, and Percentage of Female Lawyers

Women	1980	1987	1993	1997	2003
Federal	5.4%	7.0%	11.1%	17.4%	21.2%
State Supreme	3.6	6.5	11.2	20.0	29.3
State Trial	2.4	7.3	8.5	9.0*	N.A.
Lawyers	8.0	13.0	19.0	25.0*	30.0
Law Degrees	30.0	40.0	45.0	47.0*	50.0

*Estimates

Sources: Martin, 1988, 1997; Allen and Wall, 1993; and McGlen and O'Connor, 1995.

than may be truly the case. Thus, even though the number of women lawyers is increasing rapidly, there is still a time lag for those in the pool to acquire the professional experience and maturity traditionally considered necessary for white males to reach judicial office. For example, in 1995, the average judge (usually a white male) sitting on a state trial court, the lowest rung on the judicial ladder, was 46 years of age on first attaining office.[7] If the male pattern for judgeships prevails with respect to age, the pool of women lawyers eligible for state trial judgeships in 1995 would have been the number of women lawyers in the state 20 years previously, an obviously small number. Yet, there is no particular reason, other than past history with white males, to assume that state trial court judges should be 46 years old instead of 36, which would significantly increase the number of eligible women.

Darcy, Welch and Clark[8] have demonstrated the importance of the role of incumbency in discouraging qualified women legislative candidates from running for election or in succeeding in gaining office if they do run. A similar impact is at work in judicial selection. Federal judges serve life-time terms. Vacancies, or opportunities for newcomers, occur only through death, resignation or Congressional creation of new judgeships. Incumbent state court judges are extremely likely to be re-elected, sometimes even running without opponents. Realistically speaking, a woman's best opportunity to become a judge is either to run for an open seat (no incumbent running) or to run for a newly created seat (no incumbent). Because of the increase in litigation in the United States, it is not uncommon for new judgeships to be created at both the state and federal levels. These new judgeships offer an opportunity for women deemed eligible. However, the obstacle for many women may be in being deemed eligible for judicial office.

Since Carter's presidency, most of his successors have made efforts to appoint women judges. This effort at the federal level has not been as prevalent at the state level, although once again "times are changing." It is quite clear that the attorneys who were selected as state court judges in the past tended to have the same general characteristics over time and across the different selection systems, with some minor variations by state or region. These general characteristics pointed to a relatively narrow political-legal career path, as well as a very restricted socio-economic pool from which state court jurists were selected. For example, in 1981 the typical state supreme court justice was a white, male, attorney who became a justice at age 53, with possibly some prosecutorial or state legislative experience and with a likelihood of previous experience as a trial court or intermediate appellate court judge. These successful candidates were also highly likely to have been born in their state and to have attended their state's law school.[9] Only 3.1 percent of these justices were female.

By 1999, 24 percent of justices were female and the composite profile had changed. Justices in 1999 were younger, less tied by birth or education to the states which they served, less likely to be former legislators and much more likely to have had prior governmental experience as prosecutors, attorneys and judges. These differences from the historical pattern of justices' backgrounds were most pronounced among women and African-American judges.[10] This is a very good sign because it suggests that the definition of eligibility has changed to include career patterns more typical of women lawyers.

CHANGING ATTITUDES IN SELECTING JUDGES

It appears likely that a broader definition of eligibility for judicial office that includes women's typical career patterns is coming about because of changing gender-based attitudes on the part of those influential in the judicial selection process. One way to test this theory is to examine the career backgrounds of women selected as judges. If women's characteristics differ from the typical male career patterns it is strong evidence of changing attitudes.

The United States has not just one judicial system but a federal system and fifty different state court systems. One of the ways in which these diverse court systems vary is the manner in which they select their judges. All federal court judges, whether trial court or appellate court members are appointed by the president and confirmed by the Senate for life. The states use several different systems to select their judges and may use different methods for higher courts than they use for lower courts.

Federal Judges

In 1976, when President Carter took office, he announced publicly his intention of appointing more women judges and openly modified the selection process to be more inclusive. This explicit affirmative action program initiated by President Carter designed to appoint more women to the federal bench added forty new United States district court and appeals court judges.[11] It also started a trend that has never ended. Although subsequent Republican presidents did not equal Carter's efforts, their appointments of women judges far outnumbered all of their predecessors except Carter. Pursuant to a campaign promise designed to capture the women's vote, President Reagan appointed the first woman ever to the United States Supreme Court. By 1992, when the next Democratic President after Carter took office, women constituted 11 percent of the federal bench. President Clinton launched a new affirmative action initiative that broke even Carter's records. Overall, less than half of Clinton's judges were white males, an amazing break with historical precedent.

Table 2 shows the number of women judges appointed by our last five Presidents and indicates the percentage of their judicial appointments that were women.

The backgrounds of women appointed to the federal bench from 1976 through 2003, by both Democratic and Republican presidents, show remarkable similarity in several respects: they were younger, less likely to have been in private law practice when appointed and more likely to have had judicial experience than men appointees.[12] Thus, the respective records on women appointments by the

TABLE 2   Women Federal Court Appointments by President

	W. Bush 2000–04***		Clinton 1992–00		Bush 1988–92		Reagan 1980–88		Carter 1976–80	
Court	%	N	%	N	%	N	%	N	%	N
District	18.0	26	28.9	88	19.6	29	8.3	24	14.4	29
Appeals	24.0	7	37.7	20	18.9	7	5.1	4	19.6	11
Supreme	-0-**		50.0	1	-0-*		25.0	1	-0-**	

*Bush made 2 male appointments to the Supreme Court and no women.

**W. Bush and Carter made no appointments to the Supreme Court.

***To March 2004.

Source: Federal Judicial Center.

five Presidents are also an indication of their willingness to break with tradition and broaden the definition of the eligible pool.

State Judges

In 1976, the same year that President Carter broke historical precedent in seeking women to appoint to the federal bench, twenty states had no women general jurisdiction trial court judges whatsoever, even though there were nearly 16,000 state and local judges in the United States. In fact, it was not until 1979 that every state had at least one woman serving as a judge.[13] The next decade saw significant change, however, with women more than doubling their numbers on state courts of general jurisdiction. This sizable increase in numbers led to only a 1.2 percent increase in the overall share of state benches held by women. This poor showing is due to a 16.4 percent increase in the total number of state judicial seats. Little is known about the career backgrounds of these new women judges. However, it is clear that women made their greatest gains in states that increased their numbers of judges, and that the ratio of increased numbers of women judges to the increased number of judicial seats is 22.6 percent.[14] This suggests that changing attitudes on the part of voters permitted women to capture a relatively high proportion of the new, open seats.

Evidence of changing attitudes is clearer with respect to state supreme courts. In 1987, only six percent of state supreme court positions were held by women[15] and 20 states had never had a women state supreme court justice.[16] In September 1997, seventy-one women justices sat in 43 states, and only seven states had no women justices.[17] By November of 2003, 98 women justices sat in 48 states, and only two states had no women justices. In fourteen state supreme courts women were over forty percent of the membership, and women were Chief Justices in fifteen states. Table 3 indicates the number of women justices on the supreme court in each state in the United States in November of 2003.

There are a number of differences between the career patterns of women justices sitting on state supreme courts in 1987 and those sitting ten years later. The

TABLE 3   States with Women State Supreme Court Justices, November 2003

States with: no women	1 woman	2 women	3 women	4 women	5 women
Indiana	Alaska	Alabama	California	New York	Washington
Oregon	Arkansas	Arizona	Colorado	Wisconsin	
	Delaware	Connecticut	Kansas		
	Hawaii	Florida	Louisiana		
	Idaho	Georgia	Massachusetts		
	Iowa	Illinois	Michigan		
	Kentucky	Maine	Nevada		
	Mississippi	Maryland	New Jersey		
	Missouri	Minnesota	New Mexico		
	Nebraska	Montana	Ohio		
	New Hampshire	North Dakota	Virginia		
	North Carolina	Oklahoma			
	Pennsylvania	Texas			
	Rhode Island	Utah			
	So. Carolina	Vermont			
	Tennessee				
	West Virginia				

more recent additions to the bench are younger (by 4 years), less likely to have attended an in-state law school, more often drawn directly from a lower court, and almost three times as likely to have had prior experience as prosecutors.[18] These figures suggest two things. First, they indicate that the definition of the eligible pool has been broadened in many states in the last ten years to include career patterns more typical of women lawyers, thereby contributing to the increase in the number of women justices selected. They also suggest that women lawyers have established a successful judicial career ladder, considerably different from that of men, moving from experience as a government prosecutor to trial court judge to appellate court judge to state supreme court justice. Interestingly, there is some indication from a study of federal court judges' backgrounds that a similar career ladder has been followed by minority judges.[19] It may be that extensive prior judicial experience persuades judicial selectors that non-traditional candidates are capable, despite the dissimilarity in their legal careers to more traditional white, male candidates.

REPRESENTATION OF WOMEN'S PERSPECTIVES

The notion of interest representation is not a simple one. Although many women might agree that women share a commonality of experience as a consequence of living in a gendered society, women are also divided, just as men are, by such characteristics as race, class, religion, income, ideology, and education. Studies of women in Congress suggest that even among women who feel an obligation to represent the interests of other women, there are differences in their interpretation of what those interests are. For example, Sue Carroll[20] demonstrates that both liberal and conservative congresswomen may see themselves as representing women's interests, even as they take opposite sides on an issue such as abortion rights.

The notion of interest representation is a particularly difficult one for judges, because the official, approved image of a judge is that of a person who is impartial and one who does not prejudge the merits of a case before hearing the evidence. What this means in a nutshell is that a good judge is supposed to put aside her or his personal feelings and values when donning the robe. The robe and all its trappings are designed to hide individual physical characteristics (some women judges find robes to be convenient maternity garb!), and in so doing, also symbolically represent the impersonal nature of the act of judging. The formal rules of the judicial game reinforce these basic expectations. The law itself, statutes and precedents, the facts of the case, the requirements of evidence, the possibility of being overturned on appeal, even the nature of the adversarial system, all restrict the freedom of judicial discretion.

Yet, political scientists continue to study judicial characteristics in the assumption that personal, social, political, ideological and economic background characteristics may have an important impact on the way judges do their jobs. The strongest evidence to support this assumption comes from studies of the United States Supreme Court. It has become almost commonplace for political pundits to refer to various Supreme Court Justices as "liberal" or "conservative." Objective studies of such features as the Justices' partisan affiliations, prior career patterns and religion have shown them to be important variables in explaining judicial decision-making.[21] It is not so clear how important judicial gender may be as an influence on decision-making.

Conventional Wisdom

There are three prevalent theories about the possible impact of judicial gender on decision-making. The first may be labeled "conventional wisdom," the second, "different voice," and the third, "gendered" or representative voice. The most conservative, and perhaps the most common, conventional view is that women judges and men judges will come to essentially the same conclusions in law, because they have similar legal education and training, and they have to operate within such institutional constraints as those itemized above. This view was expressed by former Justice Jeanne Coyne of the Minnesota State Supreme Court when she stated that most of the time: "a wise, old woman will reach the same conclusions as a wise, old man." The earliest studies of gender and judicial behavior by-and-large supported this conventional wisdom that women would behave no differently than men judges when confronted with similar cases. For example, the handful of studies conducted in the 1970s and early 1980s concluded that although there were minor differences between men and women trial court judges in their sentencing decisions, these differences were not statistically significant.[22]

A glance at Table 1 alerts us to the very small number of women judges during the time period these studies were conducted. We also know that women judges were widely dispersed throughout the fifty states and often sat as the only representative of their gender in their judicial district. In fact, in 1979, at the founding meeting of the National Association of Women Judges, many women reported that they had never before met another woman judge. Tokenism theory may help explain those early findings. Tokenism theory says that token women conform, either because selection methods in male-dominated institutions, such as the judiciary, favor women who follow the male model, or because tokens recognize the futility of non-conforming actions against the odds of male-entrenched norms. Thus, the failure of these early studies to find gender difference could be explained by the very low number of women judges, and their isolation from other women judges.

Different Voice

In the 1970s a new controversial stream of scholarship labeled feminist jurisprudence developed in the nation's law schools. These scholars were fascinated by psychologist Carol Gilligan's claims that women speak about moral issues in a "different voice," a voice of care and connectedness versus the male "voice" of universal values and hierarchically ordered values.[23] In this literature men are characterized as more "instrumental" and women as more "contextual" in their modes of thinking and feeling. It is suggested that women lawyers and judges, because of either biological or culturally induced differences in moral thinking, will bring a different perspective to the law, will employ different legal reasoning, and will seek different results from the legal process.[24] What this new jurisprudence might eventually look like is not yet clear. Political scientist Judith Baer[25] argues convincingly that the presence of enough women lawyers and judges conscious of women's interests and willing to innovate in legal and constitutional doctrine offers the possibility of achieving meaningful sexual equality in American law.

Judicial politics scholars have seized upon this "difference" theory and there have been multiple studies in recent years testing for the presence of a "different voice" among women judges.[26] It is important to understand that this different voice is defined as a *feminine* voice, not a *feminist* voice. Thus, "femaleness," not partisanship, ideology, race, or class is the key ingredient in different voices. This different voice ought, therefore, to be discernible in cases as seemingly far removed from feminist concerns as search and seizure[27] and environmental policy.[28] Most of these studies have failed in their attempts to find some over-reaching pattern on the part of women judges to make decisions in line with connection, community or context, yet they also commonly find that in a narrow range of cases raising issues of gender, racial and employment discrimination women judges may be found more often than men on the side of the claimant. It is also important to note that different voice theory is not without its methodological and substantive critics. Many of these critics point out the dangers in "difference" thinking for the continued progress of women's rights. For example, Supreme Court Justice Sandra Day O'Connor, commenting on such research, opined "gender differences currently cited are surprisingly similar to stereotypes from years past." Others point out the problems of stressing the commonality of all women's experience, to the exclusion of genuine differences, particularly those of race and class.

Gendered Voice

With the failure of the different voice theory the issue remains how to account theoretically for gender differences in judicial decision-making that some studies have found. For example, Allen and Wall[29] found that women on state supreme courts are more likely than men to be the most pro-female members of their court on women's issues. A study in Florida found that in contested custody appeals, all-male appellate panels were more likely to rule in favor of fathers than mothers, but mixed-gender panels showed no favoritism for either parent.[30] A study of Clinton's first-term appointees found that both women and black judges were more supportive of minority claims than were men or white judges.[31]

It seems likely that some of the differences in findings between the earliest studies in the 1970s and more recent studies in the 1990s can be attributed to differences in the types of women who were drawn to judicial office during the two time periods.[32] When United States Supreme Court Justice Ginsberg went to law school in the 1950s there were only nine women in her class of more than five hundred. She recalls the Dean of Harvard Law holding a reception for those nine women, and then asking them one-by-one to explain what they were doing at the law school occupying a seat that could have been filled by a man! It seems likely that enormous pressure would have been put on those new women lawyers, and potential judges, to conform to the conservative expectations of the legal profession. Since Ginsberg's student years, there have been important changes in the composition of the legal profession. More women are going to law schools, and more women have become lawyers. Perhaps one of the most striking aspects of the 1970s was the phenomenal growth in the number of women law students. For example, when Idaho Chief Justice Linda Trout entered her state's law school in 1974, her class of women was three times as large as the previous three years combined. Those earliest women judges were educated in law schools in which they were an obvious minority and subject to all the pressures of tokens; today women constitute close to one-half of all law students, and no longer have to justify their presence. These women were also educated after the 1960s women's rights movement and the extensive social changes in gender roles that followed. It may be that this new generation of women judges will feel freer to develop their own voice and behavioral differences between men and women judges may emerge more clearly in the future than in the past.

One way in which these differences could emerge is with women judges providing a counterbalance to male-dominated perspectives. Feminist legal scholars contend that law itself is male.[33] That is, that the legal system, the legal language and style of legal reasoning used to support the law has historically been founded on the basis of the life experiences and values of privileged, educated white men. Furthermore, these are the same men who have administered and interpreted the law in its application to women and others. Thus, male-based perspectives, images and experiences are typically seen as the norm. For example, men are the norm in equality law. A woman, in order to pursue equal pay in the workplace must first prove that she is similar (if not identical) to a male worker who is receiving more pay than is she. The dilemma for women in low-paying, sex-segregated jobs, like nursing, is that there are few comparable male workers to measure their equality against. Since the majority of women work in sex segregated occupations, the law gives them little recourse even though these occupations uniformly pay less than most male-dominated occupations.

Gender Bias. Although accusations of gender bias by individuals and groups are widespread in many areas of life in the United States, perhaps only in the court system has its prevalence been so fully documented. Beginning in 1983, with the creation of the New Jersey Supreme Court Task Force on Women in the Courts, more than 50 state and federal judicial circuits have contributed to a gender bias task force movement.[34] After extensive hearings, surveys and data collection, these task forces have uniformly concluded that the presence of harmful gender bias in the courts is undisputed. This bias ranges from disrespectful treatment of women attorneys, witnesses, and litigants (and sometimes even women judges) to biased case outcomes. Perceptions and experiences of unfairness differ significantly between men and women attorneys and judges. As one might expect, women are more likely to perceive gender bias. This observation applies to both women judges and women attorneys. In Mississippi, for example, 85 percent of male judges believed that male attorneys received no preferential treatment before the courts, whereas only 38 percent of female judges reached that conclusion. A large majority of both women and men judges believed that this biased treatment did not unfairly impact the outcome of the cases these attorneys were litigating. Yet, women judges (16.7%) were more likely than men judges (9.1%) to believe that biased treatment *did* unfairly impact the outcome of cases.[35]

Counterbalance. In 1979, a national organization of women judges was created with the avowed purpose of promoting the selection of more women as judges and of gathering together the far-flung women judges from around the nation in an annual conference so that they might build a "sisterhood on the bench." This organization, the National Association of Women Judges (NAWJ), spearheaded the gender bias task force movement, and many of its members chaired or worked behind the scenes to insure its success.

A study based on a national survey of women judges[36] concluded that women judges in general, and NAWJ members in particular, might, under appropriate circumstances, undertake behavior specifically designed to represent a woman's unique perspective. Respondents claimed a variety of representative behaviors from off-the-bench efforts, such as urging women attorneys to run for judgeships, to on-the-bench efforts to change the law with respect to women and children, such as in divorce and domestic violence decisions. It is easy to see that if women judges are more likely to perceive gender bias against women in the courts, and if they believe in the fundamental legal principles of justice and fairness, then they might feel obligated to redress any unfair imbalance in how men and women are treated. It is symbolically important that the newsletter of the NAWJ is titled **"Counterbalance."** The empirical question remains, is what women judges say they do in the survey above, what they really do? That is, do they decide cases raising issues of gender bias in a gendered manner?

Definition of Women's Interests. Goldstein[37] asserts that there are at least four different kinds of disadvantage faced by women in our society: 1) they are penalized if they fail to conform to societal notions of appropriate gender behavior; 2) gendered behavior by women, such as child care, is devalued; 3) women face discrimination when fulfilling their biological roles, such as pregnancy; and 4) women endure various forms of sexual violence. She concludes that feminist goals require policies that would self-consciously redress these disadvantages. Thus, for example, divorce policy ought to rectify property settlements so that they do not systematically penalize the primary caretaker of the children, typically the wife/mother.

Carroll[38] defines women's rights as "those issues where policy consequences are likely to have a more immediate and direct impact on significantly larger numbers of women than of men." Wisconsin Supreme Court Justice Shirley Abrahamson offers a working definition which she uses herself: "a self-consciously critical stance toward the existing order with respect to the ways it affects different 'women as women.'"

Thus, it seems that a representative voice is also a gendered voice. In order for this voice to represent women's interest it must ask "the woman question." That is, it must ask how the law fails to take into account the experience of women, and how existing legal standards may disadvantage women. Such a view, for example, would look beyond "gender-neutrality" in property divisions and child custody/support issues in divorce cases. It would acknowledge that the greater earning capacity of men condemns women to unequal living standards post-divorce and joint custody may fail to serve the interests of the primary care-giving parent, typically the mother.

Representative Voice. A series of studies by Martin and Pyle focusing on family law decisions in state supreme courts has concluded that women judges do, indeed, have a distinctive voice that represents a counterbalance to the male perspective in cases related to divorce, child support, child custody, property settlements, alimony, etc. They call this a "representative voice." Their longitudinal study of the Michigan State Supreme Court[39] found that both Republican and Democratic, white, women justices were likely to transcend party lines and vote with their sister judges to uphold the position of the woman litigant in divorce cases about 60 percent of the time. African-American and white men also crossed party lines to vote together to uphold the position of the man litigant about 55 percent of the time. Their study in 2001 found similar results when the Michigan study was expanded to include Wisconsin and Minnesota state high courts. In their third study,[40] 32 states' highest courts and 450 judicial votes were examined, and additional variables were added. This larger, integrated model included factors relating to the judge's personal characteristics and measures of the state's political environment. Again, the results showed a tendency for gender to be the primary predictor of judges' votes. For example, of the 14 votes cast by women on courts with three women justices, 93% sided with the interest of the women litigants regardless of political party.

Sample Cases from Representative Voice Studies.   Below are summaries of some typical cases examined in the 2003 study above.

Divorce.   A man and his wife divorce after 25 years of marriage, during which she was a stay at home mother with four children. They agree in the divorce settlement that he will give her alimony until such time as she might remarry. They further agree that the alimony will increase proportionately as his income increases, but will not exceed 30 percent of his income, and that the alimony will decrease by $1 for every $3 she earns over $1,000 per month. Eight years later, after his remarriage and subsequent birth of two more children, he goes to court to reduce his alimony payments. He states that because his income has risen steadily over the years, the alimony payments exceed her modest needs, and in any case, she could choose to make her part-time job a full-time job and thereby provide more for her own needs. She responds that the alimony is only 25 percent of his income so does not violate their agreement, and that it is none of his business whether she spends the alimony or invests it. A split court decides in her favor.

Child Support.   A man failed to pay court-ordered child support for over two years. His ex-wife took him to court. He claimed inability to pay, due to being unemployed. The trial court determined that he had made no effort to find employment, although he appeared to have some means of support as he did pay rent and feed and clothe himself. He was found in contempt of the court order for child support. A divided state high court reversed his conviction, saying that he had been justified in thinking that he did not have to pay child support when he was voluntarily without employment because he relied on an earlier case in which the court had said that voluntary unemployment was a defense against claims for alimony. The court admitted that the earlier case had not dealt with child support, and said that in the future contempt cases could be brought against other parents who willfully avoid employment and then don't pay child support. The dissent pointed out that the man certainly should have known that he could not avoid child support payments by avoiding employment, because there was a state law to that effect.

Child Custody.   An impoverished and distraught mother was urged by her former father-in-law, in a time of turmoil, to sign a paper allowing him to adopt her children. Her former husband had failed to pay court-ordered child support, her small business was bankrupted due to a flood, she was disabled by an automobile accident and unable to work. As a consequence of her impoverishment, her utilities were cut off, and she was unable to buy groceries or other necessities for herself and her children. In the desperation growing out of her bad luck, she turned to her former father-in-law, who, she claims, had been a father figure to her. He proposed to adopt the children, and she reluctantly signed a consent to adoption form. After less than 3 months, before the adoption was final, she repented of that action, and asked that the adoption proceedings be stopped. She took the position that she had not voluntarily signed the form and that her signature had been obtained under duress, by fraud and other unconscionable conduct. The majority of the state high court held that she had not been tricked or lied to and that she had no right to change her mind. The dissent claimed that in a moment of grave distress, she had made a mistake in signing a paper that gave up her rights to raise the children she bore and loved and that after she saw the truth, she acted to preserve her family and rectify that mistake. The dissent further claimed that the court should allow that mistake to be corrected, "not simply condone the powerful subduing of the weak."

CONCLUSION

Although the percentages of female judges have yet to meet those of female lawyers, their numbers show a significant increase in the last decade. The numbers of females enrolling in law school and a definition of judicial eligibility more inclusive of women's unique legal careers suggests that we may expect even greater increases in the eligible pool of women judicial candidates in years to come. As more women judges take office, we may also expect that this new generation of judges will have careers and personal backgrounds that reflect the unique career patterns of women lawyers more closely than did earlier women judges.

Results from studies done in the 1970s and early 1980s suggested that men's and women's similar legal training and socialization as lawyers minimized any potential gender differences in judicial behavior. However, more recent studies from the 1990s indicate that, as women's numbers move beyond the token stage and as younger females educated after the women's movement become judges, differences based on gender emerge more clearly. Research on this new generation of women judges suggests that these gender-based differences in experience may contribute to a widening gap between the behavior of men and women judges.

This gap is most discernible with respect to decisions in family law/divorce cases, and a strong case can be made that women are presenting a counterbalance to the biased male perspective historically embedded in the law. There seems little doubt that both men and women judges speak with a gendered voice in these decisions, with men favoring the perspective of the male litigants and women favoring the perspective of the female litigant. There are several reasons why a gendered voice may be better heard in divorce law than elsewhere. First, divorce law presents an opportunity for a greater exercise of judicial discretion than many other areas of case law, in part because of its focus on individual case facts, and its lack of broader political significance. Second, if a judge's personal experiences impact his or her perception of case facts as is generally claimed, then rare indeed is the judge whose life has not been impacted in some way by these issues. Finally, divorce law presents some of the most stark contrasts between male and female perspectives and experiences.

The implications for widespread changes in our system of justice as a consequence of increased numbers of women judges are unclear. At present, it would seem that a gendered voice, although undoubtedly significant, is relatively limited in its scope. For example, although state trial court judges often deal with issues of family law: divorce, child custody, property settlements, child support, spousal maintenance, etc., federal and state high court judges rarely do.

NOTES

1. Marianne Githens, "Getting Appointed to The State Court: The Gender Dimension," *Women and Politics,* 15 (1996) pp.1–23.

2. Hannah Pitkin, *The Concept of Representation,* (Berkeley: University of California Press, 1967) p. 60.

3. Beverly Cook, "Women Judges: The End of Tokenism," in Laura Crites and Winnifred Hepperle (Eds) *Women, the Courts, and Eqality.* (Newbury Park, CA: Sage 1987), pp. 84–105.

4. Marianne Githens, "Getting Appointed."

5. Elaine Martin, "Here Come the Judges: An Analysis of State-Based Influences on the Selection of Women as Judges," *Midwest Political Science Association Conference,* Chicago (1996).

6. Phyllis Coontz, "Gender Bias in the Legal Profession: Women 'See' It, Men Don't," *Women and Politics,* 15 (1995) pp. 1–22.

7. Robert Carp and Ronald Stidham, *Judicial Process in America,* 3rd ed. (CQ Press 1996).

8. Robert Darcy, Susan Welch and Janet Clark, *Women, Elections and Representation,* 2nd ed, (University of Nebraska 1994).

9. Henry Glick and Craig Emmert, "Selection Systems and Judicial Characteristics: The Recruitment of State

Supreme Court Judges," *Judicature* 70 (1987) pp. 228–235.

10. Elaine Martin and Barry Pile, "Gender and Racial Diversification of State Supreme Courts," *Women and Politics* 24 (2002) pp. 35–51.

11. Elaine Martin, "Gender and Judicial Selection: A Comparison of the Reagan and Carter Administrations," *Judicature,* 71 no. 3 (1987), 136–142.

12. Elaine Martin, "Gender and Judicial Selection"; Elaine Martin "Gender and Presidential Judicial Selection: Carter, Reagan, Bush, and Clinton" *Southern Political Science Association Conference,* Atlanta, GA, November 2001; Sheldon Goldman and Elliot Slotnick, "Clinton's First Term Judiciary: Many Bridges to Cross," *Judicature,* 80(6) pp. 254–273.

13. Larry Berkson, "Women on the Bench: A Brief History," *Judicature,* 65 (1982) pp. 286–293.

14. Elaine Martin, "Here Come the Judges: An Analysis of State-Based Influences on the Selection of Women as Judges," *Midwest Political Science Association Conference,* Chicago (1996).

15. Elaine Martin, "State Court Political Opportunity Structures: Implications for the Representation of Women." American Political Science Association, Washington D.C. (Aug. 29–Sept. 1, 1988).

16. David Allen and Diane Wall, "Role Orientations and Women State Supreme Court Justices," *Judicature* 77 (1993), pp. 156–165.

17. Elaine Martin, "Glass Ceiling or Skylight: Women State Supreme Court Justices," Southern Political Science Association Conference, Norfolk, VA (November 1997).

18. Elaine Martin, "Glass Ceiling."

19. Sheldon Goldman and Elliot Slotnick, "Clinton's First Term Judiciary: Many Bridges to Cross," *Judicature,* 80(6) pp. 254–273.

20. Susan Carroll, "Representing Women: Congresswomen's Perceptions of Their Representational Roles," in Cindy Simon Rosenthal (ed) *Women Transforming Congress.* (University of Oklahoma Press 2002).

21. Neal C. Tate, "Personal Attribute Models of Voting Behavior of U.S. Supreme Court Justices," *American Political Science Review,* 75 (1981) p. 355; Jeffery Segal and Harold Spaeth, *The Supreme Court and the Attitudinal Model.* (Cambridge University Press 1993).

22. Herbert Kritzer and Thomas Uhlman, "Sisterhood in the Courtroom: Sex of Judge and Defendant in Criminal Case Disposition," *The Social Science Journal* 14 (1977) pp. 77–88.

23. Leslie Goldstein, *Feminist Jurisprudence: The Difference Debate.* (Rowman and Littlefield 1992).

24. Judith Resnik, "On the Bias: Feminist Reconsiderations of the Aspirations of Our Judges," *Southern California Law Review* 61 (1988) p. 1877.

25. Judith Baer, "How Is Law Male? A Feminist Perspective on Constitutional Interpretation," in *Feminist Jurisprudence,* ed. Leslie Goldstein. Lanham, MD (Rowman and Littlefield 1992).

26. David Allen and Diane Wall, "Role Orientations and Women State Supreme Court Justices," *Judicature* 77 (1993), pp. 156–165; Sue Davis, "The Voice of Sandra Day O'Connor," *Judicature* 77 (1993) pp. 134–139; Sue Davis, Susan Haire and Donald Songer, "Voting Behavior and Gender on the U.S. Courts of Appeal," *Judicature,* 77 (1993) pp. 156–165; Elaine Martin,

"Women on the Bench: A Different Voice?" *Judicature* 77 (1993 a) pp. 126–128.

27. Donald Songer, Sue Davis and Susan Haire, "A Reappraisal of Diversification in the Federal Courts: Gender Effects in The Courts of Appeals, *Journal of Politics,* 56 (1994) pp. 425–439.

28. Donald Songer and Crews-Meyer, "Does Judge Gender Matter? Decision Making in State Supreme Courts," *Social Science Quarterly* 81 (2000) p. 75.

29. David Allen and Diane Wall, "Role Orientations and Women State Supreme Court Justices," *Judicature* 77 (1993), pp. 156–165.

30. Vicki Jackson, "What Judges Can Learn From Gender Bias Task Force Studies," *Judicature,* 81(1) (1997) pp. 15–21.

31. Jennifer Segal, "The Decision Making of Clinton's Nontraditional Judicial Appointees," *Judicature* 80 (1997) p. 279.

32. Elaine Martin, "Glass Ceiling"

33. Martha Chamallas, *Introduction to Feminist Legal Theory* (New York: Aspen Publishers 1999).

34. Richard Kearney and Holly Sellers, "Sex on the Docket: Reports of State Task Forces on Gender Bias," *Public Administration Review* 56 (1997) p. 587.

35. John W. Winkle and Justin Wedeking, "Perceptions and Experiences of Gender Fairness in Mississippi Courts," *Judicature* 87 (3) (2003) pp. 126–134.

36. Elaine Martin, "The Representative Role of Women Judges," *Judicature* 77 (3) (Nov/ Dec 1993b).

37. Leslie Goldstein, *Feminist Jurisprudence.*

38. Susan Carroll, *Women as Candidates in American Politics* (Indiana University Press 1985).

39. Elaine Martin and Barry Pyle, "Gender, Race and Partisanship on the Michigan State Supreme Court," with Barry Pyle, *Albany Law Review* 63 (2000), pp. 1205–1236.

40. Elaine Martin and Barry Pyle, 2003. "Judicial Bias or Counterbalance? A Test of 'Representative Voice' Theory," Midwest Political Science Association Conference, Chicago Il, April 2003.

FURTHER READING

Baer, Judith A. 1999. *Our Lives Before the Law: Constructing a Feminist Jurisprudence.* New Jersey: Princeton University Press.

Chamallas, Martha. 1999. *Introduction to Feminist Legal Theory,* New York: Aspen Publishers.

Epstein, Cynthia Fuchs. *Women in Law,* 2nd ed. Urbana: University of Illinois Press, 1993.

Goldstein, Leslie. *Feminist Jurisprudence: The Difference Debate.* Savage, MD: Rowman and Littlefield, 1992.

Martin, Elaine (ed). *Women on the Bench: A Different Voice?* Symposium issue, *Judicature,* 77 (3) (1993).

"Proceedings of the National Association of Women Judges 1990 Annual Meeting" *Women's Rights Law Reporter,* vol. 13, no. 1, Spring, 1991.

8

★ ★ ★ ★ ★ ★ ★ ★ ★ ★ ★ ★ ★ ★   **8**   ★ ★ ★ ★ ★ ★ ★ ★ ★ ★ ★ ★ ★ ★

Public Policy:
The Feminist Perspective

Public policy in this country significantly influences the lives of American women. Joan Hulse Thompson examines congressional action on two proposals for helping working families, the Family and Medical Leave Act (FMLA) and the Family Time Flexibility Act (FTFA), both sponsored by congresswomen in leadership roles with the Congressional Caucus for Women's Issues. President Clinton signed the FMLA in 1993, and the Supreme Court affirmed its authority in 2003; in contrast the Republican House leadership acknowledged certain defeat and pulled the FTFA from the House floor in spring 2003. The conflicts over these bills illustrate both the impact of women in the House and the ongoing battle between interest groups representing business and labor organizations. Thompson points out that when the Democrats controlled the House of Representatives, the Congressional Caucus for Women's Interests (CCWI) was a bipartisan organization able to advance an activist legislative agenda. Since the Republicans took control of the House in 1994, the CCWI has lost its office in the Rayburn House Office Building and become a less ideological organization.

Although numerous laws have been passed prohibiting sex discrimination in various areas of public policy, Ruth Bamberger finds that the insurance industry still retains sex as a classification in determining the price of insurance products. Is this practice unfairly discriminatory? The author maintains the Supreme Court has answered this question within limitations, namely, some justices, as well as judges in the lower courts, maintain that their decisions in no way intend to revolutionize the insurance industry. Over the past 30 years, civil rights and women's groups have chipped away, through legislation, regulations, and litigation, the industry's use of the sex classification. The latest target of attack is in prescription benefits, where numerous insurance policies do not cover prescription benefits for birth control, while at the same time including drugs like Viagra. The author concludes that, at best, the Supreme Court has changed public policy in insurance sex discrimination with restraint, though at some point it might have to act as final arbiter in deciding whether pricing by sex classification is unfair.

Challenged from all sides, Roberta Ann Johnson argues, affirmative action, nevertheless, continues to live on as a highly charged issue. This article (1) defines affirmative action, (2) details the development of federal affirmative action guidelines, (3) describes Supreme Court decisions and congressional responses to affirmative action, (4) describes how the states and the lower courts have become battlegrounds on the issue of affirmative action, (5) considers the ways in which affirmative action is a woman's issue, and (6) considers the future of affirmative action.

Working Women and Their Families: The Family and Medical Leave Act versus The Family Time Flexibility Act

Joan Hulse Thompson

My name is Liberia Johnson. In 1978, I was employed by a retail store in Charleston, South Carolina. . . . I became pregnant. . . . I tried to work because the income was so important to my family. My doctor told me that I was hyper-tensive and I had a thyroid problem. . . . If I did not stop working I would have a miscarriage. . . . The store manager . . . told me my job would be there after my baby was born. . . . I left at three months pregnant. I had a difficult pregnancy. I was in the hospital three times because I almost lost my baby. When I had my baby, I went and got my six weeks check up and the same day I went back to the store and asked for my job. . . . There was a new manager and he told me I don't have a job.[1]

My name is Teri Martell. . . . I have two full time jobs (in 2003) . . . first wife . . . and mother of two sons, Donny, age 7 and Eric, age 10. . . . I am also employed at Eastman Kodak as an Electrician and Instrumentation Mechanic . . . and am now the major source of income and health care benefits for my family. My commute . . . is 1 hour and 15 minutes, *one way*. . . . (Fortunately) . . . Kodak has allowed me to . . . work 4 10-hour days Monday through Thursday. . . . (However, sometimes getting my job done means) working overtime during emergencies and scheduled shutdowns on our film manufacturing machines. Because I am the major source of my family's income, I choose to work even on my regular scheduled days off, (including some) Saturdays and Sundays. My children get many more days off than I . . . (for) Columbus Day, Veterans Day, Martin Luther King Day, Teacher Conferences, and . . . for snow. . . . (My husband) is self-employed so. . . . it would be a great help (for me) to have a bank of hours to use for these situations. . . . Money is very important and the main reason I work. But . . . the decision to permit comp time instead of overtime pay should be left to me and my employer to decide—not the federal government.[2]

President George H.W. Bush vetoed the Family and Medical Leave Act (FMLA) that Liberia Johnson supported, in July 1990 and again in September 1992. However, once President Bill Clinton assumed office he signed the measure on February 5, 1993 and called for its expansion during his presidency. President George W. Bush has not advocated the repeal of the FMLA his father opposed, but like Teri Martell he supported the Family Time Flexibility Act (FTFA, HR 1119) in the 108th Congress. Women's policy proposals, including both these bills, are entangled in the confrontation between Republicans and business associations versus Democrats and labor organizations over federal employer mandates. These bills are part of the continuing debate that so often divides the parties and the nation over the role of the federal government in the working lives of women and men.

Congressional hearings seek to demonstrate the need for legislative action with testimony from experts and from public witnesses, like the two women quoted above. Witnesses like Ms. Johnson and Ms. Martell can play a brief, but significant, role in building support for legislation. According to a veteran committee staff member, anecdotes are "the only thing that move people. A good public witness draws the rapt attention of the members."[3] Since they seek to convince members of Congress that legislation is needed to remedy an injustice, the more heart-wrenching their stories the better for the bill's sponsors.

When the Democrats held the majority in the House of Representatives, they arranged hearings on legislation to require that some private employers and all government agencies provide family and medical leave for eligible employees or face lawsuits in federal court. Former Congresswoman Pat Schroeder (D-CO), then Democratic Co-Chair of the Congressional Caucus for Women's Issues (CCWI), originated the FMLA in 1985. Congresswoman Judy Biggert (R-IL) is the prime sponsor of the FTFA that she first introduced in 1995, after the Republicans won the majority of the House of the Representatives for the first time in 40 years. Biggert was the Republican Co-Chair of the CCWI in the 107th Congress from 2001–2003.

Advocates for the FMLA included the Partnership for Women and Families (then the National Women's Law Center) and the foremost labor organization, the AFL-CIO. Biggert's allies on the FTFA include the Society for Human Resources Management (SHRM) and the primary organization for both large and small business interests, the U.S. Chamber of Commerce. Congresswoman Biggert, flanked by three other Republican Congresswomen, announced the introduction of the FTFA into the 108th Congress on March 6, 2003. The bill had more than 65 co-sponsors including seven more Republican women and at least two Democratic congressmen, but no Democratic women.

Former Republican congresswomen Olympia Snowe of Maine and Marge Roukema of New Jersey were initially reluctant to support the FMLA, but later helped negotiate compromises that enabled it to pass in the House and Senate in 1990 and 1992, even though it failed both times to survive Bush's veto. Gaining support from Democratic congresswomen for the FTFA amendments to the Fair Labor Standards Act (FLSA) will be very difficult, however, because that labor law was enacted as part of the New Deal under President Franklin Delano Roosevelt to, in his words, "protect workers unable to protect themselves from excessively low wages and excessively long hours." The labor union representative at the March 2003 hearing included this quote in her testimony to remind Democrats of the critical importance of the FLSA enacted in 1938.

The FTFA is modeled on a labor law that has applied to federal employees since 1978 and to all public employees since 1985. The issue that divides the political parties is whether or not permitting private employers the same flexibibilty now available to government agencies will undermine the 40-hour workweek standard. On March 12, 2003, Houston Williams, Chairman and CEO of PNS, Inc., a member of the Chamber of Commerce Board of Directors and of the Small Business Council, told the Education and Workforce Committee that the New Deal regulations were old and outdated:

> When the FLSA was enacted, the workforce consisted mostly of men. It was atypical for households with young children to have both parents work outside of the home. But today, a greater percentage of employees who work overtime are women, there are more dual-wage earner couples in the workforce, and there are more single mothers in the workforce. These demographic changes in the workforce are a major reason why today many more employees view time off as valuable as, or more valuable than, cash payments for overtime work.

At the same hearing, Ellen Bravo, Director of 9 to 5, the National Association of Working Women labor organization, expressed labor's determined oppostion to the Family Time Flexibility Act, because in her words it "would make it harder for workers to gain either time or flexibility." While the proposal suggests that employees will usually get to choose when to take their comp time, "the reality (is) that most workers have no say in their hours or working conditions . . . (and that) current law (including the FSLA) isn't being enforced." Low wage workers would be unlikely to file lawsuits if they were routinely denied the right to choose when to use comp time or pressured to choose comp time instead of overtime pay. For instance, according to Ellen Bravo, "Denise in Milwaukee . . . works as many overtime hours as she can . . . (Because) her low pay doesn't cover the bills without the extra time. (If HR 1119 is enacted)," the foreman (will choose) who gets those overtime assignments and if she doesn't agree to time off instead of pay, Denise knows she simply won't be chosen."

The 9 to 5 organization argued, in addition, that employers could already allow workers to stay late or come in early at some point in a particular week in order to be able to take time off for a child's scheduled school event that same week, and while some do it, most do not. "Cash overtime (payment) is something an employee is free to use at will. Accrued comp time, on the other hand, loses its value to the employee any time the employer retains discretion to deny the leave." Therefore, according to Ellen Bravo, "What Denise needs is a higher minimum wage, not an erosion of the Fair Labor Standards Act Overtime Protections," which were intended to discourage mandatory overtime by making it relatively expensive.

WOMEN IN CONGRESS AND THEIR CAUCUS

Congresswomen were generally outsiders in the House starting with the first woman who entered it in 1917. However, after the 2002 midterm elections the Democrats in the new Congress selected Nancy Pelosi (D-CA) to be the House Democratic Party Leader and the Republicans voted Deborah Pryce (R-OH) their new Republican Conference Chairman, the third ranking Republican in the House. Both were the highest ranking women ever chosen by their parties for leadership positions and Pelosi is in line to become Speaker of the House, whenever the Democrats again hold a majority. On June 1, 2004, former Georgetown law professor Stephanie Herseth won the South Dakota House seat in a special election bringing the number of women in Congress to an all-time high of 63 in the House. Of that number, three women serve as Delegates, and there are 21 Republicans and 42 Democrats.

While a few women were committee leaders earlier, it was not until the 1980s that any women were invited to join either party's powerful yet informal social and political groups, such as Democratic Speaker Sam Rayburn's Board of Education or the Republican Chowder and Marching Society founded by former presidents, then House members, Richard Nixon and Gerald Ford. As women politicians, congresswomen have often been isolated from the social network of male politicians and from that of more traditional women outside of politics.

A former congresswoman suggested that they needed a support group explaining the significance of such social organizations, as follows:

> Members who don't or can't participate in them are like the kid in college who has no one to study with; no one to exchange ideas with to get a broader idea of what's going on in the class; no one to work with to get the right kind of "vibes" about the course and the teacher. It takes longer for that kid to understand what is going on and often that student is never as good as he or she could be.[4]

The Congresswomen's Caucus, founded in 1977 by Elizabeth Holtzman (D-NY), Margaret Heckler (R-MA), and Shirley Chisholm (D-NY), had both social and policy goals. All the members were committed to the Equal Rights Amendment and to increasing the number of women in public office. Frequent meetings provided an opportunity for "conviviality, affection, and good feelings."[5] Bipartisanship strengthened the organization's claim to speak for women nationally, but the Congresswomen's Caucus was not the first such organization, although its focus on member, rather than constituency, characteristics was unusual.

Paralleling the growth of special interest groups in the larger society, caucuses have flourished in the House. The Democratic Study Group was first in 1959. There were thirteen caucuses in 1974, over 100 in 1990, and, despite House rules changes, by 2003 nearly 300 caucuses.[6] Caucuses are voluntary associations of House members formed to help fulfill goals of representation, personal power, policy promotion, and reelection. Members from constituencies dependent upon the maritime industry formed the Port Caucus, those with steel mills joined the Steel

Caucus, and so forth. Caucuses gather and distribute information, seek to influence congressional agendas and may attempt to build policy coalitions. Former Speaker Newt Gingrich (R-GA) rose to power in the House as leader of an ideological caucus, the Conservative Opportunity Society, founded in 1983.

Whether congresswomen initially felt that they should represent women nationally, most soon realized that if they did not speak for women no one else would.[7] However, not all congresswomen believe that the problems of women can best be addressed at the national level. Because they favored state, local, or private initiatives, most Republican congresswomen and some Democrats were out of step with the underlying liberal perspective of the Caucus. After the election of President Reagan, the Congresswoman's Caucus expanded its influence and financial resources by admitting like-minded congressmen to the organization late in 1981. The following year the organization took on its new name, the Congressional Caucus for Women's Issues, and established an executive committee of congresswomen to set policy. Although some congresswomen were not affiliated, the group grew from a membership of 10 to 150 by 1994 with 42 congresswomen and 108 congressmen. In 1993 when the FMLA became law, male members of CCWI chaired 14 House committees and 44 subcommittees with ranking positions on 3 committees and 2 subcommittees. Having men in CCWI in the 103rd Congress also had the effect of increasing its representation on the five committees that form an oligarchy of power in Congress from 15 seats to 66 seats.[8]

Furthermore, when Family and Medical Leave passed the House for the third and final time, CCWI male membership included the Speaker, Majority Leader, Majority Whip, Democratic Caucus Chairman, and the Chairman of the Rules Committee. Although neither party leaders nor committee chairs can assure congressional passage, it did help women's issues to have publicly committed supporters in high places within the Democratic leadership. Then after the midterm election of 1994, the Republican Party took control of the House and instituted major administrative reforms including the abolition of legislative service organizations, a form of internal caucus created in 1979 and permitted to have separate staff and office space in House office buildings.[9]

The CCWI, therefore, lost its prime office space on the 4th floor of the Rayburn House Office building and the former Caucus staff moved off Capitol Hill to continue developing legislative information for Congress and the public as a new non-profit, non-partisan organization called Women's Policy, Inc (WPI). Its newsletter, *The Source,* is available free online at http://www.womenspolicy.org/ and its mission is to provide objective information on issues related to women and their families. WPI sponsors briefings, designed for Members of Congress and congressional staff from both parties and also open to the public, on domestic and international issues, such as: Work and Family Health, Violence Against Women in Conflict Situations, and Employer Provided Benefits. In the 108th Congress, Shelley Moore Capito (R-WV) and Louise McIntosh Slaughter (D-NY) chaired the CCWI organization, which cosponsored WPI's Capitol Hill briefings as well as sponsoring its own issue briefings.

POLICY DEVELOPMENT BY THE CAUCUS

Attempts by the Congresswomen's Caucus to build coalitions or "to fashion and implement legislative strategies were . . . infrequent and superficial."[10] However, the year the Caucus invited congressmen to join, it became the House coordinator for the Economic Equity Act, a package of bills initiated by then Senator David Durenberger (R-MN) in response to the fate of the Equal Rights Amendment. During President Ronald Reagan's first term, public opinion polls indicating that he was much less popular with women than with men prompted the media to focus attention on this new Gender Gap to the benefit of the CCWI. Republican congressmen feared the women's vote and Democrats in Congress were anxious to exploit their potential advantage. Child support enforcement and pension reform legislation, both included in the Economic Equity Act, were enacted before the 1984 election.[11]

After President Reagan's landslide reelection victory over former Vice President Walter Mondale and his running mate Caucus leader Geraldine Ferraro (D-NY), a CCWI staff member reflected "feminists are just poison"[12] on the Hill as of 1985. CCWI Director Anne Radigan then explained: "On Capitol Hill, legislators reacted negatively to the failure of the Democratic presidential ticket and its feminist adherents. Where only a few weeks earlier politicians had beaten a path to their doors, now feminist women's groups found themselves and their agenda held at a cool and measured distance."[13]

In order to advance women's economic issues in the 99th Congress, the CCWI Co-Chair Pat Schroeder adopted a new strategy of describing legislative proposals as "pro-family" rather than for women. The plan was to seize the politically popular label from conservatives and the religious right. The FMLA even bridged the politically divisive abortion issue by making it more economically feasible for women to continue an unplanned pregnancy. By the 1988 presidential election, both Republican George H.W. Bush and Democratic nominee Michael Dukakis of Massachusetts were talking about family policy proposals, including both parental leave and childcare.

During the first Bush's administration, the FMLA was joined on the House agenda by new women's equity legislation developed with CCWI. The Women's Health Equity Act, first introduced in July 1990 and enacted under Clinton in June 1993, increased research efforts on breast and ovarian cancer, menopause, osteoporosis, contraception, and infertility. The Violence Against Women Act, first introduced in 1990 and enacted with the crime bill in 1994, expanded rape shield laws, created federal offenses for interstate spousal abuse, and provided funds for rape crisis shelters, additional police, prosecutors, and victim advocates. In 2000, the U.S. Supreme Court invalidated a section of the Violence Against Women Act in *U.S. v. Morrison* (529 U.S. 598) declaring that the Congress did not have the power to open state courts to civil lawsuits from women against their alleged rapists.

Although abortion has been the driving issue for most feminist groups since the mid-1980s, CCWI had primarily an informational, rather than advocacy, role on abortion rights until January 1993. The 1992 elections added twenty-two new pro-choice women to the Executive Committee while two pro-life caucus congresswomen did not return to the House. The new Executive Committee therefore voted overwhelmingly to support the Freedom of Choice bill to codify the *Roe v. Wade* Supreme Court decision. In the 103rd Congress, CCWI committed itself to removing restrictions on abortion funding and including abortion services in health care reform advocated by then President Clinton. In the 108th Congress (2003–2005), however, CCWI was much less politically homogenous and therefore took no formal position on abortion, although inevitably it and/or family planning came up in almost every briefing sponsored by WPI and co-sponsored by CCWI, regardless of topic.

Congresswomen are now leaders of their respective political parties, represented on every committee, and they reflect the full spectrum of opinions on current issues, including both sides of the abortion conflict. While congresswomen certainly serve the interests of their constituents and work within their political party organizations, many do still have personal ties to other women in the House and share special concern for women and children. Cynthia Hall, WPI President, observes that, "when the Co-Chairs and members of CCWI are united, as they have been over the issues of sexual assault in the military and assuring educational and economic opportunities for women in Afghanistan and Iraq, the Congressional Caucus for Women's Issues definitely draws public attention and is effective."[14]

PROS AND CONS OF GENDER NEUTRALITY

According to then CCWI Executive Director Anne Radigan, the caucus in 1985 had long been committed to supporting gender-neutral legislation. Therefore, an FMLA bill for parental, not maternity, leave was introduced. Protective laws, such as weight-lifting restrictions, had been used to keep women out of higher paying, non-traditional jobs. Mandatory maternity leave, by treating pregnancy as a special condition, could well lead to further workplace discrimination against women, such as a reluctance to hire or promote a woman who might become pregnant.

The Pregnancy Discrimination Act (PDA), an amendment to Title VII of the Civil Rights Act of 1964, was enacted in 1978 with support from the Congresswomen's Caucus in response to a 1976 U.S. Supreme Court decision. The decision, *General Electric Co. v. Gilbert* (429 US 124), interpreted the previous statute as permitting employers to treat pregnancy differently from other medical conditions with respect to health insurance and leave policies. Under the PDA, women unable to work due to pregnancy or childbirth would have to be treated the same as other employees unable to work for medical reasons. The statute was gender neutral, but it left millions of women unprotected because their employers provided no health insurance or disability benefits. It also ignored the bonding needs of newborn infants and their families.

The year that PDA became federal law, the California legislature enacted a mandatory state maternity leave program covering all employers in the state. However, that 1978 law was challenged in 1983 by a private employer who claimed that the state statute was reverse discrimination against males and violated the federal mandate for gender neutrality. In 1984, this argument was successful in federal district court, but it was reversed on appeal in 1985 and vanquished in a 1987 U.S. Supreme Court decision, *California Federal Savings and Loan v. Guerra* (479 U.S. 272).

While the issue was before the courts, Representative Howard Berman (D-CA), who had sponsored the state law while a member of the California legislature, considered sponsoring a bill at the national level that would mandate maternity and some paternity leave. He had the support of many California feminists who believed that "since women alone bear children they are at an indisputable disadvantage compared to working men and require an edge to help them remain competitive in the workplace."[15]

Berman asked for the assistance of the Partnership for Women and Families (then the Women's Legal Defense Fund), but when it convened the lawyers who had fought for PDA, along with a newly hired CCWI staff attorney, to look for a way to respond to the initial trial court decision they strongly disagreed with Berman. To fill the coverage gap and recognize the needs of women and their families, without abandoning the principle of gender neutrality, they developed a broad policy mandating parental leave for both parents and medical disability leave for all workers. Wendy Webster Williams, a law professor at Georgetown University who worked on the gender neutral PDA, argued that so-called protective laws that "distinguish between the sexes were—eventually, perhaps inevitably—turned around and used against women."[16] Congressman Berman agreed to abandon his efforts in favor of this approach and the Partnership for Women and Families working with the CCWI decided to focus their proposal on mandating unpaid leave rather than the paid family leave programs prevalent in Europe.

A more narrowly drawn bill for pregnant women with a small paternity leave, to encourage a greater role for fathers in the care of newborns, would have had an easier time gaining support. Making parental leave optional for either parent enabled opponents to score points with such remarks as, "This is ludicrous in the extreme. I don't need 18 weeks (later reduced to 12) off if my wife has a baby."[17] Including all those temporarily medically disabled increased the cost of the bill to employers and, therefore, their resolve to oppose it. A Republican Senator from Minnesota, who was usually a dependable ally on women's issues, expressed concern in 1990 that the costs of temporary medical leaves and leaves for the care of sick family members were "virtually untested in the private sector"[18] and therefore very difficult to predict. Although the 2003 Family Time Flexibility Act is not an employer mandate with associated costs, it is gender neutral like FMLA. It is written to allow employers to offer both women and men comp time arrangements instead of overtime pay.

CHARGES OF ELITISM AND DAMAGING (DE)REGULATION

Choosing to make the mandated leave of FMLA unpaid kept the cost down and made the policy self-policing, but at the price of raising difficult issues of social class. Women's groups, like other interest groups, are composed primarily of members from the middle class and above. They are potentially vulnerable to charges of insensitivity to the real problems of working class women when their organizations engage in conflicts over abstract principles of equality. That was why both the public witnesses at the October 1985 initial FMLA hearing were African American. One of Pat Schroeder's concluding remarks expressed her pleasure that, while "The bill looks like it is for 'Yuppies,'" the hearing had demonstrated that "It's for everyone." Demonstrating universality was clearly one of the goals of the congresswomen, the caucus staff, and the women's groups when they planned the initial hearing. Congresswoman Biggert similarly brought forward a blue-collar workingwoman, Terri Martell quoted above, in order to counter expected criticism that her bill would provide greater benefits to employers and highly skilled workers than to most hourly workers and their families.

Nevertheless, 9 to 5 made exactly that claim against FTFA in the testimony quoted above and FMLA opponents described the advocates of the FMLA as "powerful special-interest groups" seeking to dictate policy against the best interests of both employers and the very employees whose interests they claimed to represent. Testimony from the U.S. Chamber of Commerce at legislative hearings on FMLA included references to the argument that, "All employees . . . will be subject to a uniform parental leave law, . . . whether they can afford to take advantage of it or not."[19] Furthermore, the business community argued that, "any mandated benefit is likely to replace other, sometimes more preferable, employee benefits . . . (such as) flextime, child-care, dental or liberalized leave benefits."[20] In 1989, a Texas Republican expressed the view that only the upper classes would be able to take the leaves while all workers would share the costs. He described the bill as "'Yuppie' welfare—a perverse redistribution of income."[21]

The mandatory nature of FMLA legislation was critical for the CCWI and could not be compromised. Supporters proclaimed that the proposal "breaks new ground in labor law"[22] and, of course, business groups opposed it for exactly that reason. Proponents could and did agree to reduce the number of weeks of leave and increase the number of employees a company must have to be covered; however, eliminating the mandatory nature of the regulation would have left nothing that women and their families could count on. But for business interests and their supporters in Congress, "Such legislation (as the FMLA) results in a loss of freedom of choice—the hallmark of our economic system."[23]

Government has regulated wages and working conditions in the private sector for decades, and Congresswoman Biggert's FTFA bill, supported by the Chamber of Commerce, can be seen as beginning the process of repealing those intrusions. The FMLA, on the other hand, embodied an extension of government regulation, which must be fought, according to the U.S. Chamber of Commerce, for the sake of maintaining the nation's international competitiveness and high rate of economic growth. Figures for employee benefit costs as a percentage of the payroll for Korea, Japan, and Taiwan were cited to show that the FMLA would put U.S. industry at a disadvantage. European nations that grant paid family leaves were praised by FMLA supporters, but criticized by the Chamber of Commerce for rates of job creation below that of the United States. The Chamber argued that the costs of mandated family leave would devastate small businesses and could even lead to discrimination in hiring, making it difficult for women of childbearing age to find employment.

To opponents, family leave was another well intentioned but misguided intervention in the employer–employee relationship. They argued that it would not serve the interests of the nation or even those of working women. Congresswoman's Biggert's 2003 proposal for the Family Time Flexibility Act is precisely the opposite of FMLA. The FTFA modifies the New Deal era overtime regulation for hourly workers with new provisions that allow employers to offer their employees the option to bank up to 160 hours of comp time with pay out available above 80 hours anytime after 30 days notice. The use of comp time, accrued at 1½ hours for each overtime hour worked, would occur via a negotiation between employer and employee such that use of comp time would come after "reasonable notice" and not "unduly disrupt the operations of the employer." All remaining banked time would be paid out within one month of the end of the calendar year.

The punishment for employer's subjecting their employees to coercion is double damages, but opponents argue that it would be difficult, probably impossible, to enforce. Opponents have also claimed that banking comp time instead of overtime pay is, in comparison to the current law, like a no-interest loan from employee to employer with no protection for the employee in the case of bankrupcy filing. Instead of getting paid 1.5 times their normal wage for working above a 40 hour week, employees would be allowed to save the compensatory hours earned to be taken as paid leave later in the year, with supervisor approval. "While like unpaid family leave, flex time favors the more well-off among hourly wage earners, even some low income women do want the option, to allow them to take time off with their families."[24]

FMLA proponents saw family leave as the next step toward a more humane society, just as child labor and minimum wage laws were fifty years before. In response to complaints about cost, prime sponsor Senator Christopher Dodd (D-CT), declared "It's mortifying that we can't offer a benefit like this that is a minimum standard of human decency."[25] Normal family life adjusts to adult employment schedules on a daily basis. Family and medical leave was developed primarily for times of transition and crisis, when accommodating the business needs of employers would cause great harm to the family. In contrast, the FTFA focuses on voluntary accommodations for ordinary schedule conflicts, but it would rewrite fundamental New Deal labor law for private sector employees. Labor is opposed to any weakening of the paid overtime mandate that could take the nation back toward the pre–New Deal assumption that employees would work a six day week, sometimes as many as 70 hours total with only one day off.

BUILDING SUPPORT FOR THE FMLA AND THE FTFA

According to then CCWI staff director, Anne Radigan, the legislative strategy for the Family and Medical Leave Act (FMLA) assumed compromise would be necessary for success. She described the CCWI plan in 1985 as follows: "At first, try to be as all-encompassing as possible, then go for as much as you can (realistically hope for), and finally get what you can."[26] Radigan worked for the CCWI leaders who tended to be pragmatic, because they wanted legislative accomplishments to claim credit for back home. Similarly, Congresswoman Biggert highlights her Family Time Flexibility Act on her Web site designed to communicate her views and accomplishments to her constituents. She has strong support for her FTFA bill from the Republican leadership in the House of Representatives, who see it as a way to demonstrate their concern for the needs of working class women and their families.

The FTFA passed the House of Representatives in 1996 and 1997, but each time it failed to pass in the Senate. Congresswoman Biggert is also the prime House sponsor for the FMLA Clarification Act which is the main vehicle for changes to FMLA regulations, including changing the interpretation of the term serious health condition and modifying intermittent leave rules. Employees now can take leave in increments as short as one hour, which can make record keeping burdensome. The Society of Human Resources Management and the National FMLA Corrections Coalition advocate changes now, but not the repeal of the FMLA employer mandate. Once enacted labor laws are very difficult to repeal.

Because public support is essential to win congressional support, the initial hearing for the FMLA and every subsequent hearing were planned with the media in mind. The first hearing had a star witness, Dr. T. Berry Brazelton, who had the charisma of a cable television star and the authority of a noted Harvard University pediatrician and author. His testimony on the importance of bonding between infants and their parents gave the bill the advantage of backing in the medical community. As hoped, he drew a feature story in *The Washington Post*. Subsequent hearings noted other potential beneficiaries, including testimony from a retail manager who recovered from cancer but was unemployed for two years, and a daughter who lost her job when she was absent caring for her father during the last weeks of his life.

After the very first committee hearing in 1985, the anxious caucus staff monitored the media coverage and was both encouraged and discouraged. Both the AP and UPI wire services carried the story but both talked about maternity leave. "What did we do wrong?" lamented Anne Radigan. "How was that connection, the language . . . misunderstood? We are talking so very clearly about parents, mothers *and fathers*." On the other hand, there was good coverage and an opportunity to build support before opposition surfaced. Reflecting on media strategy three years later, Anne Radigan recalled that "most reporters covering the issue gave the bill a favorable spin."[27]

By 1989, *Congressional Quarterly* was referring to the FMLA as "a key item on the agenda . . . of organized labor."[28] At the first hearing in 1985, the labor union prospective came from a man who prefaced his remarks with the question, "What's an official of a macho male coal miners union doing in a place like this?" He then described the parental leave proposal that the coal companies refused to accept in national contract talks in 1984, the growing number of women in coal mining, the changing family patterns in mining communities, and the special hardships facing rural families when their children are seriously ill. Medical treatment for cancer, for instance, is available only in major cities, requiring time off from work for travel to hospitals as far as 200 miles away.

Although his stories were emotionally compelling, the United Mine Workers spokesman made it clear that he was coming to Congress, because the union had been unable to get parental leave through in contract negotiations. In a sense, he was asking Congress to circumvent the collective bargaining process, because mandatory benefits allow unions to focus their bargaining on other issues. Union support, while necessary for committee approval, was less important for enactment than the media coverage that could build support within the general public and therefore in the full chamber.

In 1985, Representative William Clay (D-MO), a black congressman and union ally, called the FMLA "preventive medicine, (because it) . . . goes to the heart of what is causing families to struggle."[29] As a cosponsor, Clay, then chairman of the Labor Management Subcommittee of the House Education and Labor Committee, proved valuable. However, his advocacy may have further strengthened the resolve of the business community. Clay was known for angry rhetoric, but not for legislative effectiveness beyond his own committee. Furthermore, the Education and Labor (renamed under the Republican majority Education and the Workforce) Committee was perceived then as a partisan, ideological committee where liberals pushed for proposals that would not win in the full House. FMLA opponents were not interested in making concessions as long as they had an ally in the White House who could defeat the proposal entirely with his veto.

EXPANDING THE FMLA COALITION AND CONFRONTING BUSINESS ORGANIZATIONS

In 1985, Schroeder's original bill provided for disability leaves, defining disability as "a total inability to perform a job, a notion of disability that disabled rights advocates had been struggling for years to overcome."[30] Substituting "medical leave" resolved the objections of the disabled and gained the support of five organizations, including the Disability Rights Education and Defense Fund. At the suggestion of then Congresswoman Roukema (R-NJ), ranking Republican on the subcommittee, the proposal was expanded in 1987 from parental to family leave by including leave to care for seriously ill, elderly parents. This inclusion brought the politically powerful American Association of Retired Persons and another group into the FMLA coalition.

Advocates recognized that women with difficult pregnancies and those who could not afford to risk losing their jobs might choose to have an abortion for financial reasons. At the first hearing on the FMLA then Congresswoman from Ohio, Mary Rose Oakar, a Roman Catholic and pro-life CCWI member, said that "nothing is more sacred than children in their formative weeks," making parental leave "a real, positive, minimum response." She also pledged, in her role as chair of the subcommittee responsible for federal employee benefits that the federal government would become a model employer and provide FMLA leaves. Congressman Dale Kildee (D-MI), also a devout Roman Catholic, added that the bill promised to be "a real vehicle for making this government pro-family." Other pro-life members, including Republican Henry Hyde of Illinois, and the U.S. Catholic Conference supported the bill. However, anti-abortion forces could not develop a maximum lobbying effort for anything other than a prohibition of abortion.

In March 1989, the House Education and Labor Committee approved amendments to add a title including congressional employees among covered workers and a section outlining special rules for instructional personnel at public and private schools. The rules for educators were negotiated by the National School Board Association, professional unions representing teachers, and other education organizations to provide employee coverage even at small schools and prevent undue disruption in classroom instruction from intermittent leaves or teachers returning at the very end of the term.

Businesses would be paying the cost of FMLA, so members of Congress would want to see evidence of business support. After questioning ten major companies about their leave provisions, Pat Schroeder and the Caucus staff attorney invited General Foods Corporation to testify at the first hearing in 1985. The company had a policy of *paid* disability and child-care leaves as part of its plan to "meet contemporary and future needs of employees," explained its representative. Male employees had been reluctant to ask for leave, she continued, but recently a "very highly placed executive" had taken parental leave to be with his new baby and "he's being looked at as the domino." Such a company had an incentive to support the FMLA. The governmental mandate would require its competitors to bear the cost of a minimal unpaid benefit, while its paid benefit package would remain attractive to prospective employees. At a subsequent hearing, Southern New England Telephone testified that their parental leave policy had enabled them to retain trained employees, avoiding costly staff turnover.

The U.S. Chamber of Commerce, the National Federation of Independent Business, and the Society for Human Resource Management, (SHRM, then the American Society for Personnel Administration) all testified against the FMLA, because of its mandatory nature and these are the same groups that have supported the Family Time Flexibility Act. SHRM states on its website that FTFA would "make small changes to an outdated law, but the impact will be tremendous. . . ." Its spokesman at the March 12, 2003 committee hearing said that "a survey found 41 percent of HR professionals in favor of amending FLSA to allow comp time in order to increase flexibilty for employees' personal needs." Since the change would be voluntary for employers, there was no need to demonstate majority support from SHRM members.

When FMLA was under consideration, congressional staff found some small business representatives to argue for the bill. These included the National Federation of Business and Professional Women's Clubs and the National Association of Women Business Owners. Congresswoman Pat Schroeder said that from small business owners in her district she heard that "parental leave policies save employers the cost of hiring and training new employees. Most of all these policies help attract the best and the brightest, and retain a valued and trusted work force."[31]

The co-sponsorship of the four subcommittee chairs with jurisdiction was sufficient for success at that initial stage in the legislative process. The primary focus during full committee consideration was the cost for business, especially small business, to continue health insurance coverage of workers on leave and to hire temporary replacements. The original bill applied to employers with five or more workers, repeated concessions raised that number to 50, provided a legal means to deny some highly paid employees reinstatement, shortened the number of weeks of leave, restricted workers to either family or medical leave during a twelve-month period, and raised the number of weeks worked to be eligible. The bill still covered some part-time as well as full-time workers, intermittent as well as continuous leave, mandated continued health benefits if offered, and provided job guarantees for family and medical leaves. Since 95 percent of all private employers have less than 50 workers, only about 5 percent of companies and 45 percent of the private sector workforce is currently covered by the FMLA mandate.

STUDYING THE IMPACT OF THE FMLA

Released in early 1987, the original annual cost estimate from the Chamber of Commerce for family leave alone was $16 billion; but this figure was based on the faulty assumptions that all workers would be replaced and that replacements would be paid more than regular workers. Under pressure, the Chamber reduced the estimated cost to $2.6 billion. After initial compromises, the nonpartisan Government Accounting Office estimated that the new bill would cost $188 million annually.[32] Based upon these figures, supporters argued that the FMLA would cost employers only $6.50 per year per eligible worker. A report, produced by the CCWI research arm and the Partnership for Women and Families, found that unemployment resulting from the absence of parental leave costs American families at least $607 million a year and costs taxpayers about $108 million a year for government assistance programs.[33]

While the Caucus saw the FMLA as a step in a new very desirable direction, opposition groups feared more costly encroachments if the bill succeeded in any form. Academic specialists, comparing the United States with other Western democracies in Europe and with Canada, pointed out at congressional hearings that in those countries payments are available to compensate for lost wages after childbirth. Realizing that such a proposal was too costly to win passage, successive versions of the FMLA provided for a commission to study ways to provide salary replacement for employees taking parental and medical leaves. Early advocates who wanted paid leaves were thus partially satisfied, since a study commission could improve prospects for a future program of leaves paid for by employers, Social Security, or some other means.

The final version of the FMLA Commission mandate, however, focused on examining the administrative and implementation costs business groups feared from the law as enacted. Issues of productivity, alternative benefits, job creation, federal enforcement, and economic growth by sector had been added to the commission mandate in response to business criticism, and the examination of paid leave provisions was greatly reduced in importance. Consideration of the needs of employees who had been covered by the original proposal, but are not eligible for mandatory leaves under the law as enacted were also added to the commission's charge. The commission report, submitted in April 1996 to a Congress dominated by FMLA opponents, reflected the fact that its bipartisan members were appointed before the 1994 Republican victory and therefore a majority were advocates of the FMLA.

CONTINUED CONFLICT OVER BUSINESS REGULATION OR DEREGULATION

The implications of enacting Family and Medical Leave actually extended beyond the narrow domain of women's issues. More ominous to the business community than the FMLA itself was the prospect that any new mandatory benefit opened the way for others to follow. Employers could be required to offer not only paid parental and medical leaves, but also health insurance to all employees and their families. Opting for a gender neutral policy meant that passage, if accomplished, would be a precedent for both governmental regulation of business and passing costs of social welfare programs on to private industry. Although this made passage more difficult, it also helped supporters attract a broader coalition of stakeholders than they would have for a narrowly drawn maternity leave bill.

President Clinton's health care reform proposal, introduced in November 1993, did include an employer mandate to cover 80 percent of the cost of health insurance for employees and their families, with government subsidies for small employers. The mandate was criticized by the U.S. Chamber of Commerce and other business representatives with the argument that more governmental regulation would cost jobs in the private sector. According to opponents, FMLA, like health care reform, was "yet another Democratic effort to regulate industry, increase the bureaucracy and set the stage for costly litigation."[34] Clinton's health reform lost public support after the insurance industry advertisements raised fears that those currently insured would have to pay more for less coverage. "From the Republican point of view, Democrats had turned a deaf ear to their longstanding warnings that a big bill could never gain broad support because there would always be more risks associated with passing it then clear gains."[35]

The 103rd Congress began with the easy passage of FMLA, which unlike health reform had bipartisan support, limited direct impact, and an incremental approach, putting off paid leave and universal coverage to the future. The potential impact of the Family Time Flexibility Act and of other overtime wage changes was a matter of partisan debate in the 108th Congress. Opponents stated that FTFA would undermine the 40 hour work week while supporters insisted it would offer valuable family time for parents who freely chose that option in preference to overtime pay. The fact that the FTFA included a 5 year sunset clause enabled proponents to argue that if workers were pressured unduly in violation of the anti coercion and anti retaliation provisions of the bill, then the law could be allowed to expire.

In April 2004, Secretary of Labor Elaine Chao presented a much broader revision of federal overtime regulations making changes to provisions in effect since 1949. These regulations were to take effect in August 2004. A previous revision proposal failed to win a majority in either the House of Representatives or the Senate in 2003 despite Republican control of both chambers. The Administration then decided to focus on gaining a precedent and exempted nurses and many other workers, which made it difficult for Democrats and their union allies to defeat the change again. Calls for roll call votes before the 2004 elections created another test of the relative strength of labor union and employer lobbyists in Congress.[36]

THE POLITICS OF CONGRESSIONAL PASSAGE

With its strong public appeal, Family and Medical Leave was viewed as a potentially powerful political issue throughout its consideration. Although not at the top of the congressional agenda until 1993, it attracted and sustained public support from 1985 until its enactment. The story of FMLA consideration between 1988 and 1993 demonstrates that party politics and media strategies were decisive, as they so often are in Congress.

The bill did not reach the floor of the House until 1990, but it was first debated on the Senate floor in 1988. Just before the presidential and congressional elections, Democratic Senators brought minimum wage increases, parental leave, and child care to the floor "in an openly partisan fashion," according to *Congressional Quarterly Almanac.* "While the Senate waited for conference reports on fiscal 1989 appropriations bills, Democrats used their power as the majority party to put on the floor all the labor and social legislation they wanted to highlight in the closing weeks before the November 8, (1988) elections."[37] No vote was taken on the bills due to a Republican filibuster.

One-third of the Senators faced reelection in the fall of 1990 and those who opposed the FMLA were not anxious to participate in another filibuster or cast a recorded vote against the family oriented bill. Then Senate Majority Leader, George Mitchell, a Democrat, worked out a deal with Senator Robert Dole, the Republican leader, to permit the FMLA to pass the Senate on a voice vote on the condition that Mitchell would schedule a vote on a constitutional amendment to make flag desecration a crime. Thus each party was able to advance an issue it hoped would work to its advantage in the coming congressional elections. Although the Senate remains a more civil place than the House, as a whole in recent years "civility (such as this mutually beneficial arrangement) has been mostly lost in Congress."[38]

An anti FMLA lobbyist, Mary Tavenner, working for the National Association of Wholesaler-Distributors, reported in 1990 that, "I had John Sununu (White House Chief of Staff) look me straight in the eye and say that the president would veto it."[39] Opponents felt secure therefore in refusing to compromise on the FMLA. After declining to meet with Republican supporters of the bill, President Bush did veto the FMLA on the last Friday afternoon before the July 4th holiday in 1990; a time when the media and the public would be least attentive.

The vetoed bill was a substitute proposal, negotiated among members just prior to House floor consideration, then under Democratic leadership. It eliminated the possibility that the same worker would be eligible for both family and medical leave, totalling 25 weeks, in one year. The cap would be 12 weeks for either or both and the small employer exemption was modified as well. Such changes made the law less burdensome for business and therefore picked up some congressional support. This revised 1990 version, which for the first time included care of a seriously ill spouse, was supported by 198 Democrats and 39 Republicans while 54 Democrats and 133 Republicans opposed it. Three planned amendments were actually withdrawn by Republicans at the request of the White House, because their passage might have made the bill more attractive and made a veto more difficult to sustain.

While the 1990 Bush veto killed the bill for that session, the issue remained for the fall congressional campaign, the next Congress and the 1992 election. In a national public opinion survey taken in June 1990, 74 percent favored a law guaranteeing up to 12 weeks of unpaid parental leave.[40] One columnist predicted that the 1990 veto of FMLA, veto number 13 for Bush, would turn out to be unlucky for the President[41] Although hardly decisive, the issue did contribute to the defeat of the first President Bush in 1992.

In 1991, Democratic Senator Christopher Dodd, the prime Senate sponsor, negotiated an additional compromise with Republican Senators Bond of Missouri and Coates of Indiana, who wanted to be responsive to business and also support pro-family legislation. This version added a provision allowing employers to deny reinstatement to their highest paid employees, if necessary to avoid "substantial and grievous economic injury to the operations of the employer" (Public Law 103-3). The bill passed both the House and the Senate in the fall of 1991, but in order to increase pressure on opponents no conference committee met until August 1992, with the spotlight on the Bush v. Clinton contest.

During the summer and fall of 1992, then Senator and Vice Presidential candidate, Al Gore, spoke movingly "of how fortunate he had been to take time off from work when his young son lay critically ill in the hospital after he was hit by a car."[42] The Senate passed the conference committee bill by unanimous consent on August 11 and the House followed suit by a vote of 241 to 161 on September 10, 1992. Advocating a new proposal to grant a tax credit to small and mid-sized companies who voluntarily granted family leave, President Bush sided with opponents who would not accept any form of mandatory leave. His veto of the FMLA was overridden in the Senate 68 to 31, but the House failed to attain the two-thirds vote necessary, voting 258 to 169, about 30 votes short.

Mother's Day, commemorated each May, has played a special role in both the FMLA and FTFA stories. In spring 1989, Schroeder said, "the worst rumor we hear up here is that the (Republican) administration will ask us to schedule the bill (for floor action) around Mother's Day and then take men out of the bill."[43] If such a Republican amendment had been proposed and succeeded, advocates of gender neutrality would have been forced to vote no on what had been their own proposal. Such poison pill amendments are an effective way to kill legislation. Instead, the Democratic Speaker arranged for FMLA to pass the House, with its gender neutrality and governmental mandate intact, just in time for Mother's Day 1990. As the supporters of the FMLA celebrated its first ever passage in the House, opponents knew President G. H. W. Bush absolutely would not sign it.

Ironically, the Republicans under the second President Bush, were planning a House vote on the Family Time Flexibility Act for a weekday near Mother's Day, 2003,[44] but a strong lobbying effort by the AFL-CIO forced the House Republican Whip to postpone the vote and finally withdraw the bill from the Floor. The Chairman of the Education and Workforce Committee along with Congresswoman Biggert supported the Whip's decision, but vowed to continue the fight to enact the FTFA sponsored by 110 members of the House and organizations including the National Association of Manufacturers, National Federation of Independent Business and the National Restaurant Association.[45]

After losing a close vote on regulations to protect workers from repetitive motion injuries in March 2001, labor in 2003 rallied their members against FTFA at the grassroots and made repeated visits to targeted Republicans. One Connecticut Republican actually withdrew as a co-sponsor of the FTFA when his constituents, who worked in hospitals and nursing homes, told him that they feared being pressured to bank comp time instead of receiving overtime wages.[46] Business lobbyists argued repeatedly that such pressure would violate the provisions of the law, but the congressman heard and responded to the fears of his constituents.

In 1993, the new Congress moved quickly through the reconsideration of FMLA with hearings in January, highlighting Clinton administration support, and

House and Senate passage early in February. On the final vote, FMLA was supported by 224 Democrats and 40 Republicans with 29 Democrats and 134 Republicans opposed. An amendment, negotiated with the Clinton administration and added in the Senate, calling for a full review of policy on homosexuals in the military marred President Clinton's first legislative victory. During the final vote on the legislation in the Senate the debate was actually about the "don't ask, don't tell" policy for the military, which got most of the media coverage as well. At his first legislative signing ceremony, President Clinton tried in vain to reclaim his presidential honeymoon by declaring that "America's families . . . have beaten the gridlock in Washington to pass family leave."

IMPLEMENTATION OF FMLA

Despite President Bush's vetoes, the concept of family leave entered the agenda of the state governments during the years it was debated in Washington. Eighteen states, Puerto Rico, and the District of Columbia have their own laws providing for some form of job protected leave for at least some workers. A few of these measures are more generous than the FMLA; the others are the same or less comprehensive. Laws in ten states provide only maternity leave, but the newer statutes are predominantly gender neutral.[47]

Experience with family and medical leave laws at the state level provided information on actual costs and benefits that was used to argue for the national approach. When finally enacted, FMLA did not supersede any provision of state law or local ordinances that provided more generous family or medical leave rights. If a state law provides for sixteen weeks of leave every two years, an eligible worker could, if family circumstances dictated, take sixteen weeks of leave one year under state law and twelve weeks the next year under FMLA. Corporations with worksites in more than one state would have preferred one federal requirement, but after the long delay in enactment, Congress refused to override benefits granted in the meantime by state legislatures. Some employers are therefore faced with both state and national standards to reconcile with guidance from the rules and regulations issued by the Department of Labor.

In the first year of implementation, the Labor Department received more than 125,000 requests for information about FMLA from employers and employees. Of the 3833 complaints it received during the first two years, over 90 percent were resolved quickly, often with just a phone call. In about 60 percent of the cases the employer was violating the act and in about 30 percent the employer was not violating the act. Less than 200 cases were pending at the end of the second year, and the department had filed eight lawsuits against employers by March 1996.[48]

Private lawsuits had also been filed and they led to a definitive appellant ruling in 1995. The interim regulations issued by the Department of Labor included a section on employee notification when leave is unforeseeable that was ambiguous about whether the employee had to specifically mention the FMLA to be protected by it. Given the U.S. Chamber of Commerce's concern during congressional passage about FMLA being a "yuppie" benefit, it is ironic that an employer pressed the courts to limit the benefits of FMLA to those who could articulate them. June Manuel, an employee of Westlake Polymers Corporation, lost her initial case, but won her job back in a Federal Circuit Court decision that quoted a floor statement by Congresswoman Roukema (R-NJ), a CCWI member and a key supporter of FMLA (*Manuel v. Westlake Polymers,* 66 Federal Reporter, at 762). The requirement for employer notification was clarified in the final Labor Department regulations to protect workers who are eligible for FMLA coverage, even if they are not aware of the law. However, "courts are split over whether the simple statement that an employee is ill constitutes sufficient notice under the FMLA."[49]

Advocates for women, such as the Partnership for Women and Families, urged the Labor Department to take steps to publicize FMLA more widely and Congress to expand its reach to more workers and seek a means of partial wage replacement. In 1997, President Clinton appeared as himself in a made for television movie entitled "A Child's Wish," about a terminally ill teenager. The movie, starring the late John Ritter as the father who needs FMLA leave to spend more time with his cancer stricken daughter, provided a vehicle for publicizing the FMLA law. In 2000, members of the public made 2833 complaints to the Labor Department alleging violations of the FMLA and the department, acting on behalf of employees, recovered almost $3 million for them[50] Unions do not have the right to bring FMLA claims on behalf of their members.

In 2002, California became the first state to enact paid family leave, allowing an estimated 13 million workers starting in July 2004 to be eligible for up to 6 weeks of paid FMLA leave over a 12 month period if their employer is covered by FMLA and they are enrolled in the state unemployment compensation disablity insurance program. The California program is paid for by employee contributions through payroll deductions. Paid leave is most likely to occur gradually; some counties have now enacted it for their employees and the federal government could serve as a model employer in the future.[51]

Congress has not enacted additional legislation and the U.S. Chamber of Commerce continues to oppose all employer mandates. It argues that "the FMLA does not expand the range of benefits available to employees; it simply locks one benefit into the package, thereby reducing the ability of employees to negotiate for other benefits they need more."[52] Although some members of the House and Senate sought to represent business interests, the U.S. Chamber of Commerce and other employer interest groups were never part of the process of negotiating the provisions of the FMLA.

As long as President Bush guaranteed a veto, the business community had nothing to fear and declined to participate in the talks that resulted in compromise provisions. Once Clinton was elected and anxious to sign the FMLA, it was too late to expect supporters to listen to corporate concerns about specific provisions. "There were lots and lots of things they could have raised," reflected Donna Lenhoff of the Partnership for Women and Families, but by maintaining their adamant opposition they lost the opportunity to shape the final statute, such as making it easier to administer or avoiding separate state granted leaves.[53]

It is not surprising then that attorney Will Aitchison called the FMLA a "badly written law" in 2003, adding that "some portions of the FMLA are clear, (but) others are confusing. More often, though, one encounters obvious 'holes' in the law—gaps that leave significant questions unanswered."[54] The rush to pass it once Clinton assumed the presidency played a part as well as the general lack of regulatory precedent for the Labor Department to follow, but interest groups on both sides did submit comments to the Department on its implementation. Congressional hearings had focused on newborns and children with cancer, but the statute was ambiguous enough that the regulations written by the Clinton administration are more inclusive. As long as the ill or injured child is under medical care and unable to participate in normal activities for more than three consecutive days (or would be without medical treatment), job protection will be available to covered employees, even if paid sick leave is not. As the women's interest groups hoped, the FMLA represents a concrete accomplishment of the feminist movement for working families, especially to the extent common illnesses as well as catasthrophic ones are covered.

In March of 2000, the U.S. Court of Appeals for the 8th Circuit decided *Caldwell v Holland of Texas Incorporated, doing business as Kentucky Fried Chicken* in favor of Juanita Caldwell, a single mother with a 3 year-old son named Kejuan. Kejuan had a severe ear infection that persisted from his initial medical evaluation on June 7, 1997 until after his surgery to remove his adenoids and tonsils and place tubes in his ears on July 17, 1997, but the employer contended that Kejuan's illness did not meet the regulatory standard set for the FMLA. On Saturday morning, June 7, his mother notified the assistant manager and missed her shift for her son's first doctor's appointment and initial antiobotic treatment. She was fired for that absence on Monday, June 9 by the store manager.

The District Court determined that Juanita Caldwell had not provided proof that met the standard of incapacity for more than 3 consecutive days and granted summary judgment to the employer, but the Circuit Court declared that in view of the medical records, "Kejuan's period of incapacity . . . may be measured over the entire time during which he was suffering from this illness and being treated for it." (8th Circuit, No. 99-2382). Kejuan's grandmother usually watched him when his mother worked, but the court considered daycare center rules excluding sick children in determining that an issue of fact existed for the trial court. The court noted that "what constitutes incapacity for a three-year-old is not directly addressed by the regulations." Without the surgery, Kejuan was at risk for serious hearing loss, but that fact was not the focus of the decision.

Another decision by the Fourth Circuit Court of Appeals (*Miller v. AT&T*, No. 00-1277, May 7, 2001) stated that influenza could qualify as a serious health condition. While the Labor Department had stated that "ordinarily the common cold, flu, ear aches, upset stomach, minor ulcers, etc. will not constitute serious health conditions," this list, which also appeared in congressional documents, means that normally these conditions will not last more than 3 days, require inpatient treatment or otherwise meet the standards for a serious health condition set by the Labor Department when it implemented the FMLA. *Miller v. AT&T* thus accepted as valid a revised opinion letter issued in 1996 by then Secretary of Labor Robert B. Reich, because the rules he defined were not clearly in violation of legislative intent and therefore within the authority of the executive branch to interpret federal law.

Fear of a controversy about abortion that would have killed the bill kept advocates from seeking more explicit language on serious health conditions during congressional consideration.[55] Employer advocates did not discuss or defend absentee policies, which set specific standards for attendance *regardless* of medical excuses. While sick leave can be abused and employers do need a dependable workforce, requiring 94 to 98 percent attendance regardless of circumstances results in the termination of people facing real family hardship. Employees, working "at will" without an employment contract, often have little job protection other than their rights under the FMLA regulations.

The CCWI and its allies presented FMLA as a means to ensure that employees faced with a family crisis would be able to keep their jobs and avoid welfare and Medicaid. Employer advocates never discussed or defended no-excuse attendance policies that allow workers with serious health conditions to be fired and become the taxpayers' responsibility. The FMLA does not require that employers allow workers paid sick leave to care for family members, because the primary focus was on job security and maintaining health care benefits. Issues of pay during leave were avoided by advocates in order to gain votes for passage. The measure was intended to be low cost and largely self policing. According to a 2000 Labor Department survey, one-third of workers on FMLA receive no pay during their leave and 40% cut their leave short for financial reasons. About 75% of those employees who do not take leave when they qualify for it cite the loss of pay as the reason. About 9% of employees go on public assistance during their unpaid family or medical leave. In the 1995 FMLA survey, about 2.2 million workers had taken FMLA during the previous 18 months, but by 2000 the figure for the same 18 month time period had more than doubled to 6.1 million.

On March 19, 2002, the U.S. Supreme Court decided the case of *Ragsdale v. Wolverine* (No. 00-6029), which unlike *Caldwell* and *Miller,* was a victory for employers. Wolverine World Wide, Inc. granted Tracy Ragsdale 30 weeks of unpaid sick leave under company policy when she needed surgery and radiation treatment for Hodgkin's disease in 1996. The company paid her health insurance premiums, but failed to give her written notice that this extended leave would include her FMLA mandated leave of 12 weeks. Without such notice, Labor Department regulations entitled her to 12 additional weeks of FMLA leave, if her medical condition still precluded her from returning to work. The Supreme Court, however, determined that prior notice would have changed Ragsdale's decision about taking leave and therefore refused to defer to the Secretary of Labor's penalty provision, concluding that mandating additional leave would be "manifestly contrary to the statute" and therefore violate the intent of Congress. The regulation might be valid, however, for cases where an employee could have made other arrangements with prompt notification.

On May 27, 2003, the Supreme Court in *Nevada v. Hibbs* (No. 01-1368) upheld the FMLA rights of state employees despite the justices prior precedents denying them the right to sue state employers for violations of the Age Discrimination in Employment Act and the Americans with Disabilities Act. Chief Justice Rehnquist wrote in his opinion for the Court that the U.S. Congress specifically applied the FMLA to the states and that it had the right to abrogate the 11th Amendment immunity of states from citizen lawsuits under its authority to enforce the 14th Amendment's Equal Protection clause already recognized as applying to gender discrimination. Although Hibbs is a husband who requested FMLA leave in 1997 to care for his wife, the FMLA is gender neutral specifically because Congress at the urging of the CCWI chose to contradict traditional societal assumptions about the roles of women. The case protected approximately 5 million state employees. Although the first President Bush, as recounted above, vetoed the FMLA twice and urged only voluntary programs in its place, his son and the Justice Department in 2003 asked the Supreme Court to side with state employees and uphold the FMLA.

The 10th Anniversary of the FMLA occurred in 2003 and provided an opportunity for advocates of the law to spotlight its impact and for opponents to again raise their concerns.[56] On January 21, 2003, the U.S. Chamber of Commerce wrote a letter to Congresswoman Biggert in praise of her legislative proposal that would modify the language of the FMLA. In it the Chamber outlined corporate objections to the Department of Labor's FMLA regulations, stating that,

> employers are compelled to ask deeply personal and invasive questions of employees seeking leave; employers are saddled with unintended administrative burdens and costs; workplace disruptions due to unscheduled and unplanned absences are common; employers must contend with unworkable notice requirements; employer policies are routinely over-ridden by heavy-handed regulations; and a decline in voluntarily provided sick and other paid leave is attributed to DOL's problematic FMLA regulations" (http://www.uschamber.com/government/letters/2003/)

In February 2003, Deanna Gelack of the FMLA Corrections Coalition, and Deron Zeppelin of the Society for Human Resource Management participated in a Roundtable discussion on Regulatory Issues before the House Committee on Small Business, Subcommittee on Regulatory Reform and Oversight, using the anniversary of passage to discuss their proposals for FMLA changes to benefit employers.

In celebration of the February 2003 10th anniversary of the signing of the FMLA, Senator Christopher Dodd (D-CT), the original Senate sponsor of the law, announced he was re-introducing an FMLA Expansion Act to extend the mandate from employers with at least 50 employees to those with 25 workers or more, and to provide grants for states to offer workers on leave partial wage replacement. In January 2003, Democratic Senate Leader Tom Daschle of South Dakota introduced a comprehensive early childhood bill that included some expansions of FMLA to serve as a statement of his party's legislative program. Congresswoman Carolyn

Maloney (D-NY) introduced companion legislation in the House that like the Senate bills would provide leave specifically for instances of domestic violence. Her bill, HR 1430 would also add domestic partner, grandparent, sibling, adult child and parent-in-law to the list of relationships that could trigger FMLA leave. Congresswoman Lynn Woolsey (D-CA) introduced the Balancing Act, HR 3780, and another companion bill in the House on February 5, 2004. She added childcare assistance programs to the expanded family leave proposals.

According to a National Public Radio broadcast on August 5, 2003, ten years after the FMLA went into effect, more than 35 million workers took job protected leave during the first decade. Most of them were women between ages 25 and 34 primarily for maternity leave or the care of sick children, but recently a rising number of FMLA leaves were requested by workers between 50 and 64 for the care of their elderly parents with serious health conditions. In 1995, the U.S. Department of Labor survey of non-government employees found that nearly half of all FMLA leaves were taken due to the employees' own health, i.e. traditional sick leave. By 2000, the proportion of leaves for the employees own health was below 40% and concern by co-workers about leaves meaning extra work for them had also declined. Non-traditional leaves for the care of an ill child or parent were too low to be recorded in the 1995 survey, but by 2000 they totalled nearly 25% of all leaves as the concept of family leave took hold.

CONCLUSION

The confrontation between business and labor over voluntary versus mandatory accommodations by employers of their employees' family lives will continue with the women in Congress playing an important role on both sides of the battle. The role of CCWI staff in helping launch FMLA, however, was unusual and not likely to be repeated, because congresswomen are now more divided on economic and social policy and no caucus is likely to regain coveted space in the congressional office buildings from which to direct a legislative effort. The old CCWI office space in the Rayburn House Office Building now belongs to the majority party leadership and it is hard to imagine officials of either party or individual members relinquishing their congressional office space for the return of legislative service organizations.[57]

Lesley Primmer, the last CCWI director and first president of WPI, observed after the passage of FMLA that "moving legislation is done by personal and committee staff primarily, with the caucus serving in an intermediate role."[58] With top leadership positions in both parties and greater committee seniority now, congresswomen no longer need the CCWI to individually influence policy development.

Furthermore, the congresswomen like women voters are split along both partisan lines and generational ones primarily over issues of economics and reproduction, so no one organization can be the voice of women voters in the House. Both parties court the women's vote by pledging to help families. The annual rotation of

CCWI co-chairs positions provides some leadership training for congresswomen and relationships between congresswomen across party lines still develop and can play an important role in the legislative process, since most new laws have at least some bipartisan congressional support.[59]

Former CCWI Director Anne Radigan once explained the goal of the women in Congress, as follows:

> To get across to the public at large that women's issues are everybody's issues. Women don't live in a vacuum, they don't exist alone, and they certainly don't exist in a "we against them" adversary relationship. Women are wives who are dependent, women are wives who are working, women are daughters who are going to school, and women are elderly parents who are vulnerable. . . . This is a family sort of prerogative. . . . Women's issues affect everyone.[60]

NOTES

1. Liberia Johnson, Joint Hearing on Disability and Parental Leave, 2261 Rayburn House Office Building, October 17, 1985, tape recorded by the author. Subsequent quotations from testimony at the same 1985 hearing will not be footnoted.

2. Teri Martell, Hearing on Family Time Flexibility Act, Subcommittee on Worker Protections, Committee on Education and the Workforce, US House of Representatives, March 12, 2003. (http://edworkforce.house.gov/hearings/108th/wp/familytime031203/martell.htm). Subsequent quotations from testimony at this 2003 hearing will be identified in the text and not footnoted.

3. Anonymous staff interview with the author for a case study of pension reform legislation, Washington, DC, July 19, 1984.

4. Irwin N. Gertzog, *Congressional Women: Their Recruitment, Integration, and Behavior,* 2nd ed. (Westport, CT: Praeger Publishers, 1995), p. 89.

5. *Ibid.,* p. 197.

6. Susan Webb Hammond, *Congressional Caucuses in National Policy Making,* (Baltimore, MD: Johns Hopkins University Press, 1998), pp. 1 & 42, and Maureen Groppe, "Got an Issue? Form a Caucus." Garnett News Service on LexisNexis, December 5, 2003.

7. Joan Hulse Thompson, "Role Perceptions of Women in the Ninety-fourth Congress," *Political Science Quarterly,* 95 (Spring 1980), p. 73.

8. The most powerful committees were: Appropriations, Budget, Ways and Means, Rules, and Energy and Commerce. See Lawrence C. Dodd and Bruce I. Oppenheimer, "Consolidating Power in the House: The Rise of a New Oligarchy," in *Congress Reconsidered,* 4th ed., (Washington, DC: C.Q. Press, 1989) pp. 48–50.

9. Hammond, *Congressional Caucuses in National Policy Making,* p. 209.

10. Gertzog, *Congressional Women,* 1st ed., 1984, p. 202.

11. Joan Hulse Thompson, "The Women's Rights Lobby in the Gender Gap Congress, 1983–84," *Commonwealth,* 2 (1988), pp. 19–35. The other side of the gender gap is higher support among men for Republican candidates.

12. Anonymous staff interview with author, October 1985.

13. Anne L. Radigan, *Concept and Compromise: The Evolution of Family Leave Legislation in the U.S. Congress* (Washington, DC: Women's Research and Educational Institute, 1988), p. 12.

14. Cynthia A. Hall, President, Women's Policy Inc., personal interview with author, Washington DC, June 7, 2004.

15. Radigan, *Concept and Compromise,* p. 8.

16. Elving, Ronald D., *Conflict and Compromise: How Congress Makes the Law,* (New York: Simon & Schuster, 1995), p. 20.

17. Macon Morehouse, "Parental, Medical Leave Bill Gets Markup in Senate," *Congressional Quarterly Weekly Report,* 47 (April 22, 1989), p. 892.

18. Morehouse, "Markup in Senate," p. 892.

19. Christine A. Russell, Director of the Small Business Center, U.S. Chamber of Commerce, "America's Small Businesses Cannot Afford Mandated Leave," public information release, no date, pp. 1–2 (obtained from its author, 1/90).

20. *Ibid.*

21. Brian Nutting, "Parental-Leave Bill Passed by Panel," *Congressional Quarterly,* 47 (March 11, 1989), 519.

22. Radigan, *Concept and Compromise,* p. 2.

23. Russell, "America's Small Businesses . . . ," p. 2. One precedent does exist. The Veterans' Reemployment Rights Act (1940) mandates up to four years of leave with job security for workers called to active military duty.

24. Anonymous staff interview with author, June 7, 2004.

25. Morehouse, "Markup in Senate," p. 892.

26. Anne Radigan, Executive Director, Congressional Caucus for Women's Issues, personal interview with author, Washington, DC, October 18, 1985.

27. Radigan, *Concept and Compromise*, p. 15. Indeed, Ms. Radigan notes that some of the reporters had a special interest in the story, because they were dissatisfied with the parental leave policies of their own employers.

28. Nutting, "Passed by Panel," p. 519.

29. "Family and Medical Leave Act of 1987 Introduced," *Update*, (former newsletter of the CCWI) February 27, 1987, p. 13.

30. Radigan, *Concept and Compromise*, p. 16.

31. "Family and Medical Leave Hearings in D.C. and on West Coast," *Update*, August 7, 1987, np.

32. "Capitol Boxscore," *Congressional Quarterly*, 47 (February 4, 1989), p. 243.

33. Roberta Spalter, Heidi Hartmann, and Sheila Gibbs, *Unnecessary Losses: Costs to Workers in the States of the Lack of Family and Medical Leave* (Washington, DC: Institute for Women's Policy Research, 1989), p. 3.

34. "Family Leave Waits for Clinton," *Congressional Quarterly Almanac*, (1992), p. 355.

35. Alissa Rubin, "Overhaul Issue Unlikely to Rest in Peace," *Congressional Quarterly*, 52 (October 1, 1994), p. 2800.

36. David Espo, "Dems Determined to Derail Overtime Plan," Associated Press Wire Service, April 28, 2004 and anonymous staff interview with author, June 7, 2004.

37. "Democrats Stymied on Parental-Leave Bill," *Congressional Quarterly Almanac*, 1988, p. 263.

38. Anonymous staff interview with author, June 7, 2004.

39. Alyson Pytte, "House Passes Parental Leave; White House Promises Veto," *Congressional Quarterly*, 48 (May 12, 1990), p. 1471.

40. A Louis Harris Associates poll of 1254 with a margin of error of plus or minus 3%. The other results were: opposed to such a law 24% and 2% unsure. Cited in *New York Times*, July 26, 1990.

41. Ellen Goodman, "Ambushing Bush on Family Leave," *Philadelphia Inquirer*, August 1, 1990, sec. A.

42. "Clinton Signs Family Leave Act," *Congressional Quarterly Almanac* (1993), p. 389.

43. "Parental-Leave Bill Moves Forward," *Congressional Quarterly*, 47 (April 15, 1989), p. 815.

44. "Buying Time: The Family Time Flexibility Act," *Atlanta Journal-Constitution*, May 4, 2003, p. 6C.

45. Sheryl Gay Stolberg, "Compensatory Time Bill Retracted in House," *New York Times*, June 6, 2003, sec. A, p. 22.

46. "'Family Friendly' Bill to Foster Comp Time Flexibility Gets Laid Off House Schedule," *Congressional Quarterly Weekly* (2003), pp. 1388–1389.

47. Donna Lenhoff and Sharon Stoneback, "Review of State Legislation Guaranteeing Jobs for Family or Medical Leaves," Partnership for Women and Families, August 1989, pp. 5–6; *New York Times*, July 27, 1990, p. A8; and "Family and Medical Leave Legislation in the States," Partnership for Women and Families, June 1991.

48. Commission on Family and Medical Leave, "A Workable Balance: Report to Congress on Family and Medical Leaves," April 1996, p. 85.

49. Aitchison, *The FMLA: Understanding the Family and Medical Leave Act: A Practical Common-sense Guide to the Nation's Family Leave Law* (Labor Relations Information System Publications, 2003), p. 84.

50. Aitchison, *The FMLA*, p. 207.

51. Anonymous staff interview with author, June 7, 2004.

52. "Comments of The United States Chamber of Commerce Regarding the Interim Regulations Implementing the Family and Medical Leave Act of 1993," provided by Nancy Reed Fulco, Human Resources Attorney, U.S. Chamber of Commerce.

53. Donna Lenhoff, General Counsel, Women's Legal Defense Fund, August 12, 1997, telephone interview.

54. Aitchison, *The FMLA*, p. 3.

55. As a practical matter it is very difficult to define serious illness. Even terminally ill patients may not be bedridden and advocates were very reluctant to create a definite list of covered conditions that would inevitably be incomplete.

56. In October 1997, the CCWI celebrated its twentieth anniversary with a gala attended by then President Clinton and Secretary of State Madeleine Albright. Ten of the fifteen founding members were present, as well as former co-chairs Patricia Schroeder and Senator Olympia Snowe.

57. Anonymous staff interview with author, June 7, 2004.

58. Primmer interview, July 28, 1989.

59. Anonymous staff interview with author, June 7, 2004.

60. Radigan interview, October 18, 1985.

FURTHER READING

Burrell, Barbara C. *Public Opinion, The First Ladyship and Hillary Clinton* New York: Garland Publishing Co., 2001.

Carroll, Susan J. *The Impact of Women in Public Office.* Bloomington: Indiana University Press, 2001.

Carroll, Susan J. *Women & American Politics, New Questions, New Directions.* Cambridge: Oxford University Press, 2003.

Costain, Anne N. *Inviting Women's Rebellion: A Political Process Interpretation of the Women's Movement.* Baltimore: Johns Hopkins University Press, 1992.

Costello, Cynthia B. and Anne J. Stone, Eds. *The American Woman 2001–2002: Getting to the Top.* New York: WW Norton Press, 2003.

Edelman, Marian Wright, *Families in Peril: An Agenda for Social Change* Cambridge: Harvard University Press, 1987.

Fried, Mindy. *Taking Time: Parental Leave Policy and Corporate Culture.* Philadelphia: Temple University Press, 1998.

Ford, Lynne E. *Women and Politics: The Pursuit of Equality.* New York: Houghton Mifflin Co., 2002.

Hammond, Susan Webb. *Congressional Caucuses in National Policy Making.* Baltimore: Johns Hopkins University Press, 1998.

Hewlett, Sylvia Ann, Nancy Rankin and Cornell West, Eds. *Taking Parenting Public: The Case for a New Social Movement.* Lanham, MD: Rowman & Littlefield Publishers, 2002.

Klein, Ethel. *Gender Politics: From Consciousness to Mass Politics.* Cambridge, MA: Harvard University Press, 1984.

Malveaux, Julianne and Deborah Perry. *Unfinished Business: The 10 Most Important Issues Facing Women Today.* New York: Penguin, 2002.

McGlen, Nancy E., et al. *Women, Politics, and American Society,* 4th edition. New York: Longman. 2005.

USEFUL WEB SITES

Members of Congress and Government Web Sites

Congressional Caucus for Women's Issues—www.womenspolicy.org/caucus/leadership.html

Congresswoman Judy Biggert (R-IL)—www.biggert.house.gov

Senator Christopher Dodd (D-CT)—www.dodd.senate.gov

Senator Judd Gregg (R-NH)—www.gregg.senate.gov

Congresswoman Carolyn Maloney (D-NY)—www.house.gov/maloney

Congresswoman Lynn Woolsey (D-CA)—www.woolsey.house.gov

U.S. Department of Labor Fact Sheet—www.dol.gov/esa/regs/compliance/whd/whdfs28.htm

U.S. Department of Labor FMLA Survey 2000—www.dol.gov/asp/fmla/chapter3.htm & www.dol.gov/asp/fmla/chapter4.htm

California Paid Family Leave—www.edd.ca.gov/direp/pflind.asp

Employer and Personnel Organizations Web Sites

U.S. Chamber of Commerce—www.uschamber.com/government/priorities.htm

FMLA Technical Corrections Coalition—www.workingforthefuture.org

Society for Human Resource Management—www.shrm.org

National Federation of Independent Business—www.nfib.com

Labor and Women's Organizations Web Sites

Women's Policy Inc.—www.womenspolicy.org

National Partnership for Women and Families—www.nationalpartnership.org

AFL-CIO Labor Union Organization—www.aflcio.org

Paid Leave Clearinghouse—www.paidleave.org

9 to 5, National Association of Working Women—www.9to5.org

American Association of University Women—www.aauw.org

Sex at Risk in Insurance Classifications? The Supreme Court as Shaper of Public Policy

Ruth Bamberger

Since the onset of the women's movement in the late 1960s, the private insurance industry has been confronted by civil rights groups, particularly feminist organizations, and government agencies over the treatment of insurance consumers whose risk potential is determined in part by sex classification. Numerous studies by congressional committees, state insurance commissions, and feminist *ad hoc* groups revealed practices whereby women in the same occupation, age, and health categories as men, were subjected to demeaning underwriting criteria, denied equal access to coverage and benefits, particularly in health and disability insurance, and charged higher prices. Sex-based prices also affected men adversely, particularly in life and in auto insurance (for young men), with higher prices charged than for women.

As a result of political pressures, most of the fifty states have adopted insurance regulations nominally prohibiting differential treatment in coverage and benefits of men and women.[1] But sex is still widely used as a classification in setting prices for individual health, life, disability, auto, and retirement insurance. Only one state, Montana, prohibits by law the use of the sex classification for any purpose, including pricing.[2] Five other states ban the sex classification only in auto insurance, where it is seen to disadvantage young men.[3] Selective prohibition of sex discrimination and inattention to the disparate economic impact of sex-divided pricing, especially on women by the insurance industry, are presently legally defensible in the absence of a constitutional presumption that the sex classification violates women's right to equal protection of the law.

The insurance industry's reluctance to forego the sex classification is a direct consequence of insurance marketing methods which use classifications to exclude some customers and price-compete for others. Actuarial tables demonstrate that women and men have different morbidity and mortality experiences, though some studies conclude otherwise.[4] The sex classification, selectively used, promotes the impression that classifications are driven by costs, not selling strategies. Most companies charge women higher prices for health, disability, and retirement plans, while men pay higher prices for life insurance, and young men pay more for auto insurance These price differences originated as sales discounts and continue to serve that function. However, in auto insurance, women's discounts cease around age twenty-five, although men at every age average more accidents than women, because their average annual mileage is higher than women's.

The Insurance Project of the National Organization for Women (NOW) has developed model legislation to eliminate the sex classification, and give the insured the option of purchasing auto insurance based on per mile driven rather than on a fixed annual rate. Women across all ages would pay lower premiums than men, because they drive fewer miles. In 2002, Texas adopted a law encouraging the per mile option; however, it is not mandatory.[5]

CRITIQUE OF INSURERS' USE OF THE SEX CLASSIFICATION

Criticisms of the insurance industry's use of the sex classification are numerous. The most basic is its acceptance of sex as an *a priori* differential. Simply stated, sex is used to justify using sex. What actuarial data tell us then is something about the average woman or man, but applications of these averages to individuals grossly distorts the reality, with unequal treatment the result.[6] Stated another way, emphasis on the sex classification allows other meaningful factors to be overlooked.

Critics also argue that continued use of the sex classification perpetuates traditional stereotypes of men and women. For example, underwriting manuals well into the 1970s labeled women as ". . . malingerers, marginal employees working mainly for convenience, and delicately balanced machines eagerly awaiting a breakdown. . . . If a woman has disability coverage, the temptation exists to replace her earnings with an insurance income once work loses its attractiveness."[7]

Finally, insurers should not use a classification scheme over which the insured have no control. Sex, like race, is an immutable characteristic, and therefore, should not be used as a basis for determining costs and coverage of insurance policies. Critics document insurance practices prior to the civil rights movement where race was casually employed as a classification. More importantly for insurers, the practice was actuarially justified because blacks have higher morbidity and mortality rates. However, race, because it was recognized as a repugnant classification placing a badge of inferiority on blacks, ceased to be used as a classification. The same constraint should apply to the sex classification, critics argue, though in some respects, racial discrimination has been more invidious than sex discrimination.[8]

The unfairness of sex as a classification can be illustrated in a directive before the European Union in late 2003. The EU Commissioner for Employment and Social Affairs submitted a wide ranging proposal to member states to eliminate the sex classification in all manner of goods and services purchased in the private sector. The Commissioner argues that "the separation of women and men into different pools leads to an unjustified difference of treatment and a resulting disadvantage for one sex or the other."[9] This proposal was tabled in 2003 because of strong negative reaction from the insurance industry; but the ministers of social affairs will be debating it in the near future. If it is adopted, pressure for such action could arise on this side of the Atlantic for U.S. insurers to do the same.

FEDERAL COURTS AND SEX DISCRIMINATION IN INSURANCE

Even though the campaign to eliminate sex discrimination in insurance has been waged largely at the state level, where the insurance industry is regulated, a major vehicle for challenging industry practice has been the federal courts via Title VII of the Civil Rights Act of 1964. The law states that it is an unlawful employment practice for an employer ". . . to fail or refuse to hire or to discharge any individual, or otherwise to discriminate against any individual with respect to compensation, terms, conditions, or privileges of employment, because of such individual's race, color, religion, sex, or national origin. . . ."[10] The Equal Employment Opportunity Act of 1972 broadened Title VII to include in the definition of employer government agencies at the state and local levels.

Since many companies and government agencies provide compensation by way of insurance products to their employees (over 80% of all employees are enrolled in employer-sponsored health, disability, and pension plans), sex-based insurance plans became a visible target for calling into question the common practice of classification by sex. Civil rights and feminist groups surmised that if the federal courts would strike down sex-based employer plans that affected large numbers of people, this would have a spillover effect on the insurance industry in its sales of individual policies. A careful examination of Supreme Court opinions in key cases provides clues about the direction of public policy in the controversy over the sex classification in insurance.

WOMEN AND THE SEX CLASSIFICATION IN DISABILITY, PRESCRIPTION, AND PENSION PLANS

Beginning in the 1970s, the Supreme Court decided several cases that have played a major role in defining the parameters of sex classification schemes in disability and pension plans. The disability cases, *Geduldig v. Aiello* (1974) and *General Electric v. Gilbert* (1976), raised the question of whether employer sponsored disability plans excluding pregnancy constituted unlawful sex discrimination.[11] In both cases, the majority of the Court upheld the plans, arguing that the pregnancy exclusion was not a sex-based classification, but a classification of "pregnant . . . and non-pregnant persons."[12]

Gedulig and *Gilbert* demonstrated the unwillingness of the Court to undo established insurance practices. The insurance industry has never considered normal pregnancy a disability, moreover, it argued in *Gilbert* that if pregnancy were included in an employee group plan, it would significantly drive up employers' costs.[13] Public reaction after *Gilbert* was so great that in 1978, Congress passed the Pregnancy Discrimination Act as an amendment to Title VII, requiring employers with disability plans to include pregnancy benefits.[14]

More recently, Title VII and the Pregnancy Discrimination Act have been used to challenge company policies that do not cover birth control in their prescription insurance plans. In 1997, the Equity in Prescription Insurance and Contraception Coverage Act was introduced in Congress for the first time. In 1999, the Senate Committee on Health, Education, Labor and Pensions held hearings on the bill; the measure had forty-two co-sponsors, but no action ensued.[15] The Equal Employment Opportunity Commission (EEOC), state legislatures, and federal courts have proved to be more effective venues for women. In 2000, the EEOC issued regulations requiring companies of fifteen or more employees to cover birth control in their prescription drug insurance plans. Through May of 2003, twenty-one states have adopted laws similar to the EEOC directive.[16]

In 2001, a federal district court in Washington state issued a ruling that if an employer (in this case, Seattle-based Bartell Drug Company) does not cover prescription contraceptives in its comprehensive health insurance plan, this constitutes sex discrimination in violation of Title VII and the Pregnancy Discrimination Act.[17] This landmark decision and the EEOC directive triggered litigation against a number of large companies, including United Parcel Service, Wal-Mart, CVS pharmacies, Dow Jones and American Airlines. (The AA plan included Viagra but not contraceptives!)[18] The Supreme Court has not been involved in any such cases, but could at some point do so, especially if lower court decisions conflict with one another.

With respect to pension plans, the Supreme Court in 1978 considered the validity of a sex differential in an employee retirement plan in *Los Angeles Department of Water and Power v. Manhart*.[19] The case involved a pension program of the LA Department whereby women made larger contributions from their salaries to the pension fund than men, on the basis that women as a class live longer than men. The Department had calculated from a study of mortality tables and its own employee experience, that women should contribute 14.84% more per monthly pay than men, since they would draw more monthly payments from the fund over their average life span. (Women live longer than men.) The Court struck down the plan on a 6–2 vote. The central argument of the majority opinion, written by Justice Stevens, was that Title VII specifically prohibits discrimination against any individual on the basis of sex, and therefore it is illegal to treat one gender group differently from the other.

Although it appears that Stevens was attacking the common insurance practice of classifying by sex, he tempered the majority opinion by stating that Title VII was not intended to "revolutionize" the insurance industry:

> All that is at issue today is a requirement that men and women make unequal contributions to an employer-sponsored pension fund. Nothing in our holding implies that it would be unlawful for an employer to set aside equal retirement contributions for each employee and let each retiree purchase the largest benefit which his or her accumulated contributions could command in the open market. Nor does it call into question the insurance industry practice of considering the composition of an employer's work force in determining the probable cost of a retirement or death benefit plan.[20]

In 1983, the Supreme Court reaffirmed *Manhart in Arizona Governing Committee v. Norris,* though by a narrower margin of 5–4.[21] The state of Arizona's retirement plan differed from the Los Angeles plan, in that employee contributions were not determined by sex, but upon retirement, women's monthly payments were lower because of their longer life expectancy. The plan provided employees with three options at retirement—a lump sum benefit, a fixed monthly payment over a specific number of years, or a lifetime annuity. Women's benefits under the first two options were the same as men's, but the lifetime annuity option gave women a smaller monthly payment than men. The litigant in the case, Natalie Norris, in opting for the lifetime annuity, would be paid $320 per month at age sixty-five, while a man in an identical situation would collect $354.

Justice Marshall, who wrote the majority opinion, reaffirmed the Court's position in *Manhart:* "We have no hesitation in holding . . . that the classification of employees on the basis of sex is no more permissible at the payout stage of a retirement plan than at the pay-in stage."[22]

In defending the retirement plan, the state of Arizona contended that Title VII was not applicable in this case, since retirement options were being offered through a third party (an insurance company) whose policies were comparable to what was available in the open market. The Court rebutted this argument by noting that when the state entered into such an agreement, it was the responsible agent for employee pension plans, and hence subject to Title VII requirements.

It should be noted that Justice Powell, who voted with the majority in *Manhart,* was on the minority side in *Norris,* precisely because the Arizona plan was provided by a third party insurer. He argued that striking down such a plan, where the insurer used actuarially sound sex-based mortality tables, amounted to revolutionizing the insurance and pension industries, which *Manhart* went out of its way to avoid.[23]

MEN AND THE SEX CLASSIFICATION IN PENSION PLANS

The Supreme Court decisions in *Manhart* and *Norris* ended discriminatory treatment for women in a prospective manner, but they did not get retroactive relief of any kind. The Court grandfathered into the future unequal payments to women already retired. Likewise the contributions made by women still employed did not apply to the ruling.

Two years before the *Manhart* decision, however, the Supreme Court was more generous with men in the settlement of a dispute over a retirement plan for Connecticut state employees. The case, *Fitzpatrick v. Bitzer* (1976), was brought by current and retired male employees of the state on the allegation that the statutory retirement plan discriminated against them on the basis of their sex.[24] The Connecticut plan allowed female employees with over twenty-five years of service to the state to retire at age fifty with full retirement benefits, while men were not eligible until age fifty-five. Reduced retirement benefits were also available to employees who left state employment before they were eligible to retire. The plan adversely affected men, who, if they left at age fifty-five, would receive less than a woman of similar age, who could already be drawing full benefits after age fifty. The Court not only struck down the retirement plan on Title VII grounds, but concluded that all retirees and survivors were entitled, under the protection of the Fourteenth Amendment, to retroactive payments dating back to the adoption of the pension program in 1939.

Surprisingly, the Supreme Court did not cite the *Fitzpatrick* decision in either *Manhart* or *Norris*. All three cases involved violations of Title VII of the Civil Rights Act of 1964, as amended in 1972. The awarding of back pay to male employees in the *Fitzpatrick* decision was rendered on Fourteenth Amendment grounds, namely, that Congress could require states to correct sex discrimination practices, even if the costs were significant.[25]

FITZPATRICK, MANHART, NORRIS AND THEIR AFTERMATH

The Supreme Court's decisions on sex discrimination in group retirement plans have had a wide impact on employer-sponsored plans. The TIAA-CREF retirement plan for college teachers and staff is a case in point.[26] The system of unequal payments to men and women retirees had been in the federal court pipeline for several years prior to *Norris* in 1983. On the same day the Supreme Court handed down its decision in *Norris,* it remanded to the appellate courts two cases challenging the TIAA-CREF plan. As a result, all TIAA-CREF participants now receive unisex benefits on annuity income payments made after May 1,1980.[27]

On the question of retroactive payments to employees, the Supreme Court, on a 9–0 vote, granted relief to all male retirees and their survivors in *Fitzpatrick,* but was less kindly disposed to female retirees in *Manhart* and *Norris*. In *Manhart,* seven justices argued against retroactive pay. Justice Stevens, speaking for the majority, alluded to a precedent in *Albemarle Paper Co. v. Moody,* where the Court established generous guidelines for awarding back pay for Title VII, but that it was not to be given automatically in every case.[28] Granting retroactivity in a case like *Manhart* would not be practical, according to Stevens, as pension plans could be jeopardized by drastic changes in the rules.[29] It was enough of a blow to employers to adapt to the Court's decision requiring equal contributions from men and women.

In *Norris,* the number of justices arguing against retroactive payments was reduced to five, while four supported some kind of retroactive relief. Justice O'Connor, whose vote was crucial in the 5–4 vote striking down the Arizona plan, did not go along with the four justices who thought that relief should apply to all benefit payments made after the federal District Court's judgment in *Norris.* O'Connor maintained, as Stevens did in *Manhart,* that the magnitude of a decision awarding retroactive relief would have the effect of disrupting pension plans.[30] In contrast, retroactive relief for male employees in *Fitzpatrick* was awarded. The Supreme Court granted men equal protection of the law under the Fourteenth Amendment in *Fitzpatrick,* but denied this protection under Title VII to women in *Manhart* and *Norris* under Title VII.

PROSPECTS FOR ELIMINATION OF THE SEX CLASSIFICATION IN INSURANCE

One immediate consequence of the *Manhart* and *Norris* decisions was the introduction of bills in Congress in the late '70s and early '80s to prohibit insurance companies nationwide from using the sex classification in determining coverage, benefits and prices. Known as the Non-Discrimination in Insurance Act in the House and the Fair Insurance Practices Act in the Senate,[31] the bills were introduced under Congress's prerogative in the McCarran-Furgeson Act,[32] and its authority to regulate interstate commerce and to legislate in matters of civil rights. While the bills received wide support from women's groups and organizations such as the American Association of University Professors, the American Association of Retired Persons, and the Leadership Conference on Civil Rights, the insurance industry waged an expensive lobby campaign to kill the proposal and was successful.[33]

Thus far, most state Equal Rights Amendments and equal protection provisions have failed to protect women against sex discrimination in insurance. The insurance industry continues to use sex in setting premium rates, despite the numerous efforts of women's organizations to reverse public policy.[34]

THE SUPREME COURT AND PROSPECTS FOR ELIMINATING THE SEX CLASSIFICATION IN INSURANCE

It would be an overstatement to say that the Supreme Court has been the primary mover and shaker in shaping public policy on sex discrimination in the insurance industry. But one could cogently argue that in the American constellation of political decision-makers, it has been a strategic actor. The Court's decisions in *Fitzpatrick, Manhart,* and *Norris* serve notice to the insurance industry that sex discrimination in insurance, especially in pricing premiums, merits greater scrutiny. At the same time, the Court has also made it clear that it will not revolutionize the insurance industry by eliminating sex as a category in the pricing of insurance products.

Women's rights and civil rights organizations must look beyond the judiciary to eliminate the practice of sex discrimination in pricing insurance products. One avenue is a reintroduced Equal Rights Amendment to the Constitution that incorporates a legislative history clearly articulating that the scope of equal rights for women and men applies to the insurance industry. Sex, just like race, would be excluded because it is unconstitutional. However, prospects for adopting an ERA faded when the time for ratification expired in 1982. In the meantime, pushing for incremental change is the best alternative, as is demonstrated in women's groups current efforts to incorporate birth control medications in prescription coverage.

NOTES

1. Primary regulation of the insurance industry rests with the fifty states. This arrangement dates back to the middle nineteenth century, when individual states legislated regulatory agencies to oversee the growing business of insurance. The McCarran-Furgeson Act, passed by Congress in 1945, reaffirmed state regulation, though not exclusively. Congress reserved for itself the authority to enact legislation under the following clause in McCarran: "No Act of Congress shall be construed to invalidate, impair, or supersede any law enacted by any state for the purpose of regulating the business of insurance . . . unless such Act specifically relates to the business of insurance." 15U.S.C. 1012(b) (1982).

2. Montana Code Ann. 49-2-309 (1983). ACLU Fact Sheet. www.aclu-mass.org/legis/S804H2534.html

3. Hawaii, Massachusetts, Michigan, North Carolina, Pennsylvania. For path-breaking work on automobile insurance sex discrimination, see Patrick Butler, Twiss Butler, and Laurie Williams, "Sex-divided Mileage, Accident, and Insurance Cost Data Show That Auto Insurers Overcharge Most Women," 6 *Journal of Insurance Regulation*, 243–284 (Part I), 373–420 (Part II), 1988. While Butler notes that men pay larger premiums from 16–25, he argues that over a lifetime, women are charged more because they drive less.

4. See U.S. Congress, Joint Economic Committee, *Hearings, Economic Problems of Women,* 93rd Cong., 1st Sess., 1973, pp. 151–220; "The Weaker Sex," *Life Notes,* National Association of Life Underwriters, April, 1974; California Commission on the Status of Women, *Women and Insurance,* 1975; ACLU Fact Sheet, *loc. cit.*

5. *National NOW Times,* Summer, 2002. www.now.org/nnt/summer-2002/cents/html. *supra,* 3.

6. An excellent example is the sex differential used in dental and vision care insurance. No medical explanations are available to verify differences in men and women. Yet the insurance industry uses the sex classification anyway, and indeed has established a differential, with the result that women pay higher rates. Robert Randall, "Risk Classification and Actuarial Tables as They Affect Insurance Pricing for Women and Minorities," in *Discrimination Against Minorities and Women in Pensions and Health, Life, and Disability Insurance.* Vol. I. U.S. Commission on Civil Rights, 1978, pp. 568, 576.

To further illustrate, studies of mortality differences by sex show a considerable overlap between men and women with respect to the age at which death occurs. For over 80% of males, one can find a matching female who died at approximately the same time. Sex is not a reliable predictor of mortality, so that it would be misleading even to talk about an average man or average woman. For reference to the debate over overlapping death rates of men and women, see Spencer Kimball, "Reverse Sex Discrimination: *Manhart,*" 83 *Amer. Bar Foundation Research Journal,* 120–23 (1979), and Lea Brilmayer et al., "Sex Discrimination in Employer-Sponsored Insurance Plans: A Legal and Demographic Analysis," *University of Chicago Law Review,* 530–31 (1980).

7. Quoted in Susanne Stoiber, "Insured: Except in Case of War, Suicide, and Organs Peculiar to Females," *Ms.,* June, 1973, p. 114.

8. Anne C. Cicero, "Strategies for the Elimination of Sex Discrimination in Insurance," *Harvard Civil Rights-Civil Liberties Review,* 211 (1985); Brilmayer et al., "Sex Discrimination . . . ," 526–29; Jill Gaulding, "Race, Sex, and

Genetic Discrimination in Insurance: What's Fair?" 80 *Cornell Law Review,* 1682 (1995).

9. Informa Publishing Group Ltd, "Equality Guaranteed—At Any Cost." *Insurance Day,* December 23, 2003.

10. 42 U.S.C. 2000e-2(a) (1).

11. *Gedulig v. Aiello,* 417 U.S. 484 (1974). This case, challenging a California state disability plan, was argued on 14th Amendment equal protection grounds. With the exception of *Fitzpatrick v. Bitzer,* 427 U.S. 445 (1976), *infra* 17, which was argued on both Title VII and 14th Amendment grounds, other federal court cases were argued on Title VII grounds only; *General Electric v. Gilbert,* 429 U.S. 125 (1976).

12. 417 U.S. at 496–497 n. 20.

13. 429 U.S. at 131.

14. Pregnancy Discrimination Act as codified at 42 U.S.C. 2000e (k) (1982).

15. National Women's Law Center, September 10, 2001. www.nwlc.org/details.cfmid=880&section=newsroom. *Employment Litigation Reporter,* "Exclusion of Prescription Contraceptives from Employer Health Plans May Violate Federal and State Laws," May 28, 2002. http://web.lexis-nexis.com/universe/document? m=a865 b7fee085abf4693576d816aef61fe.

16. Joanna Grossman, "Insurance Coverage for Birth Control: The EEOC Speaks." *Findlaw's Legal Commentary.* http://writ.news.findlaw.com/grossman/2001-0102.html. PR Newswire, "Women in Illinois Finally Get Fair Insurance Coverage for Contraceptives . . . ," May 29, 2003. www.prnewswire.com.

17. *Erickson v. Bartell Drug Co.,* 141 F.Supp. 1d 1266 (W.D. Wash., 2001).

18. *Employment Litigation Reporter, loc.cit.;* Nell Smith, "Suit Wants Wal-Mart to Pay for the Pill, Birth Control Not in Health-Care Plan," *Arkansas Democrat-Gazette,* October 6, 2002, p. 69.

19. *Los Angeles Department of Water and Power v. Manhart,* 435 U.S. 702 (1978).

20. *Ibid.,* 717–18.

21. *Arizona Governing Committee v. Norris,* 463 U.S. 1073 (1983).

22. *Ibid.,* at 1081.

23. *Ibid.,* at 1099.

24. *Fitzpatrick v. Bitzer,* 427 U.S. 445 (1976). The significance of this decision was first described by Ruth Weyand, who was a senior attorney with the federal Equal Employment Opportunity Commission. See the 14th *National Conference on Women and the Law Sourcebook* at 303–04 for Weyand's list of Title VII pension cases that ended early retirement pay discrimination against men with back pay before the retirement pay discrimination against women was ended without back pay.

25. A U.S. District Court's opinion on attorney's fees stated that the *Fitzpatrick* settlement would eventually cost Connecticut almost $400 million over forty years. 445 *F. Supp.* 1338, 1343 (D. Conn., 1978).

26. *Teachers Insurance and Annuity Association v. Spirt* and *Long Island University v. Spirt,* 691 F. 2d 1064, 463 U.S. 1223 (1983); *Peters v. Wayne State University,* 691 F. 2d 235, 463 U.S. 1223 (1983).

27. For a complete summary of TIAA-CREF action after *Norris,* see *News from TIAA-CREF,* October 9, 1984.

28. *Albermarle Paper Co. v. Moody,* 422 U.S. 405 (1975).

29. 435 U.S. at 718–23.

30. 463 U.S. at 1109–11. Five years after *Norris,* the Supreme Court ruled that the state of Florida did not have to pay $43.6 million in retroactive payments to male state employees whose spouses shared in their pension plans prior to *Norris.* At dispute in this case was a plan where male employees with spouses were paid less than female employees with spouses on the basis that female spouses lived longer than the male spouses of female employees. *Florida v. Hughlan Long,* 56 *U.S. Law Week.* 4718–25 (1988).

31. For the House version of this legislation, see *Non-Discrimination in Insurance Act of 1983: Hearings on H.R. 100 Before the Subcommittee on Commerce, Transportation, and Tourism of the Committee on Energy and Commerce,* 98th Cong., 1st Sess. 1–15 (1983). H.R. 100 was significantly weakened through the adoption of an amendment that would exempt sex discrimination in individual private insurance contracts. For the Senate version of this legislative proposal, see *Fair Insurance Practices Act: Hearings on S. 372 Before the Committee on Commerce, Science, and Transportation,* 98th Cong., 1st Sess., 2–16 (1983).

32. *supra,* 1.

33. The campaign cost the industry almost $2 million. A group called the Committee for Fair Insurance Rates was financed by thirty-three companies for the expressed purpose of "educating" the public about the adverse consequences of H.R. 100 and S.372. Common Cause, *NEWS,* Sept. 21, 1983; *National Underwriter (Life and Health Edition),* Oct. 1, 1983, p. 2.

34. The National Organization for Women maintains an office in Washington committed to eliminating sex discrimination in insurance. Dr. Patrick Butler is Director of the NOW Insurance Project.

FURTHER READING

Abraham, Kenneth S. *Distributing Risk: Insurance, Legal Theory, and Public Policy.* New Haven, Conn.: Yale University Press, 1986.

Baird, Karen L. *Gender, Justice and the Health Care System.* New York: Garland Publishers, 1998.

Benston, George J. "The Economics of Gender Discrimination in Employee, Fringe Benefits: *Manhart* Revisited." *University of Chicago Law Review* 49 (1982), 489–542.

Benston, George J. "Discrimination and Economic Efficiency in Employee Fringe Benefits: A Clarification of Issues and a Response to Professors Brilmayer, Laycock, and Sullivan," Brilmayer, Lea et al. "The Efficient Use of Group Averages as Non-Discrimination: A Rejoinder to Professor Benston." *University of Chicago Law Review* 50 (1983), 222–279.

Butler, Patrick et al. "Sex-Divided Mileage, Accident, and Insurance Cost Data Show That Auto Insurers Overcharge Most Women." *Journal of Insurance Regulation* 6 (1988), 243–284, 373–420.

Comptroller General of the United States. *Economic Implications of the Fair Insurance Practices Act.* Report to Sen. Orrin Hatch et al., GAO/OCE-84-1, April 6, 1984.

Jerry, Robert H. II. "Gender and Insurance." in Conway, M. Margaret et al. *Women and Public Policy.* Washington D.C.: Congressional Quarterly Press. 1994, pp. 102–123.

Law, Sylvia A. "Sex Discrimination and Insurance for Contraception." *Washington Law Review* 73xxx (1998). www.crlp.org/pub_art_sylvialaw.html.

Marks, Alexandra. "Legal Battles Over Contraceptive Equity." *Christian Science Monitor.* Dec. 4, 2003, p. 1.

U.S. Commission on Civil Rights. *Discrimination Against Women and Minorities in Pensions and Health, Life, and Disability Insurance.* Vol. 1, 1978.

WEB SITES

American Civil Liberties Union-Mass. www.aclu-mass .org.

Employment Law Information Network. www.elinfonet.com.

Equal Emp. Opportunity Com. www.eeoc.gov/docs/decision-contraception.html.

Family Planning and Reproductive Health Assn .www.nfprha.org.

National Organization for Women. www.now.org.

National Women's Law Center. www.nwlc.org.

Planned Parenthood. www.plannedparenthood.org.

Affirmative Action and Women

Roberta Ann Johnson

Challenged from all sides, affirmative action, nevertheless, continues to live on as a highly charged issue. Debate about affirmative action has often been heated and emotional. It has generated discussions about "merit";[1] it has buried academics in Department of Labor statistics,[2] it has absorbed lawyers and historians in interpretation of congressional intent;[3] it has bogged down the public policy experts with implementation matters;[4] and it has stimulated hotly debated referenda.[5]

In what ways has a policy of affirmative action assisted women to become more fully integrated into schools, training programs, and jobs? We will explore that question by examining the history and future of affirmative action policy. This article will (1) define affirmative action, (2) detail the development of federal affirmative action guidelines, (3) describe Supreme Court decisions and congressional responses to affirmative action, (4) describe how the states and the lower courts have become battlegrounds on the issue of affirmative action, (5) consider the ways in which affirmative action is a woman's issue, and (6) consider the future of affirmative action.

AFFIRMATIVE ACTION DEFINED

Affirmative action is a generic term for programs that take some kind of initiative, either voluntarily or under the compulsion of law, to increase, maintain, or rearrange the number or status of certain group members, usually defined by race or gender, within a larger group. When these programs are characterized by race or gender preference, "especially when coupled with rigorously pursued 'goals,' [they] are highly controversial because race and gender are generally thought to be 'irrelevant' to employment and admissions decisions" and are "immutable characteristics over which individuals lack control."[6]

AFFIRMATIVE ACTION AND FEDERAL GUIDELINES

Significant moves to prohibit discrimination in the public sector began in the late 1930s and early 1940s, according to David Rosenbloom, who describes a series of executive orders, starting with the Roosevelt administration, that called for a policy of nondiscrimination in employment.[7] However, it is President John F. Kennedy's executive order, issued March 16, 1961, that is usually seen as representing the real roots of present-day affirmative action policy.[8] Executive Order 10,925 required government contractors to take affirmative action and established specific sanctions for noncompliance.[9] Nevertheless, even the order's principal draftsperson admitted that the enforcement process led to a great deal of complainant frustration.[10]

Before another executive order would be issued, civil rights exploded onto the public agenda. A march on Washington held on August 28, 1963, brought 200,000 black and white supporters of civil rights to the Capitol. In response to this and other demonstrations, and as a result of shifting public sentiment, President Kennedy sent a civil rights bill to Congress; it was passed in 1964, after his assassination. The Civil Rights Act of 1964 included in its provisions Title VI, which prohibited discrimination on the basis of race, color, or national origin by all recipients of federal funds, including schools, and Title VII, which made it unlawful for any employer or labor union to discriminate in employment on the basis of race, color, religion, sex, or national origin. Title VII also created the Equal Employment Opportunity Commission (EEOC) for enforcement in the private sector.

The following year, 1965, President Lyndon B. Johnson issued Executive Order 11,246 barring discrimination on the basis of race, color, religion, or national origin by federal contractors and subcontractors.[11] On October 13, 1967, it was amended by Executive Order 11,375 to expand its coverage to women. One major innovation of the order was to shift enforcement to the secretary of labor by creating an Office of Federal Contract Compliance (OFCC). Starting in 1968, the government established the enforceability of the executive order with legal action[12] and, for the first time, issued notices of proposed debarment (contract cancellation) using its administrative process.[13]

Prodded to be more specific about its standards, the OFCC began to spell out exactly what affirmative action meant in the context of the construction industry, and that became a model for all affirmative action programs.[14] During this period, President Richard Nixon played the role of champion of affirmative action, saving LBJ's executive order.

In 1968 the OFCC focused on blacks in the construction industry. The result was the Philadelphia Plan, which was developed in three stages. First, the OFCC required preaward affirmative action plans from low bidders in some labor market areas, like Philadelphia. But because there were no guidelines for acceptability, the industry pressured Congress, which stimulated an opinion from the comptroller general, who recommended that the OFCC provide minimum requirements and standards by which programs would be judged. The second or revised Philadelphia Plan was then developed. It required that contractors submit a statement of "goals" of minority employment together with their bids, which took into account the minority participation and availability in the trade, as well as the need for training programs. On September 23, 1969, the Labor Department issued its third and final set of guidelines for the Philadelphia Plan after having determined the degree to which there was discrimination in construction crafts. This final plan established ranges within which the contractor's goals had to fall and recommended filling vacancies and new jobs approximately on the basis of one minority craftsman for each nonminority craftsman.

The comptroller general found the revised plan illegal on the ground that it set up quotas. But the attorney general issued an opinion declaring the plan to be legal and advised the secretary of labor to ignore the comptroller general's opinion. The comptroller general then urged the Senate Subcommittee on Deficiencies and Supplementals to attach a rider onto its appropriations bill prohibiting the use of funds to pay for efforts to achieve specific minority employment goals. The Nixon administration lobbied hard in the House and succeeded in eliminating the rider. On reconsideration, the Senate also defeated the rider, and the Philadelphia Plan was saved.

In 1971 the Department of Labor issued general guidelines that had the same features as the Philadelphia Plan, making it clear that "goals and timetables" were meant to "increase materially the utilization of minorities and women," with underutilization being spelled out as "having fewer minorities or women in a particular job classification than would reasonably be expected by their availability. . . ."[15] The 1971 Department of Labor guidelines, called Revised Order 4, were to govern employment practices by government contractors and subcontractors in industry and higher education.

Hole and Levine, in *Rebirth of Feminism,* document the initial exclusion of women from the guidelines. In 1970 Secretary of Labor Hodgson even publicly remarked that he had "no intention of applying literally exactly the same approach for women" as was applied to eliminate discrimination against minorities.[16] However, because of publicity and pressure by women's groups, by April 1973 women were finally included as full beneficiaries in the Revised Order 4.

What is important about the Philadelphia Plan and the Department of Labor guidelines is that they established not only the principle but also the guidelines for the practice of affirmative action that other civil rights enforcement agencies and even the courts would follow.

During the 1970s, administrative changes strengthened affirmative action. The Office of Management and Budget enlarged and refined the definition of *minority group* and, under President Carter, affirmative action efforts were consolidated. By executive order on October 5, 1978, the OFCC went from overview responsibility, whereby each department had responsibility for the compliance of its own contractors (with uneven results), to consolidated contract compliance, whereby the OFCC was given enforcement responsibility over all contractors;[17] overnight, 1600 people who had been working for other departments were now working for Labor. The expanded program now was called the Office of Federal Contract Compliance Programs (OFCCP).

During the 1980s, there were attempts to weaken affirmative action. The Reagan administration publicly and continually criticized goals and timetables, calling them quotas.[18] By 1982 the OFCCP's budget and number of workers were significantly reduced. By 1983, while President Reagan used attitudes toward affirmative action as a litmus test to successfully reorganize the U.S. Commission on Civil Rights, his attempt to rescind or revise Executive Order 11,246 by specifically prohibiting numerical hiring goals was successfully stopped by opposition from within his own administration.[19] Nevertheless, during these years, the administration whittled away at the policy. In 1983 it instituted changes within the OFCCP that affected the agency's case determinations and remedies, although by January 1987 some of these changes were rescinded. On January 21, 1987, Joseph N. Cooper, director of the OFCCP, quit his job in protest. In an interview, he spoke candidly about the "number of officials in the Labor Department and elsewhere in the Administration who were intent on destroying the contract compliance program."[20]

While President George Bush, during his four-year term, was no friend to affirmative action, he seemed to oppose it for tactical political reasons rather than because of strident political ideology. Even Democratic President Bill Clinton, at first, seemed gun-shy when it came to affirmative action. Clinton abandoned Lani Guinier, his choice for director of the Civil Rights Division of the Justice Department, when she was portrayed by the media as the "quota queen." Although this characterization was untrue, Clinton quickly disassociated himself from Guinier and withdrew his nomination in the interest of maintaining his own centrist image.

Clinton seemed to have a change of heart during his second term in office. Affirmative action became a "friend of Bill's" by the end of 1997. This gave the issue and the president a lot of publicity. For example, when President Clinton hosted the first in a series of Town Hall meetings on race relations in Akron, Ohio, he created what newspaper reporters called "the most dramatic moment of the meeting" when he engaged in a heated exchange with the only outspoken opponent of affirmative action at that meeting. After the session, the Akron audience, consisting of college students, civic leaders, and business executives, was criticized for not including more divergent opinions on affirmative action. Within weeks, the president arranged for an official and well publicized White House meeting with some well known opponents of affirmative action. Another example of Clinton's well publicized support of affirmative action was his engagement with the issue at his long year-end presidential press conference on December 16, 1997. Affirmative action continued to be a much discussed public policy issue for Americans partially because President Clinton was publicizing and spinning it.[21] The topic came up but was not a major issue during the 2000 presidential campaign. Many voters were unable to discern any differences between Democrat Al Gore's "affirmative action" and Republican George W. Bush's "affirmative access."[22] Largely because of this confusion, as well as the relatively minor attention the candidates paid to affirmative action, few voters used this issue as the deciding criterion in casting their votes.

THE *BAKKE* DECISION AND OTHER COURT DECISIONS

Affirmative action policy for student admissions has its own unique history. The source is Title VI of the Civil Rights Act of 1964 and Title IX of the Educational Amendments of 1972, not Executive Order 11,246. Title VI *requires* affirmative action steps to be taken in admissions *only as a remedy* for past discrimination. However, most minority affirmative action admission programs were self-imposed.[23] Title IX (subpart B, section 106.17) of the Educational Amendments of 1972, which prohibits *sex* discrimination, also calls for affirmative steps to be taken to remedy "past exclusion." A case having to do with minority affirmative action in admissions became the most well known and celebrated test of the principle of affirmative action.

Justice Lewis Powell announced the *Bakke v. University of California* Supreme Court decision to a hushed courtroom on the morning of June 28, 1978. He said, "We speak today with notable lack of unanimity." In fact, the 154 pages of judicial text presented *six* separate opinions and *two* separate majorities.[24]

Allan Bakke wanted to be a medical doctor. In 1973, at age thirty-three, while employed as a full-time engineer, he applied to a dozen medical schools, one of which was the University of California—Davis, and was turned down by all of them. The next year, after a second rejection from the twelve medical schools, Bakke sued the University of California in the California Court system, claiming that Davis's use of racial quotas was what had excluded him from medical school.

The *Bakke* case was not a strong one for those who supported affirmative action. On trial was an admissions program that reserved 16 of its 100 places for minority students (Blacks, Hispanics, and Asians), which looked like an admissions "quota" system. Furthermore, the Davis Medical School was founded in 1968, so the school could not claim that affirmative action was a remedy for past years of discrimination.

In this case, fifty-eight amicus curiae briefs were filed, and "The Court seemed less a judicial sanctum than a tug of war among contesting lobbyists."[25] When the dust cleared, the Court found a way both to admit Allan Bakke, now age thirty-eight, to the Davis Medical School and to defend the practice of affirmative action. By a 5–4 margin, the Court rejected the Davis program with a fixed number of seats for minorities; but also, by a different 5–4 margin, the Court accepted race-conscious admissions as being consistent with the Constitution and with Title VI.[26]

OTHER COURT DECISIONS AFTER *BAKKE*

Two cases that followed *Bakke, Weber* in 1979 and *Fullilove* in 1980, helped clarify the legal picture on affirmative action. In a 5–2 decision in *Weber* (two Supreme Court members did not participate), it was ruled permissible under Title VII for the private sector voluntarily to apply a compensatory racial preference for employment.

Brian Weber was an unskilled laboratory employee at the Gramercy, Louisiana, plant of the Kaiser Aluminum and Chemical Corporation. In 1974, while blacks made up 39 percent of Gramercy's general labor force, at the Kaiser plant, only 2 percent of the 273 skilled craft workers were black. Kaiser instituted a training program for its unskilled workers, earmarking half the trainee openings for blacks until the percentage of black craftspeople corresponded to their proportion in the labor force. Weber had more seniority than some of the blacks chosen for the program. The Court, however, argued that Kaiser's affirmative action program was a reasonable response to the need to break down old patterns of segregation.

The following year, in *Fullilove,* the Supreme Court decided, 6–3, that a congressional affirmative action program, a 10 percent set-aside of federal funds for minority business people, provided in the Public Works Employment Act of 1977, was also permissible under the Constitution.

Fullilove v. Klutznick was decided during the summer of 1980.[27] Chief Justice Burger wrote the majority opinion, which found the "limited use of racial and ethnic criteria" constitutionally permissible when its purpose was to remedy the present effects of past racial discrimination. With this case, Father Mooney suggests that, with certain qualifications, the Supreme Court legitimized affirmative action as a policy for U.S. society.[28] But not so when it came to layoffs.

In 1984, when layoffs were concerned, the Court shifted from its permissive view on classwide "race conscious remedies." On June 12, 1984, the Supreme Court issued its decision in *Firefighters Local Union No. 1784 v. Stotts,* which focused on the extent to which seniority systems may be overridden as part of court-ordered relief to remedy discrimination in employment. It was a 6–3 decision.

Carl Stotts was a black firefighter in the Memphis, Tennessee, Fire Department. He brought a class action lawsuit into federal district court in 1977, alleging discriminatory hiring and promotion practices in the department. This resulted in a consent decree in 1980 requiring that the percentage of black employees in each job classification be increased to the proportion of blacks in the local labor force.

The next year, because of budget problems, the city began to make plans to lay off firefighters on a seniority basis (last hired, first fired). "Black firefighters asked the court to prohibit the layoff of black employees. The court ordered the city not to apply its seniority policy in a manner that would reduce the percentage of blacks in the department. The case was appealed to the Supreme Court."[29]

The Supreme Court said that the seniority system could not be disregarded in laying people off and that although there was protection for actual victims of discrimination, "mere membership in the disadvantaged class was an insufficient basis for judicial relief."[30] In other words, a seniority system could be used to lay people off even though many blacks would be the first to go. The same was true in *Wygant v. Jackson Board of Education,* which was decided May 19, 1986.

In *Wygant,* nonminority teachers in Jackson, Michigan, challenged their terminations under a collective bargaining agreement requiring layoffs in reverse order of seniority unless it resulted in more minority layoffs than the current percentage employed. This layoff provision was adopted by the Jackson Board of Education in 1972 because of racial tension in the community that extended to its schools. In a 5–4 decision, the court said that this system of layoffs violated the rights of the nonminority teachers even though (unlike the case of *Stotts*) it was a part of their collective bargaining agreement. Powell, writing for the Court, argued that he could not find enough to justify the use of racial classifications.[31] Affirmative action was not as important as seniority when it came to layoffs.

Nevertheless, the "principle" of affirmative action actually survived in the majority's opinion in *Wygant.* The Court again affirmed that under certain circumstances policies using race-based classifications were justified. It was just that, for the majority, these were not the right circumstances. Marshall's words written in his dissenting opinion ring true: "Despite the Court's inability to agree on a route, we have reached a common destination in sustaining affirmative action against constitutional attack."[32] His assessment was to be proved correct in the February 25, 1987, case *U.S. v. Paradise,* and in the March 25, 1987, case *Johnson v. Transportation Agency, Santa Clara County.*

In a 5–4 decision, in the *Paradise* case, the Court upheld a federal district court judge's order requiring Alabama to promote one black state police trooper for each white trooper from a pool of qualified candidates. Justice Brennan wrote the plurality opinion justifying the affirmative action program because of the "egregious" nature of previous bias against blacks. Justice Powell, in a concurring opinion, emphasized that the "quota" did not disrupt seriously the lives of innocent individuals; Justice Stevens's concurring opinion emphasized that the Court-imposed plans fell within the bounds of reasonableness, whereas the dissenters emphasized the undue burden the plan placed on the white troopers.

In the *Johnson* case, six of the nine Supreme Court Justices approved of Santa Clara county's affirmative action program. In 1978 Santa Clara's transit district's board of supervisors adopted a goal of a workforce whose proportion of women, minorities, and the disabled equaled the percentage of the country's labor force at all job levels. Women constituted 36.4 percent of the relevant labor market, and although women made up 22.4 percent of the district workers, they were mostly in clerical positions, with none in the 238 skilled jobs. In 1979 Diane Joyce and Paul

Johnson competed, along with five others who were all deemed "well qualified," for the job of dispatcher, a skilled position. They had all scored over 70, the passing grade, in an oral examination conducted by a two-person panel. Johnson tied for second with a score of 75, and Joyce ranked third with 73. After a second interview, first Johnson was chosen, but then, because of affirmative action considerations, Joyce got the job. Johnson sued, contending that he was better qualified. In 1982 a judge ruled that Johnson had been a "victim of discrimination." The Reagan administration joined attorneys for Johnson and appealed to the Supreme Court.[33]

Justice William Brennan, in writing for the Court, put its stamp of approval on voluntary employer action designed to break down old patterns of race and sex segregation. "'Given the obvious imbalance in the skilled craft category' in favor of men against women, Brennan said, 'it was plainly not unreasonable . . . to consider the sex of Ms. Joyce in making the promotion decision.'" Brennan called the affirmative action plan "a moderate, flexible case by case approach to effecting a gradual improvement in the representation of minorities and women in the agency's work force."[34] Justice Antonin Scalia responded with a scathing dissent, emphasizing the burden that falls on the "Johnsons of the country," whom he called "the only losers in the process."[35]

THE COURT AND THE PUBLIC ARE DIVIDED ON AFFIRMATIVE ACTION

The Supreme Court remained divided on affirmative action, and by a bare majority the Court supported affirmative action for purposes of hiring and promotion, but not to determine layoff lists. A Gallup Poll conducted in June 1987 following the *Johnson* decision showed that the public also continued to be divided on the issue of affirmative action and that the majority of those polled continued to be opposed (see Table 1).

TABLE 1   Affirmative Action Ruling—*Johnson v. Transportation Agency, Santa Clara County, CA,* 480 U.S. 616

	Approved	Disapproved	No Opinion
National	29%	63%	8%
Democrats	37	54	9
Republicans	22	74	4
Independents	27	64	9
Men	26	66	8
Women	32	59	9
Whites	25	67	8
Blacks	56	34	10
Hispanics	46	47	7

Source: George Gallup Jr., "Little Support for High Court Ruling on Hiring," *San Francisco Chronicle,* June 15, 1987.

Eight years in the White House allowed President Reagan to accomplish, with judicial appointments, what he was not able to do with judicial arguments. When Supreme Court justices retired, he used his power of appointment to add conservatives Sandra Day O'Connor and Antonin Scalia to the bench—and he appointed conservative William H. Rehnquist to be chief justice. Even so, as we have seen, affirmative action programs continued to win majority Court approval through 1987. Then, however, when Justice Powell, the "swing" vote, retired, and Reagan replaced him with conservative Anthony M. Kennedy, the Court was packed for the next affirmative action case.

On January 24, 1989, the Supreme Court announced its decision on the *Richmond v. Croson* case. The Court ruled, 6–3, that a 1983 Richmond, Virginia, ordinance that channeled 30 percent of public works funds to minority-owned construction companies violated the Constitution. Justice O'Connor, who wrote the majority opinion, argued that "laws favoring blacks over whites must be judged by the same constitutional test that applies to laws favoring whites over blacks"— namely, that classifications based on race are suspect and have to be scrutinized very carefully.

In scrutinizing this case, O'Connor did not see the necessary evidence of past discrimination that would justify using race-based measures. Black people made up 50 percent of the Richmond population, she noted, and although there was a "gross statistical disparity" between "the number of prime contracts awarded to minority firms and the minority population of the city of Richmond," still, she argued, this case does not "constitute a prima facie proof of a pattern of practice of discrimination." The appropriate pool for comparison is not the general population but the "number of minorities qualified to undertake the task," and O'Connor pointed out that the city did not know exactly how many minority business enterprises (MBEs) there were in the relevant market that were qualified to undertake prime or subcontracting work in public construction projects. Even if there were a low number of MBEs, she argued, maybe it was not because of discrimination but because of "black career and entrepreneurial choices." "Blacks may be disproportionately attracted to industries other than construction."[36]

Justice Thurgood Marshall, in his dissent, found it "deeply ironic" that the majority did not find sufficient evidence of past discrimination in Richmond, Virginia, the former capital of the Confederacy. "Richmond knows what racial discrimination is; a century of decisions by this and other Federal courts has richly documented the city's disgraceful history . . . ," he wrote, and Marshall defended, again, the use of race-conscious measures to redress the effects of prior discrimination.[37]

The *Richmond* case did not end the debate, but perpetuated the uncertainty surrounding affirmative action plans. Now such plans could stand only if they could survive strict judicial scrutiny—for example, if they were adopted to eliminate "patently obvious, egregious discrimination that can be linked to the deliberate acts of identifiable parties." Mere numerical disparities would not be enough. Experts predicted that the lower courts would be flooded with challenges to affirmative action by white plaintiffs.[38]

OTHER CASES THAT INFLUENCED AFFIRMATIVE ACTION

On June 5, 1989, the court again decided a case that would affect affirmative action policy. In *Wards Cove Packing v. Atonia,* the court ruled, 5–4, that plaintiffs who are not employers have the burden of proving whether a job requirement that is shown statistically to screen out minorities or women is a "business necessity." The case redrew the ground rules unanimously established by the Court in 1971, which prohibited not only employment practices *intended* to discriminate but also practices that had discriminatory *impact.*

The plaintiffs in this case were non-whites—Filipino and Alaskan native cannery workers who were channeled into lower-paid unskilled jobs. Noncannery jobs were filled by the company with predominantly white workers who were hired in Washington and Oregon. With these statistics showing disparate impact, and consistent with precedent, the lower court asked the salmon canneries to justify, on grounds of "business necessity," the business practice of flying in whites for managerial jobs and hiring local non-whites to work in the cannery. Justice Byron White, writing for the majority, overturned eighteen years of precedent. He said that the cannery business did not have to prove anything. It was up to the non-white cannery workers to disprove the company's claim that there was no discrimination.

Justice John Paul Stevens, in his dissent, called the decision "the latest sojourn into judicial activism," accusing the majority of "[t]urning a blind eye to the meaning and purpose of Title VII. . . ."[39]

One week after the *Wards Cove* decision, the court dealt an even more lethal blow to affirmative action. In *Martin v. Wilks,* five members of the court ruled that whites may bring reverse discrimination claims against judge-approved affirmative action plans. This meant that consent decrees, which settle many discrimination suits and had been thought to be immune from subsequent legal attack, were now fair game.

The *Martin v. Wilks* case had its roots in the early 1970s, when a local chapter of the National Association for the Advancement of Colored People (NAACP), supported by the federal government, sued the city of Birmingham, Alabama, on the grounds that blacks were being discriminated against in hiring and promotion in the city's fire department. Several years later a settlement was reached, although the union representing the "almost all white work force" objected to the settlement at the hearing.[40] The Federal District Court "approved the settlement and entered a consent decree under which blacks and whites would be hired and promoted in equal number until the number of black firefighters approximated the proportion of blacks in the civilian labor force." A few months later, fifty white firefighters sued the city, claiming discrimination. The Federal District Court dismissed the suit. In 1987 the Eleventh Circuit Court overturned that dismissal, a decision inconsistent with those of every other circuit court, and reinstated the white firefighters in the city of Birmingham; a group of black firefighters appealed to the Supreme Court.

Chief Justice William Rehnquist wrote the majority opinion, in which he agreed with the Eleventh Circuit Court, arguing that a decree could be binding only on parties who had been part of the original lawsuit. "Outside groups" could not be required to join such a suit, and if they were not bound by the decree, they could sue. Justice Steven's dissent pointed out that the Court's decision "would subject large employers who seek to comply with the law by remedying past discrimination to a never-ending stream of litigation and potential liability. He called the results 'unfathomable' and 'counterproductive.'"[41]

The next year, the Court rendered a decision supporting affirmative action. By a bare majority, the Supreme Court supported an affirmative action program in *Metro Broadcasting Inc. v. Federal Communications Commissions,* defending Congress' right to provide affirmative action for minorities and women in issuing broadcasting licenses. But, the composition of the Supreme Court was changing through retirements. Five years later, of the five justices favoring affirmative action in this case, only one, Justice John Paul Stevens, was still on the Court.

RESPONSES TO THE COURT DECISIONS

These decisions of the Court stimulated two important responses during the early 1990s. First, across the country, lawsuits were filed by white male workers who now had standing in the Court to allege that they had suffered reverse discrimination because of affirmative action programs, even programs that were court-imposed or that resulted from full trials. The effects were felt from San Francisco[42] to Birmingham.[43] The second important response to the Court's decisions came from Congress.

For six months, civil rights organizations and their congressional allies worked together to prepare legislation that would basically reverse three of the Supreme Court decisions, two that related to affirmative action, the *Wards Cove* case, "in which the Court ruled that . . . the plaintiff has the burden of proving that an employer had no business reason for a practice with discriminatory effects," and the *Martin v. Wilks* case, "in which the Court held that Court-approved affirmative action plans can be challenged as reverse discrimination. . . ."[44] The proposed legislation would also reverse another civil rights (but non-affirmative action) case, *Paterson v. McClean Credit Union,* "in which the Court ruled that an 1866 law prohibiting racial discrimination in contracts applies only to hiring agreements, not to on-the-job discrimination."[45]

The civil rights bill's sponsors, Senator Edward Kennedy (D-MA) and Representative Augustus Hawkins (D-CA), were confident about getting the majority necessary to pass the law. The challenge, which kept them negotiating behind closed doors, was to line up the sixty Senate cloture votes needed to shut off debate and to get the sixty-seven votes to guarantee override of a possible presidential veto. This civil rights bill, because it dealt with more subtle issues like "burden of proof" and "right to sue," was not as "sexy" as, for example, the Voting Rights Act, and the fear was that the supporting public might be less attentive to its fate.[46] Nevertheless, the White House watched closely.

At the end of May 1990, reporters were describing the "tough test" faced by the Bush administration. Although the president originally had warned he would veto the civil rights bill, by spring he was backing off from his threat. There seemed to be two reasons for his change of heart. First, it appeared that many Republicans in the Senate were ready to break with the White House to support the bill. The president's veto might not be sustained. The second reason for the president to look for compromise was his concern about his reelection. President Bush was eager to court the African American vote in 1992; in mid-1990, he had a 56 percent black approval rating and was the most popular Republican president among blacks since Dwight Eisenhower.[47] A compromise on the civil rights bill seemed likely. Thus, in 1990 it appeared that a committed pro–civil rights core in Congress and a pragmatic White House would help important elements of affirmative action to survive. But in the fall of 1990 President Bush vetoed the civil rights bill, and Congress was unable to override his veto. That December, Robert Allen, chairman of AT&T, arranged a private dinner between top business and civil rights leaders. A coalition of 200 top CEOs, the so-called Business Roundtable, voted to continue these talks, and both sides agreed to have lawyers meet to try to "hammer out their differences." Saving affirmative action and the civil rights bill now seemed probable.

The Bush administration, however, was unhappy with the prospect of such a compromise. Preparing for the presidential campaign of 1992, GOP strategists believed that a Republican anti–affirmative action position would be very effective and that a compromise bill would dilute the Republican political advantage on the quota issue. Therefore, the White House proceeded to destroy the business civil rights negotiations. Roundtable members were warned that their talks undermined business support for the president's version of a civil rights bill, and Chief of Staff John Sununu personally drummed up opposition among smaller companies. The White House campaign was blunt and vicious. Even Robert Allen came under personal attack from conservative columnist Pal Gigot in the *Wall Street Journal* because of his involvement. The participants who had seemed so hopeful buckled under the political pressure.[48] Then, a turn of events that no one could have predicted, made the passage of the congressional act virtually inevitable.

In Louisiana, an avowed racist and self-described Klan member, David Duke, became the Republican candidate for Senate. This represented a serious problem for the Republican party, which wanted desperately to disassociate themselves from him. Continuing with an anti–civil rights position, therefore, became problematic for Bush because such a position would seem too similar to Duke's position. Bush reversed himself on the civil rights bill; by the end of 1991, President Bush was on record supporting the civil rights legislation, and he signed it into law.

The Republican Party sought and failed to make affirmative action a *decisive* election issue in 1996. After the election, however, the issue continued to divide the two parties and exacerbate the problems inherent in the United States system of divided government. In 1997, President Clinton nominated Bill Lann Lee, a California attorney who supports affirmative action, to head the Justice Department's Civil

Rights Division. For months, Senator Orrin Hatch (R-Utah), Senate Judiciary Commit-tee Chair, and other Republican senators who objected to Lee's affirmative action position were successful in blocking a Senate confirmation vote. President Clinton circumvented their actions by nominating Lee as "Acting" Head of the Civil Rights Division after the Senate had recessed. But the controversy continued. "Lee's nomi-nation, which was hardly seen as controversial when it was made . . . evolved into a high profile clash over affirmative action, as well as an epic Washington power struggle between the Democratic White House and the Republican Senate."[49]

Meanwhile, the Supreme Court continued to make decisions that struck down affirmative action programs; nevertheless, the Court never struck down the *principle* of affirmative action. In 1995, in *Adarand v. Pena,* the High Court over-turned its *Metro Broadcasting* decision. In *Adarand,* the Court decided on the va-lidity of a program that benefitted minority- and women-owned highway construction businesses. The court held differential treatment because of racial or ethnic origin inherently suspect, and said that the government can adopt affirma-tive action programs only when it can demonstrate that they correct real and pre-sent discrimination.

In November 1997, the Supreme Court was prevented from deciding a case scheduled on their docket to be argued just six weeks later. The case originated in Piscataway, New Jersey. Eight years earlier, in a move to reduce the number of business school teachers, the Piscataway School District laid off on the basis of race Sharon Taxman, a white teacher, instead of Debra Williams, a black teacher who they deemed to be equivalent. Civil rights advocates worried that this was not a strong case for affirmative action. In fact, they feared that the Supreme Court might use it as a vehicle to declare affirmative action unconstitutional. In a surpris-ing move, the Piscataway School District paid Taxman $430,000 to settle her case and thus avoid its being heard by the Supreme Court. Civil rights groups con-tributed most of the settlement money. Like the *Wygant* case described earlier, in Piscataway, women teachers were pitted against each other when the operative af-firmative action basis was race.[50]

In 2003, the Supreme Court decided another landmark affirmative action case, *Grutter v. Bollinger,* concerning the admissions policy of the University of Michigan Law School.[51] Barbara Grutter, a white female applicant, had been rejected for ad-mission. Upon finding out that African-Americans and other racial minorities were accepted with lower overall admissions scores, she sued, alleging that she was a victim of illegal discrimination. Grutter's attorney argued that Michigan's "point sys-tem," wherein admissions departments award points for a variety of student charac-teristics, including race, was functionally identical to the quota system ruled unconstitutional in *Bakke*. The court was split 5–4, with Justice Sandra Day O'Con-nor casting the deciding vote. The majority found that point systems were not the same as quotas. Points were, afterall, also awarded based on geographic informa-tion, as well as family educational, and financial background. Moreover, the court found that the academic and social benefits of a diverse student body comprised a state interest compelling enough to warrant special considerations.

LOWER COURT CHALLENGES TO AFFIRMATIVE ACTION

The educational system has been especially hard hit by anti affirmative action law suits. In 1996, the Supreme Court left intact a ruling that threatened affirmative action programs at state run colleges in three states, Texas, Louisiana, and Mississippi. Although the Clinton administration, nine states, and the District of Columbia all filed amicus briefs supporting affirmative action in the case of *Texas v. Hopwood,* the Supreme Court let stand the lower court's decision, which effectively reversed the *Bakke* decision in those three states.

Affirmative action programs in school districts across the country are also being challenged in Court. In San Francisco, a 1982 Court supervised consent decree limiting the student enrollment of any ethnic group in each San Francisco school to 40 percent, is being challenged by Chinese American parents. The parents claim the policy denies their children admission to the kindergarten of their choice as well as to prestigious Lowell High School. In addition, in Boston, parents have sued the oldest American public school, Boston Latin, because of the school's affirmative action policy guaranteeing a certain number of Latino and black seats; in Arlington Virginia, the lower court has already ruled that using racial preferences to admit preschoolers to three magnet schools violated the Constitution; and in Houston, Texas, parents are suing the school district because their children were denied admission to a magnet school, Lanier Middle School, due to racial caps on enrollment.[52] Just as the lower courts are a central arena for affirmative action policy, states are also making policy.

State Action

Much of the current public conversation, legislative debate, and referenda activities on affirmative action are taking place in the states. While the Supreme Court has never rejected affirmative action principles, some states have tried and succeeded in outlawing affirmative action. California's successful attempt, via a referendum, has been the most well publicized. In November 1996, 54 percent of the California electorate voted in favor of proposition 209, what the proponents called the California Civil Rights Initiative. The Proposition prohibited the implementation of race- and gender-conscious affirmative action programs. As a result of the passage of "Prop 209," state-required affirmative action programs are now banned in California. However, in 1997, opponents of affirmative action in Houston, Texas, failed to get the same results. In November, a referendum simply asked voters if they wanted to end the city's affirmative action programs. Decisively, voters said "No."

Of course, the Texas vote did not put the issue to rest in other states. By January 1998, the state of Washington's opponents of affirmative action collected more than enough signatures to put the affirmative action issue on their November 1998 ballot. Their "Initiative 200," modeled after California's Proposition 209, was approved with 58 pecent of the vote.[53] There has since been debate as to how to desegregate school districts and to increase minority enrollment at state universities without using racial data.

In Florida, Governor Jeb Bush defused growing tensions over a proposed anti–affirmative action initiative by pushing for a separate plan to sharply restrict racial preferences in education and government contracts.[54] His "One Florida" plan, approved by the Florida Board of Regents, eliminated affirmative action from all state university admissions programs. In its place, the One Florida plan guaranteed state college acceptance to the top 10 percent of every high school's graduating class. Supporters of this policy have noted that over several years, minority enrollment has remained steady despite the absence of racial preferences. These cases suggest that it is likely that many of the future changes in affirmative action will be made at the state level. Moreover, clear answers will continue to be sought on the effects of such ballot measures on diversity.

AFFIRMATIVE ACTION: A WOMAN'S ISSUE

In only three of the major Supreme Court decisions were women the beneficiaries of the affirmative action programs in question. The *Johnson* case was specifically about the promotion of a woman in a program that provided affirmative action for women and minorities and the *Metro Broadcasting* case, and the *Adarand* case that overturned it, concerned programs whose beneficiaries were both women and minorities. All the other major Supreme Court cases concerned only minorities as beneficiaries. Not surprisingly therefore, the public is more likely to connect affirmative action to racial and ethnic minorities than to women. But affirmative action very clearly relates to women, in fact, women's very inclusion as beneficiaries came as a result of the efforts of women in politics.

In the beginning stages of affirmative action, women's rights organizations, such as the National Organization for Women (NOW) succeeded in getting women to be included as affirmative action beneficiaries. In 1967, when President Johnson amended the affirmative action Executive Order to include women, he did so as a response to their successful lobbying efforts; and in the early 1970s, when the rules of affirmative action were first being developed by the Department of Labor, it was only after women's groups effectively challenged and lobbied Labor that women, in 1973, became fully included in government guidelines.

However, the aim of affirmative action is the redistribution of benefits and opportunities. Has the program benefited women? Even with the Department of Labor guidelines, there is no guarantee that women as a protected class will be included in affirmative action pools, which are up to each employer to define.

As beneficiaries, industrywide figures consistently have painted a mixed picture for employed women under affirmative action. For example, Goldstein and Smith analyzed minority and female employment changes in over 74,000 separate companies between 1970 and 1972. They compared contractor and noncontractor companies with a presumption that federal contractors are more likely to conform to affirmative action goals. What they found surprised them.

Although, as expected, black males did economically better in employment in contractor companies between 1970 and 1972, so did *white males.* The big losers during these years were white women. Between 1970 and 1972, before the OFCC revised guidelines included women, white women not only showed no employment gains, they showed significant employment losses. In fact, white women's losses were equal in magnitude to the significant gains made by white males.[55]

Under the revised guidelines, it appears that the effect of including women in the federal affirmative action program, as a protected class, is mixed. From 1967 to 1980, for white women, "Rough stability prevailed over this period in their wages relative to white men," according to Smith and Welch. Sociologist Paul Burstein suggests an interesting explanation, rarely considered by economists, to account for why white women have not experienced a large wage advance under the 1972 guidelines. As a group, their "seeming decline" in income is probably due to the steady influx of relatively inexperienced female workers into the labor force. Women as a group are better off, but their average income drops.[56] The story on wages for black women is different. Between 1967 and 1980 the largest wage advances were achieved by black women, who went from earning 74 percent of the wage of similarly employed white women in 1967 to almost complete racial parity in 1980.[57] It has been suggested that "part of the reason for nonwhite women's gains . . . may be their having been so badly off initially that their jobs and incomes could improve considerably without posing any real threat to the normal workings of the economy."[58]

In a National Bureau of Economic Research paper, Jonathan Leonard studied the effectiveness of affirmative action for the employment of minorities and women.[59] Focusing on the period between 1974 and 1980, he also compared *contractor and noncontractor* establishments. Leonard compared the mean employment share of targeted groups and controlled for establishment size, growth, region, industry, occupation, and corporate structure. He found that members of protected groups grew faster in contractor than in noncontractor establishments, 3.8 percent faster for black males, 7.9 percent faster for other minority males, 2.8 percent for white females, and 12.3 percent for black females.[60] This suggests that affirmative action programs benefit black women and tend to help white women, though not as much as they benefit minorities.

When Leonard focused on the effect of compliance reviews—that is, the role they played over and above that of contractor status—he found that they advanced black males by 7.9 percent, other minority males by 15.2 percent, and black females by 6.1 percent. It *retarded* the employment growth of whites (including white women). Thus, he concluded, "*with the exception of white females,* compliance reviews have had an additional positive impact on protected group employment beyond the contractor effect."[61] His data also show that white women were not benefiting from affirmative action when it came to promotions.[62]

Leonard suggests an explanation for why white women's position in contractor companies has not improved significantly compared with noncontractor companies. It is that these women have so flooded the employment market that they have been hired in *both* contractor and noncontractor companies. As he says, "female [employment] share" has "increase[d] at all establishments because of the supply shift. . . ." Thus, his comparison of contractor and noncontractor hiring does not show the general large increase in white women hired. His explanation seems plausible considering the clear increase in the number of women employed, which is reflected by Bureau of the Census data for the period between 1970 and 1980.[63]

Although it appears that not all women have benefited directly from affirmative action, there are many specific cases where women (including white women) have directly benefited from an affirmative action approach. Affirmative action, with its emphasis on numbers and parity, can indirectly benefit women (including white women) because it inevitably shifts our focus from rhetoric to results. Thus, in some areas, such as academic admissions (which falls under Title IX protection), public scrutiny was all that was necessary to make possible a large redistribution of places to all women. Quoting McGeorge Bundy, Wilkinson wrote, "Since 1968 the number of women entering medical schools has risen from 8 percent to 25 percent of the total. A parallel increase has occurred in law schools. No constitutional issue is raised by this dramatic change, . . . the women admitted have had generally competitive records on the conventional measures."[64] By 2001, the number of women applying to law school surpassed fifty percent for the first time and the American Bar Association noted that more women than men actually entered law school.[65]

Even though they score competitively and have been highly successful, I am arguing that affirmative action has helped women get admitted to professional schools by focusing public attention on admissions criteria and admission results. In this context let us remember a Charlotte Perkins Gilman line in a poem that focuses on Socialist change. "A lifted world lifts women up," she wrote.

Thus, there is a mixed answer to the question "Does affirmative action benefit women?" Nonwhite women seem to have most clearly benefited directly from the program, but all women may be benefiting indirectly. Might affirmative action be a women's issue for reasons other than women's benefits?

Perhaps affirmative action could be seen as a woman's issue, in the tradition of social feminism, because it calls for a fairer distribution of social benefits. Of course, I am not suggesting that women be insensitive to the catalog of arguments, some of them practical, that have been made against affirmative action.[66] What I would suggest is that women (and men) be wary of falling into the trap of characterizing affirmative action as the "opposite" of a merit system. It is not. After all, proportionality is used even to select justices on the Supreme Court, where there may be a Jewish seat, a southern seat, a black seat, and now seats for two women.[67]

The major issue raised by affirmative action is not merit but redistribution. Allan Bakke's arguments were made against a special program benefiting minorities. Over and over he raised the flag of "fair competition," but Davis Medical School had another special program, which Bakke did not complain about—the dean's special admissions program "under which white children of politically well-connected university supporters or substantial financial contributors have been admitted in spite of being less qualified than other applicants, including Bakke."[68] Thus, the Bakke issue is not, and never was, special programs. The issue is who will be benefiting from these special programs—and that is a matter not of merit but of politics. And the country remains divided over this political question.

THE FUTURE OF AFFIRMATIVE ACTION

While the judicial system and state initiatives seem to be chopping away at the legal status of affirmative action, the public remains divided on the issue, and the national debate over affirmative action continues.

In December 1997, the *New York Times*/CBS News conducted a survey, asking virtually the same questions about affirmative action that they had been asking the public for over a decade. Since 1985, their surveys showed an erosion of support for "preferences" with a big drop in support in the late 1980s. Respondent's views on preferences for women were just as negative as their views on preferences for blacks. For example, in response to the question on preferential treatment, "Do you believe where there has been job discrimination in the past, preferences, in hiring and promotion should be given?" the response relating to blacks was almost the same strong negative one as the one relating to women; 37 percent respondents were for preferences for women, 35 percent were for preferences for blacks; 51 percent were against preferences for women, 52 percent were against preferences for blacks.

How can affirmative action have a future given such strong opposition to affirmative action preferences? While the *New York Times*/CBS News poll revealed strong opposition to preferential treatment, the survey also showed a public very much committed to diversity and the goals of affirmative action.

The polls revealed that a vast majority of the public does not want to see affirmative action abruptly ended. Only 12 percent want to see it "ended now" while 40 percent want it "phased out over the next few years" and 41 percent want affirmative action continued for the foreseeable future.

Furthermore, a large majority want special efforts to continue. Fully 63 percent favor "special education programs to assist minorities in competing for college admissions," and 69 percent favor "government financing for job training for minorities to help them get ahead in industries where they are underrepresented." As the *New York Times* summarizes it, "Asked what society should do with 'affirmative action programs giving preference to some minorities, people were much more inclined to say that they should be maintained or revised than they were to say that they should be abolished."[69] Americans seem to want to level the playing field. Fully 69 percent polled favor the continuation of anti-discrimination laws. Thus, it is clear that the majority of Americans want some elements of affirmative action to continue as a part of public policy. However, the public debate will likely focus more on black and Latino men and women and less on white women.

This is a revised version of an article that appeared in the Journal of Political Science, vol. 17, Nos. 1 and 2 (Spring 1989). Reprinted with permission. The author would like to acknowledge David Leong, a student at the University of San Francisco, for his assistance.

NOTES

1. See Allan P. Sindler, *Equal Opportunity: On the Policy and Politics of Compensatory Minority Preferences* (Washington, DC: American Enterprise Institute for Public Policy Research, 1983).

2. See Jonathan S. Leonard, "The Effectiveness of Equal Employment Law and the Affirmative Action Regulation," Working Paper No. 1745, NBER Working Paper Series, National Bureau of Economic Research, November 1985 (unpublished).

3. See Thomas Sowell, *Civil Rights: Rhetoric or Reality?* (New York: William Morrow, 1984); and James E. Jones Jr., "The Bugaboo of Employment Quotas," *Wisconsin Law Review,* 5 (1970) p. 341.

4. Daniel C. Maguire provides the most complete compendium of practical "problems" in *A New American Justice* (New York: Doubleday, 1980).

5. The most widely discussed state initiative on the affirmative action issue is California's Proposition 209, passed by the electorate November 5, 1996.

6. Arval A. Morris, "Affirmative Action and 'Quota' Systems," Commentary, 26 Ed. *Law Report,* 1985.

7. David H. Rosenbloom, *Federal Equal Employment Opportunity Politics and Public Personnel Administration* (New York: Praeger, 1977), p. 60; see also James E. Jones, "Twenty-one Years of Affirmative Action: The Maturation of the Administrative Enforcement Process under the Executive Order 11,246 as Amended." *Chicago Kent Law Review,* 59 (Winter 1982); pp. 66–122; Paul Burstein, *Discrimination, Jobs, and Politics* (Chicago: University of Chicago Press, 1985), pp. 8, 13.

8. *U.S. Federal Register,* March 6, 1961, 26, pt. 2: 1977.

9. Rosenbloom, *Federal Equal Employment Opportunity Politics,* pp. 67–69.

10. Jones, "Twenty-one Years," p.f. 72.

11. *U.S. Federal Register,* 30, pt. 10: 12319.

12. In *U.S. v. Local 189,* United Papermakers and Paper-workers, 290F2d 368, and Crown Zellerbach Corp., 282F Supp. 39 (E. D. La. 1968) "the government sought an injunction against the union's interference with the company's contractual obligations under Executive Order 11,246. . . ." *Ibid.,* p. 83.

13. There are many who criticize the way affirmative action has been implemented. For an overview, see Leonard, Working Paper No. 1745, and Leonard, "Affirmative Action as Earnings Redistribution: The Targeting of Compliance Reviews," *Journal of Labor Economics,* 3 (3) (July 1985), pp. 380–384; see also James P. Smith and Finis Welch, "Affirmative Action and Labor Markets," *Journal of Labor Economics,* 2 (April 1984), pp. 285–286, 298.

14. Leonard, Working Paper No. 1745, p. 4.

15. Sowell, *Civil Rights,* p. 41.

16. Judith Hole and Ellen Levine, *Rebirth of Feminism* (New York: New York Times Book Company, 1971), p. 46; see also Morris Goldstein and Robert Smith, "The Estimated Impact of the Antidiscrimination Program Aimed at Federal Contractors," *Industrial and Labor Relations Review,* 29 (4) (July 1976), pp. 523–543.

17. Interview with Joseph Hodges, assistant regional director, Office of Federal Contract Compliance, U.S. Department of Labor, Region IX, February 6, 1987.

18. See, for example, Joann S. Lublin and Andy Pasztor, "Tentative Affirmative Action Accord Is Reached by Top Reagan Officials," *Wall Street Journal,* December 11, 1985, p. 4; and Robert Pear, "Rights Chief Assails Hiring Goals as Failure," *New York Times,* November 1, 1985, p. 19.

19. Lublin and Pasztor, "Tentative Affirmative Action Accord."

20. Kenneth B. Noble, "Labor Dept. Aide Quits in Protest Over 'Lip Service' to Jobs Rights," *New York Times,* January 21, 1987; see also "Job-Bias Official Quits Labor Post," *Washington Post,* January 21, 1987.

21. Peter Baker, Michael A. Fletcher, "Clinton Runs a Town Hall Talk on Race," *San Francisco Chronicle,* December 4, 1997, pp. 1, 17; Marc Sandalow, "Focus on Race as Clinton Meets Press," *San Francisco Chronicle,* December 17, 1997, pp. 1, 19.

22. Michael C. Dorf, "Gore's Affirmative Action versus Bush's Affirmative Access: Why Color-Blindness Still Won't Work," November 1, 2000. From *Find Law's Legal Commentary* web site (12 April 2004): http://writ.news.findlaw.com/dorf/20001101.html

23. Interview with Paul Grossman, head of the Attorney's Division, Office for Civil Rights, U.S. Department of Education, Region IX, February 6, 1987.

24. Christopher F. Mooney, S.J., *Inequality and the American Conscience* (New York: Paulist Press, 1982), p. 5.

25. J. Harvey Wilkinson III, *From Brown to Bakke: The Supreme Court and School Integration* (New York: Oxford University Press, 1979), p. 255.

26. *Ibid.,* p. 301. Since Justice Powell was the "swing" vote, "An irony of Bakke, wrote Washington attorney and civil rights activist Joseph Rauh, was that 'Affirmative action was saved by a conservative Southern justice.'"

27. Mooney, *Inequality,* p. 101.

28. *Ibid.,* p. 103.

29. United States Commission on Civil Rights, *Toward an Understanding of Stotts,* Clearinghouse Publication 85, January 1985, p. 2.

30. *Ibid.*

31. *Wygant v. Jackson Board of Education* in *United States Law Week,* 54 (45) (May 20, 1986), pp. 4480f.

32. *Ibid.,* p. 4489.

33. David G. Savage, "Landmark Ruling Upholds Job Preferences for Women," *Los Angeles Times,* March 2, 1987, pp. 10, 22.

34. *Ibid.,* p. 22. See also "Caveats Reversed in Workplace Equality," Insight, *Washington Times,* April 27, 1987, pp. 8–12.

35. *Ibid.,* "Caveats Reversed."

36. Linda Greenhouse, "Court Bars Plan Set up to Provide Jobs to Minorities," *New York Times,* January 24, 1989, pp. 1, A12; Sandra Day O'Connor, "Excerpts from Court Opinions in Voiding of Richmond's Contracting Plan," *New York Times,* January 24, 1989, p. A12.

37. Thurgood Marshall, "Excerpts," *Ibid.,* p. A12.

38. Linda Greenhouse, "Signal on Job Rights," *New York Times,* January 25, 1989, pp. 1, A9.

39. Linda Greenhouse, "Court, Ruling 5 to 4, Eases Burden on Employers in Some Bias Suits," *New York Times,* June 6, 1989, pp. 1, A24; "Excerpts from Court Opinions about Job Rights," *New York Times,* June 6, 1989, p. A24.

40. Linda Greenhouse, "Court 5–4, Affirms a Right to Reopen Bias Settlements," *New York Times,* June 13, 1989, p. A7.

41. *Ibid.*

42. Martin Halstuk, "White Cops' Suit Alleges Bias in S.F. Promotions," *San Francisco Chronicle,* September 26, 1989, p. 1.

43. Ronald Smothers, "Ruling on Firefighter Is Debated in Alabama," *New York Times,* June 14, 1989, p. A18.

44. Susan Rasky, "Rights Groups Work on Measure to Reverse Court's Bias Rulings," *New York Times,* December 30, 1989, p. A11.

45. *Ibid.*

46. *Ibid.*

47. Larry Martz, Ann McDaniel, and Bill Turque, "Bush's Pledge: 'I Want to Do the Right Thing,'" *Newsweek,* May 28, 1990, pp. 20, 21.

48. Bob Cohn and Thomas M. DeFrank, "A White House Torpedo," *Newsweek,* April 29, 1991, p. 35.

49. Marc Sandalow, "Lee Gets Acting Rights Position," *San Francisco Chronicle,* December 12, 1997, pp. 1, 11; "Senators Suggest Lee Must Leave in 120 Days," *San Francisco Chronicle,* December 20, 1997, p. 3.

50. Louis Freedberg, "Settlement Scuttles Test of Affirmative Action," *San Francisco Chronicle,* November 22, 1997, pp. 1, 12; Barry Bearak, "Civil Rights Groups Criticized for Avoiding a Decision," *San Francisco Chronicle,* November 22, 1997, p. 12.

51. "Split Ruling on Affirmative Action;" and "Following the Case: *Barbara Grutter v. Lee Bollinger, et al., From NPR Archives* Web site (13 April 2004): http://www.npr.org/news/specials/michigan/

52. Louis Freedberg, "Oldest School Faces Modern Controversy," *San Francisco Chronicle,* December 11, 1997, pp. 1, 12.

53. "Washington State I-200," November 28, 2001. From *Affirmative Action and Diversity Project* Web site (14 April 2004): http://aad.english.ucsb.edu/pages/I-200.html

54. "Florida and Affirmative Action," August 2000. From *Affirmative Action and Diversity Project* Web site (14 April 2004): http://aad.english.ucsb.edu/pages/florida.html

55. Goldstein and Smith, "Estimated Impact."

56. Burstein, *Discrimination,* p. 148.

57. James P. Smith and Finis Welch, "Affirmative Action and Labor Markets," *Journal of Labor Economics,* 2 (2) (April 1984).

58. Burstein, *Discrimination,* p. 150.

59. Leonard, Working Paper No. 1745.

60. *Ibid.,* p. 10.

61. *Ibid.,* p. 11.

62. *Ibid.,* p. 17.

63. See, for example, a study by Cynthia M. Taeuber and Victor Valdisera, *Women in the American Economy,* Current Population Reports, Special Studies Series P-23, No. 146, U.S. Department of Commerce, Bureau of the Census, p. 23, which focuses on occupations with major employment gains for women and shows that in many of the male-dominated fields, the percentage of women employed rose sharply.

64. Wilkinson, *From Brown to Bakke,* pp. 262–263.

65. Allie Gilmore, "Women Law Apps Top Fifty Percent," April 6, 2001. From *Student Life, Washington University in St. Louis* Web site (14 April 2004): http://www.studlife.com/main.cfm?include=detail&storyid=64624.

66. The best list of arguments against affirmative action is in Maguire, *A New American Justice,* pp. 31–39.

67. Wilkinson, *From Brown to Bakke,* p. 269.

68. Charles Lawrence III, "The Bakke Case: Are Racial Quotas Defensible?" *Saturday Review,* October 15, 1977, p. 14.

69. Sam Howe Verhovek, "In Poll, Americans Reject Means But Not Ends of Racial Diversity," *The New York Times,* December 14, 1997, p. 18.

FURTHER READING

Bergmann, Barbara R. *In Defense of Affirmative Action.* New York.: Basic Books, 1996.

Cahn, Steven M. *Affirmative Action and the University: A Philosophical Inquiry.* Philadelphia: Temple University Press, 1993.

Greene, Kathanne W. *Affirmative Action and Principles of Justice.* New York: Greenwood Press, 1989.

Jones, James E., Jr. "The Bugaboo of Employment Quotas," *Wisonconsin Law Review,* 5 (1970), p. 341.

Maguire, Daniel C. *A New American Justice.* New York: Doubleday, 1980.

Mooney, Christopher F., S. J. *Inequality and the American Conscience.* New York: Paulist Press, 1982.

Orlans, Harold, and June O'Neill. "Affirmative Action Revisited," *Annals of the American Academy of Political and Social Science,* 523 (September 1992), pp. 144–158.

Rosenfeld, Michel. *Affirmative Action and Justice: A Philosophical and Constitutional Inquiry.* New Haven, CT: Yale University Press, 1991.

Sindler, Allan P. *Equal Opportunity: On the Policy and Politics of Compensatory Minority Preferences.* Washington, DC: American Enterprise Institute for Public Policy Research, 1983.

Skrentny, John David. *The Ironies of Affirmative Action.* Chicago, IL: University of Chicago Press, 1996.

Sowell, Thomas. *Civil Rights: Rhetoric or Reality?* New York: William Morrow, 1984.

Thernstrom, Stephan, and Abigail Thernstrom, *America in Black and White: One Nation, Indivisible.* New York: Simon & Schuster, 1997.

United States Commission on Civil Rights. *Toward an Understanding of Stotts.* Clearinghouse Publication 85, January 1985, p. 2.

Wilkinson, Harvey J. III. *From Brown to Bakke: The Supreme Court and School Integration.* New York: Oxford University Press, 1979.

Women, Empowerment, and Cultural Expression

We have explored the issue of women in politics. We began with a theoretical component; moved to political attitudes, voting, and elections; looked at women and government; and continued with an analysis of women and national policy. We began with theory and conclude this volume with practice. In our concluding chapter, we look at three essays. The first essay focuses on an analysis of a feminist women's health clinic that has existed in three distinct forms over the past three decades. The second essay explores the role of women in the military. The final essay deals with the relationship between coffee, coffeehouse cultures, political discourse, and gender.

Kathleen P. Iannello's article highlights the third-wave feminist perspectives on power. The author argues that over the past two centuries women in America have been working toward the goal of obtaining greater power in the personal as well as public spheres. The first wave of feminism held as its prize the right of American women to participate in the political process, equal with men, in the act of voting. The second wave of feminism began with "consciousness-raising" groups in the 1960s and also was successful in obtaining power. Collaboration was a cornerstone of second-wave feminism in the practice of consensual organization. The goal of collaboration in consensual structure was to empower women as part of a group and to share knowledge and information that served to advance the cause of the group. The notion of leadership was the group, and women gained power through this participation and group identity. The author argues that third-wave feminism, taking form in the 1990s, has just begun to make its contribution to women's progress with regard to power. This article maintains that the story of the transition from second- to third-wave organization can be told through specific examples. The author uses an analysis of a feminist women's health clinic that has existed in three distinct forms over the past three decades. Based on the health clinic case, it seems that third-wave feminists seek the individual opportunity to explore, experiment, and focus on their own career development. The feminist struggle in the third wave becomes a personal one.

The women's movement has seen the removal of many obstacles for females—obstacles that crossed political, economic, social, cultural, and legal boundaries. One significant change, and one that brings forth emotional arguments on both sides, extends to the role of women in the military. D'Ann M. Campbell maintains that American women have played many roles in wars from the Revolution to today. Her article focuses on the changes, which she explains century by century, with special attention to the major wars, when change happened fast. Today, some women even serve in combat roles and combat units. What has not changed is that women continue to be in the minority in organized American military units. Thus, the author concludes the majority of women in today's American military service remain outsiders looking "in."

Our final article examines the often-complex relationships between coffee, coffeehouse cultures, and gender, along with how these relationships have shifted historically. Elizabeth A. Kelly concludes with a look at the countercultural institutions that have emerged in the last two decades that draw on the traditions of free speech and cultural and political criticisms that were integral to the coffeehouse cultures of centuries past. The author describes the feminist community organizing and the cultural work since the late 1960s that has often centered around coffeehouses, sometimes in tandem with feminist bookstores and other forms of cultural expression. She describes two feminist coffeehouses and the political struggles attached to building alternative social and cultural institutions that prioritize women and their concerns or needs. Let us further examine female empowerment and how female attitudes and tactics can bring about change.

The Political Is Personal: Third-Wave Feminist Perspectives on Power

Kathleen P. Iannello

Over the past two centuries women in America have been working toward the goal of obtaining greater power in the personal as well as public spheres. The first wave of feminism held as its prize the right of American women to participate in the political process, equal with men, in the act of voting. This goal was realized with the passage of the 19th Amendment to the Constitution in 1920, after decades of struggle in which many women sacrificed their personal lives to obtain public credibility and the power of voice in our democracy. Women were scorned, jailed and even subjected to physical violence in leading the fight to expand the voting franchise.[1]

The second wave of feminism began with "consciousness-raising" groups in the 1960s and also was successful in obtaining power. While their legislative goal of an Equal Rights Amendment (ERA) failed, they won a woman's right to "choose" regarding abortion (*Roe v. Wade*). They also made possible women's advancement in the military, corporate America, college and professional sports, institutions of higher learning, the U.S. Congress, and State Legislatures as well as other governmental positions. While second-wave feminists were obtaining power they were also engaged in redefining it. Rather than recreating the oppressive, dominating nature of power that permeated male hierarchies, second-wave feminists sought to "empower" others through forms of shared leadership and consensual decision making.[2]

Reprinted by permission.

Third-wave feminism, taking form in the 1990s, has just begun to make its contribution to women's progress with regard to power. Third-wave feminism can be described as individual, multicultural and sexual. It is individual in the sense that it reflects personal direction and a multiplicity of conflicting views—so much so that a notion of "sisterhood" is called into question. If any sense of sisterhood has formed, it is through multiracial alliances that did not exist in the second wave of feminism.[3] Third-wave feminism is sexual in that it focuses on the pleasures of womanhood through sexual freedom. An example of this new sexuality is reflected in popular culture through television shows such as *Sex and the City,* where female characters explore issues of female sexual freedom across both gender and generational lines. In fact, there is a debate as to whether third-wave feminism is more likely to be located in popular culture than in academic settings.[4] Nonetheless it is true that youth subcultures are providing a nurturing environment for the intersections of feminist consciousness through music, print and Internet technologies.[5]

> Third-wave feminism owes its ideological premises slightly less to feminism than to Generation X. Although its unswerving focus on sexist oppression clearly identifies the third wave as feminist, it sometimes appears to be the only common ground it shares with feminism; the shape it otherwise assumed is entirely consistent with [what has come to be known as] the Generation X mold. . . .[6]

Obviously third-wave feminism has already been empowered through the successes of the first and second waves. Those two movements drew strength from, as a means for organization, the notion of women's shared experiences in the private sphere of family—the only sphere in which women had a legitimate "socially acceptable" place as wife and mother. In the second wave, feminists coined the phrase "the personal is political."[7] This meant that out of women's experiences in the private sphere of family and home came issues of public importance—questions of power. As Sara Evans explains in her book *Tidal Wave:* "Under this banner, the movement politicized issues that had long been deemed outside the purview of 'politics,' including sexuality, domestic violence, and the exercise of authority within the family. It also confronted the ancient association of men and maleness with public life (politics and power) and women and femaleness with domesticity (personal life and subordination)."[8]

There is no question that second-wave feminism opened the door to public life for women; however there are still issues of discrimination and exclusion as evidenced by the "glass ceiling." The "glass ceiling" means that women are unable, in significant numbers, to attain the highest positions in business and politics as well as other professions such as law and medicine.[9] In addition, there is still much to be achieved with regard to women's power within the family. While women go off to work and pursue their professions, upon arriving home their day is often just beginning. This is called "the second shift."[10] It is reported that women still perform 70 percent of the housework and are still considered the primary caretakers of children. While women have achieved equity in some aspects of the public sphere, clearly less ground has been gained in the private sphere of family and home.[11] The question is: how are third-wave feminists building on the foundation of previous movements in continuing to gain power for women in both the public and private spheres?

WHERE HAVE WE BEEN: SECOND-WAVE FEMINISM AND CONSENSUAL PROCESS

As stated earlier, second-wave feminists not only wanted to obtain greater power but also redefine it. In forming their own feminist organizations or as feminists moving into the world of work, women of the second wave did not accept the hierarchical/patriarchal system that already existed. They wanted to form organizations that were "leaderless" in the name of equality and the common good. They wanted to bring women into the public sphere in a distinctly female way, accentuated by group process and consensus.[12]

Many second-wave feminists argued that power, defined as domination, was perpetuated through hierarchical structures. They advocated building alternative forms of organization through which they could eliminate the structural factors that created and maintained leaders and followers. This called for a redefinition of power as a basis for new, consensual structure. This meant a change from power as *domination* to power as *empowerment* or the ability to accomplish or achieve mutual goals.[13] The consciousness-raising groups of the 1960s and 1970s were a first attempt at building alternative organizations. While they succeeded in raising consciousness they were not non-hierarchical. According to Jo Freeman's account of their experiences, there was a "tyranny of structurelessness," meaning that *no structure* gave way to the development of *informal* leaders—individuals who gained power due to media attention or personal characteristics.[14] A lack of decision-making process opened the door to unaccountable leadership. What they learned from this experience was that non-hierarchy had to be carefully *structured*. This discovery led second-wave feminists to create a decision-making process that was able to maintain non-hierarchical structure: consensual organization.

Organizations that operate consensually share *all* decision making within the group. The smaller and more homogeneous the group, the easier it is to reach *consensus* on issues of varying importance. In a consensual organization the entire membership discusses an idea until everyone can endorse it. There is no voting. Voting is thought to waste time because it creates winners and losers, meaning that those who lose today will return another day to fight their battle again. Consensus avoids this kind of confrontational decision making because decisions are inclusive of all views and the product of lengthy and often creative discussion.

As second-wave feminist organizations evolved, some of them modified their consensual structure in order to focus their energies on the most important issues. This modified consensual structure characteristically developed "coordinator groups," smaller groups within the organization charged with the responsibility of decision making on routine matters.[15] In general, the distinction made between routine and critical decisions became very important to the survival of these groups. Routine decisions were those that did not change the direction or overall goals of the group and instead were considered important to the daily operation of the organization. Critical decisions were retained for the entire group, as these decisions could well determine their overall mission. This modified consensual structure enabled these organizations to retain their core commitment to non-hierarchy while being more efficient with their internal resources.

There were many consensual and modified consensual organizations that thrived during the second wave of feminism. These organizations were appropriate to the culture of feminism and ground-breaking for their time. Health clinics, peace groups and women's studies programs were often organized this way.[16] As a result of their commitment and example, consensual decision making is found in many organizations today. Even large bureaucracies and corporations that are clearly hierarchical have now incorporated consensual practices within sublevels of their organizations.

WHERE WE ARE GOING: THIRD-WAVE FEMINISM AND COLLABORATIVE LEADERSHIP

Along the way in this discussion of feminism and decision making the question of gender-related values surfaces. That is to ask: is there something about being female or socialized to "female values" that leads to identifiable behavior in organizations? There is much today in the social-psychological literature, as well as the literature of political science that answers this question in the affirmative.[17] According to this literature, women, more so than men, will encourage non-confrontational styles of decision making. For example, recent studies of women's behavior in state legislatures provide evidence to support this theory. Women tend to seek out networks through which they can test new ideas and build support for new legislative initiatives before formally introducing them. Men are more likely to propose new initiatives first, then later engage in argument in order to build support. As one male legislator explained, he preferred to "develop my own solution to a problem, have it drafted, drop it in the hopper and watch everyone scream."[18]

Women's collaborative nature has long been a factor in American feminism. As far back as the Revolutionary War women collaborated in organizing boycotts of tea and other British goods. This early collaboration gave women their first opportunity to make claims for citizenship—the early seeds of first-wave feminism and the fight for the right to vote.[19] The Women's Strike for Peace (WSP) in the early 1960s was an example of women's collaboration in forming a spontaneous "un-organization," as they liked to say, focused on reducing the threat of nuclear war.[20] WSP also unintentionally used the strength of "female culture" to disarm the infamous House Un-American Activities Committee (HUAC) and the communist witch hunt conducted by Senator Joseph McCarthy.[21] Indeed numerous examples of women's collaborative political behavior exist throughout American history.

Collaboration was a cornerstone of second-wave feminism in the practice of consensual organization. The goal of collaboration in consensual structure was to empower women as part of a group and to share knowledge and information that served to advance the cause of the group. The notion of leadership *was* the group and women gained power through this participation and group identity.

A STORY OF TRANSITION: CONSENSUAL PROCESS TO COLLABORATIVE LEADERSHIP

The story of the transition from second- to third-wave organization can be told through specific examples. One such example is provided through analysis of a feminist women's health clinic that has existed in three distinct forms over the past three decades. The clinic was formed in 1972 by community members as a non-profit organization, "in response to the need for safe, legal abortion services for . . . women." Its mission statement indicated the goals of the organization as follows:

> To provide high quality, cost-accessible, health care for and by women that includes but is not limited to gynecological and abortion services.
> To empower women by informing them medically and politically and by training women healthworkers.
> To be a women-operated business striving for consensual power-sharing and equality of worker input in major policy decisions.
> To have our business structure be seen as a working model for other interested groups.[22]

In the first two decades, the health collective went through two major organizational and structural changes. At the time of its inception, the organization was established with a staff that made decisions about the day-to-day operation of the clinic. There was a separate (outside) board composed of community members, which met with the staff every two weeks to make major policy decisions. As the staff members explain, "This was helpful in the beginning, as a broad range of experience and opinions were needed." However, by the end of the first two years, the board had become what the staff described as a "technical legality," and was dissolved.[23]

At this point the full staff became the board as well, and all staff members participated in all decision making, according to consensus. The staff/board met weekly at that time and made all routine as well as critical policy decisions, including the hiring of staff and determination of salaries. At this point in their development, the staff decided that all salaries would be the same for all members. In terms of jobs and tasks, as they explained, "The philosophy of the collectivity involves the idea that each staff member should ideally be trained to do any given task. Most staff members rotate positions of counselor, coordinator and phone counselor. Training programs are arranged for staff to learn more specialized tasks such as lab work, administrative skills and physician assistant skills."[24]

After the first ten years of operating in this fashion, the health collective once again changed or modified its structure. Members reported that there were two major reasons for a change: (1) a need to make the "business" of the organization more efficient and (2) a need to recognize, through position and salary, the expertise of certain members. The structure that developed out of these needs was one in which there were three coordinators who had responsibility for areas such as personnel, medical, and business matters. These tasks had been delegated to them by the full staff. The women in the organization described how the coordinator positions evolved from the expertise some women brought with them when they joined the clinic. For instance one member who had worked in another medical organization, brought with her knowledge of medical protocol. She eventually became the medical coordinator.

It is also important to note that when expertise was lost, through the departure of a member, the position the member held was dissolved. For example, a woman who brought "political and communication" skills to the organization became outreach coordinator. When she left the organization, the outreach coordinator's position was dissolved. While coordinator positions did not rotate, coordinators made an effort to share knowledge and information with the rest of the group. While this new structure brought with it some differentiation as to position and salary, the full staff still made policy decisions in these areas. The full staff met once a month to consider critical policy questions, with routine decisions delegated to coordinators.

Within the women's health collective, individual members said they joined because they were looking for a female-managed business where they expected to find a supportive work environment, more flexible working hours, and coworkers who really understood the members' needs both inside and outside the workplace. In short, these individuals expressed a commitment to a distinctly woman-centered environment which benefited the organization's members/employees as well as their clients. Upon being hired, new employees needed to be trained in consensual decision making in order to join the group.

One of the most significant aspects of the women's health collective was the way the organization was able to recognize "ability" or "expertise" within its membership and then utilize it to the benefit of the entire group. In most traditional organizations, ability or expertise reflects increased knowledge on the part of individuals. Ultimately knowledge equals power and power results in hierarchy. This was not true in the modified consensual organization. Coordinators, who had more knowledge than the average member on a particular subject, were *delegated* responsibility from the entire staff. Yet they also had a responsibility to educate the remaining staff in a specific area of routine work, such as medical protocol. This structure was a model of nonhierarchy that demonstrated the concept of empowerment. This meant that organization members became enriched or gained personal power through the expertise of others or, in other words, through the group

process. Maintenance of nonhierarchy in this organization was also impressive because of the external constraints: the health collective had to interact with, and in
some instances be dependant on, an external environment that included medical,
political and economic hierarchies.

Modified consensual structure thus became the hallmark of the second
decade in this organization's evolution. In a modified consensual structure members are keenly aware of the distinction between critical and routine decisions. Decisions that are "critical" have the potential for changing the direction of the
organization. Those that are "routine" are important to the operation of the organization on a daily basis but are not likely to raise significant questions about
changes in overall policy. Critical decisions are reserved for the entire membership
of the organization, while routine decisions are delegated horizontally.

In the health collective, it was the coordinators and their respective committees who made decisions about problems they were close to and had information
about. It was recognized that routine decisions had the potential for becoming critical. In the event that they did, they were reconsidered by the entire group. In hierarchical organizations, only those at the top, with varying degrees of input from
lower levels, make critical policy. In a modified consensus routine decisions are
delegated horizontally to those who have an interest in making them. While such
delegation can involve additional responsibility, authority, and expertise, it does
not result in a super-ordinate-subordinate relationship. The health collective relied
more on the "process" of the organization, including trust among members, to
avoid the development of hierarchy.

While the most important defining element of this structure was the reserving
of critical decisions for the entire membership, and the outward delegation of routine decisions to the few, other aspects of the internal environment were important
to the maintenance of nonhierarchical structure. These aspects are best described
by the term *process* which includes the concepts of consensus and empowerment.
Without the trust among members that is fostered through consensus decision
making and the conscious effort to avoid domination, hierarchy would be difficult
to avoid. In this way, the political ideals of the members and the ideological commitment to nonhierarchy are vitally important. A "culture" of consensus must be established. Central to this culture is the *outward,* not downward, delegation of
routine decisions to the few and the reserving of critical decisions for the entire
membership. Other important elements of the model include (1) recognition of
ability or expertise rather than rank or position, (2) the notion of empowerment as
a basis of consensual "process" and (3) clarity of goals that are arrived at *through*
this consensual process.

In the late-1990s, growing market pressures began to make operation of this
nonprofit health collective increasingly difficult. The rising costs of running a medical clinic, including the skyrocketing costs of malpractice insurance, led the
women in this organization to reevaluate their position. Additionally, others in the
community were thinking about forming a new women's clinic that would be affiliated with Planned Parenthood. These women did not want to work in competition

with the existing health collective, so the two groups decided to work collaboratively toward new goals. In 1972 the women of the original health collective had been pioneers in their community, founding one of the first woman-run abortion clinics in the country. They again wanted to be pioneers in providing health care to women at the start of a new century.

The pioneering idea that carried them forward was based on collaboration: a notion of "seamless" care for women. What is "seamless" care? Most commonly women have a primary care physician as well as a gynecologist. Additionally they may see a naturopathic physician (alternative medicine) and also a psychiatrist, particularly for issues related to the mental and physical effects of menopause. The idea of "seamless care" brings these practitioners under one roof so that they can coordinate patient care and end the fragmented care that once existed.[25]

What did this merger mean for the health clinic and its modified collective? As one of the former coordinators explained, "the modified collective died a natural death. The decision to merge with Planned Parenthood came through consensus, so the original organization was true to its 'process' right to the end."[26] The new clinic that formed took with it the nearly 30 years of expertise from the old clinic as well as much of its staff. A few staff members moved into positions with the regional administrative office of Planned Parenthood, which is located nearby in another community.

Staff members at the regional office are educated in a particular style of organization known as "the learning organization." The concept of "the learning organization" derives from the work of Peter M. Senge. In his book, *The Fifth Discipline,* Senge defines the learning organization as "an organization that is continually expanding its capacity to create its future."[27] The core principles of the learning organization are: personal mastery, mental models (internal images), shared vision and team learning.[28] This kind of organization thrives on collaboration, a quest for continual learning and an environment that provides "the enabling conditions for people to lead."[29] The organization commits itself to the well-being of its members, rejecting authoritarian aspects of hierarchy. While this model of organization was not created by feminists, just as feminists did not "create" consensual organization, it provides them with an example of how to pursue leadership in a supportive environment. This environment includes encouraging organization members to see their connectedness to the world, to be compassionate and to develop a commitment to the whole organization.[30]

It is not yet evident that the values and goals of "the learning organization" have taken hold in the new planned parenthood health clinic. The specific goals of the new clinic are to fill the need for personalized conventional and natural health care for women. They remain committed to a model (as health care providers) that respects all women in providing a comprehensive range of gynecological services. This includes medical (abortion pill) and surgical abortion. The organization has three doctors, a site manager, two nurse practitioners, a nurse and some administrative support for a total number of 17 people. In theory, the site manager is charged with the task of "running" the organization. In this case the site manager is someone who worked for 25 years with the former clinic and describes herself as a relational/transformational leader. However, she reports that those leadership qualities do not appear to be as valued by her co-workers in the new organization.[31]

She cites two reasons for this. One is that she sees a generational change in the interests of younger women who were part of the old clinic and the second is that the old clinic kept "physician culture" on the outside. With regard to the younger women, she describes them as not as politically motivated or invested as those who had been at the old clinic for over ten or fifteen years. She describes these women as more interested in building their own careers than building the organization. She does not mean this as a criticism, but rather as an observation that these women came of age at a less politically threatening time in terms of women's reproductive rights. Their commitment to the organization is based on each member's individual career and not grounded in politics.

With regard to "physician culture," she refers to the change in dynamic or power-relations that enter an organization when doctors are part of the internal culture. Even though the doctors in the new clinic refer to themselves as feminists, they do not subscribe to the consensual process of the old clinic. Instead, they are willing to collaborate with other doctors, but have not yet demonstrated collaboration with the rest of the staff. The site manager reports that the younger staff members of the new clinic are comfortable with the doctors "in control" of the clinic because they see that the knowledge they will gain from working with the doctors will benefit/advance their careers. She also points out that the new clinic has not yet had time to "settle," and that new forms of leadership and the qualities of a learning organization may yet emerge. Whether or not that happens, the women of this clinic are still "pioneers" in their vision of patient-centered "seamless care." This mission, in and of itself, is an example of collaborative leadership.

Based on the health clinic case it seems that third-wave feminists seek the individual opportunity to explore, experiment and focus on their own career development. Further, the concept of individual *leadership* is quite opposite the notion of a collaborative process utilized in the consensual organizations that served the second wave of feminism so well. Consensual organization, in rejecting individual leadership, required conformity and sought individual power through "oneness" with the group. Feminist leadership in the third wave is collaborative but individually focused. Third-wave leadership is mindful of hierarchical boundaries but not bound by hierarchical minds—nor is it restrained by consensual process. Third-wave feminism presents the *opportunity* for leadership, the ability to reestablish "self" as the subject.

HOW THE POLITICAL BECOMES PERSONAL

What can be accomplished in the name of feminism when centering on "self"? In the public sphere third-wave feminists have the opportunity to shatter the glass ceiling. Due to the successes of second-wave feminism, many more women have reached higher levels in corporations, law firms, and government. Now that the link between hierarchy and patriarchy is not as strong as it once was, young women may have a new platform from which to launch their own careers. Young women will be empowered in a new era of feminist thinking that legitimates female careerism. One way to think of it is that they have a running start in reaching the top and much more legitimacy in making the attempt.

In the private sphere of home and family, third-wave feminists have their work cut out for them. Second-wave feminism brought attention to the significant differences in the way men and women have been socialized to think and act with regard to home and family. Surprisingly even women who thought themselves more "liberated" came to realize that they too were invested in the powerful social norms underlying the belief that men should be the "breadwinners."[32]

Presumably second-wave feminists have been able to raise sons, and daughters, to think differently about men's and women's roles in the home. However, given current data on housework, these feminist-generational changes have not yet had a significant impact.[33] Thus another important objective of third-wave feminism is to shed light on the psychological and social development of children, especially boys, as an important early investment toward equality in the home.

A focus on male development represents quite an "about face" from at least one part of the second-wave movement, the radical separatist feminists, who sought women's equality through severing ties with men. Third-wave feminism asserts all aspects of womanhood including the legitimacy of relationships with men.[34] Further, third-wave feminism endorses the value in exploring men's roles and the ways in which society dictates that men must be breadwinners and other "myths" that have been the result of what William Pollack terms "the boy code," in his book *Real Boys*. The "boy code" is the way in which boys are socialized to be tough, to not express or feel emotion, to pretend that everything is fine when they feel pain, loneliness or anger. As Pollack states:" The Boy Code puts boys and men into a gender straightjacket that constrains not only them but everyone else, reducing us all as human beings and eventually making us strangers to ourselves and to one another—or, at least, not as strongly connected to one another as we long to be."[35]

New research by psychologists like Pollack emphasizes the need to rescue our boys from these myths just as the need to rescue girls is so clearly articulated in Mary Pipher's book *Reviving Ophelia*.[36] If boys can be raised to feel comfortable expressing a full range of emotion and escape the solitary and otherwise "tough" aspects of the boy code, they can grow into men who can engage in full and equal domestic partnerships. If girls can be raised to be resilient and less affected by the patriarchal images and expectations of popular culture, they will be empowered to approach relationships with confidence and a strong sense of self.

The work of both Carol Gilligan in *A Different Voice* and Mary Pipher in *Reviving Ophelia* describes the ways in which adolescent girls "stop being and start seeming."[37] This means that girls lose their sense of self that has been so clear and natural up until this adolescent period and begin to conform to the expectations of popular culture and the patriarchy that surrounds them. Pipher argues that girls must strive to retain their "centered self," which is compassionate, nurturing and empathetic—but not empathetic to the point of lost identity.

Much of the rest of women's development is about rediscovering themselves as the subject of their own lives. So far, one of the great contributions of third-wave feminism is its challenge that each young woman define feminism to include herself.[38] This challenge may hasten young women's ability to discover their "centered self," or a kind of internal compass. Thus the feminist struggle in the third wave becomes a personal one. The successes of the first and second waves empowered all women in the public sphere. Even if women have not yet attained the most powerful positions in business, government or the law, at least the "road map" is there. But where is the "road map" in the private sphere? The third-wave feminist quest for personal power may be the most difficult of all. As one young writer in New York city explains:

> It is really an inner struggle that we are fighting now and we are coming to understand that you can't picket your own inner voices. How do we keep ourselves from obsessing over unrealistic expectations about career achievement and our personal lives? Why can't we kick the fear of not pleasing people? Why do we wage war on our own bodies? Feminism in its pop culture, widely-held definitions doesn't give us answers to these questions. . . . So after all this work of our predecessors and contemporaries: the suffragettes, the bra burners, even the girl power rock stars, there is still an unbelievably narrow balance beam which a "successful" woman must gracefully perch on. All of us twenty-somethings are teetering, trying to curl our tired feet around the notions of what is not enough and what is too much. Move too far to the right and you are gluttonous, not the kind of good young women who is thinking about the world and how to save it. Move too far to the left and you are a lamb, unable to assert yourself, a throwback too preoccupied with how others fare and not enough about your own advancement. And the worst part, the most stress inducing, is that we precariously fight to get our balance here with a crowd of spectators watching our every move, our very own panopticon of judging eyes. The crowd is filled with our employers and co-workers, potential lovers and friends, our families, and the jury foreman: the brazenly critical voices in our own heads. . . . Feminism, as it exists now, hasn't articulated how to stop the eternal performance.[39]

NOTES

1. Nancy E. McGlen, Karen O'Connor, Laura van Assendelft and Wendy Gunther-Canada, *Women, Politics, and American Society*, 3rd ed. (New York: Longman, 2002), p. 38.

2. Kathleen Iannello, *Decisions Without Hierarchy*, (New York: Routledge, 1992), pp. 121–123.

3. Amanda D. Lotz, "Communicating Third-Wave Feminism and New Social Movements: Challenges for the Next Century of Feminist Endeavor," *Women and Language*, 26.1 (2000): 141–170.

4. Rita Alfonso and Jo Trigilio, "Surfing the Third Wave: A Dialogue Between Two Third Wave Feminists," *Hypatia, Vol. 12 No. 3 (1997)*.

5. Ednie Kaeth Garrison, "U.S. Feminism—Grrl Style! Youth (Sub) Cultures and the Technologies of the Third Wave," *Feminist Studies*, (Spring 2000): 141–170.

6. Organization for Research on Women and Communications, "Isn't It Ironic? The Intersection of Third-Wave Feminism and Generation X," *Women's Studies in Communication* 24 (2001): 137.

7. Jennifer Baumgardner and Amy Richards, *ManifestA*, (New York: Farrar, Straus and Giroux, 2000), p. 284.

8. Sara M. Evans, *Tidal Wave*, (New York: Simon & Schuster, Inc., 2003), p. 3.

9. McGlen, et al., pp. 222–224.

10. Arlie Russell Hochschild, *The Time Bind*, (New York: Henry Holt and Co., 1997), p. 6.

11. McGlen, et al., p. 310.

12. Iannello, p. 35–49.

13. Lydia Sargent, *Women and Revolution* (Boston: South End Press, 1981), p. 7.

14. See Jo Freeman, *The Politics of Women's Liberation* (White Plains, NY: Longman, 1975).

15. Iannello, p. 80.

16. Kathleen Iannello, "Anarchist Feminism and Student Power: Is This Any Way to Run a Women's Studies Program?" in Lois Lovelace Duke, *Women in Politics* 2nd edition (Upper Saddle River, NJ, 1996), pp. 340–350.

17. Belle Rose Ragins and Eric Sundstom, "Gender, and Power in Organizations: A Longitudinal Perspective," *Psychological Bulletin*, 105 (1989), pp. 51–88.

18. Cindy Simon Rosenthal, "Determinants of Collaborative Leadership: Civic Engagement, Gender or Organizational Norms?" *Political Research Quarterly*, 51 no. 4 (Dec. 1998), p. 852.

19. Linda K. Kerber, "May All Our Citizens Be Soldiers and All Our Soldiers Citizens: The Ambiguities of Female Citizenship in the New Nation," in Jean Bethke Elshtain and Sheila Tobias (Savage MD: Rowman & Littlefield, 1990), pp. 89–103.

20. Amy Swerdlow, "Motherhood and the Subversion of the Military State: Women Strike for Peace Confronts the House Committee on Un-American Activities," in Jean Bethke Elshtain and Sheila Tobias (Savage MD: Roman & Littlefield, 1990), pp. 10.

21. Swerdlow, p. 18.

22. Organization mission statement, women's health collective, p. 1.

23. Interviews with health collective members 1986–1987.

24. *Ibid.*

25. Lorilee Schoenbeck, Cheryl A. Gibson and M. Brooke Barss, *Menopause*, (New York: Kensington Publishing Corp., 2002), Preface.

26. Interview with former coordinator who now works for Planned Parenthood, June 2003.

27. Peter M. Senge, *The Fifth Discipline*, (New York: Doubleday, 1990), p. 14.

28. Senge, p. viii.

29. Senge, p. 140.

30. Senge, pp. 170–171.

31. Interview with site manager, June 2003.

32. Jean Potuchek, *Who Supports the Family: Gender and Breadwinning in Dual-Earner Marriages* (Palo Alto: Stanford University Press, 1997), pp 1–18.

33. Hochschild, pp. xvii–xxv.

34. Baumgardner and Richards, pp. 34–44.

35. William Pollack, *Real Boys*, (New York: Henry Holt and Company, 1998), p. 6.

36. Mary Pipher, *Reviving Ophelia*, (New York: Ballantine Books, 1994), p. xi–xiv.

37. Pipher, pp. 1–15. See also, Carol Gilligan, *In a Different Voice*, (Cambridge: Harvard University Press, 1982).

38. Jennifer Drake, "Third-Wave Feminisms," *Feminist Studies*, (Spring 1997), p. 97.

39. Courtney E. Martin, "Juggling Our Own Expectations, "unpublished manuscript, July 2003.

FURTHER READING

Baumgardner, Jennifer and Amy Richards. *ManifestA*. New York: Farrar, Straus and Giroux, 2000.

Evans, Sara M. *Tidal Wave*. New York: Simon & Schuster, Inc., 2003.

Hochschild, Arlie Russell. *The Time Bind*. New York: Henry Holt and Co., 1997.

Iannello, Kathleen. *Decisions Without Hierarchy*. New York: Routledge, 1992.

McGlen, Nancy E., Karen O'Connor, Laura van Assendelft and Wendy Gunther-Canada. *Women, Politics, and American Society*, 3rd ed. New York: Longman, 2002.

Pipher, Mary. *Reviving Ophelia*. New York: Ballantine Books, 1994.

Pollack, William. *Real Boys*. New York: Henry Holt and Company, 1998.

Potuchek, Jean. *Who Supports the Family: Gender and Breadwinning in Dual-Earner Marriages*. Palo Alto: Stanford University Press, 1997.

Senge, Peter M. *The Fifth Discipline*. New York: Doubleday, 1990.

Inside or Outside? Women's Role in American Military History

D'Ann M. Campbell

American women have played many roles in wars from the Revolution to today. The changes are explained century by century, with special attention to the major wars, when change happened fast. Today, some women even serve in combat roles and combat units. What has not changed is that women continue to be in the minority in organized American military units. Thus the majority of women in today's American military service remain outsiders looking "in."

This essay explores the relationship between women and the American military which has changed radically over the years; some of the key developments are highlighted. Since wartime always adds urgency and speeds up the process of transformation, we will concentrate on times of emergency and warfare.[1]

THE COLONIAL ERA AND THE AMERICAN REVOLUTION

European women and men, side by side, fought when Native American tribes attacked their settlements. Harrowing stories of captivity, like Mary Rowlandson, *The Sovereignty and Goodness of God, Together, with the Faithfulness of his Promises Displayed Being a Narrative of the Captivity and Restauration of Mrs. Mary Rowlandson* (1682), attested to the penalty for failure.[2] By the time of the American Revolution, thousands of women accompanied the Continental Army of George

Washington and the various state militias that maneuvered against the British. They performed three major roles. The so-called "Women of the Army" performed duties as medics, nurses, assistants in artillery units, or served as support staff who handled cooking, cleaning, and uniform repair. Polly Cooper, an Oneida Indian, was sent by her tribe to help feed soldiers at Valley Forge in 1777–78. Second, a few hundred women like Deborah Sampson served side by side with men; a few disguised themselves as men and fought as men. Still others served in warships, acted as spies and scouts, and brought support to frontier outposts. Third, handfuls of women served in local military units primary to defend their homeland. The Americans did not allow known prostitutes to accompany their troops.[3] While some women were hired for the logistical work, wives of officers understood it was their duty to accompany their husbands and volunteered to care for them and their units. An example is Sarah Osborn, who accompanied her husband and the Continental Army to Yorktown and witnessed the surrender of the British troops. Still other women in the first category served as spies or water carriers for the colonial militia. Spies attended functions of Loyalist families and relayed information to the Continental Army. A group of women also served as "Molly Pitchers" and lugged pitchers of water to cool down the canon barrels after they were fired. Private Joseph Martin provided an only eyewitness account describing a Molly Pitcher who seemed nonchalant when an enemy cannon ball bounced "directly between her legs without doing any other damage than carrying away all the lower part of her petticoat." She apparently joked about it not hitting her a little higher and went back to her job. The most famous Molly Pitcher was Margaret Corbin, who briefly took over command of an artillery battery when her officer husband was killed. She herself was wounded, received a pension at the end of the war, and is now buried at West Point.[4] While a few women were in harm's way during the American Revolution, most worked behind the lines and were "attached" to Washington's army or were serving "with" not "in" the army. Washington himself wanted to professionalize his army and get rid of the women, but the camps would be too unsanitary without them. Such women stood outside the norm in all American wars down to World War Two.

THE CIVIL WAR

Gender roles grew more distinctive during the 19th century, with women increasingly assigned to domestic roles as wife, mother, and housekeeper. Professional military service was not a high prestige role for American men, in sharp contrast to Europe and Japan. Temporary voluntary service in the militia in times of crisis, such as the War of 1812 and the War with Mexico, was prestigious. Service as an enlisted man was very low prestige, and a large fraction of the army comprised recent Irish and German immigrants or "John Smiths" who were escaping something.[5] Officers' wives followed their husbands from post to post, creating their own closed society; otherwise women were few in the military world.[6] In the

War of 1812 and again in the Civil War some women disguised themselves and fought as soldiers and sailors. A certain proportion were uncovered and expelled when they were wounded; probably most returned home undetected. One such woman whose letters survived was Sarah Rosetta Wakeman who first enlisted as Pvt. Lyons Wakeman.[7] The Civil War called out a need for spies, with women using their gender to deflect suspicious sentries. Rose O'Neal Greenhow spied for the Confederacy, was imprisoned twice and released. Another rebel spy wrote her memoir, *Belle Boyd in Camp and Prison*.[8] By this time it was unacceptable for wives of officers to accompany their husbands too closely. A few women worked around the army camps as cooks and laundresses, and were often derogatorily called "camp followers," a term suggesting casual prostitution.[9]

The Civil War saw female nurses for the first time play major roles. A decade earlier Florence Nightingale had pioneered the nursing role for British women during the Crimean War, and already the Germans had created an important niche for military nurses. Nursing had not yet emerged as a legitimate occupation for American women, but the wartime emergency clearly required urgent action to save men's lives. Many nurses served the Confederacy, but they were never well organized. The Yankees were nothing if not superb organizers; their most important instrument was the quasi-official U.S. Sanitation Commission. Jeanie Attie has revealed the gender-based tensions inside the Sanitary Commission, as the male leadership pushed their modernizing national vision, while the women volunteers thought in terms of supporting the menfolk of their family and community. Dorothy Dix, with a well established reputation in mental health nursing, became superintendent of U.S. Army nurses in July 1861. She trained some 180 women, including Louisa May Alcott, for medical duty. Despite her quiet demeanor she had a forcible personality that had little tolerance for fools or impediments, male or female. Alcott served for only three weeks until she contracted typhoid fever and permanently ruined her health. Her experience was the base for the best-selling *Hospital Sketches* (1863).[10] The book juxtaposes heartbreaking scenes in the wards with Alcott's outrage at the mismanagement of the bureaucracy. Dix's operation staffed hospitals well behind the front lines. Some nurses such as Clara Barton operated outside organizational channels, either eager to serve closer to the battlefield or unwilling to subordinate themselves to either the Sanitary Commission or Dix's Department of Female Nurses. In all, almost 20,000 women served in hospitals during the Civil War.[11] A few women served as medical doctors, most notably Mary Edwards Walker. Walker, a certified medical doctor, started as an unpaid volunteer but by 1863 won an official appointment as assistant surgeon. She was captured by the Confederates on one such adventure and was imprisoned until she and two dozen other Union doctors were exchanged for Confederate doctors. was released in an exchange of prisoners.[12] The majority of women on and near battlefields were trained and untrained nurses and nurse's aides. A permanent nurse corps became a possibility only in the 1890s, when the overseas war with Spain showed the necessity of a professionally trained cadre of nurses who could be sent anywhere in the world where they were needed.

WORLD WAR I

From 1900 to 1920 women played leadership roles in the drive for woman suffrage, and in the pacifist movement to outlaw war.[13] President Woodrow Wilson effectively handled the pacifists by explaining he had a plan to end all wars—by fighting now. Once America declared war, policymakers made special efforts to enlist the support of women. The Food Administration under Herbert Hoover successfully appealed to housewives to conserve meat and fats and minimize food waste so that vast quantities of American food could ship to Europe. (Hoover did not mention the goal of enabling France and Britain to draft more of its farmers for combat duty.) Middle class women excelled in the area of volunteer activities, responding to calls for patriotism and the urgent need to end the war quickly so that their menfolk could return safely from abroad. The YWCA, women's clubs, women's colleges, and most importantly, the Red Cross, appealed to women to volunteer on the homefront and overseas. Red Cross chapters exploded from 267 local chapters in early 1917 to over 2300 by that summer. Over eight million women labored at chapter sites to make medical and clothing supplies for soldiers. They hand-rolled bandages—not because it was efficient but because it added a personal touch and energized their patriotism. Still others volunteered in canteens, in munitions factories and as aides at military camps and assembly points.[14]

Sixteen thousand civilian women shipped out to France with three million soldiers as part of the American Expeditionary Force (AEF). They worked at stereotypically female jobs such as nurse's aide, physical therapist, dietician, relief worker, clerk and librarian. Civilian agencies such as the Red Cross and Salvation Army coordinated their women staffers handling welfare and canteen work among American soldiers and sailors overseas.[15] The Navy Department exploited a loophole in legislation and created a new category of service, Yeoman (F). It enlisted over 12,500 women in the reserves to handle clerical and storekeeper duties. The Marines followed suit and enlisted 305 women reservists. The Coast Guard allowed some women to enlist during wartime to occupy clerical billets.[16] While women reservists in the Navy and Marines did the same work for the same pay and benefits as men in yeoman and storekeeper billets, the Army refused to allow any military status for any women workers except for nurses. When the AEF urgently needed experienced telephone operators, a contingent of 223 women nicknamed "Hello Girls," shipped over. They were civilians who wore official-looking uniforms while under contract with the Signal Corps in France. The Quartermaster Corps also hired civilian women for duty in France. Almost sixty years later women who had served with the Army were retroactively granted military status.[17]

Since the Spanish American War where nurses had played a critical role but as civilian contractors, American policymakers had slowly grown to accept that nurses were needed for future wars. In 1901, Congress took the next step and created the Army Nurse Reserve Corps. In 1908 Congress added a Navy Nurse Reserve Corps. Unsure whether to have women serve as civilian employees or as military reservists, Congress made these nursing corps into quasi-military units. These nurses were neither officers nor enlistees; they wore officers' uniforms but never had command authority over men. What was most important is that finally women were organized in military units on a permanent basis. By 1920, the status of the nursing corps was clarified and nurses now held "relative rank" which meant that they were officially officers but did not receive the same pay or benefits that men did at that rank. This vague status would persist for nurses until they gained equal status in 1944. Thus at the turn of the twentieth century, American nurses were organized and prepared to serve in future conflicts. The first test came about a decade later with the advent of the Great War. In a manner of months the nurse corps expanded from a few hundred to over 21,000 Army nurses and 1,500 Navy nurses. Several hundred Army nurses, on loan to the British, went to France in the summer of 1917. Eventually Army nurses would serve in 198 stations in the 48 states as well as Hawaii, Puerto Rico, France, England, Belgium, Italy, and Siberia. Three hundred women died while in service; some were killed when a hospital was shelled but most succumbed during the influenza epidemic of 1918. A few young women who tasted military service during the Great War would be selected as leaders in the next world war, including Yeoman (F) Joy Bright Hancock, who directed the Navy's WAVES, and Florence Blanchfield who was appointed Superintendent of the Army Nurse Corps in 1943. In 1947 Colonel Blanchfield became the first woman commissioned in the Regular Army.[18] The enthusiastic support women provided for the war effort Over There and Over Here demonstrated that effective service in the national cause no longer required combat. Coupled with the Progressive plan to purify politics by adding a large female electorate, this new sensibility guaranteed the passage of woman suffrage in 1920. The women had earned their political equality by wartime service.

WORLD WAR II

What was the most efficient way to have women involved in the armed forces? Between the wars only the nurses remained in uniform but awareness of the wartime experience led Army planners to envision a women's corps in the next war. Once America entered the war and began working closely with Allies, generals became impressed with the success of the British in fielding large numbers of women in uniform. Magazines and newsreels featured Princess Elizabeth in her military uniform serving with the Auxiliary Territorial Service (ATS).[19] The Pentagon realized that total warfare necessitated the total use of womanpower. Many women were effectively deployed as civilian workers in munitions factories and indeed inside the Pentagon itself. The military leaders were, however, wanted to issue commands to men and women who had enlisted and had to follow orders regardless. When in 1942 it came time to create a women's army corps, Congresswomen Edith Nourse Rogers could not find sufficient backing for the creation of a reserve unit which would give women the same military status as male reservists. Reluctantly, she sponsored the compromise bill that created the Women's Auxiliary Army Corps (WAAC) giving women a military status that was distinctly inferior to men. However the inequality was resented by the women and did little to mollify the minority of men who wanted no women around whatsoever. The Navy went through the same debate but with a push from Eleanor Roosevelt decided to create a women's naval reserve that put women on the same legal and pay status as male reservists. They formed the WAVES (Women Accepted for Volunteer Emergency Service). The Coast Guard, a basically civilian agency with dual humanitarian and military roles, operated under Navy command during the war and in November, 1942, set up the U.S. Coast Guard Women's Reserve, nicknamed the SPARS (from the Coast Guard motto Semper Paratus). The Marines were first on the beach but last to create a woman's corps in February, 1943; their women reservists had no official nickname. Realizing its previous mistake, Congress replaced the WAAC in June 1943 with the Women's Army Corps (WAC). The women were now inside each service with the same status as men.[20]

The Pentagon wanted white women only, but political intervention from the Secretary of War and the White House overruled them. While the Navy saw no need for black women in general to serve in the military (and little need for black men either), the Army authorized a quota of 10 percent black women (but never exceeded 6 percent); they served in all-black WAC units and lived in segregated barracks. Late in the war the President forced the Navy to take 70 black Waves; they were not segregated. In addition, after a drumbeat of political pressure, especially from Eleanor Roosevelt and the NAACP, one WAC black unit was sent overseas. The 6888th Central Postal Battalion handled postal duties in England and France in 1945.[21]

In all 350,000 women served as Waacs, Wacs, Waves, Spars, Women Marines and nurses. Enticing women to join arguably the most masculine of professions was no easy selling job. Government posters portrayed beautiful women in striking uniforms who were getting a once in a lifetime opportunity to travel and serve. One slogan that had to be dropped was "free a man to fight." The men in safe support billets did not want to be reassigned to combat, nor did their womenfolk. The Wacs thus were a genuine threat. Army Air Forces, least bound by hoary tradition, offered women the greatest variety of jobs. One thousand served in the WASP (Women Airforce Service Pilots), with civilian status. Their mission was to ferry bombers and other warplanes from the factories to the embarkation points. They never flew in combat, but the duty was hazardous and thirty-nine were killed in crashes. In 1977 the Wasps were retroactively given military status.[22] Whichever branch in which they served and wherever they served, the servicewomen confounded the myth that they were unsuited for military life. Indeed, they mastered military language and customs, thrived at marching, accepted the discipline, excelled at their jobs and enjoyed the experiences.[23]

Unlike its Allies, the United States neither drafted women nor placed them in combat roles.[24] The closest policymakers came when President Roosevelt asked Congress for permission to draft nurses in 1945. Nearly half of the eligible civilian nurses in the country had already joined the Army or Navy Nurse Corps, the highest service rate by far of any occupational group, male or female. Plans for the invasion of Japan envisioned hundreds of thousands of casualties who would need the services of even more nurses. A Cadet Nurse Corps was in operation training thousands of young women for eventual military duty. Before Congress acted, Japan surrendered. Ironically, many Black nurses were available but could not be enlisted because of strict quotas. The Army Nurse Corps allowed handfuls of black women to join but they could only serve as nurses to black soldiers or POWs. The Navy rejected all black nurses until 1945, when President Roosevelt demanded that some be admitted.[25]

The U.S. Army in 1942 undertook an experiment to see how well mixed-gender crews could handle anti-aircraft guns. They outperformed the all-male crews, leading some generals to demand women for combat roles in fighting the German Luftwaffe. However the Army Chief of Staff, George Marshall, vetoed the idea. Public opinion was not ready for American women in combat, and such a move might reduce the recruitment of women for non-combat roles. America had drawn the gender line. Meanwhile British, Canadian, German and Russian women fought in anti-aircraft batteries.[26] Anti-aircraft units might be bombed but they certainly would not be captured, relieving generals of the fear their women would be captured and abused by the enemy. Nurses were not so lucky; after the Japanese seized the Philippines, 80 women nurses became POWs. The Japanese badly abused, tortured and killed captured nurses from Australia and elsewhere, but were not so brutal toward the Americans.[27]

Soldiers, sailors, marines and airmen, if asked if women should be in the military, would shake their heads. Yet once they met and served with such women many changed their attitude. According to one Army report, the unfavorable comments dropped from 90 percent before WACs arrived to 28 percent after several months in the station. In Australia favorable comments increased from 30 percent to 70 percent in soldiers' correspondence from the time the Wacs arrived in May 1944 to the time they disembarked in August 1945. The holdout minority, however, had the power to poison public opinion by spreading ugly false rumors about female sexuality—the women were whores or lesbians. (In reality, the servicewomen were far less sexually active than the servicemen, and rather less active than their sisters on the homefront.) Favorable observations about the performance of particular Wacs or Waves were unable to neutralize the poison.[28] As a result all the women's corps screened their volunteers carefully and dismissed any women deemed to exhibit "loose morals" or who became pregnant.[29] Venereal disease was far more prevalent among servicemen than servicewomen, for example, yet even a single case or rumor could cause long-term damage. A nationwide underground slander campaign painting all women soldiers as sexually promiscuous began in 1943, at about the time of increased government publicity emphasizing how badly women were needed to release men for combat. Canadian and British servicewomen experienced similar smear campaigns. The Pentagon called in the FBI to see if any of the rumors were true or if they could have been planted by Nazi agents. They determined that American servicemen were inventing and spreading these rumors. The Army recruiting campaigns never fully recovered, and all services suffered a major setback in recruiting women.[30]

On the homefront women played a critical role in producing the avalanche of munitions that won the war. Millions of women had been pulled out of housework and school. Many policymakers assumed they were serving "for the duration" and that traditional patterns would return after the war. Most formal restrictions on women holding certain jobs were indeed permanently dropped. Women were no longer eliminated from gaining employment because of age. Women teachers were not automatically required to quit once they married. Bank tellers and grocery store clerks—formerly male bastions—suddenly became predominantly female occupations. With the GI Bill most colleges and graduate programs became heavily male-dominated. Munitions factories shut down and laid everyone off; when the plants reopened to make civilian products they hired mostly men, especially male veterans. Female veterans legally had the same preferences in hiring, but in practice often found men were preferred. With the sexual rumors still stigmatizing the woman's branches, many veterans simply remained quiet and did not claim their rights under the GI Bill. The domestic ideal of companionate marriage—with the husband as the breadwinner—proved more attractive to women than the extra pay they could earn in factories. They had done their patriotic duty at the drill press during the emergency and now wanted a quiet family life.[31]

In such an environment, what would policymakers want for women inside or outside the postwar military? Senator Margaret Chase Smith of Maine defined the postwar debate explaining that "They either need these women or they do not."[32] If the armed forces *did* need women, then these women were needed on active duty as well as in the reserves: both or neither. On the military side, Generals Omar Bradley and Dwight Eisenhower led the fight to have women's corps remain a permanent part of the postwar military. They had WACs working for them in Europe and argued that a small permanent corps of women was needed to avoid the waste of time re-creating a women's corps during future wars. Their views were reflected in the Women's Armed Services' Integration Act of 1948.[33] The so-called "Integration Act" did not truly integrate women in various military branches since women would still serve in a separate woman's corps. The legislation limited women to two percent of the active duty military, limited the number who could ever attain senior rank, and barred women from achieving flag rank (that is, they were not allowed to become generals or admirals). There were also unequal policies in terms of enlistment requirements and dependency benefits. Pregnancy meant an honorable discharge. Thus the policy was set: permanent all-female units, with equal pay for women *inside* the military.

POST WORLD WAR II 1948–1967

The post World War II history of women in the military saw long periods of little activity interrupted by wars that quickened events and helped dissolve barriers to women's full participation in the armed forces. The Secretary of Defense set up an advisory committee, Defense Advisory Committee on Women in the Services

(DACOWITS) with 50 civilian members. The number and proportion of women in the services remained small—the 2% quota was never reached. Servicewomen, especially nurses, served in support roles near the front lines in the two major conflicts in this period, Korea and Vietnam. About 7,500 women were stationed in Vietnam at one time or another, along with two million men.[34]

1967–2004

During the height of the Vietnam War in 1967, the Pentagon became anxious to find qualified soldiers to handle increasing complex service duties. Racial barriers were lowered; Hispanics were recruited; the largest remaining pool of talent was womanpower. The Pentagon worked with Congress to increase promotion possibilities, remove the 2% ceiling and allow each of the services to set ceilings. Women were moving inward from the far periphery. In the next two decades thirty-four women achieved flag rank as generals or admirals. The prejudice against allowing women to command men broke down as women took command of hospital ships, military intelligence units, military police detachments and training bases. Efforts were made to minimize the risk women would ever be captured by the enemy; combat and service in combat support units remained closed. By 1970 the women's corps director's offices were eliminated. With the ending of the draft in 1972 the automatic inflow of young men declined, and the numbers and proportion of servicewomen in the all-volunteer military steadily rose. Analysts doubted whether All-Volunteer Force could have survived the 1970s without women. Absent the women directors there was a danger that women's issues might be ignored, so advisory committees were added and DACOWTIS was strengthened. America's allies in Europe lagged well behind the United States in using women, but they did form a Committee on Women in the NATO forces in 1977; by 1983 the Veterans Administration added an Advisory Committee on Women.[35]

The 1970s pulled servicewomen closer to the center; it was a watershed as important—and more successful—than World War Two. In 1972 collegiate ROTC programs started to enroll women who received training and scholarships, and were eligible for officer commissions in the reserves on the same terms as men. By 1978 all of the women's corps were disbanded.[36] In 1978, the Navy, obeying a federal court order, finally allowed women to become seafarers on non-combat vessels. Starting in 1974 the U.S. Merchant Marine Academy enrolled women as cadets. The Military Academy at West Point tried unsuccessfully to argue that since it trained combat officers and women were prohibited from combat that they should not allow female cadets. Upon close investigation, policymakers discovered that many cadets entered support units, not combat units. By 1976 all of the military academies were forced to drop their gender barriers. The academies had recently dropped their informal racial barriers and discovered that non-white cadets had equal or higher performance scales on athleticism and eagerness for combat. The first women graduated in 1980 in the face of intense hostility from a fraction of the male cadets who ridiculed the weaker upper body strength of women and feared their own military prowess and self-esteem were in doubt if women could perform alongside them.[37] Virginia Military Institute and The Citadel were state (not federal) institutions, and their cadets had civilian ROTC status. About a third of their graduates received military commissions. They furiously resisted the admission of women but as state agencies they had very weak legal cases, and finally submitted to a Supreme Court ruling in 1995.[38] Allowing women to volunteer for non-combat roles was acceptable to Americans, but at the time the line was drawn against either drafting women or allowing them to volunteer for combat missions. A furious debate erupted in the 1970s regarding an Equal Rights Amendment that would guarantee legal equality to women. It finally failed because the conservative opposition argued it would mean the drafting of women, and most supporters of equal rights were reluctant to draft women on an equal basis with men.[39]

The Army experimented with training mixed gender units for combat support positions and policy leaders carefully watched public opinion polls.[40] The tide turned in 1990–91 in the first Iraq War (Desert Shield and Desert Storm) as the American public saw that there was no longer a clear battlefield zone and realized women serving in combat support units were in harm's way. Army Specialist Melissa Rathbun-Nealy of the 233rd Transportation company was the first woman POW; she was held thirty-four days. Rathbun-Nealy explained that she was treated well in part because the Iraqis told her she was a hero, "as brave as Sylvester Stallone and as beautiful as Brooke Shields." The second woman POW, Major Rhonda L. Cornum, an Army flight surgeon, was on a rescue mission in 1991 when her Apache helicopter crashed. The Iraqis sexually molested her. Five women were killed in action, twenty-one wounded in action, and two became POWs.[41]

After watching the servicewomen's performances during the Persian Gulf War, Congress repealed the laws forbidding the Navy and Air Force servicewomen from sailing on combat vessels or flying combat planes. The legal barriers were down, but military leaders would now be *allowed* but not be *forced* to employ women in combat roles. Quickly a Presidential Commission on the Assignment of Women to Armed Forces was created. Its recommendations were mixed; not a ringing endorsement for opening more combat slots for women.[42] DACOWITS advice was critical in allowing women to volunteer for combat. Conservatives groused that it was a bastion of feminism that undermined national readiness, but even they had to admit the military needed its women.[43] The U.S. Coast Guard, part of the Department of Transportation at the time, not the Defense Department, was under no legal requirements for its assignment of women. Its strong humanitarian ethos and rescue mission appealed to women and its men were more likely to welcome the Coast Guard's efforts to move women up from desk jobs and support roles to front-line positions of authority. In 1977, it began assigning women to sea duty and a year later removed all restrictions and sent mixed gender crews to their ships. In April 1979, LT (jg) Beverly Kelly became the first women to command an American warship, the Coast Guard cutter Cape Newagen.[44]

Almost two decades later, in February 1992, 890 new Navy recruits at Orlando Naval Training Center became members of the first mixed-gender recruit companies (530 men, 360 women). That same year, the Navy selected the first women to serve the roles of a command of a squadron, a command at sea, and a Naval astronaut. Not to be left on the ground, the Air Force began training women to fly a wide range of aircraft and had women fill instructor positions even for aircraft that they themselves could not legally fly in combat missions. By 2001, the Coast Guard flew through another ceiling by using female helicopter pilots.[45] By 2004 only a few restrictions remained: women were not deployed in submarines, in tanks or in infantry units.

Debates on the compatibility of military service with motherhood and sexuality continued to roil the waters. In 1990 *Newsweek* reported that some troops dubbed Desert Storm "A Mom's War."[46] In actuality, it was more of a Parents' War than any other war in history. Previous wars were fought primarily by young, single men who volunteered or were drafted for the occasion. Most fathers had been exempted from the draft, even during the world wars. Most fathers who were drafted were normally assigned to non-combatant duty because America did not want war orphans. The all-volunteer military was now much older, better-paid, career oriented, married with children, with expectations that the command would give high priority to the issues of family support.[47] Pregnancy also created scrutiny and concern. Some women reservists deployed before they discovered that they were pregnant, still others became pregnant while overseas. Rumors abounded that thousands of women were being sent back because they were pregnant. The media had a field day and dubbed the ship which returned pregnant women to the United States, the "Love Boat." In the real world approximately 5–10% of servicewomen are pregnant at any given time.[48]

In 1991 Navy aviators sponsored an off-duty wild and raunchy "Tailhook" party with support from senior officers. Two admirals were forced to retire because of their cover-up of the scandal, which revealed an intensely sexual, anti-female sensibility among combat pilots.[49] Episodes of sexual harassment even sexual assault continue to surface every year, despite repeated commands from senior authorities to stop immediately. The Air Force Academy discovered that 19% of the women cadets had been victims of sexual assault by male cadets. However four out of five did not report it. Pentagon investigators uncovered a tolerant attitude toward male offenders, and a harsh one toward whistleblowers, who risked being accused of wrecking unit cohesion and acting like crybabies instead of warriors. The four top commanders at the Academy were transferred to other jobs in the Air Force.[50] Individual women in the academies, reserves and on active duty continue to find a hostile environment caused by the fervent belief of about one-fifth of servicemen that women do not belong in the military.[51]

In the past few decades the percentage of women in the armed forces has increased to double digits in the academies and in the service branches. Women are so well integrated that neither service units nor combat support units could operate without them. However that is a command perspective and misses the day to day psychological interactions. As sociologist Rosabeth Moss Kanter has convincingly argued, until women reach a critical mass, about a third of each unit, they are outsiders and are perceived as tokens—not individuals—perhaps even sexual objects rather than teammates.[52] By 2000 women reached the 30% threshold at the Coast Guard Academy. Furthermore the Coast Guard has numerous maritime missions and its humanitarian life-saving activities have proven especially attractive to women. This helps explain why the Coast Guard avoided a culture of harassment, and suggests for the next decade women in the other military service will remain outsiders.

NOTES

1. Two histories span the centuries: Jeanne Holm, *Women in the Military: An Unfinished Revolution* (Novato, CA: Presidio Press, 1993); Linda Grant DePauw, *Battle Cries and Lullabies: Women in War from Prehistory to the Present* (Norman: University of Oklahoma Press, 1998). More focused is M. C. Devilbiss, *Women and Military Service, History, Analysis, and Overview of Key Issues* (Maxwell: Air University Press, 1990), online at http://www.maxwell.af.mil/au/aul/aupress/Books/B-44/html/b44chl.htm. An excellent scholarly history is Susan Godson, *Serving Proudly: A History of Women in the U.S. Navy* (Annapolis: U.S. Naval Institute, 2002).

2. Full text is online at http://www.gutenberg.net/etext97/crmmr10.txt. For background see "Early American Captivity Narratives" at http://guweb2.gonzaga.edu/faculty/campbell/enl310/captive.htm

3. Holly A. Mayer, *Belonging to the Army: Camp Followers and Community during the American Revolution* (Columbia: University of South Carolina Press, 1996); Linda Grant DePauw, "Women in Combat: The Revolutionary War Experience," *Armed Forces and Society* 7 (Winter 1981): 209–226; Linda Grant DePauw, *Founding Mothers: Women of America in the Revolutionary Era* (New York: Houghton Mifflin, 1975); Walter Hart Blumenthal, *Women Camp Followers of the American Revolution* (New York: Arno Press, 1974). Deborah Sampson received a pension as Robert Shurtliff of the 4th Massachusetts Regiment. At one point Sampson removed a musket ball from her thigh for fear that a doctor might discovered her identity. Lucy Freeman and Alma Bond, *America's First Woman Warrior: The Courage of Deborah Sampson* (New York: Paragon House, 1992). For the ideological context see Linda K. Kerber, *Women of the Republic: Intellect and Ideology in Revolutionary America* (Chapel Hill: University of North Carolina Press, 1980). During the War, many women worked for Loyalists, British and Hessian forces, and some for the French. See Don N. Hagist, "The Women of the British Army during the American Revolution." *Minerva Quarterly Report on Women and the Military* 13, 2 (Summer 1995). On the European background see Barton C. Hacker, "Women and Military Institutions in Early Modern Europe: A Reconnaissance," *Signs: Journal of Women in Culture and Society*, 6 (Summer 1981) pp. 643–671.

4. "Sarah Osborn, A Soldier's Wife, Relates How She Accompanied the Continental Army to Yorktown" (1781), and "Private Joseph Martin Provides the Only Contemporary Account of "Molly Pitcher" (1778), in John Whiteclay Chambers and G. Kurt Piehler, eds. *Major Problems in Military History* (Boston: Houghton Mifflin Co. 1999), pp. 70, 73–74. See also Charles E. Claghorn, *Women Patriots of the American Revolution* (New York: Rowman & Littlefield, 1994), which provides 600 brief biographies.

5. Edward M. Coffman, *The Old Army: A Portrait of the American Army in Peacetime, 1784–1898* (New York: Oxford University Press, 1986).

6. Ellen McGowan Biddle, *Reminiscences of a Soldier's Wife* (Mechanicsburg: Stackpole Books, 2002); Sandra Myers, ed., *Cavalry Wife—The Diary Of Eveline M. Alexander 1866–1867* (College Station: Texas A&M Press, 1977).

7. See Lauren Cook Burgess, ed. *An Uncommon Soldier: The Civil War Letters of Sarah Rosetta Wakeman, alias Pvt. Lyons Wakeman, 153rd Regiment, New York State Volunteers, 1862–1864* (Pasadena, MD: Minerva Center 1994); Deanne Blanton and Lauren N. Cook, *They Fought Like Demons: Women Soldiers in the Civil War* (Baton Rouge: Louisiana State University Press, 2002); Elizabeth D. Leonard, *All the Daring of the Soldier: Women of the Civil War Armies* (New York: Penguin Books, 2001); S. Emma E. Edmonds, *Memoirs of a Soldier, Nurse and Spy: A Woman's Adventures in the Union Army* (De Kalb: Northern Illinois University Press, 1999.

8. *Belle Boyd in Camp and Prison* (1865) is online at http://docsouth.unc.edu/boyd/menu.html

9. For further studies of women's roles during the Civil War see the general classic work Mary Elizabeth Massey, *Bonnet Brigades: American Women in the Civil War* (New York: Knopf, 1966); and C. Vann Woodward, ed., *Mary Chestnut's Civil War* (New

Haven: Yale University Press, 1986); Charles East, ed., *Sarah Morgan: Civil War Diary of a Southern Woman* (New York: Touchstone Books, 1992). For scholarly analysis see Drew Gilpin Faust, *Mothers of Invention: Women of the Slaveholding South in the American Civil War* (Chapel Hill: University of North Carolina, 1996); and Catherine Clinton, Nina Silber, eds., *Divided Houses: Gender and the Civil War* (New York: Oxford University Press, 1992). On women on the homefront see George C. Rable, *Civil Wars: Women and the Crisis of Southern Nationalism* (Urbana: University of Illinois Press, 1989); Margaret Ripley Wolfe, *Daughters of Canaan: A Saga of Southern Women* (Lexington: University Press of Kentucky, 1995); Elizabeth D. Leonard, *Yankee Women: Gender Battles in the Civil War* (New York, W.W. Norton & Co. 1994); Bell Irwin Wiley, *Confederate Women* (Westport, CT: Greenwood, 1975).

10. The book is online at http://digital.library.upenn.edu/women/alcott/sketches/sketches.html

11. Jeanie Attie, *Patriotic Toil: Northern Women and the American Civil War* (Ithaca: Cornell University Press, 1998). Judith Ann Giesberg, *Civil War Sisterhood: The U.S. Sanitary Commission and Women's Politics in Transition* (Boston: Northeastern University Press 2000) shows that the Sanitary Commission was a critical link between antebellum evangelical religious reforms and postwar movements such as the WCTU and suffrage crusades. For primary documents see http://www.netwalk.com/~jpr/index.htm. For other nurses see David Gollaher, *A Voice for the Mad: The Life of Dorothea Dix* (New York: Free Press, 1994); Stephen B. Oates, *Woman of Valor: Clara Barton and The Civil War* (New York: Free Press, 1995); John R. Brumgardt, ed., *Civil War Nurse: The Diary and Letters of Hannah Ropes* (Knoxville: University of Tennessee Press, 1980), reveals Ropes' close observation of hospital conditions and efforts to achieve reforms over the course of a year. See also Harold Elk Straubing ed., *In Hospital and Camp: The Civil War Through the Eyes of Its Doctors and Nurses* (Mechanicsburg: Stackpole Books, 1993); Cornelia Hancock, *Letters of a Civil War Nurse: Cornelia Hancock, 1863–1865* (Lincoln: University of Nebraska Press, 1998).

12. Elizabeth D. Leonard, *Yankee Women* Chapter 3; Leonard Berlow, "Mary Walker: Only Woman to Win the Medal of Honor," *Time Magazine* (September 1980) pp. 60–61. Walker also supervised a hospital of women prisoners. In 1865 she became the first woman—and only—to be awarded the Congressional Medal of Honor. It was later rescinded and then re-awarded. Note that Medal at the time was not nearly as important or symbolic as today.

13. Harriet Hyman Alonso, *Peace as a Women's Issue: A History of the U.S. Movement for World Peace and Women's Right* (Syracuse: Syracuse University Press, 1993). See the online documents in "How Did Women Activists Promote Peace in Their 1915 Tour of Warring European Capitals?" at http://womhist.binghamton.edu/hague/doclist.htm

14. Lettie Gavin, *American Women in World War I: They Also Served* (Niwot, CO: University Press of Colorado, 1997); Barbara Steinson, *American Women's Activism in World War* (New York: Garland, 1982); Dorothy Schneider and Carl J. Schneider, *Into the Breach: American Women Overseas in WWI* (New York: Viking Press, 1991); Foster Rhea Dulles, *American Red Cross* (New York: Harper & Brothers, 1950). Taking a contrarian view, John F. Hutchinson. *Champions of Charity: War and the Rise of the Red Cross* (Boulder: Westview Press, 1997) complains that in every country the Red Cross (and Red Crescent) societies promoted national war aims and by making medical services more efficient, made warfare itself more efficient.

15. On AEF see Susan Zeiger, *In Uncle Sam's Service: Women Workers with the American Expeditionary Force, 1917–1919* (Ithaca, NY: Cornell University Press, 1999); Addie W. Hunter and Kathryn M. Johnson, *Two Colored Women with the AEF* (New York: G.K. Hall, 1997).

16. Godson, *Serving Proudly;* Linda L. Hewitt, *Woman Marines in World War I* (Washington, D.C.: History and Museums Division, Headquarters U.S. Marine Corps, 1974); Jean Ebbert and Marie-Beth Hall, *The First, the Few, the Forgotten: Navy and Marine Corps Women in World War II* (Annapolis: Naval Institute Press, 2002), see also Jean Ebbert, Marie-Beth Hall, and Edward Latimer Beach, *Crossed Currents: Naval Women from WWI to Tailbook* (Washington, D.C.: Batsford Brassey Inc., 1999). The term "reservist" is misleading because all women reservists were on active duty. They were deactivated by 1919 and by 1925 the loophole had been closed. For the U.S. Coast Guard see John A. Tilley, "A History of Women in the Coast Guard" online at http://www.uscg.mil/hq/g-cp/history/h_womn.html

17. Mattie E. Treadwell, *The United States Army in World War II, Special Studies, the Women's Army Corps* (Washington: Office of the Chief of Military History, 1954) is the outstanding official history of the WAC and should not be missed; the full text is online at http://www.army.mil/cmh-pg/books/wwii/Wac/index.htm For recent scholarship see D'Ann Campbell, *Women at War With America: Private Lives in a Patriotic Era* (Cambridge, MA: Harvard University Press, 1984), Chap 1.

18. Sarnecky, *U.S. Army Nurse Corps;* Joy Bright Hancock, *Lady in the Navy: A Personal Reminiscence* (Annapolis: Naval Institute Press, 1972); Doris M. Steiner, *In and Out of Harm's Way: A History of the Navy Nurse Corps* (Washington D.C. Navy Nurse Corps Assn. 1996); Godson, *Serving Proudly.*

19. For a good overview see Shelford Bidwell, *The Women's Royal Army Corps* (London: Leo Cooper, 1977).

20. Campbell, *Women at War With America,* Chapter 1; D'Ann Campbell, "Fighting with the Navy: Women's

Experiences in World War II," *New Interpretations in Naval History* (1993), 343–360; Treadwell, *Women's Army Corps;* Godson, *Proudly Serving;* Lt. Col. Pat Meid, "Marine Corps Women's Reserve in World War II," Historical Branch, G-3 Division Headquarters, U.S. Marine Corps, (Washington: Marine Corps, 1964).

21. Treadwell, *Women's Army Corps,* Ch. 30 online at http://www.army.mil/cmh-pg/books/wwii/Wac/ch30.htm; Brenda L. Moore, *To Serve My Country, To Serve My Race: The Story of the Only African American WACs Stationed Overseas during World War II* (New York: New York University Press, 1996). See also Charity Adams Early, *One Woman's Army: A Black Officer Remembers the WAC* (College Station: Texas A & M University Press, 1989); Martha S. Putney, *When the Nation Was in Need: Blacks in the Women's Army Corps during World War II* (Metuchen, NJ: Scarecrow Press, 1992). See also Ulysses Lee, *The Employment of Negro Troops* (Washington: Center for Military History, 1966), online at http://www.army.mil/cmh/books/wwii/11-4/chapter14.htm#b6

22. Wasps flew planes and therefore were most like men in combat, which has led to an extensive literature. See Sally V. Keil, *Those Wonderful Women in Their Flying Machines: The Unknown Heroines of World War Two* (New York: Atheneum, 1979); Jean Hascall Cole, *Women Pilots of World War II* (University of Utah Press, 1992); Molly Merryman, *Clipped Wings: The Rise and Fall of the Women Airforce Service Pilots (Wasps) of World War II* (New York: New York University Press, 1998).

23. See D'Ann Campbell, "Servicewomen of World War II," *Armed Forces and Society* 16 (Winter 1990) pp. 251–270 and Campbell, *Women at War With America,* Chapter 1. For letters and memoirs see Anne Bosanko Green, *One Woman's War: Letters Home from the Women's Army Corps 1944–1946* (St. Paul: Minnesota Historical Society Press, 1980); Alieen Kilgore Henderson, *Stateside Soldier: Life in the Women's Army Corps 1944–1945* (Columbia: University of South Carolina Press, 2001); Judy Barrett Litoff and David C. Smith, eds. *We're in the War Too: World War II Letters from American Women in Uniform* (New York: Oxford University Press, 1994; See also, Brenda L. Moore, *Serving Our Country: Japanese American Women in the Military during World War II* (Newark: Rutgers University Press, 2003); D'Ann Campbell, "The Regimented Women of World War II," in Jean Elshtain and Sheila Tobias, eds., *Women, Militarism, and War* (Rowman & Littlefield, 1990), 107–122. For comparative perspective see John Costello, *Love, Sex and War: Changing Values 1939–1945* (London: Collins, 1985).

24. On the possibility of drafting Wacs, see Treadwell, *Women's Army Corps,* ch 13 online at http://www.army.mil/cmh-pg/books/wwii/Wac/ch13.htm#b12.

25. See Mary T. Sarnecky, *A History of the U.S. Army Nurse Corps* (Philadelphia: University of Pennsylvania

Press, 1999); Godson, *Serving Proudly.* More details on nurses appear in Evelyn Monahan and Rosemary Neidel Greenlee, *And If I Perish: Frontline U.S. Army Nurses in WWII* (New York: Knopf, 2003); Diane Burke Fessler, *No Time for Fear: Voices of American Military Nurses in World War II* (Lansing: Michigan State University Press, 1977); Barbara Brooks Tomblin, *GI Nightingale: The Army Nurse Corps in World War II* (Lexington: University Press of Kentucky, 1996); Doris M. Steiner, *In and Out of Harm's Way: A History of the Navy Nurse Corps* (Washington: Navy Nurse Corps Assn., 1996).

26. D'Ann Campbell, "Women in Combat: The World War II Experience in the United States, Great Britain, Germany and the Soviet Union," *Journal of Military History* 57 (April 1993) pp. 301–323 online at http://members.aol.com/DAnn01/combat.html; Treadwell, *Women's Army Corps,* ch. 17 online at http://www.army.mil/cmh-pg/books/wwii/Wac/ch17.htm#b2; see also Reina Pennington, *Women, and War: Soviet Airwomen in World War II Combat* (Lawrence: University Press of Kansas, 2002); Anne Noggle, *A Dance with Death: Soviet Airwomen in World War II* (College Station: Texas A&M University Press, 2002). For Russian memoirs see Kazimiera J. Cottam ed., *Defending Leningrad: Women Behind Enemy Lines* (Nepean, ON, Canada: New Military Publishing, 1998).

27. Evelyn Monahan and Rosemary Neidel Greenlee, *All This Hell: U.S. Nurses Imprisoned by the Japanese* (Lexington: University Press of Kentucky, 2003); Elizabeth Norman, *We Band of Angels: The Untold Story of American Nurses Trapped on Bataan by the Japanese* (New York: Bantam Books, 2001); Dorothy Still Danner, *What a Way to Spend a War: Navy Nurse POWs in the Philippines* (Annapolis: U.S. Naval Institute, 1995).

28. Campbell, *Women at War with America,* Chapter 1; For treatment of lesbians in the military see Allan Berube, *Coming Out Under Fire: The History of Gay Men and Women in World War Two* (New York: Free Press, 1990); Mary Ann Humphrey, *My Country, My Right to Serve: Experiences of Gay Men and Women in the Military, World War II to the Present* (New York: Harper Collins, 1990); see also Randy Shilts, *Conduct Unbecoming: Lesbians and Gays in the U.S. Military: Vietnam to the Persian Gulf* (New York: New York University Press, 1990).

29. The majority of women dismissed for pregnancy were married and the rates were much lower than for same age women on the homefront. In the Army the pregnancy discharge rate was seventeen per thousand women in 1943, forty-nine per thousand in 1944, and sixty-eight per thousand in 1945. To discourage abortions women were discharged if they were or had been pregnant. See Treadwell, *Women's Army Corps,* ch 25, online at http://www.army.mil/cmh-pg/books/wwii/Wac/ch25.htm

30. Campbell, *Women at War with America,* Chapters 1 and 2 compares the differences in perceptions among servicemen between nurses and non-nurses in WWII and the tendency to be protective of "their" women. See also Leisa D. Meyer, *Creating GI Jane, Sexuality and Power in the Women's Army Corps During World War II* (New York: Columbia University Press, 1996); Treadwell, *Women's Army Corps,* ch. 11 online at http://www.army.mil/cmh-pg/books/wwii/Wac/ch11.htm; Ruth Roach Pierson, "Ladies or Loose Women: The Canadian Women's Army Corps in World War II," *Atlantis* 4 (1979): 245–266. On male gender perspectives see Samuel Stouffer et al., *The American Soldier: Combat and Its Aftermath* (Princeton, 1949), 2:131–34; Joshua S. Goldstein, *War and Gender* (New York: Cambridge University Press, 2001); and William Arkin and Lynne R. Dobrofsky, "Military Socialization and Masculinity," *Journal of Social Issues* 34 (1978) pp. 151–68.

31. Campbell, *Women at War with America,* Chapter 4; Keith W. Olson. *The GI Bill, the Veterans, and the Colleges* (Lexington: University Press of Kentucky, 1974); Susan Hartmann, *The Home Front and Beyond: American Women in the 1940s* (Boston: Twayne Publishers, 1982); Treadwell, *Women's Army Corps,* ch. 36. Online at http://www.army.mil/cmh-pg/books/wwii/Wac/ch36 .htm

32. Janann Sherman, "'They Either Need These Women or They Do Not' Margaret Chase Smith and the Fight for Regular Status for Women in the Military," *Journal of Military History* 53 (January 1990), pp. 47–78; Sherman, *No Place for a Woman: A Life of Senator Margaret Chase Smith* (Rutgers: Rutgers University Press, 2000); Treadwell, *Women's Army Corps,* pp. 740–749 online at http://www.army.mil/cmh-pg/books/wwii/Wac/ch36 .htm

33. Bettie J. Morden, *The Women's Army Corps, 1945–1978* (Washington: Center for Military History), is the excellent official history. It is online at http://www .army.mil/cmh-pg/books/wac/. See also Godson, *Serving Proud;* Treadwell, *Women's Army Corps;* Technically, women in the U.S. Air Force (WAF) were from the beginning airmen and officers rather than WAF airmen and WAF officers.

34. Sarnecky, *U.S. Army Nurse Corps;* Frances Omori, *Quiet Heroes: Navy Nurses in Korea* (New York: Smith House, 2001); Elizabeth Norman, *Women at War: The Story of Fifty Women Nurses Who Served in Vietnam* (Philadelphia: University of Pennsylvania Press, 1990); Judith Bellafaire, "Called to Duty: Army Women During the Korean War Era," *Army Center of Military History* 2,2 (Spring 2001): 19–27; Olga Gruhzit-Hoyt, *A Time Remembered: American Women in the Vietnam War* (Novato, CA: Presidio Press, 1999); Keith Walker, *A Piece of My Heart: The Stories of 26 Women Who Served in Vietnam* (Novato, CA: 1986); Spurgeon Neel,

Medical Support of the U.S. Army in Vietnam 1965–1970 (Washington: Department of the Army, 1991), ch. 12, online at http://history.amedd.army.mil/booksdocs/ vietnam/medicalsupport/frameindex.html; Bobbi Hovis, *Station Hospital Saigon: A Navy Nurse in Vietnam 1963–1964* (Annapolis: Naval Institute Press, 1992).

35. See Bettie J. Morden, *The Women's Army Corps, 1945–1978* (Washington: Center for Military History, 1990) ch. 10 online at http://www.army.mil/cmh-pg/books/wac/chapter10.htm; Curtis L. Gilroy et al., "The All-Volunteer Army: Fifteen Years Later," *Armed Forces & Society* (1990): 329–50; Robert F. Lockman, and Aline O. Quester, "The AVF: Outlook for the Eighties and Nineties," *Armed Forces & Society* 2 (Winter 1985): 169–82; Frank N. Schubert and Theresa L. Kraus, eds., *The Whirlwind War: The United States Army in Operations DESERT SHIELD and DESERT STORM* (Washington: Center for Military History, 1995), ch. 9, online at http://www.army.mil/cmh-pg/books/www/ www9.htm

36. Morden, *The Women's Army Corps, 1945–1978* ch 13, online at http://www.army.mil/cmh-pg/books/wac/ chapter13.htm; Holm, *Women in the Military,* Devilbiss, *Women and Military Service.*

37. The best coverage is Judith Hicks Stiehm, *Bring Me Men and Women: Mandated Change at the U.S. Air Force Academy* (Berkeley: University of California Press, 1981). See also Carol Barkalow with Andrea Raab, *In the Men's House: An Inside Account of Life in the Army by One of West Point's First Female Graduates* (New York: Poseidon, 1990); Kathleen P. Durning, *Women at the Naval Academy: The First Year of Integration* (San Diego: Navy Personnel Research and Development, 1978); John Lowell, *Neither Athens Nor Sparta?* (Bloomington: Indiana University Press, 1979); Robert F. Priest and John W. Houston, *Analysis of Spontaneous Cadet Comments on the Admission of Women. No 76–104,* Washington, DC: Office of Institutional Research, 1976; Office of the Chief of Naval Operation, *Navy Women's Study Group: An Update Report on the Progress of Women in the Navy* (Washington, DC: Chief of Naval Operations, 1990); Alan G. Vitters and Nora Scott Kinzer, *Report of the Admission of Women to the U.S. Military Academy (Project Athena)* (Washington, D.C.: Department of Behavioral Sciences and Leadership, 1977); D'Ann Campbell, "Lessons on Gender Integration from the Military Academies," in Francine D'Amico and Laurie Weinstein, eds. *Gender Camouflage: Women and the U.S. Military* (New York University Press, 1999), 67–79.

38. See Laura Fairchild Brodie, *Breaking Out: VMI and the Coming of Women* (New York: Pantheon Books, 2000); Philippa Strum, *Women in the Barracks: The VMI Case and Equal Rights* (Lawrence: University Press of Kansas, 2002); a woman cadet who enjoyed VMI tells her story in Nancy Mace with Mary Jane Ross, *In*

the *Company of Men: A Woman at The Citadel* (New York: Simon and Schuster, 2001). For a stinging feminist attack on the Citadel see Catherine S. Manegold, *In Glory's Shadow: Shannon Faulkner, The Citadel, and a Changing America* (New York: Knopf, 2000).

39. Jane J. Mansbridge, *Why We Lost the ERA* (Chicago: University of Chicago Press, 1986).

40. Morden, *The Women's Army Corps, 1945–78*, ch. 13 online at http://www.army.mil/cmh-pg/books/wac/chapter13.htm#b4; Schubert and Kraus, eds., *The Whirlwind War*, ch. 9, online at http://www.army.mil/cmh-pg/books/www/www9.htm

41. D'Ann Campbell, "Combatting the Gender Gulf," *Temple Political & Civil Rights Law Review* 2,1 (Fall 1992), pp. 63–91; Department of Defense, *Conduct of the Persian Gulf Conflict, Final Report to Congress 647* (1991); Rhonda Cornum as told to Peter Copeland, *She Went to War: The Rhonda Cornum Story* (Novato, CA: Presidio Press, 1992).

42. Presidential Commission on the Assignment of Women in the Armed Forces. *Women in Combat: Report to the President*, November 15, 1992 (Washington: Brassey's, 1993); Campbell, "Combatting the Gender Gulf."

43. See the DACOWITS homepage at http://www.dtic.mil/dacowits/; Conservatives set up the "Center for Military Readiness" with a homepage at http://cmrlink.org/; for a flavor of their hostility see Brian Mitchell, *Weak Link: The Feminization of the American Military* (Chicago: Regnery, 1989) and his *Women in the Military: Flirting with Disaster* (Chicago: Regnery, 1998). Despite the evidence to the contrary from a series of wars in the Mideast, the antifeminist conservatives continue to predict that American units will be massacred in future wars because women degrade the performance of combat units.

44. Grace Lichtenstein, "Oh, the Captain, She's a Lady," *New York Times* (Aug. 26, 1979); John A. Tilley, "A History of Women in the Coast Guard" at http://www.uscg.mil/hq/g-cp/history/h_womn.html. See also "Women & the U.S. Coast Guard" http://www.uscg.mil/hq/g-cp/history/Women%20Index.html

45. Campbell, "Combatting the Gender Gulf," pp. 67–68; See also Estelle McDoniel, *Registered Nurse to Rear Admiral: A First for Navy Women* (Austin: Eakin Publications, 2003).

46. Melinda Beck et al., "Our Women in the Desert," *Newsweek* (Sept. 10, 1990) p. 2.

47. See the resources online at the Military Family Resource Center website at http://www.mfrcdodqol.org/reseval.cfm and Military Family Research Institute, "Deployment and Family Separation: An Annotated Bibliography" online at http://www.mfri.purdue.edu/pages/research/annotated_bib.html

48. Mady Wechsler Segal, "The Argument for Female Combatants" in Nancy Goldman, ed., *Female Soldiers—Combatants or Noncombatants: Historical and Contemporary Perspectives* (Westport, CT: Greenwood Press, 1982).

49. William H. McMichael, *The Mother of All Hooks: The Story of the U.S. Navy's Tailhook Scandal* (New York: Transaction, 1997); Jean Zimmerman, *Tail Spin: Women at War in the Wake of Tailhook* (New York: Doubleday, 1995).

50. Cathy Booth Thomas, "The Air Force Academy's Rape Scandal," *Time Magazine* (March 10, 2003), online at http://www.time.com/time/magazine/story/0,9171,1101030310-428045,00.html; for the details see "Report of the Panel to Review Sexual Misconduct Allegations at the U.S. Air Force Academy," (Washington: 2003) which is online at http://www.dod.mil/news/Sep2003/d20030922usafareport.pdf; for an in-depth study of a telling episode see D'Ann Campbell, "The Spirit Run and Football Cordon: A Case Study of Female Cadets at the U.S. Military Academy," in Elliott Converse, ed. *Forging the Sword: Selecting, Educating and Training Cadets and Junior Military Officers in the Modern World* (Chicago: Imprint, 1998), 237–47. For feminist approaches see Cynthia Enloe, *Does Khaki Become You? The Militarization of Women's Lives* (London: Pandora Press, 1988); Jean Bethke Elshtain and Sheila Tobias eds., *Women, Militarism and War* (Savage, MD: Rowman and Littlefield, 1990); and Stiehm, *Arms and the Enlisted Woman* (Philadelphia: Temple University Press, 1989).

51. Laura L. Miller, "Not Just weapons of the Weak: Gender Harassment as a Form of Protest for Army Men," *Social Psychology Quarterly* 60 (March 1997) pp. 32–51, reported that some servicemen believe that organized feminism has made women dominant in the military. They see men as an oppressed minority which has a right to fight back with guerilla tactics. See also Juanita M. Firestone and Richard J. Harris, "Sexual Harassment in the U.S. Military: Individualized and Environmental Contexts," *Armed Forces & Society* 21 (Fall 1994), pp. 25–43.

52. Rosabeth Moss Kanter, *Men and Women in the Corporation* (New York: Basic Books, 1993); Karen O. Dunivin, "Gender and Perceptions of the Job Environment in the U.S. Air Force," *Armed Forces and Society* 5 (1988), pp. 80–85.

FURTHER READING

Campbell, D'Ann. *Women at War with America: Private Lives in a Patriotic Era.* Cambridge, MA: Harvard University Press, 1984.

DePauw, Linda Grant. *Battle Cries and Lullabies: Women in War from Prehistory to the Present.* Norman: University of Oklahoma Press, 1998.

Devilbiss, M.C. *Women and Military Service, a History, Analysis, and Overview of Key Issues.* Maxwell: Air University Press, 1990, online at http://www.maxwell.af.mil/au/aul/aupress/Books/B-44/html/b44ch1.htm.

Enloe, Cynthia. *Does Khaki Become You? The Militarization of Women's Lives.* London: Pandora Press, 1988.

Godson, Susan. *Serving Proudly: A History of Women in the U.S. Navy.* Annapolis: U.S. Naval Institute, 2002.

Holm, Jeanne. *Women in the Military: An Unfinished Revolution.* Novato, CA: Presidio Press, 1993.

Morden, Bettie J. *The Women's Army Corps, 1945–1978.* Washington: Center for Military History 1990, online at http://www.army.mil/cmh-pg/books/wac/chapter 13.htm#b4

Sarnecky, Mary T. *A History of the U.S. Army Nurse Corps.* Philadelphia: University of Pennsylvania Press, 1999.

Stiehm, Judith. *Arms and the Enlisted Woman.* Philadelphia: Temple University Press, 1989.

Treadwell, Mattie E. *The United States Army in World War II, Special Studies, the Women's Army Corps.* Washington: Office of the Chief of Military History, 1954.

Grounds for Criticism: Coffee, Passion, and the Politics of Feminist Discourse

Elizabeth A. Kelly

More than one-third of the world's people drink coffee today, but coffee has never been merely a beverage. Three centuries or so have gone by since it became an overnight rage among the fashionable and witty in cities across Europe. Jürgen Habermas, among others, has drawn attention to the role played by coffeehouses in the formation of a bourgeois public sphere in the late eighteenth century. Indeed, the role of the coffeehouse as a bastion of free speech had far-reaching implications: Coffee and the establishments serving it played an integral role in the founding of the United States and continue to provide arenas where discourses of resistance and alternatives to established "politics as usual" may take place. The GI coffeehouse movement, for example, promoted resistance to U.S. involvement in the Vietnam Conflict; places like Chicago's Mountain Moving Coffeehouse, established over twenty years ago and still operating today, have been focal points for the development of a feminist "women's culture" and served as safe spaces for the articulation of feminist and lesbian–feminist political thought.

This article will explore the relationship between coffee and political discourse, paying particular attention to the role of coffeehouses as alternative public spheres. It will also examine the often complex relationships between coffee, coffeehouse cultures, and gender, along with how these relationships have shifted historically. Considered by turns as cure-all or the "devil's brew," the common

I am grateful to Uma Narayan, Jacqueline Taylor, and Linda Hillman for their careful readings, encouragement, and insights. Michael Forman, Carl Larsen, and John Martin also deserve thanks for reading and commenting on an earlier version of this article and for providing the moment of its "conception."

people's drink or the liquor of the elite, object of disdain or cause for celebration, coffee has seldom failed to elicit one emotion that perhaps best explains its powerful political impact: passion. I will argue that such emotions, often overlooked by political theory, indeed stand at the center of a critical theory of coffee drinking.

ORIGINS OF COFFEE

The origins of coffee drinking are shrouded in mystery; legends abound, but there is little factual evidence to show precisely when people began to drink this seductive brew, let alone who first concocted it. Remarkably similar accounts from Arab chronicles credit either King Solomon or the Prophet Muhammad with first "discovering" coffee. As the story goes, the great man interrupts a journey to visit a town whose inhabitants suffer from a strange, unnamed illness. On command from the Angel Gabriel, he roasts coffee beans and prepares a beverage whose curative powers are truly miraculous; the townsfolk recover completely after taking only a few sips.[1] Another tale has the dreaming Prophet visited by an angel, who commands Muhammad to fetch a bowl of water to a nearby field. When the water stops moving, a sign from Allah will appear. The next morning, Muhammad carries out these instructions: When the water in the bowl is still, he kneels in prayer. A shrub appears before him, and a voice commands him to taste its fruit. Obeying, he experiences a great surge of energy and leaves the field refreshed. The fruit, of course, is the coffee bean.[2]

A variation on the "discovery" theme centers on the dervish Omar, who is awakened one midnight by a huge apparition, the spirit of his long-dead mentor, which guides him to a coffee tree. Omar and his disciples at first attempt to eat the berries; they then try to soften them in water. When this fails, they drink the liquid in which the berries have been boiled. Shortly thereafter, victims of an epidemic of itching rampant in Mocha come to consult with Omar and are cured after drinking the brew. Their gratitude allows Omar to enter Mocha with honors; he becomes the patron saint of coffee growers, owners of coffeehouses, and coffee drinkers alike.[3]

Perhaps the most commonly told story of coffee's origins is that of the "dancing goats." Here Kaldi, a young Ethiopian goatherd, is depressed. Weary of searching for greener pastures and faced with a flock of tired, hungry goats, he rests, unable to move on. The herd begins to nibble sweet red berries off nearby bushes; suddenly all the goats begin behaving very strangely. The oldest billy goat kicks up his heels, cavorting ecstatically; the others quickly join him in a manic dance. Startled, Kaldi, decides to try the berries himself. He, too, begins leaping giddily about the hillside, his troubles forgotten. A passing monk is astonished to see shepherd and flock dancing about the meadow; he samples the berries, and invites other monks to join in. That night during prayers, the monks all feel remarkably alert. They spread news of the amazing discovery throughout the religious community;

the fame of the coffee berries—and the beverage brewed from them—spreads throughout the land.[4]

It seems safe to say that whoever the first coffee drinkers may have been, they experienced sensations ranging from exhilaration to religious ecstasy. None of the serious histories of coffee I looked at in the course of preparing this essay contains any mention—whether couched in terms of legend or fact—of the possibility that a *woman* may very well have been the first to hit on the concept of roasting, grinding, and brewing coffee beans into a beverage. This is peculiar, because women have historically been responsible for roasting, brewing, stewing, and fermenting all sorts of substances in the course of preparing food and drink. Given the highly gender-specific ways in which coffee has been both utilized and symbolized—from the days of dervishes and dancing goats down through the present—it is perhaps not surprising.

EARLY HISTORY OF COFFEE AND COFFEE DRINKING

Once legends of origin are dispensed with, coffee's history becomes much more prosaic. The practice of roasting coffee beans probably began around the thirteenth century, when the drink appears to have become popular in connection with Sufi Muslim religious practices. It was first widely used in the Yemen, but soon spread to Mecca and Medina. References to the beverage are found in scientific literature, philosophical tracts, folklore, and religious texts. The eleventh-century physician and philosopher Avicenna wrote that coffee "fortifies the members, cleans the skin, dries up the humidities that are under it, and give an excellent smell to the body." Another Islamic physician claimed that "it is by experience found to conduce the drying of colds, persistent coughs and catarrh, and to unblock constipation and provoke urination; it allays high blood pressure, and is good against smallpox and measles." He added a cautionary note that adding milk to the brew might "bring one in danger of leprosy." By the end of the fifteenth century, Muslim pilgrims had extolled coffee's restorative powers throughout the Islamic world. While the beverage remained one of the crops of the nocturnal devotional services of the Sufi religious order, those who were less spiritually inclined found it a pleasant stimulus to talk and sociability. Here, the coffeehouse was born.[5]

COFFEEHOUSE CULTURE IN SIXTEENTH-CENTURY ISLAM

The story of how coffee drinking fueled a democratic fad for coffeehouse culture across Europe during the seventeenth and eighteenth centuries, especially in England, is familiar. It has often been told in relation to demands for freedom of speech and freedom of the press, which were central to the politics of an emergent bourgeois public sphere. However, the historical and political antecedents of Euro-pean coffeehouses in sixteenth-century Islam are far less well known. The actual preparation of the beverage differed depending on the cultural context, but in fifteenth-century Mecca and Cairo coffee's popularity—along with its tendency to encourage people to speak freely as they gathered in public places—was not just noteworthy but highly politically charged and acutely gender-specific.

In the Arab world, coffeehouses were essentially Muslim establishments, whose clientele was therefore exclusively male. They served as practical alterna-tives to the proscribed taverns where wines and other alcoholic beverages were served. With wine and other fermented drinks forbidden under Islamic law, local water often scarce and brackish, and goat's milk barely palatable, coffee was a per-fect thirst quencher. It was served and drunk hot, but generally savored slowly; this all but demanded stationary, relatively protected places of consumption, where patrons could take their time, and which in turn served as the perfect setting for talk and socializing with others. Gaming, dancing, music, and singing—activities frowned upon by the strictest followers of Islam—went on in the coffeehouses, along with freewheeling social, political, and religious discussions. All of this was viewed by the authorities with suspicion, and many Islamic officials saw coffee as subversive. It gathered people together; it sharpened their wits and loosened their tongues; it stimulated political arguments and, at least potentially, fomented revolts.

In 1511 an official in Mecca, whose office apparently combined aspects of consumer advocacy and protection with the enforcement procedures of a vice squad, put coffee on trial. He convened a meeting of religious scholars who heard evidence from physicians regarding the putatively detrimental effects of coffee drinking and from religious leaders and government officials regarding the immoral and impious behavior of coffeehouse denizens. For a brief time the sale and con-sumption of coffee were banned in the city. However, the sultan turned out to be a coffee aficionado; within a year the official who had instigated the ban had been removed from his post, and coffeehouses once again flourished. However, in 1525–1526 a more serious incident surrounding coffee took place in Mecca, where a distinguished jurist, Muhammad ibn al-'Arraq, succeeded in closing down the cof-feehouses for nearly two years.[6]

A similar pattern of opposition to coffeehouses and coffee drinking emerged in Cairo, where attempts were made to ban all coffee in 1532–1533 and where riot-ing broke out in the streets on several occasions during 1534–1535 when authori-ties attempted to shut down the coffeehouses. Here, again, secular and religious leaders were suspicious of the potential threats to their authority symbolized by nocturnal gatherings where people spoke freely and critically on any and all issues. These fears were real and sometimes took substantive form. In Istanbul, in 1633, Sultan Marat IV ordered all coffeehouses tom down on the pretext of fire preven-tion; they remained closed, "desolate as the heart of the ignorant," until the last quarter of the century. Perhaps the most remarkable, and definitely the most sav-age, example of the sporadic attempts to prohibit coffee drinking was seen in Turkey, where the grand vizier banned coffee outright in 1656. For a first violation of the ban, the punishment was the cudgel; for a second, the offender would be sewn into a leather bag and thrown into the Bosphorus, where the straits claimed many souls.[7]

Attempts to curtail coffee drinking or coffeehouse culture proved futile, however, over the long run. Throughout the Arab world, social life had been permanently and irrevocably altered by the ever-growing use of coffee, for in cities, towns, and villages, a previously unknown *public* institution—the coffeehouse—had grown up around the production and sale of this commodity. Talk, whether in the form of casual banter or passionate literary disputes and political arguments, was central to the new institution, as was a certain egalitarian spirit. The traveler Pedro Teixeira reported that in Baghdad coffee was "prepared and sold in public houses built to that end; wherein all men who desire it meet to drink it, be they great or mean."[8] In place of newspapers or other public forums, coffeehouses had quickly become places where information of all kinds, from place gossip to the latest trades in the market, could be exchanged simply by world of mouth. At least one Islamic critic bemoaned the way in which coffeehouse patrons "really extend themselves in slander, defamation, and throwing doubt on the reputations of virtuous women. What they come up with are generally the most frightful fabrications, things without a grain of truth in them."[9] This complaint retains its resonance today, although the sports bar or health club locker room might come more readily to mind as places where tall tales of male sexual prowess or conquest may be routinely overheard.

INTRODUCTION OF COFFEE IN EUROPE

The introduction of coffee to Europe, most likely through Venice and other Italian port cities, recapitulated many of the patterns that had been set in Arab lands a century or so earlier. In Europe, as in Islam, coffee drinking initially had religious connotations; in both cases the practice quickly gave rise to the public institution of the coffeehouse, which was often viewed with suspicion by authorities, if not deemed downright subversive of the state. A relatively egalitarian ethic, free speech, and the exchange of news and information also prevailed as the fad for coffee caught on in areas where both the beverage and the institutions it encouraged had previously been unknown. At first European Christians were skeptical about what was seen as a "pagan brew." Italian priests attacked the beverage virulently and successfully petitioned Pope Clement VIII in the hope that he would place coffee under papal interdiction throughout Christendom. The priests argued that coffee was the drink of the devil. Satan, they reasoned, had forbidden the Muslim infidels the use of wine (central to the Christian sacrament of Holy Communion), supplying them instead with his "hellish black brew." The pope, however, found the pungent aroma of the cup of coffee brought before him as evidence of this diabolical intrigue to be utterly irresistible. After tasting the drink, he pronounced it delicious and declared that it would be dreadful to let the infidels have exclusive use of the beverage. Pope Clement turned the tables on Satan by baptizing coffee on the spot. Thus sanctified, coffee no longer required an apothecary's prescription; ordinary people flocked to try the drink, which was sold on street corners throughout Italy.[10]

With this incident, we see a striking connection to the legends surrounding coffee's origin; clearly, the perceptions of the beverage's magical or medicinal properties have something to do with how its advent, whether in the Arab world or some chamber deep within the Vatican, is culturally remembered. In both contexts, religion, spirituality, and much medical healing were clearly and emphatically defined as exclusively male preserves—even, in many cases, at the expense of long-standing traditions of female dominance in these realms.[11] Thus it is particularly interesting that when coffee makes its appearance in Europe, it does so only after receiving papal approbation—in essence, recapitulating the earlier Islamic legends. In both cases, spiritually enlightened males get the credit for discovering, sanctioning, or sanctifying coffee drinking.

In 1650 the first European coffee house opened in Oxford, England, "at the Angel in the parish of St.-Peter-in-the-East."[12] It took another ten years before coffeehouses became truly popular in the university town, but complaints about them grew as their popularity increased. Neither the university nor the coffeehouses springing up in its environs welcomed women, either as scholars or as customers. By 1661 Anthony Wood opined that scholarship was in decline, since "nothing but news, and the affaires of Christendom is discoursed off and that also generally at coffee houses."[13] Roger North held that "the Scholars are so Greedy after News (which is none of their business) that they neglect all for it . . . a vast loss of Time grown out of a pure Novelty; for who can apply close to a subject with his Head full of the din of a Coffee House?"[14] By 1677 the vice chancellor of the University was ordering coffee sellers not to open after evening prayers on Sundays, but he opined that "at five of the clock they flocked all the more" to their favorite haunts. Three years later, a Puritan mayor attempted to close the coffeehouses down entirely on Sundays, but it seems highly unlikely that this edict was ever enforced, let alone obeyed.[15]

POPULARITY OF COFFEEHOUSES IN LONDON

Nowhere were coffeehouses so popular as in London, where the first one had opened in 1652. By 1700 there were about 3000 coffeehouses in the city, which at the time had a population of around 600,000; this works out to an almost unbelievable ratio of one coffeehouse for every 200 people. Coffeehouses represented a spectrum of interests, ranging from commerce to politics and literature. They generally opened off the street and were rather crudely furnished, with tables and chairs scattered about a sanded floor. Eventually booths were added and the walls covered with broadsides and newspapers of all kinds, playbills, handbills, and posters. Macaulay described the company at the famous literary establishment, Wills,' as consisting of "earls in stars and garters, clergymen in cassocks, pert templars, sheepish lads from the Universities, translators and index-makers in ragged coats."[16] Here, classes mixed more freely than they might elsewhere; no one who could put a penny on the bar was excluded. All were welcome in these centers of male networking; all, that is, except women.

Coffeehouses arrived on the London scene along with Puritan rule; they were especially suited to the social climate of the day, offering an antidote to taverns and alcoholism. One approving entry into the pamphlet wars that raged shortly after the advent of coffeehouse culture praised "this coffee drink" for having "caused a greater sobriety among the Nations," and added, by way of explanation: "Whereas formerly Apprentices and clerks with others used to take the morning's draught in Ale, Beer, or Wine, which, by the dizziness they Cause in the Brain, made many unfit for business, they use now to play the Good-fellows in this wakeful and civil drink."[17] While tea and chocolate were also available in the coffeehouses, alcoholic drinks were not; sobriety and moderation were the order of the day, and rules governing the behavior of coffeehouse patrons were prominently displayed on the walls of these establishments. Manners mattered in these places, although it is doubtful that all of the posted regulations were followed to the letter.[18]

Even allowing for a gap between theory and practice when it came to rules and regulations, the democratic character of the English coffeehouse and the sobriety encouraged there were significant at a time when the bourgeoisie was newly organizing as a class. Progressive ideas were in the air, and the coffeehouse as a public space where such thoughts could be aired was as novel a concept as coffee was a beverage. Here, as Habermas and others have noted, *men,* not only could meet to talk over the issues of the day but also begin to articulate a critique of the theory and practice of absolutist domination. Eventually these expressions of "public opinion" legitimized by rational consensus among relatively equal citizens would take on a political dimension of their own, as the bourgeoisie deployed this new, critical public sphere as a revolutionary instrument of class emancipation. The public sphere, insofar as it served to build public opinion in support of values like free speech, democracy, or the rule of law, also served to protect individuals from arbitrary actions of the state, and to mediate between the state and civil society. New technologies allowed newspapers, journals, and books to be produced cheaply and quickly; these media became more widely available than ever before, facilitating lively political debate and opposition—much of which, of course, took place in coffeehouses. The bourgeois public sphere may thus be seen as an arena where democratic discourse was not only available—at least to a limited extent—but, especially as exemplified by English coffeehouse culture, could flourish.[19]

GENDER POLITICS OF COFFEEHOUSE CULTURE

Joan Landes's contention that Habermas's notion of the "bourgeois public sphere" was essentially, and not just contingently, masculinist, bears mention here. Landes takes Habermas to task for not paying adequate attention to the way in which the eighteenth-century public sphere, described in outline here, was shaped by gendered categories and overtly sexist strategies, such as Rousseau's ideology of republican motherhood. The equation of "men" and "citizens" is thus not generic, for the public sphere was just as exclusive of women as the coffeehouse—whether located in fifteenth-century Cairo or eighteenth-century London.[20]

Clear evidence of this was seen in 1674, when unhappy wives published *The Women's Petition against Coffee.* The authors of this pamphlet declared that it was unhealthy for men to be spending so much time away from their homes. Men who became addicted to coffee, they argued, were becoming "as unfruitful as the deserts, from where that unhappy berry is said to be brought." The women complained that they were being neglected by their husbands, whose enjoyment of coffeehouse society placed "the whole race . . . in danger of extinction."[21] Especially interesting here is the way in which women's resentment of coffeehouses would appear to stem less from their exclusion from these male preserves than from the way in which the coffeehouse drew husbands and fathers away from the home (and the marriage bed). Coffeehouses, like taverns, were comfortable retreats from the responsibilities of family life, where men could both reduce the time and attention spent on domestic affairs and fritter away scarce financial resources, leaving less available for family needs. Not only did these public spaces exclude women; they also competed with women and domestic life for the time and money of men. Thus an interest in politics and public life could often provide a convenient excuse for men to hang out in such places, shirking their family responsibilities.

The gender politics of coffeehouse culture allow us to ask whether the political "fraternity" encouraged within the bourgeois public sphere of the eighteenth century resulted from something more than the mere exclusion of women. In spending long hours at the coffeehouse discussing the affairs of the day, men were withdrawing from the demands of family life at a time when the family constituted the basic economic unit of society. Thus women's responsibilities for domestic affairs and the household economy were only increased in the absence of men. Perhaps the democratic discourse of the new public spaces was built not just on the exclusion of women and the creation of specifically gendered categories like "republican motherhood," but also at the cost of increased anxiety and family labor on the part of wives, mothers, and daughters.[22]

COFFEEHOUSES, POLITICAL DISCOURSE, AND REVOLUTION

The coffeehouse played an integral role in revolutionary politics on the North American continent as well as in Europe. European settlers brought coffee with them to the colonies throughout the seventeenth and early eighteenth centuries. Four years after the British took control of Dutch New Amsterdam in 1664, coffee had eclipsed beer as the preferred breakfast drink of New Yorkers. In Boston the

Green Dragon Coffee House, founded in 1697, would in later years be named the "headquarters of the Revolution" by no less than Daniel Webster. At the Green Dragon John Adams, Paul Revere, and others reportedly planned the Boston Tea Party, which made coffee drinking a patriotic act. Another Boston coffeehouse, the Bunch of Grapes, provided the stage for the first public reading of the Declaration of Independence. New York's Merchants Coffee House, located at the southeast corner of Wall and Water Streets, served as another focal point for revolutionary politics. The Sons of Liberty met there on April 18, 1774, to repel a shipment of tea arriving on a British ship; a month later citizens gathered there to draft a letter calling for a "virtuous and spirited Union" of the colonies against Great Britain, along with a congress of deputies—which would become the First Continental Congress. After the Revolution, the coffeehouse continued to play a political role, most notably hosting a huge reception on April 23, 1789, in honor of President–elect George Washington. Coffee was thus bound up, in the early days of the Republic, with a revolutionary politics of liberty and critical public opinion.[23]

Women were, for the most part, excluded from this political community, despite the fact that prewar boycotts and the need to quarter and provision the revolutionary army had politicized household economies before and after independence was declared.[24] Indeed, women had mounted public actions to police local merchants who hoarded scarce commodities in Poughkeepsie. Philadelphia, and elsewhere. On at least one occasion, coffee played a central role in such activity. In July, 1778. Abigail Adams reported to her husband, John, that "a Number of Females, some say a hundred, some say more, assembled with a cart and trucks, marched down to the Ware House" of an "eminent, wealthy, stingy Merchant" who was believed to be hoarding coffee in Boston. When the merchant refused to deliver the keys, "one of them seazd him by his Neck and tossed him into the cart . . . he delivered the keys . . . they . . . opened the Warehouse. Hoisted out the Coffee themselves, put it into trucks and drove off. . . . A large concourse of Men stood amazed silent Spectators."[25] By the end of the war, however, such patriotic activity on the part of women would be deflected into benevolence, with service and reform societies directing women's energies back into the private world of home and family.

Much the same state of affairs prevailed in Europe, although in the case of the French Revolution, comparable women's riots were more desperate, frequent, and violent; the issue was bread, not the luxury of coffee or tea.[26] The historian Michelet described coffee as "the great event which created new customs, and even modified human temperaments," ascribing to the beverage the intangible and spontaneous flow of wit characteristic of the age of the philosophes—but this was entirely gender-specific. Coffeehouse culture flourished in France after the famous Café Procope opened its doors in 1689. Located across from the Comédie Francaise, this establishment attracted authors, actors, dramatists, and musicians, along with philosophers and politicians. Voltaire, who is rumored to have consumed over seventy cups of coffee a day, was a frequent patron. So were Rousseau, Diderot, Beaumarchais, and—during the days of the Revolution—Marat. Robespierre, and

Danton. As in England, French coffeehouse culture emphasized temperance, luring customers away from the taverns and wine sellers.[27]

The café society central to the revolutionary public sphere remained relatively intact throughout the nineteenth and early twentieth centuries in France, but by the end of the eighteenth century coffeehouse culture in England had all but vanished. For the wealthier classes, select "gentlemen's clubs" became the preferred place to assemble in the company of one's social peers: the poorer and less exclusive establishments reverted to their earlier roles as taverns or chop houses, and a new fad for drinking tea eclipsed the coffee-drinking habit. As the public life of coffee declined in England, it found new favor on the domestic scene in Germany, as a breakfast and afternoon drink in middle-class homes.

Coffee was not unknown in Germany. Its use, however, had ambivalent connotations, notably the notion that coffee drinking made men and women sterile, which spared a movement aimed at preventing women from drinking the brew. In 1732 Johann Sebastian Bach composed a "Coffee Cantata," inspired by his love of the brew, which includes the aria "Ah! How sweet coffee tastes! Lovelier than a thousand kisses, sweeter far than muscatel wine! I must have my coffee." The fact that Bach had two wives and fathered twenty children also tended to give the lie to claims regarding coffee's putative links to sterility. We are left wondering, however, just what the mothers of these children might have felt about any of this.[28]

In 1777 Frederick the Great of Prussia attempted to ban coffee consumption by ordinary citizens. Annoyed with the large sums of cash that were flowing to foreign coffee merchants, he declared:

> It is disgusting to note the increase in the quantity of coffee used by my subjects and the amount of money that goes out of the country in consequence. Everybody is using coffee. If possible, this must be prevented. My people must drink beer. His Majesty was brought up on beer, and so were his officers. Many battles have been fought and won by soldiers nourished on beer; and the King does not believe that coffee-drinking soldiers can be depended upon to endure hardships or to beat his enemies in case of the occurrence of another war.[29]

Retired soldiers were recruited as "coffee smellers" to go about arresting anyone caught secretly roasting or brewing the beverage, while physicians were encouraged to tell their patients that drinking coffee would make them sterile. This move of Frederick's generated numerous expressions of passive and active resistance. The public's desire for coffee however, won out in the end. Yet in Germany, coffee drinking became a private, domestic activity; coffee replaced flour soup or beer at breakfast and took on a new, gender-specific dimension as the focus of socializing among women in the afternoons. Breakfast coffee retained vestiges of the public functions of the coffeehouse, marking the start of the working day. After a cup or two in the morning, people were alert and ready to face the business day. In the nineteenth century the newspaper, another émigré from the coffeehouse, was added to this ritual. But the real impetus for the spread of coffee's popularity in Germany came from women of the new burgher class.

WOMEN AND "COFFEE CIRCLES" CULTURE

Recently arrived from the countryside, freed from work in the fields, townswomen gathered to drink coffee in the afternoons at one another's homes. The *Kaffeekränzchen,* or "coffee party," (literally "coffee circle") was entirely a women's affair; it demanded the relative freedom and leisure attached to the bourgeois cult of domesticity. Amaranthes's *Frauenzimmerlexikon,* the "Woman's Lexicon," defined it as "a daily or weekly gathering of several closely acquainted women, each taking her turn as hostess, and in which the members divert and amuse themselves with drinking coffee and playing *Ombre* [a popular card game of the day]." One way to "read" the significance of these gatherings is to suggest that women approached them with a passion that must be seen as compensation for their exclusion from other, more public, domains. In many respects, afternoon coffee parties served as a sort of exclusively female parallel to the exclusively male socializing of coffee-houses and taverns, often becoming the objects of ridicule. Indeed, to this day the word *Kaffeeklatsch* ("ladies gossip circle") retains extremely pejorative—and heavily gendered—connotations.[30] An alternative interpretation, however, might focus on the fact that women might simply have found the company of other women more interesting and stimulating than mixed company.[31]

Without romanticizing the women's coffee parties, it is important to protest the prevailing portrait of them as venues for trivial (i.e., domestic) gossip, especially as contrasted to images of coffeehouses as places where important (i.e., public) speech and activity would prevail. This serves to obscure the reality of how much time spent in taverns or coffeehouses—male preserves of "publicity"—was likely devoted to forms of "male" gossip, or conversations about sports, sexual conquest, tall tales, and the like, instead of (or, more charitably, in addition to) the serious political discourse that is often spoken of by theorists of the bourgeois public sphere. Perhaps there is something threatening to men in the image of women getting together and talking among themselves. The language is, indeed, replete with pejorative synonyms for "girl talk": *gab, gossip, chat, chitchat, chatter, babble, prattle,* and *hen party* are only a few of the terms used to devalue women in their verbal interactions. But perhaps this is not so much a matter of male fear as it is a question of women's internalization of second-class status. As Deborah Cameron notes, "Men trivialize the talk of women not because they are afraid of such talk, but in order to make women themselves down-grade it. If women feel that all interaction with other women is a poor substitute for mixed interaction and trivial compared with the profundities of men's talk, their conversations will indeed be harmless."[32]

Even more is at stake here than the use of language—powerful though language may be as a cultural significator of power and power-structured relationships. Ambivalence and anxiety about women's leisure time seem to have accompanied the rise of the bourgeois family; derogative responses to women's coffee parties may have been one manifestation of bourgeois male concerns in this regard. On the one hand, a wife's leisure may be taken as a positive reflection of her husband's status and affluence. On the other, however, this newfound leisure might give rise to a whole new set of worries about what "mischief" women might get up to if they have too much free time on their hands. Such concerns would eventually be borne out when Betty Friedan's germinal analysis of a "feminine mystique" emerging among middle-class women was published in the United States—a century after women's coffee parties were all the rage among the German bourgeoisie.[33]

COFFEE'S CHANGING ROLE IN TWENTIETH CENTURY

The movement of coffee out of the public sphere and into the private realm of the bourgeois family and its imitators in nineteenth-century Germany was paralleled in the United States, where, by the start of the twentieth century, the beverage had been thoroughly domesticated. Indeed, its gendered connotations underwent a further transformation when coffee drinking was promoted by the Women's Christian Temperance Union (WCTU) as an alternative to the alcoholic beverages that were readily available in saloons across the nation. The American Public Health Association supported the WCTU, claiming that there was "a physiological antagonism between coffee and alcohol, as well as between coffee and opium," and designating coffee a healthy stimulant, "much favored by brain workers," as well as an antimalarial agent.[34] Female reformers of the Progressive Era often suggested founding coffeehouses in the slums as a means of displacing saloons. They looked favorably on the popularity of coffeehouses among Jewish and Italian immigrants, whose sobriety was noteworthy compared with that of many other immigrant groups. In the early 1900s, Jane Addams praised these working-class cafés as the "Salons of the Ghetto" and cited them for "performing a function somewhat between the eighteenth century coffee house and the Parisian café."[35]

The public sphere of the coffeehouses—whether in medieval Islam or eighteenth-century London and New York—had been an exclusively male domain. Throughout the twentieth century in the United States the domestic use of coffee would become something of a feminized cultural icon, central to the spread of commodity goods and consumer capitalist culture. George Lipsetz analyzed coffee's changing role as a cultural icon in a case study of the women's roles in the CBS network television show *I Remember Mama,* which consistently ranked among the top ten programs during its eight-year run in the 1950s. Both this production and a 1948 feature film of the same name were inspired by a collection of short stories by Kathryn Forbes entitled *Mama's Bank Account,* as were a Broadway play and radio performance. The stories, and their various media interpretations, dealt with Norwegian immigrant life in the years before the Great Depression. Lipsetz contrasted the role of coffee drinking in the movie and the television series, which was (not incidentally) sponsored by Maxwell House Coffee.[36]

In the motion picture one of "Mama's" teenage daughters was permitted to join her parents in a cup of coffee after she proved herself as an adult by rejecting a showy dresser set and accepting a piece of family jewelry for her high school graduation gift. The young woman's rejection of consumer goods in favor of traditional values was seen by moviegoers as praiseworthy. However, this was turned upside down in the television series, where tradition served only to legitimate the purchase of more and more consumer goods, and the family story became a lure to bring the audience commercial messages from the program's sponsor. As Lipsetz put it, "The product becomes a member of the Hansen family, while tradition and emotional support become commodities to be secured through the purchase of Maxwell House coffee."[37]

Coffee was cast in the dramatic narratives of the show in a variety of ways. Mama and Papa drank it together in the kitchen; it served as a means of calming down rambunctious children, as a spark for women's conversations, or as an excuse for having company; it facilitated clear thinking and problem solving. Perhaps more importantly, its magical attributes served to draw viewers toward other commodities seen in an equally respectful, if not quite so consistently magical, light.[38] A fundamental connection was established between the warmth of these nostalgic scenes of idyllic family life and the impetus of a consumer capitalist economy toward ever-expanding commodity purchases. In the context of the television series, the domestication of coffee drinking stands in sharp relief as an example of the subsumption by the "culture industry" of the critical public sphere of political discourse formerly found in coffeehouse culture. This iconography demonstrates the extent to which the industry's attendant forms of "publicity" and "entertainment" have come to serve as stand-ins for free speech and cultural critique.

Indeed, contemporary coffee advertisements would seem to demonstrate that coffee today has moved almost totally out of the public sphere and into the realm of privacy and intimacy. Television commercials for Folger's Coffee, for instance, evoke "traditional" family values far more insistently (and effectively) than any of the speakers at the 1992 Republican National Convention. In a typical spot we see the young African American soldier returning home, duffle bag over his shoulder, to share a cup of coffee with Mom in the family kitchen along with an affectionate hug—and "masculine" toss of a football—with a kid brother. In another, a young white woman returns home after college, and, by taking over the chore of making morning coffee, demonstrates that for all her education she still aspires to be "just like mom." Every December the handsome young son returns, we know not from just where—perhaps an Ivy League college?—his arms filled with brightly wrapped packages. The presents get put under the Christmas tree before he awakens his delighted family with the aroma of a pot of freshly brewed Folger's. Images are, indeed, often more powerful than words!

In this context it is also important to think of the unfolding heterosexual romance portrayed in a recent, ongoing series of commercials for Taster's Choice instant coffee or the call to "celebrate the moments of our lives" by drinking General Foods International Coffees. The latter ads often display various forms of female bonding, with sisters or former college roommates drinking coffee while engaging in nostalgic conversation. These relationships between women are depicted as either emphatically asexual or prophetically heterosexual, as when college pals reminisce about the handsome waiter at a European café. They are indicative of the confinement of female discourse, and especially the "symbolic speech" of female sexuality, to domesticity within an overarching framework of compulsory heterosexuality.[39] Indeed, coffee drinking is often equated with women making time for themselves in the midst of competing demands: An instant cappuccino, one ad implies, can make the conflicting demands of children, housework, a profession, and caring for elderly relatives melt away to nothing—and in just "an instant." Only rarely do we see coffee advertised in more "public" settings, notably the Folger's commercials that show diners in fancy restaurants drinking instant coffee that's been "switched" for a freshly brewed beverage. And even then the domestic message is clear: "I'll serve this at home" is, explicitly or implicitly, the tag line spoken by these putatively surprised patrons.

It might seem, in the United States at least, as if the pendulum had swung entirely from one side to the other, from a heavily male (public) sphere of coffeehouses and coffee drinking to a specifically female (private) realm of idyllic domesticity where coffee is just one of many commodities to be purchased and consumed. Indeed, it would not be difficult to develop a wholly negative, one-sided critique in the style of Horkheimer and Adorno, where the golden (masculine) age of the coffeehouse is valorized at the expense of a debased (feminine) mode of domestic coffee drinking. But such a critique would ignore the ways in which vestiges of the older traditions not only remain in contemporary society but on occasion have been manipulated consciously by members of progressive social movements in ways that subvert both the established "culture industry" and the gendered distinctions of the "public" and "private" spheres.

COFFEE AND ALTERNATIVE SOCIAL AND CULTURAL INSTITUTIONS

Countercultural institutions have emerged in the last two decades that draw on the traditions of free speech and cultural and political criticism that were integral to the coffeehouse cultures of centuries past. Indeed, these institutions may be situated in a context of political discourse that includes the café societies of Bohemian Paris at the turn of the twentieth century and Weimar Germany after the First World War.[40] The GI coffeehouse movement was a focal point, on and around a number of military installations, for organizing against the Vietnam Conflict. By the early 1970s, some peace protestors had shifted their efforts away from college campuses to military bases around the country. At Mountain Home Air Force Base in Idaho, for example, peace workers "opened a coffeehouse for GIs in an abandoned theater downtown; they called it the Helping Hand. They had meetings that advised enlisted personnel how to assist the antiwar movement. They published an antiwar newspaper for the base, began counseling GIs on how to file for conscientious-objector status, and opened a small library of radical books."[41] Comparable efforts were made across the country, with coffeehouses springing up in the vicinity of almost every major military base. Over a hundred underground newspapers would be published, often in conjunction with coffeehouse activities. For a while there was even talk of unionizing the military. In at least some cases, these initiatives involved discussions of class relationships (between middle-class and working-class peace organizers and between civilians and GIs) and confrontations with feminist issues that sparked difficult and lively debates.[42]

Since the late 1960s, in cities and towns across the United States, feminist community organizing and cultural work has often centered around coffeehouses, sometimes in tandem with feminist bookstores and other forms of cultural expression. While some of these businesses have been relatively short-lived experiments in collectivity and other alternatives to capitalist organizations, others have survived and continue to do so despite an often hostile economic climate. In Chicago, for example, the Mountain Moving Coffeehouse celebrated its twenty-fifth anniversary in 1998. Its very name connotes the political struggles attached to building alternative social and cultural institutions—it is no easy task to "move the mountains" of entrenched sexism and homophobia that militate against feminist organizational agendas prioritizing women and their concerns or needs.

Technically speaking, Mountain Moving is set somewhat apart from the "tradition" of coffeehouse culture, not just in that it provides a space for feminist/ lesbian cultural expression but also because this space is not permanently devoted to the consumption of coffee or any other comestibles. Rather, Mountain Moving Coffeehouse has met on Saturday nights in space made available by at least two Chicago churches. Coffee, tea, soda, and sweets are served at intermissions or before and after programs, and are somewhat incidental to the featured events. At large-drawing concerts, the bulk of the audience never leaves the sanctuary space of the church to visit the third floor of the building where the library and refreshments are available. Smaller events, such as a popular crafts fair held during the December holiday season, take place entirely on the third floor, and in these instances coffee is more integrated. In addition to sponsoring a variety of ongoing reading, discussion, and support groups for women and children, with an emphasis on lesbian political issues, Mountain Moving Coffeehouse has brought a wide range of cultural programming to Chicago's feminist community (at affordable prices). A typical month includes events ranging from comedy to folksingers to a jazz duo, along with showings of artwork by differently abled women.

Despite its departures from more conventional forms, the heart of traditional coffeehouse culture has been retained insofar as Mountain Moving's clientele sustains a lively alternative to more mainstream forms of information sharing, community support, and entertainment. The importance of countercultural institutions such as this should not be underestimated. In addition to providing safe spaces for critical discourse and cultural events, they are places where symbolic speech, represented by styles of dress, bodily presentation, and other nonverbal forms of behavior, may find free expression. For some women this freedom to "speak" symbolically is a luxury unavailable in other venues of everyday life.

A young woman who is a recent graduate of college where the author teaches poignantly expresses the importance of such symbolic speech and the need for places where it may be freely and safely articulated. She describes herself as "a walking stereotype of a young 'Generation X' lesbian" who is a "regular" at Mountain Moving events, saying, "I look like a twelve-year-old boy—short hair, no makeup, no dresses, no skirts, definitely no high heels; when people aren't sure they assume I'm male." She is frequently the object of homophobic verbal assaults on the streets of Chicago, but at coffeehouse events she looks "like everyone else." At Mountain Moving there are no "gender police" to call her to account for transgressing standards of "feminine" appearance or behavior, so she can feel comfortable just being herself. Coffeehouse events serve to remind her that she is not "alone in the world"; she feels empowered "to know that there's a group of people trying to move the mountain together, and not just me." When she was first coming out as a lesbian in Chicago, "it was really affirming to be surrounded by other lesbians, given that there's so much homophobia in the 'real' world." She still sees the coffeehouse as a place where she is guaranteed community and conviviality: "It's as if I'm a battery that runs down in the real world, but I can go to Mountain Moving and get recharged."[43]

Lynette J. Eastland spent several months studying Twenty Rue Jacob, a feminist coffeehouse and bookstore in Salt Lake City, Utah. She described her experiences as a participant–observer in this ethnographic study, citing the importance of everyday relationships to the coffeehouse community:

> The days I liked the best were those heavily loaded with people. . . . Sometimes they purchased something, but most often these days were primarily socially oriented. We would sell a lot of cups of coffee, some lunches and maybe a record or two. The women would greet each other warmly with hugs and smiles and catch up on the news of each others' lives. Some would come in to check the bulletin board and posters for local activities . . . or to see who was there, but mostly they came to pass time with one another, to find a friendly face.[44]

Here, it would seem, the exclusively male atmosphere of the eighteenth-century coffeehouse has been irrevocably altered by the social and political needs of women "customers"; while the gender specificity may have been inverted, traditions of free speech, public information, and sociability have been retained.

Indeed, in some instances, the explicitly political connections have been positively exploited. Eastland recounts how a typical day at Twenty Rue Jacob might include a scene such as the following, which involved

> two young women who came in early afternoon and ordered two cups of coffee. They were obviously upset and isolated themselves from the few people gathered around the counter . . . they asked to speak to [the manager, who] pulled up a chair and sat down. The two women held hands across the table as they talked. Both appeared very young, very attractive and were wearing dresses and high heels. . . . They needed the name of a lawyer, they said, who would be sensitive to their problem. They were being threatened by the ex-husband of one of the women, who said he

would take [her] child away if they continued to see each other. They were confused and afraid and needed help.

The manager of the coffeehouse supplied the women with the name and phone number of an attorney; while we do not know "the rest of the story," it is clear that Twenty Rue Jacob played an integral role in making available to patrons information that might otherwise be unavailable or difficult to obtain from "mainstream" sources. Once again, echoes of past traditions linger, though with a twist.[45]

Oppositional and progressive coffeehouse cultures such as the two described here represent viable alternatives to the commodity culture of the mass media and serve as reminders of how it may still be possible to create public spheres where critical political discourse may be sustained in troubled times. Perhaps more importantly, as the vitality of feminist coffeehouses today would tend to indicate, such publicly discursive moments can be recreated in ways that inform a new generation of citizens. Here the links between the passions stimulated by coffee drinking and free speech undertaken in public association not only reach back through time of medieval Islam or the Enlightenment but also stretch forward to an as yet unimagined future. For those who prize a good cup of coffee along with democracy and passionate critical discourse, there may yet be hope.

NOTES

1. Aytoun Ellis, *The Penny Universities: A History of the Coffee-Houses* (London: Secker and Warburg, 1956), p. 3; Ralph S. Hattox, *Coffee and Coffeehouses: The Origins of a Social Beverage in the Medieval Near East* (Seattle: University of Washington Press, 1985), p. 12.

2. Ellis, *The Penny Universities*, p. 17.

3. Claudia Roden, *Coffee* (New York: Penguin, 1977), p. 20; David Joel, and Karl Schapira, *The Book of Coffee and Tea* (New York: St. Martin's Press, 1982), pp. 5–6.

4. Sara Perry, *The Complete Coffee Book* (San Francisco: Chronicle Books, 1991), p. 7; Roden, *Coffee*, p. 20; Schapira, *The Book of Coffee and Tea*, p. 6.

5. Norman Kolpas. *A Cup of Coffee* (New York: Grove Press, 1993), p. 14; Hattox, *Coffee and Coffeehouses*, pp. 22–28; Perry, *The Complete Coffee Book*, p. 7; Roden, *Coffee* p. 20.

6. Hattox, *Coffee and Coffeehouses*, p. 37.

7. *Ibid.*, pp. 32–39; Roden, *Coffee*, p. 21.

8. Hattox, *Coffee and Coffeehouses*, p. 93.

9. *Ibid.*, p. 101.

10. Perry, *The Complete Coffee Book*, p. 8; Roden, *Coffee*, p. 21; Schapira, *The Book of Coffee and Tea*, p. 9.

11. David F. Noble, *A World without Women: The Christian Clerical Culture of Western Science* (New York: Knopf, 1992). esp. pp. 3–39.

12. Ellis, *The Penny Universities*, p. 19.

13. *Ibid.*, p. 24.

14. *Ibid.*, p. 27.

15. *Ibid.*, p. 24.

16. Quoted in Roden, *Coffee*, p. 28.

17. Quoted in Edward Robinson, *The Early English Coffee House, with an Account of the First Use of Coffee* (1893) (Christchurch, Hants.: Dolphin Press, 1972), p. 117.

18. *Ibid.*, pp. 109–110.

19. Jürgen Habermas. *The Structural Transformation of the Public Sphere: An Inquiry into a Category of Bourgeois Society*, trans. Thomas Burger with the assistance of Frederick Lawrence (Cambridge, MA: MIT Press, 1989).

20. See Joan B. Landes, *Women and the Public Sphere in the Age of the French Revolution* (Ithaca, NY: Cornell University Press, 1988), pp. 7, 129.

21. The Women's Petition Against Coffee, representing to publick consideration the grand inconveniences accruing to their sex from the excessive use of that drying, enfeebling liquor. Presented to the right honorable the keepers of the library of Venus by a wellwiller. London, 1674.

22. Thanks to Uma Narayan for this insight. On the family as an economic unit, see Laurel Thatcher Ulrich,

Good Wives: Image and Realty in Northern New England, 1650–1750 (New York: Oxford University Press, 1982).

23. Kolpas, *A Cup of Coffee*, p. 22.

24. Linda K. Kerber, *Women of the Republic: Intellect and Ideology in Revolutionary America* (New York: Norton, 1986), p. 35.

25. L. H. Butterfield (Ed.) Abigail Adams to John Adams, July 31, 1778, *Adams Family Correspondence* (Cambridge, MA: Belknap Press, 1963), II, p. 295, quoted in Kerber. *Women of the Republic,* p. 44.

26. *Ibid.,* p. 44.

27. Roden, *Coffee,* p. 25.

28. Perry, *The Complete Coffee Book,* p. 17; Josh Glenn, "Coffee Time," *Utne Reader,* November/December 1994, p. 62.

29. Roden, *Coffee,* p. 22.

30. Wolfgang Schivelbusch, *Tastes of Paradise: A Social History of Spices, Stimulants, and Intoxicants,* translated from the German by David Jacobson (New York: Vintage Books, 1993), p. 69.

31. See, for example, Carroll Smith-Rosenberg, "The Female World of Love and Ritual Relations between Women in Nineteenth-Century America," *Signs,* 1 (1) (1975), pp. 1–29.

32. Deborah Cameron, *Feminism and Linguistic Theory,* cited in Jane Mills, *Womanwords: A Dictionary of Words about Women* (New York: Free Press, 1989), p. 44. See also Dale Spender, *Man Made Language,* 2nd ed. (New York: Pandora, 1991), p. 106–108.

33. Betty Friedan, *The Feminine Mystique* (New York: Norton, 1963).

34. "The Abuse of Alcohol from a Sanitary Standpoint," *American Kitchen Magazine,* 5 (1) (April 1896), p. 33, quoted in Harvey A. Levenstein, *Revolution at the Table: The Transformation of the American Diet* (New York: Oxford University Press, 1988), p. 99.

35. Jane Addams, "Immigration: A Field Neglected by the Scholar," *The Commons,* January 1905, p. 16.

36. George Lipsetz, "Why Remember Mama? The Changing Face of a Women's Narrative," in *Time Passages: Collective Memory and American Popular Culture* (Minneapolis: University of Minnesota Press, 1990), pp. 77–96.

37. *Ibid.,* p. 89.

38. *Ibid.,* p. 90.

39. Adrienne Rich, "Compulsory Heterosexuality and Lesbian Existence," *Signs,* 5 (4) (1980), pp. 631–660.

40. See, for example, Georges Bernier, *Paris Cafes: Their Role in the Birth of Modern Art* (New York: Wildenstein, 1985); and Henry Pachter, "Expressionism and Café Culture," in *Weimar Etudes* (New York: Columbia University Press, 1982).

41. Randy Shilts, *Conduct Unbecoming: Gays and Lesbians in the U.S. Military* (New York: St. Martin's Press, 1993), p. 152.

42. See Ellen Willis, "Radical Feminism and Feminist Radicalism" in Sonya Sayres, et al (Eds.), *The 60s without Apology* (Minneapolis: University of Minnesota Press, in cooperation with Social Text, 1984), pp. 111–112.

43. Suzy Stanton, personal communication, October 20, 1994. Suzy is a 1994 graduate of De Paul University. At De Paul, she was instrumental in founding an organization for lesbian, gay, and bisexual students and for developing and administering a survey of homophobic attitudes on campus—no mean feats at a Catholic institution of higher education.

44. Lynette J. Eastland, *Communication, Organization and Change within a Feminist Context: A Participant Observation of a Feminist Collective* (Lewiston, NY: E. Mellen Press, 1991), p. 176.

45. *Ibid.,* pp. 184–185.

FURTHER READING

Eastland, Lynette J. *Communication, Organization and Change within a Feminist Context: A Participant Observation of a Feminist Collective.* Lewiston, NY: E. Mellen Press, 1991.

Kerber, Linda K. *Women of the Republic: Intellect and Ideology in Revolutionary America.* New York: Norton, 1986.

Landes, Joan B. *Women and the Public Sphere in the Age of the French Revolution.* Ithaca, NY: Cornell University Press, 1988.

Rich, Adrienne. "Compulsory Heterosexuality and Lesbian Existence," *Signs,* 5 (4) (1980), pp. 631–660.

Smith-Rosenberg, Carroll. "The Female World of Love and Ritual: Relations between Women in Nineteenth-Century America," *Signs,* 1 (1) (1975), pp. 1–29.

★ ★

Contributors

Denise L. Baer is a political scientist and consultant living in the Washington, D.C. area. In 2004, she was the Director of Campaign 2004, The Washington Center's Special Academic Seminars-on-site at the Democratic and Republican Conventions. Dr. Baer is a national expert in political party organization, and has been to the 1988, 1992, 1996, 2000, and 2004 Democratic and Republican conventions. She served as an American Political Science Congressional Fellow for the House Democratic Caucus under Rep. Steny Hoyer and also worked for Rep. David Price, a former political scientist. Dr. Baer has published books and articles on women and politics, community mobilization, and political parties and organizations, including an elite study of convention delegates. She has taught at the Ray C. Bliss Institute at the University of Akron, Northeastern University, American University and George Washington University, where she currently teaches. As a consultant, she has worked with a variety of national women's organizations, including the National Women's Political Caucus, the National Congress of Black Women, and the Women's Campaign Fund, and has expertise in campaign and leadership training, gender-specific programs, girls and delinquency and domestic violence. She has consulted with other organizations, including the National Democratic Institute, the National Governor's Association, and government agencies including the Department of Justice and the Office of Juvenile Justice and Delinquency Prevention. She holds a Ph.D. in political science from Southern Illinois University-Carbondale.

Ruth Bamberger is professor emeritus of political science at Drury University, Springfield, MO. She has researched extensively in the area of sex discrimination in insurance since it became a major public policy issue in the mid-1970s. She has authored papers on the topic, which have been presented at the annual meetings of the American Political Science Association, Southern Political Science Association, the Midwest Political Science Association, and the Southwestern Social Science Association. In 1981, Dr. Bamberger was granted an honorary research fellowship at the University of Durham, England, where she researched sex discrimination in insurance in the British system.

Irene J. Barnett is a policy analyst with the U.S. General Accounting Office's (GAO) Education, Workforce, Income Security Issues team. Her research interests include gender politics, assisted reproductive technology policy and comparative healthcare policy.

Sarah Brewer is the associate director of the Women & Politics Institute at American University. She completed her Ph.D. from American University in 2003. Her dissertation, titled "Gender and Political Vocation: Women Campaign Consultants," explores the significance of gender in political vocations in general, using the campaign consulting industry as a case study. Her publications include, "Gender-Bias in Elections for County Office in the South: Additions to the Gender Role Hypothesis," in *Social Science Quarterly* and "Women Political Consultants: Who Are They, Where Are They? in *Campaigns & Elections*. She is also a co-author of an edited anthology of classics in Women and Politics. She is the Program Director for the NEW Leadership DC Program, a week-long political leadership training program for women who attend the 12 colleges and universities in Washington, D.C.

Charles S. Bullock, III, is the Richard B. Russell Professor of Political Science at the University of Georgia. Among his co-authored and co-edited books are *The New Politics of the Old South* (2003), *Elections to Open Seats in the U.S. House* (2000), *Implementation of Civil Rights Polity* (1984), *Coercion to Compliance* (1976), *Law and Social Change*

(1972), and *Runoff Elections in the United States* (1992) which won the Southern Political Science Association's V.O. Key Book Award as the Best Book on Southern Politics. He is past president of the Southern Political Science Association and past chair of the American Political Science Association's Legislative Studies Group.

Cynthia Burack is associate professor in the Department of Women's Studies at The Ohio State University. She is the author of *The Problem of the Passions: Feminism, Psychoanalysis, and Social Theory* and *Healing Identities: Black Feminist Thought and the Politics of Groups,* and the co-editor (with Jyl J. Josephson) of *Fundamental Differences: Feminists Talk Back to Social Conservatives.* She is currently writing a book on the Christian Right.

D'Ann M. Campbell is Dean of Academics at the U.S. Coast Guard Academy. While simultaneously serving as a professor of history, her 25+ year administrative career includes service as Interim President of White Pines College, Vice President of Academic Affairs at two institutions and dean at two others. Campbell served as Distinguished Visiting Military History Professor at the U.S. Military Academy (West Point) from 1989–1991. Her doctorate is from the University of North Carolina, Chapel Hill (1979). Her book *Women at War With America: Private Lives in a Patriotic Era* (Harvard, 1984) was a comprehensive treatment of women's roles in WWII. She has authored over three dozen articles on women in American history including "Women in Combat: The World War II Experience in the United States, Great Britain, Germany, and the Soviet Union,." *Journal of Military History* 57 (April 1993): 301–323.

Nancie E. Caraway is an award-winning political scientist and feminist scholar/activist with twenty years of leadership experience in human rights and social justice initiatives. Her 1992 book, *Segregated Sisterhood: Racism and the Politics of American Feminism,* was co-recipient of the American Political Science Association's Schuck Award for best book on women and politics. An experienced journalist and reporter as well, she has served as a public intellectual, writing on topics such as: multicultural identities and politics, post-colonialism and Native Hawaiian rights, the nature of power and privilege in a globalizing world, and the challenge of political activism within postmodern frames. She is an international expert on globalization and human trafficking, having participated in major UN global and Asian fora on the topic: Women Waging Peace, Harvard Kennedy School 2000; Asian Regional Initiative Against Trafficking, Manila 2000; The Second World Congress Against Child Commercial Exploitation, Yokohama 2001; Freedom Network conference "Is the New Human Trafficking Law Working?" New York 2003; and served as expert consultant at the Seminar on Cross-Border Trafficking, Centre for Feminist Legal Research, New Delhi, India, January 2004.

Cal Clark is a professor of Political Science at Auburn University. He received his Ph.D. from the University of Illinois and previously taught at New Mexico State University and the University of Wyoming. He is the author of *Taiwan's Development,* co-author of *Women in Taiwan Politics, Comparing Development Patterns in Asia,* and *The Social and Political Bases for Women's Growing Political Power in Taiwan,* and co-editor of *Democracy and the Status of Women in East Asia.*

Janet M. Clark is professor and chair of the Political Science/Planning Department at the State University of West Georgia. She holds the Ph.D. degree in Political Science from the University of Illinois, Urbana-Champaign. She is co-author of *Women, Elections, and Representation; The Equality State: Government and Politics in Wyoming; Women in Taiwan Politics;* and *The Social and Political Bases for Women's Growing Political Power in Taiwan.* She is a former editor of *Women & Politics,* a quarterly journal, and has published articles and book chapters on political participation.

Kathleen P. Iannello is an associate professor of Political Science at Gettysburg College in Gettysburg, Pennsylvania, where she teaches courses in American Politics and Feminist Political Theory. She is the author of *Decisions Without Hierarchy* and is currently researching and writing a book on women, decision making and third-wave feminism.

Hedy Leonie Isaacs, who graduated from Rutgers University with a Ph.D. in Public Administration, is currently a Lecturer of Public Administration and Public Policy at the University of the West Indies, Department of Government-Mona Campus.

Roberta Ann Johnson is professor of Politics and director of the public service minor at the University of San Francisco (USF). She was the recipient of the USF College Service Award in 2003. She earned her Ph.D. in political science at Harvard University and is the author of numerous journal articles and book chapters on American society and politics and is author of *Whistleblowing: When It Works-And Why,* published by Lynne Rienner; *The Struggle Against Corruption: A Comparative Study,* 2004, with Palgrave at St. Martin's Press; and *Puerto Rico: Commonwealth or Colony?* with Praeger.

Elizabeth A. Kelly is associate professor of Women's and Gender Studies at DePaul University, where she served as director of the Women's and Gender Studies Program for six years. Her book, *Education, Public Knowledge,* *and Democracy* (Westview, 1995) received the Michael Harrington Award from the New Political Science section of the American Political Science Association. She is currently collaborating with Frida Kerner Fuman and Linda Williamson Nelson on *Three Lives: Women Speaking Across Difference* (forthcoming from Rowman and Littlefield).

Jennifer L. Lawless is assistant professor of Political Science and Public Policy at Brown University. She received her Ph.D. from Stanford University in 2003. She has published a series of articles about symbolic representation, political ambition, and gender stereotyping in the electoral process. Her work has appeared in *American Journal of Political Science, Political Research Quarterly, Legislative Studies Quarterly,* and *Women and Politics.*

Susan A. MacManus is the Distinguished University Professor of Public Administration and Political Science in the Department of Government and International Affairs at the University of South Florida. She is the author of *Young v. Old: Generational Combat in the 21st Century* (Westview Press), *Targeting Senior Voters: Campaign Outreach to Elders and Others With Special Needs* (Rowman & Littlefield, 2000), editor of *Mapping Florida's Political Landscape: The Changing Art & Politics of Reapportionment & Redistricting* (Florida Institute of Government, 2002), and co-author, with Thomas R. Dye, of *Politics in States and Communities,* 11th ed. (Prentice-Hall, 2003). Her research on women in politics—candidates, office holders, activists, voters—has been published in *Social Science Quarterly, Public Administration Review, Journal of Politics, Women and Politics, Urban Affairs Quarterly, National Civic Review,* and the *Municipal Year Book,* among others. She chaired the Florida Elections Commission from 1999–2003.

Elaine Martin is a professor at Eastern Michigan University in Ypsilanti, Michigan. She teaches courses in judicial politics, women in politics, and public administration. She has published extensively on the subject of gender and the judiciary.

Maureen Rand Oakley is assistant professor of Political Science at Mount Saint Mary's University in Emmitsburg, Maryland. Her research focuses on state policy change, reproductive policy, and gender and political attitudes. She recently authored an article, in *Politics and Policy* (September 2003) entitled, "Abortion Policy and Abortion Rates: Has Abortion Policy Been Successful?" She teaches courses in state and local politics; research methods; gender, race and politics; biomedical policy and American politics.

Karen O'Connor is a professor of Government and Director of the Women & Politics Institute at American University. She has written extensively about women and the law, women and politics, and American politics. She is the past president of the Women's Caucus for Political Science and the Southern Political Science Association.

Karen L. Padgett holds a Masters of Public Administration degree from the School of Public and International Affairs at the University of Georgia. She interned for the Georgia State Senate's Transportation Committee and worked as a Legislative Analyst for Ford Motor Company's Southeastern Governmental Affairs office.

Brittany Penberthy is a recent graduate of the University of South Florida where she was a member of Pi Sigma Alpha, the National Political Science Honor Society, and a research assistant to Dr. Susan A. MacManus.

Sarah Poggione received her Ph.D. from the Pennsylvania State University in 2001. She is currently an assistant professor in Political Science at Florida International University. Her research and teaching interests include women and politics, state legislative politics, and quantitative research methods. Her current research projects include investigating the effects of legislative structure and women's representation on the content of state welfare policy, examining state legislators' strategies for influencing bureaucratic policy making, and exploring the electoral implications of men and women's legislative behavior. Her research has been accepted for publication in *Legislative Studies Quarterly* and *Political Research Quarterly.*

Jennifer Ring is professor of Political Science, and former Director of Women's Studies at the University of Nevada, Reno. She received her doctorate from the University of California, Berkeley, and is author of *The Political Consequences of Thinking: Gender and Judaism in the Work of Hannah Arendt* (1997); *Modern Political Theory and Contemporary Feminism: A Dialectical Analysis* (1991); journal articles, reviews and chapters in collected volumes in political theory and feminist theory, including most recently chapters on Arendt for *Holocaust Literature,* and John Stuart Mill for the Oxford volume, *Political Thinkers: From Socrates to the Present.* She is currently at work on a book on American sports and the construction of gender, which focuses on the significance of women's exclusion from baseball.

Carolyn Ellis Staton was appointed as Provost and Vice Chancellor for Academic Affairs at The University of Mississippi June 1, 1999. In 1977 she joined the faculty of the School of Law and in 1993–94 served as Interim Dean of the Law Center. In 1994 she became Interim Associate Vice Chancellor for Academic Affairs, and in 1996 she became Associate Provost. She received a B.A. from Tulane University, an M.A. from Columbia University, and a J.D. from Yale Law School. Formerly, she was in private practice in New York and was an Assistant United

States Attorney in the District of New Jersey. She was also a Fulbright Fellow in Germany, teaching at the University of Frankfurt and the University of Munich. For eight years, she served as Reporter on Evidence for the Mississippi Supreme Court Advisory Committee on Rules, drafting the evidence laws for the State of Mississippi. She is the author of books and articles on evidence, criminal procedure, and sex discrimination. She was the first recipient of the Outstanding Mississippi Woman Lawyer Award in 1995. She served on the Secretary of Defense's Defense Advisory Committee on Women in the Services (DACOWITS) from 1993–96, and served as vice-chair from 1995–96. She also served on the Board of Advisors of the Naval Postgraduate School from 1997–2004.

Gertrude A. Steuernagel is professor of Political Science at Kent State University. Her teaching interests include women and politics and political theory. She is the co-author of two Congressional Quarterly Press books: *Women and Political Participation* and *Women and Public Policy*. She also has research interests in the areas of disability policy and women and health policy.

Sean M. Theriault is assistant professor of Government at the University of Texas at Austin. He is the author of *Power of the People: Congressional Competition, Public Attention, and Voter Retribution* (Ohio State University Press, 2005). He has also published on a variety of subjects including the Pendleton Act of 1883, the Compromise of 1850, issue framing, and congressional careers. His work has appeared in *Journal of Politics, Legislative Studies Quarterly, Presidential Studies Quarterly,* and *American Politics Research.*

Joan Hulse Thompson is associate professor of Political Science and department chair at Arcadia University. She served as an American Association of University Women Foundation Fellow at the Congressional Caucus for Women's Issues in 1983. She was an American Political Science Association Congressional Fellow in 1985–1986. She teaches courses on American politics and public law, including a course on Congress and another on gender roles and family policy issues.

Robert P. Watson is associate professor of Political Science at Florida Atlantic University. He has written or edited twenty books and published over 100 scholarly articles and chapters on such topics as the presidency, first ladies, civil rights, elections, environmental policy, bureaucracy, and U.S. politics. He has been interviewed by CNN, MSNBC, *USA Today,* and dozens of other media outlets. He has appeared on C-SPAN's *Book TV* program; served as a visiting fellow-scholar with numerous universities and presidential sites including the Truman Presidential Library and Mount Rushmore National Memorial. He directed the first-ever *Report to the First Lady,* which was presented to Laura Bush, Lynne Cheney, and their aides after the 2001 presidential inauguration. He serves on the boards of several presidential foundations and scholarly journals, and is the founding editor of the journal *White House Studies.*

Sara J. Weir is an associate professor and chair of the Political science Department at Western Washington University. She teaches courses in the fields of public policy and women in politics. She recently published an edited volume (with Constance Faulkner) *Voices of a New Generation: A Feminist Anthology* (Boston, MA.: Pearson Education, Inc, 2003). She is currently working on a memoir documenting her experience with childhood cancer and a book on women governors.

Lois Duke Whitaker is professor of Political Science, Georgia Southern University in Statesboro. She is the author of many pieces on women and politics and on U..S. national government, including a co-edited volume with James MacGregor Burns, William Crotty, and Lawrence Longley, *The Democrats Must Lead: The Case for a Progressive Democratic Party.* Her research interests also include mass media and politics, and state and local government. Currently, she is working on a manuscript featuring civil rights activists and their contributions to the civil rights movement in the Deep South. She has taught at the University of South Carolina, Columbia; the University of Alabama, Tuscaloosa; the University of San Francisco; Clemson University; and Auburn University, Montgomery. She is a past president of the Women's Caucus for Political Science: South; is a past president of the South Carolina Political Science Association and the Georgia Political Science Association; and a past Program Vice-President for the League of Women Voters of South Carolina. She is the recipient of the Clemson University Chapter of the American Association of University Professors (AAUP) Award of Merit for distinctive contributions to the academic profession (May 1992). She presented a paper and participated in the Oxford Roundtable on Women's Rights held in the Lincoln College of the University of Oxford, Oxford, England, March 28-April 2, 2004.

Thomas E. Yatsco is a senior analyst-in-charge of Strategic Issues at the U.S. General Accounting Office (GAO) in Washington, D.C. In this position he leads Congressional studies on crosscutting issues such as intergovernmental relations, government management, and performance indicators, and the nation's policy, fiscal, and regulatory challenges. He has also held positions at the U.S. Department of Health and Human Services and the National Council on Aging. In addition, he has authored other book chapters on health care and long-term care issues as well as intergovernmental relations.